THE TIMES

HISTORY OF

WAR

THE TIMES

HISTORY OF

WAR

TIMES
BOOKS

HarperCollins*Publishers*
77-85 Fulham Palace Road
Hammersmith
London W6 8JB

First published by HarperCollins*Publishers* 2000

1 3 5 7 9 10 8 6 4 2

© HarperCollins *Publishers* 2000

ISBN 0 00 472338 4

Editor: Ian Drury
Consultant Editor: Richard Brooks
Cartographic Editor: Martin Brown
Maps: Peter Harper and Cosmographics
Design: Rod Teasdale

Printed in Great Britain by Bath Press

Picture Credits

The Publishers would like to thank the following
organizations and individuals for providing photographs:

Richard Brooks: 63, 72, 74, 84, 86, 88, 96, 101, 102, 103,
105, 107, 108, 109, 116, 124, 126, 129, 141, 142, 143, 144
(x2), 148, 150, 156, 157; British Library: 50, 51, 59;
Bunbury Collection: 67, 133, 147, 159, 171; Werner
Forman Archive: 24, 25, 43, 56; Peter Foster: 233; Ken
Guest: 244; Imperial War Museum: 152 (x2), 153, 160,
161, 163, 168, 174, 175, 176 (x3), 179, 180 (x2), 181, 182,
183, 184, 185, 186, 187, 195 (x2), 198, 200, 201 (x2), 203
(x3), 208, 209, 210, 212, 215, 217, 218, 224, 228, 230, 231
(x2), 247 (x2); Mary Evans Picture Library: 20, 21, 29, 35
(x2), 40, 48 (x2), 49 (x2), 52, 54, 95; Musée de la Marine:
99; National Maritime Museum: 83, 90, 93, 98; Royal
Marines Museum: 162, 172, 189, 235, 250; Scala: 8 (x2), 9,
10, 13, 14 (x2), 17, 19, 22, 26 (x2), 28 (x2), 30, 31, 32, 33,
34, 38 (x2), 44, 45, 46, 62, 64, 65, 75, 76, 77, 79, 80,125;
US Air Force: 229, 240 (x2), 241, 249; US Army: 242; US
Marine Corps: 243; US National Archives: 137, 139, 196,
197, 205, 217, 220, 223; US Navy: 191, 227, 241, 249.

Contents

Introduction

ABOVE: A lurid illustration of the Huns' invading Europe in the 5th century. The Huns were defeated at the Catalaunian Fields near Troyes in 451, but invaders from the East would menace Europe until the 17th century.

TOP RIGHT: Prussian troops of the Napoleonic Wars. Uniforms were pioneered in ancient times, but reached their most splendid during the 18th and 19th centuries.

ABOVE RIGHT: Part of Trajan's Column shows Roman soldiers fortifying their positions. Their mastery of field works and siege techniques enabled the Romans to overcome any opponent with a fixed base that they could attack.

The intention of this book is to reveal how warfare developed from ancient civilizations to the beginning of the 21st century. It is a complex story. Of all historical disciplines, the study of military history is perhaps the most multi-faceted. Political, economic, social, religious, cultural, technological, agricultural and even meteorological factors have shaped the way nations fight. The outcome of some wars have been determined by decidedly non-military elements. Conversely, purely military factors have often had profound political and social consequences.

When renaissance writers rediscovered the literature of the ancient world, their military contemporaries seized upon Greek and Roman instruction manuals and studied the careers of Classical commanders. They put the lessons of the past into practical use, re-introducing uniforms and drill. Many military precepts are basically common sense, but their rendition in Latin lent authority. Since the 17th century, Julius Caesar's self-serving, but illuminating *De Bello Gallico* has been carried on campaign by many a general seeking to emulate him.

Can the wars of the past illuminate those of the future? A succession of military historians have claimed to identify certain immutable principles of war, citing examples from ancient times up to the time they were writing. Yet the greatest military analyst, Karl von Clausewitz, deliberately focused on the wars of his own age. His analysis is a weighty tome, best known for his observation that war is 'the continuation of politics with the addition of other means.' Not every deduction he made has the universal application he sought, but no other author has approached his ability to distil the eternal truths that govern wars between nation states.

This history of war reveals how and why warfare has evolved. Boundaries between eras of history are always contentious, but by focusing on the differences between the periods under discussion, the authors highlight the features that distinguish successive phases. At the beginning of the 21st century, our world is dominated by rapid technological progress. It may come as a surprise to discover how, in the past, war could change radically despite weapons technology remaining static.

The first modern military historian, Hans Delbrück, discovered some grievous errors in the study of ancient and medieval history. Generations of historians had accepted the numbers quoted in ancient sources as gospel. Yet the army of Xerxes could not possibly have numbered the millions described by Herodotus. A quick glance at 19th century marching tables revealed that an army of over 2 million marching on Thermopylae would have its vanguard in Greece and the wagons still at Susa.

Delbrück's application of contemporary military thought to Greek and Roman history improved our perception of the ancient world. However, other attempts to view military history through modern eyes have had the opposite effect. Delbrück himself is one of many historians who took a jaundiced view of medieval armies. As Jan Honig argues in chapter 2, medieval soldiers should be judged on their own terms; they neither fought nor thought in Clausewitzian terms. Fortunately for them, they never encountered enemies that did. Other warriors would not be so lucky: the Aztecs and Incas were successful in their

own terms, but the Spanish fought by different rules. The Conquistadors may have reached the New World with new technology, but had neither the numbers nor the technological advantage to overcome whole empires. Yet they won.

The 'military revolution' of which the Conquistadors were the earliest visible export, endowed European powers with a strategic reach that would eventually encompass the globe. China developed walled cities at much the same time as the ancient Near East; until the middle ages, the empires of Asia fielded similar armies to those of the Classical Mediterranean world. Yet, their story is told briefly because, for reasons examined in chapters 3 and 4, they did not evolve beyond this. Since it was steam frigates that penetrated the Yangtse, rather than junks that entered the Thames, developments in Europe demand greater coverage.

Dramatic changes in Europe's warmaking capability were followed by political and social upheaval. Asked for his opinion of the French revolution, the late Deng Xiaoping quipped that 'it was too early to tell'. Certainly, the French revo-lution had far reaching military consequences: the 'nation in arms' would transform the world.

Today, political history has allegedly reached a hiatus. Liberal democracy is no longer challenged by the ideologies of Communism or Fascism. At the same time, the evolution of 'smart' weapons and 'push-button warfare' mark an end to the era of industrial warfare that began in the late 19th century and reached its apogee in the Second World War. Whether it signals an end to war itself is less certain. Civil wars in Rwanda and the Balkans during the 1990s expose the uncomfortable truth that superior firepower remains the ultimate guarantee of life and liberty, if not happiness. They also indicate that the barbarization of warfare associated with Nazi racism and Communist inhumanity has not ceased with the disappearance of these extremist ideologies.

Forecasts that war had become too expensive and would ruin modern economies were made on the eve of the First World War. Promises that international peace-keeping forces would impose a 'new world order' were broken in the 1930s as the League of Nations faltered. Post-war interventions by the United Nations have only a marginally greater success rate. It remains to be seen if the public opinion that triggered recent operations will support the long term commitments these entail: garrisoning turbulent regions and perhaps partitioning nation states.

At the dawn of the 21st century, many nation states are being undermined by regionalism and supranational organizations. The military implications are examined at the end of chapter 10. However, Mao Zedong's statement of the obvious, 'power grows from the barrel of a gun' is as true today as when he masterminded the Chinese revolution. In the short-lived republic of South Vietnam, US-supplied tanks were nick-named 'voting machines' because their presence on the streets of Saigon usually presaged a change of government. It remains the disagreeable truth that armed force is still the final arbiter of national and international politics. Even in today's 'global village' it seems prudent to walk quietly — and carry a big stick.

ABOVE: The uniforms actually worn on campaign by British soldiers in the 19th century often bore little relation to the red-coated finery of home service dress. Captain Atkinson's sketch of troops during the Umbala campaign in 1857 shows the men wearing 'Havelocks', lengths of cloth to protect the back of the neck from the sun, later associated with the French Foreign Legion. White tropical uniforms were soon dyed 'khaki', which eventually became the official colour of the combat uniform.

Chapter 1 The First Military Empires

RIGHT: The roots of organized warfare go back to hunting, and early weapons were based on hunting weapons and farm implements. Specialization can be identified by the second millennium BC with the introduction of defensive equipment (helmets and body protection) and purpose-built items from chariots to siege engines. These Assyrian archers wear jackets variously interpreted as cotton-padded or metal scales.

Warfare is as old as humanity. In prehistory it was mankind against the environment in a conflict of survival. It is possible, but undocumented, that the first warfare was between competing species of man; there is tentative archaeological evidence that Cro-Magnon and Neanderthal groups fought over resources. The first clash between modern man was probably over hunting territory, women, or candidates for ritual sacrifice. These early "battles" were primarily warrior versus warrior encounters, based on group hunting tactics.

Warfare had been conducted for millennia before the first recorded battle took place, at Megiddo (Armegeddon), during the late 15th century BC. The battle was fought by specialized military units fighting in formation, with a command structure to control them. How warfare evolved from that first hunter's clash into recognizable armies remains unknown. By the time of the Pharaohs, warfare had become an instrument for gaining power, not just resources. Better organized political structures used military force to conquer their neighbours.

The types of forces built by a society were a reflection of its economic structure. Nations that evolved in open regions tended to develop mobile units based on chariots and, later, horses. Their armies were extensions of an economy based on animal husbandry. They tended to emphasize missile weapons, in particular the bow. In the Scythian and Persian armies, mounted archers used an extension of herd control techniques to bury their enemies in a cloud of arrows.

Armies created by subsistence farming cultures tended to emphasize shock combat and short-range missile weapons, such as the javelin. Their weapons were extensions of farm implements. They developed dense formations of foot soldiers whose numbers and body armour enabled them to close with an enemy and defeat them in massed, hand-to-hand combat.

The truly outstanding armies of this early period, such as the Assyrians, Egyptians, and Macedonians, went one step beyond massing a lot of men on a battlefield. They were combined arms armies. These armies were organized to use the entire spectrum of specialized units at the right place at the right time. The asymmetrical use of tactical formations was the height of generalship. Every tactical formation had a vulnerability, and applying the correct combinations to exploit the chinks in an opponent's unit composition often brought decisive victory. The most famous generals of the ancient world were masters of combined arms warfare; Alexander the Great, Hannibal, and Scipio Africanus made their reputations in this way, setting examples for all the future generations of leaders and armies.

RIGHT: The formidable defences of Tiryns, typical of the fortresses built in Bronze Age Greece. Mycenean fortifications were improved c.1250 BC but all such citadels were sacked or abandoned by the end of the 12th century BC.

ABOVE: **A Roman wall painting commemorates the most famous ruse in military history: the Trojan Horse. Walled cities appeared in the second millennium BC but siege techniques took many centuries to evolve beyond a blockade calculated to starve them into surrender. It is unlikely Troy withstood a ten-year siege: it may have been an unusually prolonged campaign or the result of several campaigns over consecutive summers.**

BELOW: **Societies capable of building cities were able to field armies, some based on part-time citizen-soldiers, others evolving into a professional warrior caste. The earliest military campaigns in recorded history established new empires in the Near East, some complete with standing armies and the first fleets.**

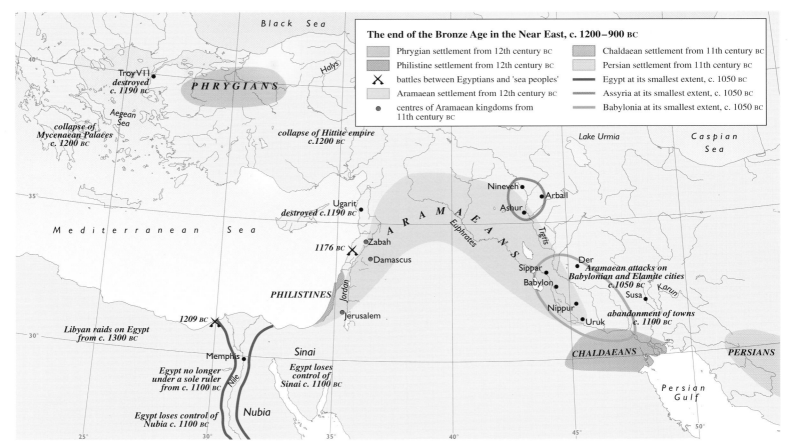

The end of the Bronze Age in the Near East, c. 1200–900 BC

Phrygian settlement from 12th century BC	Chaldaean settlement from 11th century BC
Philistine settlement from 12th century BC	Persian settlement from 11th century BC
✕ battles between Egyptians and 'sea peoples'	Egypt at its smallest extent, c. 1050 BC
Aramaean settlement from 12th century BC	Assyria at its smallest extent, c. 1050 BC
● centres of Aramaean kingdoms from 11th century BC	Babylonia at its smallest extent, c. 1050 BC

Black Sea

Troy VII
destroyed c. 1190 BC

Halys

PHRYGIANS

Aegean Sea

collapse of Mycenaean Palaces c. 1200 BC

collapse of Hittite empire c.1200 BC

Lake Urmia

Caspian Sea

Nineveh ● Arbail

A R A M A E A N S

Ugarit
destroyed c.1190 BC

Ashur

M e d i t e r r a n e a n   S e a

Euphrates

Tigris

1176 BC ✕ Zabah

● Damascus

Der
Aramaean attacks on Babylonian and Elamite cities c.1050 BC

Sippar

Babylon

Susa

Karun

PHILISTINES

Jordan

Nippur

abandonment of towns c. 1100 BC

● Jerusalem

● Uruk

1209 BC ✕

Libyan raids on Egypt from c. 1300 BC

Memphis ●

Sinai

Egypt loses control of Sinai c. 1100 BC

CHALDAEANS

PERSIANS

Egypt no longer under a sole ruler from c. 1100 BC

Nile

Nubia

Persian Gulf

Egypt loses control of Nubia c. 1100 BC

Egyptian and Hittite Warfare

The first military campaigns for which enough evidence survives took place in the Middle East. Egypt, Assyria, Hatti (the Hittites), and the Persians were the main protagonists. From the ascendancy of Sumer, in southern Mesopotamia, around 2500 BC, we have indications of warfare with large numbers of troops. Sumerian armies had both un-armoured skirmishers, wielding javelin-like spears and battle axes, as well as helmeted, close order infantry arranged in rows of heavy spears. The Sumerians also fielded a clunky forerunner to the war chariot. Pulled by what appears to be the Middle East version of today's donkey, these functioned as mobile platforms for archers.

Two major developments occurred around 1500 BC: the military use of the bow and the horse. The combination of both produced armies with excellent mobility (on open ground – and relatively long-range killing capabilities. These two inventions turned Middle Eastern armies away from the massed, armoured infantry that Greece was to develop, and towards a mobile, missile-based force. From 1200 BC, when it was introduced to Egypt by the mysterious "Sea Peoples", the chariot became the key weapon system, one that would remain in service for a thousand years.

The main users of chariots were the Egyptians who, in the 2nd millennium BC, under such pharaohs as Thutmoses III and Ramesses II, achieved their pinnacle of military power. The worth that the Egyptians held in the chariot is illustrated by the large numbers of representations of pharaohs driving chariots through piles of enemies. The chariot itself was a small platform, meant to hold an archer and his driver (the only one with any protection), and pulled by a two-horse team. While the art of bending wood had progressed enough to produce excellent wheels, the chariots were burdened with fixed wheels and an inadequate turning radius. Later on, the chariot would be countered by cavalry and even well-trained light infantry.

Egyptian power began to grow around 1600 BC, when she began to attempt to expand her borders to the north east. The first "known" battle – Megiddo _ occurred in the early 15th century BC, when Thutmoses III shattered an alliance of various opponents. His victory allowed Egypt to extend its borders to its greatest extent in history, as far north as Syria and as far east as the Euphrates. However, its campaigns into the north aroused the fear of another nation, centred in what is now Anatolia in Turkey: the Hittites.

The Hittite army had similar chariots to the Egyptians, but some were heavier, with a crew of three. Advancing into modern Syria, a Hittite army under King Suppalliliumus, marched to confront the Egyptian Pharaoh Akhenaten. Akhenaten died, and his daughter Ankhsenamun (widow of Tutenkhamun) bought off Suppalliliumus by her offer to marry one of his sons. It seemed like too good an offer to refuse, a Hittite prince a heartbeat from the pharaonic throne. It was. Two Egyptian ministers had the Hittite prince assassinated at the border, and the war was on again.

The eventual result was the battle of Kadesh in 1282 BC. Ramesses II was intent on stopping Hittite forays into western Syria and destroying the army of the

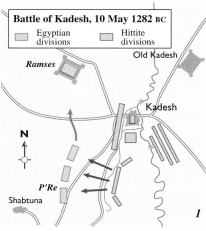

Battle of Kadesh, 10 May 1282 BC
Egyptian divisions Hittite divisions

1

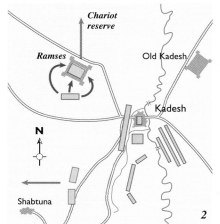

2

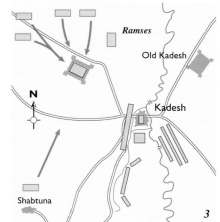

3

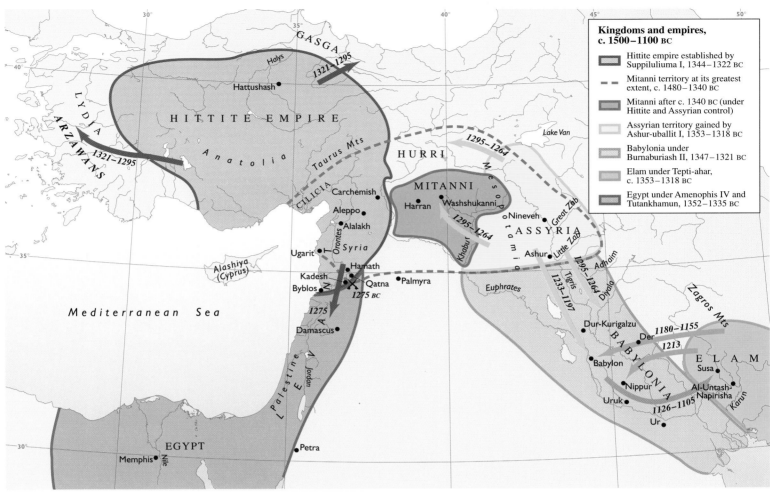

Kingdoms and empires, c. 1500–1100 BC

- Hittite empire established by Suppiluliuma I, 1344–1322 BC
- Mitanni territory at its greatest extent, c. 1480–1340 BC
- Mitanni after c. 1340 BC (under Hittite and Assyrian control)
- Assyrian territory gained by Ashur-uballit I, 1353–1318 BC
- Babylonia under Burnaburiash II, 1347–1321 BC
- Elam under Tepti-ahar, c. 1353–1318 BC
- Egypt under Amenophis IV and Tutankhamun, 1352–1335 BC

Hittite king, Muwatallish. Both armies relied on a chariot corps as the striking force, with waves of tightly packed foot soldiers following. Most infantry sported shields, spears and a curved slashing sword. A large number of bowmen were arrayed behind the spearmen. Ramesses's army comprised four major divisions: Amun, Re, Ptah and Set (the latter, using the coast road, did not participate), plus two groups of "auxiliaries", probably on loan from Levantine allies. Ramesses marched into central Syria, where the Hittite army waited hidden behind the city of Kadesh. As the Amun division started to

make camp on the west bank of the Orontes, the Hittite army splashed across the river and overran it. The chariots then turned south to face the oncoming division of Re which, still marching along the road, was hit from the flank by more Hittite chariots. A disaster was imminent. However, Ramesses and his personal chariot guard managed to regroup the Amun division, while the Ptah division arrived from the south and their allies from the west. The Hittite charioteers stopped in the Amun camp to loot, and Muwatallish never moved his infantry to the west side of the Orontes. With Ramesses at their head, the Egyptians smashed the Hittite chariots, forcing Muwatallish to take refuge inside Kadesh.

It is the first battle for which the outline of events is known, and it anticipates many features of subsequent actions, not the least of which was the way both commanders claimed victory. The result was a non-aggression treaty.

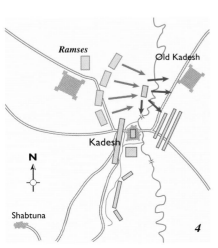

RIGHT: **Use of the chariot spread to Anatolia where the Hittites developed into a powerful state that ultimately destroyed the Mitannians. Lands were granted by the king in return for military service and a military aristocracy was established. Written treaties were made (and broken) and war was often preceded by a written ultimatum.**

4

Egyptian campaigns in Syria and Palestine

- northern limit of campaigns of Tuthmosis I (1507–1494 BC) and Tuthmosis III (1490–1436 BC)
- boundary between Egyptian and Mitannian zones of influence at the end of the reign of Amenophis II (1438–1412 BC)
- boundary between Egyptian and Hittite zones of influence at the end of the reign of Akhenaten, 1347 BC

Assyria and Persia

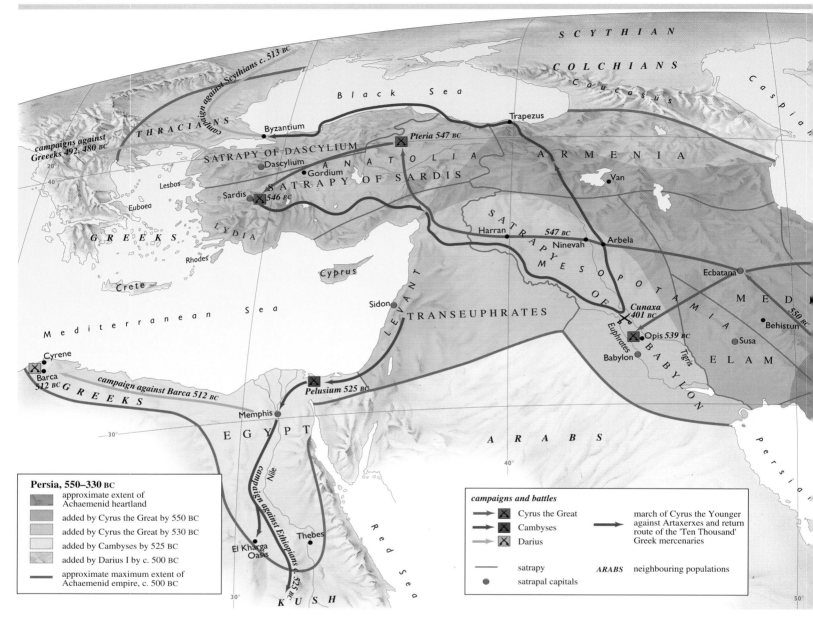

Persia, 550–330 BC

- approximate extent of Achaemenid heartland
- added by Cyrus the Great by 550 BC
- added by Cyrus the Great by 530 BC
- added by Cambyses by 525 BC
- added by Darius I by c. 500 BC
- approximate maximum extent of Achaemenid empire, c. 500 BC

campaigns and battles

- Cyrus the Great
- Cambyses
- Darius
- march of Cyrus the Younger against Artaxerxes and return route of the 'Ten Thousand' Greek mercenaries
- satrapy
- satrapal capitals
- *ARABS* neighbouring populations

In about 1200 BC new invaders descended on the eastern Mediterranean. The Hittite kingdom collapsed, the city states of Syria were wiped out, and the Egyptians lost all their lands east of and including the Sinai. The 'Sea People', as the Egyptians called them, were the forerunners of the Hellenistic society that would appear in another 500 years. They wore plumed helmets, wore armour, and fought with long, slashing, swords. Egypt barely survived the onslaught. The only power to be unaffected was the kingdom of Assyria in Mesopotamia.

Over the next 500 years Assyrian armies, led by such kings as Tiglath-pileser, Sargon, Shalmaneser, Sennacherb and Ashurbanipal conquered and ruled a great empire. Their campaigns prefigured those of the Mongols in terms of their treatment of losers; their ruthlessness was unparalleled in history to that time. Originally, the Assyrian army was made up of citizen/farmer volunteers. However, as the nation expanded, a professional standing army evolved, fed by involuntary

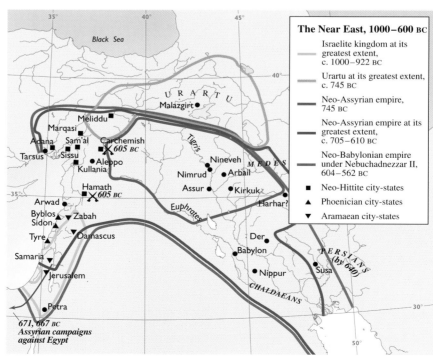

The Near East, 1000–600 BC

- Israelite kingdom at its greatest extent, c. 1000–922 BC
- Urartu at its greatest extent, c. 745 BC
- Neo-Assyrian empire, 745 BC
- Neo-Assyrian empire at its greatest extent, c. 705–610 BC
- Neo-Babylonian empire under Nebuchadnezzar II, 604–562 BC
- ■ Neo-Hittite city-states
- ▲ Phoenician city-states
- ▼ Aramaean city-states

671, 667 BC Assyrian campaigns against Egypt

LEFT: The later Assyrian Empire dominated the region with an army that included cavalry as well as chariots and improved siege techniques that enabled them to overrun the walled cities of Judea. A state policy of terror served to intimidate their enemies into surrender: cities that resisted were razed to the ground, their populations exterminated.

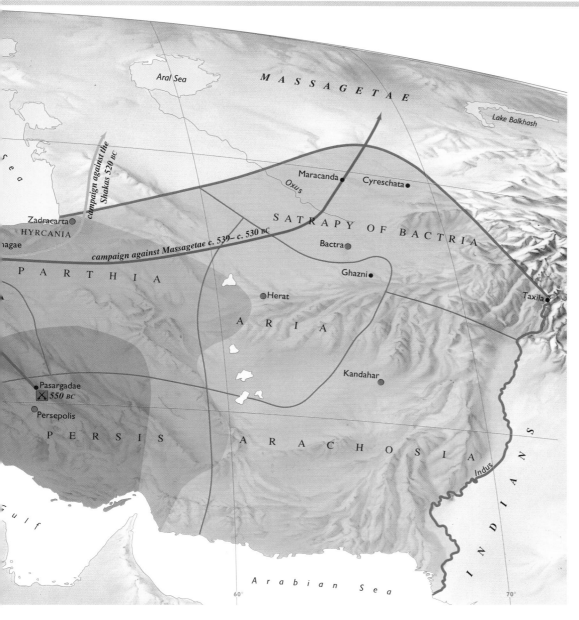

foot. The area of Persian origin was mountainous, where horses were virtually unknown. But the Persians had the ability to adopt and adapt. The elite force in their army was not the chariot wing but "The Immortals", the King's personal guard of 10,000 infantry, so-named because the division was always kept up to strength. The Immortals, however, were not the heavy infantry emerging in Greece, but more moderately-armoured spear and bow with better uniforms.

Persian foot soldiers expanded the kingdom to the west, but when the Persians turned east to conquer the Lydians, the cavalry of the latter dealt them a severe lesson. Cyrus was able to overcome the Lydian cavalry only through use of his camels; the Lydian horses hated camels on sight and did their best to get out of their way. After absorbing the lessons of the Lydian campaign, the Persians increased their own cavalry, often combining it with chariots. Infantry went from atop the military hierarchy to mercenary status, especially as the spread of the kingdom gave Persia an almost endless source of manpower.

By the time King Darius turned his attention to Europe, the Persian army consisted of cavalry and chariots with mercenary and levied light infantry providing a continual shower of arrows in support. The Persian cavalry was the best of its time, but the light infantry was levied from usually reluctant allies. In the 5th century BC the Ionian city states revolted against their Persian overlords, supported by several cities on mainland Greece. The result was a confrontation between the Greek citizen armies of hoplite farmers, and Persia, with its light cavalry and foot. Within 175 years, the Greeks ruled the western world and Persia had ceased to exist.

ABOVE: Cyrus the Great carved out an empire that continued to expand under his successors. The Persians adapted from an infantry-based army to an all-arms force in which heavy cavalry was combined with professional bow- and spear-armed foot soldiers. Having conquered the Near East, the Persians turned to the Greek city states of the eastern Aegean.

recruits from the conquered peoples. The Assyrians controlled almost the entire Middle East by the 7th century BC, from Egypt to the Taurus mountains, from Sidon and Tyre to the capital of the Medes, Susa, just north of the Persian Gulf.

Assyria's armies relied upon speed and missile fire. While their chariots and small cavalry contingents were their main striking weapons, they still used infantry as a second wave of assault. The majority of the army consisted of bow or spear-armed foot. Both wore helmets and chest armour, with most of their protection coming from huge shields, taller than the soldiers, held by shield-bearers. Archaeological evidence shows late Assyrian infantry carrying smaller, circular shields and sporting heavier armour.

At the battle of Qarqar, in present-day southern Syria, an Assyrian army under Hadadezer, governor of Damascus, augmented by contingents from Hamath, Israel, Syria, Palestine, and even some Arab tribesmen (on camels) numbered over 60,000 infantry, 1,200 horse, and 4,000 chariots. This is a large number, but

most scholars take it as reliable, indicative of the great strength the Assyrians could muster. Assyria reached its zenith in the beginning of the 7th century BC, before it imploded, with no little help from the powers it had previously trampled, plus new powers from the east: Babylon and the Medes. The fall of Nineveh, in 612 BC, signalled the death knell for this remarkable society. The disintegration of Assyria left the field open for four smaller powers to fight over the remains: Babylon, which had some success under Nebuchadnezzer; Egypt, which was in decline; and two eastern mini-powers, Lydia and Media.

The power of the Median kings was usurped from within by the Persian faction, led by the man who would later be known as Cyrus the Great. Cyrus seized the throne in 550 BC, and conquered Babylon and Lydia; Egypt would have to wait a few years. Within a decade or so, Persia was the superpower of the Middle East, the Persian kingdom one of the largest in the known world. Persian tactics were originally missile-oriented and on

RIGHT: King Ashurbanipal (c.668-c.626) extended the Assyrian Empire to cover most of the modern Middle East and established a splendid capital at Nineveh. The Assyrian army evolved from warrior-farmers into a fulltime, professional force, capable of legendary cruelty.

The Greek and Persian Wars

ABOVE: The Athenian statesman Themistocles inspired the creation of fleet powerful enough to challenge the Persians and their allies at sea. While King Leonidas made his epic stand at Thermopylae, a largely Athenian navy held off the Persian fleet at Artemisium. Themistocles held the Greek coalition together long enough to destroy the Persian fleet at Salamis

RIGHT: The relief on this sarcophagus commemorates the scramble for the ships that concluded the Battle of Marathon. Defeated by the unexpected Greek charge, the Persian army re-embarked in considerable disorder, hotly pursued by the Greeks. The dramatist Aeschylus fought in the battle; his brother was killed trying to board one of the beached Persian transports.

In Greece, only Sparta fielded what would be called a standing, professional army. The other city states relied on a citizen call-up. Wars between these states were between militia armies intent on protecting their farmland. Forces were usually less than 10,000 men. The Greek military system relied on the hoplite, an armoured infantryman so named for his shield, the *hoplon*. Soldiers were protected from head to shins by bronze armour, stronger than the penetrating power of most missile and hand weapons. Cavalry, unsuited to the rocky terrain, was usually limited to small detachments used to guard the flanks. Light infantry, such as archers, were rare and were little more than armed camp followers.

A hoplite battle consisted of two opposing lines of similarly armed infantry rushing at each other in the *ephodos*, the charge, with one side or the other yielding under the stabbing spears and shield-pushing of the opponent. Since the clash of the hoplites was the key tactical moment of the battle, reserves, which took strength away from the charge, were counter-productive. The commanding general lined up all of his men, intermixed any archers or slingers he did have, divided his few cavalrymen between his two flanks, and then led them, personally, into battle.

The Persian military was optimized for the open spaces of Southwest Asia, where speed and manoeuvrability won battles. The Persian Army consisted of foot archers and mounted javelin-armed cavalry with the occasional chariot. The strongest arm of the Persian war machine was its cavalry, which included many varieties, from swift-riding archers to armoured lancers. Given its training and experience, Persian cavalry was far superior to that of the Greeks, but Persian infantry was ill-equipped to stand toe-to-toe with hoplites.

The Persian Empire continued to expand under Darius I, conquering the Greek city state colonies in Anatolia (modern day western Turkey). In 500 BC these cities rose in revolt, appealing to their mother cities in Greece to give them aid. Athens and Eretria sent a small naval contingent. Darius' navy defeated the Greek squadrons at the Battle of Lade (494 BC) and his army put several of the cities to the torch.

Darius despatched an expeditionary force to punish Athens and Eretria. His forces were said to be several hundred thousand strong, a ludicrous claim yet one still sometimes repeated. Recent historical opinion credits the Persians with an army little stronger than the Greeks, perhaps 20,000 including the ships' rowers, with some 7,000 combat troops including about 1,000 cavalry. The Persian problem was not numerical inferiority but keeping its army supplied, which is why the Persian army travelled with a huge escort of galleys on its seaward flank as it marched into Thrace, towards Greece.

The Persian forces captured Eretria, then shipped their army to a beach on the Marathon plain, 19 miles from Athens, near a convenient road that lead to the city. Forewarned, the Athenian army arrived just after the Persians had debarked and occupied a narrow valley, Vrana, that flanked the Persian route of advance to the city. The valley also offered the Athenians protection against the Persian cavalry. Since the valley was wider than their battle line, they used wooden abatis to extend their defensive positions on each side. If the Persians tried to march overland toward Athens, the Athenians would fall on their flank. If the Persians tried to re-embark and advance by sea, the Athenians could attack them at their most vulnerable. The Persians were left with two options: fight,

Greece and the Persian wars, 490–479 BC

- Persian empire, 497 BC
- Ionian territory reconquered by Persia 497–494 BC
- Persian reconquests under Mardonius 492 BC
- neutral and pro-Persian states
- Greek allies
- → route of Mardonius's army, 492 BC
- → Mardonius's fleet, 492 BC
- --- route of expedition led by Datis and Artaphernes, 490 BC
- → route of Xerxes's army, 480 BC
- --- route of Xerxes's fleet, 480 BC
- X Persian victory
- X Greek victory
- X indecisive battle

LEFT: In his account of the invasion, Herodotus grossly inflated the size of the Persian army, which he also credited with greater professionalism than the citizen-soldiers of the city-states. The Spartans were the only 'regular' troops in the Greek alliance. In fact, it is unlikely that the Persians enjoyed a significant numerical advantage. Greek civilization was saved by inventive tactics at Marathon and by the Athenian naval construction programme that ended Persian maritime supremacy.

or wait for the city to be betrayed to them by traitors in their pay.

Herodotus says the Greeks charged swiftly, limiting the effect of Persian archery. The missile volleys of the Persian archers should have defeated the hoplites, if the hoplites stood and received them. But the Athenians covered the gap too quickly for the Persians to loose many volleys, and hoplite armour was resistant enough to keep the battle line cohesive. The Persian centre, high quality Persian infantry regulars who were probably better armoured than the majority, defeated the thinned out Athenian centre. However the Athenians triumphed on both wings, re-formed, and destroyed the Persian centre.

The victorious Athenians only managed to capture seven ships; a rearguard action by the Persian cavalry covered their escape. The Persian cavalry may not even have been present at the battle's beginning.

This theory rests on the fact that the opposing armies had occupied their positions for three days, with resultant depletion of supplies for the Persians. It is possible that the Greek attack began as a consequence of the Persian cavalry having left to forage, only to return after the battle was almost over.

Internal conflict delayed the Persian riposte until 480 BC when a new King of Kings, Xerxes, led a new expedition to avenge Marathon. Xerxes chose to take a large army, probably numbering around 40-50,000 men, overland across the Dardanelles. Again, a large naval force protected its sea line of communication.

Most Greek cities in the north surrendered without a fight. In the south, a Hellenic league, with Sparta as its leader, sent a land and naval force to buy time to prepare fortifications on the isthmus. At Thermopylae 300 Spartans held off the entire Persian army for several days and an

inconclusive naval battle took place off Artemisium. The Spartan delaying force, under their king, Leonidas, was wiped out to the last man; the galley fleet withdrew when its land flank was uncovered.

The Persians marched into a poorly defended Athens, which they sacked. But their fleet was lured into closed waters near the island of Salamis and destroyed by the Athenian and Corinthian navies. With its logistic support destroyed, the majority of the Persian army withdrew to Asia while some 20-25,000 men remained behind near Plataea. In 479 BC a Hellenic army representing most of Southern Greece defeated the Persians in a confused battle where the superior Greek hand-to-hand fighting skills won the day. The Persian rout was then completed by their defeat at Mycale. With the Persians out of Europe the Spartans returned home, while an appeal from the Ionian Greeks to Athens created the Delian League.

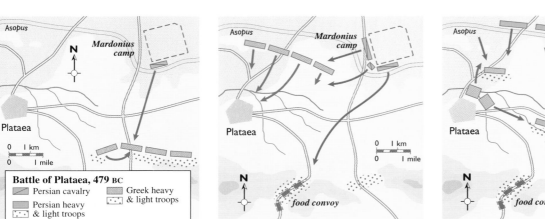

Battle of Plataea, 479 BC
- Persian cavalry
- Persian heavy & light troops
- Greek heavy & light troops

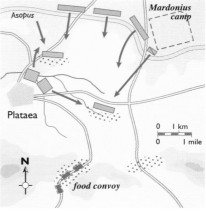

LEFT: The Persian and Greek armies were equally matched at Plataea, indeed, the Greeks may well have enjoyed numerical superiority. The armies remained in close proximity for about two weeks, each trying to tempt the other to attack at a disadvantage or force the enemy to retreat through lack of supplies. A Persian attempt to cut off the Greek water supply brought on the decisive clash, but their commander perished in the attack and the Persian army was routed.

The Peloponnesian War

RIGHT: Mutual suspicion between the Spartan and Athenian alliances led to war in 431 BC, but neither side could score a decisive victory until Athens lost the bulk of her navy in an ambitious operation against Syracuse. Thucydides' contemporary account of the war presents this defeat as poetic justice: the previous year, the Athenian assembly ordered the citizens of Melos to be massacred after their surrender.

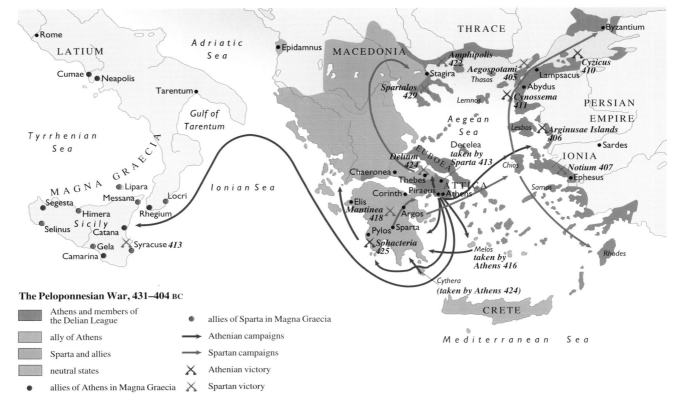

The Peloponnesian War, 431–404 BC

▨ Athens and members of the Delian League	● allies of Sparta in Magna Graecia
▫ ally of Athens	→ Athenian campaigns
▫ Sparta and allies	→ Spartan campaigns
▫ neutral states	✕ Athenian victory
● allies of Athens in Magna Graecia	✕ Spartan victory

BELOW: On their third attempt, the Syracusan army extended a defensive wall past the Athenian siege lines, preventing the total blockade of the city. Spartan general Gylippus then trapped the Athenian fleet within the great harbour and the besiegers found themselves cut off. The surrender and enslavement of the expeditionary force was a catastrophe for Athens and her fleet never recovered its qualitative advantage.

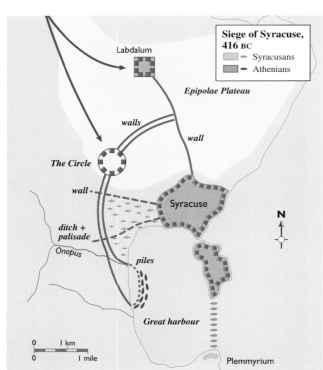

Siege of Syracuse, 416 BC

▫ Syracusans
▨ Athenians

The war between the Peloponnesian League, led by Sparta, and the Delian League, led by Athens, pitted a land power against a sea power. The asymmetric nature of the conflict helped prolong hostilities for 25 years. Since the end of the Persian Wars, the Delian League had evolved into the Athenian Empire. Athens collected tribute from its allies who were bound to her by treaty. Athens maintained a fleet of 300 triremes, the professional-ism of Athenian steersmen and rowers enabling the fleet to develop the trireme ram into the primary weapon system of the ship. This allowed Athens to win the majority of its battles, even when outnumbered. The Peloponnesian League's naval forces relied on boarding, which gave their heavier ships an advantage in closed waters, but nearly always led to defeat in open waters. They were outnumbered, with some 90 triremes from Corinth and another 60 provided by the other allies.

The Peloponnesian League could muster some 30-35,000 hoplites, more than twice as many as Athens. At its core was the Spartan army, the only profession-al army in Greece, but Sparta depended on the helot (serf) population to sustain it. This serf labour pool required surveillance by the *Krypteia* (secret police) and pre-vented Sparta from deploying more than two thirds of its strength on campaigns for fear of a helot revolt.

Athens and its port, Piraeus, were enclosed by fortifications, the Long Walls. Assault techniques in this period were incapable of carrying fortifications by force and Athens could not be starved into submission while its fleet controlled the Aegean. The first phase of the war (The Archidamian War) saw the Spartan army invade Attica every year, while the Corinthian navy attempted to break out of the Gulf of Corinth. The Athenian admiral, Phormio, operating from Naupactus, defeated a succession of Corinthian sorties and prevented Corinth from maintaining its economic links to colonies in Italy. Athens established a base at Pylos on the western coast of the Peloponnesus. Sparta landed a small army on an adjacent island (Sphacteria), but Athenian naval forces isolated them. After a series of failed nego-tiations, Athenian naval forces were able to project superior Athenian land forces onto the island, destroying the majority of the Spartan force and capturing the survivors.

Negotiations followed, culminating in the Peace of Nicias in 421 BC, but it was no more than an armistice. Many of Sparta's allies became disaffected and formed a new league with Argos. At the Battle of Mantinea (418 BC), Sparta won the one and only large hoplite battle of the Peloponnesian War when it defeated an Argive-led army which included an Athenian contingent. This victory, plus the Athenian invasion of Sicily, prompted a renewal of hostilities.

For reasons that can only be speculated, Athens launched a pre-emptive attack on Syracuse, a potential Spartan ally. The Syracusan navy (potentially 80+ triremes), if combined with extant Peloponnesian naval forces, could have contested Athenian naval superiority. However, divided and incompetent command led the Athenians to lose their main advantage: their fleet. The fact that the Athenians could launch the original expedition and subsequently reinforce it without hin-drance from the Peloponnesian league tes-tifies to their control over the western sea routes to Sicily. But the loss of 160 Athenian and 56 allied triremes in the con-fined waters of Syracuse harbour equal-ized the naval forces available to both sides for the first time in fifty years.

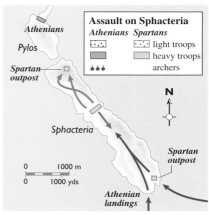

Assault on Sphacteria

Athenians	Spartans	
⠿	⠿	light troops
▨	▨	heavy troops
♦♦♦		archers

Athenians

Pylos

Spartan outpost

Sphacteria

N

| 0 | 1000 m |
| 0 | 1000 yds |

Spartan outpost

Athenian landings

LEFT: The Battle of Sphacteria was a small scale Athenian victory: the Spartans had only 440 hoplites on the island. Yet their defeat by a mixed force of Athenian hoplites and skirmishers (peltasts) demonstrated that even the best hoplites could be beaten by a combination of shock action and missile fire. The surrender of 292 Spartan soldiers was a political disaster.

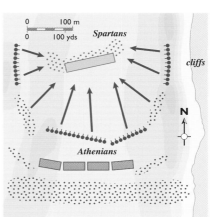

| 0 | 100 m |
| 0 | 100 yds |

Spartans

cliffs

N

Athenians

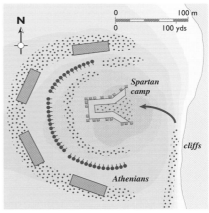

N

| 0 | 100 m |
| 0 | 100 yds |

Spartan camp

cliffs

Athenians

Sparta was able to establish sea contact with Persia and Syracuse. Based on a Syracusan expeditionary force and Persian gold, Sparta was able to establish a series of fleets in Western Asia Minor that contested Athens' sea lines of communication across the Aegean and the Hellespont. Although Athens had lost naval superiority and had suffered a series of political upheavals at home, its superior tactical prowess enabled the navy to win a series of naval battles over an eight-year period. Yet these were not enough; Athenian allies rebelled and ceased paying tribute, further weakening the Athenian navy. In 405 BC the Athenian fleet, maintaining its eastern sea lanes in the Hellespont, was destroyed while beached and Athens surrendered a year later when faced with imminent starvation.

LEFT: The great Athenian statesman Pericles (c.495-429 BC) ordered the construction of the 'long walls' between Athens and Piraeus. The Spartan army was unable to storm the defences and the superior Athenian navy kept the city supplied by sea. This lopsided and protracted war continued until the Athenians's catastrophic defeat in Sicily.

Alexander the Great

RIGHT: At the Battle of the Issus in 333 BC, the Persians slipped past the Macedonian invaders to occupy a strong position astride Alexander's lines of communication. However, Alexander attacked and broke through the Persian army at the head of his cavalry. He headed for Darius, who fled the field as his army disintegrated.

BELOW: The meteoric career of Alexander brought the Macedonian army to the limits of the known world. In ten years of unceasing warfare, he led his men to victory over the Persian army, the cities of Phoenicia, mountain tribes and Scythian horsemen. That his empire would not outlive him was evident before his death: false news of his demise triggered several revolts prior to his fatal sickness at Baghdad.

Wars between the Greek city states continued after the Peloponnesian war until the northern state of Macedon overwhelmed a Theban-led coalition at the battle of Chaeronea in 338 BC. The Macedonian king, Philip II, had won a decisive advantage by combining his infantry with missile-armed skirmishers and a cavalry force trained for shock action. Philip modified the phalanx, deepening the formation and arming the men with longer spears, and changed its tactics too. In hoplite battles the clash of the infantry was the decisive moment, but the Macedonian phalanx did not engage until the enemy army's wings had been attacked by Philip's cavalry, the Companions. Armed with lances and wearing armour, the Companions charged home instead of relying on archery like Persian cavalry.

Philip planned to invade Persia, but was assassinated in 336 BC. Two years later, his son Alexander III led the Macedonian army into Asia, on a one-way journey that won him the reputation of the greatest field commander of the Ancient world. He shattered a Persian army led by local satraps in western Asia Minor, personally leading a headlong cavalry charge that nearly cost him his life. Ironically, the most serious opposition at the battle of the Granicus came from Greek mercenary hoplites. Alexander had them all killed.

Alexander's communications with Macedon were vulnerable to the Persian fleet, which was also capable of supporting revolts within Greece. His own navy was inferior, so he led the army against the coastal cities of the eastern Mediterranean.

King Darius III of Persia arrived in 333 BC, outmanoeuvring Alexander to occupy a strong defensive position astride his lines of communication. The Persian flanks were protected by the sea on one side and mountains on the other, and the river Pinarus flowed across their front. However, Alexander forded the river upstream and led his cavalry in another charge that broke into the rear of the Persian army, while his phalanx made a frontal attack that cost it dearly. The

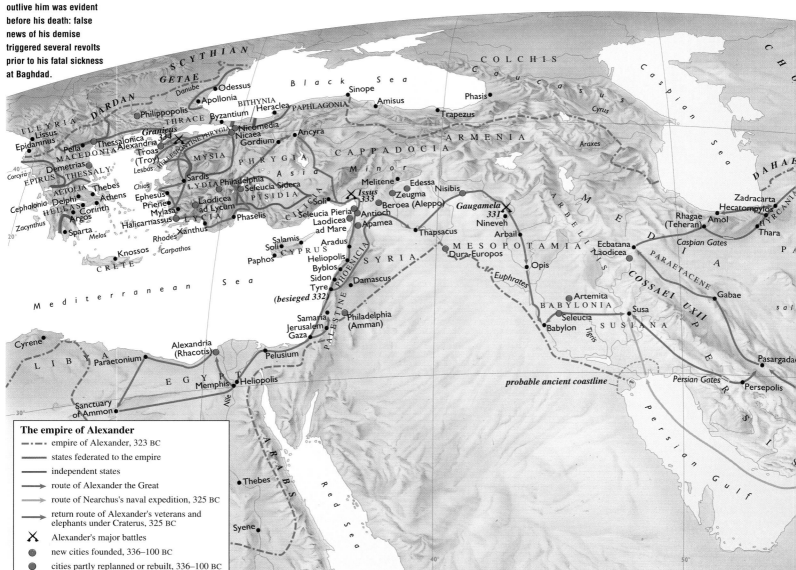

The empire of Alexander

- –·–·– empire of Alexander, 323 BC
- ——— states federated to the empire
- ——— independent states
- ——▶ route of Alexander the Great
- ——▷ route of Nearchus's naval expedition, 325 BC
- ——▶ return route of Alexander's veterans and elephants under Craterus, 325 BC
- ✕ Alexander's major battles
- ● new cities founded, 336–100 BC
- ● cities partly replanned or rebuilt, 336–100 BC

Macedonian cavalry struck out for Darius himself, who fled the field, and the Persian army disintegrated.

Darius abandoned his family and his treasury. Alexander was pleased to look after them both. As he advanced down the Mediterranean coast, most cities surrendered. Tyre resisted but fell after a seven-month siege that revealed there was more to Alexander's military techniques than leading cavalry charges. The Macedonian mastery of siegecraft was demonstrated again at Gaza, which fell in two months. The Persian Empire began to fracture. Its provinces included a wide variety of races, subject peoples with no particular allegiance to the Persian Achaemenid dynasty. Egypt's cities surrendered to Alexander and he founded the last dynasty of pharaohs, which ended with Cleopatra VII.

In 331 BC Alexander marched into the heartland of Asia for a final confrontation with Darius. The Persian king had raised and equipped another army. Many of his cavalrymen were armoured and equipped with lances. There was an attempt to train more infantry to fight like hoplites, but the army still contained a high proportion of missile-armed skirmishers, mounted and on foot. Viciously armed chariots and a dozen war elephants added an exotic touch.

At the battle of Arbela (or Gaugamela) on 1 October 331 BC, Alexander led the Companion cavalry in a charge aimed directly at Darius and the Persian centre. Historians have continued to credit Darius with the unfeasible quantities of soldiers conjured up by ancient chroniclers — figures of 200,000 men are quoted in all seriousness. Whether the Persian battle line extended past either flank of Alexander's army because Darius had more troops, or his army was simply less concentrated, will never be known. What is recorded is that Alexander led his Companions directly against Darius and the Persian centre, while the phalanx advanced in echelon; the full weight of the Macedonian attack struck the Persian left and centre while the Persian right wing was checked by light cavalry. Darius escaped the swords of the Companions but not those of his own nobles; he fled the field, pursued for some months by Alexander until assassinated by Bessus, the satrap of Bactria.

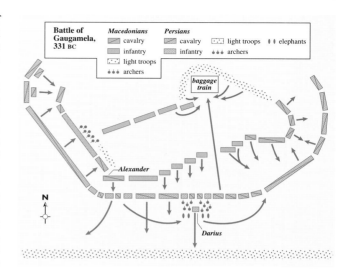

Alexander devoted the next ten years to conquering the farthest reaches of the Persian Empire. His hardest moments occurred in modern day Afghanistan where he fought off a Scythian invasion and quelled a local rising in a savage two-year campaign. Fixed point defences combined with flying columns of 'search and destroy' guerrilla bands anticipate much later counter-insurgency wars. He invaded north west India where he was resisted by King Porus and an army based on war elephants and bow-armed infantry. At the battle of the Hydaspes river (326 BC), Indian elephants faced off the Macedonian cavalry on the right flank, but Alexander broke around Porus's left to rout the Indian forces from the rear; all this while the phalanx was being chewed up by elephants, a performance watched closely by Alexander's generals, soon to become enthusiastic users of war elephants themselves.

Alexander's army mutinied within two months of this, his final victory. After more than ten years on campaign, it turned for home, sustaining heavy losses during a nightmare march across the Gedrosian desert (southern Iran). Alexander had conquered most of the classical world. He intended to attack the rest, projecting invasions of Carthage and Italy too, but in 321 BC Alexander died of fever, or possibly poison. He was 33-years old.

ABOVE: **Darius fielded the most exotic military units his empire could provide at the Battle of Gaugamela: scythed chariots, war elephants and camel-mounted archers. His main body consisted of cavalry supported by large numbers of infantry skirmishers, but the Macedonian cavalry triumphed again and Darius fled for a second time.**

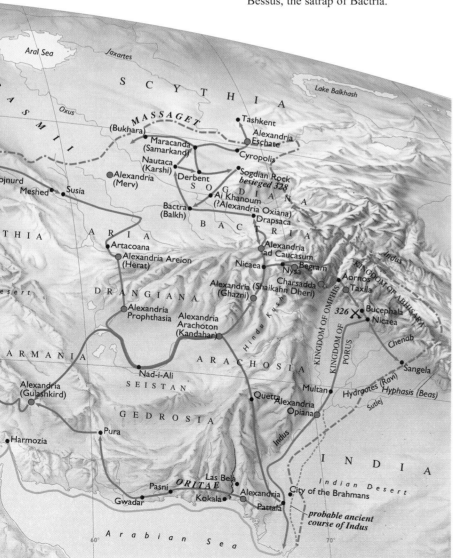

LEFT: **A military genius with insatiable appetites, Alexander was planning to conquer the western Mediterranean when he died, possibly assassinated by members of his own court. He had become an oriental despot, executing several of his long-serving officers including Parmenio, commander of his Companions.**

The Successor Wars

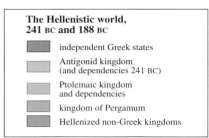

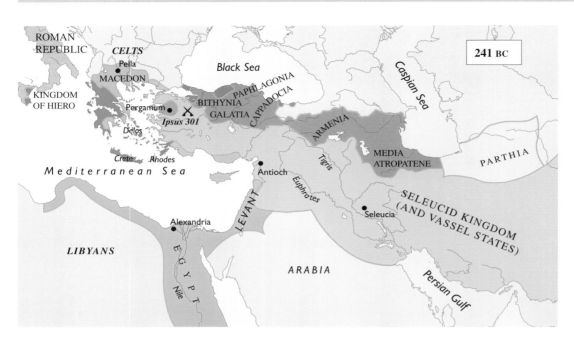

The Hellenistic world,
241 BC and 188 BC

	independent Greek states
	Antigonid kingdom (and dependencies 241 BC)
	Ptolemaic kingdom and dependencies
	kingdom of Pergamum
	Hellenized non-Greek kingdoms

ABOVE: Antigonus 'one eye' was killed at the battle of Ipsus in 301 BC, ending the most serious attempt by one of Alexander's generals to control the entire empire. By the time the last of the original 'successors' was killed in 280, Alexander's empire had fractured into many states. The most powerful were based on Egypt, the old Persian heartland and Macedonia itself.

Alexander's sudden death precipitated a series of wars that only ended with the arrival of Roman power in the region. Alexander's generals (the *Diadochoi*, or Successors) fought to inherit if not his throne then at least an empire of their own.

Nearly a dozen of his former commanders made a bid for power. All perished. By the assassination of Seleucus, the last of Alexander's officers, in 280 BC, three main successor states emerged: Macedon, Egypt, and the Seleucid kingdom that stretched from the eastern shores of the Mediterranean to Baghdad. Numerous independent city states and smaller kingdoms established themselves in the process.

The major armies fought in the Macedonian style, with some regional variations. The phalanx formation was deepened. Elephants were employed, with greater enthusiasm than tactical success; likewise scythed-wheeled chariots. The many battles of this era were between combined arms armies fighting on even terms. Battles were not determined by tactical superiority or better weaponry but by numbers, leadership, luck – and not infrequently treachery.

Over a century after Alexander's death, the Egypt of the Ptolemys and the Seleucids in the Middle East/Syria were at war over the ports and cities that were part of Coele-Syria, the modern-day Mediterranean Middle East. In 218 BC, fresh from suppressing a series of eastern rebellions, the Seleucid kingdom's young ruler, Antiochus III, invaded Coele-Syria and marched against Egypt. Polybius credits Ptolemy with 70,000 infantry, of which almost 50,000 were supposed to be heavy infantry phalangites. A more reasonable number is a total force of some 55,000 men, with 25,000 phalangites. Ptolemy force-marched up the coast to assume an excellent defensive position just south of the ancient city of Raphia (near modern-day Sabot). He deployed on flat ground between a series of shifting dunes and sand ridges that would prevent his army being outflanked, negating the effect of Antiochus' excellent cavalry and numerical superiority in elephants.

Antiochus moved his army into position opposite the Egyptian array, where, in mid-spring 217 BC, they stood eyeball to eyeball for almost a week, each trying to figure out how to counter-balance the other's deployment. Both armies had about a 10:1 ratio of infantry to cavalry, a major change from the days of Alexander, but, while Antiochus had some 12,000 more foot soldiers, most were skimishers of dubious quality. The Egyptian phalanx, reinforced by 8,000 Greek-Macedonian mercenaries, outnumbered the Seleucid phalanx by 5,000 men. According to Polybius, the phalangite superiority enabled Ptolemy to use double-depth formation for his heavy infantry, turning them into virtual squares. This is possible, but Ptolemy still had to maintain enough frontage to keep his army

RIGHT: The war elephants of the Indian ruler Porus made an enormous impression on the Macedonians. Alexander's successors imported war elephants for their own armies, using them as a screen to hold off enemy cavalry or to break up enemy infantry formations.

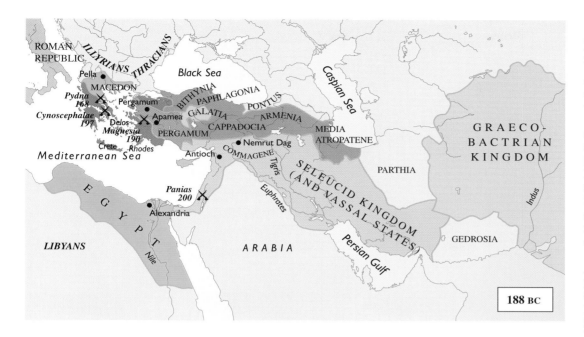

188 BC

Selucid horsemen, who cut into the scattering Egyptian cavalry and left wing infantry. By the time Antiochus arrived with his bodyguard to fight Ptolemy himself, almost the entire Egyptian left wing was in flight. Assuming that Ptolemy was with them, Antiochus took off in hot pursuit.

Meanwhile, the Egyptian right wing swung into action. Thessalian heavy cavalry and Gallic/Thracian infantry struck the Seleucid cavalry in the flank while the Ptolemaic Greek mercenary heavy infantry slammed into Antiochus' Arab and eastern light infantry. The Seleucid left collapsed. (What, if anything, the elephants on this flank did remains unknown.) Ptolemy ordered forward his phalanx.

None of this would have occurred had Antiochus and his victorious cavalry been present to attack the Egyptian infantry from the rear. But they were chasing the broken Egyptian left. By the time Antiochus realized what was happening, it was too late. His phalanx had no protection on its right, and marauding Egyptian cavalry on its left. To make morale worse, the line of heavy infantry approaching them was visibly lead by king Ptolemy, while the Seleucid leader was nowhere in sight. The Egyptian phalanx made short work of the Seleucid phalanx. Antiochus returned to the battlefield to find his whole army in flight.

From a military point of view Raphia shows all the elements of the Macedonian system in action. Politically, it left Palestine in Egyptian hands while Antiochus devoted his considerable energy to further campaigns in Bactria, Arabia and as far east as the Punjab.

ABOVE: Macedonian intrigues with the Carthaginians during the Second Punic War were not forgotten in Rome which declared war on Philip V in 200 BC. The Macedonians were defeated in 197 and again in 168. Between the Macedonian wars, Rome intervened in the eastern Aegean where smaller states allied with her against Antiochus III, ruler of the Seleucid empire. Antiochus was defeated at Magnesia in 190, the success of cavalry under his own command failing to stop the legions demolishing his phalanx.

anchored against the dunes. Deepening his phalanx would have shortened his line, exposing his army to flank attacks by the superior Seleucid cavalry.

Antiochus' plan, it appears, was to kill Ptolemy. He deployed his army in a line opposite the Egyptians with each individual group deployed to counter-balance the opposing, similar group. The only exception was to place his Royal Squadron of cavalry at an angle, somewhat forward of his right flank. This was done to allow it to sweep out and around the Egyptian left-wing cavalry and strike at Ptolemy, parading up and down the line with his martial

sister, Arsinoe. Each army's line stretched approximately 3.5 miles.

Antiochus' plan went too well. The vaunted Seleucid elephant corps comprised 102 Indian elephants, split between both flanks, as opposed to the 73 North Africans of Ptolemy, similarly divided. The Indians were bigger than their African counterparts, and more aggressive. Their size made it difficult for the Africans' riders to reach the Indians' riders with their spears and javelins. The Indian elephants of Antiochus' right wing thundered across the intervening ground and routed their opponents. The Indians were followed by

RIGHT: Ptolemy II (285-246 BC), consolidator of the dynasty founded by Alexander's general, Ptolemy Soter. The dynasty survived until Ptolemy XIV was murdered by his sister and intended wife, Cleopatra. Her liaison with Mark Anthony linked Egypt to the losing faction in a Roman civil war.

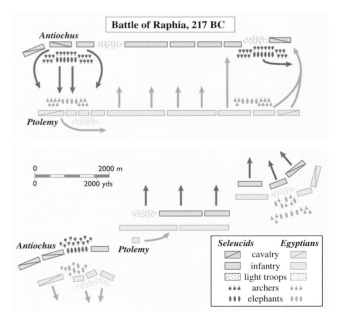

ABOVE: The Battle of Raphia involved two Macedonian-style armies, both supported by war elephants. Antiochus dispensed with the subtleties of combined arms tactics and charged straight for Ptolemy, who wisely took cover behind his infantry. Antiochus pursued the Egyptian left wing off the field while the Egyptians did the same to his left wing. Meanwhile Ptolemy led his phalanx forward to crush his enemy's centre before Antiochus returned.

The Punic Wars

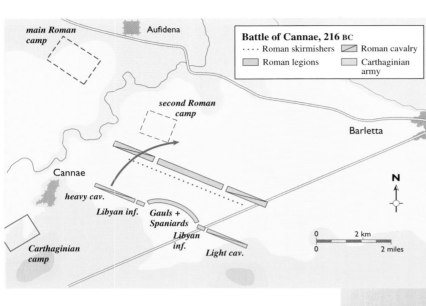

Battle of Cannae, 216 BC
···· Roman skirmishers   ▨ Roman cavalry
▧ Roman legions   ▨ Carthaginian army

main Roman camp

Aufidena

second Roman camp

Barletta

Cannae

heavy cav.

Libyan inf.

Gauls + Spaniards

Libyan inf.

Light cav.

Carthaginian camp

N

0   2 km

0   2 miles

ABOVE: Although outnumbered, Hannibal annihilated the Roman army at Cannae by enveloping the legions with his superior cavalry. The legions proved little more flexible than the monolithic phalanxes of the Successors. Once surrounded, they were unable to manoeuvre and were overwhelmed. However, this most decisive of military victories failed to produce a political breakthrough: Rome did not give up and even recruited freed slaves into new legions.

TOP RIGHT: Scipio Africanus (237-183 BC) was one of the greatest Roman generals. In the Second Punic War he took the war to the enemy in a brilliant campaign in Spain, ultimately invading Africa to defeat Hannibal himself in 202. His adopted grandson razed Carthage to the ground in 146 BC.

By the 4th century BC, Rome had extended its power to southern Italy. Rome, Carthage and the Macedonian successor state of Epirus vied for control of Sicily. Epirus fought Rome from 281-272 BC when King Pyrrhus died; he defeated Rome's armies, but at such heavy cost the expression 'Pyrrhic victory' was coined. The First Punic (from the Latin *Punicus* or Phoenician/Carthaginian) War lasted from 265-242 BC. Rome conquered Sicily, but an invasion of North Africa met with disaster. After a period of uneasy peace, the two powers clashed over control of Spain in 219 BC and Hannibal led his army towards the Alps.

Hannibal beat the Roman armies at the Trebbia and Lake Trasimene, leading Rome to adopt a defensive policy championed by Fabius, but a populist consul, Varro, claimed the nobility were prolonging the war for their own profit and that he could end it now. This 'political general' led 80,000 Roman infantry against 50,000 Carthaginians, of which half were Gallic auxiliaries. Doubling the depth of their formation, the Romans formed a mass which should have been unstoppable. Hannibal's only advantage lay in his cavalry: 10,000 horsemen against 6,000 Romans. Unlike Alexander the Great, who left his infantry to advance according to a pre-planned timetable while he charged at the head of his cavalry, Hannibal remained in the centre where he could coordinate the battle. The Carthaginian cavalry disposed of the Roman horse, re-organised, then fell on the rear of the Roman phalanx, bringing it to a standstill. The Carthaginian centre held, albeit at heavy cost. Then Hannibal attacked the Roman infantry in both flanks with his Carthaginian infantry.

The Roman legions at Cannae were unable to manoeuvre as discrete units. The legion was an administrative organisation; its division into sub-units made the Roman infantry less prone to disorder than the monolithic Macedonian phalanx, but they were only trained to go forward. There was no drill by which the Roman infantry could cut their way out. A determined few struggled clear, but the rest were slaughtered. Survivors were sold as slaves, lucky ones ransomed by their families, others to be found twenty years later working the fields in Crete and Syria.

In his history of Rome, written with access to memoirs by both sides' senior staff, Polybius breaks his narrative after Cannae. He inserts an explanation of Roman political institutions, the source or perhaps the expression of Rome's hidden strength. Rome had the political will to survive fifteen years of campaigning in Italy. New legions were raised, the city resorting to the recruitment of freed-slaves such was the pressure on manpower. Rome's fortifications were formidable; it was impossible for Hannibal to storm the city. The Fabian strategy was tried again, and this time the Romans persisted with it; keeping their army close to Hannibal's, but never risking battle. The Romans habitually fortified their camp, nullifying the

Carthaginians' cavalry superiority. Isolated detachments of Carthaginians were attacked, the Romans retiring behind their fortifications if pressed. Rome could replace its losses in such skirmishes, but Hannibal could not. The few Italian cities that had deserted Rome came to regret it, the fate of Capua anticipating that of Carthage. The Roman navy prevented reinforcements reaching Hannibal by sea. Hannibal's brother marched an army overland from Spain, but Hannibal only learned of the attempted reinforcement when Hasdrubal's severed head was tossed into his camp. The Romans had concentrated in north Italy and destroyed Hasdrubal on the banks of the river Metaurus.

Rome's superior manpower enabled a second front to be opened; sustained by Roman naval superiority, new armies were deployed to Spain where they drove out the Carthaginians. This 'indirect approach' stampeded the Carthaginian senate into negotiations. An armistice was arranged and Hannibal's army sailed home. Its arrival stiffened the Carthaginians' resolve,

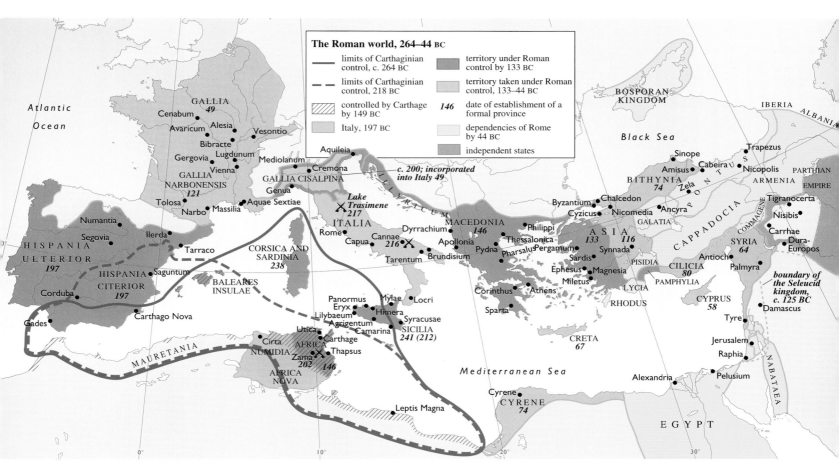

and a final battle took place near the small town of Zama. Publius Cornelius Scipio won the sobriquet 'Africanus' for this, his most famous and important victory.

At Zama, Scipio followed Hannibal's example and directed the battle rather than charging sword-in-hand like Alexander. Both commanders kept troops in reserve, feeding them into the front-line when they judged the time was right. The Roman cavalry beat Hannibal's, and their intervention in the infantry battle was decisive. The Roman infantry was a far more capable instrument than the inflexible mass that Hannibal lured to destruction at Cannae. The first line (*hastati*) fought well in advance of the second (*principes*), which functioned as a separate echelon rather than pressing forward at the first contact. The individual sub-units (maniples) manoeuvred to avoid the war elephants

with which Hannibal opened the battle, before closing up again to engage the Carthaginian infantry.

Zama demonstrated how far the art of war had progressed since Alexander. Both commanders directed their armies rather than plunging into the fray themselves. The use of reserves, infantry in separate waves rather than a monolithic phalanx, and the ability of cavalry to rally after combat and resume the fight, represented the summit of ancient military capability.

In 146 BC, the Romans ended 150 years of hostilities with Carthage by storming the city. The survivors were sold as slaves and the city demolished. The Carthaginian language was eventually lost and only the writings of later historians shed any light on Carthage's military institutions and its most famous general, Hannibal.

ABOVE: Over 20 years of intermittent war with Carthage left Rome in control of Sicily by 242 BC but the house of Barca proved implacable: Hannibal and his brothers were sworn to eternal hatred of Rome. With the silver mines of Spain in their hands, the Barcas recruited large numbers of mercenaries to bolster the limited resources of their city state. Hannibal campaigned the length of the Italian peninsula, but Rome endured to mount a counter-invasion of Spain and then North Africa itself.

BELOW: The Roman army triumphed at Zama, absorbing the charge of the war elephants and defeating the Carthaginian cavalry. Hannibal's infantry were eventually overwhelmed and the city was obliged to make peace on any terms.

THE ARMY OF THE ROMAN REPUBLIC

Roman Legions owed their size and organization to the days when the Roman army was a citizen militia. Legions were not tactical units like 19th century battalions: they were administrative organisations. In battle, all the legionaries present combined to fight in a phalanx, but not the monolithic formation of the Greek city states. It was divided into three echelons. The first six ranks were supposed to be the youngest (the *hastati*); these and the next six ranks (the *principes*) were armed with a heavy javelin. The final three ranks (the *triarii*) were theoretically the veterans, the heads of households the city state could not afford to lose.

These distinctions were retained until the end of the republic, but they ceased to be relevant during the Second Punic War. Legions were raised at such a pace, two every year from 215 to 212 BC, that the *triarii* were no more veterans than the teenage conscripts of Napoleon's Young Guard. The terminology of Rome's original militia remained in use, but the soldiers no longer returned to their farms at the end of a campaigning season. Scipio's legions at Zama were professional soldiers, hardened by ten years' campaigning in Spain.

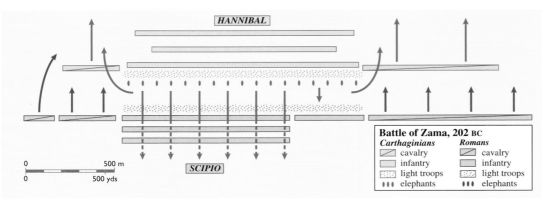

HANNIBAL

SCIPIO

0 — 500 m
0 — 500 yds

Battle of Zama, 202 BC
Carthaginians   *Romans*
▨ cavalry   ▨ cavalry
▨ infantry   ▨ infantry
▨ light troops   ▨ light troops
♦♦♦ elephants   ♦♦♦ elephants

Chinese Warfare

Chinese central governments faced two main challenges: maintaining internal security from usurpation and defending against nomadic horse armies, such as the Hsiung Nu (known to us as the Huns) and, later, the Mongols. The first identifiable dynasty (c.1766 BC) was a theocratic state supported by a Bronze Age army that was similar to its peers in the west. Archaeological evidence suggests a Shang army was composed of around 3,000 to 5,000 bow- and spear-armed foot soldiers. By the end of the dynasty, Shang armies had added a striking force of chariots through which the Shang dominated their weaker neighbours (at least in the north; China became China, as we know it, under the Qin.). China and Egypt started using chariots at almost the same time: 1200 BC.

Over the course of the next 2,000 years states such as the Shang used military force to create a central government controlled by the nobility. Successive regimes descended into corruption or were beset by natural disasters until they were dismembered by rival warlords. Periods of 'warlordism' ended when one leader conquered enough of his enemies to form a new core state. The nature of the cycle makes it difficult to separate the one dynasty from another.

Until the 5th century BC, the primary weapon system was the chariot. It was usually a two-wheeled, three-man fighting platform consisting of a driver, an archer, and a halberd-armed warrior. It probably began as a ceremonial vehicle and mobile command post, and evolved into a missile and shock platform. Five chariots constituted the primary tactical formation, and five squads

(25 chariots) comprised a brigade, usually supported by 25 to 150 infantrymen. Chariots were expensive to build and maintain, confining them to the nobility. As early as the Shang, infantry used the composite bow, augmented by spear-armed auxiliaries. Infantry formed the missile base from which the chariot forces manoeuvred to launch shock attacks. Cavalry was a supporting arm to the chariot forces and did not come into its own until the 3rd century BC.

At that time, Emperor Qin (of the Qin dynasty) shaped Chinese cavalry into a mobile strike force that shunted the chariots to secondary status.

The Shang lasted about 500 years as the strongest power in pre-Qin China, until supplanted by the Zhou in c.1150 BC. Under the Zhou there were no significant changes in military strategy although armour and weapons improved. The sword was introduced around 771 BC. The erosion of Zhou power resulted in the various vassal states breaking free of central government control and initiating a period called the 'Spring and Autumn' (722-481 BC). Early armies in this period were built around chariot forces numbering in the hundreds (occasionally up to 1,000) supported by up to 10,000 infantry. Total dynastic – and would-be dynastic – military assets seem to be rather small, at around 4,000 chariots and 40,000 infantry each.

The Spring and Autumn period divided China into seven major states and 15 lesser ones. After 500 BC iron weapons were in common usage. During the 'Warring States' period (450-222 BC) armies grew much larger, ironically because of improved economic conditions. The growth in massed infantry armies led to the development and widespread use of the crossbow during the 4th century BC. Commercial centres became increasingly heavily fortified. They were the crucial campaign objectives. Siegecraft techniques and technology matched the improvement in fortifications and sieges became a regular feature of military operations.

By the end of the ancient period, caval-

The Warring States and the unification of China

- ⊔⊔⊔ defensive walls with dates of first construction. Rebuilt by Ch'in after 220 BC
- original Ch'in territory, 350 BC
- Ch'in expansion before 300 BC
- other major states with dates of annexation by Ch'in
- new areas annexed by Ch'in after unification

HSIUNGNU
c. 300 BC
to Chao 300 BC
290 BC
annexed 222 BC
CHAO *369 BC* WEI YEN
c. 352 BC
annexed 228 BC CH'I
annexed 221 BC
JUNG
213 BC
c. 300 BC HAN *WEI* *450 BC*
annexed 225 BC LU
CH'IN CHOU
HAN SUNG TENG
annexed 230 BC
C H 'U YÜEH
SHU *(to Ch'u* *333 BC)*
incorporated 316 BC *annexed 223 BC* *annexed 223 BC*
Yangtze
P A
c. 209 BC
TIEN
213–11 BC
211–09 BC MIN-YÜEH

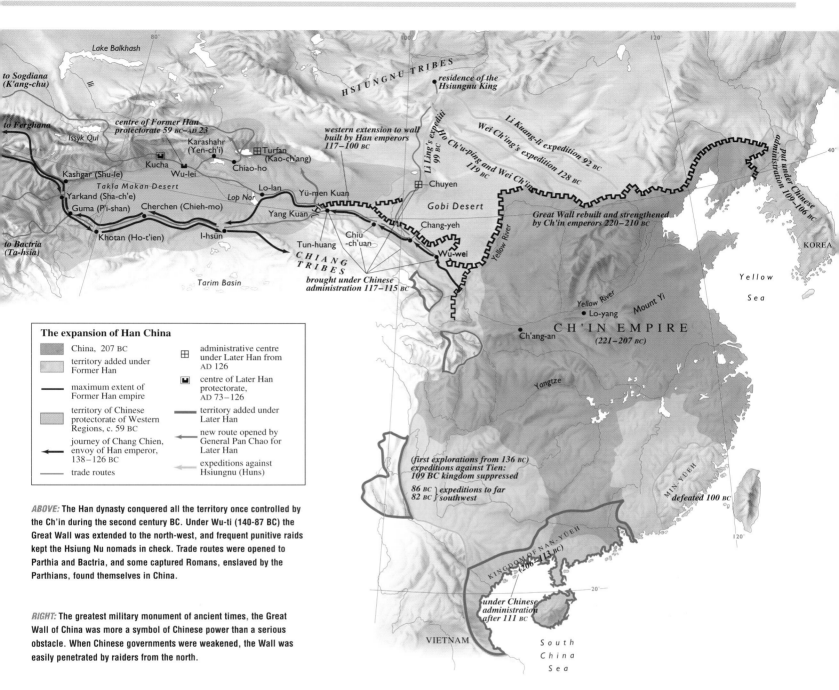

The expansion of Han China

▨ China, 207 BC	⊞ administrative centre under Later Han from AD 126
▨ territory added under Former Han	▣ centre of Later Han protectorate, AD 73–126
▬ maximum extent of Former Han empire	
▨ territory of Chinese protectorate of Western Regions, c. 59 BC	▬ territory added under Later Han
➤ journey of Chang Chien, envoy of Han emperor, 138–126 BC	⬅ new route opened by General Pan Chao for Later Han
▬ trade routes	⬅ expeditions against Hsiungnu (Huns)

ABOVE: The Han dynasty conquered all the territory once controlled by the Ch'in during the second century BC. Under Wu-ti (140-87 BC) the Great Wall was extended to the north-west, and frequent punitive raids kept the Hsiung Nu nomads in check. Trade routes were opened to Parthia and Bactria, and some captured Romans, enslaved by the Parthians, found themselves in China.

RIGHT: The greatest military monument of ancient times, the Great Wall of China was more a symbol of Chinese power than a serious obstacle. When Chinese governments were weakened, the Wall was easily penetrated by raiders from the north.

ry had achieved dominance. Cavalry techniques were copied from the Steppe horsemen with whom Chinese armies frequently had to deal. Cavalry freed the armies from seeking level ground upon which to operate their chariots. The increased mobility of the new cavalry armies augmented by armoured infantry changed Chinese warfare into its medieval counterpart. Combat became more an engagement of manoeuvre, and armies were capable of fighting over more diverse terrain. The massed use of the crossbow and horse archer (learned from the Mongolians) saw Chinese battles dominated by missile engagements; Persian-style, as opposed to western, shock-oriented combat. Despite the local touches of colour, along with differing societal mandates, Chinese warfare closely paralleled that of the Mediterranean world during the same period.

Naval Warfare in the Mediterranean

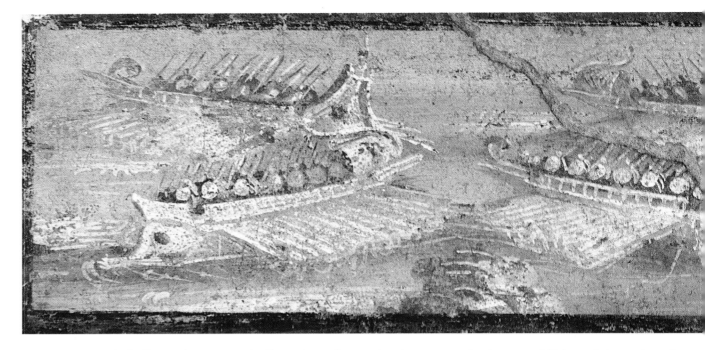

Until the spread of railways, the transport of both trading goods and armies would usually be quicker by water than by land. Minoan Crete fell to invaders from the mainland c.1400 BC. Some 200 years later, a Greek army sailed to Troy to begin the first and most famous siege in western history. By around 700 BC the Phoenicians had the first dedicated warships; earlier vessels had doubled as merchantmen or troop carriers, easily converted from one role to the other. Experience bred greater skill in seafaring and naval construction and stimulated the design of oar-propelled warships. Independent of the wind, these narrow-beamed ships had the manoeuvrability and acceleration to force an action with lumbering sail-driven merchant ships.

By shipping two banks of oars, one above the other, the Phoenicians developed the bireme. By the 5th century BC this had been largely superseded by the triple-banked trireme. Early warships were costly to operate; they demanded large numbers of specially-trained men and their design was so specialized they could serve no other purpose. At the time of Marathon, even Athens, a city state dependent on the sea, could not muster more than 20 triremes. It was not unknown for cities to borrow triremes from their allies, and with both warships and skilled oarsmen in short supply, the Ionian cities secured concessions from the Persian Empire in return for the use of their squadrons. When, ten years after Marathon, the Persians launched a second invasion of Greece, they were understandably confident. The Persian soldiers, battle-hardened conquerors of an already vast empire, were accompanied by a large fleet of perhaps 400 warships. It came as a disagreeable surprise to encounter a Greek fleet of similar size off Artemisium. For a second time, Athens had been blessed with a far-sighted leader. Themistocles had persuaded the citizens to spend the profits from their new-found silver mines on a massive programme of naval construction. The Athenian navy held off the Persian fleet while 300 Spartan soldiers passed into legend at Thermopylae.

In ancient naval warfare there was seldom any advantage standing on the defensive. Triremes were built with reinforced prows, and a skilled crew could ram an

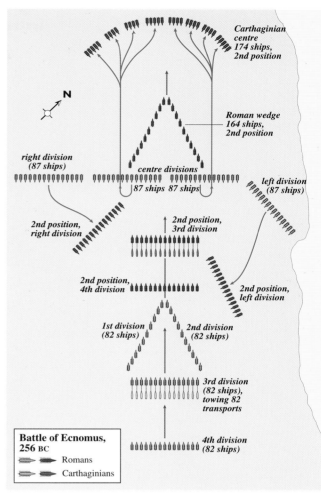

Battle of Ecnomus, 256 BC
Romans
Carthaginians

Carthaginian centre 174 ships, 2nd position

Roman wedge 164 ships, 2nd position

right division (87 ships)

centre divisions 87 ships 87 ships

left division (87 ships)

2nd position, right division

2nd position, 3rd division

2nd position, left division

2nd position, 4th division

1st division (82 ships)

2nd division (82 ships)

3rd division (82 ships), towing 82 transports

4th division (82 ships)

Punic War (264-241 BC), Polybius tells how the Romans built their first warship by reverse-engineering a captured Carthaginian vessel, and trained rowers to man it on mock-ups ashore. The Roman fleet relied on boarding rather ramming, which required more skilled seamanship. Successive fleets were lost in storms, but they persevered with Roman fortitude and won. In fact, the Romans were no strangers to the sea; their alliance of Italian city states included many coastal cities and their own city crest was a galleon. They achieved naval superiority during the first Punic War, and maintained it during the Second Punic War (218-202 BC). If Polybius' story has any basis, it may be that the Romans copied a Carthaginian warship because it was superior to their existing types.

By 31 BC, when the battle of Actium decided the Roman Civil War in favour of Octavian (later Augustus), the quinquireme was the standard battleship of the ancient Mediterranean. Larger vessels, including some behemoths of legendary proportions, had been tried, but proved too cumbersome. Lighter warships, some relying as much on their sails as their oars proved of greater value, and would play a greater role as Roman naval power waned in the absence of organized opposition (although it would be periodically revived to tackle piracy). During the following centuries of the *Pax Romana,* warships all but vanished from the Mediterranean.

enemy, sheering off its oars or penetrating the fragile hull. Alternatively, they could grapple and board an opponent, swordsmen swarming aboard, while archers picked off enemy officers and steersmen. However, by offering battle in the Bay of Eleusis, the Athenians lured the Persian fleet to defeat. The Greek crews lacked the experience of their opponents, their triremes were heavier and less manoeuvrable, but they were able to concentrate on the leading Persian squadrons as they entered the bay. Caught in a bottleneck, the Persians had no room to exploit their superior seamanship. A flanking attack by their Egyptian squadron was similarly defeated by Corinthian triremes on the western side of Salamis, and the Persian warships withdrew in confusion.

All major sea battles in the ancient Mediterranean took place inshore. Oar-powered warships demand large crews and triremes could only carry a few days' provisions. Rowing is thirsty work, and the fleets put ashore each night for food and water. This made it difficult to impose a blockade; Pompey's fleet failed to stop first Caesar then Mark Anthony crossing the Adriatic in 48 BC. Fleets were vulnerable when beached for the night, a weakness highlighted during the Peloponnesian war when the Athenian navy was annihilated at Aegospotami in 405 BC. Lysander, the Spartan commander, massacred the Athenian oarsmen. Athens had demonstrated extraordinary powers of economic recovery in nearly 30 years of conflict, but while the city might be able to rebuild ships, trained seamen were irreplaceable. Athens surrendered.

Warships grew larger during the fourth and third centuries BC. Roman and Carthaginian fleets used quadriremes and quinquiremes, with four and five banks of oars respectively. In his account of the first

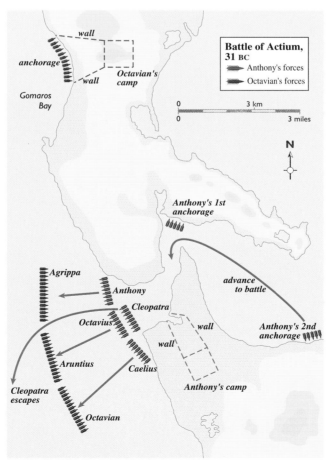

Battle of Actium, 31 BC
Anthony's forces
Octavian's forces

wall
anchorage
wall
Octavian's camp
Gomaros Bay

0   3 km
0   3 miles

N

Anthony's 1st anchorage

Agrippa
Anthony
Cleopatra
Octavius
Aruntius
Caelius
Cleopatra escapes
Octavian

advance to battle

wall
wall

Anthony's 2nd anchorage

Anthony's camp

LEFT: The final battle of the civil war following Caesar's murder was fought off the Greek coast at Actium. Cleopatra's squadron broke through the enemy centre, but she hoisted sail and escaped to Egypt with the treasury. Mark Anthony's flagship was a gigantic warship with multiple banks of oars, but most ships on both sides were quinquiremes, the standard Roman warship since the Second Punic War.

ABOVE: A Roman invasion fleet of 330 vessels sailed for Africa but was intercepted off Sicily by 350 Carthaginian ships. The Romans won the battle, capturing 64 enemy ships and sinking 30 for the loss of 24 of their own. Both the Carthaginian admiral and one of the two Roman consuls were later tortured to death by the Carthagininan authorities.

Rome and the Successor kingdoms

LEFT: The small successor kingdom of Epirus fought Rome from 281-272 BC, but King Pyrrhus's army suffered such heavy losses in the course of his victories that the expression 'Pyrrhic victory' was coined. And his army was far closer to the original Macedonian model than those of a century later.

RIGHT: Lucius Cornelius Sulla (138-78 BC) became dictator of Rome from 82 to 79 BC. As a military commander, he presided over the final destruction of the Macedonian system, defeating the king of Pontus and an army packed with exotic elements such as scythed-wheeled chariots and elephants.

While Rome was busy destroying Carthage, the successors of Alexander's *diadochoi* had been constantly at war with each other in an attempt to expand the mini-kingdoms they had carved out by the end of the First Successor War. Greece saw over a 100 years of constant warfare to determine, usually by might, whom was to sit on the Macedonian throne. The Seleucids, based in Syria, were either trying to expand their lands south, into Egypt, or north, into the vacuum of Asia Minor created by the end of the Achaemenid Persian Empire. And, in Egypt, the Ptolemys, content with ruling as pharaohs, spent much effort maintaining the status quo.

In doing so, all of the Successors continued the Macedonian system. Unfortunately, they decided to magnify the elements they felt made it powerful, often ignoring that Alexander used his army in true combined arms fashion. In Greece, the phalanx became, if anything, even more rigid and inflexible, and in the Levant, use of mercenaries and elephants diluted whatever power the infantry had. At the massive battle of Raphia (217 BC) the Seleucids and the Ptolemaic Egyptians fielded 50,000+ men each, in a battle line stretching over three miles. Both forces included a substantial mercenary element, plus hordes of lightly armed irregulars,

and a spectacular formation of war elephants. The battle line was so long that the commanders had no adequate means of using all their forces, and the battle degenerated into a sectional affair, with one section simply charging its opposite. While Rome learned from each engagement it fought, the Successors, in a constant effort to go one up on their brethren kings, simply diluted the power of the system they inherited.

At the end of the Punic Wars, Rome controlled the Western Mediterranean. Under the guise of protecting Roman interests, she now turned east. From about 200 BC to the middle of the 1st century Rome waged a series of wars against the Eastern Mediterranean powers, and aspirant powers, that eventually led to its total control of the Mediterranean. And in facing the armies of the Successors, Rome set in motion the final confrontation between the two systems: legion versus phalanx.

The first confrontations were with the Macedonians. In the constant warfare between claimants to the Macedonian throne, virtually all of the battles, such as those at Sellasia in 221 BC and Mantinea in 207 BC, pitted one army's phalanx against the other's. Small contingents of cavalry and light auxiliaries were present but had little ultimate effect.

During the Punic Wars, Rome made

extensive efforts to keep the ambitious Philip V, the Macedonian king, from allying himself with Carthage. At one point (Elis, 208 BC) they even sent a legion in support of Philip's enemies, the Aetolian League. When the Punic Wars ended, Philip began to cast covetous eyes on expanding into Asia Minor. So far, the Rhodians, Pergamenes and other Aegean island states had kept Philip from gaining control of the sea lanes. To keep the Macedonians in place, Rome sent a consular army (complete with 20 elephants) to Greece, eventually reinforced by an additional 10,000 Aetolians.

The two armies stumbled on each other at Cynoscephalae (a ridge shaped like a dog's head) in 197 BC, one of the few battles in the ancient world where the two sides did not deploy and gaze unfondly at each other for hours. For most of the battle Philip's doubled phalanxes (the "more is better" theory of warfare) more then held their own. However, when the Macedonian left advanced to take advantage of its success, the Romans moved a small force into the breach and fell on the Macedonian rear. Philip's army was shattered, as were his dreams of hegemony in Greece. Despite the Roman victory, it was not clear which system was better.

To the south, the Seleucid king, Antiochus III, seeing Macedon and

Rome's attentions directed elsewhere, decided it was time to move into Asia Minor, in force. To help him with his plans, Antiochus went so far as to hire Hannibal, whose under-use by the Seleucids was one of the reasons for the campaign's failure. All of this alerted Rome's Rhodian and Pergamene allies, and it all came to a head in 190 BC. Antiochus' army was moving up the western coast of Asia Minor. In an attempt to support it by sea, the Syrians lost two large naval battles to the Roman allies (at Side and Myonessus) and were, thus, forced to fight at Magnesia, where the Romans handed Antiochus' polyglot army a thrashing. The glory days of the Seleucids were over, as was exhibited 30 years later when she lost Judea to the guerrilla armies of Judah Maccabaeus.

While the Maccabaeans were busy confounding the Seleucids, the Macedonians, this time under Philip's son, Perseus, started making trouble again. The Greeks still favoured the Macedonian system, despite the three major victories by the Roman legions at Beneventum, Cynoscephalae and Magnesia. In the first two, the terrain had greatly favoured Roman flexibility; in the latter, the Seleucids may have used the Macedonian system but they manned it with inferior troops and confused it with chariots and too many auxiliaries.

The battle at Pydna (168 BC), a standard set-piece linear battle, proved a decisive Roman victory. It also sounded the death knell for the Macedonian system.

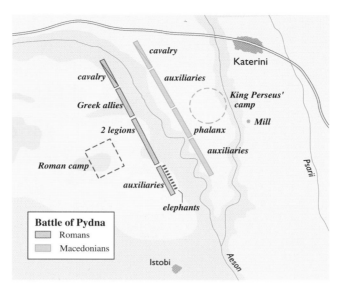

Battle of Pydna
- Romans
- Macedonians

Some 80 years later, Mithridates VI of Pontus decided to test the Roman mettle. The Pontines advanced into Greece, under Archelaeus, with a Macedonian-style army of some 65,000 men. Facing him at the pivotal battle of Chaeronea, in 86 BC, was the infamous Dictator of Rome, Sulla, with only 23,000 men. But Archelaeus' army was the dregs of the Macedonian system—chariots, hordes of light troops, and a phalanx anchored by slave infantry. Despite outflanking the Romans, the Pontines were crushed. It had become obvious that a Roman legion could defeat anything but a superior trained and commanded Macedonian army.

LEFT: Perseus, son of Philip V of Macedon, challenged the power of Rome, bringing on one of the last formal battles between the Macedonian pike phalanx and the Roman legions. The phalanx mowed down some of the Romans' allies, but it became disordered on rough ground. The superior articulation of the legions enabled them to exploit the resulting gaps in the Greek formation. Once past the fearsome rows of pikes, the Romans' superior swordplay brought victory.

BELOW: Titus Quinctius Flaminius defeated the Macedonian army of Philip V, largely thanks to one of his tribunes who managed to attack the victorious enemy right wing in the rear.

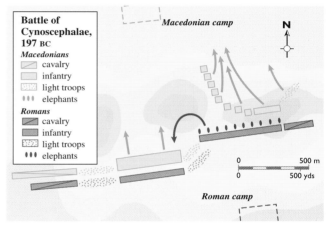

Battle of Cynoscephalae, 197 BC
Macedonians
- cavalry
- infantry
- light troops
- elephants
Romans
- cavalry
- infantry
- light troops
- elephants

LEFT: Alexander the Great's empire fractured into some mighty successor states, but one by one they were defeated by Rome. One of the last to succumb was the small state of Pontus, whose final ruler, Mithridates VI ordered one of his mercenaries to kill him after his ramshackle army was shattered by the legions.

The Gallic Wars

The evolution of the Roman army from citizen militia to professional long service force continued after the end of the Second Punic War. By the end of the 2nd century BC the legion had been reorganized into ten sub-units (cohorts) and included a unit of skirmishers and a small force of cavalry. The Roman camp was a key part of the manual: Roman armies would march early and stop early. By mid-afternoon, the legion was constructing a fully-walled camp for the night. The Romans became so good at this, as well as at building roads and bridges, that their methods of campaigning were years ahead of their northern neighbours, the Gauls.

Rome had been subjected to frequent invasions from the north. The Gauls had come within a stone's throw of Rome in 386 BC and two major battles, Sentinum (295 BC) and Telamon (225 BC), had been fought in recent memory. The fear of yet another invasion was one of the moving forces of Roman Republican frontier strategy. The Gauls were conglomerations of aggressive tribes, most of which had set-

tled in what is now France and Germany. Some moved as far south as the Po Valley. Warfare was a way of life, bravery in battle a sure road to elevation in the tribal hierarchy. As a result, the Gauls could be most impressive and difficult foes, especially with their furious initial charge, which could sweep all before it. The Romans called it *furor*, and they feared its effect mightily.

The Gauls not only eschewed armour in battle; they often wore no clothes at all. Their main weapons were swords, javelins and throwing axes. Gallic cavalry could be effective, but was used more for transporting light infantry than for shock action. They also had chariots, rickety two-wheeled, fixed-axle vehicles that were more a mode of transport than a weapons system. The main Gallic tactic was the all-out, frontal charge. Working themselves into a frenzy, they would launch the entire horde right at the enemy. It could work to devastating effect. But Gallic armies were very brittle; if the initial charge failed they went home to fight another day.

The legion was trained to withstand exactly what the Gauls threw against it. Discipline kept Roman soldiers in place even when confronted by the Gallic *furor*. It was this aspect of the Roman system, as well as their superiority in armament, that triumphed over the Gallic charge.

The Gauls Caesar met in the 1st century BC were the same tribes the Romans had encountered in Italy in the 3rd century BC. Their armies still used *furor*, although their weapons and armour had improved. However, they were still a light army, with not enough cavalry to make a difference. Despite Caesar's efforts to gather votes at home by putting a spin on how fearsome they were, in his famous book *de Bello Gallico*, it is obvious that Caesar had little trouble smashing three large Gallic armies: the Helvetii at Bibracte; the Nervii, et al., at the Sabis; and the Germanic tribes under Ariovistus, somewhere west of the Rhine. In none of these battles did the Gauls or Germans significantly outnumber the Romans. Of interest in respect of the latter is that the legendarily ferocious German cavalry of the era - actually a system in which light cavalry and light infantry fought as one, an idea we see many times in years to come - was nowhere to be found during this battle. With Caesar, it is always more interesting what he does not say than what he does.

Caesar's Gallic campaigns involved several naval ventures. In order to neutralize the Armorican tribes, Caesar built a fleet of Liburnian biremes from scratch and engaged in a full-scale battle with the smaller, sail-driven ships of the Veneti. The Veneti were superior sailors, but no match for boarding parties of legionaries, and when the wind died down, they were annihilated. By clearing the northern waters of the Veneti, Caesar was able to launch his invasions of Britain. The Britons were Gauls, with similar armies that made great use of chariots. Ultimately, Caesar could not establish a solid base from which colonization could grow. The best Caesar could say was that he was there first.

The climax of the Gallic Wars, the epic siege of Alesia, demonstrated the formidable engineering skills of the Roman legions. With Vercingetorix holing up in the hilltop village of Alesia, Caesar constructed 26 miles of parallel walls; one set to keep Vercingetorix in, the other to keep his friends out. The Gauls had no siege skills. They also did not have the 250,000 men in the relief force Caesar claims in his account. The logistics of assembling and feeding such a huge army were far beyond the ability of the Gallic chiefs. The military genius on display at Alesia was in the Roman preparations for the assault of the relief force. The battle simply reflected the merit of the works. Caesar's thrilling narrative should be read in light of his desire for permanent public office.

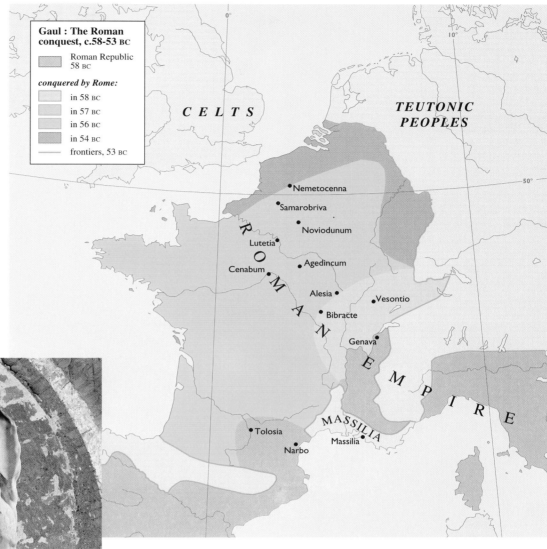

Gaul : The Roman conquest, c.58-53 BC

Roman Republic 58 BC

conquered by Rome:
in 58 BC
in 57 BC
in 56 BC
in 54 BC
frontiers, 53 BC

CELTS

TEUTONIC PEOPLES

Nemetocenna
Samarobriva
Noviodunum
Lutetia
Cenabum
Agedincum
Alesia
Vesontio
Bibracte
Genava
Tolosia
MASSILIA
Massilia
Narbo

ROMAN EMPIRE

ABOVE: Divided among themselves, the Gallic tribes were defeated one after another by the Romans. Caesar exploited their inability to maintain a large army for any length of time. Avoiding battle in the early stages of a campaign, Caesar went over to the offensive as the Gauls began to disperse. He probably outnumbered the tribal armies by the time they met on the battlefield, something he was determined to conceal in his published account of the wars.

BELOW: Vercingetorix, chief of the Arveni tribe in central Gaul, waged a 'scorched earth' policy against Gallic tribes that allied themselves to Rome. Caesar besieged him at Gergovia, but had to break off the siege to deal with another revolt. In 52 BC he besieged him at Alesia (Alise-Sainte-Reine) where he defeated another Gallic army that attempted to raise the siege. Vercingetorix led many attempts to break out, but was ultimately obliged to surrender.

ABOVE: Celtic freedom crushed beneath the Roman boot: a Gaul commits suicide after killing his family. Such romanticized images endure, despite the fact that the Gallic tribes were a slave-owning society dominated by a small cadre of noble families. However, the final campaigns were conducted with great ruthlessness, both sides allowing the civilian population of Alesia to starve to death in 'no man's land'.

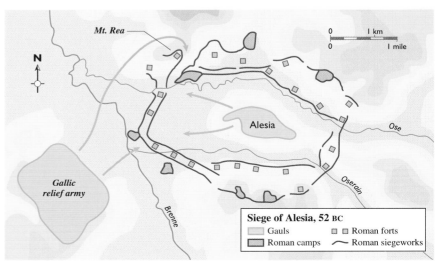

Mt. Rea

N

Alesia

Gallic relief army

Ose

Oserain

Brenne

Siege of Alesia, 52 BC

Gauls
Roman camps
Roman forts
Roman siegeworks

The Limits of Roman Power

RIGHT: Domitian (ruled 81-96) gave the Roman army its first pay rise since Augustus and remained popular with the soldiers, if not the senate until his assassination. His capture of the Taunus region helped secure the frontier along the middle Rhine. His campaigns against Dacia were to be completed by Trajan, the son of Domitian's short-lived successor, Nerva.

RIGHT: The Parthians were a Scythian people that conquered the Near East between 250 and 130 BC. Their armies consisted mainly of horse archers, whose ability to shoot behind them gave rise to the expression 'Parthian shot'. A core of heavily armoured lancers (cataphracts) stood ready to charge, once the arrow storm had depleted the enemy ranks and disordered their formation.

By the end of the 2nd century BC, Gallic migrations in northern Europe had pushed some of the 'Germanic' tribes towards the expanding Roman frontier. The foremost of these were the Teutons and Cimbri, who, in the 15 or so years before 100 BC, migrated over most of Europe. In 113 BC, they came into contact with Rome, winning four victories against small, poorly lead Roman armies. Period scribes put it all down to the huge numbers of Germans, up to 300,000 in one army, numbers to be taken with a bit more than a grain of salt. When it counted, however, the Romans crushed first the Teutons, at Aquae Sextiae, and then the Cimbri, at Vercellae. Nevertheless, the halt to German aggression was temporary, as Caesar and the emperors were to find out.

German tribal armies were first cousins of their Gallic counterparts. However, the Germans tended to be much bigger than the Romans, who were impressed by the height of the average Gaul. Several Roman sources have the Cimbri gloriously armed, with gilded breastplate and helms that would make a *daimyo* green with envy. Archaeological evidence is to the contrary. They had a few swords and virtually no armour. What they did add to the tactical mix was a method of attack Romans called 'the wedge'. A section of Germans would charge in a solid block with the idea of concentrating effort and energy at one point. Against mediocre troops, or other tribes, this could be a most effective tactic. Against veteran legions, it proved useless. Nowhere was this better demonstrated than at the battle of Vercellae. King Beorix, his Cimbri, and the German wedge could do little against the implacability of the Marian legion.

Both the Numidians, in Africa, and the Parthians, in the regions east of Syria, were similar in their approach to warfare. Both armies consisted almost entirely of light cavalry, and the Romans had great difficulty countering them. Numidian light cavalry had been a key element of Carthaginian armies and, afterwards, of Roman forces. Numidians excelled at a hit-and-run style of warfare. Their cavalry would charge up to an enemy line of infantry, discharging their javelins as they got near, then wheeling and galloping away. If the infantry, stung by too many spears, moved out to challenge them, they swooped in, isolated the rash few, and hacked them to pieces.

The Romans, lacking cavalry suitable to handling this tactic, usually went on the defensive. When attacked by masses of light, missile-throwing cavalry, the legions formed into 'square', so as not to be out-flanked. They used their shields to protect them against the missile fire, adopting the *testudo* (tortoise) formation. If a Roman army was not too far from its base camp, it could, slowly, make its way back with minimal losses. The more and the better the contingent of Roman cavalry, the more able it was to take the offensive.

Against the last King of Numidia, Jugurtha, who had revolted against Roman attempts to turn him into a puppet, the Roman legions came close to being picked apart but their discipline, just enough cavalry to make a difference, and Marius' leadership, provided Rome with two victories – and Jugurtha in chains.

Against the Parthians, they had less success. The Parthians perfected the 'Parthian shot', the ability of their cavalry to fire accurately while galloping away. They were so adept at hit-and-run that a large consular army under Publius Crassus

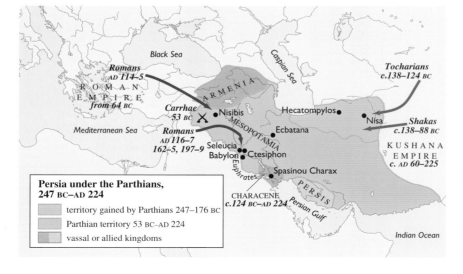

Persia under the Parthians, 247 BC–AD 224

- territory gained by Parthians 247–176 BC
- Parthian territory 53 BC–AD 224
- vassal or allied kingdoms

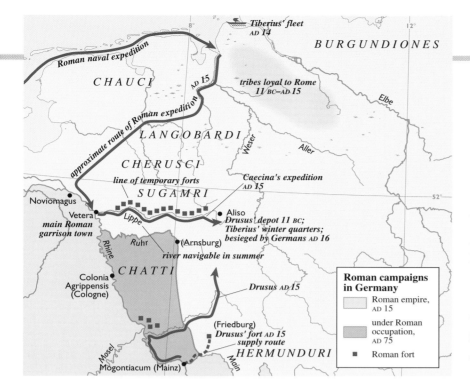

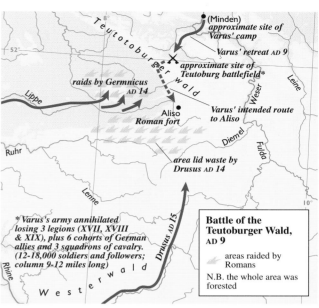

Roman campaigns in Germany

▨	Roman empire, AD 15
▨	under Roman occupation, AD 75
■	Roman fort

Battle of the Teutoburger Wald, AD 9

⚜ areas raided by Romans

N.B. the whole area was forested

* Varus's army annihilated losing 3 legions (XVII, XVIII & XIX), plus 6 cohorts of German allies and 3 squadrons of cavalry. (12-18,000 soldiers and followers; column 9-12 miles long)

ABOVE: Unlike the Gallic tribes, the semi-nomadic Germans had no fixed bases for the Romans to attack. Animal herds were their main source of food so there were no grain stores for the Romans to seize. However, by exploiting the rivers and the coast, the Romans were able to launch a series of summer campaigns, their armies sometimes over-wintering at a temporary base established at Aliso. Tribes were bribed or bullied into alliance with Rome, but their long term loyalty could only be ensured by an immediate military presence.

ABOVE: Rome's most famous defeat in Germany occurred in AD 9 when Varus's three legions were wiped out during their retreat to the fort at Aliso. Roman vengeance followed: Germanicus led a punitive expedition in AD 14 and Drusus launched a two-pronged assault the following year. The Roman frontier seemed set to reach the Elbe, but Tiberius halted the war, afraid of that victorious generals might emulate Caesar and return to Rome to seize power.

(triumviral associate of Julius Caesar, but a wealthy aristocrat of mediocre military talents) was picked to death and destroyed at Carrhae. Crassus' fate put Rome off any advance east of Syria for generations. His army was surrounded by Parthian cavalry in flat, arid terrain, with few supplies and little cavalry. Even worse, it was far away from its base and had no camp in the vicinity. Such a situation was the weak link in the legion armour. While, like most infantry, it fought best on level ground, its manoeuvrability was internal. It was thus better suited to terrain that could define its flanks and protect them against light cavalry tactics. In the face of unusual tactical systems, the legionary armies needed a leader with vision, not a political hack. Rome soon had a number of capable commanders, but the legions became increasingly loyal to them and not the senate and people of Rome.

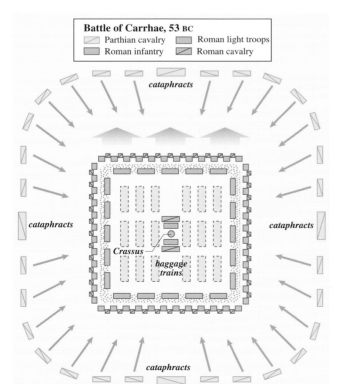

Battle of Carrhae, 53 BC

▨ Parthian cavalry		▨ Roman light troops
▨ Roman infantry		▨ Roman cavalry

LEFT: Marcus Crassus invaded Parthia without authority, gambling on a victorious foreign adventure to bolster his political position. His army was intercepted by a Parthian force commanded by Surena, an equally hedonistic general who went to war with a personal baggage train of 200 wagons and a harem. Subjected to incessant showers of arrows, the Romans suffered heavy losses and began to retreat. Crassus tried to buy his way out, but the Parthians killed him during negotiations then slaughtered his army. Surena was later murdered by his own king, afraid that the victor would seize the throne for himself.

ABOVE: Hadrian (76-138) succeeded Trajan in 117 and soon embarked on the construction of the famous wall that marked the frontier between Roman Britain and the tribal territories to the north.

The Fall of the Republic

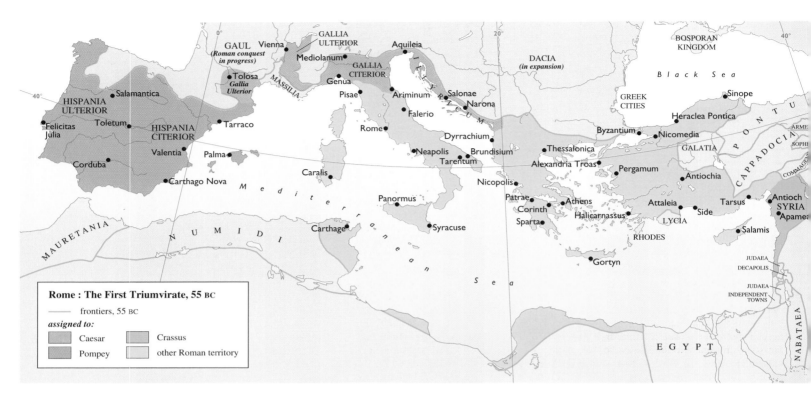

Rome : The First Triumvirate, 55 BC

— frontiers, 55 BC
assigned to:

◼ Caesar   ◼ Crassus

◼ Pompey   ◼ other Roman territory

ABOVE: By the first century BC constitutional politics were all but over: power in Rome depended on money and soldiers. The first triumvirate divided the growing empire between Julius Caesar, Marcus Crassus and Gnaeus Pompey in 60 BC. Crassus was killed in Parthia in 53 and Caesar declared war on Pompey and the senate in 49 BC, crossing the river Rubicon which divided the province of Gaul from Italy. The ensuing civil war was fought in Italy, Spain, Greece and North Africa until Caesar emerged victorious.

RIGHT: Marcus Brutus conspired with veteran general Gaius Cassius to organize the most famous assassination in political history. Julius Caesar had emerged victorious from the five year civil war he initiated in 49 BC; his murder triggered a succession struggle that would not be concluded until 31 BC. The Republican constitution was doomed.

The evolution of the Roman army from citizen militia to long service professionals delivered victories against every opponent in the Mediterranean world. In the hands of Marius, and later Caesar, the legions dealt savage blows against tribal armies of northern Europe. However, the republican political institutions, that caught the attention of Polybius when he sought to explain the rise of Rome, were subverted as politics became increasingly personalized. The success of one faction was followed by the proscription - mass execution - of its enemies, who sought and often achieved vengeance in the same manner. In the process, the armies became the ultimate arbiters.

After Caesar crossed the Rubicon to initiate his bid for supreme power, senatorial limitations on the armies became irrelevant. The numbers of Romans under arms rose to staggering proportions in the ensuing civil wars. There were battles involving more than twenty legions at a time, almost as many as Rome fielded at the height of the Second Punic War. For the next 150 or so years, most of the major battles involved legions fighting other legions, with some 'time outs' to fight Germans in the north and to subdue rebellions in the east.

In 49 BC Caesar's army faced one loyal to Pompey (Cnaeus Pompeius) in Spain. Caesar outmanoeuvred his opponents, cutting them off from their water supply and forcing a surrender. Caesar disbanded the defeated legions, gaining some recruits in the process, then returned to Italy. Although Pompey's fleet was present in the Adriatic, Caesar shipped his army to the Balkans to attack Pompey at Dyrrhachium (Dubrovnik). Five months of manoeuvre

and counter-manoeuvre followed, the rival armies fortifying their positions with Roman thoroughness until Pompey, cut off from his supplies, launched an attack that broke through Caesar's lines. Caesar regrouped in Thessaly, Pompey followed and the rival armies fought a pitched battle at Pharsalus in August 48 BC.

Caesar had eight legions to Pompey's eleven, but Caesar's army was severely depleted. The comparative numbers, if you take Caesar literally, were about 45,000 Pompeians to 22,000 Caesarians, plus a 7:1 Pompeian superiority in cavalry. Some historians doubt these figures. There is no concrete proof either way, but Caesar was probably outnumbered by a large margin. However, Caesar's legions were better trained and more experienced; only two of Pompey's legions were anything approaching veteran. Pompey had labelled himself 'the Great' after his conquests in the east, but his army commanders openly disagreed with his strategy. Caesar was blessed with some extremely capable officers, such as Marcus Antonius (Mark Anthony).

The battlefield was well defined and restrictive on each flank, with a river at Caesar's left and rocky hills on the right. Despite the numbers, Caesar's frontage was about the same as Pompey's, as he had stretched his front line cohorts out to make sure he was not outflanked. His biggest problem was Pompey's marked superiority in cavalry. Pompey placed virtually all of his cavalry on his left, under the command of Caesar's old lieutenant, Titus Labienus.

He planned to advance his front line of legions, pinning Caesar in place, at which point his superior cavalry would sweep around Caesar's right flank, overrun Caesar's cavalry, then fall upon the rear of Caesar's infantry. It was a good plan, but Caesar recognized what was likely to happen. He employed his cavalry merely as a screen. Caesar stole a march on Pompey and advanced his own legions to pin Pompey's. Then, as Labienus advanced his cavalry Caesar's horse galloped to the rear, revealing a 'refused' line of some half dozen cohorts, standing right in Labienus' line of charge. Cavalry do not do well when charging infantry head-on, and the Pompeian cavalry became disorganized after charging into such a surprise. As they attempted to withdraw and reform, Caesar's cavalry attacked and destroyed them, a smaller force of horsemen in good order defeating a larger force in disorder.

Meanwhile, Pompey's legions made little progress against Caesar's veterans and, when their cavalry streamed to the rear, they turned and fled too. Pompey fled to Egypt where he was murdered by his associates who inspired Ptolemy XII to attack Caesar in Alexandria. A siege ensued, broken by Caesar's allies from Pergamum and Ptolemy was killed in the ensuing battle. Caesar returned to Alexandria where he enjoyed a notoriously warmer reception from Ptolemy's sister, Cleopatra.

Caesar was murdered in 44 BC. Mark Anthony and Caesar's 18-year-old nephew Gaius Julius Caesar Octavianus (Octavian) defeated the assassins, but fell out themselves ten years later. Octavian's victory at Actium, the last major naval battle of the ancient world, made him sole ruler of Rome. In 27 BC he was granted the title Augustus by the Senate and the republic's transformation into an empire was all but complete. Some of his successors would inherit the role of emperor, but many more achieved it the same way Octavian did: by force of arms.

Battle of Pharsalus, 48 BC
- Caesar's forces
- Pompeius' forces

Antonius · Lentulus · Cn. Domitius · Scipio · Pompeius' camp · P. Sulla · L. Domitius · Labienus · Pharsalus · Enipeus · N

ABOVE: **Caesar transported his army from Italy to Greece despite the presence of a fleet loyal to Pompey. After prolonged siege warfare around Dyrrachium he withdrew to Thessaly. Pompey pursued, but his army was destroyed at Pharsalus: Caesar's reserve cohorts routing his cavalry on the right flank.**

ABOVE: **Mark Anthony defeated Caesar's assassins, Brutus and Cassius, at Philippi. However, it was a battle won more by his legionaries than any great generalship. His subsequent campaign in Parthia failed to avenge Crassus and his desertion of his own fleet at Actium set the seal on a dubious military career.**

LEFT: **Cleopatra and her son Caesarion, commemorated on a frieze. Egypt's most famous queen had commanded one naval expedition that ended in shipwreck off Libya before she led her fleet to Greece in support of Mark Anthony.**

The decline of the Roman Legion

By the reign of Septimius Severus (193-211), the factors that led to the decline of the Roman military system were in place. Ironically, it was this capable emperor who inadvertently triggered the events that would culminate with the fall of Rome 250 years later.

At the end of the 2nd century, the Roman army was still based on legions little different from those the early emperors had led. But Rome, itself had changed. Outlying, provinces had previously looked to the city of Rome for strength and guidance. By the early 3rd century, social and economic power had devolved to the provinces. Citizenship was extended to most peoples within the Empire and the importance of Rome itself diminished. This affected the legions, most of which were not only stationed on the frontiers but were now allowed to settle where they served, raise families and take jobs. This major change, initiated by Severus was stimulated by the decline in the Roman fiscal system. Roman currency was so debased by his reign, partly because of a decline in the availability of precious metals, that cash payments to soldiers became increasingly difficult.

Integration with local communities had a corrosive effect on the legions' military quality. Legionaries held jobs outside the military, often becoming part-time farmers and living with their families. The fearsome discipline of the legion disappeared, and with it, the legions' advantage over 'barbarian' forces. By the beginning of the 4th century, the legion had completely disappeared. Instead, the Roman army consisted of *palatini, comitatenses*, and *limitanei*. The *palatini* were the emperor's guard, assigned by merit from provincial regions, replacing the Praetorian Guard. The *comitatenses* were the field army, politically crucial because imperial succession was so often by assassination or military coup. The emperor needed a large army around him at all times. An expanded form of

the *comitatenses* were the *pseudocomitatenses*, *comitatenses* that were sent to the frontiers if local forces failed to contain an invasion. On the frontier, and composing the greater majority of Roman soldiers, were the *limitanei*, the legionnaires-turned-farmers and burghers — effectively a militia. The headcount for each of these new legions — as they

were still called that on the lists — was about one-third of a 1st century legion, or less. Hence their rapid multiplication. Whereas Septimius Severus has 33 legions in the field, by the end of the 4th century there were 175 of these smaller formations.

Thus, while the number of troops available to Rome sometimes rose to 500,000, they were less effective against stubborn foes such as Persia and the restless outer German tribes, Goths, Vandals, et al.. Previously, barbarian tribes had supplied auxiliaries to boost the prowess of the legion; now it was these same auxiliaries who provided the backbone. The army was no longer a club for Roman citizens fighting for the idea of Rome. It was German, Hun, Saracen, Armenian and whatever tribes the emperor could enlist. By the 3rd Century, most barbarian tribes still understood the futility of engaging in an open-field, set piece battle with the Roman army, even a mediocre Roman army. It was for this reason that most barbarian armies were raiders, although there were some bent on conquest.

Barbarian infantry was armed mostly with spear and shield, with some throwing axes or javelins too. Swords were rare, archers few, and armour only for the chieftains. The tribes had neither the resources nor the skilled artisans ,manufacture to produce armor. Cavalry was the best part of a barbarian army, and ranged from heavy, shock troops with swords to the usual lightly-armed scouts. The all-for-

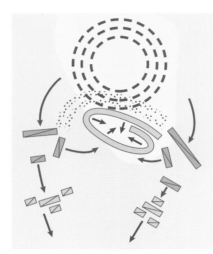

Battle of Adrianople, AD 378

Goths		Romans	
tribesmen		infantry	
cavalry		cavalry	

waggon laager

Emperor Valens

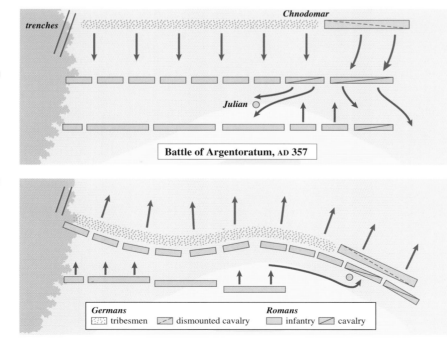

trenches

Chnodomar

Julian

Battle of Argentoratum, AD 357

Germans		Romans	
tribesmen	dismounted cavalry	infantry	cavalry

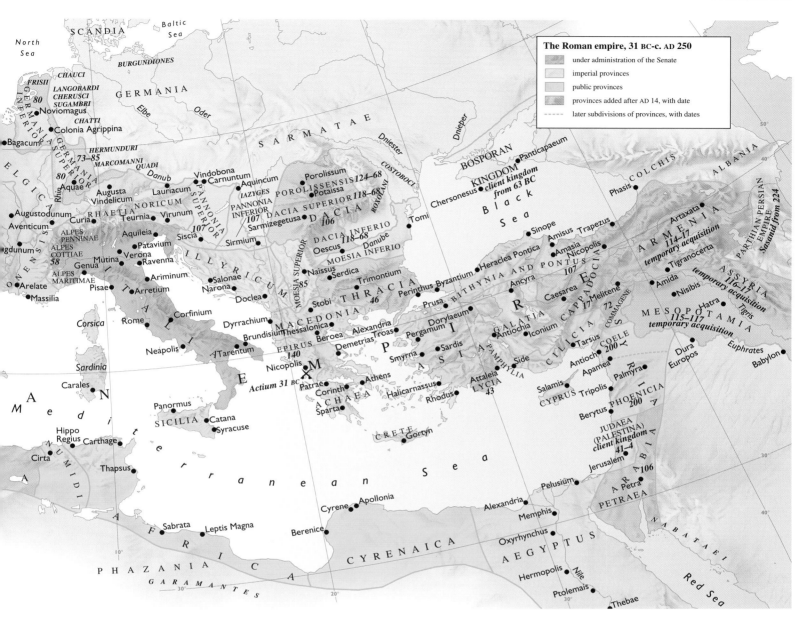

The Roman empire, 31 BC-c. AD 250

- under administration of the Senate
- imperial provinces
- public provinces
- provinces added after AD 14, with date
- later subdivisions of provinces, with dates

one charge by a dense throng of tribesmen was still the main tactic. One tactical development in this period was the Romans' adoption of the bow. The latter-day legions included a significant quantity of archers, to rain arrows on the masses of unprotected barbarians.

Two major battles towards the end of the 4th century illuminate the changes that time and policy had brought. At Argentoratum (or Strasbourg) in 357, Emperor Julian routed an army of German tribes under King Chnodomer. The methods of both armies reflect the maxim that 'the more things change, the more they remain the same'. Julian's army was deployed in two lines, with the fully armoured *clibanarii* (heavy cavalry) and supporting horse archers on the right, opposite the still-feared German cavalry. The front line of infantry was predominately ersatz 'legions' recruited from the Germanic citizen-tribes. The second line had several regular legions, *pseudocomitatenses*: it was this rear line that destroyed Chnodomer's Germans, after they had chased off the Roman cavalry and then broken through the centre of the first line.

The Germanic army was composed of 15,000 to 30,000 tribesmen, arrayed as usual in one big line. It relied on the impetus of its initial charge to shatter the Roman line. Significantly, both sides gave forth the legendary German war cry as battle commenced. The Roman infantry wore armour and fought with sword and shield like the old-style legions; not as tactically adept as Caesar's veterans, it was backed by an increasing proportion of horsemen during the 4th century.

The expansion of the cavalry, and especially the *clibanarii*, enabled several Roman expeditions to the East, and especially against the Persians, to gain more success than failure. The hit-and-run tactics of eastern horse-archers were less effective against Rome's new armoured cavalry force. As would be shown by the Magyars and the Mongols during the next millennium, such light cavalry could be devastating, but could checked by disciplined heavy cavalry.

By the time of the disaster at Adrianople in 378, the Goths and Vandals sensed Rome's strategic weakness, and had aspirations beyond raiding. At Adrianople, an over-eager Roman army under Emperor Valens, seeking to rid Thrace of the Goths forever, attacked the Gothic lager only to be driven back by Gothic cavalry, enveloped, and then smashed. Historians used to dawn of the 'cavalry era' from this battle, since the Roman army was destroyed by mounted Goths. However, it is also the case that the impetuous and inept Emperor Valens, plunged into battle without waiting for his second army to arrive. The Gothic commander Fridigern made the most of his opportunity.

The increasing power of cavalry stemmed not from any significant increase in its own capability, but to the gradual disappearance of trained infantry. Disciplined foot soldiers could usually, if not always, stand up to good cavalry. But by the end of the 4th century, Rome's 'legions' were no more than a local militia; cavalry dominated the battlefield and both arms were largely recruited from 'barbarian' allies.

ABOVE: **By the end of the republic, Rome had conquered all major states except Parthia. Cross-border raids by Germanic or Dacian tribes were discouraged by bribery or punitive expeditions. Some emperors continued to wage wars of conquest: Trajan added several short-lived provinces in the east, Severus campaigned into Scotland. Others, like Vespasian and Hadrian, were content to consolidate.**

Chapter 2 Men on Horseback 400–1500

The key military phenomenon which unifies this long period of over a thousand years is the rise and decline of 'chivalry'. This small military elite dominated European society not only militarily, but also socially, politically, economically and even culturally for centuries. It still lives on in the public imagination as the armoured knight on horseback. Mounted combat was indeed one of its defining characteristics and celebrated by medieval literature. However, these full-time warriors engaged in a wide range of military activities.

The knight has not had a good, military press. Although his individual martial prowess was never in doubt, military historians like Hans Delbrück (1848–1929) and Sir Charles Oman (1860–1946) derided his tactical and strategic abilities. Their view, perpetuated through reprints of their works, was that the very idea of knighthood was inimical to the art of war. They presented the knight as only interested in personal glory and lacking the discipline for force to be used in an organized sense, in the pursuit of common tactical and strategic designs.

This view is outdated. The objective of the following chapter is to illustrate the essence and quality of medieval warfare. A proper understanding of medieval warfare, however, must start with a recognition that medieval war was fought in a context very dissimilar to modern war. Not only was the material world different, but, more importantly, so was the mental world. Wars were fought for other reasons. Wars were seen first, not as a continuation of politics by other means, but as the continuation of justice by other means. Second, wars were a business venture from which the participants expected—and had the right to expect—to gain personally. Medieval war was, as a result, not dominated by a quest for decisive battle, but by strategies and tactics that aimed to pursue rights and profits.

RIGHT: Constantine I (c.280-337) transferred the imperial capital to Byzantium, which he renamed after himself in 330. His eastern empire would survive for over a thousand years, but political infighting in the west saw would-be emperors employing barbarian allies that would eventually seize power for themselves.

OANNES·ACVTVS·EQVES·BRITANNICVS·DVX·AETATIS·S
AE·CAVTISSIMVS·ET·REI·MILITARIS·PERITISSIMVS·HABITVS·EST

The Dawn of the Middle Ages

LEFT: Restored in a fanciful way in the 19th century by the architectural historian Viollet-le-Duc, the city walls of Carcassonne include a number of towers and wall sections of late Roman origin. Many Gallo-Roman cities retained their walls and tried to keep them in a state of repair. Roman fortifications remained a key element in the medieval military landscape, although, over time walls (if not the ground plan) did change beyond all recognition, as other sections of the walls of Carcassonne indicate.

4093. — CITÉ DE CARCASSONNE. *Montée de la Porte de l'Aude.*

In the course of the 5th century, a flood of Germanic and other tribes brought down the Western Roman Empire. In 407, Britain was abandoned. Gaul and North Africa were lost before the middle of the century. All of Spain was gone by 484. During the last quarter of the century, the heart of the Empire, Italy, was taken over by the Ostrogoths.

In many ways, the defeat of the Western Empire was surprising; the Eastern, or Byzantine, Empire survived fitfully for another 1,000 years. In numbers, organization, tactics and strategy, the 'barbarians' were far inferior to the Romans. The tribes were quite small, typically comprising 10–30,000 able-bodied men, whereas the Roman army in the West may have consisted of up to 300,000 men at the beginning of the 5th century, with another 300,000 guarding the East. In the critical years between 407 and 410, when the Visigoths, Vandals, Alans and Sueves attacked the Empire at the same time,

these tribes probably fielded a grand total of 60,000 warriors.

Tribal battlefield tactics consisted of an all-or-nothing shock charge—a glaring contrast with the complicated evolutions of which the legions were capable. Attracted by the wealth of cities, the tribes lacked the ability to conduct sieges and they usually relied on surprise or just plain luck to take a town. Without the bureaucratic and logistical infrastructure of the Empire, tribal strategy was often guided by

The Frankish kingdom, 511

Frankish territory at the beginning of Clovis's rule, 481

controlled by Syagrius before the Frankish conquest

conquered by Clovis by 497

conquered by Clovis, 507

boundaries between the kingdoms of Clovis's sons from 511

frontiers, 511

dates are those of Frankish conquest

LEFT: Clovis founded the Frankish empire. From modern-day Belgium and northern France Clovis launched raids against the Visigoths in Aquitaine, the Gallo-Roman remnant of the Roman Empire under Syagrius, the Burgundians and the Alamans. His plundering and occasional battles created a 'Frankish' empire, based not on conquest but on the acceptance overlordship and the payment of tribute. The looseness of the Empire is illustrated by the penetration of Germanic words into the local languages. Rule was an ephemeral, constantly contested, superimposition over existing societies.

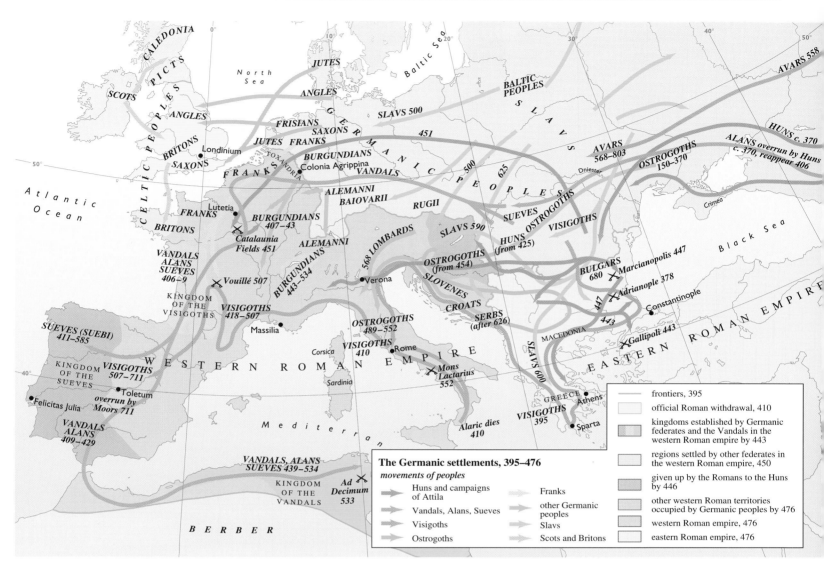

The Germanic settlements, 395–476

movements of peoples

Huns and campaigns of Attila	Franks
Vandals, Alans, Sueves	other Germanic peoples
Visigoths	Slavs
Ostrogoths	Scots and Britons

frontiers, 395

official Roman withdrawal, 410

kingdoms established by Germanic federates and the Vandals in the western Roman empire by 443

regions settled by other federates in the western Roman empire, 450

given up by the Romans to the Huns by 446

other western Roman territories occupied by Germanic peoples by 476

western Roman empire, 476

eastern Roman empire, 476

their members' stomachs. Wandering tribesmen plundered the Roman countryside in small, vulnerable groups. Yet, Roman armies, which had succeeded century after century in destroying waves of invaders in climactic battles, failed in the 5th century.

Why did the tribes emerge victorious? With threats all along the imperial frontiers, the invasions had to be resisted first of all locally. Thus the relative balance of forces did not favour the Romans as much as the overall, absolute balance suggested. But, more importantly, the Empire proved easy to fragment. Institutionally and ideologically, the Empire turned out to be too weak for its citizens to feel forced or obliged to provide the taxes and manpower necessary to defeat the invasions. All too often, regions faced the invaders in isolation. Historians have noted a curious lack of will, a state of paralysis almost, that seems to have gripped the Empire. Many cities, for example, that could have withstood a siege, failed to summon the necessary resistance. The invaders, on the other hand, utilized their military potential more efficiently. Favouring their morale and effectiveness was the fact that they consist-

ed of peoples-in-arms: all able-bodied men were fighters, unified by a common desire to escape the primeval forests of central Europe and acquire the riches of the empire.

After an enormous plundering spree, which left few parts of the Empire unaffected, the tribes settled in the Empire. In general, they did not displace the local population, but supplanted local elites, indirectly proving that their numbers were limited. As indicated by the boundaries of Germanic and Slavic languages which persist to this day, they only became dominant in the border territories, along the Rhine and Danube, where there was a longer history of invader-Roman interaction. Their small numbers explain why Germanic rule was often ephemeral and the boundaries of their kingdoms constantly shifting.

Fascinated and impressed by the Empire, the 'barbarians' tried hard to become Romans. As they acquired Roman titles and functions from the waning imperial powers, the legalistic framework in which wars took place was one of competing claims of succession to the Empire, in whole or in part. Also important was the idea that victory in war was a sign of

Divine approval. For many chieftains and their followers, conversion to Christianity was clinched by the perception that the Christian God was a 'God of hosts' who provided the ultimate aid in their just pursuit of worldly power. To them, an integral part of victory was the acquisition of loot. Wars were not about the conquest of territory with a view to its long-term exploitation; wars provided immediate profit in the form of plunder. If there was a longer-term perspective, it usually went no further than the annual extraction of tribute from defeated enemies.

The Frankish king Clovis (born 466; ruled 481–511) provides an excellent example of all this. His very name meant 'glory by combat' and his spectacular success in war was interpreted as a sign of divine favour (he converted to Christianity) which also brought him recognition from the Romans. The Byzantine emperor Anastasius made him consul after his victory over the Alamans in the battle of Vouillé in 507. Nonetheless, his victories did not usually consist of battles, which he fought rarely, but of bountiful yearly raids of plunder deep into the territory of his enemies.

ABOVE: Descending from the primeval forests of central and eastern Europe, the invaders were attracted by the wealth of the empire. Once over the frontier, the tribes plundered vast swathes of territory; living off the countryside, they had to stay on the move. Intense looting destroyed the administrative infrastructure of the Western Empire. The tribes' casualty rates were very high. The Vandals (who covered the most ground of all) crossed to North Africa in 429 with only 16,000 men, of which 4,000 constituted the remnants of three other tribes.

The Arab Conquest

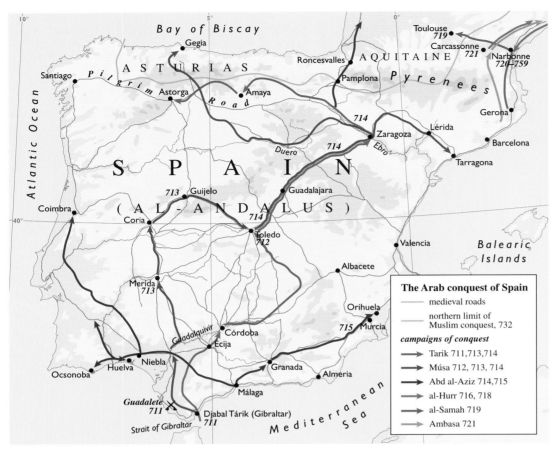

The Arab conquest of Spain

— medieval roads
— northern limit of Muslim conquest, 732

campaigns of conquest

→ Tarik 711,713,714
→ Músa 712, 713, 714
→ Abd al-Aziz 714,715
→ al-Hurr 716, 718
→ al-Samah 719
→ Ambasa 721

ABOVE: In a great feat of maritime adaptation, the Arabs fanned out across the Mediterranean. In the Eastern Mediterranean, they struggled with the Byzantine fleet for many centuries. But after the Byzantines abandoned North Africa in 699, they began to dominate the Western Mediterranean. Their raiding became particularly fierce in the 9th century. From bases on the coast, they attacked deep inland, even plundering the monastery of St Gallen north of the Alps. This was a period of great anarchy and confusion for the Christian shores, made worse by the appearance of the Vikings.

The speed of the 7th century Arab conquest still astonishes. The Prophet Muhammad established himself in the Arabian peninsula in little more than ten years. After his death in 632, his follower Abu Bakr completed the conquest of the peninsula in two years. His successor moved into Egypt, Syria, Mesopotamia and beyond. By 669, Arab forces had briefly laid siege to Constantinople. Before the century was out, they had penetrated deep into Persia, knocked at the gates of the Byzantine Empire in Asia Minor and stood poised at the Straits of Gibraltar to move into Visigothic Spain.

This was achieved without any superiority in numbers, armament, organization, tactics and discipline over their enemies. However, their main opponents, the Byzantines and Persians had been greatly weakened by their interminable wars. Secondly, the Visigoths, Persians and Byzantines were not closely integrated with the populations they ruled. For many it made no difference who their rulers were. Once defeated, one regime was easily replaced by another. Moreover, the Arabs were usually quite lenient in their treatment of conquered peoples. They

required no conversion to Islam, only tribute, often at a rate lower than the tax burden imposed by the old regime.

Arab armies had a number of strengths. The traditional motive of lust for loot was reinforced by religious enthusiasm. Islam offered entry into paradise to those who died for the faith. Also, Islam had an egalitarian streak which opened up the way for new talent. The early Arab conquest saw the emergence of a large group of first-rate military leaders. Being on the attack with armies largely on horseback, they also possessed

the twin advantages of initiative and mobility. Their knowledge of the desert enabled them to attack the old empires from a new direction. The Byzantines in North Africa had never previously contended with an enemy that could move swiftly across the desert and attack from almost any point.

Nonetheless, conquest happened almost by accident. The standard operation was the *razzia*, or raid. Rather than returning home every year, the Arabs, like the Vikings a little later, established armed camps along the way of their major expeditions from which they systematically launched further attacks. Famous examples with a long and distinguished future were Fustat in Egypt (which later grew into Cairo) and Basra in Iraq. Shorter-lived establishments were Qairawan, founded south of Carthage in 670, Cyzikos, just south of Constantinople (674-677) and Fraxinet, near Marseilles (c. 894-972). The camps emphasized that the new conquerors were outsiders.

The Arabs achieved another major feat in taking to the seas. Already in the 650s they began to mount raids across the Mediterranean. In the 9th century, the raids multiplied and led to long-term presences on Sardinia, Sicily, and Crete, as well as the Italian mainland and southern France. Although raiding across the Mediterranean continued for centuries, the hold on the lands across the sea proved tenuous with the rise of new powers, such as the Normans in Sicily.

Arab expansion appears to have stopped

The Arab Conquest

▇ growth under Mohammed
▇ growth under Abu Bakr (632–4)
▇ growth under Omar (634–44)
▇ growth under Othman (644–56) and Ali (656–61)
▇ expansion of Umayyad Caliphate (661–750)
▇ expansion under the early Abbasids (750–850)

○ military camps/ new cities
→ routes of advance
638 date of Muslim conquest
-- - principal trade routes

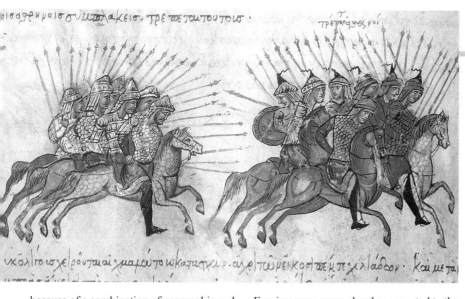

in France is often ascribed to the decisive Frankish victory in the battle of Poitiers on 25 October 732. This is extremely doubtful. Not only do we not have enough primary sources from the period to really warrant such a claim — no contemporaries saw it as decisive — we do know that Arab raids did not cease for quite some time after the battle.

The Arabs also fell prey to their own internal bickering. Created by a group of enterprising individuals, there was no strong central power. Instead, the size of the empire provided opportunities for the establishment of new dynasties, who soon began to quarrel with each other. In time, their divisions handed opportunities to other waves of enterprising individuals, from Western Christendom and the Byzantine Empire, to try and turn the tide back.

LEFT: An eleventh century Byzantine illustration shows Byzantine and Arab cavalry in battle.

because of a combination of geographic and socio-political factors. In Spain, Asia Minor and Armenia, the Pyrenees, Taurus and Caucasus mountains marked the limit; in the east, the vast expanses of inner central Asia put a (temporary) halt to expansion. Desert, steppe and high plain were the most congenial terrain. In addition, north of the Pyrenees and beyond the Taurus mountains, the rulers of the Frankish and Byzantine

Empires were more closely connected to the local populations than had been the case with the peoples the Arabs had already conquered. Resistance stiffened and establishing a permanent presence became more difficult. The end of Muslim expansion

LEFT: The Arab conquest spread like wildfire across the Middle East and North Africa. Through the establishment of a network of armed camps, they took their raiding strategy progressively further, away from their heartland. Eventually they established a network of bases all around the Mediterranean and deep into Central Asia. Almost by accident, the Arabs had, within a century, brought down the Persian and Visigothic empires and seriously weakened Byzantium by taking Syria, Egypt and North Africa.

43

The Byzantine Empire

RIGHT: Byzantine soldiers in a scene depicting Justinian's court. Much of the territory he conquered was lost during the 7th century, but the development of the *themes* reduced the impact on the army. Offering soldiers land instead of wages allayed the recruitment crises that chronic shortages of money had created.

The Byzantine Empire grew out of the partition of the Roman Empire by the Emperor Diocletian in 293. The division was made mainly for military reasons. Separate sectors, with their own armies and command structure, were intended to make the defence of the frontiers more effective. The Eastern Empire was not as hard hit by invasions as the West in the 5th century and managed to survive until the great and final siege of its capital, Constantinople, by the Turks in 1453. There were two main reasons for its long life, albeit as a shadow of its former self after the 11th century: geography and military organization.

The territorial core of the empire was Asia Minor, shielded by sea on three sides and the Taurus Mountains in the east. Despite many raids, these barriers protected a great reservoir of manpower, agriculture and taxes until the Seljuk Turks broke through permanently in the 11th century. Without comparable physical barriers, the Balkans were more difficult to defend. Nonetheless, the Byzantines tried and, for significant periods of time, managed to hold on to the Danube as a frontier.

The Byzantines inherited a well-educated military. Its core consisted of long-serving, well-paid conscripts. They were led by an elite that read and wrote an extensive military literature. The elite regularly reformed the military, partly in response to having to deal with different and changing enemies, and partly to adapt to the changing resources of the Empire. Cavalry became the key element in Byzantine armies. The proportion of cavalry in the field armies increased from about 20 per cent in late Roman times to a third or more by the 10th century. A small minority of these were heavy cavalry. Since most of the army's time was spent on dealing with raids, often by mounted invaders, or mounting raids of its own, cavalry offered increased flexibility.

Paying the army proved as much of a headache as fending off invaders. The chronic problem of raising sufficient tax money for wages led to a subdivision of the Empire into 'themes' in the mid-7th century. Each theme could raise a field army from soldiers who were given local land grants in return for military service. The land grant provided the soldier not only with a steady source of income, but also gave him a stake in the defence of the

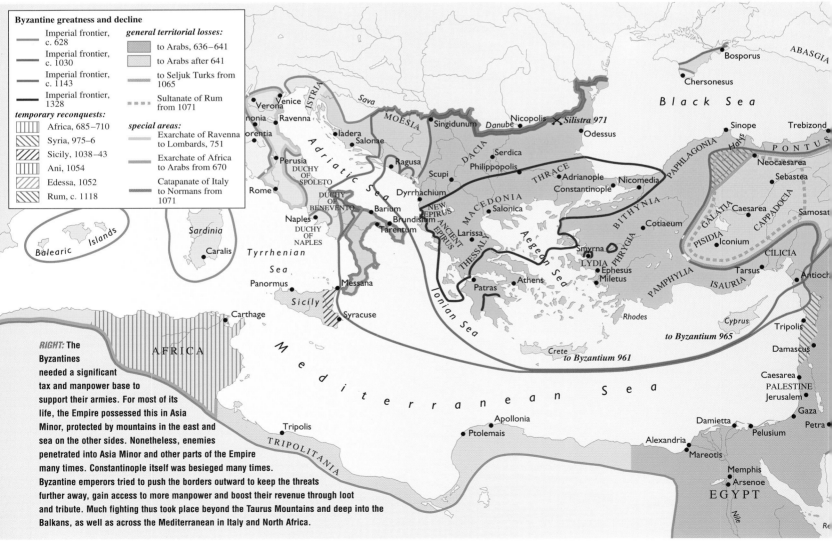

Byzantine greatness and decline

Imperial frontier, c. 628	
Imperial frontier, c. 1030	
Imperial frontier, c. 1143	
Imperial frontier, 1328	

temporary reconquests:
Africa, 685–710
Syria, 975–6
Sicily, 1038–43
Ani, 1054
Edessa, 1052
Rum, c. 1118

general territorial losses:
to Arabs, 636–641
to Arabs after 641
to Seljuk Turks from 1065
Sultanate of Rum from 1071

special areas:
Exarchate of Ravenna to Lombards, 751
Exarchate of Africa to Arabs from 670
Catapanate of Italy to Normans from 1071

RIGHT: The Byzantines needed a significant tax and manpower base to support their armies. For most of its life, the Empire possessed this in Asia Minor, protected by mountains in the east and sea on the other sides. Nonetheless, enemies penetrated into Asia Minor and other parts of the Empire many times. Constantinople itself was besieged many times. Byzantine emperors tried to push the borders outward to keep the threats further away, gain access to more manpower and boost their revenue through loot and tribute. Much fighting thus took place beyond the Taurus Mountains and deep into the Balkans, as well as across the Mediterranean in Italy and North Africa.

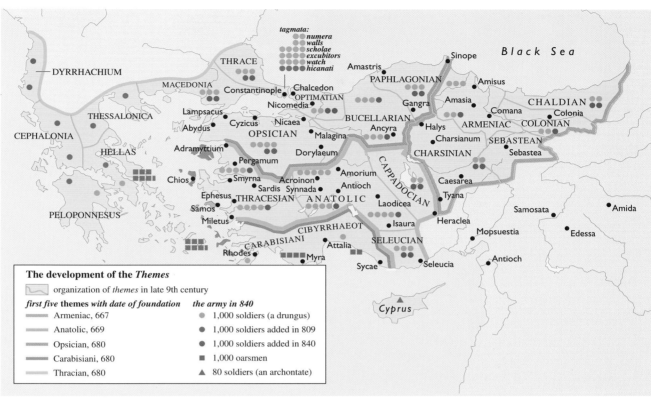

RIGHT: The successes of the Byzantine Empire depended in large part on its superior ability to raise, train and maintain armies. The organization of the Empire into *themes* from the mid-7th century onwards, stabilized recruitment problems. In effect, the *themes* militarized the state, by creating a capacity for an equitable mobilization of manpower from all over the Empire as well as a defence in depth.

The development of the *Themes*

organization of *themes* in late 9th century

first five themes *with date of foundation*

Armeniac, 667
Anatolic, 669
Opsician, 680
Carabisiani, 680
Thracian, 680

the army in 840

● 1,000 soldiers (a drungus)
● 1,000 soldiers added in 809
● 1,000 soldiers added in 840
■ 1,000 oarsmen
▲ 80 soldiers (an archontate)

Empire, or at least of that region. Although it helped reduce financial pressures, the problem with the themes was that it made thematic armies independent from the state. This encouraged military uprisings, which came with particular frequency from the Opsician Theme around Constantinople. The Byzantine Empire never really found a way to solve its internal instability and the propensity of its army to take over power. Attempts to reduce the dependence on land as the main remuneration, such as in the 'tagmata' of the 8th century, required money — which was always in short supply. Another solution, difficult to avoid with the shrinking of the Empire, was the use of mercenaries, such as the Varangians. They were often drawn from erstwhile enemies of the Empire. Their salaries, however, did not always buy total loyalty.

The military success and longevity of the Empire is nevertheless remarkable. It often found itself fighting two- and even three-front wars. The Empire contracted and expanded at regular intervals. The most celebrated period of expansion was under Justinian (527–565), when his generals Belisarius and Narses repeatedly defeated the Persians, destroyed the Vandals in North Africa and forced the Ostrogoths in Italy into submission. Justinian even managed to take territory from the Visigoths in Spain. The Byzantines generally maintained a presence in Italy, but they permanently lost the western Mediterranean with the growth of Muslim naval power in the 7th century. Byzantine and Muslim fleets tussled for control over the eastern Mediterranean for centuries. Muslim suc-

cesses included, from 674 to 677, the establishment of a base at Cyzikos in the Sea of Marmara, very near to Constantinople, as well as sieges of Constantinople itself, notably in 669 and 716-717, and the seizure of Crete in 828.

The Byzantine fleet enjoyed a long period of success. Byzantine possessions continued to dot the Italian and Balkan coasts, even when much of the interior was lost. The same was true for Asia Minor after the Seljuk Turks arrived in the 11th century and permanently breached the eastern defences. This defeat ultimately spelled the end of the Empire. Its territory began to contract to such an extent that it could no longer support adequate defences. In the late 13th century, when the rise of the Ottoman Turks began in Bythinia, just across the Bosporus, the writing was on the wall. The Turks gradually tightened the nose. In the 1340s, on the invitation of a pretender in one of the interminable struggles for the Byzantine throne, they crossed into the Balkans. Soon only Constantinople's walls delimited the borders of the once powerful empire.

RIGHT: Emperor Justinian I (ruled 527-565) oversaw the most dramatic strategic counter-offensive undertaken by Byzantine armies. Persia was humbled, Italy and North Africa reconquered and a bridgehead established in Spain.

The Carolingian Empire

The Carolingian Empire was founded on and brought down by war. The early rulers — Charles 'the war hammer' Martel (r. 714–741), Peppin the Short (r. 741–768) and the greatest of all, Charlemagne (r. 768–814) — were outstanding warlords. They established and expanded their authority by offering their followers booty and land in return for military service. Virtually every year of their reigns, the Carolingians led their armies in major military campaigns, gradually turning the direction of the campaigns outward, away from the pacified and renewed *Imperium Romanorum.* Saxons, Avars, Lombards, Moors and Bretons all suffered the depredations of the Franks, year after year. As these peoples realized that it was better to be inside than outside the Empire, they began to submit and thus, particularly under Charlemagne, the Empire expanded greatly.

However, this form of empire-building carried the seeds of its own downfall. Not only were the personal abilities of the ruler critical, there was also a continuous

Viking, Magyar and Saracen invasions

→ Saracen attacks
→ Magyar attacks
→ Viking routes
✕ battles

● Viking bases
✱ main Viking raids (with dates)
▨ areas most affected by Saracen raiders (with dates)
▨ areas most affected by Magyar raiders (with dates)

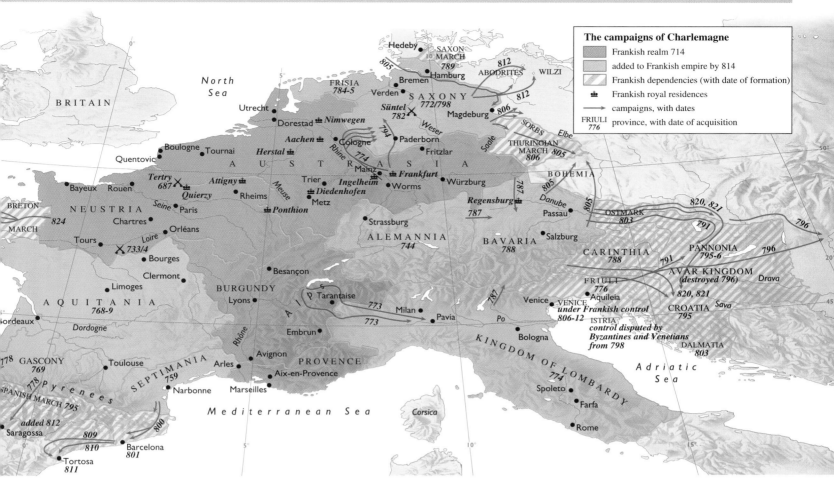

The campaigns of Charlemagne

Frankish realm 714

added to Frankish empire by 814

Frankish dependencies (with date of formation)

Frankish royal residences

campaigns, with dates

FRIULI
776 province, with date of acquisition

requirement for new lands to plunder. After the submission of the Saxons and the Avars, the Franks found campaigning further east unrewarding. In the south, in Italy, geography stopped expansion, while in Spain, a strong Moorish presence made it difficult. The distances armies needed to cover to reach their enemies increased. For armies that needed to be mobilized anew for each campaign from all over the Empire, more and more time was taken up by profitless travel.

The size and success of the Empire reinforced a process of social and military stratification that had begun when the Germanic tribes settled within the borders of the old Roman Empire. They underwent a slow metamorphosis from peoples-in-arms into a society in which only a minority fought while the majority worked the land. Over time, most rank-and-file 'barbarians' merged with the local peasant populations who, as in Roman days, remained unused to military service. As they struggled to produce the meagre food surpluses common to Medieval agriculture, the peasantry were dominated and exploited by a rising military elite. By living off the agricultural surplus and by gaining additional income from war, these warriors could afford to train as well as acquire better military equipment, particularly armour and horses, thereby steadily widening the qualitative gap. Cavalry became more important in Frankish

armies, not so much because of their value in combat (this came later), but because mobility in the large empire was useful.

Historians have debated the size of Charlemagne's armies, with estimates ranging from 5,000 to 50,000. Much depends on one's evaluation of how far the stratification process had proceeded by the late 8th century. In theory, there existed a vast pool of manpower. The ruler had the right to call up for unlimited service all free, able-bodied men, who had to equip themselves at their own expense. Yet the need to deploy on the borders and the greater value of well-armed, mounted (and thus wealthy) individuals drove numbers downwards. Nonetheless, armies contained a sizeable infantry element, recruited from imperial territories close to the theatre of operations.

With fewer opportunities for plunder and with weaker military leadership, the Carolingian Empire faltered under Charlemagne's son, Louis the Pious. Instead of channelling their energies outwards, the warrior nobility started fighting amongst itself. The collapse of central power was hastened by the quarrelsome division of the Empire, according to Frankish custom, among Louis' three sons in 840 and by a wave of Viking, Magyar and Muslim raids.

Viking attacks began in 834 and only let up by the late 10th century. Between 899 and 955 the Magyars launched 33

major expeditions from the east against Germany, Italy, France and even Spain. At the same time, Muslims repeatedly attacked Italy and the south of France. The success of these raiders did not in the first place depend on superior weaponry, tactics or strategy. Rather, initiative and mobility were the key. The raiders could choose the time and place of attack. The mounted Magyars and the ship-borne Vikings and Muslims were also highly mobile. The flat-bottomed Viking ships, moreover, allowed deep penetration into Europe via rivers.

Just as with the late Roman Empire, the response to these attacks from all directions was a local one. Many cities and monasteries — prime targets for the plunderers — were refortified. Local strongmen received an opportunity to distinguish themselves. In the east, a strong Saxon dynasty organized the defence of the Holy Roman Empire (greatly benefiting from the old Carolingian organization of the border into numerous military districts, or marches). In 955, Otto, later nicknamed the Great, defeated the Magyars on the Lechfeld and slaughtered so many that major attacks ceased for almost a century. In the west, numerous territorial principalities emerged, some, such as Flanders and Normandy under dynasties with Viking connections. Yet even strong rulers found it difficult to extend their power because of a new development in warfare: the rise of castles (see p50).

ABOVE: Charlemagne's campaigns were once interpreted as grandly conceived multi-pronged invasions, but they were repeatedly aimed at the same enemies, often with an interval of one or more years, suggesting that their total overthrow may not have been a key objective. More important was the acquisition of loot. Allowing the enemy time to recover increased the pickings next time round. Subdivision of the army was necessary because that made it easier to live off the land.

The Age of Chivalry

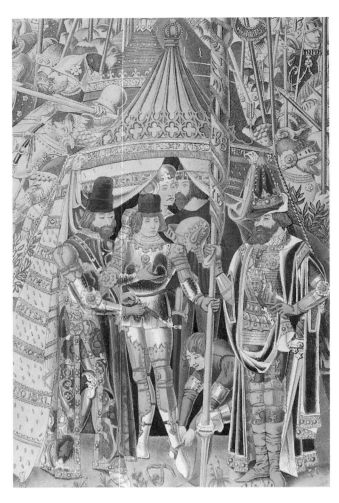

ABOVE: **The ceremony
of knighthood endorsed
a warrior caste with the
specific blessing of the
church. Medieval
campaigns were
influenced by religious
sentiment to a degree
that makes modern
analysis difficult.**

The word 'chivalry' denoted both a class or 'order' in society and a code of conduct. The elite which regarded itself as chivalrous emerged in France during the 11th century and spread across Western Europe. The term, which is derived from the French word *cheval*, indicates that the horse was a key attribute of this new class and one that distinguished them from society at large. The members of chivalry were known, in English, as knights. Although they fought as often on foot as on horseback and castles marked them out as much as their horses, their self-image was intimately tied up with the horse.

Chivalry was a surprising product of the extreme political fragmentation that Europe suffered with the collapse of Carolingian public order. Power became vested in a multitude of local strongmen who jealously guarded their recently acquired right to use force and administer justice. The symbols of these rights and the embodiment of their independence were the castle and the war-horse. Paradoxically, despite a lack of political unity, they developed a common outlook on life and war.

The definition of chivalry was greatly helped by the Church. The Church suffered considerably from the collapse of public order. The depredations of a rapacious knighthood in the 10th and early 11th centuries gave rise to a movement called the 'Peace of God' in the south of France.

Central to the movement was the call on knights to protect the unarmed, that is clerics and common people. Top clergy and top nobility, as well as, unusually for the Middle Ages, the common people, organized mass demonstrations that were surprisingly effective. This evolved into the more ambitious aim of establishing a 'Truce of God' which banned all fighting between Christians on certain days of the week. The net effect of these movements was to 'Christianize' knighthood: promoting the idea that knights, if they fought, must to do so respecting certain rules — and in the service of Christendom. By the end of the 11th century this idea culminated in the supreme Christian enterprise of the Crusade (see p54). The Church offered remission of sins for those who would fight to liberate and defend the Holy Land. The astonishing achievements of the Crusades provide an example of the appeal of Christian ideals on chivalry.

The three key elements that epitomized the code of chivalry were quite secular in nature. The first, *fidélité*, or loyalty, came in three basic forms: domestic, feudal and political. The political loyalty owed to the king was the weakest. Stronger than the political was the feudal bond of loyalty between vassal and lord. The strongest by far, however, were ties based on kinship and household connections. The nucleus in the chivalric warrior society was the family 'gang'. The gang was held together and enlarged through the second fundamental element of chivalry, *largesse*, or generosity. Winnings in war and tournaments had to be passed out to the gang members. The more successful a knight was as a fighter, the larger and more loyal his following. Success in war (and tournaments) had to be acquired the right way. A true knight therefore displayed *prouesse*, or prowess. He fought according to the rules, valiantly and fairly. He did not kill — at least not his noble opponents — but captured them for ransom. The code of chivalry was essentially a pragmatic code of conduct in which self- and group-interest were paramount. The relative lack of idealism and emphasis on materialistic motives made the medieval reality of chivalrous behaviour very different from modern notions.

Chivalry was fostered in war and, in peacetime, in tournaments. Tournaments emerged in France in the middle of the 11th century and experienced their greatest popularity in the 12th century. They were true war games. Two armies opposed each other with the aim of driving each other from the field and acquiring as much

booty, in the form of equipment and horses, and ransom from captured opponents as possible. They were relatively unbloody events, largely thanks to the excellent protective armour that the knight by then possessed. Tournaments provided a first-rate training-ground for the real thing. It was here that the great new battlefield tactic of the 11th century, the massed mounted shock charge, could be practised. Even sieges could be part of them. Tournaments were indistinguishable from war proper where loot and ransom were also the prime objectives. In the only battle fought by a French king in the 12th century, at Brémule on 20 August 1119, the chronicler Orderic Vitalis wrote that of the 900 knights engaged only three were killed, but scores captured and ransomed.

Chivalry moulded a class, which dominated society through violence, into a homogeneous group with shared values. Chivalry made Europe, not more peaceful, but more ordered as war was fought according to widely accepted rules. Their codes of conduct would influence the conduct of war for generations to come.

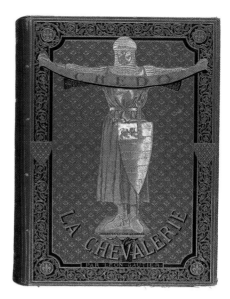

ABOVE: An allegorical representation of the Chivalric ideal, one that continued to evolve long after the Middle Ages. The medieval reality of chivalry was very different from its later romantic manifestations.

ABOVE: A 14th century knight in full panoply. The sheer cost of a knight's equipment helped limit numbers: their specially bred war-horses changed hands for sums that could buy a small castle. Contrary to later myth, the weight of medieval armour was well distributed and knights could vault horses and turn somersaults in a suit of armour.

LEFT: Emperor Maximilian knights the French warrior Claudius de Barre c. 1500. The end of the Middle Ages did not see the end of the knightly class (see p 60). Chivalry adapted to new technology while remaining politically dominant.

RIGHT: The frequency and spread of the Peace of God movement in the late 10th and early 11th century. In an attempt to combat the anarchy that ensued from the collapse of Carolingian public order, an alliance of bishops, high nobility and common people organized mass gatherings. The key value that they initially called attention to was the Christian duty of the strong to protect and respect the weak and unarmed. Less successfully, the movement subsequently tried to obtain acceptance that Christians should not fight on certain days. Although knights were quite receptive to the idea that rules should be obeyed in war, they were less enthusiastic about a ban on the activity they regarded as critical to their being.

The Peace of God Movement in France until 1031

- - - - - approximate boundary of dioceses

– – – approximate boundary of ecclesiastical provinces

✝ archbishopric

participation in the Peace of God Movement

6-7	
5-6	number of times
3-4	Peace of God proclaimed
1-2	

Castles and Sieges

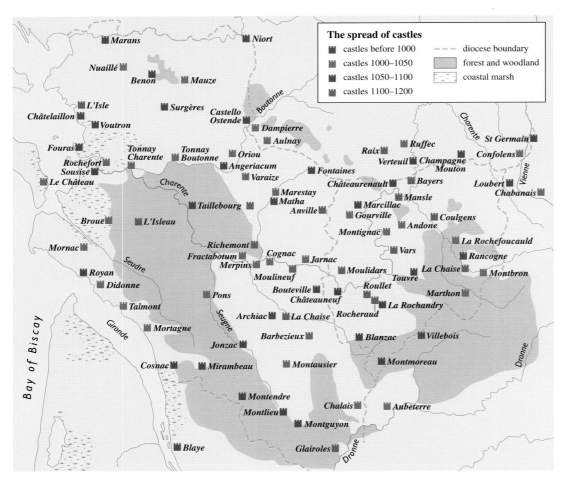

The spread of castles

- castles before 1000
- castles 1000–1050
- castles 1050–1100
- castles 1100–1200
- - - - diocese boundary
- forest and woodland
- coastal marsh

more straightforward methods. First of all, besiegers could try to avoid the use of force by instigating treason or offering bribes. If a castle or town resisted, the quickest method of attack was storming. Scaling the walls, however, made the attackers highly vulnerable and, if there was little or no surprise, this could be very costly. Also, as time wore on, walls became higher, making them more 'scale-proof'. In the early days of wooden motte and bailey castles, the next most obvious weapon was fire. When wood was replaced by stone and brick, fire was still used against the gates. In response, intricate defensive designs were developed, like receding the gate between towers, protecting it with an iron guard (or *portcullis*) and drawbridge, and building protruding platforms above the gates from which could be thrown stones and other objects, including in times of extreme need, the lord's furniture.

If storm and fire failed, the next method was mining. Although much more time-consuming, success was also virtually guaranteed. The high, heavy walls of castles and towns were highly vulnerable to collapse when undermined. However, mining required an army to stay in one place for an extended period — as did the usually most time-consuming method, starvation. For armies that usually lived off the land, that was very difficult as they soon

Castles appeared in the 10th century and dramatically multiplied in the 11th *after* most Viking, Magyar and Muslim raiding stopped. Older fortifications, common since prehistoric times, were usually quite large and meant to protect a local community. Castles, on the other hand, were generally small and designed to protect only the local strongman and his 'gang'. The early common design was the so-called motte and bailey castle, consisting of a wooden tower on top of a small mound (the motte) surrounded by a moat and towering over a small courtyard (the bailey). Wood, because of its susceptibility to fire, was replaced by stone from the late 11th century onwards.

Next to campaigns of plunder, the attack and defence of castles became the dominant feature of medieval warfare. The success of the castle can be explained by the ease with which they could be defended. Garrisons were small: half-a-dozen to a dozen fighting men were common complements until the end of the Middle Ages. Castles relied for their defence, not on manpower, but on the strength of their design and the difficulties associated with siege warfare.

Siege engines were not as critical in medieval siege warfare as is commonly believed. Although stone-throwing engines and siege towers retained as strong a hold on the medieval as the modern imagination, they were rarely a match for

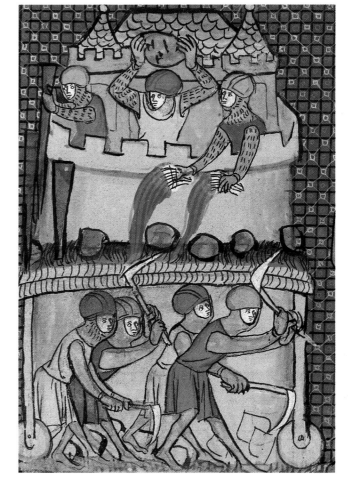

LEFT: Several siege techniques in action: a miner picks at the wall, while knights climb siege ladders, supported by archers who keep the defenders' heads down. In reality, ladders were positioned with the tops below the parapet, making it hard for the defenders to push them down.

BELOW: A castle only dominated the ground on which it stood. Its projection power depended on the size of its garrison, but these were very small. The main function of a castle was to provide a place where a lord and his followers found protection: hence the inhospitable places in which castles were often built. With the growth of royal power, particularly in England, they became a key element in the exercise of that power. The castles that Edward I built in Wales did not so much conquer the region, but provided a ring of bases from which raids could be launched into the Welsh interior. They were positioned on the coast so that they could easily be supplied and reinforced. The conquest of Wales, like that of any other region, required leaving the castles and fighting for it in the countryside.

exhausted local resources. With the development of effective gunpowder artillery by the beginning of the 15th century, sieges became easier. Concentrating gunfire at a single, low point of the wall had the same effect as the time-honoured method of mining. Artillery spelt the end for castles and, by the end of the century, they were superseded by new designs that were more gunpowder-proof.

A striking feature of medieval warfare was the extent to which it was subject to rules and rituals. This was nowhere more apparent than in siege warfare. The set of laws regarding siege warfare started from the premise, provided by the Bible in Deuteronomy XX, 14ff., that in towns or castles that had resisted 'all males' should, on surrender, be 'put to the sword' and 'the loot divided among the army'. This harsh principle, meant to induce immediate surrender, was tempered by the equally uncompromising principle that immediate surrender constituted treason to one's own party, which was also punishable by death. As a result, an intricate body of customs emerged by the late Middle Ages that allowed resistance and surrender under certain circumstances. In the typical siege of Harfleur in 1415, the English king Henry V, for example, allowed the besieged formally to ask the king of France to relieve them. The town would surrender if a French relieving army failed to turn up within a set period of time to do battle with Henry. Thus Henry and the king of France could both show magnanimity: Henry because the town surrendered and the French king because he had been notified of the town's plight and, by failing to relieve it, absolved it of treasonous behaviour. To modern eyes, this is curious behaviour, compromising Henry's security by letting the enemy know his dispositions and intentions.

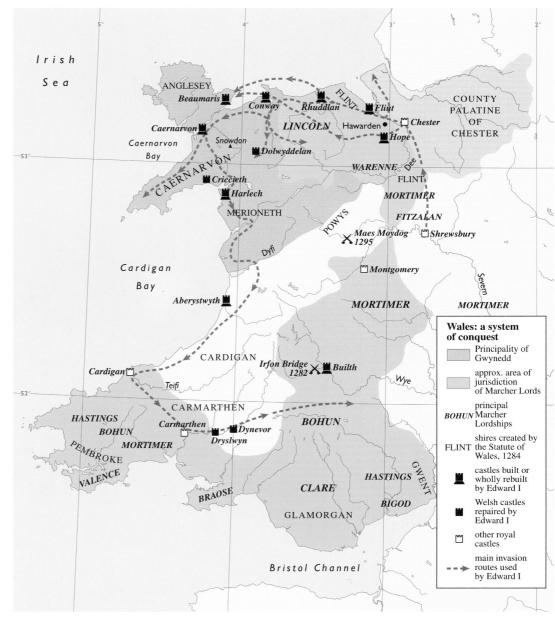

Wales: a system of conquest

- Principality of Gwynedd
- approx. area of jurisdiction of Marcher Lords
- **BOHUN** principal Marcher Lordships
- FLINT shires created by the Statute of Wales, 1284
- castles built or wholly rebuilt by Edward I
- Welsh castles repaired by Edward I
- other royal castles
- main invasion routes used by Edward I

Pitched Battle

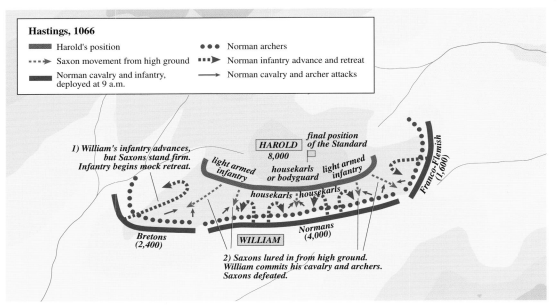

Hastings, 1066

▬▬▬ Harold's position

▪▪▪▪➤ Saxon movement from high ground

▬▬▬ Norman cavalry and infantry, deployed at 9 a.m.

●●● Norman archers

■■■➤ Norman infantry advance and retreat

───➤ Norman cavalry and archer attacks

1) William's infantry advances, but Saxons stand firm. Infantry begins mock retreat.

HAROLD 8,000

final position of the Standard

light armed infantry

housekarls or bodyguard

light armed infantry

Franco-Flemish (1,600)

housekarls · housekarls

Bretons (2,400)

WILLIAM

Normans (4,000)

2) Saxons lured in from high ground. William commits his cavalry and archers. Saxons defeated.

ABOVE: The English army formed a densely-packed shield-wall that resisted Norman archers, infantry and even a series of cavalry charges. But when part of the duke's army fell back, the English broke ranks in pursuit. William rallied his knights and overwhelmed the disordered English. In hard fighting, punctuated by a number of Norman feigned flights, Harold was killed and the English fled. The battle between the two claimants for the English throne is depicted in the accounts of the time as a divine judgement.

RIGHT: Clovis, pagan king of the Franks, invokes God's help in defeating the Germans. He converted to Christianity after his victory, as he promised his wife Clothilde.

Pitched battles were rare in the Middle Ages. William the Conqueror, for example, fought all his life, but only conducted two battles: Val-des-Dunes (1047) and Hastings (1066). The Hundred Years' War did not lack skirmishes, but there were only three major, royal battles: Crécy (1346), Poitiers (1356) and Agincourt (1415). This was not so much the result of military incompetence or of primitive military organization, as is often alleged, but more one of fear.

Battle between the major protagonists in a conflict was feared as a divine judgement, as an 'ordeal'. In a society that believed that history was developing according to a divine plan and that saw war as a continuation of justice by other means, battle was believed to be an institution which revealed the will of God. As in the Old Testament

battles, God would side with the righteous, not with the strong (as in the case of David and Goliath). However, no side had justice entirely on its side since no Christian was entirely without sin. God, moreover, might decide, if not to exact punishment for an old sin, to test one's faith. The trial of battle was not to be undertaken lightly.

Battle, when it occurred, was highly ritualized. Generally, the protagonists agreed a time and place in advance (hence *pitched* battle). The preparation for the fight was accompanied by religious ceremony. The party that went into the battle of Axspoele in 1127, for example, as penitents, with hair shorn, wearing hair shirts under their armour and praying, was awarded the victory. The losing side was believed to have been defeated because of their failure to follow comparable religious protocol. After battle, a victor was expected to demonstrate his victory by staying in possession of the field for three days and nights, rather than pursue his enemy.

The key actor in battle by the 11th century was the knight. The popular image of the medieval knight depicts him as a vainglorious individual, unwilling to submit to any kind of discipline, who engaged in mounted single combat and who wore such extraordinarily heavy armour that he was virtually unable to move. This picture is riddled with misconceptions.

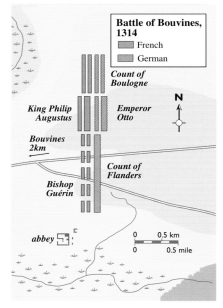

Battle of Bouvines, 1314

▬ French

▬ German

Count of Boulogne

King Philip Augustus

Emperor Otto

N

Bouvines 2km

Count of Flanders

Bishop Guérin

abbey

0   0.5 km

0   0.5 mile

ABOVE: Some 1,200 French knights, supported by perhaps 5,000-6,000 foot soldiers, encountered Otto's 1,300-1,500 knights and 7,500 foot soldiers. The French arrayed themselves in better order and more quickly. The knights on the French right flank routed Otto's Flemish allies, capturing the count of Flanders. Both royals had a brush with death. While Philip was saved by his household, Otto had to flee. Few knights were killed, but many were captured. Like Hastings, contemporary sources stress that this royal battle was a divine judgement and that the combatants took great care in observing the correct formalities.

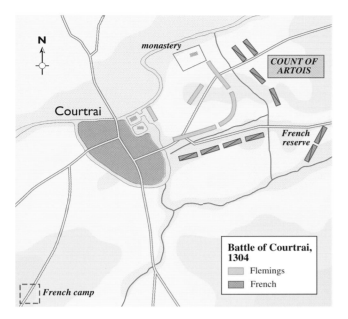

ABOVE: Some 8,000-10,500 Flemish city militia drew up behind two brooks to avoid the worst effects from French crossbow fire. This also denied the 2,500 French nobles the space to develop the force of their charge. Some 2,000 French knights crossed over and charged, but failed to make headway. When the Flemish began to push the French back, the count of Artois committed his right-wing reserve, but with even less room for manoeuvre across the brook, that charge failed as well. As a fight between social unequals, neither side expected quarter. For the loss of a few hundred men, the Flemish killed more than 1,000 French nobles.

ABOVE: The Battle of Neville's Cross in 1346 saw a Scottish invasion of England roundly defeated. King David II of Scotland was taken prisoner and joined the king of France in the Tower of London to await the payment of his ransom. The phrase 'a king's ransom' was not coined lightly: the sums involved could beggar national treasuries as the English had discovered when King Richard I was captured on his way home from the Crusades. Unfortunate noblemen and monarchs could languish for a decade or more while their families or countries raised the cash to buy their liberty.

First, combat armour (of which very little survives in museums) was relatively light. A suit of mail, which was the standard body protection in the 11th and 12th centuries, weighed 10 to 12 kg. In addition, the helmet was a little over 1 kg and a sword 2 kg. A full suit of plate armour by the 15th century was heavier — weighing some 25 kg — but had the advantage of a better weight distribution over the body, whereas the full weight of a mail coat rested on the shoulders. Good armour allowed a knight, as the sources tell us, to stand on his head or to jump on his horse unaided. Such agility was critical in combat.

Second, a knight did not only fight on horseback. Much of his time was spent on foot. How else could he have defended or besieged a castle? Even in battle, particularly in the later Middle Ages, he fought regularly on foot. Nonetheless, the mystique of the knight, propagated already in the Middle Ages, projected an image of cavalry combat being elevated over all other forms.

The key battle tactic developed by the knight was the mounted shock charge. This was only invented in the 11th century and not, as is often believed, at the time of the introduction of the stirrup in Western Europe in the 8th century. Although the stirrup helped keep the rider in the saddle on the impact of the charge, more was needed than a simple new technology. (Incidentally, the equally important deep saddle with the raised cantle and pommel was only introduced in the 10th century.)

The mounted shock charge was only effective if practised en masse. Possessing only the technology was not enough; a supportive society and ideology were critical. The Bayeux Tapestry, which depicts the battle of Hastings, shows the early form of the shock charge. The skills required were practised in another great invention that emerged after the middle of the 11th century: the tournament.

Knights, in other words, fought, not as individuals, but in units. These were based on feudal and kinship bonds. Knights fought, first of all, with their household. Secondly, vassals (that is, knights who held a piece of land, a fief, from a lord in return for military service) fought with their feudal overlords. Because virtually every knight was caught in the web of kinship and feudalism, an extensive network of ready-made military units and command structures existed.

Finally, infantry was invariably present in medieval armies. Foot soldiers usually outnumbered the knights by five, or even ten, to one. Their role, however, was defensive, providing a base around which the knights could form into their compact charge formation and, after the battle developed, to seek protection or catch their breath. Infantry also defended the loot, euphemistically known as 'the baggage train', that accompanied armies, and guarded the enemy knights that were captured for ransom. Only in the late Middle Ages did infantry begin to be used offensively.

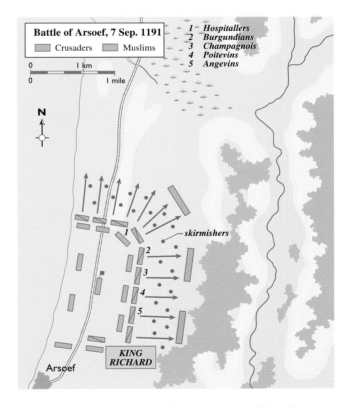

ABOVE: Marching from Acre to Jaffa, a Crusading army under Richard 'Coeur de Lion', met the army of Saladin. Richard advanced with infantry and crossbowmen protecting the cavalry from Muslim archers. The right flank was protected by the sea, the left by cavalry, so that they and the cavalry in the centre could sally forth to beat off attacks or, God willing, smash the main body of the enemy. On 7 September, Saladin's forces closed in but were shattered by three successive charges.

The Crusades

The Crusades were the most ambitious military operations undertaken by the Christian West in the Middle Ages. Beginning in 1095, with the preaching of a crusade by Pope Urban II, and ending in 1291, with the loss of the last outpost in Palestine, Christian warriors attempted to restore Jerusalem and the surrounding Holy Land to Christianity. First and foremost, the Crusades were the expression of an idea. All the material motives usually ascribed to crusaders — lust for power, land and loot — were secondary to the religious idea, the liberation of Jerusalem. Since the material motives could have been satisfied much closer to home, without an arduous journey across inhospitable lands and seas, it required considerable conviction for the tens of thousands of crusaders to undertake the dangerous and expensive expedition. Nonetheless, land and loot were important subsidiary motives. Both provided an attractive and expected bonus to the spiritual salvation offered by the Church.

The crusaders have often been criticized for their lack of unity. The army of the First Crusade (1096–1099) started out with perhaps 4,500 knights and 30,000 foot soldiers. It not only suffered serious casualties in an astonishingly high number of 12 battles and four sieges before reaching Jerusalem, but also lost significant numbers to the ambitions of such leaders as Baldwin, Bohemond of Taranto and Raymond of Toulouse who sought to create principalities around Edessa and Antioch. The army that took Jerusalem may have counted only 1,200 knights and 12,000 infantry. The new principalities, however, served an important purpose by providing strategic depth to the defence of the new kingdom of Jerusalem. Since the major Muslim power base in the 12th century lay in the Baghdad area, attacks on Palestine would come from the north, via the fertile crescent stretching from the Euphrates and Tigris across to the Syrian and Palestinian coasts.

To what extent all this was conscious crusader policy remains debatable, but the crusaders had — or soon developed — some strategic sense. They started to avoid the difficult land journey to and from

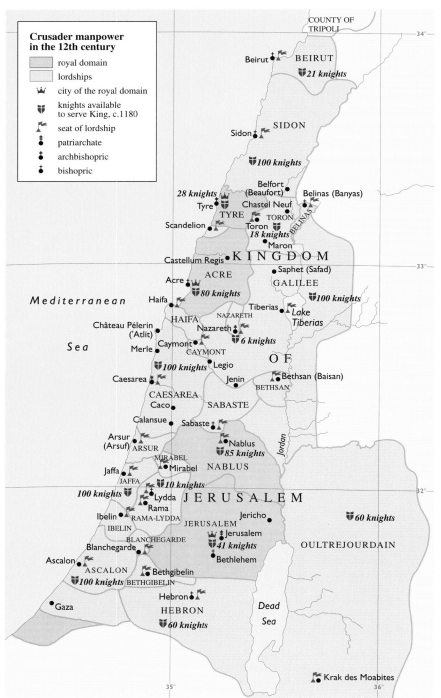

ABOVE: Richard I 'Coeur de Lion' lands at Acre, the first Crusading king to reach the Holy Land with his army intact and without owing a fortune to Venetian shipping agents. Behind his heroic image lay a shrewd strategic mind.

Palestine and, instead, travelled by sea. Sea travel became much easier with the booming trade conducted by the Italian city states with the Levant, thus providing an example of the interaction between war and trade. When the centre of Muslim power shifted to Egypt in the 13th century, the direction of the later Crusades (the Fifth, 1217–1221, and Sixth, 1248–1254) changed accordingly. The best sources of plunder automatically led to strategically important areas and provided good locations for settlement and the development of trade. This can even be said in a perverse way (because it turned on a Christian empire) about the Fourth 'Crusade' (1202–1204), which was diverted onto the rich prize of Constantinople.

The Crusades have often been depicted

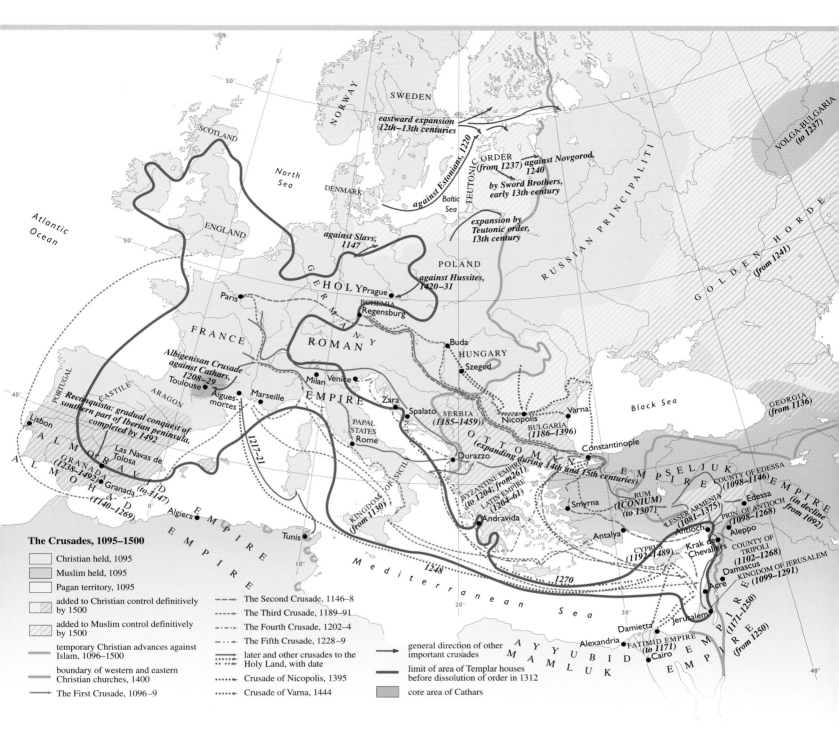

The Crusades, 1095–1500

- ☐ Christian held, 1095
- ▨ Muslim held, 1095
- ☐ Pagan territory, 1095
- ▨ added to Christian control definitively by 1500
- ▨ added to Muslim control definitively by 1500
- — temporary Christian advances against Islam, 1096–1500
- — boundary of western and eastern Christian churches, 1400
- → The First Crusade, 1096–9
- --- The Second Crusade, 1146–8
- ···· The Third Crusade, 1189–91
- ·–·– The Fourth Crusade, 1202–4
- ·· – ·· The Fifth Crusade, 1228–9
- ⇒ later and other crusades to the Holy Land, with date
- ···· Crusade of Nicopolis, 1395
- ···· Crusade of Varna, 1444
- → general direction of other important crusades
- — limit of area of Templar houses before dissolution of order in 1312
- ▨ core area of Cathars

as an exercise in mindless slaughter — even genocide. This is an exaggeration. The same laws of war were applied as in Western Europe. Notorious events, like the slaughter of the inhabitants of Jerusalem in 1099 — unacceptable though they may be to us— were admissible under the rules at the time. On the whole, it is striking to what extent the crusaders and Muslims cooperated, even to the extent of ransoming each other as in the case of King Louis IX of France who was captured in Egypt in 1249. The customs of knightly warfare were hard to break, even in the fight against the infidel.

The most effective defence of the Holy Land was a system based on the combination of castles with a mobile, field army. The crusaders built many castles and other fortifications. In the Kingdom of

Jerusalem alone some 162 fortified sites have been identified. However, on its own, a castle was a 'sitting duck'. Without the threat of relief by a field army, a Muslim force could, in principle, take as long as was necessary to take the crusader castles one by one. Mobilizing armies proved a difficult challenge. Crusaders settled only in limited numbers. The four principalities (Edessa, Tripoli, Antioch and Jerusalem) could raise only perhaps 2,000 knights in total. Perhaps some 10,000 foot soldiers could be added from the ecclesiastical foundations and cities. Even if these could all have been mobilized at the same time (which never happened), such numbers were inadequate for a sustained defence. One lost battle could easily lead castles to fall like dominoes — as indeed happened

after the battle of Hattin in 1187.

Battles were generally fought against the background of a siege. They involved a pattern of tactics very similar to that practised in Europe. The key was the shock charge by the heavily-armed knights. In the Middle East the timing and pace of the charge was, if anything, more critical than in Western Europe. As the Muslims relied principally on the tactic of harassing the Franks with their horse archers so that they would become so agitated that they launched into an early, uncontrolled charge, self-control was essential. The Franks had to let the Muslims get close enough, in sufficient numbers, that they could be caught with a sudden charge. This worked well at Arsuf, for example, but failed equally often, as at Hattin.

ABOVE: The Crusades were the longest distance military operations undertaken in the Middle Ages. They involved large armies by medieval standards, but considering the geographical space they were operating in, their numbers were puny. The crusaders fortified themselves across modern-day Syria, Lebanon and Israel which gave their kingdom some strategic depth.

The Mongol Invasions

ABOVE: A 16th century Indian illustration depicts the storming of a Persian city by the Mongols. Infamous for their policy of terror, the Mongols actually followed rules of siege warfare little different from those prevailing in western Europe.

The Mongol Empire, created by Chingiz Khan (?1167-1227) and his successors in the 13th century, was unique in terms of its geographical size. By 1280, it was the largest continuous land empire in history. However, in terms of military and political techniques employed, the Mongols were far less original. Raids by mounted nomads from the central Asian steppes had started around the middle of the first millennium BC. Attracted by the wealth of the emerging Chinese empire, the nomads mounted plundering raids. At times, they moved further afield, towards the west. In the 5th century, for example, Europe was ravaged by the Huns, while from the 11th century onwards, Turkish tribes moved into the Middle East.

The relative strength of the nomadic tribes was founded on numbers, mobility and weaponry. Like the Germanic tribes that brought down the Roman empires, they were peoples-in-arms. They could mobilize their manpower more efficiently than the more stratified Chinese, Central Asian and Middle Eastern empires, as well as the later medieval European monarchies. With every able-bodied man on horseback, they could move very quickly and seek to surprise and overwhelm their enemies with concentrated force. However, their numbers have often been exaggerated. Mongol armies do not appear to have been much larger than 100,000 men; nevertheless an enormous force by medieval standards. Tactically, their main weapon was the composite bow, which in combination with mobility, was used to harass the enemy from a distance, wearing him out before moving in for the kill. Not surprisingly, the hunt provided the male nomad with the perfect training for war from an early age.

Nomad strategies and tactics had their weaknesses. They were effective in cross-border raids that sought plunder. But their horses needed vast grazing areas for fodder. The heart of the Chinese empire and many areas in the Middle East (or, for that matter, Western Europe) were unsuited to armies were every fighter was accompanied by up to five horses. Also, nomadic cavalry armies were ill-suited for siege warfare — a necessary skill if the urbanized empires on their periphery were to be subjected on a more permanent basis. As a result, nomad attacks were a recurring, but mostly transitory phenomenon.

The unparalleled success of the Mongols was due to a rigorous exploitation of traditional nomad military strengths, plus three additional factors: leadership, organization and divided opponents. Chingiz Khan must have been an unusually skilful leader. A minor noble, he exploited the openness of Mongol tribal and inter-tribal career structures to those who excelled in satisfying the cravings for loot by nomad rank-and-file and top leaders alike. Careful choices of blood-brothers and allies (as well as some Chinese subsidies) further advanced his position. By 1206, he was the pre-eminent leader of the Mongolian tribes.

Although his name is synonymous with cruelty, Chingiz was usually magnanimous in victory. Opponents who had incurred his just wrath, like the Mongol tribe who kidnapped his wife and the Khwarazm-shah who murdered and humiliated his ambassadors in 1218, could expect little mercy. The Eurasian law of siege was applied uncompromisingly. Cities which resisted were laid waste. However, Chingiz' ambitions, when they began to turn on the world, required a lot of manpower. Those who acknowledged his overlordship, whether willingly or by force, were often incorporated into the army. The need for non-Mongol troops became even greater with

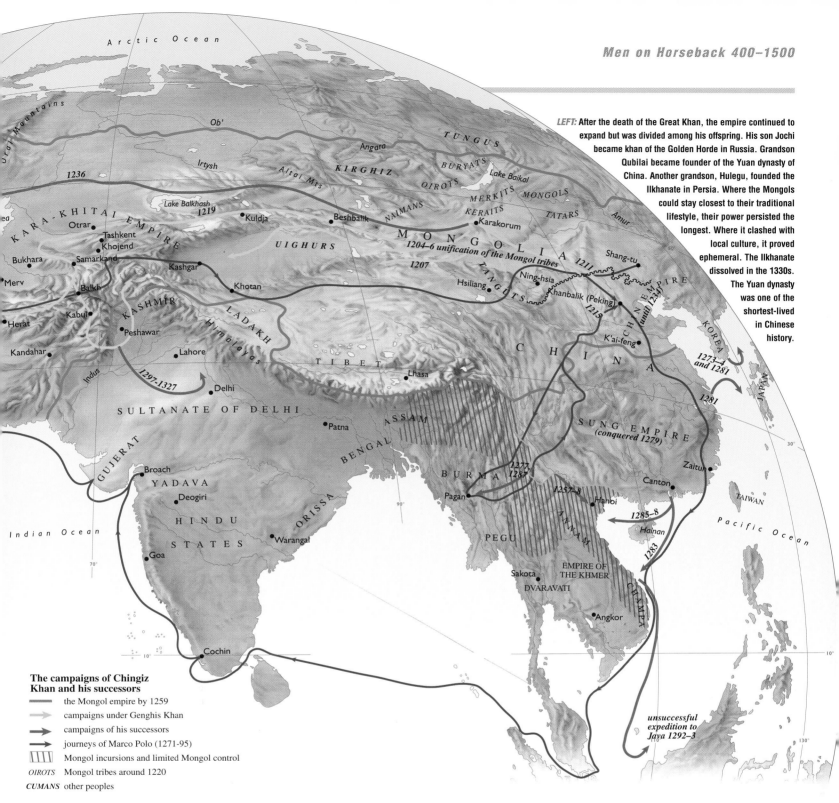

LEFT: After the death of the Great Khan, the empire continued to expand but was divided among his offspring. His son Jochi became khan of the Golden Horde in Russia. Grandson Qubilai became founder of the Yuan dynasty of China. Another grandson, Hulegu, founded the Ilkhanate in Persia. Where the Mongols could stay closest to their traditional lifestyle, their power persisted the longest. Where it clashed with local culture, it proved ephemeral. The Ilkhanate dissolved in the 1330s. The Yuan dynasty was one of the shortest-lived in Chinese history.

The campaigns of Chingiz Khan and his successors

--- the Mongol empire by 1259
⟶ campaigns under Genghis Khan
⟶ campaigns of his successors
⟶ journeys of Marco Polo (1271-95)
|||| Mongol incursions and limited Mongol control
OIROTS Mongol tribes around 1220
CUMANS other peoples

the penetration of China and the Middle East. Local forces, especially siege engineers and even infantry, became an integral part of their armies.

Much is made to this day of Mongol military organization which, with its subdivision of the army in units of tens, hundreds, thousands and, particularly of the division-like ten-thousand-strong *tünmens*, seems to presage modern military rationality. More importantly, subdued peoples were broken up and integrated into the Mongol army, ignoring their old affiliations. Significant members of their elites often ended up in the imperial guard, which functioned both as a supreme reward and as a reservoir of hostages. The imperial guard summed up how the loyalty of the army as a whole was assured:

through terror and opportunity. The Mongols offered such opportunity for advancement, adventure and plunder as few armies have in history. But lack of loyalty was punished pitilessly.

The Mongols became victims of their own success. Once the Mongol tribes were united, new greener pastures, full of riches and reward, had to be found or else they would revert to their old, squabbling ways. The length of the list of Mongol successes makes its enumeration tedious. Each year of Chingiz' reign and those of his successors, one or more massive campaigns were organized. Conquest, however, was more a by-product of success than an objective. The more successful a plundering campaign, the more likely the suffering locals would seek submission.

Once accepted, the campaigns had to move on. The process of submission was much helped by the divisions among their enemies. China, the toughest, richest and most irresistible opponent, was divided into three parts: the Hsi-Hsia, the Chin and the Sung empires. In Central Asia, a new empire, the Khwarazm, had only just emerged and was not yet consolidated, while in the Middle East and eastern Europe, different dynasties and principalities vied for pre-eminence. All these could be taken on in turn.

The empire did not last. Quickly divided among various branches of Chingiz' family, they could only rule by co-opting the local elite. As a result, the Mongols soon 'went native' and disappeared among the local populations.

The Hundred Years' War

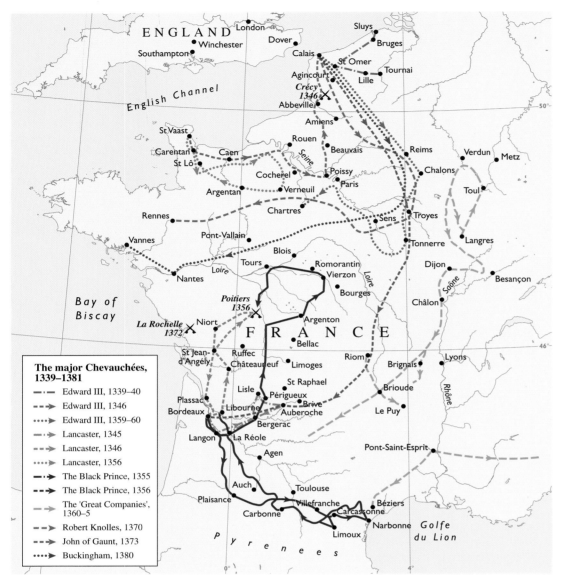

The major Chevauchées, 1339–1381

- —·— Edward III, 1339–40
- —·→ Edward III, 1346
- ••••→ Edward III, 1359–60
- —·→ Lancaster, 1345
- —·→ Lancaster, 1346
- ••••→ Lancaster, 1356
- —·→ The Black Prince, 1355
- —·→ The Black Prince, 1356
- —→ The 'Great Companies', 1360–5
- —·→ Robert Knolles, 1370
- —·→ John of Gaunt, 1373
- ••••→ Buckingham, 1380

ABOVE: In the first half of the Hundred Years' War, English armies criss-crossed the French countryside like giant lawn-mowers, laying waste everything in their path. These operations were aimed at damaging the French king's economy and calling into question his ability to protect his subjects, while simultaneously satisfying the desire for plunder on the part of the English nobility.

The major war of the later Middle Ages, the Hundred Years' War between France and England, has all the key characteristics of medieval warfare. Named much later and actually lasting longer (from 1337 to 1453 by the most common count), most campaigns revolved around the acquisition of plunder and battle was usually avoided. At the core, it was a struggle about justice, centring on feudal rights and obligations. As a vassal of the king of France for the territory of Aquitaine, the king of England owed his fellow king, among other obligations, the key feudal duty of military service. This infringed on the sovereign independence of the English king's foreign policy. Relations were further complicated by the fact that inhabitants of Aquitaine had their ultimate court of appeal, not in London, but Paris, thus allowing for the lawful interference by French kings in Aquitaine. Finally, as French nobles, the kings of England had long-standing claims to many other lands in France as well.

The king of England, Edward III, short of advocating a fundamental rewriting of feudal law (which was against all contemporary understanding of the law), could only solve the conflict by becoming king of France. Edward did have a claim to the French throne through his mother, but, throughout his life, he hesitated in the face of this enormous challenge. The French king, in turn, had to dispossess Edward of his fief. Neither king was strong enough to achieve his goal. At the same time, both protagonists were lawfully obliged to go to war. When not defending against English incursions, French strategy was to whittle down English possessions in France through a long war of harassment and siege. In the end, it succeeded. By 1453, the war was to all intents and purposes over when the English had lost all possessions but Calais.

English strategy went through a more convoluted process. Edward III started by organizing raids into France, called *chevauchées*, which, by plundering the countryside, sought to make the French king more accommodating regarding the constitutional position of Aquitaine and perhaps also force him to restore other for-

mer English possessions in France. An important, additional advantage of this strategy was that it satisfied the craving for loot and ransom of English chivalry. The war was generally profitable for the English nobility who (like his nobles had Charlemagne 600 years earlier) saw Edward and his son, the Black Prince, as great rulers because of their prowess in leading them in annual campaigns of plunder. The war, however, was not resolved this way and, perhaps, it was not meant to be as it suited both king and nobles to continue the good fight.

The *chevauchées* were subject to strange conventions. Although the English were habitually shadowed by mostly larger French armies, neither side usually showed much inclination to do battle — even though battle, to modern strategists at least, could have settled matters quickly and decisively. Instead, the French allowed the English to march through France unscathed and did not attempt to surprise and destroy them. The English, on their part, clearly did not expect any such unchivalrous acts and did not often hesitate to spread out their armies in vulnerable groups to plunder the countryside. This indicates that a battle between royals was considered a very special solemn occasion, that had to be arranged by mutual consent in advance. The ordeal (in its original meaning of judgement) of battle, however, was so feared that neither side let it come to it, except for only three occasions in a hundred years.

After a long series of militarily ineffective (and thus contested) rulers, Henry V's accession to the throne in 1413 marked a new phase. Like Edward III, he began with a *chevauchée* in 1415, but then embarked on the systematic reconquest of his ancestral land of Normandy. The war, in another departure, was legitimated by a claim to the French throne. Henry, competent though he was, benefited enormously from the strife within the French ruling house, led by the mentally troubled Charles VI. In 1420, he struck the ultimate deal: he married the French king's daughter and extracted the promise that their son would inherit the kingdom of France. However, his premature death in 1422 changed everything. He was succeeded by his 9-month-old son, who grew up feeble-minded like his grandfather. The long and tragic reign of Henry VI saw the loss of the war.

Both dynasties were extremely fearful of battle. The kings, or their immediate proxies, the crown princes, only met in the field three times: at Crécy in 1346, at Poitiers, ten years later, and, finally, at Agincourt in 1415. Although they shadowed each other on their *chevauchées*, and even drew up for battle a number of times, they more often than not judged the risks of battle's divine judgement too high and did not engage. Indeed, two of the three

French defeats forced the French to sign peace treaties that were so humiliating they were never kept.

Much has been made of the success of the English longbow. However, it was not a war-winning weapon. Reliance on this defensive weapon on the battlefield gave the initiative to the French; its victories also depended on the French bungling their attack. The English were fortunate that their opponent failed to get it right three times in a 70-year period. When the French, who did try to learn from their mistakes refused to engage in battle and concentrated on the ultimately more important siege warfare, the English 'wonder weapon' was of little use.

The French plan for Agincourt (see diagram) indicates how their tactical thought, if not their luck, improved over time. The standard English deployment included archers on the wings and dismounted men-at-arms (that is, the armoured knights and squires in the middle). The French would develop a three-pronged attack. One thousand or more mounted men-at-arms would charge the English on their right flank and break them up. At the same time, cross-bowmen, backed up by foot soldiers, would advance on both flanks to fix and harass the English archers. As a coup-de-grace, a small force of 200 mounted men-at-arms would attack the English baggage train in the rear. Such an attack had the great advantage of distracting English attention, since the baggage contained the loot they had diligently collected, as well as their horses. The two cavalry units were each backed up by a force of varlets with spare horses and who could also provide a protective screen and rescue force for the cavalry, if necessary. Finally, the two battles in the centre allowed the French to either widen or shorten their front line to match the deployment of the English men-at-arms.

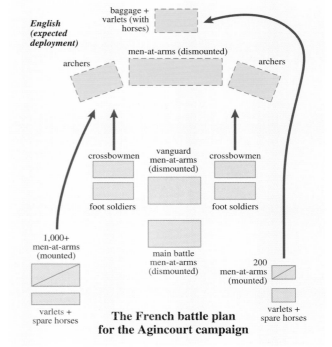

The French battle plan for the Agincourt campaign

Edward III's campaign, 1339 (below)

✳	village plundered
⊚	main town plundered
•	town not destroyed
⊙	main town not destroyed
⟶▷	route of Edward III's army
——	boundary of diocese
----	main routes
▧	woodland

The End of the Middle Ages

The later Middle Ages was a period of great military change. It is often claimed that chivalry withered and died with the rise of infantry and gunpowder weapons. Closer to the truth is that chivalry adapted and, despite all innovations and the increased diversification of armies, continued to dominate warfare.

The major change in infantry was its offensive use. The Swiss exemplified this development. Their compact formations famously defeated the duke of Burgundy, Charles the Bold, in the battles of Morat, Granson and Nancy in 1476-77. However, Charles, that supposed epitome of outdated chivalry, as well as his knightly contemporaries, knew that the Swiss and other infantry formations had a fundamental weakness. Swiss success depended on the impact of tightly-packed units of pikemen, backed up by halberdiers. Their density (10,000 men formed a square of only 60m^2) made them highly vulnerable to the effects of firepower. Fifteenth century armies thus became combined arms formations. Foot soldiers with crossbows or longbows, and increasingly gunpowder weapons, protected by noble armoured men-at-arms on foot, were to stop attacks by infantry or cavalry. Heavy cavalry waited in the wings for the knock-out blow. Although the proportion of nobles in armies dropped, they continued not only to hold the leadership positions but also remained the decisive weapon.

Keeping up with military developments became tougher for the military elite. Armour evolved rapidly. In the first half of the 14th century, a suit of mail began to be covered by plates. In the 15th century, the made-to-measure full suit of plate armour became the desirable standard. An arms race had developed in response to the increased use of bows. Crossbows, in particular, were very powerful after the introduction of steel bows and mechanical means for drawing them. (Longbows were much less powerful as they were made of

wood and depended on muscular power.) The ultimate in armour, a full suit made of steel, was nonetheless fairly effective in stopping arrows. Armour became heavier although never as heavy as is commonly believed, and required even better, specially bred horses. Also, the term 'man-at-arms', the common term for the heavy cavalry man, actually denoted a mounted unit of at least three men and four horses: the cavalry man proper, a more lightly armed varlet, and a page. One or more archers were also often added. Although everyone received wages, war was an expensive business for the individual noble who was expected to pay for his own equipment and support his followers.

The conquest of Holland and Zeeland by Duke Philip of Burgundy affords an interesting example of late medieval strategy in action. He wrested Holland and Zeeland from his cousin, Countess Jacqueline of Bavaria, in a war lasting from 1425-8. The protagonists began by winning over the cities, strategically critical in highly urbanized Holland. Philip was fortunate that only Gouda, Oudewater and Schoonhoven supported Jacqueline. Rotterdam, Delft, Leiden, Haarlem and Amsterdam came out for the duke and he garrisoned them. Philip then blocked the waterways used by Jacqueline's supporters to raid the countryside. Blockhouses (as they were called) were built at the key locks at Leidsendam and Alfen and ships, with garrisons, moored on the main rivers, the Ijssel, Lek and Merwede. The final campaigns sought to cut off supplies to Jacqueline's strongpoints. A pact with the duke of Guelders was reinforced by expeditions up the Vecht and Eem rivers. The Vecht was shut after taking the castle of Utermeer and the Eem blocked by a massive garrisoned ship. Jacqueline submitted soon after.

Battles continued to be a rare occurrence throughout the period. Soldiers (as they could be called now as they were overwhelmingly salaried) were far more likely to spend their days, like their ancestors, on garrison duty, in sieges and in raids. In short, they conducted what were called 'small wars' or more prosaically 'wars over cows' (*guerre aux vaches*). Strategically, there was no revolution. Geoffrey Parker has claimed that the introduction of effective artillery in the 15th century saw a brief period of decisive warfare. The strength of medieval forti-

A Burgundian battle plan from Sep. 1417

Swiss deployment

archers — men-at-arms — archers

lines of attack

archers + crossbowmen

archers + crossbowmen

main battle men-at-arms (dismounted)

40–60 paces

1,000 men-at-arms (mounted) + varlets

2 units of 16–20 mounted 'wise and valiant' knights who are to stop those in front from fleeing or fill the gaps

an arrow shot

400 men-at arms (mounted)

300 archers

LEFT: As in the battle plan for Agincourt, the key to victory was the heavy cavalry. A solid base of dismounted men-at-arms was to hold the centre. Archers and crossbowmen would fix the enemy while cavalry on the flank mounted an attack at a suitable point in the enemy line. Just in case, a mounted reserve is kept 'an arrow shot' behind the main battle. Interesting is the concern by John the Fearless, duke of Burgundy, that men-at-arms from his vanguard and main battle might defect. Anyone withdrawing was to be stopped by a small unit of 16-20 'wise and valiant' knights.

RIGHT: Charles' ideas — from just before he was defeated and killed by the Swiss — show the evolution of the combined arms army by the late Middle Ages. Firepower, still in the form of archers, was now a key ingredient of all armies, not just the English. Even the infantry had pikemen mixed with early firearms and crossbows. The cavalry, deployed in depth, was still meant to be the decisive arm. There was even an attempt to include artillery in the field army.

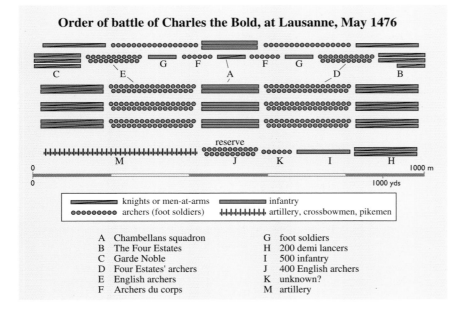

Order of battle of Charles the Bold, at Lausanne, May 1476

C — E — G — F — A — F — G — D — B

reserve

M — J — K — I — H

0 — 1000 m
0 — 1000 yds

	knights or men-at-arms		infantry
	archers (foot soldiers)		artillery, crossbowmen, pikemen

A	Chambellans squadron	G	foot soldiers
B	The Four Estates	H	200 demi lancers
C	Garde Noble	I	500 infantry
D	Four Estates' archers	J	400 English archers
E	English archers	K	unknown?
F	Archers du corps	M	artillery

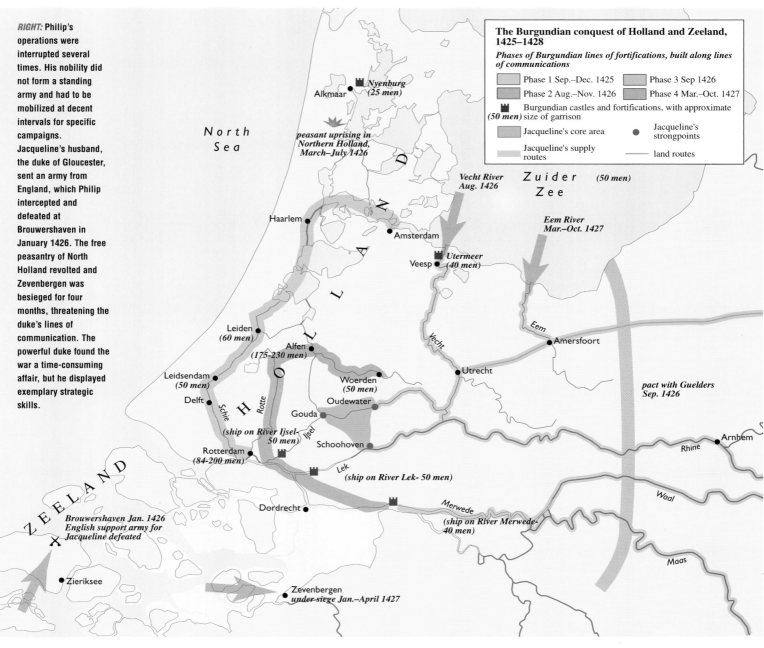

RIGHT: Philip's operations were interrupted several times. His nobility did not form a standing army and had to be mobilized at decent intervals for specific campaigns. Jacqueline's husband, the duke of Gloucester, sent an army from England, which Philip intercepted and defeated at Brouwershaven in January 1426. The free peasantry of North Holland revolted and Zevenbergen was besieged for four months, threatening the duke's lines of communication. The powerful duke found the war a time-consuming affair, but he displayed exemplary strategic skills.

The Burgundian conquest of Holland and Zeeland, 1425–1428

Phases of Burgundian lines of fortifications, built along lines of communications

- Phase 1 Sep.–Dec. 1425
- Phase 2 Aug.–Nov. 1426
- Phase 3 Sep 1426
- Phase 4 Mar.–Oct. 1427
- Burgundian castles and fortifications, with approximate **(50 men)** size of garrison
- Jacqueline's core area
- Jacqueline's supply routes
- Jacqueline's strongpoints
- land routes

fications — high walls — was suddenly turned into a critical vulnerability. Directing cannon fire at the lower part of walls would make them collapse under their own weight. In this way, he argued, the Moors lost Spain, the Turks took Constantinople in 1453, and the French drove the English out of Normandy in the 1450s and conquered Italy in the 1490s. The design of a new type of artillery-resistant fortification by the late 15th century — the low, thick-walled brick bastions and later the '*tracé italienne*' — closed this window of opportunity.

Closer inspection reveals that the cannon, like the longbow, was not a 'wonder weapon'. The details of the campaigns in Normandy, Spain and Italy show a role for artillery, but as one element in a process characterized by traditional siege and campaign techniques. The critical factor was that the organization for war, particularly in France, improved. War could be fought on a

more permanent basis and more intensively (such as the Burgundian conquest of Holland and Zeeland). The French monarchy as no other exploited war as an opportunity for raising taxes and taking the first steps towards building a standing army. The monarchy had a comparative advantage over the other forces in society when it came to meeting the rising costs of war. Only monarchs could afford the wages, larger and more numerous garrisons, and the constant updating and improvement of fortifications, armour and firearms. Over time, this self-reinforcing mechanism led to the rise of the modern state, first in France and then elsewhere in Europe. But the wars of the new monarchies still took time. There were few battles. And war continued to be about the pursuit of rights, though increasingly of kings alone, and profit for all; war as a continuation of politics by other means lay in the future.

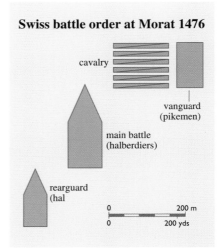

Swiss battle order at Morat 1476

cavalry

vanguard (pikemen)

main battle (halberdiers)

rearguard (hal

0   200 m
0   200 yds

LEFT: The disposition of Burgundian troops at Morat shows that their commander, Duke Charles the Bold, knew, at least in theory, how to defeat the Swiss. The idea was to catch them in a fire zone of archers and artillery, then finish them off with cavalry. However, after his men had been waiting in full battle order for most of the day, the duke gave the order to stand down. Then, with the knights out of their armour and the archers away from their fortified positions, the Swiss appeared out of a nearby forest. The Burgundians were routed.

The 16th century saw a decisive shift in the military balance between East and West. Europe in 1500 lay at the mercy of Asian nomads, as it had since the fall of Rome. The invasions of the Ottoman Turks would be the last Asiatic incursion into Central Europe until 1945. Contemporaries perceived a military revolution, caused by infantry armies and artillery, which swept away the castles and 'knightly' armies that had dominated warfare for a thousand years. European political plurality encouraged military innovation, sparking off a period of relentless change in tactics and weaponry.

The cheapness of infantry armed with handguns allowed Western European states to create the largest armies seen since Roman times. Military leaders rediscovered classical patterns of tactics, drill, and fieldworks. Spain formed permanently embodied units resembling modern tactical units: the *colunela* (battalion) and *tercio* (brigade). The Spanish square dominated European battlefields until the Dutch and Swedes developed all-arms tactics that combined firepower and shock action. This military renaissance, however, failed to increase the pace of operations. Modernized fortifications, mounting their own guns on a low bastioned trace, reimposed traditional constraints on the speed and scope of field operations. Atrocious roads could not meet the logistical demands of siege warfare. Wars remained a slow process of attrition.

War at sea changed dramatically, after 2,000 years of continuity. Galleons driven by sails and armed with broadsides of heavy guns replaced oar-driven galleys dependent on ramming and a few axially-mounted guns. Europeans used galleons and firearms against less well-equipped societies overseas. Some non-European powers imitated or bought in European techniques, but generally lacked the social infrastructure needed for their consistent or effective use.

The Italian Wars

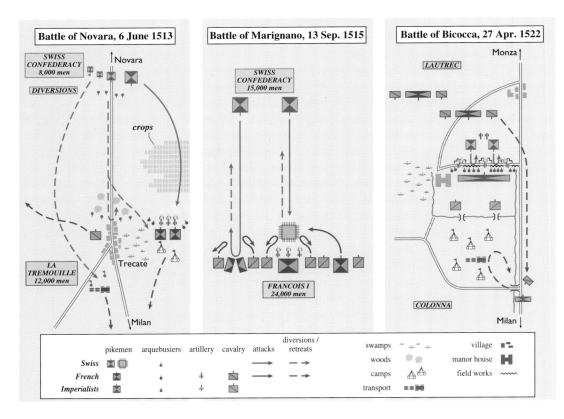

| Battle of Novara, 6 June 1513 | Battle of Marignano, 13 Sep. 1515 | Battle of Bicocca, 27 Apr. 1522 |

SWISS CONFEDERACY 8,000 men — DIVERSIONS — Novara — crops — LA TREMOUILLE 12,000 men — Trecate — Milan

SWISS CONFEDERACY 15,000 men — FRANCOIS I 24,000 men

LAUTREC — Monza — COLONNA — Milan

		pikemen	arquebusiers	artillery	cavalry	attacks	diversions / retreats		swamps		village	
Swiss									woods		manor house	
French									camps		field works	
Imperialists									transport			

ABOVE: Armies caught in the open could not resist the ferocious rush of Swiss pike men, but Novara was the last Swiss success in the old style. Their enemies learned to halt the pike squares with cavalry or fieldworks, and shoot them down with massed artillery and arquebus fire.

The rediscovery of classical Greek and Roman thought, known as the Renaissance, affected warfare as well as painting, literature, and architecture. Fifteenth century Italy had the most sophisticated culture in Europe. Its well-developed economy supported the most mature military institutions. Wealthy city states blended military professionalism and civil administration to secure political stability, and for a while the military capability of great powers. Italy's disunity and wealth, however, were an irresistible temptation to her neighbours. The obstacles around Italy gave no security. Mountain ranges like the Alps make poor defensive barriers, while the sea provided a highway for Spanish intervention. Italy's geographical position at the intersection of great power rivalries made the peninsula a military proving ground.

The strategic logic of the Italian Wars is hard to follow. The French suffered repeated disasters pursuing their claim to the kingdom of Naples, an area untenable without naval superiority, which they rarely had. French and Swiss armies regularly exposed themselves to defeat by sheer carelessness. After the initial shock of barbarian vigour wore off, the calculating strategic style of the *condottieri*, the military entrepreneurs of the *Quattrocento*, reasserted itself, although military historians still echo Machiavelli's derision of their 'bloodless' strategy. Like the *condottieri*, rational commanders preferred manoeuvre to combat, unless they had the enemy at a disadvantage.

The Italian Wars saw unprecedented tactical ferment. Italy lay at the crossroads

RIGHT: The refreshingly succinct political theorist, Niccolo Machiavelli was also a military pundit. Alert to the dangers of dependence on mercenaries, he argued for Italian cities to train politically reliable citizen soldiers. Like many writers of the military renaissance, he drew many of his examples from ancient history.

of regionally distinctive military traditions, from which the wars would create a single European tactical consensus. The French invaders had the best heavy cavalry and field artillery in the world. The offensive capability of Swiss pikemen, rare in medieval infantry, inspired imitation by German *Landsknechts*. Spanish armies who traditionally relied on infantry quickly adopted the pike, and replaced their crossbows with the arquebus or Hackenbusche. This combined a curved butt, a trigger and cock, so handgunners could now aim while firing. The arquebus was the key weapon of the military renaissance. Requiring little training, the arquebus was readily transferable across national borders, unlike the pike which the French never mastered. It revolutionized the soldier's equipment and killed regardless of social class or armour. The rapid spread of mass-produced handguns fuelled the growth of armies, paid for by loans and higher taxes. The proportion of infantry carrying firearms rose steadily, from 30% at Venice in 1548 to 60% in the Spanish army of 1600. Commentators in the 1590s thought hand-to-hand combat a rarity. The pike was retained to deter cavalry, or push home an attack already decided by fire. Paradoxically the arquebus, a weapon unknown to the ancients, encouraged linear tactics consciously based on those of the Romans. In the absence of drill and trained cadres, however, these were slow to realize their potential.

The battles of the Italian Wars show the development of the new European tactical consensus, as the arquebus transformed the dominant mode of combat from shock to attrition. The opening battle at Fornovo (6 July 1495) recalled the chivalric past.

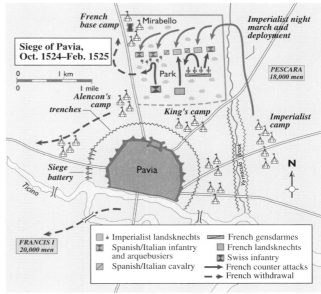

Siege of Pavia, Oct. 1524–Feb. 1525

0 1 km	
0 1 mile	

French base camp · Mirabello · Imperialist night march and deployment · Park · PESCARA 18,000 men · Alencon's trenches · King's camp · Imperialist camp · Siege battery · Pavia · Venecula Brook · Ticino · FRANCIS I 20,000 men

- ■♦ Imperialist landsknechts
- ⊠ Spanish/Italian infantry and arquebusiers
- ▨ Spanish/Italian cavalry
- ▭ French gensdarmes
- ■ French landsknechts
- ⊠ Swiss infantry
- → French counter attacks
- ⇢ French withdrawal

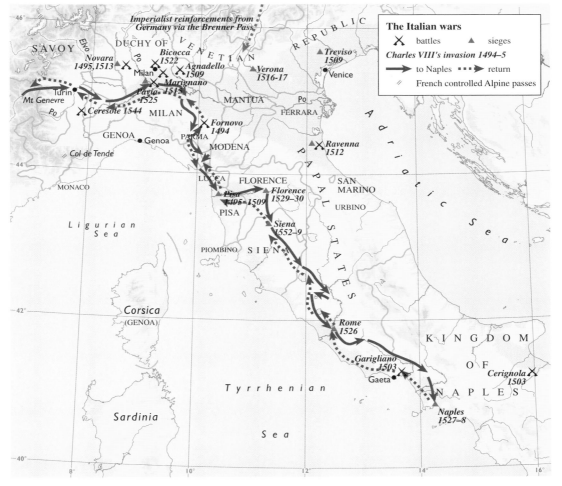

ABOVE: King Charles VIII of France enters Florence during his invasion of Italy 1494-5. His retreat was intercepted by the Hapsburg forces. French heavy cavalry won the ensuing battle at Fornovo, but most subsequent battles were determined by gunfire.

The Italian wars

- ✕ battles
- ▲ sieges
- Charles VIII's invasion 1494–5
- → to Naples
- ⇢ return
- ∥ French controlled Alpine passes

ABOVE: Pavia confirmed the invulnerability of fortifications defended by artillery, and the superiority of Spanish arquebusiers over French gensdarmes. The result was so decisive that Pavia would be the last major battle in Italy until Ceresole, twenty years later.

LEFT: Renaissance Italy lay between competing power centres: France, Spain, Turkey, and the Empire. Foreign armies used the peninsula as a proving ground, testing novel combinations of shock and fire weapons in numerous battles. Strategy remained rudimentary, however, driven by French obsessions with Lombardy and Naples.

French gensdarmes rode down similar Italian heavy cavalry, disordered by an unexpectedly flooded stream. Cerignola (April 1503) saw the first combination of arquebus and fieldworks to checkmate heavy cavalry, but at Ravenna (11 April 1512) cannon appeared to be the antidote to Spanish trenches. Field artillery played a decisive battlefield role for the first time, although it was the French heavy cavalry who clinched victory by penetrat-ing the Spanish defences to take their infantry in the rear. Novara (6 June 1513) and Marignano (13/14 September 1515) revolved around Swiss attempts to fore-stall the deadly combination of field artillery and heavy cavalry, but Bicocca (27 April 1522) vindicated the Spanish defensive school. Prosper Colonna, a typ-ically cautious *condottiere*, placed pike-men close behind his entrenched arque-busiers, to win the handgun's first major victory. Pavia (24 Feb 1525) confirmed the tactical dominance of firearms, this time in the open. Furious cavalry charges failed to break Spanish pikemen support-ed by arquebusiers, who shot down the French nobility around their king. So deci-sive was the Spanish victory that the French exchanged their crossbows for the arquebus. Battles became a rarity, Pavia serving as a stock excuse for commanders wishing to avoid action.

Artillery and Fortresses

Spread of the military renaissance
- ⚏ 1490–1540
- ⚏ 1540–60
- ⚏ 1560–1600
- ⚏ 1600 onward
- —— Holy Roman Empire

ABOVE: Bastioned fortresses first appeared in Italy, and soon spread to France and the Netherlands. Outlying areas were slower to apply the new principles: Henry VIII of England built circular forts in the 1540s, and bastions only reached Poland in the 1630s.

The mobile siege train of bronze guns with which Charles VIII invaded Italy was more destructive than gigantic medieval bombards had been. Traditional masonry fortresses that had withstood years of siege fell in 1495 after a few hours bombardment. Renaissance Italians, however, were well equipped to respond to the challenge, with skills in map-making, surveying, and geometry acquired from the great architectural projects of the *Quattrocento*. Their military engineers designed a new lower style of artillery fortress protected by earth ramparts, capable of withstanding prolonged bombardment. The spread of the Trace Italienne across Europe can be seen as a litmus test of the progress of the military renaissance, but the new fortifications were more than symbols. Their scale and the problems they posed were themselves potent causes of military change.

Late 15th century artillery achieved a form unchanged until the Industrial Revolution. Breech-loading guns built up from iron hoops gave way to cast bronze muzzle-loaders of increased accuracy and power. Wheeled carriages replaced the bombard's immobile sledge, the piece balanced on a pair of trunnions for easy elevation. Together wheels and trunnions enabled gunners to lay their pieces accurately for both line and range. Wheeled carriages could deploy directly from the line of march, and in emergencies move about the battlefield. However, the misuse of artillery at Bicocca and Pavia, where assaulting troops masked their own guns, obscured the offensive potential revealed at Ravenna and Marignano. Field armies relied instead on the arquebus, supplemented from the 1520s by the musket, a mobile wall piece light enough for one man to carry. Heavier guns were confined to the defensive, where their embarrassing variety mattered less. Charles V, Holy

Roman Emperor and King of Spain, inherited fifty different calibres, from 98-pounders downwards. Like every artillerist of the period, from Francis I of France to Gustavus Adolphus of Sweden, he rationalized. The Spanish army of 1609 had 48-, 24-, 12-, and 6pr guns, calibres that would remain standard until the 1850s.

The essential component of the new fortifications was the bastion, a low broad gun platform whose flanking fire swept the ditch and curtain wall that connected separate bastions in a unified defensive trace. At first medieval town walls were hastily upgraded, earth piled against them from an expanded moat, their towers cut down into gun positions. Later, whole cities were refortified in the new style, earth ramparts revetted in brick to resist both rain and cannon balls. Elaborate outworks developed. Earth piled up beyond the ditch formed a glacis to reduce the vertical target presented by the ramparts. The first ravelin appeared in 1497: a free-standing triangular work used to defend gates, or placed in front of the curtain to thicken up the crossfire around the bastions. Sentinels patrolled a covered way along the outer edge of the ditch. The single skin of the medieval town wall had given way to a complex system of defence in depth, each layer swept by flanking fire.

Fortresses like Verona restored the strategic advantage to the defender. Formal siege techniques replaced Charles VIII's brisk bombardments. In 1522 Prosper Colonna revived the Roman practice of circumvallation and contravallation to isolate the besieged and secure the besiegers against relieving armies. Wise besiegers directed attacks against a bastion, rather than the curtain, which was swept by the deadliest flanking fire. Covered by artillery and sheltered by gabions, sappers zigzagged forwards in constant fear of sorties and enfilade fire, until close enough to dig a trench parallel to the covered way as the forming up area for an assault. If the attackers gained a foothold, the defenders could still seal off the compromised sector with improvised barricades.

Artillery fortresses encouraged the growth in armies. Their bastions mounted numerous guns which kept besiegers at a distance, demanding more men to complete investments. Sieges consumed vast stores of guns and ammunition, and prolonged campaigns unseasonably. In 1552 men froze to death in the trenches before Metz. New fortifications frustrated hopes that Charles V's personal union of Spain and the Holy Roman Empire would unite Europe under the Hapsburgs. Charles V invaded Northern France in the 1540s, but fortresses built by expatriate Italian engineers barred his path. Charles V's failure to crush France ensured that Europe remained divided politically, the essential condition for the competitive innovation that drove the military renaissance.

RIGHT: Pendennis castle in Cornwall was built by Henry VIII in a style made obsolete by the *Trace Italienne*. However, it was modernized to the new style during the English Civil War. Some of the 17th century artillery positions were later used for anti-aircraft guns during the Second World War.

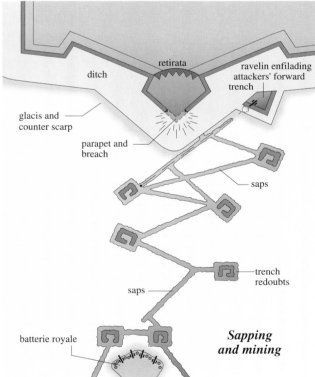

Sapping and mining

ABOVE: Artillery fortifications demanded scientific siege techniques. Defending cannon forced attackers to take cover in trenches, while sapping close enough to the defences to establish a battery within breaching range, or attach a miner to the *escarp*. Trench redoubts were an early attempt to protect the sappers against sorties.

The Trace Italienne

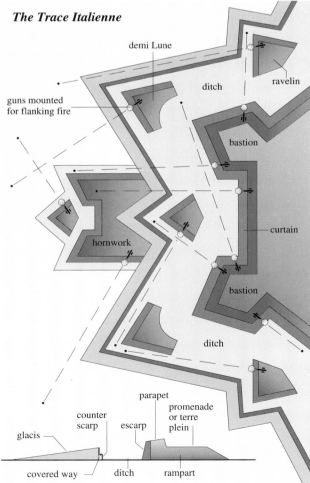

LEFT: Renaissance fortresses protected themselves against artillery fire with massive earth walls and a sloping glacis, and mounted their own guns in bastions to cover the curtain and ditch with flanking fire. The result was expensive, but much harder to capture than its medieval predecessors.

Suleiman the Magnificent and the Ottoman Threat

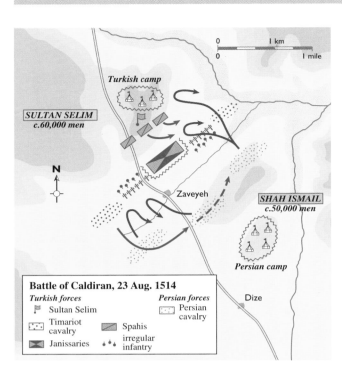

SULTAN SELIM *c.60,000 men*

Turkish camp

N

Zaveyeh

SHAH ISMAIL *c.50,000 men*

Persian camp

Dize

Battle of Caldiran, 23 Aug. 1514

Turkish forces		*Persian forces*	
Sultan Selim		Persian cavalry	
Timariot cavalry	Spahis		
Janissaries	irregular infantry		

ABOVE: Ottoman armies used similar tactics against Hungarians, Mamelukes, and Persians, supplementing the standard wagon laager of steppe warfare with cannon and professional infantry. This firebase broke up enemy attacks, and provided a rallying point for the swarms of Turkish light cavalry.

The main threat to the military renaissance lay outside Europe. The Ottoman Empire more than doubled in size during the early 16th century and under Suleiman the Magnificent (1520-66) overran Hungary. Turkish corsairs raided as far west as Spain. Distance limited Ottoman expansion, however, while their military institutions stagnated.

The Ottoman Empire followed a different military model to Western Europe. The Sultan ruled a monolithic state. His refusal to recognize other rulers as equals provoked conflict with Christian and Muslim powers alike. Turkish armies reflected this centralization of authority. A standard operational approach avoided the tactical debates that crippled the Hungarian army before Mohacs (29 August 1526). The Turks combined a strategic offensive, carrying devastation deep into enemy territory, with a tactical defensive. Janissaries, a professional infantry force armed with missile weapons, formed the core of a Turkish battle line, behind a line of wagons or cannon chained together. Feudal Timariot cavalry extended the flanks in a crescent, while Spahis of the Sultan's household cavalry acted as a reserve. Irregular troops screened the Turkish position, and drew the enemy into a frontal attack. Once the enemy was disordered by pursuit, or broken by the Janissaries' fire, the Turks counter-attacked with Spahis or cavalry placed in ambush beyond the flanks. Turkish tactics combined the defensive power of infantry and guns with the fluidity and resilience of nomad light cavalry. They changed little between Kosovo in 1389 and Kerestes in 1596. The Turks adopted firearms, but these were neither essential nor a Turkish monopoly. The system worked as well against the Hungarians at Mohacs who had guns, as against the Persians at Chaldiran (23 August 1514) who did not.

F R A N

NAVARRE

40

PORTUGAL

Madrid

Rosas 1543

Palamos 1543

Barcelona

S P A I N

A R A G O N

Minorca *1536*

Majorca

Ibiza

0

Tangier•Gibraltar
Ceuta

Melilla

Algiers *1541*

Bug 155

SULTANATE OF MOROCCO

Oran *1563*

A L Ottom fro

The Ottoman Empire, c. 1550

	Ottoman Empire c. 1550

battles

X	Ottoman victory	X	Christian victory

sieges

	Ottoman capture		successful Christian defence
	Ottoman raids		
	Venetian fortified towns		
	Christian counter-attacks		

Selim I's expedition to Persia, 1514

	route		area of concentration

Selim I's expedition to Egypt, 1516–17

	route		area of concentration

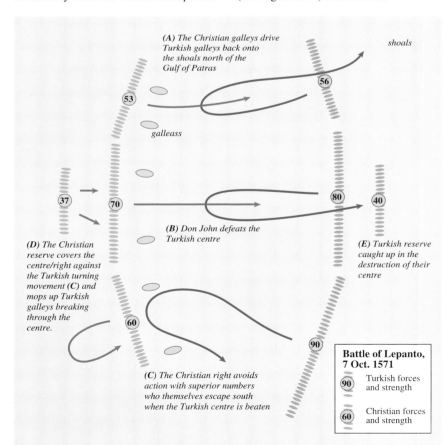

(A) The Christian galleys drive Turkish galleys back onto the shoals north of the Gulf of Patras

shoals

56

53

galleass

37 70

80 40

(B) Don John defeats the Turkish centre

(D) The Christian reserve covers the centre/right against the Turkish turning movement (C) and mops up Turkish galleys breaking through the centre.

(E) Turkish reserve caught up in the destruction of their centre

60

90

(C) The Christian right avoids action with superior numbers who themselves escape south when the Turkish centre is beaten

Battle of Lepanto, 7 Oct. 1571

90	Turkish forces and strength
60	Christian forces and strength

RIGHT: The Christian powers failed to exploit Lepanto, but it confirmed the result of the siege of Malta. Ottoman fleets were excluded permanently from the Western Mediterranean. The greatest victory of the oared galley that had dominated inland seas for two thousand years, Lepanto was also the last.

The Sultan's absolute power of life and death and the inspiration of Islam forged a discipline unknown in other armies, whose disunity was a major factor in Ottoman success. Treachery contributed to the Mameluke defeat at Mercidabik (24 August 1516). Less than half the Hungarian army turned up for Mohacs, while Hungarian renegades accompanied Suleiman to Vienna in 1529. The most crucial defection was that of France. Hapsburg-Valois rivalry diverted Charles V from defending Vienna, and destabilized the Mediterranean. Turkish galleys were short-range vessels with large crews and fragile hulls. A French alliance allowed them to winter in Marseilles, and raid the Spanish and Italian coasts, turning the Hapsburg flank when the Danubian front stabilized in the 1530s. The capture of Malta would have perpetuated the Turkish naval presence in the Western Mediterranean. However, the island's new fortifications and hard fighting by the Knights of St John, the last of the Crusading Orders, halted the Ottoman

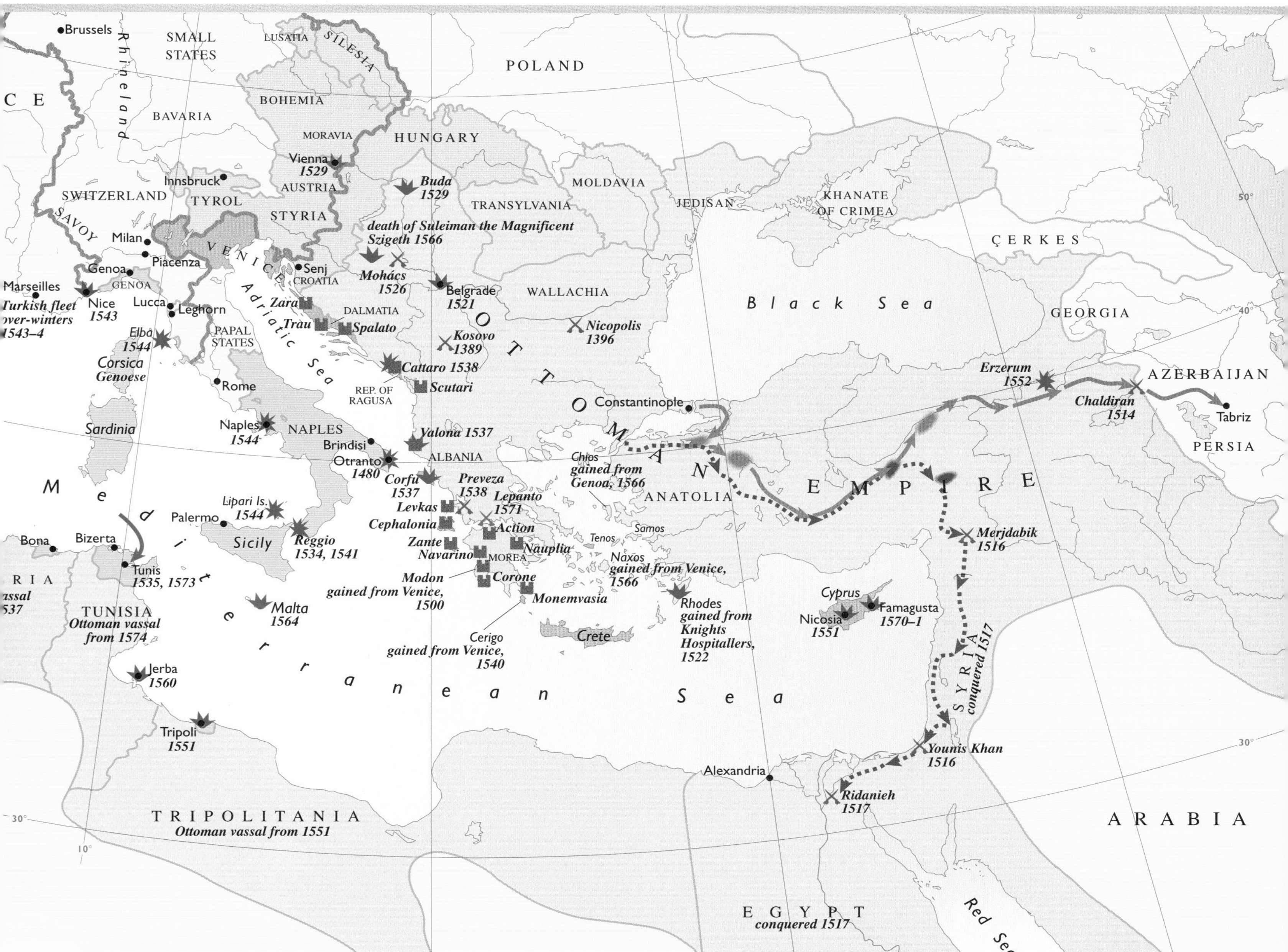

advance in 1564. At the Battle of Lepanto (7 October 1571) a coalition of Christian naval powers ended the Turkish maritime challenge. Turkish siege trains could no longer move by sea, restricting future offensives.

Lepanto was the largest naval action since Actium. Tactically unsubtle, it showed the relative decline in Turkish military capabilities. The Christians had more armour, and outranged scimitar and bow with pike and arquebus. Their 1,800 cannon outclassed the Turks' 750 poor quality guns. The Turks also failed to respond to military developments ashore. The combination of Janissaries and light cavalry defeated poorly articulated Hungarian and Mameluke armies, but was immobile, tactically inferior to veteran pikemen supported by arquebusiers. Military critics of the 1590s recommended Western armies to seek battle against the Turks, who would run away once the Janissaries were beaten. The latter had become effete, a hereditary military class, more interested in palace revolutions than the drill that restored mobility to Western infantry. Like other command economies, the Ottoman Empire responded slowly to technical change, depending on renegade Europeans to design and operate its artillery.

Geography and political centralization limited Ottoman expansion. The Sultan's personal household troops were the basis of Turkish invincibility, and he could only fight on one front. The gains of a campaign might be lost next year, when the Sultan was absent on another frontier. As the Empire grew, it could no longer obtain a decision in the short campaigning season when grass was available. Vienna was saved by its distance from the centre of Ottoman power in Constantinople. Suleiman took the field in May 1529, but the siege did not open until October, and ended a fortnight later with the first snow. Turkish armies could not fight in winter; horses died, and Janissaries mutinied. A predominantly cavalry force easily overran the open spaces of Hungary and Syria, but suffered heavy losses in the mountains of Styria and Armenia. Bastioned fortifications defied the Turks' energetic but unscientific siege techniques. Rhodes surrendered for want of gunpowder, and Famagusta through treachery. Sieges were the essential test for all 16th century armies, pitched battles becoming as scarce in the East as in the West. Abortive sieges at Vienna and Malta mark the maximum reach of the Ottoman Empire. Suleiman died of dysentery during the siege of Szigeth (Aug-Sep 1566), ending the most serious external threat to Europe for 400 years.

ABOVE: The Ottoman Empire expanded rapidly in the early 16th century, exploiting weak and divided opposition. After the 1520s increased distances from the centre of power at Constantinople to the frontiers prevented further expansion, while tactics and fortifications developed in Italy proved superior to stereotyped and inflexible Turkish methods of war.

The Limits of the Military Revolution

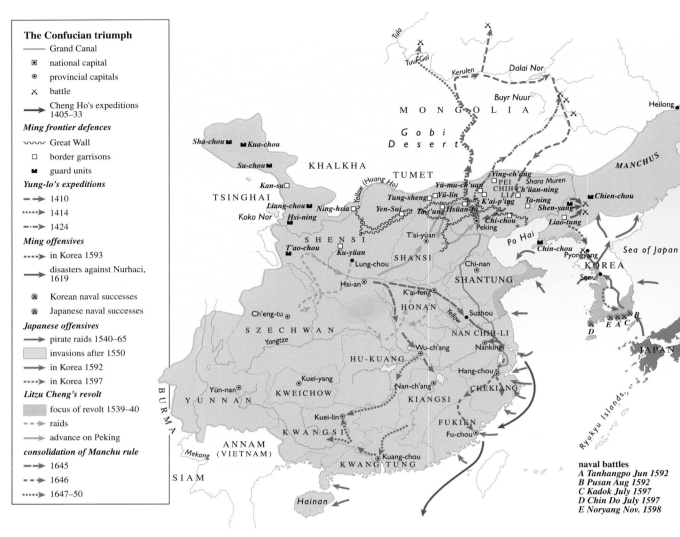

The Confucian triumph

- —— Grand Canal
- ▣ national capital
- ⊙ provincial capitals
- ✕ battle
- ➝ Cheng Ho's expeditions 1405–33

Ming frontier defences
- ⌇⌇⌇ Great Wall
- ◻ border garrisons
- ◾ guard units

Yung-lo's expeditions
- – ➤ 1410
- ••••➤ 1414
- –•➤ 1424

Ming offensives
- ••••➤ in Korea 1593
- ➝ disasters against Nurhaci, 1619
- ⊗ Korean naval successes
- ⊗ Japanese naval successes

Japanese offensives
- ➝ pirate raids 1540–65
- ▭ invasions after 1550
- ➝ in Korea 1592
- ••••➤ in Korea 1597

Litzu Cheng's revolt
- ▦ focus of revolt 1539–40
- – – ➤ raids
- ➝ advance on Peking

consolidation of Manchu rule
- – ➤ 1645
- – ➤ 1646
- ••••➤ 1647–50

naval battles
A Tanhangpo Jun 1592
B Pusan Aug 1592
C Kadok July 1597
D Chin Do July 1597
E Noryang Nov. 1598

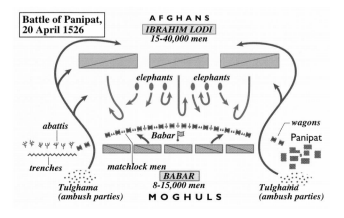

Battle of Panipat, 20 April 1526

AFGHANS
IBRAHIM LODI
15–40,000 men
elephants   elephants
abattis
trenches   matchlock men   Babar   wagons   Panipat
Tulghama (ambush parties)   BABAR 8–15,000 men   Tulghama (ambush parties)
MOGHULS

The largest states of the early modern world lay in the Far East. Ming China and Mughal India were regional superpowers, limited only by major geographical obstacles: the sea, the Mongolian desert, or the Himalayas. They possessed gunpowder weapons, but these reinforced existing military patterns, preventing the type of change seen in the West.

Chinese and Indian military establishments ran into millions, but structural weaknesses limited effectiveness. The Hindu caste system prevented sowars doing menial jobs usually undertaken by troopers. The Mughal army with which Babar seized control of Hindustan in 1526 was a lean outfit, hardened by campaigns in Central Asia. His successors' armies, like all Indian armies, were swollen by hordes of camp followers, perhaps twenty to every fighting man. Such mobile cities overawed India's well-cultivated plains, but were logistically unsustainable in the Deccan or Himalayan foothills. The Mughal combination of Rajput lancers with matchlockmen and gunners of the imperial household remained effective, however, as long as the Emperor took a personal interest in their administration.

Ming China, with its bureaucratic tradition, had permanent training camps to prepare provincial units for expeditions or service on the northern border, but standards of training and equipment declined in the 16th century. Attempts to recruit competent leaders by examination failed, educated Chinese despising military service. Unpaid garrisons took up banditry or farming. Raids from Mongolia imposed a stifling burden. The aggressive forward policy of the early 15th century cost three times the Emperor's annual revenue, but subsequent withdrawal behind the Great Wall deprived the Ming of influence and vital intelligence. Famine and banditry destabilized late Ming society to the point where only an external force could restore order. The Manchu, like the Mughals, were an army of occupation. Socially conservative, they had no taste for destabilizing military innovation.

The Chinese had invented gunpowder weapons in the late 13th century, but the speed and strategic flexibility of their nomadic opponents outweighed theoretically superior weaponry. In the disastrous T'umu campaign (July–August 1449) 20,000 Mongols wiped out a Ming army of half a million, and captured the Emperor, in a series of ambushes and harassing actions reminiscent of Carrhae. A Ming offensive in 1619 outnumbered the Manchu three-to-two, but their more agile opponents exploited a central position between separate Ming columns to destroy them piecemeal. Tactically Ming handgunners had no time to fire before Manchu horsemen overran them. Suspicious of weapons identified with a defeated regime, Manchu armies of the 1840s would be armed much as they had been in the 1650s.

Firearms played a more significant role in Mughal victories. At Panipat (20 April 1526) and Khanwa (16 March 1527) Babar fortified his front with cannon and matchlockmen, but he depended as much on generalship as superior technology.

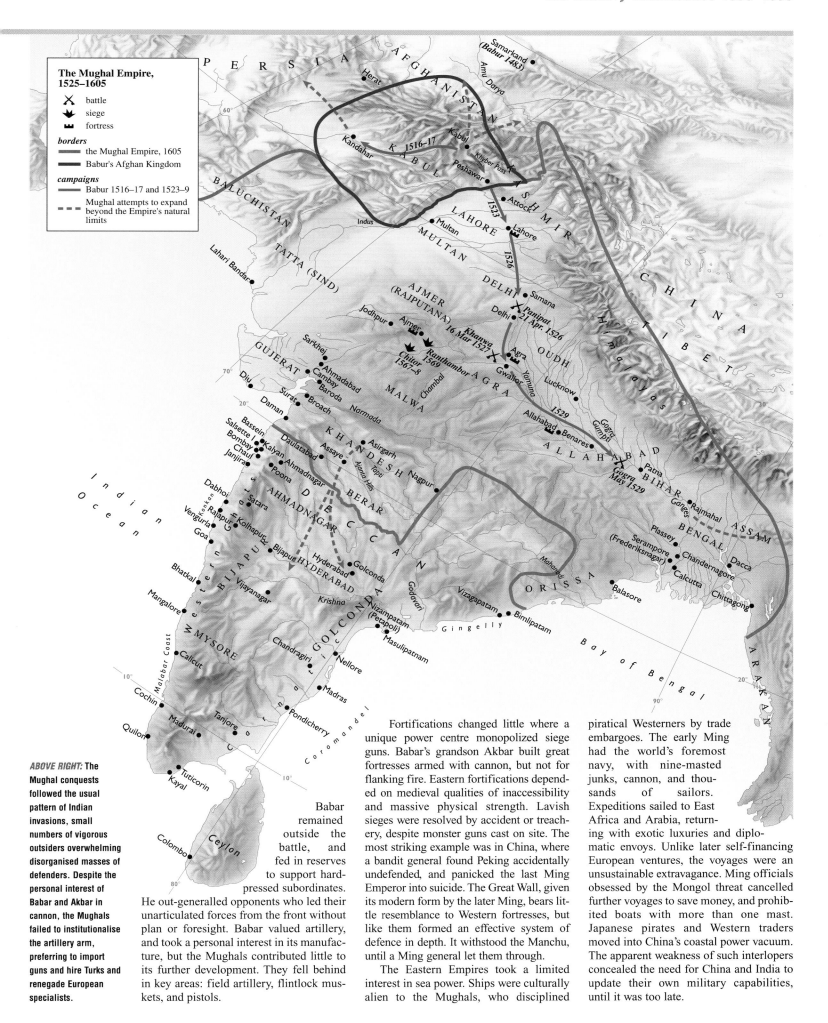

The Mughal Empire, 1525–1605

✕ battle
✦ siege
♛ fortress

borders
— the Mughal Empire, 1605
— Babur's Afghan Kingdom

campaigns
— Babur 1516–17 and 1523–9
--- Mughal attempts to expand beyond the Empire's natural limits

ABOVE RIGHT: The Mughal conquests followed the usual pattern of Indian invasions, small numbers of vigorous outsiders overwhelming disorganised masses of defenders. Despite the personal interest of Babar and Akbar in cannon, the Mughals failed to institutionalise the artillery arm, preferring to import guns and hire Turks and renegade European specialists.

Babar remained outside the battle, and fed in reserves to support hard-pressed subordinates. He out-generalled opponents who led their unarticulated forces from the front without plan or foresight. Babar valued artillery, and took a personal interest in its manufacture, but the Mughals contributed little to its further development. They fell behind in key areas: field artillery, flintlock muskets, and pistols.

Fortifications changed little where a unique power centre monopolized siege guns. Babar's grandson Akbar built great fortresses armed with cannon, but not for flanking fire. Eastern fortifications depended on medieval qualities of inaccessibility and massive physical strength. Lavish sieges were resolved by accident or treachery, despite monster guns cast on site. The most striking example was in China, where a bandit general found Peking accidentally undefended, and panicked the last Ming Emperor into suicide. The Great Wall, given its modern form by the later Ming, bears little resemblance to Western fortresses, but like them formed an effective system of defence in depth. It withstood the Manchu, until a Ming general let them through.

The Eastern Empires took a limited interest in sea power. Ships were culturally alien to the Mughals, who disciplined piratical Westerners by trade embargoes. The early Ming had the world's foremost navy, with nine-masted junks, cannon, and thousands of sailors. Expeditions sailed to East Africa and Arabia, returning with exotic luxuries and diplomatic envoys. Unlike later self-financing European ventures, the voyages were an unsustainable extravagance. Ming officials obsessed by the Mongol threat cancelled further voyages to save money, and prohibited boats with more than one mast. Japanese pirates and Western traders moved into China's coastal power vacuum. The apparent weakness of such interlopers concealed the need for China and India to update their own military capabilities, until it was too late.

The French Wars of Religion

The French Religious Wars were part of a general European struggle between Catholic and Protestant. Their duration and inconsequential savagery resemble modern ideological conflicts where political modalities defy military logic. The obdurate resistance of Paris to a legitimate but Protestant king suggests the popular engagement of modern sectarian struggles. Nevertheless the Wars illustrate how the military renaissance transformed the medieval man-at-arms into the type of cavalryman who lasted until motorization replaced the horse.

The French Religious Wars arose from a triangular struggle between the Crown and two factions, the Catholic League and Protestant Huguenots. Both sought to control a royal government weakened by the struggle with the Hapsburgs, and a succession of minors. The Huguenots lacked the siege guns to complete victories won by their superior cavalry, but held too many towns themselves for the League to take them all. Protected by salt marshes or mountains, Huguenot redoubts at La Rochelle and in the Cevennes only fell to a revived royal government in the late 1620s. The crushing Huguenot defeat at Moncontour (3 October 1569) should have

BELOW: The Wars of Religion lacked stable fronts or clear lines of operation. Like 20th century ideological conflicts they took their shape from atrocities, local rivalries, and foreign interventions. Widespread gangsterism and mutual distrust prolonged hostilities that served little rational purpose.

ended the war then, but the local nature of the struggle reduced the significance of battles. Warlordism was endemic. Local gentry perpetuated instability for amusement and profit. The primacy of religious over national feeling encouraged and legitimized foreign intervention, which sustained the combatants whenever domestic support faltered.

Shifting patterns of intrigue made nonsense of strategy in a war where victorious armies broke up in disagreement until renewed sectarian outrages provoked fresh fighting. Henry of Navarre went off after Coutras (20 October 1587) to visit a favourite mistress. Despite such vagaries, the rational strategic style of the *condottieri* persisted. Marshal Tavannes, the veteran Royalist commander in the Moncontour campaign, avoided action until he caught the Huguenot army strung out on the line of march. He only attacked then because the season was late, and the enemy's wavering pikes suggested poor morale. The great Duke of Parma derided Henry of Navarre as a captain of light dragoons, but the Huguenots' cautious manoeuvres during Parma's march on Rouen showed both sides could play a devious game. Henry's strategy trapped

ABOVE: Muzzle-loading pistols could be reloaded on horseback, but it was a cumbersome business. Reiters often went into battle with half-a-dozen loaded weapons. Their firepower enabled them to shoot down pike-armed infantry.

Parma's starving army in a bend in the River Seine, the Spaniards only escaping by an inspired bridging operation across tidal waters, under the noses of a Protestant flotilla.

The infrequency of battles in the later Italian Wars devalued traditional heavy cavalry. They were useless for sieges, and worn out by campaign duties like reconnaissance or raiding. The old French companies of gensdarmes from the Hundred Years War were in decline before the Religious Wars, as great nobles opted for the comforts of civilian life. In their place appeared less heavily armoured cavalry carrying firearms, known as Reiters from the area of their origin. German heavy cavalry had often been worsted by French gensdarmes, and readily adopted the *pistala*, a single handed arquebus that appeared in the 1540s. Such cavalry had a dual capability: they could ride arquebusiers down in the open, or shatter unsupported pike formations with their pistols. Reiters were vulnerable while reloading, and their skirmishing tactics known as the caracole encouraged unenthusiastic soldiers to fire uselessly at long range. Formations six to eight deep wasted the rear ranks, but were easier to control than a traditional shallow line of gensdarmes. Henry of Navarre's pistoleers at Coutras gave attacking lancers a close range volley, and smashed through their disordered line sword in hand.

Infantry had become the dominant arm in Italy, but cavalry could still exploit the tactical discontinuity between marching and fighting order. Infantry could resist

Huguenots and the League

- ■ Catholic strongholds
- ■ Huguenot strongholds
- ✗ Catholic victories
- ✗ Huguenot victories
- ▲ Catholic sieges
- ▲ Huguenot sieges
- ✳ Catholic outrages
- ✳ Huguenot outrages

foreign interventions
- ➡ by Spain
- ➡ by Protestant powers

Map labels: English Channel; Arques 21 Sep. 1589; Amiens; La Fere; 1592; English 1562, 1592; Rouen 1591–2; St Denys 10 Nov. 1567; Laon; Paris: Massacre of St Bartholomew 1572, Murder of Henry III 1589; 1591; 1567; 1562 German mercenaries 1569; Massacre of Vassy 1562; Ivry 14 Mar. 1590; 1567, 1590; Dormans 10 Oct 1575; Dreux 19 Dec. 1562; Paris; Meaux 1572; Corbeil; Meaux: Huguenots try to seize Royal Family 1567; Chartres 1591; Melun; Montereau; Troyes 1572; 1562 1567; Orléans 1563; Angers 1572; Tumult of Amboise 1560; Blois: Murder of Duke & Cardinal de Guise 1588; Sancerre; Fontaine-Française 9 Jun 1585; Saumur 1572; Tours; Loire; Moncontour 3 Oct. 1569; Bourges 1572; 1569–1570; La Charité-sur-Loire; Dijon; Saône; Poitiers 1569; FRANCE; La Rochelle; Geneva 1570; Bay of Biscay; St-Jean-d'Angély 1569; 1569; Cognac; Jarnac 13 Mar. 1567; Angoulême; Lyon 1572; Loire; Rhône; Coutras 20 Oct. 1587; Bordeaux 1572; Bergerac; Privas; ALPS; Negrepelisse; Millau; Alès; Uzès; Montauban; Albi; St-Affrique; Nîmes; Orthez 24 Aug. 1569; Toulouse 1572; Castres; Pau; Navarrenx; Pyrenees; Golfe du Lion; SPAIN

RIGHT: Individual campaigns displayed high standards of generalship and manoeuvre. Henry IV was unable to force Parma to fight at a disadvantage, but refused to do so himself, despite his personal preference for reckless cavalry charges.

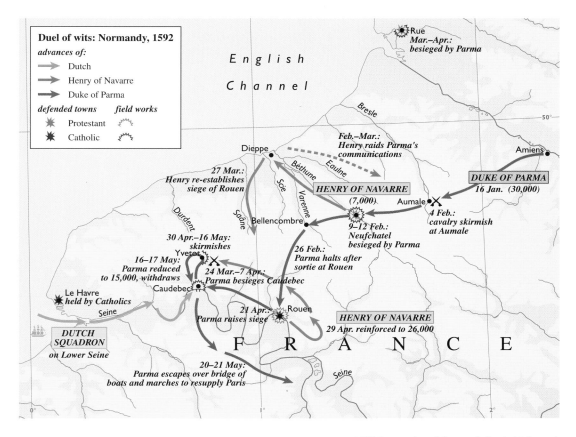

Duel of wits: Normandy, 1592

advances of:

→ Dutch
→ Henry of Navarre
→ Duke of Parma

defended towns   *field works*

✱ Protestant   〜
✱ Catholic   〜

English Channel

Rue
Mar.–Apr.:
besieged by Parma

Bresle

Feb.–Mar.:
Henry raids Parma's
communications

Amiens

Dieppe

27 Mar.:
Henry re-establishes
siege of Rouen

Béthune
Eaulne

HENRY OF NAVARRE
(7,000)

Aumale ✗

DUKE OF PARMA
16 Jan. (30,000)

Scie
Varenne

4 Feb.:
cavalry skirmish
at Aumale

Bellencombre

9–12 Feb.:
Neufchatel
besieged by Parma

Durdent
Saône

30 Apr.–16 May:
skirmishes

Yvetot ✗

16–17 May:
Parma reduced
to 15,000, withdraws

Caudebec

24 Mar.–7 Apr.:
Parma besieges Caudebec

26 Feb.:
Parma halts after
sortie at Rouen

Le Havre
held by Catholics

Seine

21 Apr.:
Parma raises siege

Rouen

HENRY OF NAVARRE
29 Apr. reinforced to 26,000

DUTCH
SQUADRON
on Lower Seine

F R A N C E

Seine

20–21 May:
Parma escapes over bridge of
boats and marches to resupply Paris

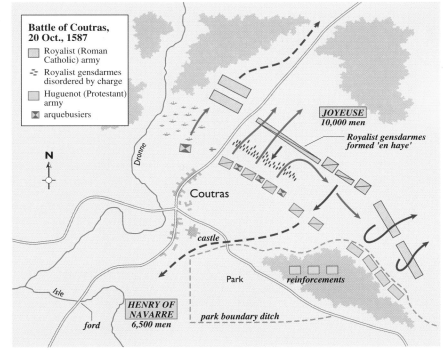

Battle of Coutras,
20 Oct., 1587

▢ Royalist (Roman Catholic) army
⫟ Royalist gensdarmes disordered by charge
▢ Huguenot (Protestant) army
⊠ arquebusiers

N

Dronne

JOYEUSE
10,000 men

Royalist gensdarmes
formed 'en haye'

Coutras

castle

Park

reinforcements

Isle

HENRY OF
NAVARRE
6,500 men

ford   *park boundary ditch*

LEFT: Coutras showed the superiority of pistol-armed cavalry over traditional lancers armed *cap-a-pie*. Cavalry and infantry fought intermixed to take advantage of favourable terrain, and provide mutual support. Unlike the battles of the Italian Wars, however, Coutras was resolved by the clash of mounted troops.

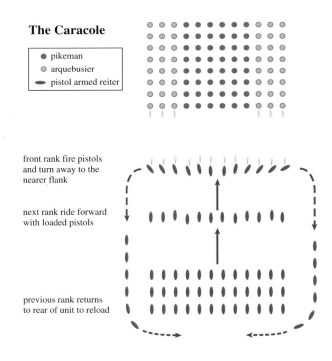

The Caracole

● pikeman
○ arquebusier
⬤— pistol armed reiter

front rank fire pistols
and turn away to the
nearer flank

next rank ride forward
with loaded pistols

previous rank returns
to rear of unit to reload

ABOVE: Deep formations of well-trained cavalry could keep up a constant fire with their wheel-lock pistols. Each rank trotted forward in its turn to fire, then fell back to reload. Theoretically vulnerable to a brisk counter-charge, caracoling horsemen had a reserve of firepower to deter attackers.

---

cavalry when suitably arrayed, but faced disaster if caught on the march by more mobile horsemen. Imperialist cavalry destroyed two thirds of a French army retiring from St Quentin (10 August 1557). France had more open country than Italy, and the haphazard circumstances of civil war suited cavalry equipped with firearms. Most of the battles of the Religious Wars were cavalry actions, the infantry hardly engaged. The Wars of Religion reversed the numerical decline of French cavalry.

From 46% in 1495 to 16% in the Metz campaign of 1552, a quarter of the forces engaged at Ivry in 1590, when Henry of Navarre smashed the Leaguers' army, were cavalry. Except for a few Spanish lancers, most of these were armoured pistoleers, now the standard European heavy cavalryman. After a thousand years the man-at-arms had lost his predominance. One of Henry of Navarre's first acts as Henri IV was to disband the surviving *compagnies d'ordonnance.*

The School of War - The Dutch Revolt

RIGHT: The matchlock musket required the soldier to have a burning length of slow match to ignite the charges. Early models were so heavy that a rest had to be provided. Pre-measured charges held in bandoliers improved the rate of fire.

RIGHT: Sample battle plans were part of the new military professionalism. Maurice standardised infantry units to form part of a geometrically consistent order of battle. Smaller regiments could afford to deploy in successive lines to provide mutual support, and cover each other's flanks.

The prosperous towns and dank swamps of the Netherlands provide a surprising setting for the next step in the military renaissance. The burghers of the Low Countries not only fought the most powerful military machine of the day, the Spanish Army of Flanders, to a standstill; they developed a new style of army, the prototype of professional military forces today.

The Dutch Revolt is a fine example of Clausewitz's analysis of the advantages of the defensive. The obstinate resistance of every Dutch town gained time for the strategic balance to shift against Spain through the action of allies and the development of Dutch sea power, which enriched the Dutch while the Army of Flanders mutinied for want of pay. Delay brought all the country's resources into play: its numerous defensible towns, dykes, ponds and difficult passages, and the inaccessible national redoubt of Holland, so waterlogged ships sailed across flooded fields to relieve Leyden (October 1573). The Duke of Alva, Spanish Viceroy in the 1560s, alienated popular support by his policy of terror. Wherever his victorious soldiers went,

they swelled the ranks of his enemies. The 'Spanish Fury' at Antwerp (October 1576) even drove the loyal Roman Catholics of the southern provinces to rebel.

The War in the Netherlands had its own rules. Lack of space reinforced the contemporary preference for sieges. Battles were uniquely scarce, after early demonstrations of the crushing superiority of Spanish arms. At Jemmingen (21 July 1568) Alva's veterans lured the rebels out of their trenches, and shot them down like wild fowl. At Gemblours (31 January

1578) Spanish cavalry killed or captured 5,000 retreating rebels, unable to defend themselves on the march. A conciliatory Viceroy exploited Gemblours to pacify the southern provinces, but the action was untypically decisive. Like other civil wars the Dutch Revolt was fought out at a local level. Small garrisons squabbled over individual villages, with no fixed front line. *'La Guerre aux Vaches'* generated widespread insecurity, and was perhaps more typical of the 16th century experience of war, than battles and marches.

The years of attrition paid off in the 1590s. Dutch forces became strong enough to launch a counter-offensive, while half the Army of Flanders was absent fighting Huguenots. The great rivers were more than military obstacles. The Dutch used barges to shift siege guns rapidly on internal lines, reducing enemy fortresses in short sharp sieges: Zutphen in seven days, Deventer in eleven, Hulst in five, and Nijmegen in six. Maurice of Nassau consolidated the Netherlands' southern border, eliminated the Roman Catholic enclave in the north east, and pushed the Dutch border fifty miles east of the River Ijssel. In 1598 the Dutch counter-offensive reached its culminating point along the modern frontier. The Army of Flanders returned, English help dwindled, and the Dutch army made little headway in the hostile open countryside of what is now Belgium.

The numerous sieges of the Revolt encouraged the scientific study of warfare. The first Spanish manuals of siegecraft appeared during the 1590s, incorporating empirically calculated range tables. Maurice of Nassau was the first commander to take a telescope up a church tower, to spy out the enemy. Young men wishing to learn the military trade took service in the Netherlands, which became known as the 'School of War'. Dutchmen replaced Italians as the leading exponents of siege warfare, inventing hornworks, demilunes, and trench redoubts to secure sapping parties against sorties. The Duke of Alva's systematic lines of contravallation defied relief attempts, although Spanish armies often depended on hunger to reduce their victims to surrender, as at

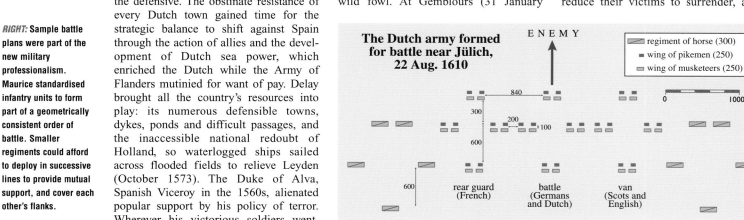

The Dutch army formed for battle near Jülich, 22 Aug. 1610

ENEMY

regiment of horse (300)
wing of pikemen (250)
wing of musketeers (250)

840
300
200
100
600

0   1000 ft

600   rear guard (French)   battle (Germans and Dutch)   van (Scots and English)

600

The Dutch Revolt 1566–1609

battles
✕ Spanish success
✕ Dutch success

sieges
▲ Spanish success/failure
✳ Spanish massacre
▲ Dutch success

Dutch defensive lines
••••••• Oude Hollandsche Waterlinie
------- River Ijssel 1605–6

regions
I Catholic redoubt in North East until 1590's
II Dutch inner redoubt
III Dutch outer redoubt
IV open cavalry country in Catholic south

support
→ Spanish
→ Protestant

BELOW: The 17th century experience of war in Western Europe was of sieges rather than battles. Superior siege techniques swung the balance in favour of attackers by the mid-1620s. Both sides could predict the progress of a siege, often resulting in surrender before a practicable breach had been made.

ABOVE: The Dutch matched the Netherlands' strategic resources against superior Spanish tactics. Numerous towns and inundations prolonged resistance, while the long frontier with Germany and the North Sea coast were always open to foreign assistance, but closed to the Spanish. Maurice of Nassau's offensives followed the fortified river lines that determined the final borders of the rebel Republic.

Antwerp, besieged from July 1584 to August 1585. The Dutch capture of Geertruidenberg in 1593 was hailed as a 'second Alesia', in reference to Julius Caesar's great siege, and the classical spirit affected the whole Dutch approach to war. Maurice of Nassau devised drill systems for his infantry from Aelian's description of Roman drill. He reduced the depth of combat formations, to make more efficient use of manpower, halving the strength of infantry companies from 150 to 80. Ten companies formed a permanently embodied regiment, which the wealthy Dutch paid through the winter. Drill and stable organization enhanced recruits' morale, allowing them to face Spanish veterans who were innocent of group training, and disbanded every autumn. Maurice made his men dig trenches, but paid them for it. Spanish troops would rather have begged in the streets. Maurice substituted the legionary for the *preux chevalier* as the ideal soldier. Modern armies would value routine above heroism.

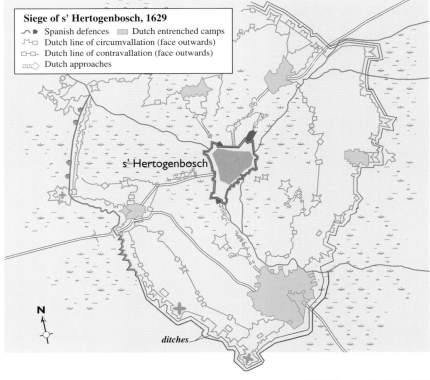

Siege of s' Hertogenbosch, 1629

⌒▶ Spanish defences ▢ Dutch entrenched camps
⊡ Dutch line of circumvallation (face outwards)
⊡ Dutch line of contravallation (face outwards)
◇ Dutch approaches

s' Hertogenbosch

N

ditches

Europe's Maritime Expansion

RIGHT: Sea power allowed the Spanish and Portuguese to dominate large areas cost effectively. Their maritime empires persisted, unlike the short-lived Chinese voyages of the 15th century. Ashore, however, local power centres, such as the Mughal Empire, and disease prevented European penetration far inland, even in South America.

ABOVE: Developments in European ship construction enabled world-wide exploration to begin, Columbus's discoveries stimulating further improvements in ship design, cartography and navigation. Ocean voyages demanded professionalism, technocrats rather than aristocrats.

During the 16th century the galley ceased to be the dominant weapon system at sea. Sailing ships armed with cannon revolutionized naval tactics, and provided their owners with a transoceanic capability. The maritime possessions of Spain and Portugal, united from 1580, formed the first empire on which the sun never set.

Medieval sea fights were boarding actions, ships defending themselves with high bulwarks and crossbows. Small breech-loading guns taken to sea in the 15th century fitted into this pattern. Unreliable gunpowder and poorly sealed breech-blocks restricted muzzle velocities, limiting early naval guns to an anti-personnel role. The castles ships carried fore and aft became higher to accommodate scores of light guns, sacrificing seaworthiness for defensive firepower. Cast bronze muzzle-loaders provided the antidote to such sea-fortresses. Stronger than iron breech-loaders, they could put a 60lb stone ball through a ship's side at 200 yards. The new guns were too heavy for upper decks, so went below, firing through gunports cut in the ship's side. Such concentrated broadsides outgunned the three bow guns of galleys, which became limited to the Mediterranean. The social effects of the new sailing warship were revolutionary. Gunnery and navigation demanded mathe-

matical knowledge, encouraging naval professionalism. Crews became homogeneous. Seamen no longer needed soldiers to fight on their ships, as sailors manned the guns. Smaller crews extended the strategic range of sailing ships, beyond that of heavily manned galley fleets.

The great explorers found their way to India and the Americas in small, unarmed caravels, but consolidated their discoveries with sailing warships. Portuguese ships were tactically superior to the Arab dhows and Ottoman galleys of the Indian Ocean. Vasco da Gama defeated the Sultan of Calicut with just eighteen ships, the largest of sixteen guns. Ashore the Portuguese faced powerful armies, and remained a minor power. The Spanish in South America were exceptional among early European imperialists in occupying large overseas territories, despite numerous and well-organized opposition. American Indian kingdoms could summon large armies of experienced warriors by systems of runners as efficient as communications in Europe. Their wood and stone weapons were not ineffective. An Aztec obsidian battleaxe could take off a horse's head, while Spanish soldiers used local quilted cotton armour. The Conquista owed little to the military renaissance, its free-booting individualism more resembling a Crusade. Cortez' army had few modern weapons:

thirteen muskets and sixteen horses. Most of his men used pikes and crossbows. Small Spanish forces, however, were highly mobile. They lived off the country, while large Inca or Aztec armies dispersed for lack of food. The latters' ritualistic conventions of war were no match for the pragmatic violence of the Spanish.

The Spanish in the New World needed efficient warships to keep out other Europeans, not to defeat the locals' dugout canoes. Spanish shipbuilders combined features of galley and caravel to produce the galleon. Its fine lines and improved sail plan provided the sea-keeping qualities needed to police an Empire. Galleons of 400-500 tons were smaller than the coastal defence gun platforms of the English navy. The largest ship in the Armada campaign would be HMS Triumph at over 1,000 tons. The Armada was the first major encounter between fleets of sailing ships. The Spaniards had much experience of amphibious operations, most recently against the Azores, but the Armada faced intractable strategic problems. Unlike the English fleet the Armada was far from home, unable to resupply or repair damaged ships. Once at sea it could not communicate with Spanish invasion forces in the Netherlands. When the Armada reached Calais, lack of a safe harbour and prevailing westerly winds prevented it

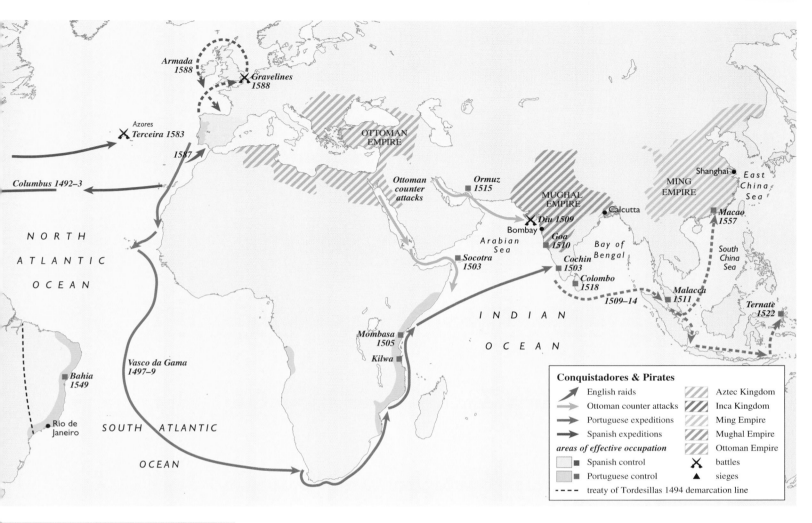

Conquistadores & Pirates

↗ English raids	◪ Aztec Kingdom
→ Ottoman counter attacks	◪ Inca Kingdom
→ Portuguese expeditions	◪ Ming Empire
→ Spanish expeditions	◪ Mughal Empire
areas of effective occupation	◪ Ottoman Empire
☐ ■ Spanish control	✕ battles
▨ ■ Portuguese control	▲ sieges
- - - treaty of Tordesillas 1494 demarcation line	

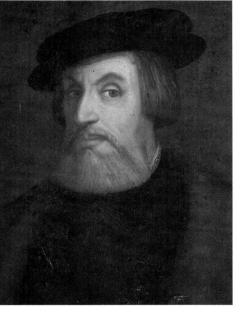

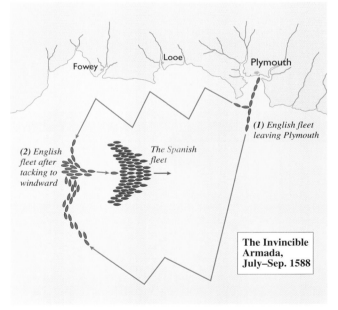

The Invincible Armada, July–Sep. 1588

LEFT: Paradoxically, the Spanish conquest of central America owed little to new technology: Cortez' expedition only had 13 muskets and his tiny force was greatly outnumbered. The destruction of the Inca Empire by another handful of freebooters led by Pizarro is equally impossible to explain in terms of any 'military revolution'. The weapons were less important than the men behind them.

LEFT: The English gained the weather gauge during the initial engagement off Plymouth, setting a pattern for future naval engagements under sail. The dense Spanish crescent formation, similar to that at Lepanto, resisted all attacks, however. Only after several days fighting had shaken the Armada's order of battle were the English able to exploit their superior gunnery.

waiting even the six days the Army of Flanders needed to put to sea.

Superior English gunnery converted strategic defeat into disaster. Spanish guns were crooked and ill-cast, an armourer's nightmare of calibres. Galleons were expected to fire a single salvo before boarding, like galleys, so lacked gunners to reload during combat. Heavy Spanish guns fired once or twice on the heaviest days' fighting. The English had recognized the tactical consequences of arming ships with heavy guns, and fought primarily by gunfire. They mounted their cannon on compact four-wheeled gun trucks, easier to handle on board ship than two-wheeled Spanish field gun carriages, increasing rates of fire and accuracy. When the Armada lost formation after the fireship attack at Gravelines, groups of English ships battered individual opponents with repeated broadsides, which the victim could not return. Damage to hulls and masts combined with storms off the Irish coast to wreck over thirty Spanish ships before they reached a home port.

The Swedish Meteor

The Thirty Years War drew together the strands of the military renaissance: the growth of armies, the rise of infantry, and the reinvention of cavalry. Gustavus Adolphus, King of Sweden, realized the potential of all these trends, creating a durable military system adopted across Europe.

The Thirty Years War began in Central Europe, but religious divisions and hostility between the Hapsburgs and the French and Dutch broadened the conflict. The unlimited aims of the Holy Roman Emperor Ferdinand II, intent on enforcing religious uniformity in Germany, made the war 'a fight between God and the Devil' with no third way. Warfare was more fluid than in the Netherlands with lower ratios of force to space and fewer bastioned fortresses, but battles remained few and indecisive. Armies were small in proportion to the area of operations, so could not force action upon unwilling opponents. Strategy focussed on logistics: subsisting the army at someone else's expense, attempts to drive the enemy into areas already plundered, or raids to divert the enemy from sensitive points. Gustavus Adolphus threatened Hapsburg Silesia to draw the Imperial General Tilly away from Magdeburg, Sweden's only ally, but Tilly's army stormed Magdeburg anyway, killing five sixths of the population.

Military forces exceeded the ability of states to support them. Armies had stood at about 25,000 until the 1530s, roughly doubled by the 1570s, and reached 100,000 in 1631-32. Less than half these numbers appeared on the battlefield, as garrisons

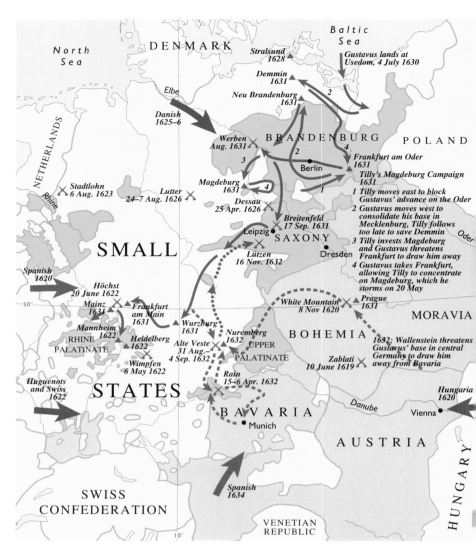

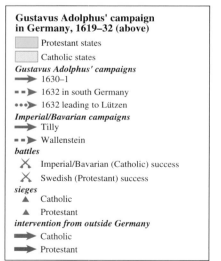

Tilly's Magdeburg Campaign 1631

1 Tilly moves east to block Gustavus' advance on the Oder
2 Gustavus moves west to consolidate his base in Mecklenburg, Tilly follows too late to save Demmin
3 Tilly invests Magdeburg and Gustavus threatens Frankfurt to draw him away
4 Gustavus takes Frankfurt, allowing Tilly to concentrate on Magdeburg, which he storms on 20 May

1632: Wallenstein threatens Gustavus' base in central Germany to draw him away from Bavaria

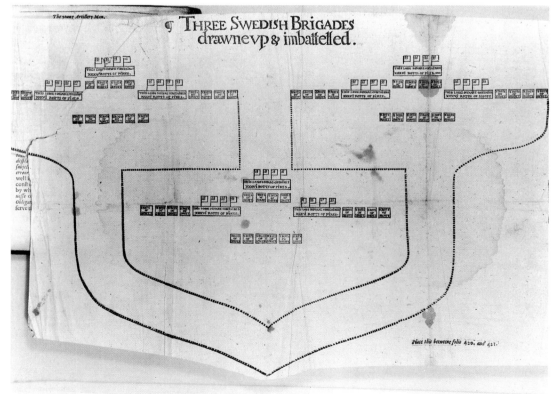

THREE SWEDISH BRIGADES drawne vp & imbattelled.

Gustavus Adolphus' campaign in Germany, 1619–32 (above)

- Protestant states
- Catholic states

Gustavus Adolphus' campaigns
- → 1630–1
- ▪▪► 1632 in south Germany
- •••► 1632 leading to Lützen

Imperial/Bavarian campaigns
- → Tilly
- ▪▪► Wallenstein

battles
- ✕ Imperial/Bavarian (Catholic) success
- ✕ Swedish (Protestant) success

sieges
- ▲ Catholic
- ▲ Protestant

intervention from outside Germany
- ➡ Catholic
- ➡ Protestant

LEFT: All arms battle, Swedish style: units of pikemen and musketeers drawn up for battle. Cavalry would form up on the flanks, with 'galloper guns' (light artillery) and additional units of musketeers.

were numerous, and wastage high. Governments competed to recruit armies beyond their means, losing operational control to military entrepreneurs like Wallenstein, the Imperialist generalissimo. Wallenstein raised whole armies, fed and equipped them from his own estates, and before his assassination appeared to threaten the position of the Emperor himself. Poor and late pay eroded military discipline. Hungry soldiers took what they needed from the civilian population, and wasted the rest, destroying the economic basis of war. Armies starved, and angry peasants murdered straggling soldiers. Officers connived at pillage, as they shared the proceeds. Strategy was subordinated to plunder. After Magdeburg, Tilly invaded neutral Saxony to resupply his army, creating the conditions for an Imperial military disaster.

Gustavus had intervened in North Germany to exclude Hapsburg influence from the Baltic. Despite Sweden's marginal location, he was well acquainted with contemporary military theory and practice, after nine campaigns. Gustavus adapted and improved Maurice of Nassau's methods. Systematic indoctrination gave his mercenaries and Swedish conscripts a cohesion that Tilly's undrilled veterans lacked. Swedish troops fought in small, mutually supporting units. They integrated fire and movement in a recognizably modern way, covering the intervals between them by fire. Like Henry of Navarre, Gustavus placed detachments of musketeers between cavalry squadrons, who were expected to charge home, as Polish cavalry had done in Livonia. Gustavus reduced the number of ranks from ten to six, then to three, achieving higher rates of fire than were possible with deeper formations. Where Maurice's musketeers retired to reload, Gustavus' fired by 'introduction', a loaded rear rank man moving to the front to fire. Swedish infantry advanced

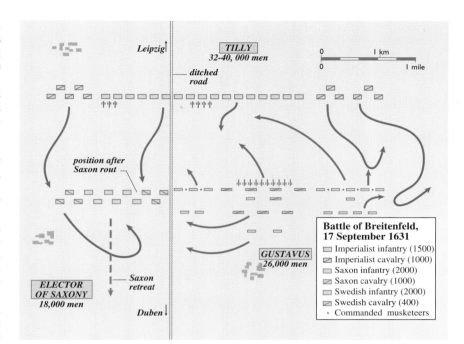

LEFT: Breitenfeld was a triumph for Gustavus' tactical system, helped by the Imperialist battle plan. Tilly sought to envelop the allied army, but his musket fringed pike squares were too slow and clumsy. Double envelopment usually fails without superior numbers or mobility.

Leipzig

TILLY
32–40,000 men

ditched road

position after Saxon rout

ELECTOR OF SAXONY
18,000 men

Saxon retreat

Duben

GUSTAVUS
26,000 men

0 — 1 km
0 — 1 mile

Battle of Breitenfeld, 17 September 1631
- Imperialist infantry (1500)
- Imperialist cavalry (1000)
- Saxon infantry (2000)
- Saxon cavalry (1000)
- Swedish infantry (2000)
- Swedish cavalry (400)
· Commanded musketeers

behind a continuous roll of fire, unless they closed up to fire a single devastating salvo, followed by a charge of pikes. Pairs of light iron 4pr guns attached to each infantry and cavalry regiment further enhanced firepower. Renaissance governments had usually avoided dangerous concentrations of military power, authorizing individual captains to raise independent companies. Gustavus created the modern military hierarchy, grouping companies in battalions permanently affiliated to regiments, some of whose successors exist in the modern Swedish Army.

Gustavus' victory at Breitenfeld (17 September 1631) was comparable with that of the legion over the phalanx; a triumph for firepower and mobility over Tilly's previously invincible masses. The Imperialist commanders were competent and energetic, but their tactics wasteful. Infantry formations thirty men deep pre-

sented a profitable target to Swedish regimental guns, while aggressive Swedish horsemen rode down Imperial Reiter-style cavalry in mid-caracole, after a salvo from supporting musketeers. Gustavus' shallow formations freed men to form a second line and a reserve. When his Saxon allies fled, the well drilled Swedes rapidly faced left, using reserve units to form a new front. This classical use of a second line to meet a tactical emergency marks the full realization of the military renaissance, making Breitenfeld perhaps the first great battle of modern times.

RIGHT: 'The Swedish Meteor', King Gustavus Adolphus of Sweden. His mastery of combined arms tactics, the use of reserves and the creation of permanent units marked the completion of the military renaissance.

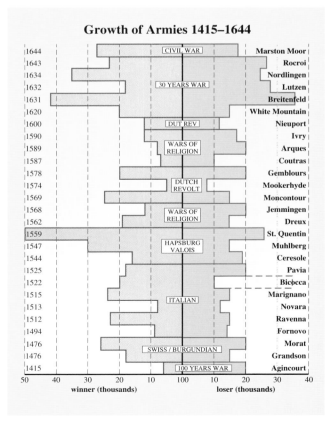

219

RIGHT: The military renaissance swelled the total numbers of men under arms, to besiege or garrison fortresses. Battlefield armies increased less, except for untypical Hapsburg coalition forces at St Quentin and Nordlingen. Numbers engaged mattered less than troop quality and doctrine. In almost half the battles shown, the losers outnumbered the winners.

Growth of Armies 1415–1644

Year		Battle
1644	CIVIL WAR	Marston Moor
1643		Rocroi
1634		Nordlingen
1632	30 YEARS WAR	Lutzen
1631		Breitenfeld
1620		White Mountain
1600	DUT REV	Nieuport
1590		Ivry
1589	WARS OF RELIGION	Arques
1587		Coutras
1578		Gemblours
1574	DUTCH REVOLT	Mookerhyde
1569		Moncontour
1568	WARS OF RELIGION	Jemmingen
1562		Dreux
1559		St. Quentin
1547	HAPSBURG VALOIS	Muhlberg
1544		Ceresole
1525		Pavia
1522		Bicocca
1515	ITALIAN	Marignano
1513		Novara
1512		Ravenna
1494		Fornovo
1476		Morat
1476	SWISS / BURGUNDIAN	Grandson
1415	100 YEARS WAR	Agincourt

50 40 30 20 10 100 10 20 30 40
winner (thousands)   loser (thousands)

The Heirs of Gustavus

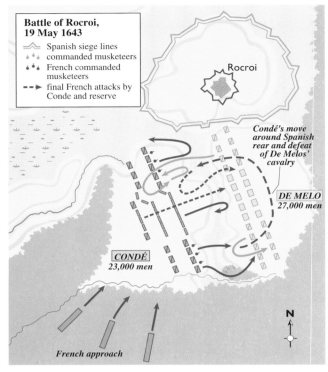

Battle of Rocroi,
19 May 1643
- Spanish siege lines
- commanded musketeers
- French commanded musketeers
- → final French attacks by Condé and reserve

Rocroi

Condé's move around Spanish rear and defeat of De Melos' cavalry

DE MELO
27,000 men

CONDÉ
23,000 men

French approach

N

LEFT: Rocroi re-established the offensive capability of well handled cavalry. Conde's battlefield control prefigured that of Cromwell at Naseby and Marston Moor. Some of his victorious squadrons pursued a broken enemy, while the rest joined the infantry battle, circling the enemy to recover disaster on the other flank.

ABOVE: Oliver Cromwell led the New Model Army to victory in the English Civil War: the combination of Swedish tactics and the ideological commitment of the soldiers produced a military machine capable of dominating the British Isles.

RIGHT: Wallenstein used field fortifications to counter his tactical weakness, in the way the Roman Army had, and stalemated Gustavus' combat strategy by adopting a logistics strategy. Starving the Swedes out of their trenches, Wallenstein forced them to fight on ground that neutralised their tactical superiority.

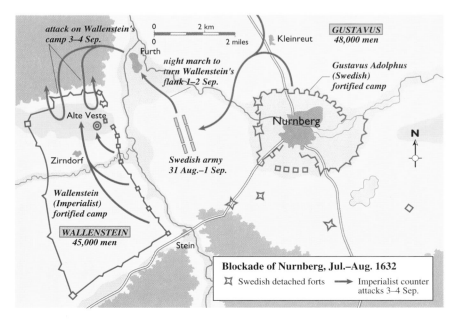

attack on Wallenstein's camp 3–4 Sep.

0   2 km
0   2 miles

Furth

Kleinreut

GUSTAVUS
48,000 men

night march to turn Wallenstein's flank 1–2 Sep.

Gustavus Adolphus (Swedish) fortified camp

Alte Veste

Nurnberg

Zirndorf

Swedish army 31 Aug.–1 Sep.

N

Wallenstein (Imperialist) fortified camp

WALLENSTEIN
45,000 men

Stein

Blockade of Nurnberg, Jul.–Aug. 1632
- Swedish detached forts   → Imperialist counter attacks 3–4 Sep.

Breitenfeld destroyed Tilly's army, but a single battle was insufficient to knock out the Empire and its Spanish allies. The Swedes, and after Gustavus' death the French, found it easier to attack the logistical basis of Hapsburg power than threaten remote political centres in Vienna or Madrid.

Gustavus did not march directly on Vienna after Breitenfeld. Despite his personal taste for action, Gustavus was as cautious as the *condottieri*, only fighting at an advantage, or from behind entrenchments. He expanded his base into the Rhineland, simultaneously reducing Imperial resources. Gustavus' ensuing campaign in South Germany, however, degenerated into an indecisive raid on Bavaria, when he failed to storm Ingolstadt's bastions. Gustavus had an army of Napoleonic proportions, but poor agricultural surpluses prevented him concentrating to dominate enemy territory. As the leader of a coalition, fighting uncivilized opponents, Gustavus lacked Napoleon's freedom to manoeuvre regardless of the interests of his allies. Wallenstein's advance against Nuremberg in July 1632 forced Gustavus to respond with a fraction of his strength (20,000 out of 150,000), or risk another atrocity like Magdeburg. Wallenstein avoided action, starving the Swedes out of their trenches. Gustavus attacked over ground unfavourable to combined arms tactics, and suffered his first defeat at the Alte Veste. Wallenstein persisted with a strategy of diversion. Raiding into Saxony, he compelled Gustavus to postpone an invasion of Austria.

The ensuing Battle of Lutzen (16 November 1632) destroyed the last Imperial army, but Gustavus' chance death in action prevented an immediate advance on Vienna. Deprived of the Swedish Hercules, Cardinal Richelieu, the French chief minister, adopted a logistical strategy, attacking the communications between scattered Hapsburg possessions in Italy, Germany, and the Netherlands. The 'Spanish Road', by which reinforcements reached the Army of Flanders from the Hapsburg Duchy of Milan, was a remarkable example of Renaissance military logistics. The troops followed routes surveyed by military engineers, skirting troublespots like Calvinist Geneva. Contractors maintained regular staging posts, or *etapes*, to limit the harm soldiers did to local communities. Henry IV cut the original Spanish Road through Franche Comte, and Dutch seapower threatened the maritime route through the English Channel, but the Spanish found another route through the Grisons valleys. A Spanish army reached South Germany to defeat the Swedes at Nordlingen (6 September 1634), but French occupation of Alsace permanently cut the Spanish Road, dashing Hapsburg ambitions for a unified Catholic Europe. Political plurality continued to ensure Europe's economic and military development, unconstrained by the command style of economy that crippled Europe's monolithic competitors in the East.

Newspapers and returning mercenaries spread the Swedish system across Europe, restoring Roman levels of tactical flexibility. Both sides in the English Civil War

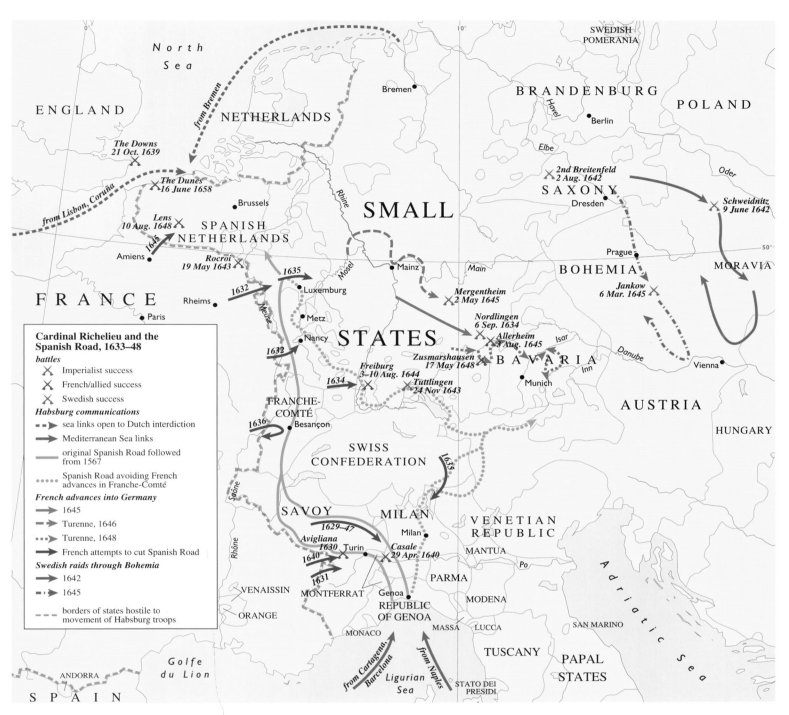

Cardinal Richelieu and the Spanish Road, 1633–48

battles

✕ Imperialist success

✕ French/allied success

✕ Swedish success

Habsburg communications

‑ ‑ ‑▶ sea links open to Dutch interdiction

➤ Mediterranean Sea links

—— original Spanish Road followed from 1567

· · · · · Spanish Road avoiding French advances in Franche-Comté

French advances into Germany

➤ 1645

➤ Turenne, 1646

· · ▶ Turenne, 1648

➤ French attempts to cut Spanish Road

Swedish raids through Bohemia

➤ 1642

‑ ‑▶ 1645

‑ ‑ ‑ borders of states hostile to movement of Habsburg troops

---

used the new tactics, the New Model Army imitating the Swedish identification of the common soldier with his cause. Trained units able to manoeuvre in face of the enemy replaced the ad hoc medieval array of individual warriors. Generals controlled rather than led their armies, consciously guided by the art of war. The Prince de Condé, French commander at Rocroi, attended Richelieu's military academy in Paris. Gustavus' mobile units made possible the grand tactical combinations of the future. Shallow formations became universal, and the pike continued its decline. Two thirds of the New Model Army's infantry carried muskets.

The battle of Rocroi finally destroyed the Spanish *tercio* as a symbol of military

power. Condé demonstrated the offensive value of cavalry against the flanks of enemy infantry, after winning the cavalry battle. The French amalgam of Dutch and Swedish tactics was flexible and hard-hitting, their *feu à volonte* killing half the Spanish infantry present. As in Alexander's and Hannibal's battles the cavalry provided the victory and the infantry the casualties. Cavalry made a comeback in the final campaigns of the Thirty Years War. An exhausted Germany could only sustain small armies, 10-15,000 strong, half of them mounted. The Vicomte de Turenne had served with Maurice of Nassau at 's-Hertogenbosch, but his rapid campaigns showed the decisive results small mobile forces could achieve against

ABOVE: **The later course of the Thirty Years War showed the primacy of politics over religion, and logistics over tactics. A French Cardinal struggled to stop Catholic Spain intervening in Protestant Germany and Holland. Turenne's militarily brilliant campaigns were finally decisive, because Germany was too exhausted for the war to continue.**

an opponent worn down by attrition. In 1646 he boldly outmanoeuvred the Imperialist forces to attack Bavaria, the Emperor's key ally, forcing the Elector of Bavaria to seek terms. In 1648 Turenne destroyed the last Imperialist army at Zumershausen (17 May 1648), and devastated a recalcitrant Bavaria. Strategic and tactical success translated into unbearable logistical pressure, to bring peace at last.

RIGHT: The Battle of the Saintes, off Domenica in 1782 was one of several naval actions resulting from Anglo-French warfare in the Caribbean. The sugar islands were of such economic value, that the British were prepared to devote greater resources to their acquisition and defence than they were to enforcing London's authority over its American colonies. Here, the French flagship *Ville de Paris* begins its epic battle against up to half-a-dozen British ships that resulted in her striking her colours by the end of the action.

Europeau states reacted to the excesses of the Thirty Years War by taking control of their armed forces. They created permanent standing armies, three times larger than in the early 17th century, but economically less disruptive. Battles became more frequent but less conclusive. Flintlock muskets and bayonets made pikes obsolete and reduced the effectiveness of cavalry, the mobile arm. There was little difference between opposing armies, uniformly equipped with musket and bayonet. This tactical homogeneity made decisive victory harder to achieve. Fortresses reached a peak of development, limiting exploitation of victory.

Wars were won by slow attrition not swift annihilation, despite the wishes of commanders. Leadership was not always unimaginative or pedantic. Skilful generals sought decisive results through improved firing systems, deception, and tactical novelties like Frederick the Great's oblique order. The spread of European mil-

itary techniques in Russia and India revealed the contemporary view of their usefulness.

Sailing warships developed rapidly, and became distinct from merchant ships. Naval forces adapted to the new weapon system, creating the first tactical manuals for a new class of professional naval offi-cers. European navies operated all over the world, while fighting each other in home waters. Sea power transformed European wars into global struggles for trade and empire.

Warfare was less destructive than dur-ing the Thirty Years War, moderated by improved logistics, the concept of honour, and increased professionalism. However, even limited wars were scarred by devasta-tions in Central Europe. There were atroc-ities in America, especially but not exclu-sively by irregular forces recruited by Britain and France. Violations of neutrali-ty took place at sea. Limited war depended upon both sides playing by the same rules.

Louis XIV's Military Hegemony

The Thirty Years War shifted the European balance of power from the bankrupt Hapsburgs to France. One sixth of Europe's inhabitants in 1660 were French. An efficient royal bureaucracy translated demographic weight into military power. French armies exploited recent tactical developments and rational strategies to make headway against major coalitions of less advanced European armies.

Michel le Tellier, Louis XIV's war minister from 1643, asserted royal control over the military proprietors of regiments and companies. Inspectors including their namesake Martinet imposed common standards of drill and equipment. Royal Intendants stamped out abuses like the false musters that allowed officers to pocket the wages of non-existent soldiers. Regular pay eliminated the mutinies typical of earlier modern armies. Regiments became permanent administrative units, as it was more economical to keep them together between campaigns than disband and reform them. Continuity squeezed out individual entrepreneurs like Wallenstein, creating a national standing army. Other states followed the French lead, a process symbolized by national uniforms adopted in the 1680s and '90s. Uniform enhanced unit cohesion; well-dressed soldiers thought more highly of themselves, and deserters could be recognized more easily. Simple badges of rank, lace upon hat or cuff, reinforced the command hierarchy, backed up by the NCO's halberd, reminiscent of the Centurion's vine staff.

Vauban, the greatest of all military engineers, reorganized France's fixed defences from 1678. He transferred resources from obsolete forts inside France to build a chain of new fortresses along the coast and frontier. Many saw service in 1870, a tribute to the soundness of Vauban's principles. Fortresses were not just defensive works. They provided a secure base for offensive action. Fed from fortress magazines French armies could pounce on some ill-protected Dutch or German province before its owners were ready for the field. The French then invited attack, well fed in their entrenched camps. All armies had adopted Gustavus Adolphus' supply system, where convoys and magazines replaced plunder, so they could subsist without continually moving. Armies could occupy provinces, not merely raid them. Military operations appeared to slow down, but had more permanent results. Louis XIV's aggressiveness inspired a Grand Alliance, alarmed by the repression of French Protestants and atrocities like the Devastation of the Palatinate in 1688-89. This formal anti-French coalition resembled later alliances bound by treaty to provide collective security. The Grand Alliance deprived Louis XIV of his early gains but slowly. The similar weapons and training of contemporary armies favoured the defence.

The French invention of the bayonet in the 1640s allowed musketeers to protect themselves against cavalry. Pikemen became redundant and had disappeared from Western armies by 1703. Flintlock muskets replaced the less reliable matchlock, reducing the number of misfires from half to one third. Except for a few grenadiers trained in bomb-throwing, European infantry now possessed a uniform armament, and adopted a simpler order of battle: two lines 300 paces apart, cavalry on the flanks, and a reserve behind the centre. Armies had more battalions to deploy, so reduced the wide intervals previously left between units. A continuous line of musketeers, five deep, maximized firepower. Opposing armies naturally formed parallel lines of battle, which only permitted a direct advance on the enemy. Attacks *à prest* with fixed bayonets might push home, but more usually became bogged down in an indecisive exchange of fire.

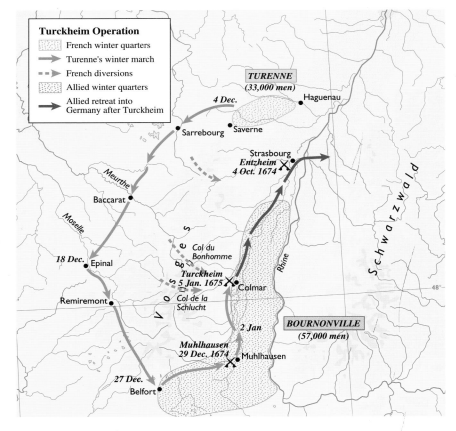

Turckheim Operation
- French winter quarters
- Turenne's winter march
- French diversions
- Allied winter quarters
- Allied retreat into Germany after Turckheim

TURENNE (33,000 men)
Haguenau
4 Dec.
Sarrebourg · Saverne
Strasbourg
Entzheim
4 Oct. 1674
Baccarat
Meurthe
Moselle
18 Dec. Epinal
Col du Bonhomme
Turckheim
5 Jan. 1675 · Colmar
Remiremont
Col de la Schlucht
2 Jan
BOURNONVILLE (57,000 men)
Muhlhausen 29 Dec. 1674 · Muhlhausen
27 Dec. Belfort
Schwarzwald
Rhine
48°

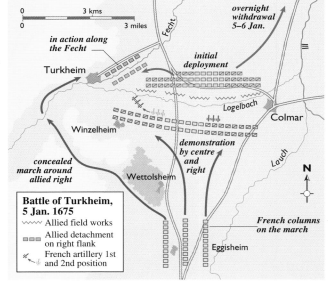

Turkheim
in action along the Fecht
initial deployment
overnight withdrawal 5–6 Jan.
Logelbach
Colmar
Winzelheim
concealed march around allied right
demonstration by centre and right
Wettolsheim
Lauch
N
Battle of Turkheim, 5 Jan. 1675
- Allied field works
- Allied detachment on right flank
- French artillery 1st and 2nd position
Eggisheim
French columns on the march
0 3 kms
0 3 miles

LEFT: Confronted with a more numerous but less energetic enemy, the aggressive master strategist Turenne manoeuvred behind a natural obstacle to compel them to fight at a disadvantage. His bold use of terrain and bad weather to achieve surprise foreshadowed similar manoeuvres by Napoleon and Stonewall Jackson.

ABOVE: The French and Imperialist armies had similar weapons and training. A frontal attack was unlikely to succeed against an opponent soundly deployed in two lines and a reserve. Turenne turned the Imperialist flank, causing their retreat, but not their destruction.

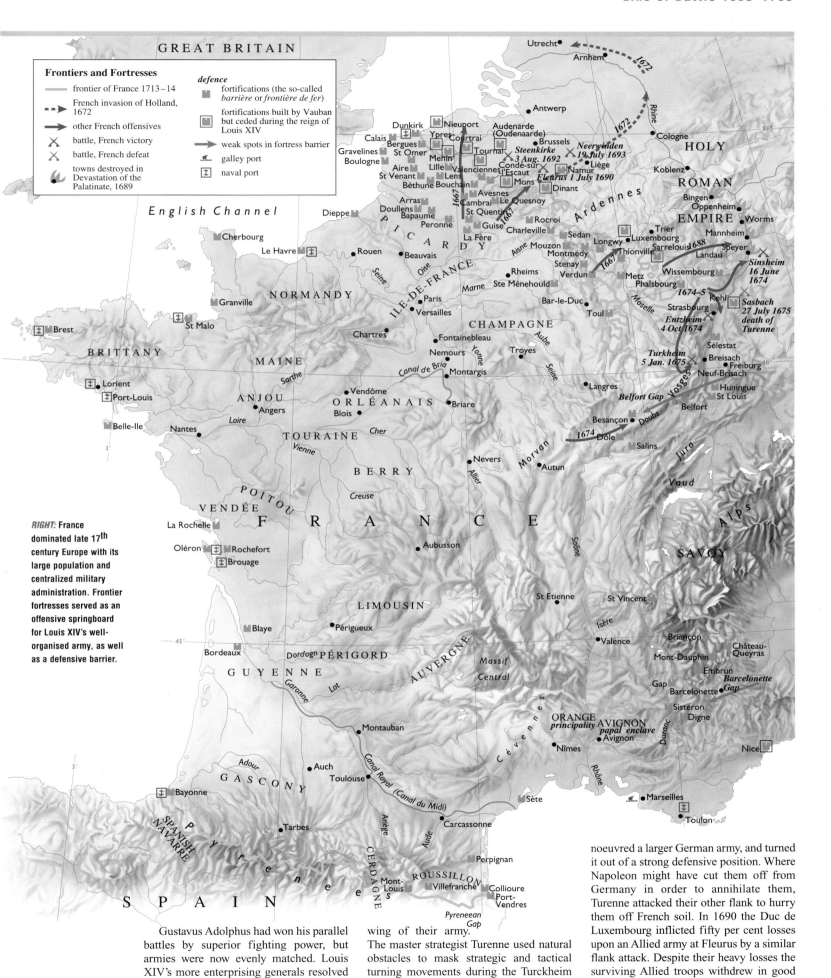

GREAT BRITAIN

Frontiers and Fortresses

frontier of France 1713–14

French invasion of Holland, 1672

other French offensives

✕ battle, French victory

✕ battle, French defeat

🔥 towns destroyed in Devastation of the Palatinate, 1689

defence

▮ fortifications (the so-called *barrière* or *frontière de fer*)

▯ fortifications built by Vauban but ceded during the reign of Louis XIV

➡ weak spots in fortress barrier

⚓ galley port

⊞ naval port

English Channel

Utrecht

Arnhem

1672

Rhine

Cologne

HOLY

Antwerp

Dunkirk   Nieuport

Calais   Ypres   Audenarde (Oudenaarde)

Bergues   Courtrai   Brussels

Gravelines   St Omer   Tournai   *Neerwinden*

Boulogne   Menin   *Steenkirke*   *19 July 1693*   Koblenz

Aire   Lille   *3 Aug. 1692*   Liège   ROMAN

St Venant   Valenciennes   Condé-sur-   Namur   Bingen

Béthune   Lens   l'Escaut   Mons   *Fleurus 1 July 1690*   Oppenheim   EMPIRE   Worms

Arras   Bouchain   Dinant   Mannheim

Doullens   Cambrai   Le Quesnoy   Ardennes   Trier   Luxembourg   *1688*   Speyer

Bapaume   St Quentin   Avesnes   Longwy   Sarrelouis   Landau   *Sinsheim*

Peronne   Guise   Rocroi   Sedan   Thionville   Wissembourg   *16 June 1674*

La Fère   Charleville   Mouzon   Metz   *1674–5*   Kehl   *Sasbach*

Dieppe   Charmes   Montmédy   Phalsbourg   Strasbourg   *27 July 1675*

Cherbourg   Rheims   Stenay   Verdun   *Entzheim*   *death of Turenne*

Le Havre   Rouen   Beauvais   *1667*   Bar-le-Duc   Toul   *4 Oct 1674*   Sélestat

NORMANDY   Marne   Ste Ménehould   *Turkheim*   Breisach

Granville   Paris   Moselle   *5 Jan. 1675*   Freiburg

Versailles   CHAMPAGNE   Neuf-Brisach

St Malo   Chartres   Aube   Langres   *Belfort Gap*   Vosges   Huningue

Brest   Fontainebleau   Troyes   St Louis

BRITTANY   Nemours   Yonne   Seine   Belfort

MAINE   Sarthe   Canal de Briare   Montargis   Nevers   Besançon   Doubs   Salins

Lorient   ANJOU   Vendôme   Briare   *1674*   Dôle   Jura

Port-Louis   Angers   ORLÉANAIS   Vaud

Belle-Ile   Nantes   Blois   Loire   TOURAINE   Cher

Vienne   BERRY   Morvan   Autun

RIGHT: France dominated late 17th century Europe with its large population and centralized military administration. Frontier fortresses served as an offensive springboard for Louis XIV's well-organised army, as well as a defensive barrier.

POITOU   Creuse   Saône   Alps

VENDÉE   La Rochelle   FRANCE

Oléron   Rochefort   Aubusson

Brouage   LIMOUSIN   St Etienne   St Vincent   SAVOY

Blaye   Périgueux   Isère   Valence   Briançon

Bordeaux   PÉRIGORD   AUVERGNE   Mont-Dauphin   Château-Queyras

Dordogn   Massif   Embrun   *Barcelonette*

GUYENNE   Lot   Central   Gap   Barcelonette   *Gap*

Garonne   Sisteron   Digne

Montauban   Durance

Adour   ORANGE   AVIGNON   Avignon

Auch   *principality*   *papal enclave*   Nîmes

GASCONY   Toulouse   Cévennes

Bayonne   Canal Royal (Canal du Midi)   Sète   Marseilles

Tarbes   Ariège   Aude   Carcassonne   Rhône   Toulon

SPANISH NAVARRE   Perpignan   ROUSSILLON

Pyrenees   CERDAGNE   Mont-Louis   Villefranche   Collioure   Port-Vendres

SPAIN   *Pyreneean Gap*

Gustavus Adolphus had won his parallel battles by superior fighting power, but armies were now evenly matched. Louis XIV's more enterprising generals resolved parallel battles by partial turning movements, outflanking the enemy with one wing of their army.

The master strategist Turenne used natural obstacles to mask strategic and tactical turning movements during the Turckheim operations of December 1673–January 1674. Scorning winter quarters, he outma-noeuvred a larger German army, and turned it out of a strong defensive position. Where Napoleon might have cut them off from Germany in order to annihilate them, Turenne attacked their other flank to hurry them off French soil. In 1690 the Duc de Luxembourg inflicted fifty per cent losses upon an Allied army at Fleurus by a similar flank attack. Despite their heavy losses the surviving Allied troops withdrew in good order, showing the resilience of the solidly drilled armies of the period.

Marlborough S'En Va-t-en-Guerre

RIGHT: The duke of Marlborough won several decisive battlefield victories, but fought many more sieges. There were so many fortresses astride communications routes and armies of the period were too small to mask them and still retain sufficient strength for a field action.

Only the most skilful generals could achieve far-reaching success within the constraints of early 18th century warfare. The Duke of Marlborough did so during the War of the Spanish Succession, by deception and variations of standard tactical procedures.

Marlborough's Blenheim Campaign was kept secret even from his allies. The march to the Danube wrong-footed hostile Franco-Bavarian forces and kept Britain's key ally, Austria, in the war. Logistical preparations even extended to replacement shoes. Marlborough extracted supplies from towns along his route by a smooth mixture of threats and promises. Payment was assured by Britain's sound war finances, symbolized by foundation of the Bank of England in 1694. His tactical victory at Blenheim broke the aura of French invincibility, and secured major Allied war aims: the Spanish Netherlands and Naples fell into Allied hands.

Marlborough's march to the Danube, (May–June 1704) and subsequent campaigns (below)

→ Marlborough's march to the Danube
- ➤ diversions
···➤ Marlborough's new communications
- -➤ Marlborough's 1708 campaign
→ Allied troops moving to join Marlborough
→ French reaction
• towns falling to Allies after Ramillies
↓ sieges
- -➤ French evacuation of Flanders after Oudenarde
---- *Ne Plus Ultra* lines forced by Marlborough, 26 July–4 August 1709

troop concentrations   *major battles*
  Marlborough   ✕ Allied success
  Allies   ✕ French success
  French

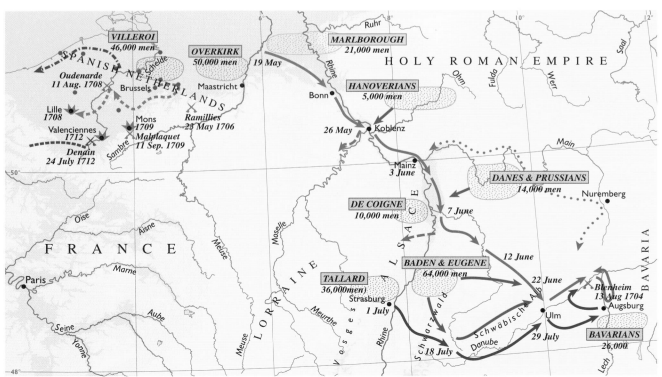

LEFT: A protégé of Turenne, Marlborough was one of the few commanders able to overcome the strategic limitations of his day. The ambiguous nature of Marlborough's manoeuvres deceived both allies and the enemy, but demanded sound logistical practice, which earned him the affection of his troops.

The Franco-Bavarian armies at Blenheim formed up separately, like the Swedes and Saxons at Breitenfeld, with cavalry in the centre. Marlborough diverted their attention to the flanks, then broke through the unstable centre with 50% more squadrons and 23 battalions to nine. Almost two thirds of the defeated armies became casualties, the highest attrition of any 18th century battle. Marlborough used the same grand tactics at Ramillies (23 May 1706). Diversions on the flanks preceded a central breakthrough, while improvised cavalry reserves moved under cover to the decisive point. Marlborough's methods became predictable. Marshal Villars inflicted heavy losses on the Allies at Malplaquet (11 September 1709): 25,000 out of 110,000 compared to 12,000 out of 80,000 French. Such heavy losses challenge common assumptions about the limited nature of 18th century war. Marlborough ruthlessly exploited the cohesion of his well-drilled infantry in suicidal holding attacks. He devastated Bavaria to force the enemy to fight. When they occupied a strong position across his own communications at Blenheim, he achieved surprise by attacking rather than tamely withdrawing.

Marlborough could risk offensive battles because tactical developments were in his favour. French successes in the 1690s made them complacent. Their cavalry forgot the headlong tradition of Condé, and broke the momentum of their charges to fire carbines. Marlborough banned such weapons, ordering his cavalry to charge sword in hand. At Blenheim five British squadrons defeated eight of elite gensdarmes, who halted to fire. French infantry kept the matchlock, and fired by ranks, slowly and ineffectively. British and Dutch platoon fire maximized the power of their flintlocks. The remorseless advance and controlled fire of Allied battalions demoralized their opponents. The flintlock's higher rate of fire compared with the matchlock permitted less deep formations, freeing men for Marlborough's battle winning attacks. These achieved a high level of inter-arm cooperation for the day. At Blenheim infantry covered the advance of Marlborough's cavalry over the Nebel. At Ramillies broken Dutch cavalry rallied behind supporting infantry. Allied infantry possessed battalion guns, the successors to Gustavus' light 4prs. Guns lacked range and mobility, so were best dispersed along the line.

Even Marlborough could not avoid the frustrations of siege warfare. In ten campaigns he fought four battles, two actions, and thirty sieges. Fortresses in Western Europe were too close together to be ignored, and armies lacked the numbers to mask them as Napoleonic generals would do a century later. The spread of outworks to keep siege guns at a distance demanded

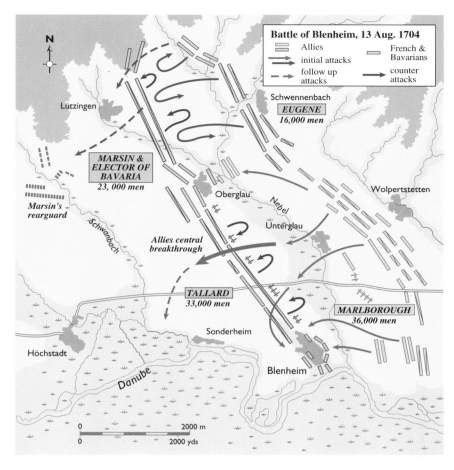

Battle of Blenheim, 13 Aug. 1704

	Allies		French & Bavarians
	initial attacks		
	follow up attacks		counter attacks

N

Lützingen

Schwennenbach

EUGENE
16,000 men

MARSIN & ELECTOR OF BAVARIA
23,000 men

Marsin's rearguard

Oberglau

Wolpertstetten

Nebel

Unterglau

Allies central breakthrough

Schwambach

TALLARD
33,000 men

MARLBOROUGH
36,000 men

Sonderheim

Höchstädt

Blenheim

Danube

| 0 | | 2000 m |
| 0 | | 2000 yds |

elaborate preparations. Vauban estimated a successful siege needed odds of ten-to-one in favour of the attackers. He laid down scientific principles of attack, to reduce the uncertainty of sieges, and their cost in time and lives. He developed the *place d'armes* to protect attackers while sapping forward, parallel trenches successively dug 600, 400, and 200 yards from the ditch.

Only at the closer range could guns batter a breach in the earth backed ramparts of a first class fortress. The siege of Lille in 1708 required eighty heavy guns, twenty mortars, and 3,000 wagonloads of stores. The siege lasted 120 days, and cost the Allies five times the casualties of the battle of Oudenarde (11 July 1708), which had made the operation possible.

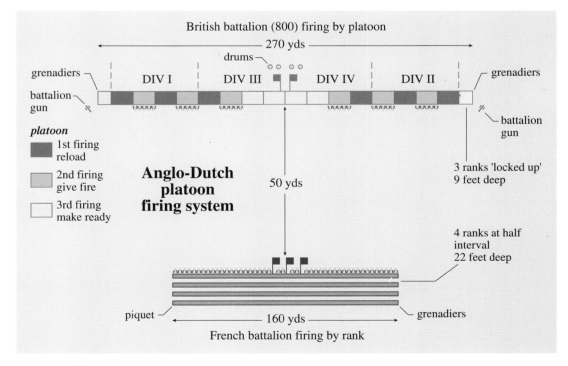

British battalion (800) firing by platoon

270 yds

drums

grenadiers

DIV I   DIV III   DIV IV   DIV II

grenadiers

battalion gun

battalion gun

3 ranks 'locked up'
9 feet deep

platoon
■ 1st firing reload
■ 2nd firing give fire
□ 3rd firing make ready

Anglo-Dutch platoon firing system

50 yds

4 ranks at half interval
22 feet deep

piquet

160 yds

grenadiers

French battalion firing by rank

The End of the Tartar Threat

While Western Europe experimented with the balance of power, the East saw a strategic revolution. The export of the military renaissance to Russia created a new power from nothing. A well-armed Russia ended forever the nomadic incursions that had terrorized Europe throughout the Middle Ages. Turkey, the most recent intruder from the steppe, rejected modern military techniques, to the advantage of a resurgent Austria.

Russia was the first Asian country to import the military renaissance wholesale, forming European style regiments in the 1630s. They made up two thirds of the Russian Army by 1682, replacing the *streltsi*, an obsolescent corps of rebellious musketeers. German loan words, such as *soldat* or *junker*, reveal the foreign inspiration of Russia's military expertise. Peter the Great crushed the *streltsi* with exemplary cruelty, before accelerating military and social change to meet a strategic challenge from Sweden. Charles XII, the youthful king of Sweden, compensated for his small army with the most aggressive tactics in Europe. His cavalry gave up armour and charged at a gallop, when even Marlborough's horse trotted into contact. Swedish infantry advanced to forty paces from the enemy without firing, fired two volleys and closed with the bayonet.

A Russian defeat at Narva (20 November 1700) showed their inability to withstand such shock tactics. Russian infantry ran about like stampeded cattle, while the Swedes, outnumbered five to one, took so many prisoners they let them go. Peter's response was to raise 50 new infantry regiments. When Charles XII invaded Russia in January 1708, advancing over the frozen rivers, the Russians avoided battle. They wore out the Swedes, destroying the countryside ahead of them. Charles' hopes of exploiting internal opposition to Peter were disappointed; the

LEFT: The Austro-Hungarian success in driving back the Turks made their light cavalry uniforms fashionable throughout Europe. Eighteenth century hussars sported outrageous moustaches and braided hair. The pelisse was worn like a cloak: a style that would endure until the First World War.

BELOW: Charles XII reached the culminating point of his Russian offensive at Poltava. Despite initial success, the outnumbered Swedish veterans could not overcome superior Russian numbers. Russia emerged as a new military power, the first successful export of the military renaissance to Asia.

RIGHT: The offensive capability of 18th century Western armies made traditional Ottoman tactics obsolete. Eugene caught a Turkish army divided by the River Theiss, and wiped out the infantry, while their cavalry watched from the other bank.

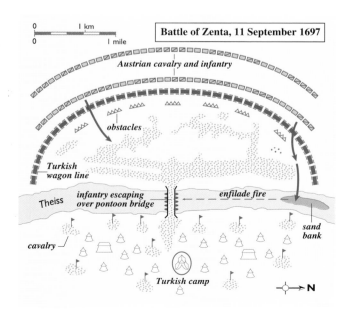

Battle of Zenta, 11 September 1697

0 — 1 km
0 — 1 mile

Austrian cavalry and infantry

obstacles

Turkish wagon line

Theiss — *infantry escaping over pontoon bridge* — *enfilade fire*

sand bank

cavalry

Turkish camp

N

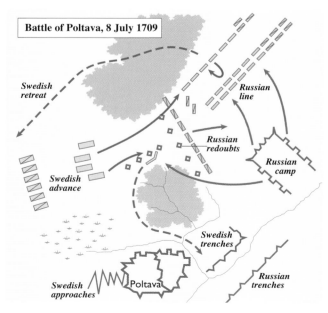

Battle of Poltava, 8 July 1709

Swedish retreat

Russian line

Russian redoubts

Swedish advance

Russian camp

Swedish trenches

Swedish approaches

Poltava

Russian trenches

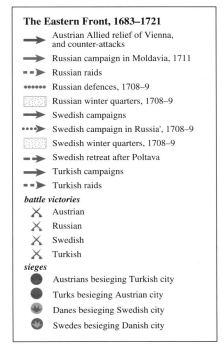

The Eastern Front, 1683–1721

→ Austrian Allied relief of Vienna, and counter-attacks
→ Russian campaign in Moldavia, 1711
--▶ Russian raids
••••▶ Russian defences, 1708–9
▒ Russian winter quarters, 1708–9
→ Swedish campaigns
••••▶ Swedish campaign in Russia', 1708–9
▒ Swedish winter quarters, 1708–9
--▶ Swedish retreat after Poltava
→ Turkish campaigns
--▶ Turkish raids

battle victories
✕ Austrian
✕ Russian
✕ Swedish
✕ Turkish

sieges
⬤ Austrians besieging Turkish city
⬤ Turks besieging Austrian city
⬤ Danes besieging Swedish city
⬤ Swedes besieging Danish city

new Russian regiments could at least suppress dissidents. At Poltava (8 July 1709) Peter destroyed Charles' attenuated army, much to the Swedes' surprise. Other powers quickly recognized the emergence of a new military power. In the 1730s a Russian army marched into Germany, and defeated a French force at Danzig. Russian and Chinese forces met in Central Asia, ending the freedom of the steppe nomads. The forcible imposition of Western military institutions upon Russia exacted a terrible price. Brutally suppressed risings became a feature of the regime. The only reliable arm of government was the army, recruited more effectively and repressively than anywhere else. The military renaissance in the West tamed the man on horseback, but in Russia's militarized society it imposed new chains.

The Ottomans, by contrast, were impervious to Western military ideas. The Turkish army remained medieval, its components distinguished by race or religion rather than tactical function: Muslim landowners provided cavalry, forced converts the elite Janissary infantry, and unarmed Christian conscripts the pioneers. European renegades manned monster guns symbolic of the inability to manoeuvre that led to the Turkish defeat at Vienna in 1683. While European armies standardized weapons, the Turks simply added flintlocks to their existing hotchpotch of matchlocks, bows, and scimitars. Tactics remained crude: a series of wild rushes intended to throw the enemy into confusion, when superior Turkish swordsmanship would allow them to cut their opponents to pieces. Once disordered, the Turks' crescent formation could not re-form. This contrasted with Western armies where group cohesion

based on constant drill had replaced individual skill at arms as the basis of military effectiveness. Attempts by Western adventurers to reform the Turkish army in the 1730s lacked social roots, and came to nothing.

Ottoman armies were no match for smaller European forces, their large numbers swelling the casualties. Only the French diversion of Hapsburg resources saved the Turks from a major Austrian counter-offensive in the 1690s. The Austrian army adopted special tactics against the Turks: portable boar spear fences to break the initial rush, and counter-attacks '*en muraille*', the infantry

and cavalry advancing and firing together like a wall. Such tactics were obsolete in Western Europe, but the Turks could not stand regular volleys. Turkish infantry were repeatedly wiped out, when their supporting cavalry ran away: at Mohacs in 1687, by Prince Eugene of Savoy at Zenta in 1697, and again at Peterwardein in 1716. Eugene's double siege and battle of Belgrade (July-August 1717) resembled the Siege of Vienna, but with a very different outcome. An Austrian army of 60,000 was flexible enough to turn and smash a relieving army of 100,000 Turks, while successfully besieging 30,000 more.

Close-hauled Line of Battle

Improved sailing warships and professionalization of Europe's navies introduced the classic age of fighting sail. The Anglo-Dutch War of 1652-54 saw more naval actions than the preceding 150 years, a trend continued in a series of maritime wars which defined the modern concepts of naval strategy.

Warships became a distinct class from merchant ships. The standard two-decker battleship carried up to 70 24pr guns compared with the merchantman's dozen 12prs. The weight and recoil of naval armaments demanded more massive timbers than freight-carrying vessels could afford. Specific warship types appeared: fast slender frigates for cruising; bomb ketches for shore bombardment; fireships for finishing off ships immobilized by battle damage or at anchor. State navies replaced ad hoc collections of impressed merchantmen, the English navy rising from 35 ships in 1649 to 151 in 1660. Naval competition was intense. A 1691 Act of Parliament required the Royal Navy to exceed the combined strength of its nearest rivals, the French and Dutch, the first example of a two-power standard. By 1762 the Royal Navy had emerged as the most powerful in the world with 84,000 men and 300 ships. Government dockyards supported the growing fleets, becoming the largest industrial enterprises in the world. The merchant fleet supplied wartime crews, supplemented by marines and unskilled landsmen, but officers had to be professional fighting seamen. Lieutenants underwent examination before receiving their commission. Half pay recognized the professional status of unemployed officers, as a permanent cadre available for service.

Large centrally directed fleets increased the number of naval battles. The English and Dutch usually adopted a combat strategy. Geography forced the Dutch to fight convoys up the Channel, past English bases at Portsmouth and Chatham. French naval strategy, with a spread of bases opening onto Atlantic waters, was more subtle, only fighting for some specific objective. French fleets avoided combat by remaining in port, where fortifications deterred blockading squadrons. An outnumbered fleet in being could influence events at sea by threatening to sortie. The Dutch had thus deterred Anglo-French amphibious operations in 1672-4. French distaste for combat could be misguided. They withdrew after the battle of Malaga (24 August 1704), although the enemy fleet was low on ammunition and cut off from its base at Gibraltar. The British responded to France's geographical advantage by developing Plymouth as a base. From 1747 a Western squadron cruised between Ushant and Scilly, to intercept sorties from Brest or Rochefort. Naval architecture reflected different national strategies. The British built slower, stronger ships to enhance sea-keeping; the

clean scientific lines of French ships made them faster, but less durable. Shallow coastal waters handicapped the Dutch when heavier rates appeared with 100 or more guns. They fell behind in the naval arms race.

Gunnery became the deciding factor in naval actions. Ships fired at $90°$ to the direction of their movement, making them vulnerable ahead and astern. The rational deployment was close line ahead to protect bow and stern, and concentrate fire. The tactical bonus of doubling the enemy line was obvious, but hard to achieve with fleets of similar mobility. Inadequate signalling systems compelled fleets to adopt

ABOVE: Admiral Byng is executed by firing squad after failing to press home his attack against a French fleet off Minorca in 1756. His judicial murder was explained by Voltaire, who observed that 'it is sometimes necessary to kill an admiral to encourage the others'. Contrary to its later image, many Royal Navy fleet actions of the period were followed by a rash of courts martial.

RIGHT: Naval warfare was a way of breaking the strategic stalemate ashore, but fleets were often too large for decisive defeat, and fleets in being imposed a new deadlock. The frequent Anglo-Dutch battles of the 1650s made way for long periods without fleet actions.

Atlantic Ocean

Bantry Bay
11 May 1689

Finisterre
3 May 1747
14 Oct. 1747

Ferrol

Vigo

Douro

Tagus

Lisbon

Madrid

PORTUGAL

S P A I N

Lagos
18–19 Aug. 1759

Cadiz

Malaga
24 Aug. 1704

Tangiers
(1661–84)

Gibraltar
(from 1704)

Cartagena

2.45 pm

Admiral Byng's defeat at Minorca, 20 May 1756

1

3
Galissonniere

A

2

wind

Byng

N

(1) British van crowds on sail to engage the French van head on.
(2) British centre (Byng) and rear close slowly on a diagonal course, still out of range.
(3) French fleet under steerage way, heeled to starboard to increase range of their port broadsides.
(4) French van withdraws downwind after crippling the lead British ships.
(5) HMS Intrepid disabled by raking fire.
(6) French flag ship and two seconds pound Intrepid and threaten to cut through the gap in the British line.
(7) British centre taken aback, unable to pass Intrepid.
(8) British rear still out of range.

4

3.20 pm

6 Galissonniere

B

5

wind

7 Byng

8

LEFT: Navies developed individual tactical styles, laid down in Fighting Instructions. Byng's personally disastrous defeat at Minorca showed the risks of even minor departures from custom. His fleet lost formation, allowing the enemy to concentrate fire on isolated British ships.

standard operating procedures. English Fighting Instructions of 1653 imitated the Dutch, who had destroyed a Spanish fleet at The Downs (21 October 1639) with line ahead tactics. Fleets approached from windward, and engaged van-to-van. The technique achieved the most spectacular naval victory for fifty years at Barfleur (28 May-2 June 1692). The battle of Toulon (22 February 1744), however, showed the dangers of depending on printed instructions. The British second-in-command

Maritime Rivalries, 1650–1760

naval bases
- Britain
- Denmark
- France
- Netherlands
- Russia
- Spain
- Sweden
- Venice

battles
as winners — **as losers**
- Britain
- Denmark
- France
- Netherlands
- Russia
- Spain
- Sweden
- Turkey
- Venice

— borders
— border of Holy Roman Empire

refused to join in an unconventional attack on the centre and rear of a Franco-Spanish fleet. Toulon and the shameful desertion of Admiral Benbow by his captains at Santa Marta (29 August-3 September 1702) suggest a lack of professional solidarity that demanded prescriptive naval tactics. British admirals spent a century seeking to resolve the contradictory requirements of tactical control and initiative. French tactics reflected their different strategic concepts. They sought action from leeward, retreating downwind when they had achieved their ulterior purpose. The French hoped to knock enemy's spars about sufficiently to prevent pursuit, knowing it was difficult to sink wooden ships. Materially inconclusive actions had significant moral results. No ships were lost at Minorca (20 May 1756), but the action convinced Admiral Byng's captains they could not relieve the British garrison on the island.

Pirates, Privateers, and Power

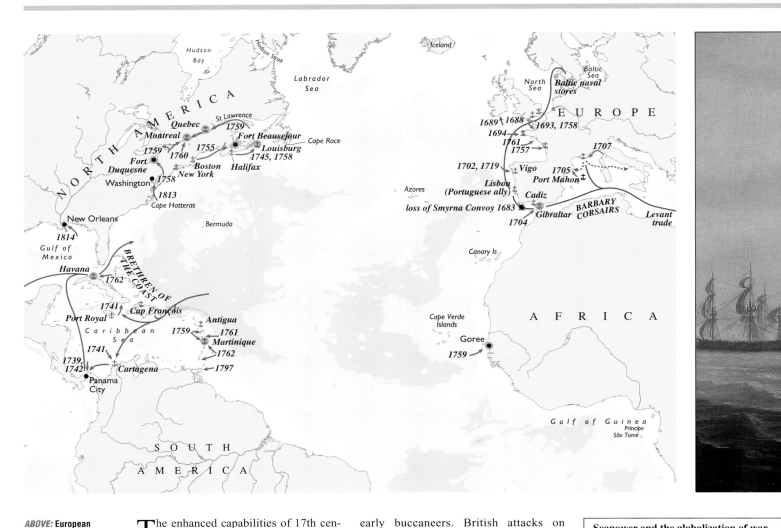

The enhanced capabilities of 17th century European navies promoted the exercise of sea power worldwide. Fleets of sailing warships bound together European and colonial rivalries, causing the first 'world wars'.

Spanish and Portuguese monopolies of trade with the Indies and America had provoked English, French, and Dutch incursions since the 16th century. Viewed by the occupying powers as pirates and smugglers, the interlopers gained respectability as officially sponsored companies and expeditions replaced the early buccaneers. British attacks on Havana and Manila during the Seven Years War were the culmination of a strategy started by Elizabethan adventurers, and articulated in Cromwell's Western Design of the 1650s. Overseas rivalries had interacted with European conflicts since Sea Beggars and Huguenots led the attack on the Spanish Main. Louis XIV saw the War of the Spanish Succession as primarily about colonial trade. The War of Jenkin's Ear in 1739 arose from Spanish harassment of British trade with South America, but spilled over into wider hostilities, involving Austria and France. Anglo-French disputes in the Ohio valley contributed to the outbreak of the Seven Years War. On the fringe of Europe, the British debated the merits of a purely maritime strategy, collecting colonies and trade, as against a continental strategy of using sea power to support European allies. A European commitment diverted ships from hunting prizes, but reduced the resources hybrid land/sea powers like France could commit to naval purposes, indirectly easing the pursuit of British objectives overseas.

Security of merchant shipping was a dividend of sea power. Land transport was prohibitively expensive, so goods travelled by sea. Navies defeated in battle reverted to the medieval strategy of

Seapower and the globalization of war (above)

— European trade routes

- - -> French interventions in Spain and Italy

— Spanish Caribbean trade routes

naval bases

‡ British/British ally   ‡ Spanish

‡ French   ‡ disputed

● captured by British expeditions

naval expeditions dependent on sea power, with year

→ British

→ Dutch (Lyme Bay)

→ French

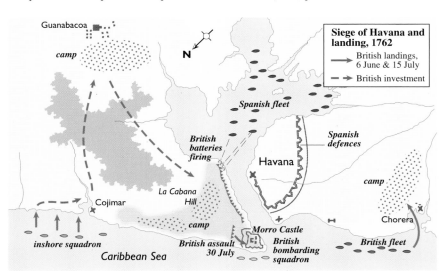

Siege of Havana and landing, 1762

→ British landings, 6 June & 15 July

- -> British investment

LEFT: The Battle of Lagos, 17 August 1759 helped end French plans to invade England using their fleets from Brest and Toulon. British naval success enabled her trade to continue during the Seven Years' War. The French merchant marine suffered catastrophic losses.

attacking trade. After Barfleur, heavy units of the French Navy participated in a systematic *guerre de course*, taking over 4,000 vessels. The Brest fleet captured 90 ships from one convoy off Cadiz in 1693. The English organized convoys from the 1660s to deter state sponsored Dutch and French privateers, and freelance corsairs operating off North Africa and the West Indies. Parliamentary legislation, such as the 'Cruisers and Convoys Act' of 1708, reflected the sensitivity of overseas trade. Active counter-measures included Blake's attack on Tunis in 1655, followed by a short-lived occupation of Tangiers. Vigorous action in American waters against the Brethren of the Coast persuaded some buccaneers to move as far away as Madagascar. Jean Bart, the great practitioner of *guerre de course* in the 1690s, hoped to divert sufficient Anglo-Dutch resources to allow a new French challenge for control of the sea. Dispersal of French warships as commerce raiders, however, allowed the British to strengthen convoy escorts, and patrol the Western Approaches. The Royal Navy swept French ships off the sea, taking 2,200 in two years (1710-12). The ruin of French trade in the 1740s helped end the War of the Austrian Succession. Great Britain, her own trade intact, was the only power not to face financial ruin during the Seven Years War.

The endurance of sailing warships allowed them to blockade enemy bases, an offensive strategy whereby a superior fleet could engage the enemy as they left harbour. Blockade countered both the privateer and the threat of invasion, which often paralysed British naval strategy. French attempts to combine the Toulon and Brest fleets for an invasion of England in 1759 led to their destruction by blockading squadrons at Lagos and Quiberon Bay. Having secured the home base, the Royal Navy took a leading part in the conquest of Canada. Most 18th century amphibious operations failed. Technical difficulties frustrated attempts to translate sea power into military leverage. The British evolved sophisticated amphibious techniques: purpose-built flat-bottomed boats, standard procedures for assault landings, and naval gun fire support. In North America the lack of roads and poverty of the country made command of the waterways essential. Moving around the defenders of Quebec by water, General Wolfe concentrated superior numbers on the Heights of Abraham for the decisive action of the campaign. The Royal Navy's ascent of the river as soon as the ice broke in 1760 consolidated the British position in Quebec. French Canadian forces surrendered, knowing that no help could arrive in face of British naval superiority off the French coast.

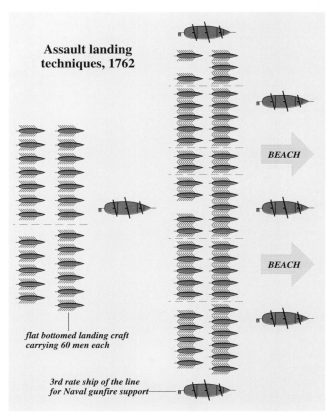

Assault landing techniques, 1762

flat bottomed landing craft carrying 60 men each

3rd rate ship of the line for Naval gunfire support

BEACH

BEACH

ABOVE: The Royal Navy developed sophisticated techniques for amphibious warfare during the 18th century. Assault landings from ship's boats supported by warships on the flanks remained standard until the 20th century.

Alternatives to Formalism

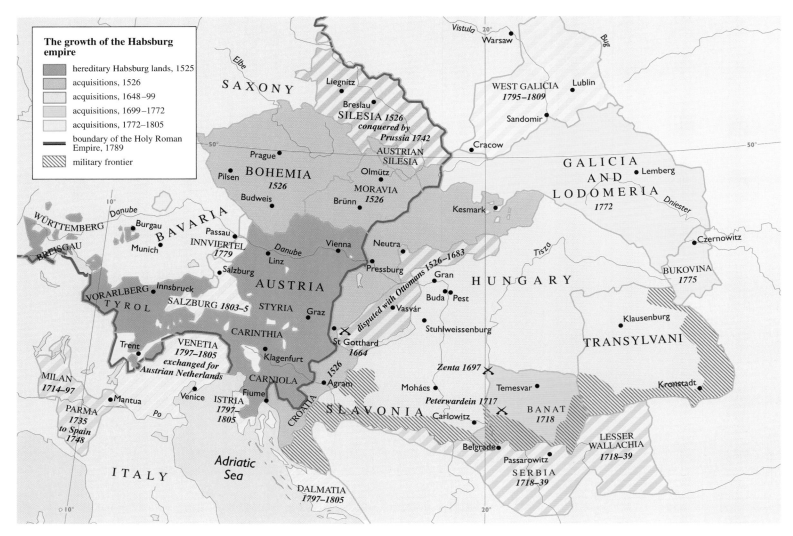

The growth of the Habsburg empire

- hereditary Habsburg lands, 1525
- acquisitions, 1526
- acquisitions, 1648–99
- acquisitions, 1699–1772
- acquisitions, 1772–1805
- boundary of the Holy Roman Empire, 1789
- military frontier

ABOVE: Austria's wars with Prussia followed 200 years of warfare against the Ottoman Empire. Croat irregular troops, long used to guard the frontier with the Turks proved highly effective against the Prussians. They could not stand up to Prussian infantry in open battle, but their guerrilla tactics drove Frederick the Great out of Bohemia.

RIGHT: Not all 18th century battles were parallel encounters between equally matched lines of fusiliers. The British maximised their offensive punch at Fontenoy by throwing a deep column against French redoubts and reserves held in depth.

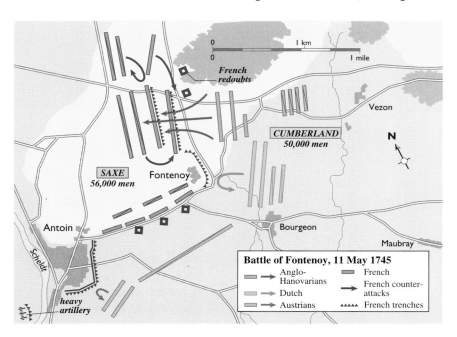

Battle of Fontenoy, 11 May 1745

- Anglo-Hanoverians
- Dutch
- Austrians
- French
- French counter-attacks
- French trenches

Eighteenth century warfare was formal, but not static. Professional officers endlessly refined the skills of their men. International competition for power encouraged European armies to improve continually. However, logistical constraints on the conduct of war remained unresolved.

Peacetime armies optimized infantry firepower by constant drill. The British perfected a walking fire technique that nearly brought them victory at Fontenoy (10 May 1745). The Prussians streamlined their soldiers' coats, gave them paper cartridges and iron ramrods, and taught them to fire five rounds a minute. At Mollwitz (10 April 1741) Prussian infantry, only three ranks deep, reversed the verdict of Rocroi. Deserted by their cavalry, they saw off both Austrian infantry and cavalry. Trained musketry dominated the battlefield. Now cavalry's only tactical opportunities were against flanks, or in pursuit of broken troops. The proportion of cavalry in European armies continued to decline: from a third in 1650, to a quarter in 1750, and one sixth in 1810.

French officers, disgusted with the slaughter at Malplaquet, turned away from conventional linear tactics. Reactionaries advocated brisk assaults by deep formations armed with pikes. Progressives encouraged individual initiative, a visionary scheme in contemporary social circumstances. Maurice de Saxe was the only reformer to put his ideas into practice. At Fontenoy he defeated British offensive fire tactics with Malplaquet-style fieldworks and a sophisticated artillery fire plan, including a dedicated reserve of twelve guns, a unique idea in the 1740s. At Roucoux and Lauffeld, Saxe took the offensive. Stripping his line to concentrate at the crucial point, he threw forward heavy columns of successive brigades in line covered by swarms of skirmishers.

The shorter front occupied by the French infantry allowed Saxe's cavalry to intervene effectively in the infantry battle.

The inspiration for Saxe's skirmishers came from outside Europe. The Austrians employed irregular troops, known as Croats, on their military frontier with Turkey. Croats guided regulars in the mountains, and protected them from Turkish snipers. In 1744 a large force of Croats harassed a Prussian army in Bohemia so effectively that Frederick the Great retreated into Silesia. The Austrians countered Prussian firepower by occupying impregnable positions, while Croats deprived them of supplies and rest. The appearance of Croats in Alsace inspired the *Legion de Grassin*, a French irregular corps that fought at Fontenoy. The British also learned about light troops outside Europe. North American Indians, used to wood fighting, were tactically superior to local militia and regular troops imported from Europe. The gradual extension of European settlement was the result of demographic not military pressure, as agriculture supported a denser population than the indigenous nomadic hunting economy. In 1755 Indians destroyed a numerically superior British force at the Monongahela. British flank guards were ineffective. The troops failed to take cover, and fell back under fire from invisible opponents. The British bunched and panicked when surrounded, losing two-thirds of their men. Subsequently, the British formed irregular corps like Roger's Rangers, who beat the Indians at their own

game. British regulars in North America lightened their equipment, cut down their hats, and learned to fight from cover. Regulars elsewhere absorbed the function of light infantry. The French disbanded the *Grassins* and trained fifty *chasseurs* per battalion. Even Frederick formed a *Jäger* battalion.

Enhanced tactical mobility did not benefit strategy. Physical limits on manoeuvre remained the same. Large armies could not disperse to subsist, as detachments lacked the command structure and mixture of arms to fight separately. Nor could they advance rapidly by a single line of operation. Inadequate roads delayed convoys, and low agricultural productivity inhibited requisitions. Armies advanced hesitantly, building up magazines as they went. One day in four they stopped to bake bread, the soldiers' staple diet, and to conduct Grand Foragings. The numerous horses that moved an army ate immense quantities of fodder, so campaigns began when the grass grew in April. By the time one side had won a battle it would be too late to do more than pick up a fortress or two, before winter allowed the beaten army to recover. The Allied reconquest of the Spanish Netherlands after Ramillies (23 May 1706) was a rare opportunity to exploit a victory at the start of the campaigning season. Nevertheless wars did cause major political shifts. Turkey was excluded from Europe and French ambitions were curbed, despite the limited capabilities of 18th century armies.

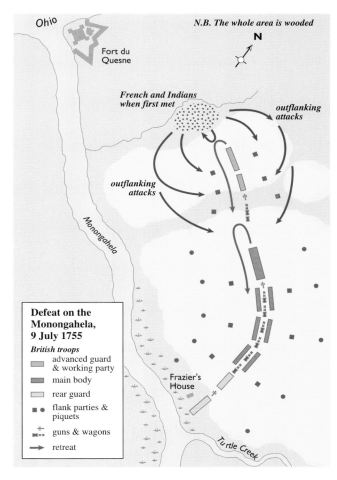

Defeat on the Monongahela, 9 July 1755

British troops

- advanced guard & working party
- main body
- rear guard
- flank parties & piquets
- guns & wagons
- retreat

LEFT: Frederick the Great relied on highly drilled infantry to outshoot his enemies. The Prussian infantry's rate of fire was unmatched and their ability to deploy so quickly enabled him to literally run rings around less well trained opponents.

ABOVE: In North America rigid lines succumbed to the elusive individualism of the wilderness. British and French infantry adapted their dress to the forests, and learned to imitate the Red Indians. The Royal Americans, formed in 1756, were the British Army's first specialist light infantry, the forerunners of true special forces.

BELOW: Some generals tried to play strength against weakness. The French Marshal, Maurice de Saxe doubled his line at Lauffeld to attack the exposed part of a defending line with heavy columns, in a precursor of Frederick's celebrated oblique order (see p96), while the French cavalry moved around the open Allied flank.

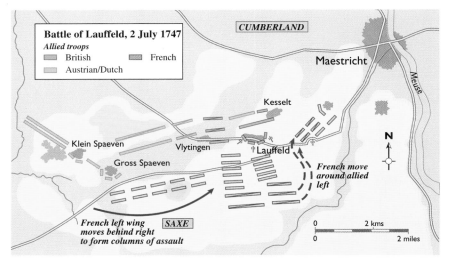

Battle of Lauffeld, 2 July 1747

Allied troops

- British
- French
- Austrian/Dutch

Frederick the Great

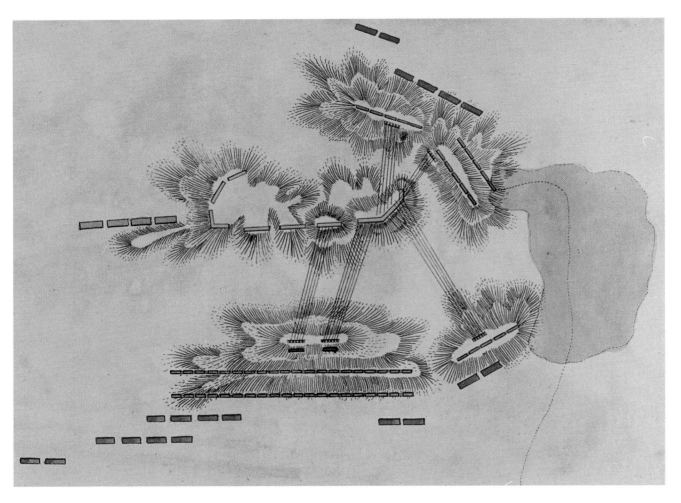

Linear tactics reached their peak in the Seven Years War. The genius of Frederick the Great and the training of his soldiers preserved Prussia from the combined efforts of Austria, France and Russia.

The Prussian army revolutionized grand tactics in the 1730s by assimilating its marching and fighting formations. Prussian infantry adopted the cadenced step, the soldiers in each tactical sub-unit all moving their left and right feet together. This allowed them to march in closed ranks, and maintain the depth of their columns. Battalions in columns of platoons at 20-yard distance could wheel right or left to form a line occupying their battle frontage. Prussian armies formed line of battle in minutes compared with the hours taken by Marlborough's straggling columns. Prussian battalions were so reliably drilled that Frederick the Great's armies could march across the enemy front, wheel into line, and go straight into an attack. This processional deployment formed the basis of Frederick's famous 'oblique order'. Previous flank attacks at Turckheim or Fleurus had involved only part of the outflanking army. Frederick continued the processional march around the enemy, to place his whole army across their flank. Prussian cavalry protected Frederick's own flanks. Trained to charge long distances at a gallop, Prussian cavalry set the standard for mounted tactics, until rifled small arms rendered the *arme blanche* obsolete in the late 19th century.

As his opponents frequently outnumbered him, Frederick advanced the stronger wing of a force first, refusing the weaker flank. The attack by regiments in echelon combined with processional deployment to create the full version of oblique order. Oblique order worked to devastating effect at Leuthen (6 December 1757), where 36,000 Prussians attacked and defeated 80,000 Austrians, inflicting almost 50% losses. Oblique order demanded absolutely consistent drill across the army. The Prussian officer corps trained from a common manual: in other armies doctrine varied from regiment to regiment. The Prussians were therefore the first totally professional army.

Frederick's opponents soon countered his turning movements. At Kolin (18 June 1757) Austrian light troops hung about the Prussian flank, provoking a premature advance. At Zorndorf (25 October 1758) encircled Russians faced about to convert

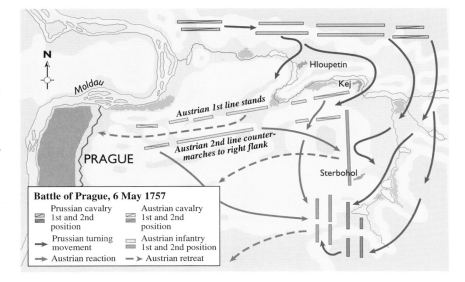

Battle of Prague, 6 May 1757

▨ Prussian cavalry 1st and 2nd position	▨ Austrian cavalry 1st and 2nd position
→ Prussian turning movement	▭ Austrian infantry 1st and 2nd position
→ Austrian reaction	--→ Austrian retreat

Austrian 1st line stands

Austrian 2nd line counter-marches to right flank

Hloupetin
Kej
Sterbohol
PRAGUE
Moldau
N

the battle into another frontal attack, with ghastly results: 35% Prussian losses against 53% Russian. All armies had improved rates of fire, making frontal attacks terribly costly. Artillery had also improved. New casting techniques made guns lighter but more effective. The Russians and Austrians reformed their artillery in the early 1750s. Their new guns outclassed the Prussians in number, range, and weight of fire, and massacred Prussian infantry at Prague and Kolin. Frederick strengthened his own artillery, deploying 12pr fortress guns at Leuthen. He broadened the capability of his gunners with field howitzers and horse artillery. Howitzers were versatile weapons, capable of lobbing shells over obstacles, such as woods or villages, or firing large calibre grapeshot at close quarters. Frederick's horse artillery formed a mobile reserve of firepower, foreshadowing Napoleon's use of reserve artillery.

The Seven Years War does not fit the stereotype of 18th century limited warfare. Prussia faced dismemberment if defeated. Frederick's pre-emptive occupation of Saxony drew in France, expanding a Central European conflict into a world war. Frederick's internal position and the tactical superiority of his army enabled him to attack his geographically dispersed enemies one at a time. He defeated a French army at Rossbach (5 November 1757), then marched 170 miles in 12 days to beat the Austrians at Leuthen. Frederick's early victories paralysed opposing generals. They were slow to exploit his absence, or their own successes. An Austro-Russian army failed to occupy Berlin, and end the war, after their victory at Kunersdorf (12 August 1759). Frederick on the other hand could not follow up his victories, as he always needed the troops elsewhere. Strategic weakness forced him into offensive battles, accepting heavy casualties to keep the enemy at bay. However, he had little choice. Prussia lacked the fortifications that limited offensives in traditional seats of war, and Frederick could not risk losing territory by defending obstacles until out-manoeuvred. As long as he controlled Prussia's revenues and received British subsidies, Frederick could hire fresh mercenaries, while even a Prussian defeat wrecked the opposing army. Despite his tactical genius, however, Frederick came to regard battles as an expedient of the unimaginative. He was saved accidentally, by the political breakdown of the opposing coalition.

RIGHT: Frederick the Great created an articulated army that could move by wings or lines, unlike previous armies, which moved as a single unit. Columns of companies at the correct distances and intervals could form line quickly to a flank, without overcrowding or leaving gaps. Such precision demanded constant drill and ferocious discipline.

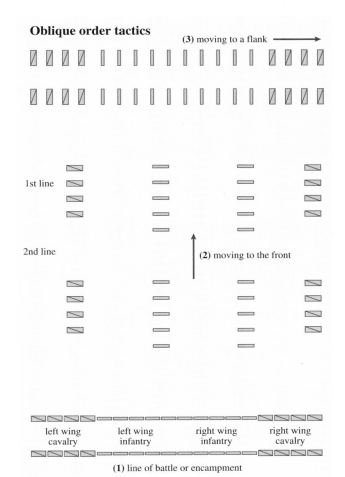

Oblique order tactics

(3) moving to a flank →

1st line

2nd line

(2) moving to the front

left wing cavalry | left wing infantry | right wing infantry | right wing cavalry

(1) line of battle or encampment

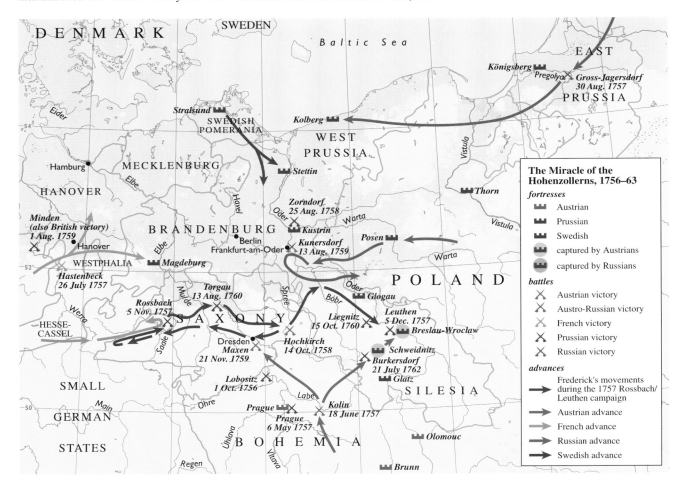

The Miracle of the Hohenzollerns, 1756–63

fortresses
- Austrian
- Prussian
- Swedish
- captured by Austrians
- captured by Russians

battles
- ✕ Austrian victory
- ✕ Austro-Russian victory
- ✕ French victory
- ✕ Prussian victory
- ✕ Russian victory

advances
- → Frederick's movements during the 1757 Rossbach/ Leuthen campaign
- → Austrian advance
- → French advance
- → Russian advance
- → Swedish advance

LEFT: Threatened by a numerically superior coalition, Frederick sought to defeat his enemies separately. He manoeuvred on internal lines and exploited the tactical superiority of his army in offensive battles. Later opponents of geographically dispersed alliances, such as the Wehrmacht or IDF, would also combine a strategic defensive with offensive tactics.

Sea power and Sepoys

European empires in Asia originated as trading posts and naval bases. Indian disunity, following the decline of Mughal power, provided an opening for France and Britain to intervene in local conflicts. The balance of naval power in the Bay of Bengal determined the course of their struggle, but it was decided by native soldiers or sepoys, organized and equipped in the European manner.

The Mughal Empire did not collapse as a result of exposure to European military techniques; internal decay invited external attack. Islamic intolerance alienated the Rajputs, the most effective component of the Mughal army, and inspired Sikh militancy. Mughal generals seized power for themselves, for instance the Nizam at Hyderabad. The Mahrathas of the Deccan, a confederacy of Hindu freebooters, frustrated the clumsy Mughal armies of the last great emperor, Aurangzeb, by their raiding strategy. After his death in 1707 they took control of northern India, even taking Portuguese bases at Bassein and Chaul. Too far from their farms to return home between raids, the Mahrathas became paid garrisons, and lost their mobility. They acquired mercenary infantry and heavy guns, to overawe recalcitrant fort owners, but failed to integrate the new tactical elements with their light cavalry. An army of Afghan heavy cavalry, armed with muskets and swivel guns on camels, inflicted a disastrous defeat on the Mahrathas at Panipat (14 January 1761). The immobile Mahratha guns were left behind, while their cavalry and infantry fought separate battles. The Afghans lacked the numbers or political support to control India and withdrew, leaving chaos from which the British would profit.

French and British coastal enclaves in India needed control of the sea for supplies and military reinforcements. Their proxim-

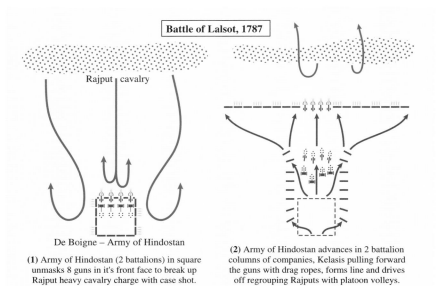

Battle of Lalsot, 1787

Rajput cavalry

De Boigne – Army of Hindostan

(1) Army of Hindostan (2 battalions) in square unmasks 8 guns in it's front face to break up Rajput heavy cavalry charge with case shot.

(2) Army of Hindostan advances in 2 battalion columns of companies, Kelasis pulling forward the guns with drag ropes, forms line and drives off regrouping Rajputs with platoon volleys.

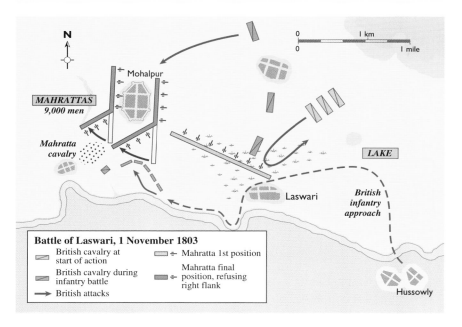

N

Mohalpur

MAHRATTAS 9,000 men

Mahratta cavalry

LAKE

Laswari

British infantry approach

Hussowly

Battle of Laswari, 1 November 1803

- British cavalry at start of action
- British cavalry during infantry battle
- → British attacks
- Mahratta 1st position
- Mahratta final position, refusing right flank

ity provoked numerous naval actions. Linear tactics prevented loss of ships, yet as in European waters inconclusive battles had disproportionate effects. A French naval victory at Negapatam (25 July 1746) allowed them to seize Madras, but British reinforcements under Boscawen saved their nearby base at Fort St George. The British then besieged the French base Pondichery, until the monsoon drove Boscawen off station. In the 1750s an outnumbered British squadron inflicted enough damage in three 'indecisive' actions, to compel the French admiral to withdraw to distant Mauritius to refit. Pondichery surrendered in 1761, having no hope of relief by sea. Naval power allowed the British to move forces between the Carnatic and Bengal. When the Nawab of Bengal occupied Calcutta in 1756, the British mounted a joint operation from Madras to retake it. A squadron of battleships then pushed 21 miles up the river Hooghly, to bombard the French factory at Chandernagore (23 March 1757). The direct application of naval power foreshadows later operations by the Royal Navy in Burma and China. Victory in India opened new strategic possibilities for the British. The 1762 expedition to Manila sailed from Madras. Calcutta developed a naval dockyard, building European-style warships in local teak.

Europeans revolutionized Indian land warfare. In the 1730s the French introduced light field guns, and trained their factory watchmen to fight with musket and bayonet, their *cipahis* defeating a Mughal successor army at St Thome (3 November 1746). The British imitated the French, depending heavily on Indian troops to extend and consolidate British rule beyond the range of their fleets. At Plassey (23 June 1757) Colonel Robert Clive defeated 50,000 Mughal-style troops with 3,200 men, two thirds of them sepoys. Traditional Indian armies had no tactical answer to well-drilled bayonets and mobile field guns firing case shot. Only the Mahrathas' strategy of retreating into ground unsuitable for artillery and harassing British communications had any success, for example at Wadgaun (February 1779). Indian princes hired European adventurers to train sepoys to fight in their feuds. The largest such force was the Mahratha Army of Hindustan: 24,000 sepoys with 130 field guns. When the British confronted the Mahrathas in 1803, they bribed their European officers to desert. Outmanoeuvred at Assaye and Laswari, the leaderless sepoys displayed a cohesion never seen in traditional Indian armies, changing front and fighting to the death. By 1805 the East India Company employed 150,000 sepoys. Britain had become a major Asian land power, combining European military techniques with Indian numbers. The new style of Indian soldier would be a mainstay of British imperial power.

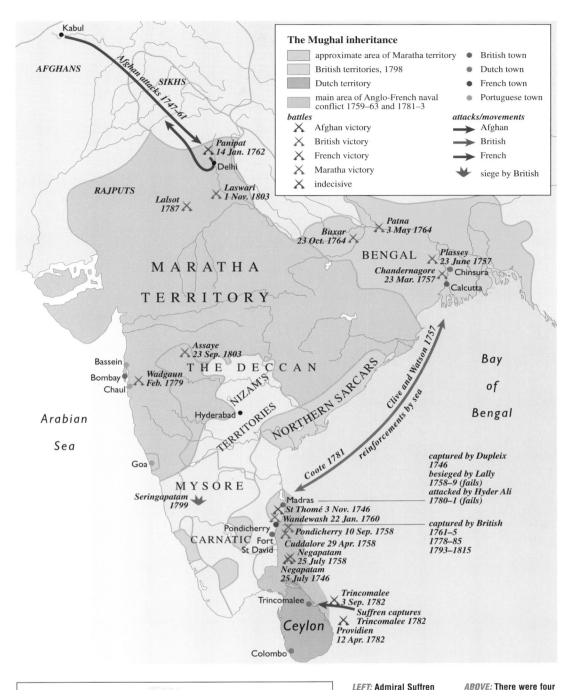

The Mughal inheritance

- approximate area of Maratha territory
- British territories, 1798
- Dutch territory
- main area of Anglo-French naval conflict 1759–63 and 1781–3

- ● British town
- ● Dutch town
- ● French town
- ● Portuguese town

battles

- ✕ Afghan victory
- ✕ British victory
- ✕ French victory
- ✕ Maratha victory
- ✕ indecisive

attacks/movements

- → Afghan
- → British
- → French
- ↘ siege by British

Kabul

AFGHANS

Afghan attacks 1747–61

SIKHS

Panipat ✕ 14 Jan. 1762
Delhi

RAJPUTS

Lalsot ✕ *Laswari* 1787 1 Nov. 1803

Buxar 23 Oct. 1764 ✕
Patna 3 May 1764

M A R A T H A

BENGAL ✕ *Plassey* 23 June 1757
Chandernagore 23 Mar. 1757 ✕ Chinsura
Calcutta

T E R R I T O R Y

Assaye ✕ 23 Sep. 1803

Bassein
Bombay ● *Wadgaun* ✕ Feb. 1779
Chaul

T H E   D E C C A N

NIZAM'S

Hyderabad ●

TERRITORIES

NORTHERN SARCARS

Clive and Watson 1757

reinforcements by sea

Bay
of
Bengal

Arabian
Sea

Goa ●

Coote 1781

M Y S O R E

captured by Dupleix 1746
besieged by Lally 1758–9 (fails)
attacked by Hyder Ali 1780–1 (fails)

captured by British 1761–5
1778–85
1793–1815

Seringapatam 1799

Madras
✕ *St Thomé 3 Nov. 1746*
✕ *Wandewash 22 Jan. 1760*
Pondicherry ✕ *Pondicherry 10 Sep. 1758*
CARNATIC Fort ✕ *Cuddalore 29 Apr. 1758*
St David ✕ *Negapatam 25 July 1758*
Negapatam 25 July 1746

Trincomalee 3 Sep. 1782
Trincomalee ● ✕
✕ *Suffren captures Trincomalee 1782*
Ceylon *Providien 12 Apr. 1782*

Colombo

LEFT: Admiral Suffren fought a series of naval actions against the British in the Indian Ocean, but he was frustrated by the indiscipline of his captains and the progressive loss of French bases in the area. His battles with Admiral Hughes were bloody affairs, the lines of battle pounding away for hours, inflicting terrible casualties, but ultimately indecisive.

ABOVE: There were four competitors to replace the Mughals: Afghans, British, French, and Marathas. Anglo-French commercial rivalry concealed the strength of the outsiders, short-sightedly seen as allies or puppets. Sea power was crucial to British success, allowing them to shuttle reinforcements between Bombay and Bengal, while French lack of naval bases settled indecisive sea battles against them.

The American Revolution

The American War of Independence is commonly seen as defying the military conventions of the day. The strategy and tactics of the war, however, were not unusual. British defeat revealed the short-comings of maritime power confronted with popular resistance on a continental scale while distracted by a strategic threat closer to home.

The British war machine of the 1770s was soundly financed, with a competent army experienced in colonial warfare and the largest navy in the world. It was defeated by a popular revolt that printed worthless paper money, created an army from nothing, and never possessed a navy beyond privateers. The initial weakness of the rebels was to their advantage, as the British government underestimated the response required. North America was simply too large to occupy with the troops available. British strategic mobility was low. They could make amphibious descents upon New York or Charleston, but once ashore lacked transport, and moved at the speed of a foot soldier. In a hostile countryside strategic combinations were risky, as shown by Howe's failure to support Burgoyne before Saratoga. British defeats became disasters, while defeated American forces had space to withdraw, protected by difficult terrain. Awareness of the relative significance of defeat for the two sides reinforced the caution imposed on the British by lack of numbers.

Cornwallis' bold operations in the Carolinas left him vulnerable to Washington's counter-stroke at Yorktown.

Political factors constrained British conduct of the war in ways familiar today. Opposition to the war within Britain was vocal. Counter-insurgency forces faced the choice between ineffective half measures and extremes that alienated moderates. Revolutionary militia dominated the countryside, their political role in suppressing Loyalist dissent exceeding their value on the battlefield. The militia symbolized the dispersal of political authority in the United States. This made for poor strategic direction of the American war effort, but increased British difficulties in suppressing a many-headed revolt. Their capture of Philadelphia, the seat of Congress, lacked the political resonance of occupying a European capital.

Tactical differences between the two sides have been exaggerated, particularly the role of the frontier rifleman. Rifles were a liability in a battle, slow to reload and lacking a bayonet. Washington was a tactical conservative, despite personal experience of Braddock's defeat on the Monongahela. He employed a German expert to train the Continental army, which relied on smooth-bore muskets and close order drill, as the US Army would after independence. Battles resembled European actions, with smaller forces, less cavalry and artillery. Troops fought in two

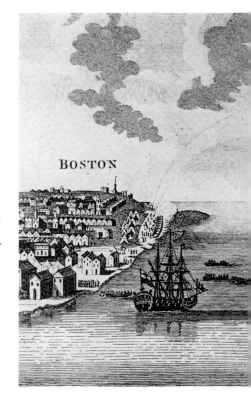

BOSTON

ranks, not three, a habit British units took home. British infantry depended on the bullet as well as the bayonet. The lack of cavalry and artillery enhanced the defensive power of infantry, who could not be turned or shelled out of positions. Cavalry

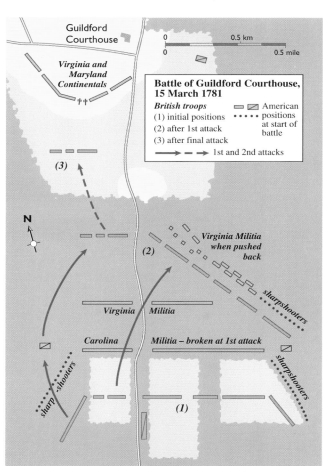

Guildford Courthouse

Virginia and Maryland Continentals

0   0.5 km
0   0.5 mile

Battle of Guildford Courthouse, 15 March 1781

British troops
(1) initial positions
(2) after 1st attack
(3) after final attack
→ — → 1st and 2nd attacks

American positions at start of battle

(3)

N

(2)

Virginia Militia when pushed back

sharpshooters

Virginia Militia

Carolina Militia – broken at 1st attack

sharpshooters

sharpshooters

(1)

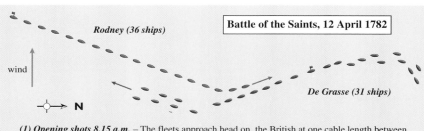

Rodney (36 ships)

Battle of the Saints, 12 April 1782

wind

N

De Grasse (31 ships)

(1) Opening shots 8.15 a.m. – The fleets approach head on, the British at one cable length between ships, the French still forming line under musketry fire. The French keep the weather gauge but are becalmed. Their van moves out of range and fails to engage the British centre.

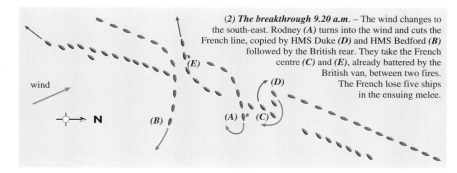

(2) The breakthrough 9.20 a.m. – The wind changes to the south-east. Rodney *(A)* turns into the wind and cuts the French line, copied by HMS Duke *(D)* and HMS Bedford *(B)* followed by the British rear. They take the French centre *(C)* and *(E)*, already battered by the British van, between two fires. The French lose five ships in the ensuing melee.

wind

N (B) (E) (D) (A) (C)

LEFT: The British won many fruitless tactical victories in America, their small forces suffering unsustainable losses for little purpose. The Americans withdrew in good order after Guildford, leaving Cornwallis to evacuate the Carolinas.

ABOVE: Peacetime economy left the Royal Navy outclassed by a hostile naval coalition. Ineptly handled squadrons suffered setbacks off the Chesapeake and at Grenada. Rodney broke with the formality of 18th naval tactics at the Saintes, showing the way for imaginative British victories in the 1790s.

were not available to follow up costly frontal assaults, as they would in Europe. American defensive capabilities and problems of exploitation imposed caution on British generals anxious not to repeat the heavy casualties suffered at Bunker's Hill at the start of the war.

Washington's success in keeping his army together deprived the British of victory, but French intervention won the war. The Royal Navy had too few resources to intimidate the rebels, or isolate North America, as it had in the Seven Years War. Ships were rotten and the best admirals politically disaffected. Many ships remained in home waters to deter a combined Franco-Spanish battle line that outnumbered the British 140 to 120. The French had no European diversions, and usurped the Royal Navy's amphibious monopoly, sending an expedition to assist the Americans. In August 1781 Washington moved superior numbers of French and American troops against Cornwallis' army at Yorktown. He urged the French fleet to concentrate off Chesapeake Bay, to cut Cornwallis' communications with British forces at New York. In the crucial battle off Cape Henry (5-9 September 1781) 24 French ships prevented 19 British from raising the siege. Sea power compelled Cornwallis to surrender (19 October 1781). The end of the land war allowed the British to focus on the naval war and a reinforced West Indies Squadron broke the mould of linear naval tactics at the Battle of the Saints (12 April 1782). Admiral Rodney broke the French line, and captured five ships, pointing the way for British naval successes in the 1790s.

Maritime vs Continental Power, 1776–82
movement of forces

→ Allied (French/American) 1776–80
⇢ Allied 1781
➡ British 1776–80
⇢ British 1781

battles

✕ Allied success
✕ British success

blockades

⛴ Allied
⛴ British

sieges

⬇ American success
⬇ British success

RIGHT: The American colonies formed an enormous theatre of war. The few British regulars were unable to suppress the numerous local irregulars, although the Royal Navy allowed them to strike at will at coastal areas. The British were defeated when a French fleet cut off supplies and reinforcements from Cornwallis' isolated army at Yorktown.

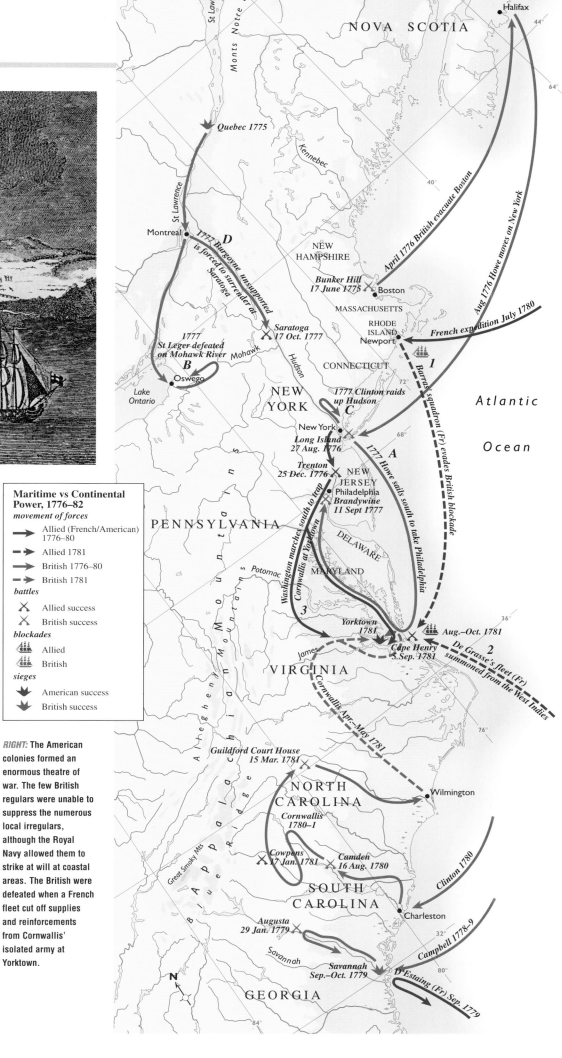

Chapter 5 Nations in Arms 1792–1815

RIGHT: **Revolutionary soldiers in the Vendée, 1794, where it took a ruthless counter-insurgency campaign to quell anti-revolutionary forces. The transformation of warfare in the wake of the French revolution owed nothing to technology: the weapons were little different from the early 18th century, but the social forces unleashed in 1789 made the 'Nation in Arms' a reality.**

BELOW: **The Battle of Grossbeeren was one of several French defeats during the 1813 campaign in Germany. Napoleon's enemies avoided him in person and concentrated against armies commanded by his marshals. The French army had lost its tactical superiority, the losses in Russia made good with juvenile conscripts, the** *Marie-Louises.*

The French Revolution empowered the state to call all citizens to its defence. The defeat of counter-revolutionary interventions revealed the formidable potential of a nation in arms. Napoleon harnessed the revolutionary armies to conquer most of Europe, making the defeated enemy pay for French victories. Napoleon's ruthless exploitation of other countries precluded lasting peace, driving other powers to mobilize popular support against him. Conservative Austrian archdukes raised *Landwehr* militia battalions in 1809. Radical Prussian officers exploited national feeling during the War of Liberation of 1813. Spain produced the first modern 'guerrilla' campaign, at the cost of lasting social and political dislocation.

The French pioneered new systems of military organization which dramatically increased the pace and violence of warfare. Operational articulation at corps and division level supplemented tactical articulation at battalion and company level. '*La Grande Tactique*' or operational art occupied the middle ground between strategy and tactics. Manoeuvres intended to destroy enemy armies became more important than single battles, which were more frequent but less individually significant. Armies could no longer refuse action, except by immediate retreat, and not always then. Staffs developed to coordinate the movement of separate Army Corps.

Conscription and enhanced agricultural productivity produced a quantum leap in the size of forces: Leipzig in 1813 was the largest battle yet fought. Armies became sufficiently numerous to mask and bypass fortresses, subordinating formal sieges to field operations. A revolution in warfare had occurred without radical technological changes, using existing means in new ways.

La Patrie en Danger

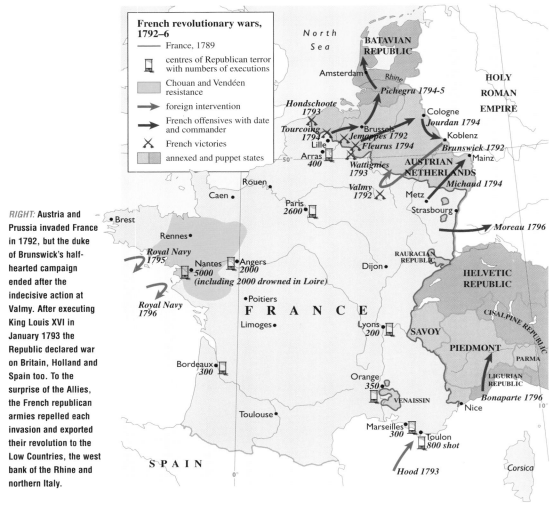

French revolutionary wars, 1792–6
— France, 1789
☐ centres of Republican terror with numbers of executions
▨ Chouan and Vendéen resistance
→ foreign intervention
➤ French offensives with date and commander
✕ French victories
▨ annexed and puppet states

The French Revolution profoundly changed the art of war. It released social forces that combined explosively with late 18th century military trends. Unlike other 'military revolutions' these were not technological in origin - there were few changes in the weapons used - but tactical.

French army officers despaired of rivalling the precision of the Prussian drill-masters who had defeated them at Rossbach (1757). Instead they exploited the native flexibility of the French soldier. Comte Jacques de Guibert proposed in 1772 that battalions should use line for fire and columns of companies for movement. Such wide, shallow columns could cover each other's flanks by fire, and move around obstacles that threw lines into disorder. Guibert integrated skirmishers with the line of battle. They screened the movement of columns unable to use their own weapons, and prepared the advance with accurate individual fire. Aimed fire was more dangerous than that of men jammed together in close order, while skirmishers presented a less vulnerable target. Dispersed skirmishers could thus achieve fire superiority over formed troops armed with similar weapons. Guibert's system became official French army doctrine in 1791, and was simple enough to learn in three months. By 1815 it had spread to all European armies, forming the basis for a new tactical consensus.

The French Army's system of all-arms divisions further enhanced tactical articulation. First formed by the Duc de Broglie in 1759, a typical division might have a dozen battalions of infantry, a regiment of cavalry, and thirty guns. Such formations could sustain an action alone until supported by other divisions marching to their support. They allowed armies to extend their frontages, probing for open flanks or gaps in the enemy lines. Able to use several roads at once, armies organized in divisions could move faster and subsist more easily. Combat became a realistic strategic aim, as a cornered enemy had no choice except to accept battle or retreat. Improved tactical articulation made individual battles less costly for both loser and winner, encouraging offensive action. Such were the advantages of divisional formations that both sides in the French Revolutionary Wars used them, although the forces of reaction rarely did so with the same energy as their opponents.

The continuous marching and fighting of Revolutionary armies was expensive. French soldiers had to forage for their food, and bivouac in the open, losing many sick. Battles were less deadly, but there were more of them: 713 battles took place in Europe between 1790 and 1820, compared with 2,659 for 1480 to 1790. Enthusiastic French armies suffered more casualties than the regular troops they defeated. Their losses were replaced by compulsion. Threatened with invasion in August 1793, the government in Paris proclaimed a *levée en masse*. Half a million Frenchmen were under arms by the end of the year, in eleven separate armies. Such numbers were hard to maintain, falling to 227,000 in 1799. Battlefield strengths rarely exceeded those of the Seven Years War; Tourcoing (18 May 1794) was exceptional. Nevertheless the increased total size of armies made it essential to feed them at the enemy's expense. A ring of annexed territories and puppet republics surrounded France by 1796, a system fundamental to Napoleon's Empire.

French expansion was slow, until Napoleon focussed Revolutionary energies. Republican armies often failed to cooperate. When Jourdan and Moreau invaded Germany in 1796, the Austrian Archduke Karl beat them in detail, and chased them back to the Rhine. However, the conquest of the Low Countries and the left bank of the Rhine in three years (1792-94) compares strikingly with Louis XIV's decades of fighting fruitlessly for the same objectives. The contrast suggests the decisive potential of Revolutionary warfare, should it be directed in a coordinated manner.

Infantry tactics of the Revolution

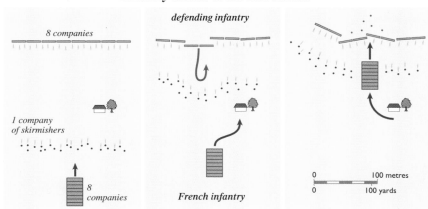

defending infantry

8 companies

1 company of skirmishers

8 companies

French infantry

0 — 100 metres
0 — 100 yards

The new tactical methods exploited a profound shift in political attitudes. War was no longer the exclusive concern of kings or governments. It demanded popular participation, if not freely given, then enforced by terror. Tactical articulation required soldiers who could be trusted not to desert when dispersed to forage or skirmish. Other European armies distrusted light infantry as socially subversive, and wished to avoid the economic dislocation caused by living off the country. They were slow to make the same demands of their soldiers and populations as the French.

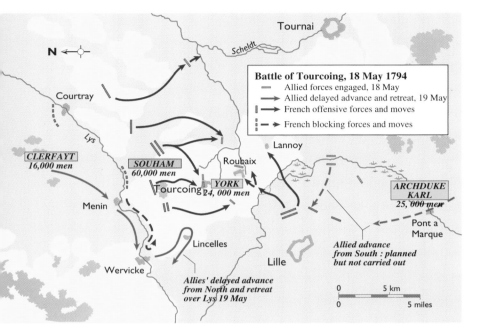

Battle of Tourcoing, 18 May 1794
— Allied forces engaged, 18 May
→ Allied delayed advance and retreat, 19 May
▮ French offensive forces and moves
▮--▸ French blocking forces and moves

CLERFAYT 16,000 men

SOUHAM 60,000 men

YORK 24,000 men

ARCHDUKE KARL 25,000 men

Allied advance from South : planned but not carried out

Allies' delayed advance from North and retreat over Lys 19 May

0 5 km
0 5 miles

ABOVE: France's revolutionary armies were famous for their rough-and-ready appearance, but they conquered the west bank of the Rhine in three years. Louis XIV spent decades failing to extend the French frontier to the Rhine. This typically tatty soldier waves a captured Austrian flag in triumph.

ABOVE: The campaigns of the 1790s saw both sides disperse their forces over wide frontages, ready to concentrate for battle. At Turcoing the French defeated the Allies in detail, acting on interior lines to concentrate against York's forces. However, both sides' losses were about 8 per cent: decisive victories proved elusive.

RIGHT: In 1796 Archduke Karl of Austria exploited his central position to defeat two French invasions of southern Germany. Jourdan was driven back and compelled to seek an armistice after the Battle of Würzburg.

Archduke Karl's German Campaign, 1796

movement of armies
→ French advance, July–August, 1796
--▸ French retreat, September– October 1796
→ Archduke Karl's advances between northern and southern wings of campaign

battles
✕ French victory
✕ Austrian victory
✕ indecisive
▦ forts

Napoleon in Italy

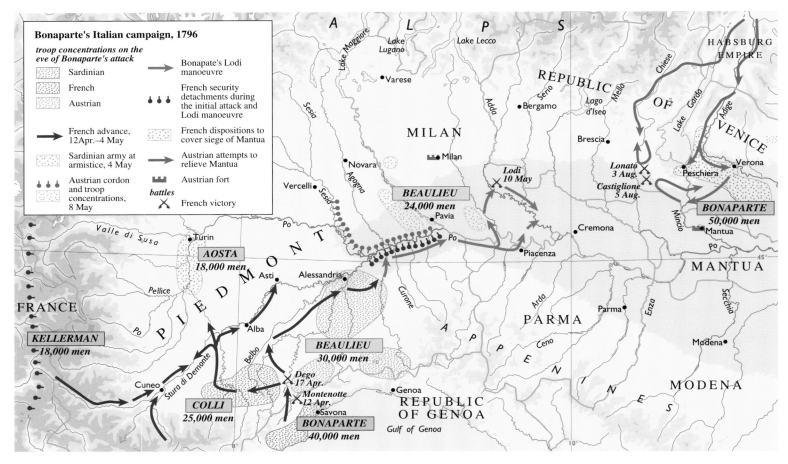

Bonaparte's Italian campaign, 1796

troop concentrations on the eve of Bonaparte's attack

Sardinian

French

Austrian

French advance, 12 Apr.–4 May

Sardinian army at armistice, 4 May

Austrian cordon and troop concentrations, 8 May

Bonapate's Lodi manoeuvre

French security detachments during the initial attack and Lodi manoeuvre

French dispositions to cover siege of Mantua

Austrian attempts to relieve Mantua

Austrian fort

battles
✕ French victory

ABOVE: In April–May 1796 Napoleon led the outnumbered French Army of Italy to victory over the Austrian and Pietmontese forces, striking at their dispersed armies and driving them from Lombardy. In August, he repeated the strategy of using a central position to defeat superior forces in turn. French losses averaged less than 10 per cent in these battles, while the Austrian armies lost a quarter of their effectives.

The Armies of the Revolution contained the seeds of Napoleon's success. Other French commanders spread their divisions evenly across the battlefront, and failed to achieve decisive results. General Bonaparte's first campaign in Italy in 1796 showed his grasp of the potential of divisional organization and skirmishing tactics. Austrian intelligence sources identified strategic expertise he had derived from Pierre Bourcet and other 18th century military thinkers. In his first campaign, Bonaparte showed the originality of his genius, defeating larger, better-equipped armies with two strategies that became Napoleonic trademarks: The Strategy of the Central Position, and The Envelopment or *La Manoeuvre sur les Derrières*.

The first allowed inferior numbers to divide a superior enemy army, and defeat its wings in detail. It worked best against allied armies, more concerned with their own safety than for their ally. The French at Tourcoing took advantage of their central position by accident. Bonaparte deliberately placed himself between the Sardinian and Austrian armies to knock Sardinia out of the war in a fortnight. Outnumbered 50,000 to 40,000, the French regularly achieved superior numbers on the battlefield, for example 11,000 to 4,500 at Montenotte. Bonaparte avoided a classical set-piece battle, but fought a series of skirmishes and tiny sieges, in which the 1791 tactics proved decisively superior. The Archduke Karl used internal lines to beat Jourdan and Moreau in Germany, but without tactical mobility his success was not decisive. In Piedmont swarms of skirmishers harried the Austro-Sardinians. Brigades advanced vigorously upon the enemy, three battalion columns deep, while light infantry crowned the heights to turn his flanks, taking masses of prisoners.

When the Austrians fell back behind the Po and Ticino, Bonaparte used his now superior numbers to implement the more ambitious *Manoeuvre sur les Derrières*. Screened by the River Po, Bonaparte gained the Austrian rear between Piacenza and Lodi, precipitating an immediate Austrian withdrawal from Lombardy. The French advanced 100 miles in two weeks, and seized Milan with enormous quantities of loot, resolving their own logistical difficulties. The crossing of the Alps in the Marengo campaign of 1800 was an even more impressive demonstration of *La Manoeuvre sur les Derrières*. The Austrians had regained

RIGHT: The coordination of French forces was illustrated at Castliglione when Fiorella's division struck the Austrian rear. The separate Austrian armies were each beaten and Napoleon claimed victory, although his enemies had succeeded in relieving Mantua and replenishing their garrison.

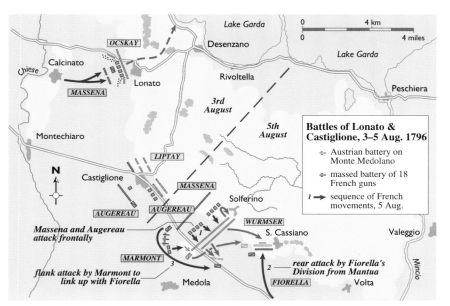

Battles of Lonato & Castiglione, 3–5 Aug. 1796

⚞ Austrian battery on Monte Medolano

▬ massed battery of 18 French guns

1 → sequence of French movements, 5 Aug.

Massena and Augereau attack frontally

flank attack by Marmont to link up with Fiorella

rear attack by Fiorella's Division from Mantua

Northern Italy, and were pressing against the French frontier on the Riviera. Bonaparte, now the French head of state, crossed the Alps behind the Austrians. The French re-occupied Milan, cutting Austrian communications, while maintaining their own through Switzerland.

Napoleon's two strategies required different resolution on the battlefield. The essentially defensive Central Position demanded offensive tactics, to defeat one enemy wing before the other could intervene. The offensive Envelopment strategy brought the advantage of the tactical defensive, as the enemy tried to fight his way out.

At Lonato and Castiglione in August 1796 Bonaparte faced encirclement by an Austrian pincer movement. A less energetic commander might have been lost, for the Army of Italy appeared to be at the culminating point of its advance: the siege of Mantua tied up 15,000 French soldiers, occupation duties absorbed another 10,000, leaving only 27,000 in the field. Bonaparte used his central position to attack each Austrian column separately in a three-day battle. Abandoning

the siege of Mantua, he concentrated every available man, even enveloping the Austrian left on the second day at Castiglione. Bonaparte retained no specific strategic reserve, the divisional system allowing him to call on any available body of troops, as necessary.

The culminating point of the 1800 Italian campaign came at Marengo. The outmanoeuvred Austrians could still supply their army by sea through Genoa. Bonaparte needed a tactical victory to confirm his strategic success. Fifty thousand French advanced on a 50-mile front, between the Alps and the sea. They prevented the Austrians escaping, but gave them a numerical advantage on the battlefield. However, the French had the advantage of the tactical defensive and the divisional system. Fresh troops came into action during the battle, to gain a narrow victory. Bonaparte's reversal of the armies' fronts had raised the stakes for the loser. The defeated Austrian commander, aware of his dangerous situation, agreed an armistice, returning most of Northern Italy to French rule.

ABOVE: An officer and private from an Austrian grenadier regiment. Sustained by British subsidies, the Austrian army resisted the French in southern Germany and Italy. Austrian victories on the Rhine were countered by Napoleon's conquest of northern Italy. His success in outmanoeuvring and destroying larger Austrian armies was to be studied at military academies for the next century.

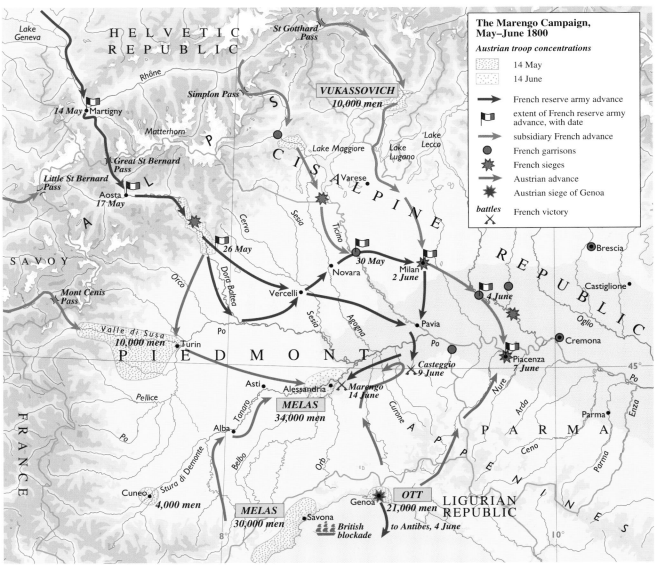

LEFT: Napoleon returned from Egypt in 1800 to find the French all but driven out of Italy. He led his army over the Alps to place his men across the Austrians' lines of communication and defeated Melas's counter-attack at Marengo. Casualties were relatively light, but the Austrians were compelled to abandon Piedmont once again.

La Grande Armée

RIGHT: Napoleon takes the surrender at Ulm: prepared for a standard eighteenth century campaign, the Austrian army was completely wrong-footed in 1805. By the time the decisive battle of Austerlitz took place in December, the Austrians had lost 60,000 men in the fortress of Ulm and Vienna had been captured with its magazines intact.

Citizen soldiers, permanently uprooted from their homes, made France a Nation of Camps, rather than a Nation in Arms. The French Army replaced the civilian Directory with its own leaders. General Bonaparte became Emperor in 1804. Lacking legitimacy, except the bayonets of his followers, Napoleon had to ensure their continued support. He plundered Europe for the benefit of the French Army, perpetuating international instability. The Grande Armée began as the Army of England, but in 1805 it turned upon Napoleon's continental rivals: Austria and Russia.

The Grande Armée was three times the size of the Army of Italy. Napoleon organized it into seven *Corps d'Armée*, which replaced divisions as the lowest level formation to include all three arms. A typical corps might have three infantry divisions, a light cavalry brigade for reconnaissance, and reserve artillery batteries in addition to those attached to each division. Heavy cavalry formed separate divisions, reserved for shock use on the battlefield. The increased size of corps allowed them to fight all day without support. Their durability enabled them to spread out to subsist. Napoleon's men lived off the country by requisition. They gave receipts for what they took, reducing the wasteful pillage of the Thirty Years War. The spread of the potato across Western and Central Europe was crucial to this streamlined logistical system. The French needed about one

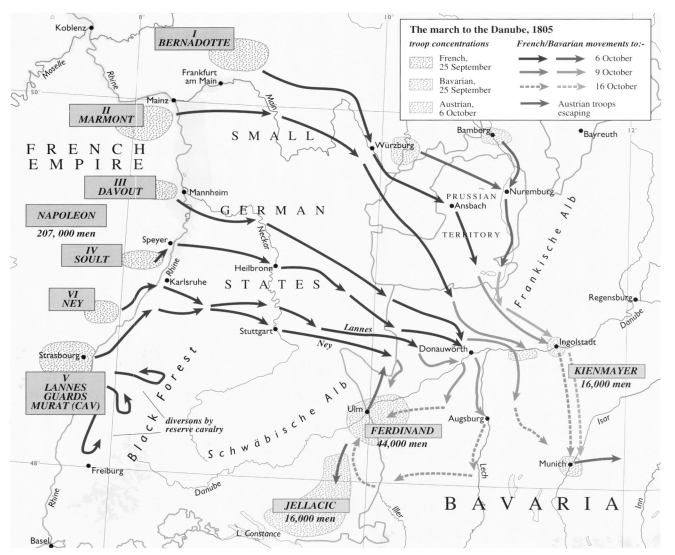

The march to the Danube, 1805

troop concentrations

French, 25 September
Bavarian, 25 September
Austrian, 6 October

French/Bavarian movements to:-

6 October
9 October
16 October
Austrian troops escaping

LEFT: Napoleon opened the 1805 campaign with a far larger army than he had previously commanded, outnumbering the enemy by 2:1. His *Grande Armée* carried little baggage, invading enemy territory at harvest time and marching far faster than the Austrians anticipated. Before they realized what was happening, the French had slipped past Ulm and Ferdinand's army was obliged to surrender.

RIGHT: At Austerlitz Napoleon tempted the cumbersome Austro-Russian army to attack his right flank, weakening its own centre. Napoleon broke through the middle of the Allied army, which broke up with 30 per cent losses. It was militarily and politically decisive: Austria sued for peace.

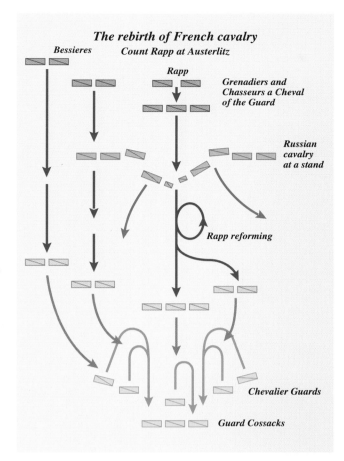

The rebirth of French cavalry
Count Rapp at Austerlitz

Bessieres

Rapp

Grenadiers and Chasseurs a Cheval of the Guard

Russian cavalry at a stand

Rapp reforming

Chevalier Guards

Guard Cossacks

ABOVE: **The Russian Guard cavalry counter-attacked Vandamme's division, but was destroyed by French Guard cavalry led by Napoleon's formidable ADC, Rapp. The well-trained French cavalry were able to charge, re-form, and charge again to defeat the clumsily handled Russians.**

eighth of the transport used by more scrupulous armies. A typical corps occupied road space roughly equivalent to a day's march, making it a logical unit to use a single road. The *Corps d'Armée* became the standard strategic building block in the great wars of the 19th and 20th centuries.

Napoleon's strategic capability far exceeded that of Louis XIV. Their armies were similar in size, but Napoleon had fewer opponents and a military system optimized by the *Corps d'Armée*. Invasions of South Germany by Marlborough or Moreau had covered a narrow front. The Grande Armée advanced with seven corps on a 100-mile front. The Austrian high command under-estimated the threat. General Mack occupied an exposed position at Ulm in Bavaria, a French ally. He expected a direct advance through the Black Forest, an illusion encouraged by the deception mea-

sures of Napoleon's cavalry screen. Meanwhile the mass of the Grande Armée swung north of Ulm, reaching the Danube between Ulm and the Austrian base at Vienna. Napoleon thought Mack would break out eastwards, south of the Danube, but some of the trapped Austrians escaped to the north east. However, 27,000 Austrians surrendered on 20 October 1805, bringing the total bag to 60,000. The manoeuvre resembled the Marengo campaign, except that Napoleon's 2:1 numerical superiority made his success much greater, a rare example of a bloodless triumph.

The Allies were unable to defend Vienna, its arsenals falling into French hands. Napoleon caught up with a combined Austro-Russian army 70 miles north of Vienna. As at Castiglione the French appeared to be at the culminating point of their offensive, 500 miles from the Rhine with half their army occupying Austrian territory. Nine years into his career Napoleon fought his first conventional set-piece battle. As always he gave the tactical encounter strategic significance. Concentrating on his left, he appeared to expose his communications with Vienna, tempting the Allies to march across his front, exposing their own flank and communications to counter-attack. The Allied army was ill-suited to complex manoeuvres, hampered by poor staff work and Russian contempt for the already defeated Austrians. Napoleon was on the defensive, and outnumbered 5:4, but he attacked as soon as the Allies were committed. Soult broke through the Allied centre on the Pratzen Heights, driving into the flank and rear of the Allied left, already fixed frontally by Davout. Napoleon had outwitted the Allies, but their defeat required hard fighting. The French owed their final success to the tactical superiority of their veterans. The Allies lost only 30% of their force, despite the complete rupture of their front. This compares with the losers' 60%

casualties at Blenheim, suggesting that even the unreformed Austrian and Russian armies were more flexible than the armies of Louis XIV. This second defeat, in the heart of his country, persuaded the Austrian Emperor to make peace. Napoleon had knocked Austria out of the war in three month's fighting.

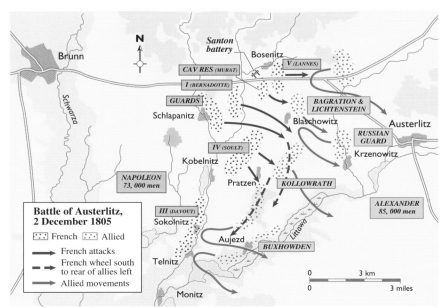

Battle of Austerlitz, 2 December 1805

⋯ French ⋯ Allied
→ French attacks
⇢ French wheel south to rear of allies left
→ Allied movements

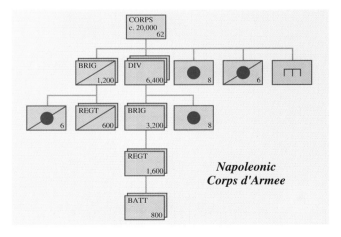

ABOVE: **The French army pioneered the use of permanently formed infantry divisions, assigned to corps d'armée with integral artillery, engineers and cavalry. These all arms formations were capable of resisting superior numbers long enough for neighbouring corps to march to intervene. On the offensive, they could concentrate and deploy faster than their enemies.**

Napoleonic Corps d'Armee

The Peak of Napoleonic Warfare

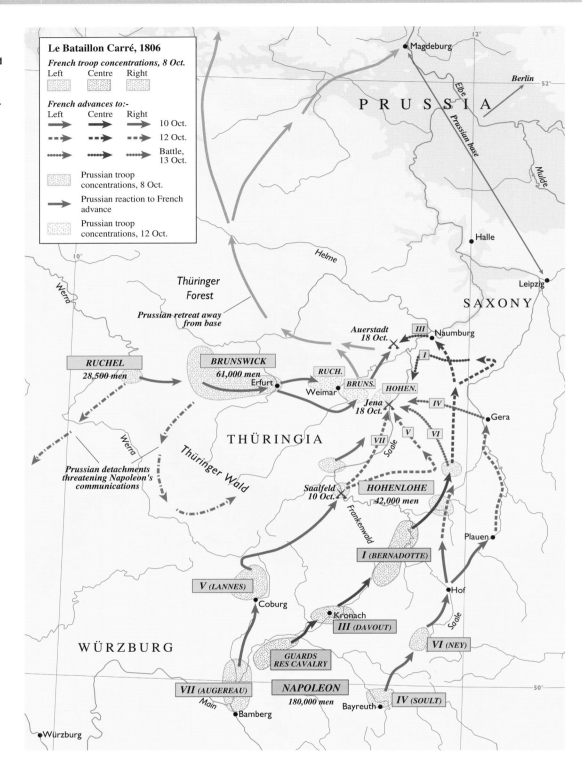

Le Bataillon Carré, 1806

French troop concentrations, 8 Oct.
Left   Centre   Right

French advances to:-
Left   Centre   Right
→ → → 10 Oct.
▸ ▸ ▸ 12 Oct.
••• ••• ••• Battle, 13 Oct.

Prussian troop concentrations, 8 Oct.

Prussian reaction to French advance

Prussian troop concentrations, 12 Oct.

The Grande Armée occupied South Germany after Austerlitz, to oversee creation of the French-dominated Confederation of the Rhine and live at the expense of the inhabitants. In response Prussia occupied Saxony and Hesse-Kassel, north of the Main. The Prussians might have embarrassed Napoleon during the Austerlitz campaign, had they exploited their position on his long northern flank, but they missed their chance. Their advanced position forward of the Elbe, their natural base, was now a liability.

Napoleon used his own position along the River Main to turn the left flank of the Prussians between Erfurt and Jena. The Grande Armée advanced in three columns, each of two corps, forming an advanced guard, two slightly refused wings, and a central reserve. Cavalry divisions covered the front and assured communication between the separate corps. These could remain well closed up as they carried enough bread and brandy for the opening days of the campaign. Napoleon expected a swift decision, after which the troops could spread out to live off the country.

Napoleon's diamond-shaped deployment became known as the *bataillon carré*. It allowed the Grande Armée to move rapidly in any direction, depending on where it found the enemy. No one corps occupied a permanent position. When Napoleon wheeled left to cut off the Prussians from the Elbe, his original Centre pushed on to become the Right. The Left concentrated at Jena, becoming the Advanced Guard as it engaged the nearest Prussian forces. The original Right wing now became the Centre, able to reinforce either wing. The manoeuvre ensured a strategic victory before Napoleon had fought a battle. The Prussians had lost the initiative, and could

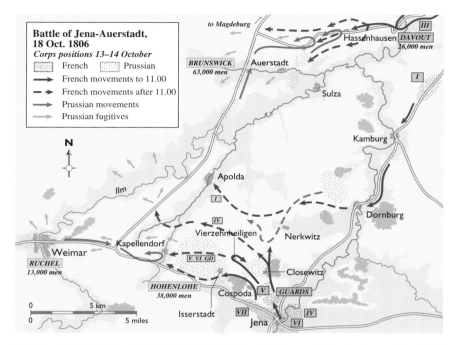

**Battle of Jena-Auerstadt,
18 Oct. 1806**
Corps positions 13–14 October

░ French	░ Prussian

→ French movements to 11.00
--➤ French movements after 11.00
→ Prussian movements
→ Prussian fugitives

to Magdeburg

III *DAVOUT* 26,000 men
Hassenhausen

BRUNSWICK 63,000 men
Auerstadt

I

Sulza

Kamburg

Apolda

I

Dornburg

IV
Vierzehnheiligen
Nerkwitz

Ilm

Kapellendorf

Weimar
RUCHEL 13,000 men

V VI GD

Closewitz

HOHENLOHE 38,000 men
Cospoda
V *GUARDS*

Isserstadt
VII
IV
Jena
VI

0 ___ 5 km
0 ___ 5 miles

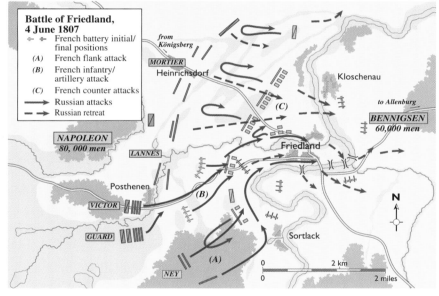

**Battle of Friedland,
4 June 1807**

⚊ French battery initial/final positions
(A) French flank attack
(B) French infantry/artillery attack
(C) French counter attacks
→ Russian attacks
--➤ Russian retreat

from Königsberg

MORTIER
Heinrichsdorf

Kloschenau

to Allenburg

(C)

NAPOLEON 80,000 men

BENNIGSEN 60,000 men

LANNES
Friedland

Posthenen

(B)

VICTOR

GUARD
Sortlack

(A)

NEY

N

0 ___ 2 km
0 ___ 2 miles

Europe, where infantry sank thigh deep in mud, and Imperial Guardsmen shot themselves rather than carry on. The Grande Armée had to fight bloody frontal actions against the traditionally obstinate Russians, whose unpredictable movements sometimes seized the initiative. A Russian descent upon a detached corps at Friedland gave the Emperor the chance of a decisive blow, against a Russian army trapped in a bend of the river Alle. Unable to manoeuvre against the Russian flanks, the French used artillery to blast a hole in their centre. Thirty guns deployed 1,600 yards from the Russian line, and advanced by bounds to sixty paces, firing case shot, the first use of a tactic common in Napoleon's later battles. Pinned against the river, Russian casualties were heavy, persuading the Tsar to seek peace. For the first time Napoleon had failed to gain the type of rapid decisive victory that he needed. The Treaty of Tilsit, signed on a raft on the River Niemen, was the high water mark of his Empire.

BELOW: Napoleon's Grande Armée *was at the height of its power in 1806. At Auerstadt, Morand's superbly drilled infantry fought in column, line, square or as skirmishers, according to the tactical situation.*

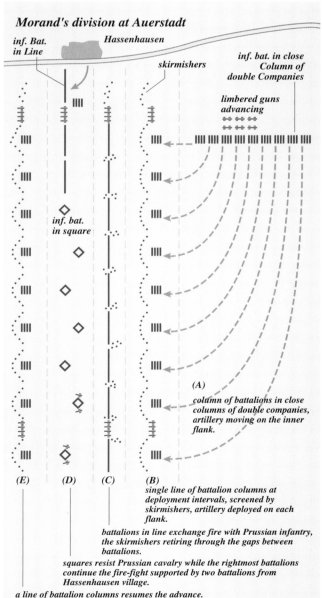

Morand's division at Auerstadt

inf. Bat. in Line   Hassenhausen

skirmishers

inf. bat. in close Column of double Companies

limbered guns advancing

inf. bat. in square

(A)
column of battalions in close columns of double companies, artillery moving on the inner flank.

(E) (D) (C) (B)

single line of battalion columns at deployment intervals, screened by skirmishers, artillery deployed on each flank.

battalions in line exchange fire with Prussian infantry, the skirmishers retiring through the gaps between battalions.

squares resist Prussian cavalry while the rightmost battalions continue the fire-fight supported by two battalions from Hassenhausen village.

a line of battalion columns resumes the advance.

not threaten Napoleon's own communications, because he was so much closer to theirs. They made a dangerous flank march across Napoleon's front to regain the Elbe, their divisions strung out along a single road unlike the French who moved by several roads on a broad front.

Napoleon's left turn brought on the double battle of Jena-Auerstadt. He concentrated at Jena, in case the Prussians tried to break out eastwards. If they beat his Right, it could fall back on the main body; if they beat his Left, Napoleon would lose his own communications. The Centre therefore reinforced the Left, making it unnecessarily powerful. Napoleon's strategic position was so strong that even his mistakes worked to his advantage. The Prussians outnumbered Davout's Corps on the right at Auerstadt 2:1 but he beat them off. Bernadotte's Corps then intercepted the Prussian withdrawal near Apolda, converting it into a rout.

On the battlefield the French maintained their tactical superiority. Most of their troops were still veterans trained at Boulogne. The Prussians adhered to Frederick the Great's linear tactics, but without his eye for ground. Prussian infantry stood in the open for hours under French skirmisher fire, until only a few files remained ineffectively loading and firing, surrounded by their dead. At Auerstadt Davout's Corps used every variant of line, column and square to hold their own, and even gain ground. The devastating consequences of the French victory made clear the implicit message of Marengo: an army losing its lines of communications and suffering a decisive defeat would be ruined.

The large French army quickly overran the small kingdom of Prussia, but resistance continued in Poland and East Prussia, with Russian help. Strategic success eluded Napoleon in the roadless wastes of Eastern

The Nelson Touch

Sea warfare in the 1790s underwent no revolution comparable to that ashore. Occasional battles and invasion scares punctuated years of blockade and privateering in a pattern familiar from the 1690s. A century of Anglo-French naval rivalry was about to reach a climax.

The French Revolution showed the irrelevance of the Nation in Arms concept to organizing a fleet in wartime. Eighty percent of French naval officers emigrated, leaving ships and dockyards in chaos. France's main naval ally, Spain, could never recruit enough trained seamen to man her extensive inventory of well-found ships. Half-trained crews could not match the rapid broadsides of well-drilled British seamen-gunners. The Allies' tactical inferiority encouraged a preference for pursuing strategic aims while avoiding a decisive battle. The Glorious First of June (1 June 1794) appeared to justify this approach. The British had the better of the fighting, but the French secured a vital grain convoy, saving the Revolution.

The Battle of St Vincent underlined the tactical value of British seamanship. Sir John Jervis exploited a gap in a Spanish fleet to achieve local superiority of numbers. Outnumbered 2:1 overall, he captured four ships, breaking off the action before numbers began to tell. Nelson repeated Jervis' tactical concentration at the Nile, against a French squadron at anchor, reversing the strategic balance of power in the Mediterranean.

Trafalgar was the culmination of this series of British successes. Nelson concentrated all his 27 ships against 23 of the combined Franco-Spanish strength of 33. He attacked in two divisions to break the enemy line, cutting off the centre and rear. Nelson had encouraged his captains to use their initiative, break through the enemy line, and engage its leeward side. This allowed them to rake their opponents at close range, and prevented the usual French tactic of disengaging downwind. The resulting attrition was devastating: 18 Franco-Spanish ships were taken or sunk. Nelson resolved the problem of ships moving at right angles to their axis of fire by attacking head-on before turning into line to open fire. A fleet manoeuvring in this way had an offensive capability similar to that of armies using battalion columns for movement and line for fire, as long as the defender's fire was too ill-directed to cripple the leading ships. A less flexible opponent could only choose between flight or destruction.

Trafalgar revealed the weakness of the French operational approach. Nelson's tactical victory resolved the strategic problem that the Royal Navy had faced since 1793. While the British successfully blockaded the French and their Hispano-Dutch allies, the latter held the strategic initiative. Secure in fortified bases from Texel to Toulon, they could break out whenever storms drove blockading British squadrons off station. The British could not tell where the escaping ships had gone, so the only safe response was to mass in the Channel to secure the home base. This might expose other strategically vulnerable points.

Napoleon's plan for the Trafalgar campaign sought to exploit this British weakness by concentrating his fleets in the West Indies. This threat to a vital economic region might

Atlantic

Ocean

Ballinamuck
1796

Bantry Bay
1796

✕ **Glorious First of June**
28 May–1 June 1794

50°

Villeneuve's return from West Indies (July 1805) and failure to join French fleet at Brest

Isle de Groix
23 July 1795

Ferrrol squadron joins Channel fleet

✕ **Cape Finisterre**
22 July 1805

21

8

●Ferrol *12*

●Corunna

●Vigo

Santander
1813

40°

1807

Lisbon● *Togus*

Douro

●Madrid

S P A I N

✕ **Cape St Vincent**
14 Feb 1797

Madeira

6

Cadiz
12 July 1801

✕Cadiz

●Gibraltar
●**British**

Cartagena

6

Trafalgar
21 Oct. 1805

✕ ✕**British**

Algeciras
6 July 1801

7

Nelson's return from West Indies and junction with Channel fleet

M O R O C C O

1797 🌀 *Canary Islands*
Tenerife

30°

Battle of Cape St. Vincent, 14 Feb. 1797

British attack, noon

British fleet passes between Spanish main body and their leeward division

British frigates

C

A

Spanish lee division raked by British fire sheers off

D

Spanish fleet apparently bears up to pass astern of British to join their leeward division

- Spanish warships
- British warships
- Rear Admiral Sir Peter Parker in HMS Prince George
- Admiral Sir John Jervis in HMS Victory
- Commodore Horatio Nelson in HMS Captain

B

HMS Culloden tacking

LEFT AND RIGHT:
At the Battle of Cape St Vincent, Admiral Jervis cut through the poorly formed Spanish line. Nelson anticipated Jervis's signal to cut off the Spanish van; the Spanish captains largely ignored their admiral's orders to double the British rear. The result was a close-range action centred around Nelson's *Captain*. Four Spanish ships were taken, two by Nelson, the superior rate of fire achieved by British gunners compensating for lack of numbers.

N

A

HMS Captain engaging the Santissima Trinidad

B

C

HMS Culloden

Spanish main body hauling their wind onto the larboard tack to escape HMS Culloden and HMS Captain

D

Sir Peter Parker's division supporting the attack on the Spanish rear

E

Sir John Jervis' division tacking in succession

The crisis– about 1PM

Spanish lee division driven of

F

Naval warfare, 1791–1814

naval bases with numbers of operational battleships
- **9** French and Allies
- **6** Spanish

naval bases with date of occupation
- *1813* British

naval interventions ashore
- French
- British

naval movemets
- French
- British

naval actions
- French victory
- British victory
- Russian victory

- **8** British blockading squadrons, March 1805 with number of battleships
- British naval concentration to cover English Channel, August 1805
- direction of prevailing winds

draw off enough British ships to give the combined fleets numerical superiority in the Channel. However, Napoleon's naval forces lacked the Grande Armée's professional quality, and he did not allow for the greater friction of war at sea, with its variable weather and erratic communications. Villeneuve at Ferrol (29 ships) proved unwilling to fight the British Channel squadron (27) to link up with French warships at Brest (21). His subsequent attempt to return to the Mediterranean gave Nelson the chance to put an end to French strategic machinations, by destroying the French fleet in combat.

The Continental System was Napoleon's admission of defeat at sea. The extent of his empire allowed him to reverse the British blockade by excluding them from European ports. His efforts to close gaps in the system exacerbated relations with non-French regions of the Empire, and alienated powerful neutrals such as Russia. The British responded by developing markets outside Europe. Maritime supremacy brought prosperity. The British subsidized opposition to Napoleon, while mounting expeditions against the periphery of the Empire, at Copenhagen, Sicily, and Spain. The Royal Navy's aggressive combat strategy had given the British strategic freedom. The limited risk strategy of the French had lost them the ability to pursue even restricted strategic goals at sea.

The Archduke and the Emperor

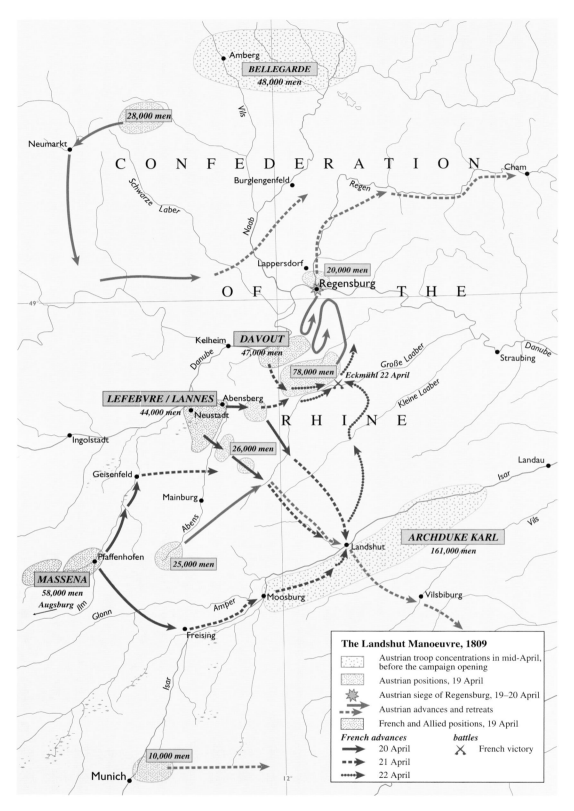

Amberg

BELLEGARDE
48,000 men

28,000 men

Neumarkt

C O N F E D E R A T I O N

Burglengenfeld

Cham

Regen

Schwarze Laber

Naab

Vils

Lappersdorf

20,000 men

Regensburg

O F   T H E

Kelheim

DAVOUT
47,000 men

Danube

Danube

Straubing

78,000 men   Eckmühl 22 April

Große Laaber

LEFEBVRE / LANNES
44,000 men   Abensberg

Neustadt

R H I N E

Kleine Laaber

Ingolstadt

26,000 men

Landau

Geisenfeld

Isar

Mainburg

Abens

Pfaffenhofen

25,000 men

Landshut

ARCHDUKE KARL
161,000 men

Vils

MASSENA
58,000 men
Augsburg

Ilm

Glonn

Amper

Moosburg

Vilsbiburg

Freising

Isar

The Landshut Manoeuvre, 1809

Austrian troop concentrations in mid-April, before the campaign opening

Austrian positions, 19 April

Austrian siege of Regensburg, 19–20 April

Austrian advances and retreats

French and Allied positions, 19 April

French advances   *battles*

→   20 April   ✕   French victory

- - →   21 April

····→   22 April

10,000 men

Munich

LEFT: In 1809 the Austrian army attacked the French forces in southern Germany, still dispersed in their winter quarters. The attempt to concentrate against Marshal Davout failed, however, and Napoleon hurried over from Paris to direct operations. The Archduke was eventually defeated at Eckmühl and withdrew, but the French no longer enjoyed clear-cut tactical superiority.

RIGHT: The Austrians demonstrated just how much they had improved at Wagram: although defeated by 6 July, with 45,000 casualties, it had been a 'near run thing' and Napoleon's loss of 34,000 cut deeply into the ranks of his veterans. The *Grande Armée* would never be quite the same again.

The Archduke Karl introduced new tactical formations that resembled the French battalion column and encouraged skirmishing. The reactionary Hapsburgs mobilized popular support half-heartedly, raising a *Landwehr* and volunteer units in Vienna. The Austrian army reached its peak strength for the Napoleonic Wars.

The Austrian attack on Napoleon's Bavarian ally without a declaration of war was symptomatic of the new circumstances. For once Napoleon did not have the initiative, and was absent in Paris. French troops were unready, deployed either side of the Danube, in separate masses around Augsburg and Nuremberg. The Austrians almost cut the Grande Armée in two by seizing a central position on the Danube, between Regensburg and Ingolstadt, but they were too slow. Napoleon took direct command on 16 April, and promptly showed the power of the *bataillon carré* on the defensive. Drawing in his flanks, the Emperor cast a net around the advancing Austrians. He broke through their over-stretched centre about Abensberg, and drove their left back across the Isar at Landshut. He then turned against the Austrian right at Eckmuhl, but the Archduke Karl narrowly escaped over the Danube. Napoleon had demanded much of his troops to rectify the ill-organized start of the campaign, and his infantry were too exhausted for pursuit. The Austrian left wing also escaped encirclement at Landshut. Enveloping columns rarely achieved what was hoped of them. Isolated behind enemy lines, they moved with a caution justified by Davout's narrow escape at Auerstadt. For the first time Napoleon failed to begin a campaign with a knockout blow comparable to Marengo, Ulm, or Jena.

Napoleon marched on Vienna, believing that occupation of the capital would bring peace. He underestimated the Austrians, and had to fight two set-piece battles outside the city, the Danube at his back. Napoleon suffered his first defeat at Aspern-Essling (21-22 May), and was

The Austrian campaign of April-July 1809 saw a change in the scale of Napoleonic warfare. The Emperor manoeuvred with customary brilliance, but the growing size of his armies stretched even his genius. At the same time the Grande Armée was losing its qualitative edge. Raw conscripts replaced the veterans of Austerlitz and Jena, eroding tactical flexibility. Allied troops replaced native Frenchmen, undermining morale.

Armies on both sides exceeded 100,000 on the battlefield, requiring more time and attrition to reach a decision. Napoleon had to fight a pair of two-day battles, at Aspern-Essling and Wagram, after five gruelling days of campaigning in Bavaria (19-23 April). The ideas of the French Revolution had spread to Germany. National antipathy to French exploitation provoked abortive risings, and even an assassination attempt against the Emperor.

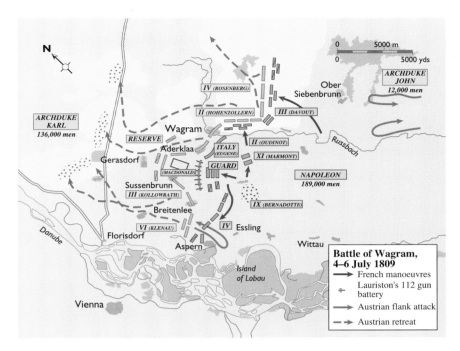

Battle of Wagram,
4–6 July 1809
→ French manoeuvres
≠ Lauriston's 112 gun battery
→ Austrian flank attack
--→ Austrian retreat

lucky to save his army. He recrossed the river in greater strength on the night of 4-5 July. Rivers make poor obstacles. Large Austrian armies twice failed to prevent the French crossing a large swiftly flowing river under their noses.

The Archduke Karl left a three-mile gap in his centre, hoping to catch Napoleon in a Cannae-style pincer movement, while the Archduke John approached from the east. Napoleon massed in a central position, shifting reserves from flank to flank, pushing his right forward to separate the main Austrian army from Archduke John. The French failed to penetrate Karl's weak centre on 5 July, and on the 6th his counter-attack nearly reached the vital pontoon bridges. Napoleon redeployed his left flank to protect them, covered by a battery of 112

guns, the largest concentration of artillery seen to date.

Napoleon's right drove the Austrian line into a vulnerable Z-shaped salient, allowing Macdonald's Corps, the last French reserve, to batter through the Archduke's centre, formed in a huge hollow square. The Archduke Karl had numerous reserves, but he used them to cover a phased retreat. A soldier of the *ancien régime*, his main aim was to preserve the dynasty. He was not a gambler like Napoleon, who was reduced to his last two regiments of Old Guard by the end of the battle.

After sixteen hours of fighting the French were too exhausted to pursue. Their casualties were enormous, 24% including 40 generals. Napoleon had not blocked the enemy retreat, as he had done before

Marengo or Jena, so the defeated Austrians escaped. The peace terms, however, cost them a fifth of their population. Even a partial defeat now spelled national ruin. The Austrian army never deployed 150,000 men again during the Napoleonic Wars, but it had showed that strategic insight and tactical ability were no longer a French monopoly.

ABOVE: Bavarian cavalry. The king of Bavaria changed sides after 1805, becoming a French ally until Napoleon's defeat in 1813 prompted another change of heart. Bavaria was attacked by Austria in 1809, initiating the first campaign that Napoleon failed to win with his usual decisiveness. However, despite heavy losses and one outright defeat, Napoleon imposed another peace treaty on Vienna by the end of the year.

The Guns of Napoleon

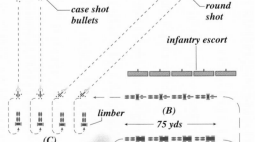

(A) Column of Route: A half battery of four guns with their ammunition waggons approaches the firing position behind natural cover. Artillery could march faster than infantry, but was strung out and incapable of defending itself.

(B) Column of Sub-divisions: The unit closes up into a gun line and waggon line, and moves rapidly into the firing position from a flank, to present a shallow target to enemy fire.

(C) Unlimbered and in action: The gunners open fire with case shot to clear their front, and with round shot to the flank. The long narrow danger space of round shot made enfilade fire particularly effective. The individual guns are well spaced to prevent accidents when firing to a flank, while the wagons take cover to the rear, in a fold in the ground.

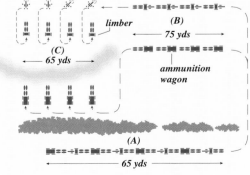

LEFT: Napoleon was a gunner by training, and massed batteries of field guns were his preferred method of execution on the battlefield. The tactical ideal was to use cavalry to force the enemy infantry into square formations, then heavy guns to engage these dense, unmanoeuvrable targets.

Tactical decline –
The massive column

MacDonald's corps (21 battalions / 8000 men)

8 battalions in line – one behind the other

7 battalions in column of companies

6 battalions in column of companies

supported by: 112 guns and 2 cavalry divisions

ABOVE: The decline in tactical skill of the French infantry led to increasingly heavy columns of foot soldiers eschewing all manoeuvre and relying on sheer weight of numbers to break through. It was in this hollow oblong formation that Marshal Macdonald led his division into the attack at Wagram: preceded by a murderous artillery barrage, he broke through, then drove off a counter-attack by Austrian cavalry.

The 'Spanish Ulcer'

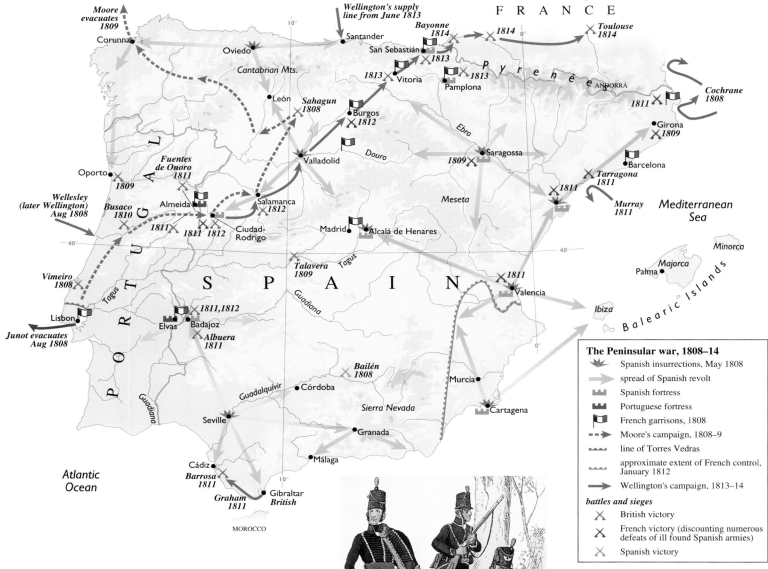

The Peninsular war, 1808–14
- ☙ Spanish insurrections, May 1808
- → spread of Spanish revolt
- 🏰 Spanish fortress
- 🏰 Portuguese fortress
- 🏳 French garrisons, 1808
- ••►• Moore's campaign, 1808–9
- •••• line of Torres Vedras
- •••• approximate extent of French control, January 1812
- ➜ Wellington's campaign, 1813–14

battles and sieges
- ✕ British victory
- ✕ French victory (discounting numerous defeats of ill found Spanish armies)
- ✕ Spanish victory

ABOVE: Napoleon's attempt to impose his brother as King of Spain triggered a war of attrition in the Peninsula. Although Spanish field armies proved brittle, the French had little answer to the ensuing guerrilla war which pitted them against another nation in arms. The British exploited their maritime superiority to sustain an army ashore, a force poised to take advantage of French weakness when Napoleon invaded Russia.

The Napoleonic military system failed comprehensively in Spain. The country is large, divided by mountain ranges that run across the path of a French invader. There was no agricultural surplus like that in Central Europe. Large armies starved. Good roads were few, hampering strategic combinations. Fortresses like Badajoz and Cuidad Rodrigo dominated such communications as there were, and could not be bypassed, giving sieges an unusual significance. A conservative and xenophobic people found ideals of liberty and fraternity unattractive, depriving the French of the political support they had received in Italy and Germany.

Elsewhere in Europe, occupation of the capital soon brought a country to order. Spanish central government was weak and local particularism ensured that resistance continued regardless of the fall of Madrid. The French occupied much of the country before fighting broke out, so had to face all the defensive resources of the country at once: the armed forces, the people, and the country itself. They suffered an unprecedented disaster at Bailén (19 July 1808); 20,000 French troops surrendered to 35,000

ABOVE: An officer and man from the 95th Rifle Regiment and (right) a soldier of the 60th Regiment. These specialist troops were equipped with the Baker rifle. Various armies of the Napoleonic wars introduced units of rifle-armed troops, but only the British enjoyed much success with them. Although far more accurate than a musket, rifles had a slower rate of fire and would not come into their own until this problem was solved.

Spanish levies. The Grande Armée became involved in a savage war of atrocity and reprisal that denied Napoleon the quick victory he needed to preserve his freedom of action elsewhere in Europe. Even so the centres of Spanish patriotic resistance would have fallen to French repression, or

the more imaginative pacification measures pursued by Suchet in Catalonia, had it not been for British intervention.

Britain's army was small, but it stopped the French finally crushing the guerrillas. They in turn prevented the French concentrating against the British. When Massena invaded Portugal in 1810, he could only use 70,000 out of the 300,000 French troops in the Peninsula. The guerrillas tied down the rest. The British commander Sir Arthur Wellesley, later Duke of Wellington, exploited British financial and maritime strength to organize a supply train of Spanish muleteers and feed his army. He avoided alienating the local population by foraging, as the French had done. When Napoleon withdrew his best troops for Russia, Wellington went on the offensive, using sea power to switch his base from Lisbon to ports in northern Spain. He thus retained his logistic advantage, despite the French shortening their own communications by retreating towards France.

British experience in North America had taught them to screen their close order lines of infantry with skirmishers, many of them locally raised. This combination neutralized French superiority on the battle-field. British commanders sheltered their main battle line from French artillery fire on the reverse slopes of hills. They exploited difficult terrain and superior numbers of light infantry, to ambush French attacks, bringing French columns under close range musketry, followed by a prompt bayonet attack. Where this failed to break the French, a costly firefight could result. At Albuera the British Fusilier brigade suffered more than 50% losses in a 20-

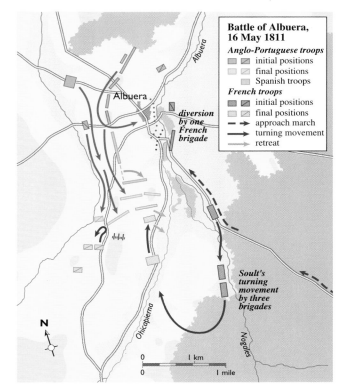

Battle of Albuera, 16 May 1811

Anglo-Portuguese troops
- ☐ initial positions
- ☐ final positions
- ☐ Spanish troops

French troops
- ☐ initial positions
- ☐ final positions
- �→ approach march
- → turning movement
- → retreat

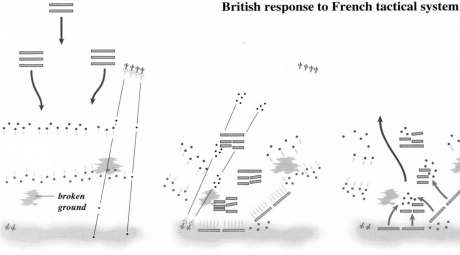

Battle of Salamanca, 22 July 1812
Anglo-Portuguese troops
- → lines of attack
- --→ concealed march of Pakenham's division and two cavalry brigades

French troops
- --→ approach march
- → counter attacks
- ⬭→ final position and retreat

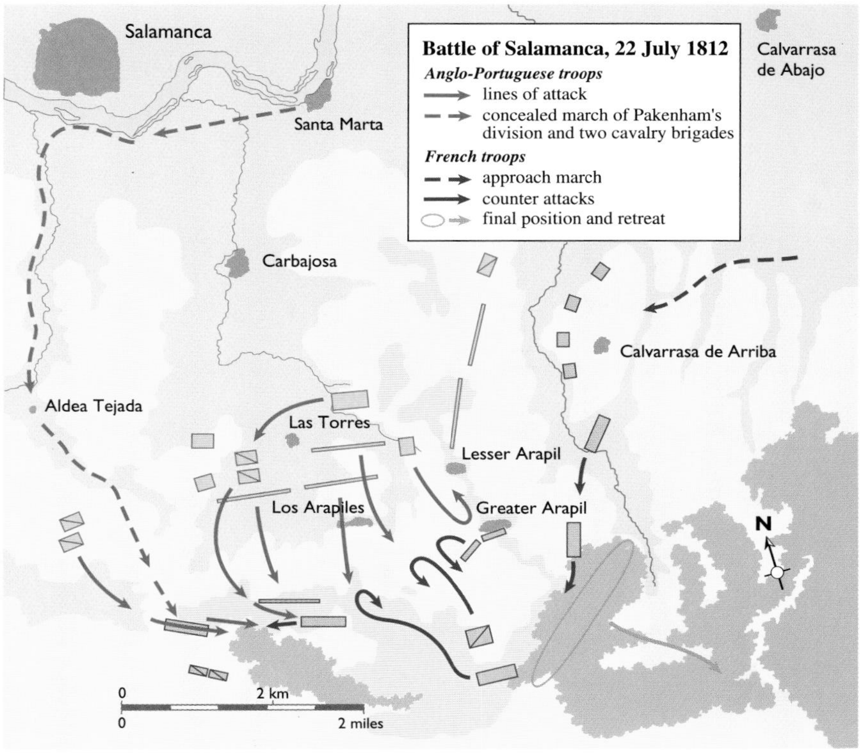

ABOVE: At Salamanca, Wellington duped the French into attacking in the mistaken belief he was retreating. Marmont's army was caught out by the British assault; he and his successor were both wounded and the leaderless French army disintegrated.

than Napoleon's strategic masterpieces at Marengo or Jena. Despite his humiliating defeat, Marmont was able to regroup his army, and drive Wellington back to the Portuguese frontier in October 1812. Wellington lacked Napoleon's unlimited reserves of manpower, so he could never risk throwing his army across the enemy's rear. He depended on a Frederician strategy of attrition to wear down French strength, assisted by the country and the guerrillas.

BELOW: Battles in the Peninsula assumed a disagreeably familiar pattern for the French: the battalion column that had brought them so many victories in central Europe was cut to pieces by British regiments fighting in 'old-fashioned' line formation.

minute exchange of fire. In the same battle French cavalry annihilated another British brigade by attacking it in flank, showing the dangers of advancing in line without cavalry support.

Unlike Napoleon, Wellington did not depend on grand strategic combinations. His methods derived from an older tradition, based on direct control of formations by the commander. Like Frederick the Great, Wellington relied on his personal eye for country to exploit enemy mistakes. Marmont had outmanoeuvred him in July 1812, forcing Wellington to retreat from Tordesillas on Salamanca. As the two armies raced side by side for a strategic river crossing, Wellington detected a gap in the French column, isolating their leading division. Within minutes he had organized an overwhelming attack on the head of the French column, not dissimilar to Frederick's demolition of the Austrian left at Leuthen. At Salamanca, however, both armies were moving, showing how dynamic battlefields had become with the general adoption of the divisional system.

Wellington had not cut off Marmont's retreat, so his victory was less decisive

British response to French tactical system

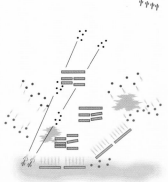
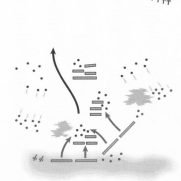

(A) The British deploy their main infantry line behind the crest of a hill to avoid French artillery fire. Their own skirmish line neutralises the French skirmishers only retiring before the advancing French columns.

(B) The broken ground forces the French columns to bunch as they approach the crest line. Here they meet a masked battery which rakes them with case shot at close range. The British infantry line advances and pours a single volley in the head and flanks of the French column.

(C) The British charge the shaken columns with the bayonet, driving them back down the slope.

The Invasion of Russia

ABOVE: **Napoleon's invasion of Russia ended with the most infamous retreat in military history and the loss of 90 per cent of his men. The Emperor hurried back to Paris, leaving his marshals to recover what they could of the army, but the spell was broken. Although Napoleon would succeed in raising new armies of conscripts, French tactical superiority was gone for good.**

All the factors that vitiated Napoleon's war in Spain applied in Russia, but to a greater degree. The sparse population produced no agricultural surplus, and was immune to Revolutionary ideals. There were few roads, all bad. It was impossible to outmanoeuvre Russian armies, or to feed the huge forces that Napoleon committed. He took three weeks' rations for 400,000 men, but after two months had yet to defeat a Russian army decisively. His own forces had lost 150,000 men from sickness and desertion, a third of their strength. The disastrous outcome of the campaign is popularly ascribed to the Russian winter, but far more men were lost during the warm summer months of 1812.

Despite his numerical advantage, Napoleon could not force the Russians to fight. An army far larger than those that had dominated Italy or Germany was lost in Russia. The Grande Armée of 1812 no more dominated the country than English raiding parties controlled France in the Hundred Years War. The size of the theatre of war made it impossible to coordinate enveloping manoeuvres against the scattered Russian forces. Lack of roads channelled Napoleon's advance down the single road to Moscow. The *bataillon carré* had no chance to throw its net around a helpless adversary. Battles at Smolensk and Valutino turned into costly frontal attacks on rearguards.

The Russians had implausibly hoped to lure Napoleon to his doom before the entrenched camp at Drissa, but its deficiencies became obvious even to the Tsar. He ordered a lengthy retreat that gave Clausewitz his classic example of how the defensive brings into play all the geographical, political, and military resources of a country. Long marches sapped the Grande Armée's strength; peace with Turkey released Russian troops from the south; patriotic feeling inspired partisans angered by French depredations.

The Battle of Borodino marked the climactic point of 20 years of Revolutionary and Napoleonic violence. Participants rated other battles as peacetime manoeuvres by comparison. Neither side showed any tactical finesse: 'the issue depended upon the exertion of power rather than the delicacy of manoeuvre or the caprices of fortune'. Napoleon let the crucial moment of the battle slip through his fingers, foreshadowing his lethargy at Waterloo. He refused to make even a limited turning movement around the Russian left, and launched a frontal attack on a Russian army, in a prepared position, at the gates of Moscow. The Russian infantry fought in dense columns that attracted heavy losses, prematurely exhausting their reserves. Much of their artillery went unused after the early death of the reserve artillery commander.

Neither side had the formal staff system needed to control the huge numbers of men deployed. Napoleon had always discouraged decentralization, while the Russian commander Kutuzov ignored the Yellow Book, the Russian staff manual of the day. Casualties were appropriately heavy. The Russians lost more men at Borodino than any other modern army suffered in one action, until the first day of the Somme in July 1916. Nevertheless the battle failed to shake Kutuzov's resolve, or that of the Tsar.

As in 1809 Napoleon mistook a capital for the enemy's centre of gravity. The fall of Moscow did not mean the collapse of Russia, which depended on the army and the will of the Tsar. When these proved unshaken, the French had no alternative but retreat. The decisive battle of the campaign was not Borodino, but Maloyaroslavets, which persuaded Napoleon to withdraw by the Smolensk road, swept bare of supplies during the advance. Poor discipline prevented sensible preparation for the retreat, and wasted such supplies as Napoleon had collected along the route, for example at Smolensk.

Kutuzov hung upon the French flank, following a logistic strategy similar to that used by the Austrians in Bohemia in 1744 against Frederick the Great. He avoided a general action, but Cossacks

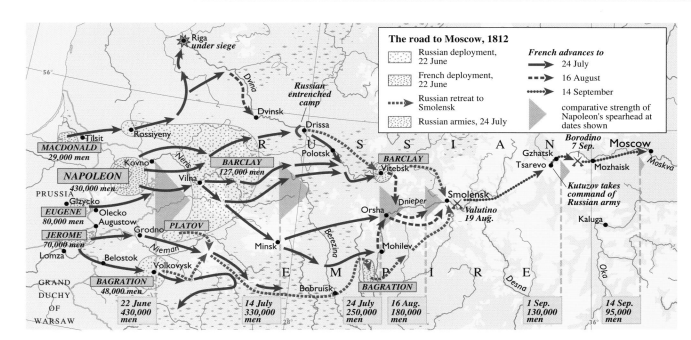

The road to Moscow, 1812

- Russian deployment, 22 June
- French deployment, 22 June
- Russian retreat to Smolensk
- Russian armies, 24 July

French advances to
→ 24 July
⇢ 16 August
····> 14 September

comparative strength of Napoleon's spearhead at dates shown

MACDONALD 29,000 men
NAPOLEON 430,000 men
EUGENE 80,000 men
JEROME 70,000 men
BARCLAY 127,000 men
BARCLAY
BAGRATION 48,000 men
PLATOV
BAGRATION
Borodino 7 Sep.
Kutuzov takes command of Russian army
Valutino – 19 Aug.

22 June 430,000 men
14 July 330,000 men
24 July 250,000 men
16 Aug. 180,000 men
1 Sep. 130,000 men
14 Sep. 95,000 men

prevented the French resting or dispersing to forage, while infuriated peasants murdered French stragglers. As in Spain the Nation in Arms had aroused a People's War.

Fresh Russian forces threatened Napoleon's line of retreat, preventing him from wintering at Smolensk. The pincers met at the Beresina. A handful of ragged heroes cut their way out of the trap, but the Grande Armée's veteran cadres were lost, making it impossible to train the next year's conscripts. The cavalry, which required years' training, never recovered from its losses in Russia. This was a serious blow for Napoleon's aggressive battlefield tactics which depended on superior cavalry and artillery to sustain his increasingly inexperienced infantry.

RIGHT: At Borodino the combination of massed artillery and clumsy infantry tactics led to the biggest loss of life in a single day's battle until the First World War. Once again, the Russians lost a third of their men and were defeated, but it was a Pyrrhic victory for Napoleon who entered Moscow at the head of a sadly depleted army.

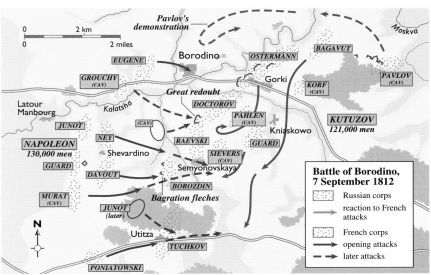

Battle of Borodino, 7 September 1812

- Russian corps
- reaction to French attacks
- French corps
- opening attacks
- later attacks

Pavlov's demonstration
EUGENE
Borodino
OSTERMANN
BAGAVUT
GROUCHY (CAV)
PAVLOV (CAV)
Gorki
KORF (CAV)
Great redoubt
DOCTOROV
Latour Manbourg
Kalatsha
PAHLEN (CAV)
KUTUZOV 121,000 men
JUNOT
(CAV)
Kniaskowo
NAPOLEON 130,000 men
NEY
RAEVSKI
GUARD
Shevardino
SIEVERS (CAV)
GUARD
DAVOUT
Semyonovskaya
MURAT (CAV)
BOROZDIN
JUNOT (later)
Bagration fleches
N
Utitza
TUCHKOV
PONIATOWSKI

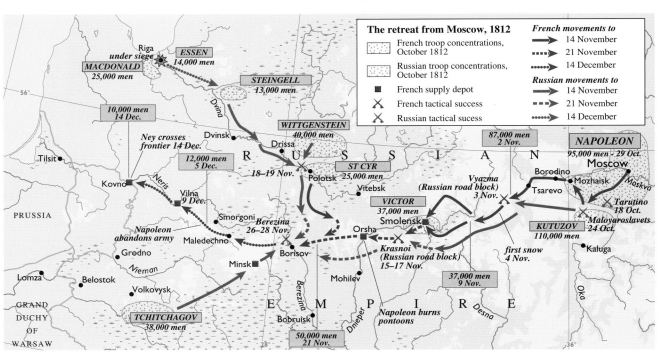

The retreat from Moscow, 1812

- French troop concentrations, October 1812
- Russian troop concentrations, October 1812
- French supply depot
- French tactical success
- Russian tactical sucess

French movements to
→ 14 November
····> 21 November
····> 14 December

Russian movements to
→ 14 November
⇢ 21 November
····> 14 December

MACDONALD 25,000 men
ESSEN 14,000 men
STEINGELL 13,000 men
WITTGENSTEIN 40,000 men
10,000 men 14 Dec.
Ney crosses frontier 14 Dec.
12,000 men 5 Dec.
ST CYR 25,000 men
87,000 men 2 Nov.
NAPOLEON 95,000 men – 29 Oct.
VICTOR 37,000 men
Vyazma (Russian road block) 3 Nov.
Tarutino 18 Oct.
Napoleon abandons army
Berezina 26–28 Nov.
KUTUZOV 110,000 men
Maloyaroslavets 24 Oct.
first snow 4 Nov.
Krasnoi (Russian road block) 15–17 Nov.
Napoleon burns pontoons
37,000 men 9 Nov.
TCHITCHAGOV 38,000 men
50,000 men 21 Nov.

The Triumph of Numbers

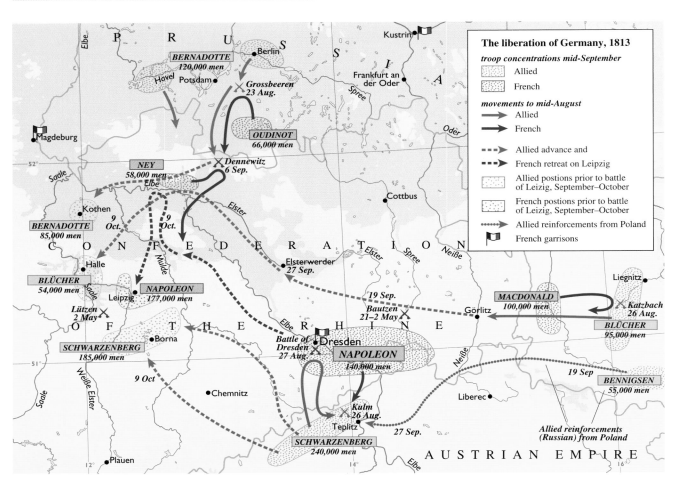

LEFT: In 1813 the Russian, Austrian and Prussian armies avoided battle with the Emperor himself whenever they could, preferring to fight his marshals. Even when Napoleon brought them to battle, his weak cavalry arm proved unable to exploit his hard-won victories.

Napoleon rejoined the remnants of the Grande Armée in April 1813, with a new army of 200,000 conscripts. His last campaign in Germany began with a string of classic victories at Lutzen, Bautzen, and Dresden. The next 12 months, however, saw the initiative pass to his enemies, as they grew in number, and found ways of surviving, if not defeating, the Emperor's devastating blows.

Critics see Bautzen as a perfectly conceived envelopment, ruined by inept sub-ordinates, but there were deeper reasons for the indecisiveness of these actions. Ill-trained French cavalry were incapable of reconnaissance, shock action, or even staying on their horses. A numerous cavalry covered Allied retreats into Silesia or, after Austria joined the coalition, into Bohemia. The Allies exploited the weakness of the strategy of the Central Position, which cannot force a reluctant enemy to fight, if he has room to withdraw. After Dresden the Allies even destroyed an incautiously pursuing French column at Kulm.

By the autumn of 1813 large armies threatened Napoleon from three sides. Allied strategy recognized Napoleon's superior battlefield skills by avoiding action with the Emperor. The Allies concentrated against his subordinates, superior numbers beating them at Grossbeeren, the Katzbach, and Dennewitz. The French had lost their tactical edge. Allied infantry were at least as good as the French conscripts at deploying skirmishers and battalion columns. Where both sides used similar weapons and tactics with equal skill, Clausewitz was right to identify numbers as the main determinant of victory. Gradually the Allies closed the circle around Napoleon, who fell back on Leipzig, a more central position than Dresden, further from Allied sanctuaries in Silesia and Bohemia. The Allies were close enough together now for mutual support in a battle. Relying on the recent harvest to feed his troops, Blücher moved west of Leipzig, surrounding Napoleon, who lacked the space to manoeuvre against one enemy force at a time. The Allies could bring their superior numbers into play.

The four-day engagement of Leipzig was the largest battle fought before the First World War. It exemplifies Clausewitz's vision of modern battle as a drawn out, smouldering process that slowly burns up armies. There was no great tac-

RIGHT: Leipzig was the largest battle of the Napoleonic wars, on a scale that even the Emperor could not control. Some 185,000 French and allied troops held off nearly 300,000 Russian, Austrian, Prussian and Swedish soldiers until the premature demoliton of the Elster bridge turned a fighting retreat into disaster. French losses were around 30,000 with another 30,000 captured; their opponents lost over 50,000 men.

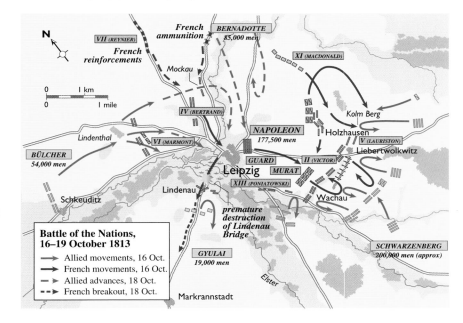

tical breakthrough at Leipzig, but the French artillery ran out of ammunition, and a whole corps of Saxons changed sides. Over half the Grande Armée escaped, showing the difficulty of annihilating a well-articulated army, but poor French staffwork led to heavy losses when the key bridge was blown up prematurely.

The brilliance of Napoleon's tactics in the 1814 campaign in France underlines the gulf between his military and political talents. He had refused reasonable peace terms in November 1813, and was not fighting for any rational political end. The Allies, on the other hand, achieved unprecedented solidarity, understanding how Napoleon's military success at Ulm, Jena, and Wagram had depended on their political disunity. Acting together the reactionary powers could achieve numerical superiority without adopting radical ideas about the Nation in Arms. Only the Prussians dramatically increased the proportion of their manpower under arms. The Austrians sidelined their *Landwehr*, while the Russians remained irremediably feudal. Numbers mattered because the discontinuous fronts of separate army corps left room for surplus numbers to operate, while improved staffwork deployed them to better effect. Radetzky had started a Staff College in Vienna, while Blücher and Gneisenau had invented a command style that would bring Prussian armies a century of victory.

Allied strategy resembled that of 1813. Three large armies invaded France, from separate directions. They requisitioned supplies freely, and carried more in wagons, making them independent of lines of communication. Their wide frontage allowed them to change their bases during the campaign, inflicting a rare strategic surprise on Napoleon. The Emperor occupied a central position between the Seine and Marne, which he skilfully exploited to

inflict heavy losses upon the Allies. During the 'Five Days' (10-14 February 1814), he scattered Blücher's army, inflicting 9,000 casualties for only 2,000 French. However, Napoleon fatally underestimated his opponents' resolve. Marching east against Schwarzenberg's communications, expect-

ing to precipitate a panic-stricken withdrawal, Napoleon left the Allies between himself and Paris. With nothing left behind them to lose, the Allies marched on Paris to dictate peace. The armies of reaction had achieved what they set out to do in 1792.

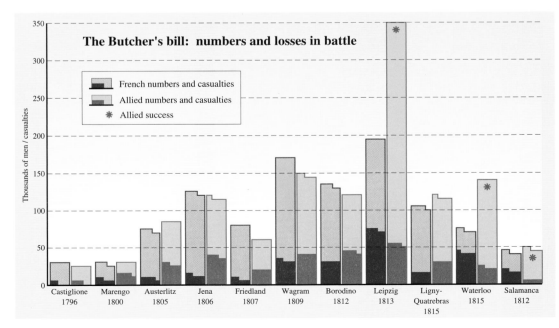

RIGHT: Increased populations and larger agricultural surpluses enabled nations in arms to field the biggest armies yet seen. Battles became far more frequent during the Napoleonic wars, but great political results seldom stemmed from a single engagement.

The Butcher's bill: numbers and losses in battle

French numbers and casualties
Allied numbers and casualties
✳ Allied success

Castiglione 1796 · Marengo 1800 · Austerlitz 1805 · Jena 1806 · Friedland 1807 · Wagram 1809 · Borodino 1812 · Leipzig 1813 · Ligny-Quatrebras 1815 · Waterloo 1815 · Salamanca 1812

ABOVE: His army reduced to more manageable proportions by catastrophic losses in Germany, Napoleon stunned his opponents in 1814 by the speed with which he struck at each invasion force in turn. However, even this tour de force could not prevent the fall of Paris and his eventual capitulation.

Napoleon at Bay, 1814

Allied approach and subsequent lines of communication, January
→ Blücher (Prussian)
→ Schwarzenberg (Russian)

advances early February
→ Blücher
→ Schwarzenberg
→ Napoleon

battles
✕ French victory ✕ Allied victory

main troop concentrations
▥ Blücher
▥ Schwarzenberg
▥ Napoleon

Allied advances, 17–24 March
-▸ Blücher
-▸ Schwarzenberg
✴ French garrison blockaded by Allies

The Hundred Days

The brief Waterloo campaign (11-21 June 1815) recapitulated the major strategic and tactical themes of the Revolutionary and Napoleonic Wars. Both sides struggled for the central position, and sought to envelop the inner flank of the divided enemy. Armies used broadly similar tactics, based around well-articulated formations of all arms. All infantry were capable of fighting in line or columns, or as skirmishers. For the first time Napoleon faced the British tactical system, which had foxed his marshals in Spain.

Napoleon had to take the initiative. Twenty years' experience had convinced the European powers that peace with Napoleon was worse than war. He invaded Belgium to knock out his most inveterate enemies, the Prussians under Prince Blücher and the British under the Duke of Wellington. The Allied armies show the contrasting styles possible within the common conventions of late Napoleonic warfare. The British fielded an essentially 18th century army, generally fighting in lines. Foreign auxiliaries supplemented scarce British infantry, still recruited on a voluntary basis. The Prussians were the most national of all the continental armies. Over a third of their units were *Landwehr*, raised outside the regular army

structure. Their tactics closely resembled the French, focussing on aggressive use of battalion columns. Unlike the British they liked to see the enemy, deploying on forward slopes where they attracted artillery fire. The British hid their troops so effectively that experienced French commanders at Quatrebras refused to advance on the thinly held crossroads until their supports arrived, and so had Wellington's.

Outnumbered almost 2:1, Napoleon naturally tried to seize a central position between Blücher and Wellington. As in 1796 the Allies' communications ran in opposite directions, so he expected them to separate when attacked. Napoleon's attempts to drive the Allies apart caused the double battle of Ligny/Quatrebras. One wing of the French held off Wellington, while Napoleon tried to crush Blücher. Problems of coordination thwarted the Emperor. His forces were much larger than in 1796, and an improvised staff was no substitute for the lost activity of his youth. The attempted envelopment of Blücher's right was bungled, allowing the Prussians to retreat as they had often done in 1813-14. If Ney had not pinned the Duke at Quatrebras, the latter would himself have struck at Napoleon's flank at Ligny.

Napoleon once more underestimated the Prussians. He failed to interpose a force between the Allied armies when he turned against the British, although the value of a central position depends on keeping the enemy apart. Blücher abandoned his communications, as he had in 1814, to join Wellington. The march illustrates Clausewitz's concept of friction in war: mud, narrow lanes, and exploding ammunition wagons delaying the troops. Blücher's Chief of Staff doubted whether Wellington would fight, and moved cautiously, waiting for his strongest but most distant corps to take the lead. Blücher's will, however, overcame all obstacles. The late Prussian arrival at Waterloo proved the more decisive for their delay.

Wellington occupied a classic defensive position at Mont St Jean. The front was short, allowing deployment in great depth. A reverse slope sheltered reserves from aimed fire, and allowed them to prepare counter-attacks unobserved. Well-built farms formed strongpoints across the front, breaking up enemy attacks. Artillery enfiladed troops attacking the British centre, from a spur on the right.

Napoleon's tactics were unsubtle. He attacked frontally in masses, as at

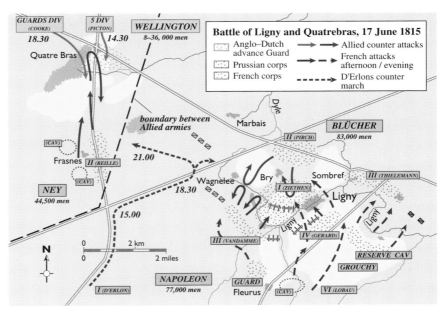

Battle of Ligny and Quatrebras, 17 June 1815

- Anglo–Dutch advance Guard
- Prussian corps
- French corps
- → Allied counter attacks
- ➔ French attacks afternoon / evening
- ⇢ D'Erlons counter march

WELLINGTON 8–36, 000 men

BLÜCHER 83,000 men

NEY 44,500 men

NAPOLEON 77,000 men

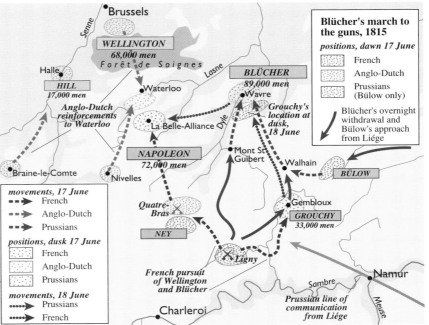

Blücher's march to the guns, 1815

positions, dawn 17 June
- French
- Anglo-Dutch
- Prussians (Bülow only)
- Blücher's overnight withdrawal and Bülow's approach from Liége

movements, 17 June
- ➔ French
- ➔ Anglo-Dutch
- ➔ Prussians

positions, dusk 17 June
- French
- Anglo-Dutch
- Prussians

movements, 18 June
- ⋯➔ Prussians
- ⋯➔ French

Borodino. The French showed none of their old flexibility. D'Erlon's Corps formed four divisional columns, the battalions in line one behind another, unable to shoot, or even see the enemy. The appearance of the Prussians drew off Napoleon's reserve, leaving no infantry to support Ney's cavalry charges against the British centre. There was little coordination between the arms, until Ney deployed horse artillery against the British squares, too late to matter.

Blücher's flank march gave him the central position. To make sure he kept it, he left a Corps at Wavre to delay Grouchy. He used his interior position not only to extend Wellington's left flank but to envelop Napoleon's right, enclosing him in a pocket between Plancenoit and Hougoumont. Napoleon's obstinately continued attacks on Wellington left no formed units to cover his retreat. Napoleon never kept a reserve against the next day, unlike the Archduke Karl at Wagram. The direction of the Prussian advance combined with Wellington's pursuit of the defeated columns of Old Guard to precipitate a rout, decisively ending one of the few truly revolutionary periods in the history of war.

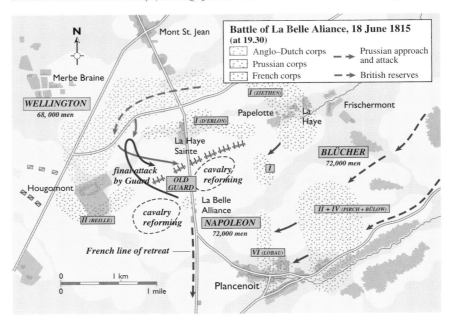

Battle of La Belle Aliance, 18 June 1815
(at 19.30)

- Anglo–Dutch corps
- Prussian corps
- French corps
- ➔ Prussian approach and attack
- ➔ British reserves

WELLINGTON 68, 000 men

BLÜCHER 72,000 men

NAPOLEON 72,000 men

Chapter 6 - The Heirs of Napoleon 1815–1905

RIGHT: The Congress of Vienna reversed Napoleon's attempt to redraw the map of Europe, but his military exploits retained a seductive glamour for generals and politicians alike. The Napoleonic ideal of short, sharp campaigns would become increasingly difficult to repeat as the century drew on.

The shadow of Napoleon loomed over the wars of the 19th century. A conservative reaction limited numbers and excluded radical officers from command, but key elements of Napoleon's system persisted: well articulated corps and divisions; flexible infantry tactics; long periods of service that isolated soldiers from civil society. Like the veterans of the Grande Armée most soldiers were professionals. Only the Prussian Army retained popular involvement in the *Landwehr*.

Clausewitz described the military consequences of the French Revolution as absolute war, but Jomini's less ominous interpretation of Napoleonic warfare attracted more attention. He played down its potentially unlimited violence, focussed on its operational mechanisms, and deprecated the horrors of People's War. The genie of the Nation in Arms could not be put back in its bottle, however. Napoleon's enduring myth lent war a spurious glamour. His short decisive campaigns afforded a misleading paradigm of future conflict.

Industrial development undermined Napoleon's military legacy. Railways, steamships, refrigeration, tinned food, and the telegraph opened new strategic possibilities. Rifles changed the balance between the arms: cavalry lost its battlefield role, but remained essential for reconaissance and raiding; artillery reverted to a supporting arm. Trench warfare made unwelcome appearances in the Crimea, America, and the Balkans, a warning obscured by short sharp wars of movement in Italy, Germany, and France.

European weapons and tactics dominated the world, except for a few fringe states. The Royal Navy's maritime supremacy made Britain the first 'world power', until new competitors appeared in the 1890s: a united Germany, the USA and Japan. By then technological changes had altered the pattern of war at sea beyond all recognition.

RIGHT: A Hungarian infantry regiment seen in the white summer uniform. Insubordinate officers and dreadful staffwork crippled the Austro-Hungarian strategy: the superior weapons and tactics of the Prussian infantry did the rest.

CONGRES DE VIENNE.

SEANCE DES PLENIPOTENTIAIRES
DES HUIT PUISSANCES SIGNATAIRES
DU TRAITE DE PARIS.

The Crimean War

RIGHT: The movement of armies and their supplies had always been faster by water than by land. The spread of the rail net across Europe would transform land communications within a generation. The Crimean War was to be the last conflict in which a maritime power could sustain a major field army at the periphery of a great land empire. Russian forces suffered terrible wastage en route to the Crimea, marching hundreds of miles over bad roads.

ABOVE: British forces deploy to defend the Ottoman Empire against Russia. Shorn of its transport department by previous defence cuts, the army nevertheless received all the blame for the subsequent debacle in the Crimea.

RIGHT: Little changed from 1812, the Russian army occupied a strong position at the Alma which it defended with traditional stubbornness. Russian counter-attacks drove back part of the British Army, but many Allied regiments had muzzle-loading rifles which gave them a tremendous advantage. The Russians withdrew after serious casualties, but the numerically weak Allied cavalry failed to convert retreat into rout.

The first major European war after Waterloo was an uncomfortable mixture of old and new. Administration plumbed depths of 18th century incompetence, while new weapons and steam power revealed the power of the Industrial Revolution.

The Tsar's ambitions in the Balkans culminated in a Russian naval attack on a much weaker Turkish squadron at Sinop (30 November 1853). Newly developed shell guns caused a 'massacre', and inspired an Anglo-French alliance to keep the Russian fleet out of the Eastern Mediterranean. Their natural war aim was to destroy the Russian Navy's dockyard at Sebastopol in the Crimea, although there were subsidiary operations in the Baltic and White Sea.

The Allies set steam-driven maritime power against Russia's pre-industrial communications. As in the Peninsula War the Allies could nourish their forces from the sea, while the Russians withered at the end of lengthy land communications. Fleets provided superior operational mobility, transporting Allied armies directly across the Black Sea, before Russian troops on the Danube could reach the Crimea on foot. It was impossible to blockade Russia, but Allied gunboats interdicted coastal traffic through the Sea of Azov which sustained Russian forces in the Crimea. Improving communications had other consequences. The telegraph paralysed French commanders with contradictory orders from Paris. Newspapers inflamed public war fever, spurred governments to ill-considered action, and compromised operational security. The world's first war correspondent made the British Commander-in-Chief a scapegoat for governmental neglect and muddle, but did heighten awareness of the human cost of war.

Crimean battles failed to match Napoleonic paradigms of brilliant manoeuvre or decisive success. All arms coordination was poor. Friction clogged armies that lacked experience or trained staffs. Battles became slogging matches where increased firepower swelled casualty lists. Smooth-bore guns were heavier than in the Napoleonic Wars: 9pr or 12pr field guns; 32pr and 68pr siege guns, their accuracy enhanced by improved manufacturing techniques.

The Alma saw the first major use of muzzle-loading rifles in battle. The Allied monopoly of the Minié rifle sufficed, with a 3:2 superiority of numbers, to drive the Russians out of a strong defensive position in a frontal attack. The Allies lacked transport and cavalry to move inland to envelop the Russians, or mount an effective pursuit. The three armies had evolved distinctive tactical styles from the Napoleonic model. The British advanced

in battalion columns while outside artillery range, then formed two lines to attack. Their shallow formations easily became disordered, and Russian counter-attacks drove them back at one point. The French used battalion columns covered by masses of skirmishers, as laid down in the 1831 Regulations, but failed to exploit their offensive potential. Massed Russian columns presented dense targets for the deadly Minié bullets, one of which might pierce five or six men.

The Russians took shelter behind improvised defences at Sebastopol, armed them with guns from the Russian fleet, and baffled the Allied armies for almost a year. Rifle pits and earthworks thrown up by Sebastopol's civilian population proved more effective than formal defences, falsifying the predictions of professional engineer officers. Trench warfare had made its unwelcome début. As in 1914-18 the defender's lines were never fully invested,

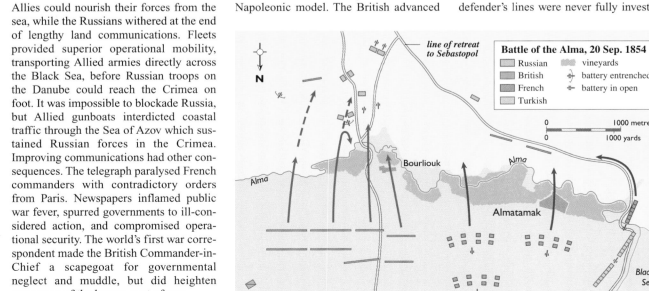

Battle of the Alma, 20 Sep. 1854

▢ Russian		▨ vineyards	
▢ British		⚑ battery entrenched	
▢ French		⚏ battery in open	
▢ Turkish			

0 — 1000 metres
0 — 1000 yards

line of retreat to Sebastopol

N

Alma

Bourliouk

Alma

Almatamak

Black Sea

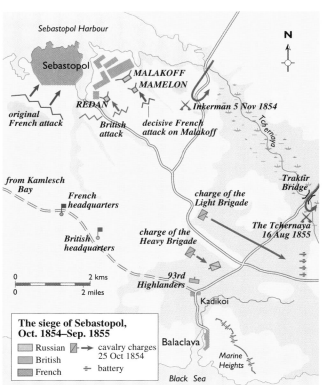

allowing in reinforcements and supplies. Mutual attrition was costly. The Royal Navy landed 140 32pr guns during the siege: 32 were destroyed, and 73 condemned as worn out. Crowding large numbers of men together caused heavy losses from disease.

The Allies' strategic offensive gave them the advantage of the tactical defensive, forcing the Russians to attack them. Battles at Balaklava, Inkerman and the Traktir Bridge underlined the Russian inability to face Allied firepower in the open. At Balaklava their cavalry refused to charge a single battalion armed with the new rifle. Inkerman was fought in a fog, but edged weapons caused only 6% of the casualties. The siege followed a pattern evocative of the First World War, including a primitive railway from the harbour at Balaklava, capable of moving 40-50 tons a day. In the sixth and final bombardment, 183 Allied guns and mortars fired 28,176 rounds in three days, an unprecedented display of firepower. Russian casualties exceeded 1,000 a day, before the Malakoff redoubt fell, persuading the Russians to evacuate Sebastopol's smoking ruins (8-9 September 1855). The Allies had won, but their armies only left the Crimea after another seven months of naval and diplomatic pressure, including the first use of ironclad warships to bombard Kinburn (16 October 1855).

ABOVE: Unable to completely invest the port, the Allies fell back on traditional siege warfare, with the heaviest guns yet seen. However, Russian earthworks proved very resilient and their defenders resolute. The Russian army's attempt to relieve the siege was beaten off in a battle most famous for the Charge of the Light Brigade and the 'Thin Red Line'.

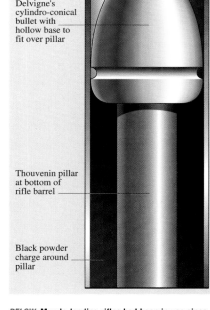

Cross-section of Minié Rifle breech

Delvigne's cylindro-conical bullet with hollow base to fit over pillar

Thouvenin pillar at bottom of rifle barrel

Black powder charge around pillar

BELOW: Muzzle-loading rifles had been in use since the 18th century, but their military value was restricted by their slow rate of fire. If a bullet was to engage the rifling, it had to be a tight fit, hence the mallet sometimes used to hammer them down the barrel. Minié solved the problem with a bullet that expanded as it travelled up the bore. The replacement of flintlocks with percussion caps made weapon vastly more reliable. The result was a substantial improvement in firepower, the consequences of which would be revealed during the American Civil War.

The Franco-Austrian War, May–July

Post-Napoleonic reaction could not stamp out all the nationalist forces released by the French Revolution. Absorbed by Austria as a defensive out-work, Italy seethed with discontent. Nationalism posed a particular threat to the multinational army of the Hapsburg Empire, the antithesis of a Nation in Arms. In 1858 France allied with Sardinia, the largest independent Italian state, to drive the Austrians from the peninsula.

Bonapartist mythology had helped the Emperor's nephew, Napoleon III, seize power. Like his uncle he needed to win a quick victory, but feared the Austrian army at Milan might overrun the outnumbered Sardinians before the French arrived. Steam power resolved both problems. Steamships carried French troops to Genoa, the passage from Toulon taking 24 hours, instead of the 20 marches previously needed. Other units went by rail to the foot of the Alps, and marched to the Sardinian railhead, pre-empting a plodding Austrian advance on Turin.

The Austrians fell back, thinking Napoleon III would envelop their left in a repeat of the 1796 Lodi manoeuvre. Instead he turned their right, boldly transferring his army 60 miles across the Austrian front by rail. Napoleon III achieved a double first, using railways not only to move his army to the theatre of war but to outmanoeuvre the enemy. The Sardinian railway net made this possible, running parallel to the frontline, through friendly territory.

The Austrians retreated to the Ticino, where they surprised the Allies by defending the river line, although French troops had already crossed further north. The result was an asymmetrical battle, fought astride the Ticino, each side trying to turn the enemy's right flank. As in the double battles of 1806 and 1815, the French had difficulty coordinating their main attack with the outflanking force, but Austrian reserves arrived too late to crush isolated French formations east of the river. Neither side's losses were decisive, but the Austrian Corps withdrew eccentrically, unlike the Prussians after Ligny, becoming too scattered to resume action the next day.

The soldiers on both sides were conscripts, but many French soldiers re-engaged, becoming long-service professionals. Austrian recruits served only a short time with the colours. Their battlefield performance reflected this, with losses of only a twelfth reducing Austrian units to hopeless disorder. Men from non-German regiments deserted in droves. Both sides used muzzle-loading rifles, but masses of fruit trees obscured the battlefield and limited their effect. Austrian reservists only received their rifles on the way to the front. They did not know how to load, let alone compensate for the weapon's high trajectory when aiming. French tactics speeded up to counteract the increased firepower of rifles. French light infantry, *Chasseurs* and *Zouaves*, became shock troops, closing rapidly with the enemy to avoid their fire effect.

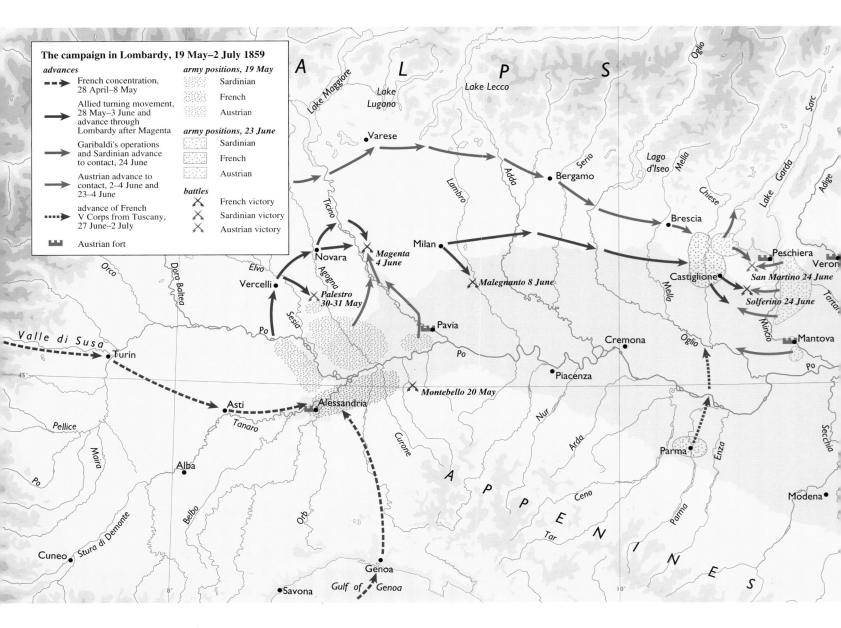

The campaign in Lombardy, 19 May–2 July 1859

advances

- **- - ▶** French concentration, 28 April–8 May
- **──▶** Allied turning movement, 28 May–3 June and advance through Lombardy after Magenta
- **──▶** Garibaldi's operations and Sardinian advance to contact, 24 June
- **──▶** Austrian advance to contact, 2–4 June and 23–4 June
- **· · · ·▶** advance of French V Corps from Tuscany, 27 June–2 July
- **♜** Austrian fort

army positions, 19 May
- Sardinian
- French
- Austrian

army positions, 23 June
- Sardinian
- French
- Austrian

battles
- ✗ French victory
- ✗ Sardinian victory
- ✗ Austrian victory

The Allies followed the Austrians cautiously. Napoleon III kept his troops closed up, avoiding further risky manoeuvres. When the Austrians launched a counter-offensive to catch the Allies off balance at Solferino, the monolithic Allied deployment made a frontal 'soldier's battle' inevitable.

In an accidental encounter, the first side to assert control over the battle is likely to win. Napoleon III went forward promptly, and ordered three French corps to concentrate against the high ground in the centre of the battlefield. The flanks had to pin their opposite numbers as best they could. Austrian corps commanders failed to support their own brigades, let alone each other. The ground was more open than at Magenta, allowing the French to use their new rifled field guns effectively for the first time. Forty guns filled the gap left by the infantry concentration on the centre. Massed in the Napoleonic style, they overpowered Austrian smooth-bore batteries before

they came into action. Rifling reduced the muzzle velocity of the new weapons, compared with smooth-bore guns. Their curved trajectory and fragmentation shells blurred the distinction between guns and howitzers, which disappeared from the inventory.

With moderate advantages in generalship and weaponry, aggressive French regulars smashed the Austrian centre at Solferino in a typical Napoleonic central breakthrough. In the absence of a turning movement the defeated army escaped over the Mincio. Casualties in the largest battle since Leipzig shocked the two Emperors into agreeing peace terms, Napoleon III fearing a repetition of Sebastopol's stalemate. French troops had muddled through magnificently, serious administrative problems escaping notice in the euphoria. The Austrians learned two lessons: the value of rifled artillery used in masses, and (more dubiously) the offensive potential of the bayonet in the age of the rifle.

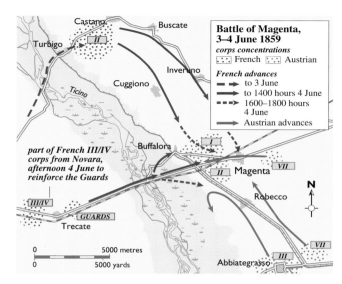

ABOVE: The French infantry did not just rely on the Minié rifle, but on dash and élan: in sad contrast to the Austrian army whose non-German regiments tended to melt away at indecent speed. The Austrian attempt to crush the French bridgehead over the Ticino collapsed in the face of furious counter-attacks. The eventual arrival of the French flanking force led the Austrians to break off the action.

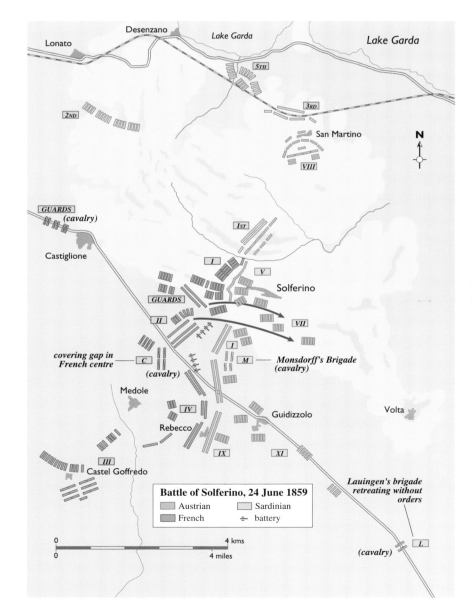

LEFT: The Austrian attack at Solferino exposed their weaknesses again: low morale in non-German units, inferior smoothbore artillery and poor coordination between their formations. Grave weaknesses in the French army went unobserved as their aggressive infantry broke the enemy centre, preceded by an artillery concentration in the Napoleonic style.

ABOVE: Napoleon III recruited an Imperial Guard of his own, the soldiers' bearskins a visible connection to the glory days of his uncle's *Grande Armée*. His army muddled through to victory in 1859, ending the Italian campaign with a complacent confidence that would be rudely shattered in 1870.

The Seven Weeks War

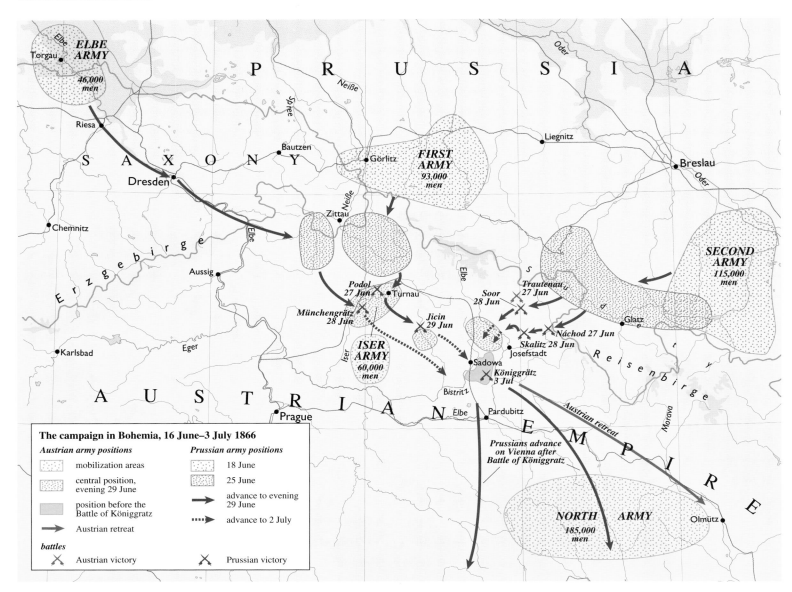

The campaign in Bohemia, 16 June–3 July 1866

Austrian army positions

(dotted)	mobilization areas
(dotted)	central position, evening 29 June
(grey)	position before the Battle of Königgratz
→	Austrian retreat

battles
✗	Austrian victory

Prussian army positions

(dotted)	18 June
(dotted)	25 June
→	advance to evening 29 June
┅➤	advance to 2 July

✗	Prussian victory

Map labels: ELBE ARMY 46,000 men; FIRST ARMY 93,000 men; SECOND ARMY 115,000 men; ISER ARMY 60,000 men; NORTH ARMY 185,000 men. Torgau, Riesa, Chemnitz, Dresden, Bautzen, Görlitz, Liegnitz, Breslau, Zittau, Aussig, Karlsbad, Eger, Prague, Podol 27 Jun, Turnau, Münchengrätz 28 Jun, Jicin 29 Jun, Soor 28 Jun, Trautenau 27 Jun, Glatz, Náchod 27 Jun, Skalitz 28 Jun, Josefstadt, Sadowa, Königgrätz 3 Jul, Bistritz, Pardubitz, Olmütz. PRUSSIA, SAXONY, AUSTRIAN EMPIRE, Erzgebirge, Reisenbirge. *Prussians advance on Vienna after Battle of Königgratz. Austrian retreat.* Rivers: Elbe, Oder, Neiße, Spree, Iser, Morava.

Armies in the Crimea and Italy minimized risk by maintaining concentration at the expense of operational flexibility. Frontal attacks at the Alma and Solferino were tactically successful, but strategically indecisive. In 1866 the Prussians broke away from Jominian concepts of strategic prudence to score a rapid and decisive victory over the Hapsburg army, then considered the best in Europe.

The architect of victory was Helmut von Moltke, Chief of the Prussian General Staff, whose relationship with King William took a step further the symbiosis between Gneisenau and Blücher. Like Clausewitz, Moltke distrusted rigid strategic theories, and saw the decisive possibilities of encirclement. Moltke was the first commander since Napoleon to regard the separation of corps as an opportunity rather than a danger. He always sought to encircle the enemy, as Napoleon had tried to do at Bautzen, and the Prussians had succeeded in doing at Waterloo.

Several factors assisted Moltke: railways and telegraphs, Prussian numerical superiority, and their General Staff.

Railways halved the time the Prussians needed to mobilize, moving their armies rapidly into defensive positions along the frontier. Telegraphs, used to run railways, could also control dispersed armies, although the orders for the decisive battle of the campaign were delivered in traditional style by a mounted ADC.

Prussia had a tradition of using reserve forces to sustain war strengths proportionately higher than those of more populous states. From 1861 Prussian infantrymen served three years with their regiment, and five in the reserves. Regiments had permanent regular cadres, and were territorial, so reservists served with familiar officers and NCOs when recalled. The system provided a mobilized army of half a million professional troops, at the financial cost of militia.

To direct these masses Moltke could rely on a body of trained staff officers, distributed throughout the army, and possessing a common body of military doctrine. They made it possible to deploy at dispersed railheads, and then launch a converging advance, in which detached Army and Corps commanders would act consis-

tently with the general intentions of the High Command.

The Austrian army that faced the Prussians concentrated in the approved fashion. In theory it could have defeated the separate Prussian armies piecemeal, but did not. Five out of eight Austro-Saxon corps were themselves beaten separately, thanks to the insubordination and inefficiency of the Austrian staff. The Austrian Army suffered 30,000 casualties, and fell back in disorder upon the fortress of Königgrätz. As the Prussians converged it became impossible for the Austrians to attack one Prussian Army, without finding the other on their flank.

The resulting battle did not go entirely to Moltke's plan. First Army was too aggressive, and was pinned down by massed Austrian artillery fire. Second Army was too slow, and failed to move east of the Elbe, to prevent the Austrians' escape. Its late arrival was decisive, however, smashing into the flank of the northernmost Austrian corps, who had left their defensive positions to join counter-attacks on First Army. The Austrians were caught

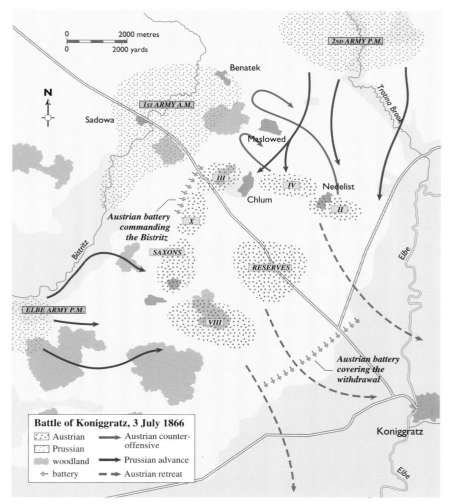

Battle of Koniggratz, 3 July 1866

⋯ Austrian	→ Austrian counter-offensive
⋯ Prussian	→ Prussian advance
woodland	
⊹ battery	⇢ Austrian retreat

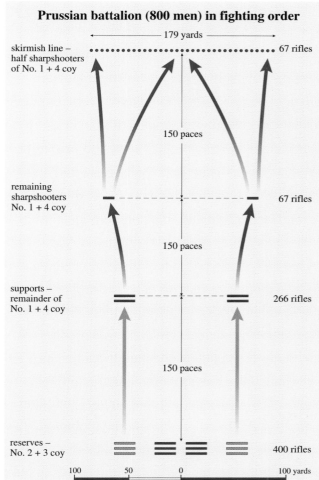

Prussian battalion (800 men) in fighting order

← 179 yards →

skirmish line – half sharpshooters of No. 1 + 4 coy — 67 rifles

150 paces

remaining sharpshooters No. 1 + 4 coy — 67 rifles

150 paces

supports – remainder of No. 1 + 4 coy — 266 rifles

150 paces

reserves – No. 2 + 3 coy — 400 rifles

100   50   0   100 yards

ABOVE: The Austrians launched repeated attacks, trying to repeat the success of the French charges in 1859. But the Prussians had the major advantage of breech-loading rifles: thin lines of fast-shooting infantry were able to repel each assault with heavy losses. The belated arrival of the German II Army caught the Austrians as their last reserves were committed to the attack. Austria's gunners covered the retreat of their army, frustrating any pursuit, but the Imperial army was shattered.

Breech mechanism of the Dreyse Rifle

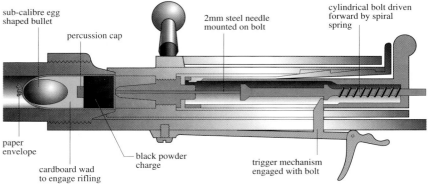

sub-calibre egg shaped bullet

percussion cap

2mm steel needle mounted on bolt

cylindrical bolt driven forward by spiral spring

paper envelope

cardboard wad to engage rifling

black powder charge

trigger mechanism engaged with bolt

ABOVE: Prussian infantry tactics divided the battalion into successive waves. Two of the four rifle companies were divided into skirmishers and two waves of supports, with the other two companies drawn up in small columns. These 'company columns' were able to take advantage of relatively minor terrain features in order to avoid losses. If the attack stalled, the front-line could be nourished from the reserves, or the columns could charge forward to restore momentum.

between the two Prussian armies, and destroyed as a fighting force.

Critics discounted Moltke's strategy, attributing Prussian success to tactical factors, especially the breech-loading Dreyse needlegun. Prussian infantry not only fired twice as quickly as their opponents; they did so lying down, presenting a much smaller target. The Austrians, misled by their experiences in 1859, launched massed bayonet assaults, which proved suicidal in face of the needlegun. Prussian infantry formed loose firing lines that took Austrian columns in a cross fire, rather as British lines had enveloped the heads of French columns in the Peninsula.

Königgrätz also showed the power of massed rifled artillery. The Austrian guns had single-handedly defeated First Army, when Second Army arrived. They then covered the retreat, many batteries fighting to the last. Prussian guns achieved little, marching too far back, and used in small numbers. Many were smooth-bore, and proved useless. Cavalry continued its decline in usefulness. Kept too far to the rear for reconnaissance, it proved ineffective in a battlefield shock role, despite suffering heavy losses. Austrian cavalry failed to report the approach of Second Army, and Prussian reserve cavalry arrived too late to mount an effective pursuit.

ABOVE: The Dreyse rifle was complex, unreliable, inaccurate but revolutionary weapon that shattered the Austrian columns in 1866. Known as the 'needle gun' because of the quixotic ignition system (the cartridge primer lies between the bullet and the charge), it was the first bolt-action rifle to enter military service. The needle often bent or broke; the breech was poorly sealed and spat burning powder grains into the firer's face and the cartridge was easily damaged. However, a battalion armed with needle guns could fire far more rapidly than one with muzzle-loading rifles, and do so lying down.

The Franco-Prussian War

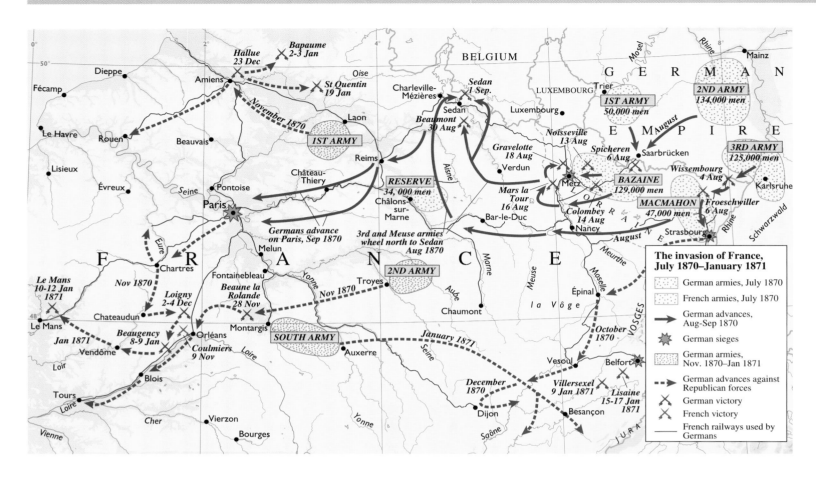

The invasion of France,
July 1870–January 1871

	German armies, July 1870
	French armies, July 1870
→	German advances, Aug–Sep 1870
✷	German sieges
	German armies, Nov. 1870–Jan 1871
---	German advances against Republican forces
✕	German victory
✕	French victory
—	French railways used by Germans

Prussia's destruction of the army of the French Second Empire in the summer of 1870 began a new military era. This time there could be no doubt that Moltke's victory was strategic, for French tactics, morale, and weapons were in many respects superior to those of the Germans.

As in 1866, Moltke used railways to occupy broad defensive positions, which served as jumping off points for a converging invasion of France's eastern provinces. Allied forces from South Germany increased his numerical superiority: 450,000 against 180,000. Prussian corps existed permanently in peacetime, but the French improvised such formations on mobilization, producing administrative chaos and strategic paralysis. As in Bohemia, Moltke laid down the general order of advance, leaving its execution to Army and Corps commanders, guided by their staff. Their movements lead to a series of battles that the high command may not have intended, but which they could exploit to their advantage. French commanders, starved of initiative by an over-centralized Napoleonic command style, failed to support each other, while German troops appeared on their flanks, marching to the sound of the guns. Between battles the more mobile Germans swept around into the French rear, forcing them to fight facing Paris.

The battle of Fröschwiller set the tactical pattern of the war. The French held a magnificent position, with splendid fields of fire for their Chassepot rifles, but the Germans trumped them with superior artillery, reorganized and re-equipped since Königgrätz. Krupp breech-loaders outranged French muzzle-loaders slightly, but there were far more of them, deployed in masses, and their percussion fuses worked at any range, unlike the French time fuses. German frontal attacks and artillery fire pinned down the French, until neighbouring corps turned the flanks of the position, enclosing the French centre in a circle of fire. French cavalry charges exceeded those of 1866 in heroism and futility; some French infantry units lost three quarters of their numbers in ferocious counter-attacks. The French rifle outranged the Dreyse, but German skirmish lines presented a dispersed target allowing them to close the range without disproportionately heavy losses.

French commanders were intellectually ill-prepared to command armies far larger than the corps they had led previously, and lacked effective staffs to help them. The weight of responsibility paralysed the experienced Marshal Bazaine, who allowed his army to be surrounded at Metz. The Paris Government ordered Marshal MacMahon, hero of Magenta, to relieve Bazaine with a turning movement that exposed his own communications. Moltke exploited his central position between the two Marshals to concentrate against MacMahon, forcing him to sur-

render at Sedan. Moltke's victories eclipsed those of Napoleon in scale, thanks to higher ratios of force to space, which made it impossible for an outmanoeuvred enemy to escape the net. MacMahon's predictable destruction shows the dangers of political demands that ignore military realities.

The Imperial army was not the French people, however. A republican government seized power after Sedan, with a conscious appeal to the Nation in Arms. By the end of the war the French had called up as many men as the Germans. Unlike the 1792 *levée en masse*, with its ex-Royalist NCOs, the *Gardes Mobiles* of 1870 lacked the regular cadres lost at Metz and Sedan. French numbers proved no substitute for skill in raising the German siege of Paris. Past besieging forces had been vulnerable to attack by relieving forces. Now the tactical superiority of the defence, coordinated by telegraph, allowed the Germans to defeat separate attacks launched from unoccupied French territory. At Coulmiers, the only

French victory of the war, the defeated Bavarians escaped with limited casualties, despite French superiority of numbers of more than 3:1.

The bitterness of the Franco-Prussian War contrasted with the moderation of the Seven Weeks War. The Germans took hostages from the beginning, while *franctireurs* murdered sentries, provoking German reprisals. The people of Paris and Strasbourg suffered starvation and bombardment. However, Bismarck limited his political ends, unlike Napoleon Bonaparte, who had threatened the very existence of his enemies. A more sinister portent of total war was the conflict between Bismarck and Moltke over control of policy in wartime. The General Staff staked claims that under less responsible leaders would lead to disaster. The rapidity and decisiveness of Moltke's success persuaded other armies to copy German methods: short service with strong reserves, permanent army corps, general staffs, even the characteristic spiked helmet.

BELOW: In agony from kidney stones, Napoleon III nevertheless took the field at the head of his army. As a Bonaparte, it was unthinkable for him to do anything else. His army was surrounded at Sedan, where he occupied the imposing chateau as his headquarters. He spent five agonizing hours in the saddle, courting death from Prussian artillery fire before accepting that his army was defeated. The failure to break out meant surrender for his army and political oblivion for him.

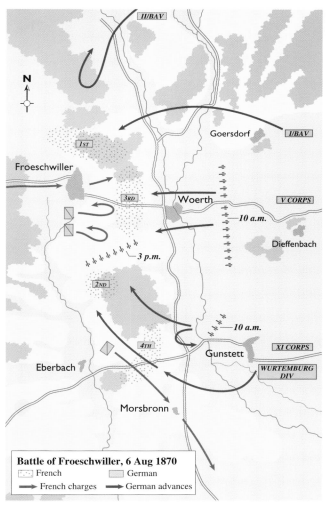

Battle of Froeschwiller, 6 Aug 1870
French   German
French charges   German advances

ABOVE: The first major action set the pattern: Prussian infantry attacks were pressed home with great gallantry, supported by their powerful artillery. Fierce French counter-attacks collapsed in the face of unprecedented firepower and the army retreated. Recriminations followed, with accusations of betrayal in the air. Within weeks, the cries of 'to Berlin' seemed very hollow.

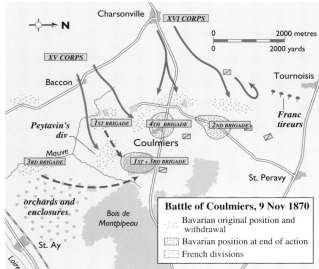

Battle of Coulmiers, 9 Nov 1870
Bavarian original position and withdrawal
Bavarian position at end of action
French divisions

ABOVE: Napoleon III was captured at Sedan, his empress fleeing the Tuileries one step ahead of the mob. But the republican administration fought on, inflicting one check on the German armies, at Coulmiers in November. However, the Bavarian forces were able to withdraw in good order as the French forces were largely composed of reservists and half-trained volunteers. The regular army languished in German prison camps.

Naval Warfare from Lissa to Santiago

RIGHT: The only major fleet action between Navarino (1827) and the Russo-Japanese War (1904-5), the action off Lissa in 1866 involved mixed fleets of ironclads and wooden ships. Gambling that long range gunnery would be ineffective, the aggressive Austrian admiral charged through the Italian line. In the ensuing melee the *Re D'Italia* was rammed and sunk, inspiring a generation of warship designers to fit rams to their ships.

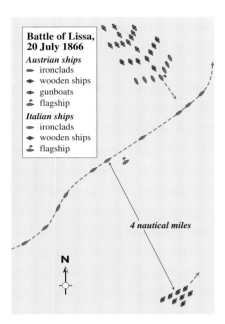

Battle of Lissa, 20 July 1866
Austrian ships
- ironclads
- wooden ships
- gunboats
- flagship

Italian ships
- ironclads
- wooden ships
- flagship

4 nautical miles

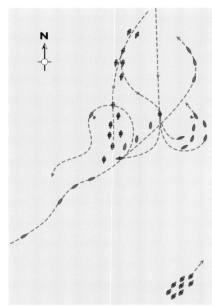

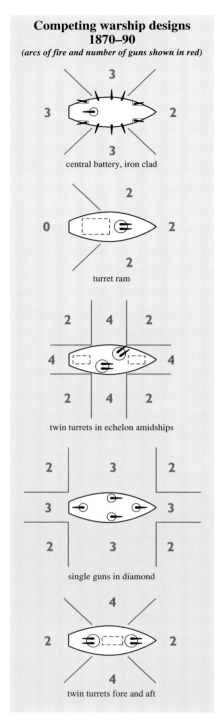

Competing warship designs 1870–90
(arcs of fire and number of guns shown in red)

central battery, iron clad

turret ram

twin turrets in echelon amidships

single guns in diamond

twin turrets fore and aft

ABOVE: The transition from broadside batteries to turret-mounted armament involved many variations and would not be settled until the eve of the First World War when superfiring turrets appeared.

Trafalgar began almost a century of British naval supremacy, consolidated by Britain's free trade policies and post-Napoleonic war-weariness. The Royal Navy's elimination of its rivals marginalized concepts like the 'struggle for command of the sea'. Industrial and naval power were still concentrated in Europe, so Great Britain's location across Europe's maritime communications with the rest of the world, gave the Royal Navy command of the Indian and Pacific Oceans as well as the Channel and North Atlantic.

Naval activity in the 19th century had more to do with exploiting command of the sea, than fighting for it. Naval forces imposed blockades, chased slavers, fired bombardments, or conveyed expeditions overseas. They even forced their way up the great rivers, into the heart of Asia and Africa. They rarely fought each other. A few naval battles happened in peripheral areas, but never challenged Britain's overarching command of the sea. That was only seriously threatened in the 1890s. The British occupation of Egypt in 1882 was too convincing a display of sea power, alienating previously complaisant powers. New naval powers emerged in Japan and America, beyond the Royal Navy's reach.

Another destabilizing factor was the revolution in maritime technology that reached its apotheosis in the 1890s. Warships that had changed unrecognizably since 1805 settled down into a pattern that remained stable into the missile age: gun-armed battleships and cruisers; torpedo-armed flotillas. Steam engines allied with the screw propeller to make ships independent of the wind. This reduced passage times by allowing ships to follow more direct routes, although the need for coal gave bases a new significance. With sailing ships seamanship had been more use in action than clever tactical ideas that were impossible to carry out. Steamships, however, lent themselves to tactical choreography.

Improved ordnance began a race between guns and armour. Shell guns made wooden ships obsolete. Naval architects armoured wooden ships, built ships entirely from iron, and then replaced iron with steel. Rifling increased battle ranges by a factor of ten, although it is doubtful whether the handful of 'monster guns' carried by battleships in the 1890s would have hit anything. At the Battle of Santiago (3 July 1898) 32 guns of 8-inch calibre or greater scored only 14 hits between them, in an action lasting four hours. Quite small ships could now sink a battleship with torpedoes. The underwater threat developed during the American Civil War, with captive mines, known as torpedoes. These became self-propelled during the 1870s, encouraging the French *Jeune Ecole* to see them as a cheap antidote to the British battlefleet. By 1900 the first submarines were in service. Armed with torpedoes they threatened to sink ships attempting to implement a close blockade like those of the Napoleonic Wars.

The overall effect of the technological revolution was unclear. Navies were slow to develop staffs, or conduct realistic exercises. The British only formed a Naval Intelligence Department in 1887, shortly after beginning annual manoeuvres. The one mid-century fleet action in the open sea was unhelpful, primarily confirming the importance of the commanders' morale. At Lissa an aggressive Austrian admiral formed his squadron in an arrowhead, to break through a line of Italian ironclads. Italian gunfire was ineffective against the armoured ships in front, which protected the wooden ships behind. In the ensuing melée the Austrian flagship rammed and sank the crippled Italian flagship. Ship designers responded to this accidental success by fitting ships with rams, and mounting guns for end-on fire. Lissa shows the danger of extrapolating tactics from a single unrepresentative example. Ranges of fleet actions would in fact increase, to avoid enemy torpedoes. Most rammings were accidental sinkings of friendly ships in peacetime.

The Battle of the Yalu River, during the Sino-Japanese War (1894-5) was more indicative of the future. Recognizably modern ships fought each other with gun

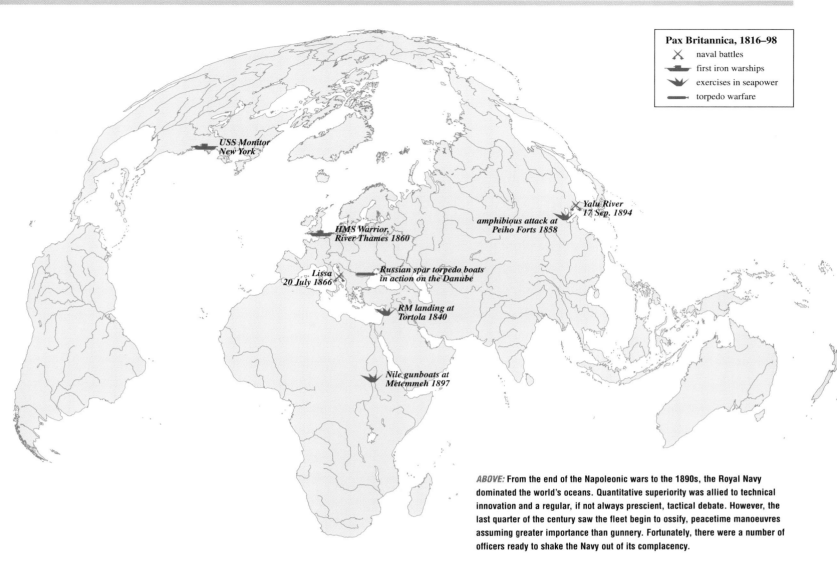

Pax Britannica, 1816–98
- ✕ naval battles
- first iron warships
- exercises in seapower
- torpedo warfare

USS Monitor
New York

HMS Warrior,
River Thames 1860

amphibious attack at
Peiho Forts 1858

Yalu River
17 Sep. 1894

Lissa
20 July 1866

Russian spar torpedo boats
in action on the Danube

RM landing at
Tortola 1840

Nile gunboats at
Metemmeh 1897

ABOVE: From the end of the Napoleonic wars to the 1890s, the Royal Navy dominated the world's oceans. Quantitative superiority was allied to technical innovation and a regular, if not always prescient, tactical debate. However, the last quarter of the century saw the fleet begin to ossify, peacetime manoeuvres assuming greater importance than gunnery. Fortunately, there were a number of officers ready to shake the Navy out of its complacency.

and torpedo, using close line ahead to achieve concentration of fire. They did not try to ram, although the Chinese battleships were designed for end-on fire. The Japanese split their squadron into fast and slow divisions, using the former's speed to concentrate fire against part of the Chinese squadron. This tactical sub-division foreshadowed Japanese use of armoured cruisers in the Russo-Japanese War, and the development of the battlecruiser. The Japanese blockaded the remains of the Chinese fleet in Weihaiwei, destroying them with torpedo attacks and land bombardment. The Imperial Japanese Navy had gained local command of the sea, the first non-European power to do so since the 16th century.

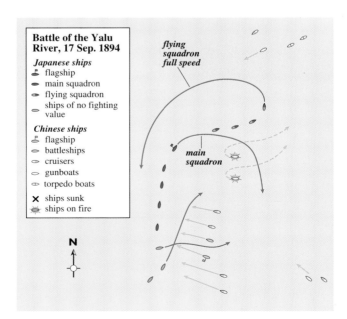

Battle of the Yalu River, 17 Sep. 1894

Japanese ships
- flagship
- main squadron
- flying squadron
- ships of no fighting value

Chinese ships
- flagship
- battleships
- cruisers
- gunboats
- torpedo boats
- ✕ ships sunk
- ships on fire

flying squadron full speed

main squadron

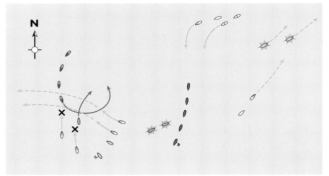

LEFT AND ABOVE: After the Empress used naval funds to decorate her palace and cement was substituted for explosive in the battleships' heavy shells, the Chinese navy was unlikely to survive an encounter with the more diligent Japanese. Both fleets employed warships built in European yards, but Japan was poised to build modern vessels of her own. Several Chinese vessels were captured in the wake of the battle and pressed into service by Japan.

American Civil War on land

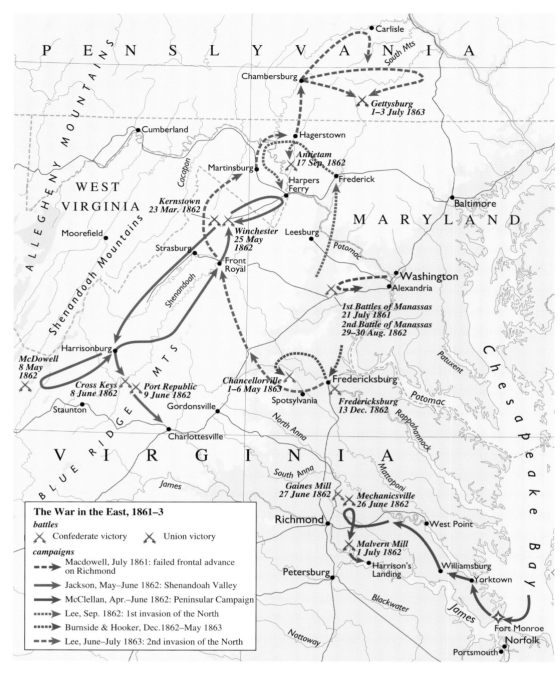

McClellan were prepared to apply Napoleonic concepts to the vast spaces of North America. They were particularly successful on the defensive. Lee's strategic manoeuvres before 2nd Manassas, Antietam, and Gettysburg all succeeded in forcing Union armies to retreat, before fighting a battle. Jackson's Valley campaign remains a classic example of strategic diversion, drawing Union reserves away from the decisive point. McClellan was less successful on the offensive, failing to reconcile Jominian principles with the strategic possibilities of a mass army, railways and telegraphs. Clinging to a single line of operations, he suffered logistical paralysis.

The Battle of Chancellorsville epitomized Lee's methods. Although acting on the strategic defensive, Lee assumed the tactical offensive in response to Union advances on the Confederate capital Richmond, uncomfortably close to the frontline. Always outnumbered, Lee made maximum use of the defensive superiority of entrenched riflemen to free sufficient forces for his offensive counter-moves. He left 10,000 men to cover his rear against 40,000 Federal troops at Fredericksburg, pinned the main Union force of 73,000 with 17,000, and sent 26,000 men around the flank to attack the Federal rear at Chancellorsville. Lee could conceal his movements in the tangled woods of North Virginia, but the boldness of his plan bordered on the reckless. The collapse of the Union commander's morale shows how a battle lost is a battle believed to have been lost. When Hooker ordered his troops to retreat, Lee's advance was faltering, while

RIGHT: A Confederate soldier, killed in the trenches at Petersburg, April 1865. To modern eyes such scenes anticipate the First World War, but too much can be read into them. Had cameras been available in the previous century, they would have recorded similar images at Yorktown.

ABOVE: The proximity of the two capitals led both sides to field their largest armies in the East. Union maritime superiority enabled their armies to base themselves at the mouth of the James River in 1862 and 1864. The Shenandoah had a dual role: as a 'back door' to the North, it was the springboard for several Southern offensives; it was also the 'bread-basket' of the South until Sheridan laid it to waste.

The duration and intensity of the American Civil War set it apart from contemporary European wars. Observers have viewed it with hindsight as one of the first modern wars. Like other wars of the mid-19th century, however, the Civil War was transitional. It looked back to Napoleonic traditions, as well as forward to the total wars of the 20th century.

The Civil War lacked the necessary conditions for swift resolution as Moltke's wars. It was an ideological conflict, releasing deep antagonisms on both sides, fought across vast distances with poor communications. The improvised armies had similar weapons and levels of training, so neither side had a qualitative edge like that possessed by the Prussians in 1866. Tactical equality and the defensive power of modern weapons forced both sides to

entrench as thoroughly as had the Romans. American infantry learned to fight in open order, and avoid frontal attacks. The Union outnumbered the Confederacy overall, but the rebels' interior position allowed them to concentrate their smaller forces against successive Union attacks. Railways were essential lines of communication in the undeveloped South, where roads did not exist, and the cotton/tobacco-based agriculture was unable to sustain large armies from local resources.

Civil War generals used railways to mount strategic concentrations far more ambitious than those attempted in Europe. In 1862, the Confederacy moved troops 500 miles from Charleston, Mobile, and New Orleans to surprise Grant at Shiloh. Both sides attempted turning movements, showing how leaders like Lee and

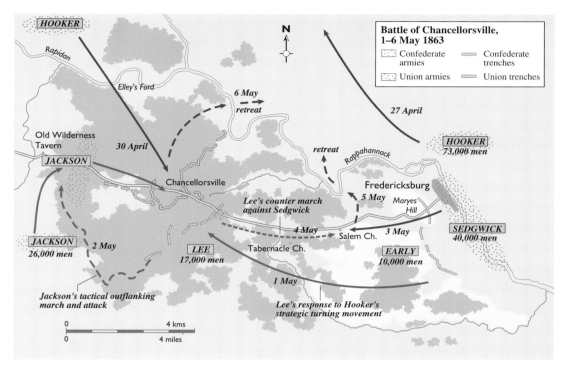

Union troops at Fredericksburg had driven back the Confederate covering force. In the absence of wireless communications, the success of an enveloping manoeuvre depended on inspired cooperation, in this case between Lee and 'Stonewall' Jackson. His death at Chancellorsville destroyed a battle winning team, and may have cost the Confederacy the Battle of Gettysburg (1-3 July 1863).

The stalemate in the East was broken by General Ulysses S Grant. He had never read Jomini, and like Moltke did not believe in universal strategic principles. Grant had shown a willingness to take risks in the Vicksburg campaign that baffled less able opponents. Against Lee, in the more confined spaces of North Virginia, Grant's attempts to turn the Confederate right resulted in a series of bloody encounter battles. Lee would not be encircled like Bazaine, but Grant would not give up, unlike Hooker. In a month's fighting (3 May-3 June 1864), both armies lost half their strength. Grant then changed his line of operations, as he had done at Vicksburg. He transferred his army across the James River to cut Richmond's rail communications with the rest of the Confederacy. He prepared this major engineering feat in such secrecy that Lee did not know of the operation until six days after it began. Friction narrowly prevented Grant winning the war at a stroke. The leading Union column stopped short of the vital railway junction at Petersburg before Confederate reinforcements arrived. The stalemated armies settled in for a nine month siege.

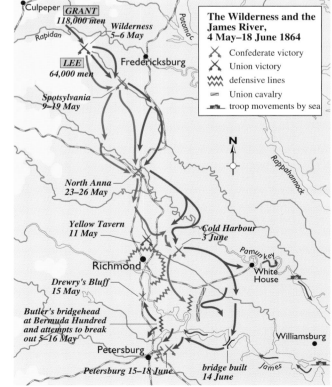

American Civil War: Naval & Economic Warfare

RIGHT: The Confederacy underwent a government-led industrial revolution during the war, but its economy was slowly strangled. Imports were choked off as the US Navy seized its ports and Union forces controlled the Mississippi. Internal communications relied on a ramshackle rail net that was soon exposed to Union cavalry raids and ultimately ripped up by Sherman's army on its march to the sea. Conversely, the Union war economy was so powerful it was exporting weapons and even building battleships to foreign accounts during the war.

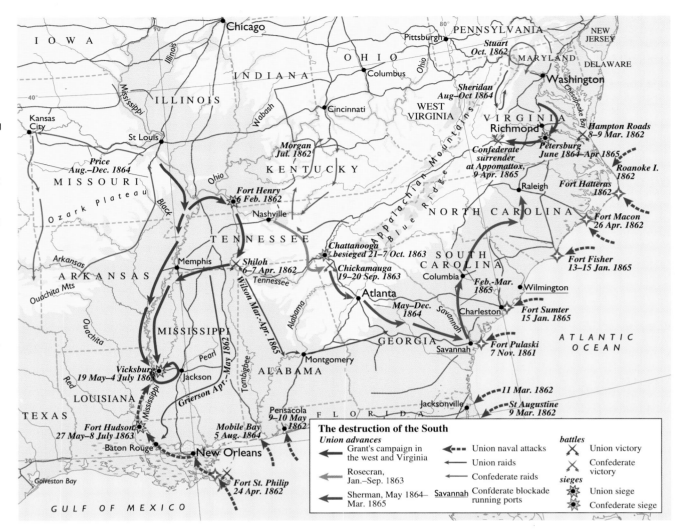

The destruction of the South

Union advances
→ Grant's campaign in the west and Virginia
→ Rosecran, Jan.–Sep. 1863
→ Sherman, May 1864– Mar. 1865

◄--- Union naval attacks
← Union raids
← Confederate raids

Savannah Confderate blockade running ports

battles
✕ Union victory
✕ Confederate victory

sieges
✳ Union siege
✳ Confederate siege

The Confederacy was too large to defeat by purely military means. Popular support for the Southern cause brought an obstinacy to the struggle, missing from contemporary European wars. Defeat of the Confederacy required a combination of pressure: military, naval, and economic.

Clausewitz had identified three strategic centres of gravity: the government, the army, and the people. Had Hooker or McClellan defeated Lee's army and occupied Richmond, they would still have faced widespread resistance across the South. By 1862 a third of the US Army was acting as an occupation force. Like other belligerents unable to occupy enemy territory effectively, the US army resorted to raids. The most spectacular was Sherman's march through Georgia to the sea. This not only inflicted economic damage on the areas traversed, but disrupted the railways that supplied Confederate armies. Sherman realized he was fighting a hostile people, and deliberately made them feel the hard hand of war. Sherman's superior numbers and his willingness to feed them from the countryside achieved astonishing strategic mobility. He turned successive Confederate positions between Chattanooga and Atlanta, and by the end of the war had carried his army to Raleigh in North Carolina.

RIGHT: The Confederates converted the hulk of the steam frigate Merrimack into an ironclad ram, intended to raise the blockade of Norfolk. Hopes that it might raid New York would never have been realized, her ancient powerplant and shallow freeboard restricting her to coastal waters, but she met her match in the bizarre shape of the Monitor off Hampton Roads on 9 March. The Merrimack's short life ended when Norfolk was abandoned by the Confederates: drawing too much water to escape up the James, she had to be blown up.

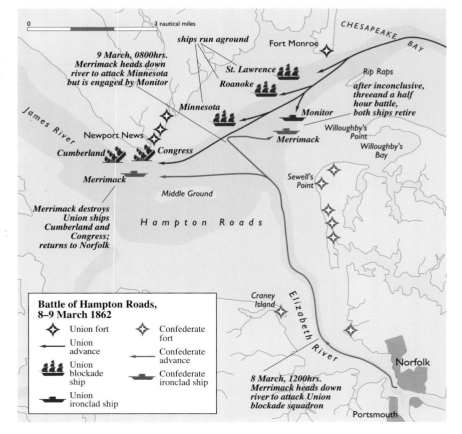

Battle of Hampton Roads, 8–9 March 1862

✦ Union fort
← Union advance
⛴ Union blockade ship
▬ Union ironclad ship

✦ Confederate fort
← Confederate advance
▬ Confederate ironclad ship

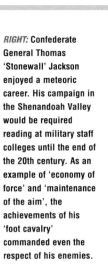

RIGHT: Confederate General Thomas 'Stonewall' Jackson enjoyed a meteoric career. His campaign in the Shenandoah Valley would be required reading at military staff colleges until the end of the 20th century. As an example of 'economy of force' and 'maintenance of the aim', the achievements of his 'foot cavalry' commanded even the respect of his enemies.

Battle of Mobile Bay, 5 Aug. 1864

Confederate
- Tennessee
- gunboats
- minefields
××× obstructions

Union
- Hartford
- Monitors
- unarmoured ships

The Confederacy was industrially weak, exchanging agricultural produce for foreign manufactured goods, including weapons. It was therefore vulnerable to naval blockade. Lack of roads and guerrilla raids on railways made rivers the most attractive lines of communication in the West. General Winfield Scott had proposed cutting the Confederacy in half by an amphibious advance down the Mississippi as early as 1861. Derided as the 'Anaconda Plan', his concept was implemented piecemeal, alongside conventional operations in the East.

The US Navy played a leading role in the capture of New Orleans in 1862, and Grant's operations around Vicksburg. Like the contemporary Royal Navy it had command of the sea, so fought few conventional ship-to-ship actions. It exploited command by supporting land operations along the coast and great rivers, or strangling the Southern economy. The US Navy carried Grant across the James River, linked up with Sherman at Savannah, and took the Atlantic coastal forts, to enforce the seaborne blockade.

Significant naval actions arose from these activities. A Confederate attempt to lift the blockade of the James River led to the first clash between armoured warships at Hampton Roads. One of them, the USS *Monitor*, was of revolutionary design. Previous armoured warships, such as HMS *Warrior* or the Monitor's opponent CSS *Merrimack*, had carried their guns on the broadside, like traditional ships of the line. The *Monitor* mounted two big guns in a revolving turret, giving a flexible arc of fire, independent of the vessel's movement. Neither ship could penetrate the other's armour, but previous fighting between *Merrimack* and conventional US vessels forcibly demonstrated the obsolescence of unarmoured ships. The *Monitor's* intervention was tactically indecisive, but it ensured the strategically decisive failure of the *Merrimack* to raise the Federal block-

ade. The Battle of Mobile Bay confirmed the difficulty of sinking armoured ships by gunfire or ramming. Forts were unable to defeat warships, the USN's armoured ships protecting their wooden vessels while running past Fort Morgan. The sinking of USS *Tecumseh* by a mine, however, suggested one antidote to armoured ships.

Mobile Bay sealed off the last Southern port, not long before Sherman began his 'March to the Sea', but the collapse of the Confederate armies in the field overtook the Union's economic strategy. Grant's efforts to turn Lee's flanks at Petersburg covered the front with 37 miles of trenches. The railway sustained both armies as Petersburg, like Sebastopol, was never surrounded. When Grant broke through the attenuated Confederate lines in March 1865, Lee was unable to disengage. American cavalry had never aspired to a battlefield role, but adopted the rifle to

pursue strategic raids and reconnaissance. They recovered the defensive firepower cavalry had lost in the 17th century, when they had focussed on a shock role. Dismounted action by Sheridan's cavalry delayed Lee's retreat long enough for Union infantry to force the Army of North Virginia to surrender at Appomattox (9 April 1865).

The American experience had limited effects elsewhere. British Army officers were taught to admire the Jominian strategy of Lee and Jackson, but Sherman had shown the future more plainly. His stark view of war as unmitigated cruelty, and his inexorable turning movements, pointed the way forward.

ABOVE: The last of the major Confederate ironclads took on a whole squadron when the US Navy broke into Mobile Bay. The *Tennessee* was eventually battered into submission after hours of close range gunnery. However, one US monitor sank in seconds after striking a 'torpedo' (a tethered mine). The drastic results possible from underwater damage led inventors to add propulsion systems to explosive devices; these weapons soon became known as torpedoes.

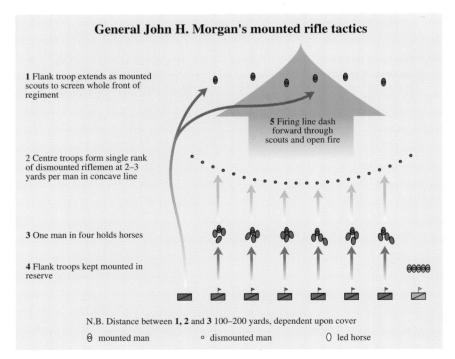

General John H. Morgan's mounted rifle tactics

1 Flank troop extends as mounted scouts to screen whole front of regiment

5 Firing line dash forward through scouts and open fire

2 Centre troops form single rank of dismounted riflemen at 2–3 yards per man in concave line

3 One man in four holds horses

4 Flank troops kept mounted in reserve

N.B. Distance between **1**, **2** and **3** 100–200 yards, dependent upon cover

⊖ mounted man   ∘ dismounted man   0 led horse

LEFT: Old-style cavalry charges had little place in the American military tradition and the few attempts in battle were not encouraging. In the Civil War, cavalry of both sides fought more like mounted infantry, using the mobility of the horse for manoeuvre, but dismounting to shoot.

The Russo-Turkish War

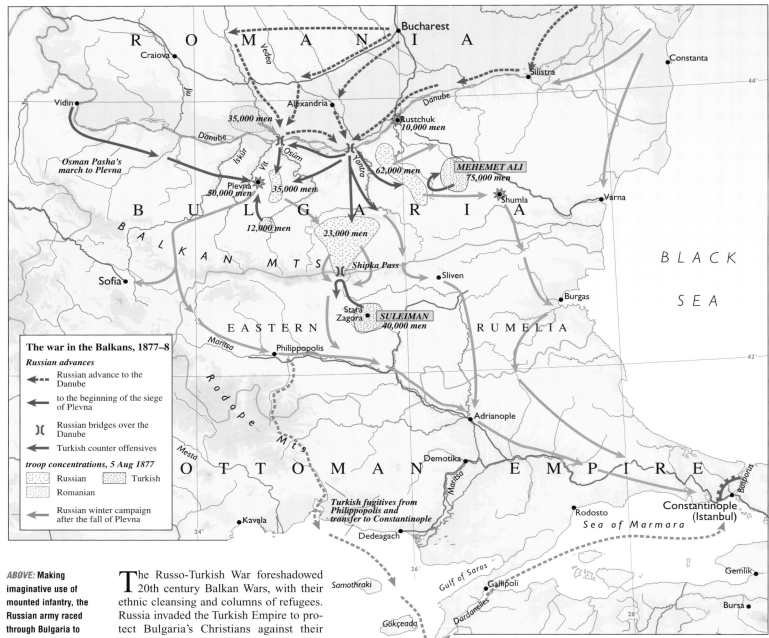

The war in the Balkans, 1877–8

Russian advances

- ◄- - - Russian advance to the Danube
- ◄—— to the beginning of the siege of Plevna
-)(Russian bridges over the Danube
- ◄—— Turkish counter offensives

troop concentrations, 5 Aug 1877
- Russian
- Turkish
- Romanian
- ◄—— Russian winter campaign after the fall of Plevna

Osman Pasha's march to Plevna

Plevna 50,000 men
35,000 men
12,000 men
23,000 men
35,000 men
62,000 men
MEHEMET ALI 75,000 men
Rustchuk 10,000 men

Shipka Pass

SULEIMAN 40,000 men

Turkish fugitives from Philippopolis and transfer to Constantinople

ABOVE: Making imaginative use of mounted infantry, the Russian army raced through Bulgaria to seize the Shipka pass, but it was unable to advance south of the Balkan mountains because a Turkish army had dug itself in at Plevna. The campaign was marked by widespread atrocities, Turkish irregulars (the infamous *Bashi-Bazouks*) preyed on Bulgarian Christians who conducted some 'ethnic cleansing' of their own against their Muslim neighbours, aided by the Cossacks.

The Russo-Turkish War foreshadowed 20th century Balkan Wars, with their ethnic cleansing and columns of refugees. Russia invaded the Turkish Empire to protect Bulgaria's Christians against their Muslim rulers, but underestimated Turkish resistance. They mobilized insufficient forces, turning a peace-keeping operation into a major war.

Turkish command of the Black Sea since 1855 forced the Russians to advance inland, over the River Danube and the Balkan Mountains. Communications were poor. The single track Romanian railway system north of the Danube was useless for troop movements. Bulgaria was economically backward, with appalling roads. Nevertheless the Russians crossed the middle Danube with 150,000 men in June 1877, their innovative use of mines and spar-torpedo boats checkmating Turkish ironclads downstream. The Russians failed to make defeat of the enemy army a key objective, believing that the mere appearance of Russian troops south of the Balkans would terrify the Sultan into giving up Bulgaria. Count Gourko led 30,000 men across the mountains in a daring raid,

creating panic in Istanbul. Turkish armies on either flank of the Russian advance were undefeated, however, while reinforcements poured into Thrace by sea. When Osman Pasha marched from Vidin to Plevna (Pleven), threatening the Danube bridgeheads, he threw the whole Russian army onto the defensive. The Russians had occupied a huge salient, 180 miles across, its most advanced point at the Shipka Pass. They could not retreat without exposing Christian Bulgarians to unspeakable reprisals. The Russians' pursuit of geographical objectives with insufficient numbers had cost them the strategic initiative, and forced them to attack Osman in a position of his own choosing.

The failure of the Russian attacks on Plevna is always taken as proof of the tactical superiority of the entrenched rifle-

man. The Russians had evidently learned nothing from the American Civil War about the need to turn the enemy out of his trenches, but they ignored every other military principle as well. They failed to reconnoitre the Turkish positions, or to launch probing attacks that would force the enemy to reveal their positions. Russian artillery never cooperated with the infantry. It fired ineffectively at long range before attacks, but never advanced to close range during them, as Prussian guns had done in 1870. Russian commanders kept inadequate reserves, preventing them from exploiting such success as there was. The first two assaults did not even have numerical superiority over the defenders.

Defensive victories like those of Osman's are rarely enough to end a war favourably. Osman failed to press his advantage, was shut up in Plevna, and starved out. The fall of Plevna in December 1877 released sufficient Russian troops to restore the momentum of their stalled advance. Crossing obscure Balkans passes on a wide front, the Russians surrounded 36,000 Turks at Shipka, and cut off their main army of 50,000 men from Istanbul. The mountains had proved a trap for their defenders. Sea power saved the Turks, moving the remains of their armies from Enez to Istanbul, covered by the guns of the British Mediterranean Fleet. Unwilling to provoke a European war, the exhausted Russians agreed terms.

The Russo-Turkish War underlined the tactical lessons of the Franco-Prussian and American Civil Wars. Turkish infantry dug themselves in, while Russian cavalry fought as mounted riflemen. Both sides used the latest breech-loading rifled artillery and small arms. Initial doubts about the fragility and complexity of such weapons, had been dispelled by their enhanced range, lethality, and reliability. In 20 years they swept away the smooth-bore musket and bayonet that had domi-

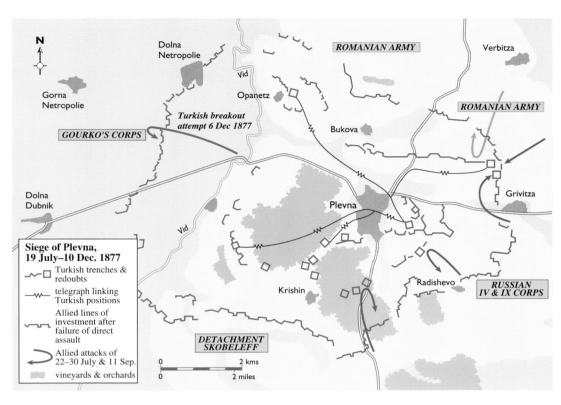

Siege of Plevna, 19 July–10 Dec. 1877

- Turkish trenches & redoubts
- telegraph linking Turkish positions
- Allied lines of investment after failure of direct assault
- Allied attacks of 22–30 July & 11 Sep.
- vineyards & orchards

ROMANIAN ARMY
ROMANIAN ARMY
Dolna Netropolie
Verbitza
Gorna Netropolie
Vid
Opanetz
Turkish breakout attempt 6 Dec 1877
GOURKO'S CORPS
Bukova
ROMANIAN ARMY
Grivitza
Dolna Dubnik
Vid
Plevna
Radishevo
RUSSIAN IV & IX CORPS
Krishin
DETACHMENT SKOBELEFF

0   2 kms
0   2 miles

The firepower revolution, 1850–90
Comparative ranges and rates of fire of infantry small arms

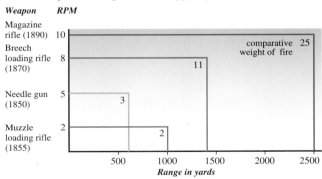

Weapon	RPM
Magazine rifle (1890)	10
Breech loading rifle (1870)	8
Needle gun (1850)	5
Muzzle loading rifle (1855)	2

comparative weight of fire 25
11
3
2

500   1000   1500   2000   2500
Range in yards

nated warfare for a century and a half. More effective weapons increased absolute losses, but long range firefights and larger armies led to lower percentage casualties. Individual regiments might lose a third of their strength, as the Prussian Guard did at Gravelotte, but the Prussian Army lost only 7.4 percent. The rifle became the main cause of wounds, reversing the Napoleonic dominance of artillery. Rifle fire caused 70% of French casualties in the Franco-Prussian War, against 25% from artillery and 5% for edged weapons. Positions were no longer carried at bayonet point, but by developing superior fire to that of the defenders. Armies dispersed to reduce losses, and dominate larger areas with their longer ranged weapons. The Russians held the 44-mile line around Plevna with 100,000 men, half the number of Germans needed for a similar front at Paris seven years earlier. To penetrate such a line was widely regarded as a purely theoretical possibility.

Colonial Warfare (1)

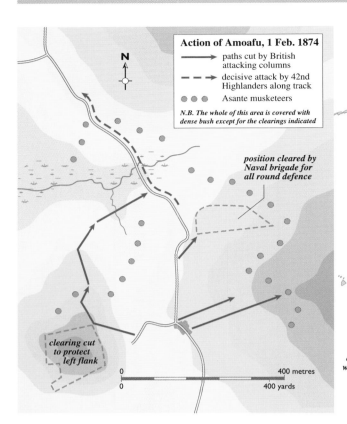

Action of Amoafu, 1 Feb. 1874

N

→ paths cut by British
attacking columns

--→ decisive attack by 42nd
Highlanders along track

●●● Asante musketeers

*N.B. The whole of this area is covered with
dense bush except for the clearings indicated*

*position cleared by
Naval brigade for
all round defence*

*clearing cut
to protect
left flank*

0   400 metres
0   400 yards

GREENLAN

ALASKA

DOMINION OF CANADA

NEWFOUNDLAND

UNITED STATES
OF AMERICA

*America's westward expansion
doomed the Plains tribes, but the
military forces employed over this
vast area were very small. On
one of the few occasions the
tribes concentrated their forces
they inflicted the shock defeat of
the Little Big Horn (1876).*

*Algeria conquered by France
in successive campaigns
from the 1830s*

MEXICO

CUBA
(occupied by USA)

BRITISH
HONDURAS

Jamaica
(Br.)

*France's attempt to install
a puppet regime in Mexico
while the USA was torn with
civil war led to a savage
guerrilla campaign against
Mexican insurgents.
Napoleon's marshals
eventually concluded the war
was unwinnable and Emperor
Maximilian was abandoned
to his fate.*

VENEZUELA

BRITISH GUIANA
DUTCH GUIANA
FRENCH GUIANA

COLOMBIA

ECUADOR

*Amoafu, 1874: The British
campaign against the Asante takes
place in dense jungle. Disease is a
greater enemy than the tribesmen.*

B R A Z I L

PERU

ACRE

BOLIVIA

PARAGUAY

C H I L E

A R G E N T I N A

URUGUAY

*The leading powers of South America
established armies on the European
pattern and used them in the same
manner to adjust their borders. Thus
Bolivia lost her coastline. Some built
modern navies too: by the 1880s Chile
had a larger and more modern fleet
than the USA.*

ABOVE: **The dense
jungle of West Africa
provided no field of fire
for superior British
weapons. Only the
extreme crudity of the
Asante's firearms saved
the British from
suffering greater
losses. As it was, the
bloody determination of
long service regulars
won through and the
Asantes' skull-strewn
capital was duly
captured and burned.
However, most of the
British force fell victim
to disease.**

RIGHT: **HMS *Shah*'s
naval brigade in action
at Ginginhlovu (dubbed
'Gin Gin I love you' by
British soldiers) during
the Zulu War. The
ability of the Navy to
form detachments for
service ashore was
invaluable in nineteenth
century colonial
campaigns.**

Colonial wars were the main source of military experience for the British, French, United States, and even Russian armies in the 19th century. Misleadingly known as 'Small Wars', such conflicts were quite different to *La Grande Guerre*, as known in Europe and North America. Western forces met a wide variety of military challenges, developing counter-insurgency techniques still used in the 1990s.

Steamships placed the world at the mercy of the mid-19th century revolution in weapons technology. Galleons and seaborne artillery had created Western seaborne empires in the 17th century. Now the West would conquer the hinterland of Africa and Asia as well. Until the Western adoption of rifled small arms in the 1850s the Islamic *jezail* had outranged the Brown Bess musket, defeating Western forces in Afghanistan and Morocco in the 1840s.

Ten years later handfuls of British soldiers, and even sailors, with Enfield rifles regularly defeated enormous numbers of rebellious Indian sepoys, who could not get within range to use their own weapons. In the second half of the century, Britain consolidated existing possessions in India and South Africa, and took a controlling interest in Egypt and the Sudan. The United States eliminated its internal frontier, while Russia absorbed most of Central Asia more or less unnoticed. The most notorious victim of Western firepower was Africa, shared out by the European powers between 1880 and 1900. France gained nearly four million square miles, a third of Africa's surface area. Only a few non-Western powers retained their independence. Japan and Ethiopia acquired Western technology, and deterred or defeated would-be predators. Siam and

Persia were saved by inter-power rivalries.

The world possessed a multiplicity of military systems in the 19th century, many of them unknown outside their own region. Few societies had adopted Western weapons and military structures, or were yet prepared to pay the social cost of doing so. The Sikhs and Egyptians followed the latest European styles of weaponry, organization, and even dress. The white Dutch farmers, or Boers, of South Africa, possessed modern weapons but only the most rudimentary organization. The Zulus combined primitive weapons with a sophisticated tactical system. The situation was not static, however. The international arms trade equipped Pathans with breech-loading rifles, and transformed the capabilities of the Chinese Army. Chinese soldiers in the 1860s had carried wooden swords and matchlocks, but by 1900 their magazine rifles and 4-inch guns outgunned the Naval Brigades landed to contain the Boxer Rebellion. The tactical methods adopted by indigenous forces were as varied as their

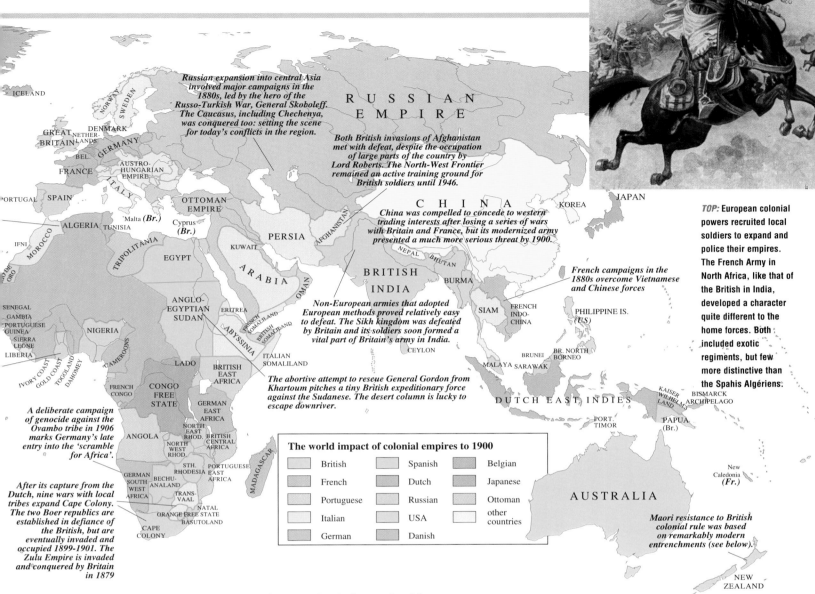

Russian expansion into central Asia involved major campaigns in the 1880s, led by the hero of the Russo-Turkish War, General Skoboleff. The Caucasus, including Chechenya, was conquered too: setting the scene for today's conflicts in the region.

Both British invasions of Afghanistan met with defeat, despite the occupation of large parts of the country by Lord Roberts. The North-West Frontier remained an active training ground for British soldiers until 1946.

China was compelled to concede to western trading interests after losing a series of wars with Britain and France, but its modernized army presented a much more serious threat by 1900.

French campaigns in the 1880s overcome Vietnamese and Chinese forces

Non-European armies that adopted European methods proved relatively easy to defeat. The Sikh kingdom was defeated by Britain and its soldiers soon formed a vital part of Britain's army in India.

The abortive attempt to rescue General Gordon from Khartoum pitches a tiny British expeditionary force against the Sudanese. The desert column is lucky to escape downriver.

A deliberate campaign of genocide against the Ovambo tribe in 1906 marks Germany's late entry into the 'scramble for Africa'.

After its capture from the Dutch, nine wars with local tribes expand Cape Colony. The two Boer republics are established in defiance of the British, but are eventually invaded and occupied 1899-1901. The Zulu Empire is invaded and conquered by Britain in 1879

TOP: European colonial powers recruited local soldiers to expand and police their empires. The French Army in North Africa, like that of the British in India, developed a character quite different to the home forces. Both included exotic regiments, but few more distinctive than the Spahis Algériens.

Maori resistance to British colonial rule was based on remarkably modern entrenchments (see below).

The world impact of colonial empires to 1900

British	Spanish	Belgian
French	Dutch	Japanese
Portuguese	Russian	Ottoman
Italian	USA	other countries
German	Danish	

organizational differences. Aggressive African tribes like the Zulus or Asante sought to encircle their opponents, but the no less redoutable Maori took refuge in fortified complexes that could withstand direct hits from 110pr Armstrong guns. The Sudanese implemented a defensive/offensive strategy, handfuls of riflemen luring their clumsy but well-armed opponents within range of concealed spearmen.

Western powers found it easiest to deal with opponents that most closely approximated to the European pattern. The Sikh Army posed the most serious threat encountered by the British in India. Once beaten in recognizably Wellingtonian style, however, the Sikhs accepted the political consequences of defeat like any normal enemy, and became trusted participants in the Raj. Less structured opponents might not possess an organized army that could be defeated in battle, or a recognizable capital to occupy afterwards. The best British commanders of the period, Lords Roberts and Wolseley, occupied Kabul and Kumase without bringing the Afghan and Ashanti Wars to a satisfactory end. The absence of any clear strategic centre of gravity enabled indigenous people to avoid

action, once they had appreciated the superiority of Western firepower. Many of them, such as the Plains Indians or the Turkomen of Central Asia were nomadic in any case. They pursued a guerrilla strategy, exploiting the poor communications and often unhealthy nature of their countries to wear out Western intruders. Disease caused almost 90% of British deaths in the Indian Mutiny (8,987 out of 11,012). The French expedition to Madagascar in 1895 lost 5,500 dead to malaria, out of 18,000. Only in the early 20th century did military medicine begin to deal with tropical disease as efficiently as the Maxim gun dealt with human opponents.

ABOVE: The accelerating pace of military technology gave colonial powers an increasing advantage over irregular opponents. Formed armies that played the colonial forces at their own game came off worst: the Sikhs and Zulus were overcome, despite the occasional upset. Nomads, or the denizens of fever-stricken jungles, were harder to tame. European armies suffered heavy losses to tropical diseases, another reason to rely on locally recruited 'native' regiments. Colonial 'small wars' provided valuable experience for several European armies, but not every 'lesson' would prove applicable to regular warfare, or even other colonial campaigns.

BELOW: The Maoris resisted the British Army from stoutly constructed positions called pahs. Sometimes they were abandoned on the eve of a bombardment that took the colonial forces weeks of labour to organize. In general, irregular forces that offered the colonial army a geographical objective would be defeated: tribal armies with no fixed base were harder to pin down.

Maori Pah 1860

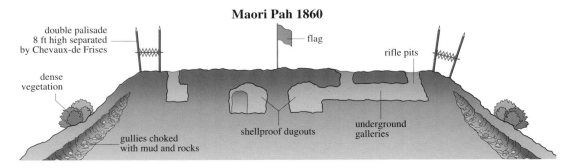

double palisade 8 ft high separated by Chevaux-de-Frises

flag

rifle pits

dense vegetation

shellproof dugouts

underground galleries

gullies choked with mud and rocks

Colonial Warfare (2): The Imperial Response

Every colonial campaign was different. British Guardsmen picked off by invisible Boer marksmen at Modder River had last seen action the year before, against Sudanese spearmen. Western forces adapted to local conditions, or suffered catastrophic defeats.

British units committed to the Zulu War had recently fought the Xhosa of Natal who possessed numerous firearms. The open order tactics appropriate against them were disastrous against the Zulu, who combined the speed of cavalry with infantry's ability to approach under cover.

The firepower of dispersed skirmishers was insufficient to halt them, while the flanks of a firing line were vulnerable to envelopment. Against such daring and mobile opponents European armies had to adopt dense formations, that were obsolete at home. Squares reduced overall firepow-

LEFT: **Royal Marines in action in Egypt in 1882, supported by an armoured train. European armies maintained an easy superiority over colonial opponents like the Egyptians, who copied European weapons and tactics, but lacked the training to use them effectively.**

RIGHT: **Bluejackets from HMS George guard a stockade in East Africa in 1895. One way of avoiding deadly tropical diseases was to land Naval Brigades, who could return to their ships before malaria took hold. The role of the mosquito in spreading fever was not understood until the 20th century.**

er, but restricted the frontage under attack, and secured the flanks. Mounted troops and transport could shelter inside. Squares were relatively immobile, so the individual units forming their sides used the usual company columns, until contact was imminent, as the French did in Algeria, with their *tête du porc* formation.

Zulu firepower was negligible, but skirmishing skills were essential against Boer and Pathan marksmen. During the First Afghan War hostile mountaineers harassed columns in the passes below, destroying an entire British army at Gandamak (13 January 1842). British and Indian troops on India's North West Frontier learned to 'picquet the heights', to keep the enemy out of range of troops moving along the valley. Such cautious tactics reduced British casualties, but made it difficult to move quickly, or achieve decisive success.

Imperial forces could not match the mobility of their enemies. Operating in agriculturally undeveloped areas with poor roads or none, they had to bring their supplies with them, restricting strategic mobility. Difficulties of supply kept imperial forces small, and forced them to detach up to 90% of their strength to protect their supply lines. Wheeled vehicles were often useless so baggage trains consisted of pack animals or human porters, straggling along narrow tracks. Imperial forces formed flying columns, partly for easier supply, and partly to catch their elusive enemies. Western tactical superiority made it safe to take such risks against opponents unlikely to exploit the advantages of internal lines. Occasionally native forces did concentrate against isolated detachments, leading to disasters like those on the Little Big Horn in 1876 or at Adowa in 1896. A battle usually favoured the imperial forces, so commanders preferred combat to manoeuvre. They needed a victory before disease, the weather, or supply problems forced them to withdraw.

The intangibility of their opponents forced colonial powers to attack economic targets, a portent of 20th century strategic trends. The British on the North West Frontier blew up towers and burned grain stores. The US Army, fresh from Sherman's March through Georgia, attacked the winter lodges of the Sioux and Cheyenne, and destroyed the buffalo. Sometimes the wish to reconcile indigenous people to imperial rule moderated economic pressure. The French in Algeria and Morocco built roads and markets to persuade tribesmen of the benefits of French rule. Colonial administrators saw military settlements as outposts of civilisation, spreading Western influence like patches of oil. At the other extreme, colonial powers divided up occupied territory with lines of blockhouses, or resettled entire populations to deprive guerrilla

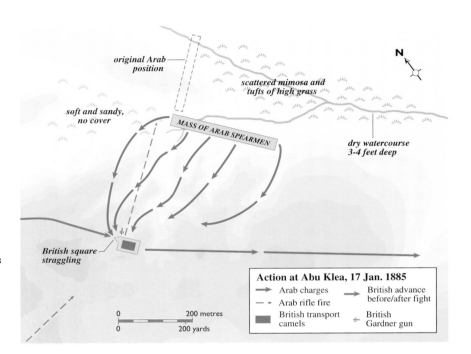

Where the Arabs broke into the square
section showing bad field of fire from rear part of left face

right face firing over the transport

left face of square

ABOVE: The British expeditionary force belatedly sent to rescue General Gordon in Khartoum was confronted by masses of very determined Dervishes. Formed in square as if to resist cavalry, the British relied on the firepower of the Martini-Henry rifle to flatten any amount of charging spearmen. The Gardner machine gun did sterling work too, its poor reputation owing more to poetry than practical experience.

RIGHT: The Arabs made excellent use of the ground and were able to ambush and break into British formations on several occasions. At Abu Klea a general massacre was averted by the right face of the square firing over the heads of their comrades. Sudanese battlefield prowess was celebrated by Kipling ('Fuzzy Wuzzy'); they broke another square at the battle of Tamai and in certain soldiers' pubs in the 1890s you could start a fight by ordering a 'pint of broken square'.

original Arab position

scattered mimosa and tufts of high grass

soft and sandy, no cover

MASS OF ARAB SPEARMEN

dry watercourse 3-4 feet deep

N

British square straggling

Action at Abu Klea, 17 Jan. 1885
- → Arab charges
- – – Arab rifle fire
- ■ British transport camels
- → British advance before/after fight
- ⊹ British Gardner gun

| 0 | 200 metres |
| 0 | 200 yards |

fighters of support. In America the great tide of transatlantic immigration swamped the native Americans. For the USA the Indian Wars were a minor distraction; for the Sioux they were a war for national survival.

Small Wars divided Western armies into colonial and metropolitan schools. The British Army had its Wolseley and Roberts rings; the US Army divided into Easterners, who got cosy staff jobs in Washington, and Westerners who fought on the Plains. In some respects colonial warfare benefited its practitioners, breathing life into decadent and over-bureaucratic home establishments. It reinforced the trend towards tactical dispersal, and built a robust self-sufficient professionalism. In other senses colonial warfare was less positive. French experience in Algeria was blamed for the disorganized staff work and strategic paralysis that led to the defeats of 1870. Some colonial soldiers neglected firepower, placing discipline or aggression above initiative or marksmanship. Artillery was of limited value in colonial wars, where cavalry retained a misleading usefulness. The colonial experience was at odds with 19th century trends, encouraging recklessness and improvisation rather than professionalism and organization.

Tete du Porc

advance guard

headquarters

section of two guns

infantry battalion in column of companies

regular cavalry regiment in column of squadrons

ammunition column

field ambulance

regimental baggage

1st brigade

irregular Arab horse

2nd brigade

formation boundaries

rear guard

ABOVE: French forces in Algeria faced a fearsome, mobile enemy and their formations also had to be adapted for all-round defence when on the march. The French Army of Africa provided some exotic units and hard-bitten officers for the defence of France in 1870, but colonial habits like closing up the columns at nightfall were of little relevance in Alsace.

Boer War

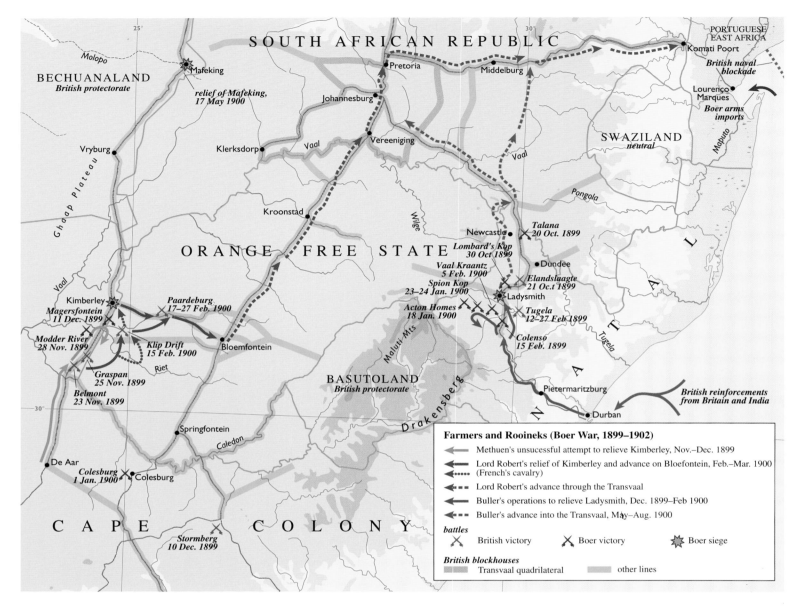

SOUTH AFRICAN REPUBLIC

PORTUGUESE EAST AFRICA

BECHUANALAND
British protectorate

British naval blockade

relief of Mafeking, 17 May 1900

Boer arms imports

SWAZILAND
neutral

ORANGE FREE STATE

Talana
20 Oct. 1899

Lombard's Kop
30 Oct 1899

Vaal Kraantz
5 Feb. 1900

Spion Kop
23–24 Jan. 1900

Acton Homes
18 Jan. 1900

Magersfontein
11 Dec. 1899

Paardeburg
17–27 Feb. 1900

Modder River
28 Nov. 1899

Klip Drift
15 Feb. 1900

Tugela
12–27 Feb 1899

Colenso
15 Feb. 1899

Graspan
25 Nov. 1899

Belmont
23 Nov. 1899

BASUTOLAND
British protectorate

British reinforcements from Britain and India

Colesburg
1 Jan. 1900

Stormberg
10 Dec. 1899

C A P E   C O L O N Y

Farmers and Rooineks (Boer War, 1899–1902)

Methuen's unsuccessful attempt to relieve Kimberley, Nov.–Dec. 1899

Lord Robert's relief of Kimberley and advance on Bloefontein, Feb.–Mar. 1900 (French's cavalry)

Lord Robert's advance through the Transvaal

Buller's operations to relieve Ladysmith, Dec. 1899–Feb 1900

Buller's advance into the Transvaal, May–Aug. 1900

battles
British victory — Boer victory — Boer siege

British blockhouses
Transvaal quadrilateral — other lines

ABOVE: The Boer War absorbed 500,000 British soldiers and echoes of it can still be heard in Army slang a century later. Once their capitals were occupied, many of the commandos fought on, relying on their mobility and the support of the civilian population to keep one step ahead of the British. Mao's revelation that guerrillas are fish in the civilian sea was already familiar to Lord Kitchener who ordered it drained. Penned in by the blockhouses, with their families dying in British concentration camps, even the 'Bitter Enders' were compelled to surrender.

The British generals of the Boer War had studied the lessons of Gravelotte and the Shenandoah Valley, but had yet to face opponents with 20th century weapons. The conflict was both a colonial war and the largest British war between 1815 and 1914. It employed almost 500,000 British soldiers, many of them reservists. For all its imperial setting, the Boer War was a total war for the Transvaal and Orange Free State who faced political annihilation if they lost. In the United Kingdom organized pacifism voiced a protest that would increasingly be heard in the new century, at least in liberal democracies.

The two decades since Plevna had completed the 19th century weapons revolution. Boer War soldiers carried small calibre magazine rifles, whose flat trajectory made them ideal weapons on the open South African veldt. Smokeless cartridge propellant did not reveal the position of defending riflemen, introducing the empty battlefield. Attackers lost the cover of the clouds of smoke previously generated by skirmish lines. Before the war was over, a British

Guards officer would propose the use of automatic rifles and armoured fighting vehicles. The war began with rapid advances by mounted Boer commandos, their mobility multiplying their initial numerical advantage. Like the French Army of Alsace in 1870, British forces deployed too far forward, in a salient, making it easy to surround them. Fortunately for the British, the Boers failed to press on to seize the ports through which imperial reinforcements would enter South Africa. The commandos sat down around Ladysmith and Kimberley, blocking the only routes for British relief attempts: the railways.

Boer firepower and fieldcraft inflicted embarrassing defeats on the British. The Boers occupied unprecedentedly wide frontages, several yards per man with no reserves. Their deep trenches were impervious to shellfire, and had secure flanks, as the British lacked the mounted troops and transport to turn them. When the British did try strategic turning movements, as at Spion Kop on the Tugela, the more mobile Boers quickly moved into a fresh blocking

position. The British took four months to build up enough forces to break through the Boer lines. On the Tugela, Sir Redvers Buller learned to support his infantry with heavy artillery fire right up to the moment they entered the Boer trenches, the prototype of the creeping barrage. On the Modder River, Lord Roberts outmanoeuvred the Boers. His cavalry division relieved Kimberley then held the retreating enemy at Paardeberg (27 February 1900) until the infantry caught up to impose a capitulation reminiscent of Lee's surrender at Appomattox.

Neither Buller nor Roberts inflicted sufficient attrition on the Boers to defeat them outright. A hard core of *Bitter-Einders* fought on after the fall of the Boer capitals at Pretoria and Bloemfontein. Logistically independent of the towns, they drew food and remounts from their family farms, and replaced weapons and uniforms at the expense of the enemy, as Che Guevara would do in the Sierra Madre in the 1950s. The British had too few mounted troops to dominate the wide spaces of

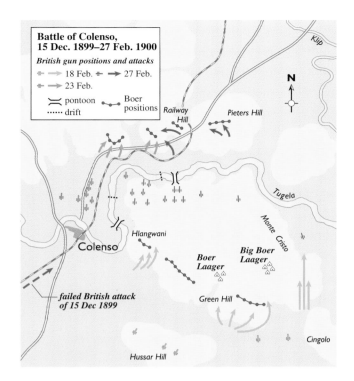

**Battle of Colenso,
15 Dec. 1899–27 Feb. 1900**

British gun positions and attacks

- 18 Feb.
- 27 Feb.
- 23 Feb.

pontoon   Boer
positions
drift

Railway
Hill

Pieters Hill

Klip

N

Tugela

Monte Cristo

Hlangwani

Colenso

Boer
Laager

Big Boer
Laager

Green Hill

*failed British attack
of 15 Dec 1899*

Cingolo

Hussar Hill

LEFT: Smokeless powder made the Boer trenches invisible and removed the smokescreen that had hitherto afforded some protection to infantry on the attack. At Colenso, British artillery deployed forward like the Prussian gunners in 1870, but the crews were shot down by concealed marksmen. Lord Roberts' only son won a posthumous VC trying to save them.

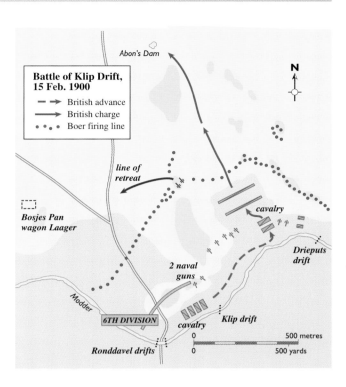

Abon's Dam

N

**Battle of Klip Drift,
15 Feb. 1900**

- British advance
- British charge
- Boer firing line

*line of
retreat*

*Bosjes Pan
wagon Laager*

cavalry

Drieputs
drift

2 naval
guns

Modder

6TH DIVISION   cavalry   *Klip drift*

Ronddavel drifts

0   500 metres
0   500 yards

ABOVE: Boer military organization was very rudimentary and their main forces proved incapable of more than a static defence. Once outmanoeuvred, Cronje's army was unable to extricate itself and obliged to surrender.

LEFT: A British armoured train in pursuit of the Boer Commando leader, Christian de Wet. His house was soon captured (his kitchen table graces the museum of the Green Howards) but he and his guerrillas proved elusive. Many British officers saw technology as the answer to both their strategic and tactical problems: Major Baden-Powell advocated armoured cars and light machine guns.

the veldt. They countered Boer mobility by building lines of blockhouses across the country, joined together by barbed wire. Mobile columns tried to pin the elusive Boer guerrillas against these obstacles with limited success. Wireless telegraphy was too clumsy to coordinate the drives. Aircraft, ideal for reconnaissance on the veldt, would not be invented until 18 months after the war ended. The war took a sinister turn with the concentration of Boer families in camps to prevent them helping their unreconciled kinsmen.

Ignorance of hygiene led to many deaths, causing an outcry in the United Kingdom, and permanently embittering Anglo-Boer relations. British recruitment of *Hands-Oppers* or surrendered Boers to hunt their kinsmen threatened to tear Afrikaaner society apart. Combined with general war-weariness this brought both sides to the peace table. Like many later guerrilla wars, the Boer War did enormous damage without producing a clear-cut victory.

As so often with colonial wars, the lessons of the Boer War were misunder-

stood. German military critics ignored the difficulties of reconnaissance on a flat plain swept by rifle fire, and attributed British problems to an effete aversion to casualties. The British Army reformed its command structure, and rewrote its drill books, but reintroduced the lance in 1909. Buller's post-war disgrace obscured the success of his fire-and-movement tactics, while the uniquely successful cavalry charge at Klip Drift created an entirely misleading impression of cavalry's offensive potential.

Russo-Japanese war (1) Pre-emptive strike

The Russo-Japanese War was the first
major conflict of the 20th century.
Often interpreted as a limited 19th century
war of manoeuvre, it had much in common
with later more absolute wars. The conflict
may have been peripheral for the Russians,
whose European commitments absorbed a
large percentage of their 4.5 million-strong
army, but the Japanese saw it as a war for
national survival. They employed all the
means at their disposal, showing how a
small power can defeat a stronger, but less
committed power.

There was no decisive victory on land.
Machine guns and barbed wire appeared in
sufficient quantities to impose tactical
stalemate, while the even balance of forces
created strategic deadlock. External
observers thought conditions in Manchuria
untypical, like the Boer War, and ignored
the conflict's wider implications. They had
some excuse. The Russian Army was unfit
to take the field, its officers ignorant of
their profession, their troops unable to
shoot. Russian staffwork and reconnaissance were poor, initiative discouraged.

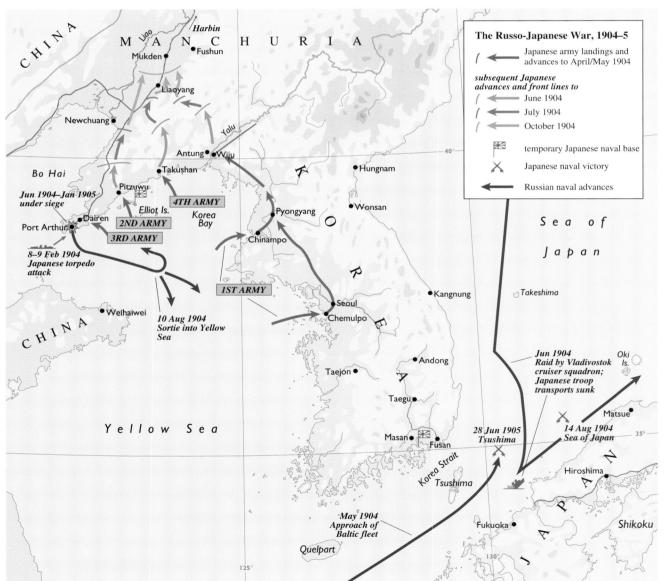

The Russo-Japanese War, 1904–5

Japanese army landings and
advances to April/May 1904

*subsequent Japanese
advances and front lines to*
June 1904
July 1904
October 1904

temporary Japanese naval base

Japanese naval victory

Russian naval advances

The total destruction of the Russian fleet contrasted with the indecisive results of the war on land. The particular strategic conditions of the Russo-Japanese War promoted an unusual interdependence between naval and military operations. As in the Crimea the theatre of war was isolated, at the end of 6,000 miles of single-track railway for the Russians, and across the Korean Straits for the Japanese. A small force fed from the sea would again exhaust the Russians. The Japanese attacked when they did to pre-empt completion of the Trans-Siberian railway, which would have swung the logistic balance in favour of the continental power. Korea is a peninsula, open to seaborne invasion, and then lacking railways or metalled roads. Japanese command of the sea countered Russian superiority on land, forcing them to divert large numbers of troops to cover possible landing places.

Russian naval forces were dispersed, their battleships at Port Arthur in the Liaotung peninsula, others in the Baltic and Black Sea Fleets. The Japanese Navy had the advantage of interior lines, encouraging them to mount a joint naval/military offensive before the Russians could concentrate in the Far East. The Japanese tipped the local balance of naval forces in their favour by a surprise torpedo boat attack on Port Arthur, followed by a close blockade by their battleships. To sustain this with steam warships, in need of frequent recoaling, they seized and fortified the Elliot Islands as an advanced base. The Japanese achieved strategic surprise by attacking without first declaring war, but found it difficult to follow-up.

The Russians tried to preserve their surviving ships at Port Arthur, while mounting a *guerre de course* with cruisers based at Vladivostock. As the French had found in the 1790s, the efficiency of a fleet kept in harbour soon declines. Mechanical breakdowns plagued Russian sorties. However, Port Arthur's forts reasserted the traditional dominance of land-based guns over ships, lost during the American Civil War. Russian mine warfare, pursued in defiance of international law, sank two Japanese battleships, forcing them to abandon their close blockade. Ironically the brilliant Russian Admiral Makarov had already fallen victim to a mine. The Japanese landed troops in Liaotung to cut Port Arthur off from Manchuria, and force the Russian Far East squadron to surrender. The first assault provoked a Russian naval sortie, leading to the Battle of the Yellow Sea. A chance shell killed the new Russian admiral, and his fleet scattered in panic. The Japanese had achieved command of the sea three months after launching most of their army across contested waters, a strategy most naval critics regarded as impossibly risky.

One casualty of Japanese risk-taking was their siege train of 11-inch howitzers,

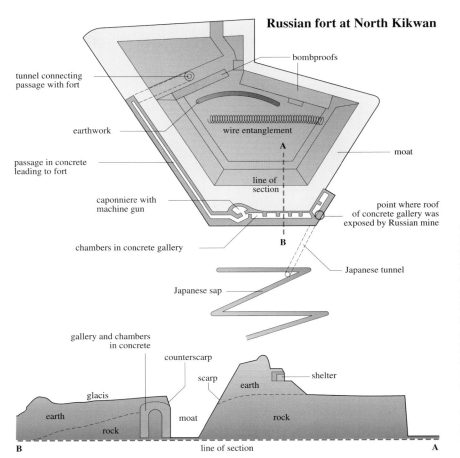

Russian fort at North Kikwan

bombproofs

tunnel connecting passage with fort

earthwork

wire entanglement

A

passage in concrete leading to fort

moat

line of section

caponniere with machine gun

point where roof of concrete gallery was exposed by Russian mine

chambers in concrete gallery

B

Japanese tunnel

Japanese sap

gallery and chambers in concrete

counterscarp

scarp

shelter

earth

glacis

earth

moat

rock

rock

B

line of section

A

LEFT: Like the battleships they protected, the Russian forts were of the latest design, not the obsolete death-traps of legend. Barbed wire, reinforced concrete and machine guns made them formidable positions to assault. Patience, bravery, and old-fashioned techniques like sapping and tunnelling eventually paved the way for a breakthrough.

intercepted at sea by Russian cruisers. The Japanese could not replace them until October 1904, after three bloody assaults on Port Arthur by unsupported infantry. The capture of 174 Metre Hill (19-24 August) cost 15,000 Japanese casualties, mostly from enfilading machine gun fire. The survivors resorted to traditional sapping techniques. Today these recall First World War trenches, but to contemporaries they were the normal accompaniment to a siege. A more convincing novelty was the

use against machine gun posts of indirect artillery fire, controlled by forward observers using telephones and captive balloons. The capture of 203 Metre Hill in December achieved the Japanese strategic aim, allowing them to sink the surviving ships of the Far East squadron with land based artillery fire. The diminished Japanese fleet returned home to prepare for the second round of the naval war. The Russian Baltic Fleet had sailed for the Far East on 15 October.

RIGHT: The base was surrounded by steel and concrete forts, connected by trenches. Infantry assaults proved terribly costly, even for the Japanese army. The loss of the Japanese siege train, sunk at sea by marauding Russian cruisers, was keenly felt. Both sides publicly mourned the death of the brilliant Admiral Makarov, killed when his flagship struck a mine. But while Admiral Togo might lament the death of a fellow Samurai, he certainly benefited from the demise of the only competent Russian leader.

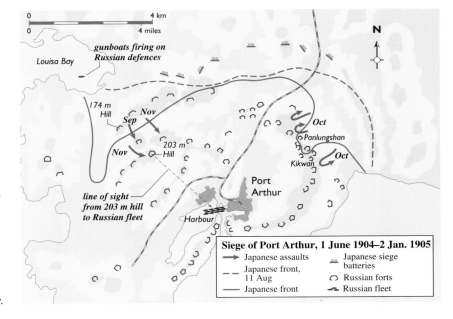

0   4 km

0   4 miles

N

gunboats firing on Russian defences

Louisa Bay

174 m Hill

Sep

Nov

Nov

203 m Hill

Nov

Oct

Panlungshan

Kikwan

Oct

line of sight from 203 m hill to Russian fleet

Port Arthur

Harbour

Siege of Port Arthur, 1 June 1904–2 Jan. 1905

→ Japanese assaults
- - - Japanese front, 11 Aug
— Japanese front

Japanese siege batteries
Russian forts
Russian fleet

Russo-Japanese War (2) Endgame

ABOVE: The Russian warships *Apraxin* and *Seniavin* after their capture by the Japanese. The Russo-Japanese naval actions were the first fleet engagements for nearly 50 years and were exhaustively studied by the world's leading naval powers. Naval technology continued to develop faster than tactical thought or communications systems.

The closing stages of the Russo-Japanese War underlined the contrast between stalemate on land and decision at sea. Contemporaries still receptive to Napoleonic ideals of decisive war ignored the former, which was truly indicative of the future, and focussed on the latter, which was not.

The Japanese could not devote all their energies to Port Arthur. They had to cover the siege against Russian troops in Manchuria, who were steadily reinforced by the Trans-Siberian Railway. Needing a quick victory, the Japanese began a converging advance against the main Russian army. Some dispersal was unavoidable for supply reasons, but a double envelopment strategy was beyond Japanese capabilities. German-trained, they imitated Moltke's strategy without his numerical superiority. At first Japanese armies manoeuvred successfully against scattered and ill-organized Russian formations. The Russian high command could not agree whether to fight forward, or await reinforcement before launching a counter-offensive to relieve Port Arthur. They pursued neither strategy properly. The Japanese regularly achieved numerical superiority in the early battles of the war, although their overall strength never exceeded that of the Russians. When the fighting fronts coalesced south of Liaoyang, the Japanese paid the price of pursuing two goals with insufficient force. They had not achieved a decisive success before Russian numbers drew ahead in September. Russian counter-offensives equally failed to break the stalemate imposed by parallel battle-fronts. The Russians made no use of the defensive strength of entrenched infantry to hold the centre, while concentrating against the enemy flanks, as Lee had done at Chancellorsville.

The Russians retreated after tied battles at Liaoyang and the Sha-Ho, not because they were routed, but because their commander believed he was beaten. General Kuropatkin had distinguished himself at Plevna, but lacked the moral strength to carry through his plans. He wore himself

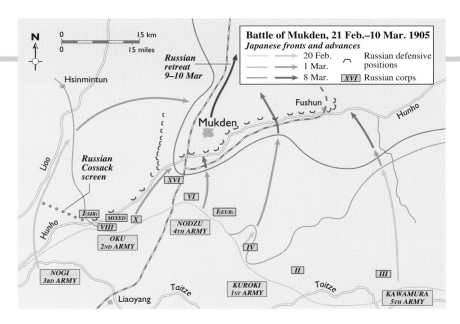

Battle of Mukden, 21 Feb.–10 Mar. 1905
Japanese fronts and advances
20 Feb.
1 Mar.
8 Mar.
Russian defensive positions
XVI Russian corps

traps was not lost on European navies. Tsushima's most significant lesson was psychological, however. It spelled the end of European supremacy at sea.

The Russo-Japanese War showed how easily a limited war might escalate. Both sides suffered enormous losses in week-long battles that made a mockery of distinctions between limited and absolute war. The Russians saw their fleet destroyed and revolution shake the Tsar's government. Even the pursuit of limited objectives need effective preparation and organization without which superior resources remain unrealized potential and losses reach catastrophic levels.

out moving restlessly about the battlefield, allowing local setbacks to sway his judgement. Marshal Oyama and his Japanese staff remained aloof from the battle, controlling events by telephone. Outnumbered 3:2, Oyama persisted with his double envelopment strategy at Mukden, employing deception to even the odds. Troops released from the siege of Port Arthur massed behind the Japanese left, unknown to the Russians, while other troop movements on the other flank drew Kuropatkin's reserves away from the true point of attack. The Japanese Third Army swept around the Russian right, to threaten the Russian lifeline, the railway. After two weeks' fighting Kuropatkin's right faced west instead of south, and two thirds of his troops were in a pocket around Mukden. He began a workmanlike disengagement, which the Japanese were unable to convert into a rout, their cavalry too few for an effective pursuit. The Japanese advance had reached its culminating point at Mukden. They had committed every man available without decisively defeating the Russian army, which regrouped still further up the railway line. The war would be ended, as it had begun, at sea.

The naval battle of Tsushima left the strategic situation unchanged, but dramatically confirmed Japanese command of the sea. Tsushima was the only fleet action fought to a finish by pre-dreadnought battleships. Like Trafalgar it was a battle of annihilation, and created similarly misleading expectations. The Battle of the Yellow Sea was a more reliable indicator of the stalemate likely between evenly balanced fleets of armoured ships. Tsushima was the product of decisively superior Japanese seamanship and gunnery which allowed Admiral Togo, hailed as the Japanese Nelson, to take the same sort of risks as his predecessor. Japanese battleships made 15 knots against the Russian nine. Togo easily crossed the Russian 'T', concentrating gunfire on the leading Russian ships. The big gun was still the dominant weapon at sea, despite mine and torpedo successes off Port Arthur. The message that old slow warships were death

RIGHT: Once the Trans-Siberian Railway was complete, Russia would be able to nourish her armies in Manchuria just as effectively as the Japanese in Korea. Japan's war took advantage of the last window of opportunity before the military balance in the region tilted against her.

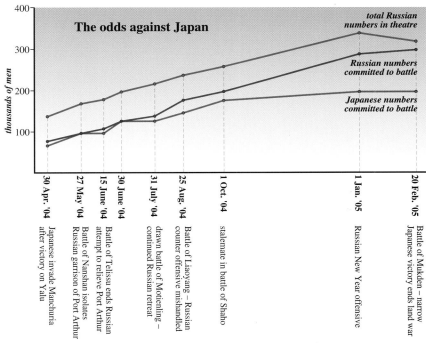

The odds against Japan

total Russian numbers in theatre

Russian numbers committed to battle

Japanese numbers committed to battle

thousands of men

400
300
200
100

30 Apr. '04 — Japanese invade Manchuria after victory on Yalu
27 May '04 — Battle of Nanshan isolates Russian garrison of Port Arthur
15 June '04 — Battle of Telissu ends Russian attempt to relieve Port Arthur
30 June '04
31 July '04 — drawn battle of Motienling – continued Russian retreat
25 Aug. '04 — Battle of Liaoyang – Russian counter offensive mishandled
1 Oct. '04 — stalemate in battle of Shaho
1 Jan. '05 — Russian New Year offensive
20 Feb. '05 — Battle of Mukden – narrow Japanese victory ends land war

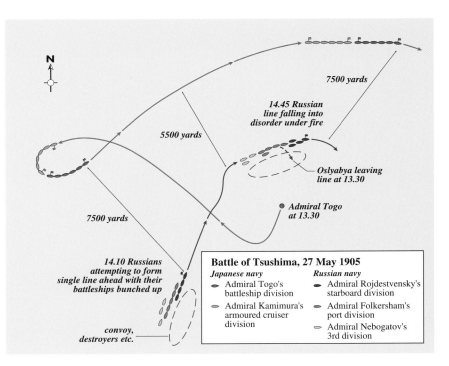

Battle of Tsushima, 27 May 1905
Japanese navy
● Admiral Togo's battleship division
◑ Admiral Kamimura's armoured cruiser division
Russian navy
◆ Admiral Rojdestvensky's starboard division
◀ Admiral Folkersham's port division
◔ Admiral Nebogatov's 3rd division

7500 yards
14.45 Russian line falling into disorder under fire
5500 yards
Oslyabya leaving line at 13.30
● Admiral Togo at 13.30
7500 yards
14.10 Russians attempting to form single line ahead with their battleships bunched up
convoy, destroyers etc.

LEFT: **Russia's Baltic Fleet sailed from Petersburg to Japan only to meet with annihilating defeat at Tsushima. Gunnery seldom produces fast results in naval actions although the some Russian battleships were so overloaded, their main armour belts were submerged and their waterline protection consequently reduced. Japanese torpedoboats finished off damaged vessels and even laid mines in the path of escaping battleships: actions studied with grim interest by British and German naval officers.**

Chapter 7 Storm of Steel 1914–16

RIGHT: The transport echelon of 1st Middlesex Regiment comes under German artillery fire during the Battle of the Marne. The range and accuracy of quick-fire artillery contributed to the 'empty battlefield' effect: both sides taking cover from the storm of steel. Command and control became very difficult because communications technology had not kept pace with the rapid increase in firepower.

The Industrial Revolution had transformed warfare by the early years of the 20th century. New means of production placed limitless quantities of unprecedentedly lethal weapons in the hands of mass armies, conscripted from Europe's ever-growing populations. Comfortable agricultural surpluses sustained forces absolutely and proportionately larger than ever before. European alliance systems and overseas empires ensured that any conflict would draw in all the powers, and spread around the world.

Military and economic developments generated high levels of force relative to the restricted frontages of European battlefields. Tactical and strategic deadlock ensued, despite operational formulae like the Schlieffen Plan, or metaphysical ones like the offensive *à outrance*. The defensive trinity of bullet, spade, and barbed wire operated on all fronts of the Great War, stalemating Allied attempts to outflank the Central Powers at Gallipoli and Salonika. Even the more open Eastern Front saw long periods of stalemate. German and Russian successes there owed more to superior organization than to Napoleonic-style manoeuvres which remained unattainable aspirations. Attrition dominated the battlefield: explicitly at Verdun, by default on the Somme.

At sea the anticipated clash of dreadnoughts never happened. Unprecedented levels of force promoted a return to the strategic stand-off of the 1690s. *Guerre de course* found new weapons: the U-boat and mine. Like gas and tanks on land these failed to resolve the impasse, meeting an effective response in the revived convoy system. Two million US troops reached Europe, untroubled by the U-boat blockade.

All powers possessed General Staffs, but none handled civil/military relations satisfactorily. The German staff misused their political power, with disastrous results. The invasion of Belgium and unrestricted U-boat warfare united the world against Germany. Distinctions between civilian and military became blurred, resulting in German atrocities in Belgium, Allied strategic bombing offensives, and the first genocide in Armenia.

LEFT: A soldier from the 1/Bedfords brings in one of nearly 40,000 wounded British soldiers on the first day of the battle of the Somme. The tragedy of 1 July 1916 still dominates British memories of the Great War, obscuring the eventual success of the British army in adapting to modern industrial warfare.

LEFT: Warfare in the 20th century began, as it ended, with unfinished business in the Balkans. Here, Austro-Hungarian troops guard a mixed column of military and civilian prisoners.

The Drift to War

The First World War was not the inevitable result of an arms race, nor was it an accident. It was the product of political choices, but military developments over the previous quarter of a century ensured a plentiful supply of inflammable material. Once ablaze it would not easily be extinguished.

The military basis for pre-war instability was the swiftness of the Wars of German Unification in the 1860s and 70s. Prussia's mixture of conscripts and professional cadres had beaten Napoleonic long service armies and the Revolutionary *levée en masse* invoked by the French Republic after Sedan. Other European states copied the Prussian pattern of cheap mass armies. Armies doubled in size after the Franco-Prussian War, outpacing the rate of population growth. Only Great Britain, secure in its naval supremacy, still relied on volunteers. The great powers resembled mistrustful travellers, brought together in a carriage by chance. If one of them put his hand into his pocket, his neighbour would get his own revolver ready to fire the first shot. All armies adopted the Prussian General Staff system. Consistently trained staff officers imposed similar patterns of weapons and doctrine across Europe. No one army had the qualitative advantage possessed by the Prussians over the ill-led French *Gardes Mobiles* of 1870.

Industrial growth provided new weapons for nations now truly in arms. Mass produced steel withstood greater forces than iron and bronze, permitting higher muzzle energies, which increased ranges and destructiveness. Field artillery pieces acquired recoil-absorbing recuperators to keep them on target between rounds. Practical rates of fire rose to eight rounds a minute, compared with two previously. Gunners could remain near their gun as it fired, sheltered by bullet-proof shields. Infantry could no longer shoot gunners down, as they had in the American Civil War. The flat trajectories of field guns were ineffective against trenches, so howitzers

reappeared, lobbing a heavier round to a shorter range. Automatic machine guns epitomized the effect of industrialization on war. Easily mass-produced, they created a large volume of accurate fire with minimal effort. Machine guns added to the vulnerability of horsed cavalry, already at a disadvantage in Europe's enclosed countryside. Motor vehicles would resolve the hiatus of the mobile arm but, like wireless telegraphy and aircraft, were scarce and unreliable in 1914.

Total mobilization appeared to demand a rapid victory, to pre-empt economic collapse. Pacifists claimed war had become impossible, but militarists responded with a cult of the offensive. Clausewitz and Moltke had seen the offensive as the weaker form of war, that is less likely to be successful, but with the stronger aim, that is more decisive. Post-Moltkeans argued that modern weapons made the offensive the stronger form, an implausible interpretation of events at Petersburg, Plevna, and Port Arthur. An offensive *à outrance* did not suit the strategic circumstances of all states, but military professionals increasingly denied the Clausewitzian primacy of politics. Absolute war had previously been moderated by political factors and the impossibility of a state deploying all its reserves at once. In 1914 offensive strategy, untempered by diplomacy, could deploy the whole of a nation's military resources instantaneously, by rail. Absolute war had become a realizable prospect, the only strategic aim the total defeat of one side. With both sides prepared to make every effort to avoid such an outcome, wars would be long and hard-fought, tending to the ruin of both sides.

The technical forces that revolutionized military weaponry also applied at sea. Precision-made heavy guns could deliver

Comparative infantry and artillery strengths, 1911

Numbers of Infantry (millions)

rifles available on mobilisation

trained reserves

Russia	Germany	France	Austria	Italy	Japan	Great Britain (not England)	United States
973,152 / 3.8m	633,000 / 4.0m	618,450 / 2.3m	420,300 / 1.6m	300,000 / 1.25m	228,000 / 1.0m	135,020 / 0.2m	39,600

Germany rejects naval holiday proposal, Britain joins Franco Russian entente

Casablanca incident, Austria annexes Bosnia-Herzegovina

Algeciras conference: Germany isolated diplomatically (except Austria)

Anglo-German Naval scare, 'We want eight and we won't wait'

Kaiser visits Tangier: First Moroccan crisis

Agadir Crisis

First Balkan War

French and Russians extend military service

Assassination at Sarajevo, outbreak of First World War

Royal Navy

number of Dreadnoughts

Imperial German Navy

The Anglo-German naval race and the countdown to war

1905 1906 1907 1908 1909 1910 1911 1912 1913 1914
Year

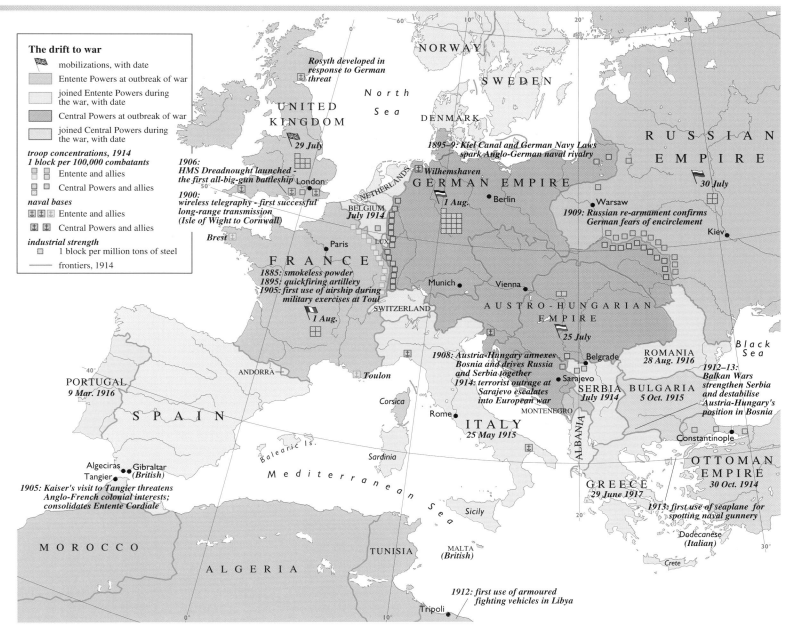

The drift to war

	mobilizations, with date
	Entente Powers at outbreak of war
	joined Entente Powers during the war, with date
	Central Powers at outbreak of war
	joined Central Powers during the war, with date

troop concentrations, 1914
1 block per 100,000 combatants
   Entente and allies
   Central Powers and allies

naval bases
   Entente and allies
   Central Powers and allies

industrial strength
   1 block per million tons of steel
   frontiers, 1914

Rosyth developed in response to German threat

1906: HMS Dreadnought launched – the first all-big-gun battleship

1900: wireless telegraphy – first successful long-range transmission (Isle of Wight to Cornwall)

1885: smokeless powder
1895: quickfiring artillery
1905: first use of airship during military exercises at Toul

1895–9: Kiel Canal and German Navy Laws spark Anglo-German naval rivalry

1909: Russian re-armament confirms German fears of encirclement

1908: Austria-Hungary annexes Bosnia and drives Russia and Serbia together
1914: terrorist outrage at Sarajevo escalates into European war

1912–13: Balkan Wars strengthen Serbia and destabilise Austria-Hungary's position in Bosnia

1905: Kaiser's visit to Tangier threatens Anglo-French colonial interests; consolidates Entente Cordiale

1913: first use of seaplane for spotting naval gunnery

1912: first use of armoured fighting vehicles in Libya

PORTUGAL *9 Mar. 1916*
SPAIN
FRANCE *1 Aug.*
UNITED KINGDOM *29 July*
NORWAY
SWEDEN
DENMARK
NETHERLANDS *July 1914*
BELGIUM *July 1914*
LUX.
GERMAN EMPIRE *1 Aug.*
RUSSIAN EMPIRE *30 July*
AUSTRO-HUNGARIAN EMPIRE *25 July*
ITALY *25 May 1915*
SERBIA *July 1914*
MONTENEGRO
ROMANIA *28 Aug. 1916*
BULGARIA *5 Oct. 1915*
GREECE *29 June 1917*
OTTOMAN EMPIRE *30 Oct. 1914*
MOROCCO
ALGERIA
TUNISIA
MALTA *(British)*
Gibraltar *(British)*
Dodecanese *(Italian)*

accurate long-range fire, centrally controlled by mechanical computers and range finders. The ineffectiveness of six-inch guns at Tsushima prompted development of the all big gun battleship. Broadsides of eight 12-inch guns enabled such ships to get the range twice as quickly as existing battleships with only four heavy guns, and concentrated twice the firepower in the same length battle line. HMS Dreadnought (1906), the first of the new type, gave a new twist to a naval race under way since the British Naval Defence Act of 1889, originally aimed at France and Russia. German Navy Laws of 1898 and 1900, inspired by the fashionable theories of the American naval writer Captain A T Mahan, refocused British naval concerns. They mended fences with France and Russia, and concentrated the Royal Navy in home waters, confirming German fears of encirclement. The British won the naval race, but the Agadir crisis confirmed Anglo-German hostility, entangling Great Britain in a European alliance for the first

time in a century. The British Army was small, but the Empire possessed enormous resources, capable of balancing the industrial power of Germany. Britain's adherence to the Entente ensured that a renewed Franco-German war would be long.

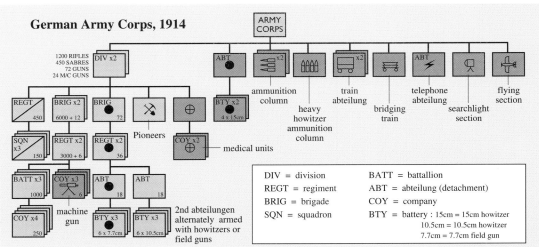

German Army Corps, 1914

DIV = division
REGT = regiment
BRIG = brigade
SQN = squadron
BATT = battalion
ABT = abteilung (detachment)
COY = company
BTY = battery : 15cm = 15cm howitzer
10.5cm = 10.5cm howitzer
7.7cm = 7.7cm field gun

ABOVE: European armies used similar weapons and patterns of organizations, but there were some significant differences. German forces included substantially more heavy artillery at corps level. Russian field armies had fewer guns because a large proportion of their artillery was installed in fortresses instead. All armies relied on flat trajectory field guns superb against troops in the open, but relatively ineffective against dug-in infantry.

The Schlieffen Plan

Historians have dissected the opening moves of the First World War endlessly, as if more effective command decisions might have ended the war by Christmas and avoided the calamity of a four-year war. Beyond the interplay of armies and leaders, however, tactical and logistical factors worked against optimistic predictions of a short, decisive war.

The driving force throughout the conflict would be the German Army. The leading military power of Europe was obsessed by fears of a two-front war against Russia and France. Count von Schlieffen, Chief of the General Staff 1893-1905, hoped to defeat France before Russia, hampered by its size, could mobilize. Regardless of international law, Schlieffen planned to launch 90% of Germany's mobile forces through neutral Belgium. They would gain the rear of the French armies and force them to attack in order to regain their communications. It is a historical cliché to compare the Schlieffen Plan with Hannibal's tactical envelopment at Cannae (216BC); Schlieffen owed more to

BELOW: Intending to replicate Napoleon's manoeuvre at Ulm, the German armies plunged through Belgium to outflank French forces along the Meuse. General von Kluck departed from the plan and wheeled his army south before reaching Paris. The French commander, General Joffre, kept his nerve and shuttled reinforcements to the Marne by rail and road.

Napoleon's strategic manoeuvre on Ulm (1805). France defeated, Germany's interior lines would become an advantage, allowing her armies to transfer rapidly by rail to the Eastern Front.

Critics have blamed Schlieffen's successor, von Moltke's nephew, for weakening the right wing, but the original plan was crucially flawed by its assumption that the enemy would behave as planned. Instead Joffre, the French Commander-in-Chief, stolidly regrouped his forces, despite catastrophic defeats in the Battle of the Frontiers (14-25 August 1914). He had no specific reserve, but moved troops by rail from disengaged parts of the front to form a new army on the outer flank of the Germans. The enveloping force was itself turned, and its centre pierced by British forces (the BEF), when aerial reconnaissance revealed a gap between the German Armies. While Joffre drove about in his personal racing car, hectoring and cajoling Army commanders, Moltke lost control. The Germans had inadequate wireless sets, and the French jammed the signals with a transmitter in the Eiffel Tower. A junior German staff officer at the front terminated one of the most momentous acts of aggression of all time, as a purely operational matter. The rightmost German Armies fell back 30 miles behind the River Aisne, where they entrenched, like American Civil War armies. By frustrating the Schlieffen Plan, Joffre had won the decisive battle of the war, and perhaps of the century.

Tactics were less flexible than in the Franco-Prussian War. Rifle and machine gun fire swept infantry away before they could establish firing lines. At Le Cateau, a rearguard action fought during the German advance, single shrapnel shells cut down whole German platoons, as if they had been pulled over by a string. After years of unrealistic peacetime manoeuvres French and German infantry bunched together under fire. Obsessed with the offensive, red-trousered French infantry attacked regardless of artillery support. German tactics mirrored their strategy. Massed infantry tried to envelop one or both of the enemy flanks, supported by massed artillery fire against the front.

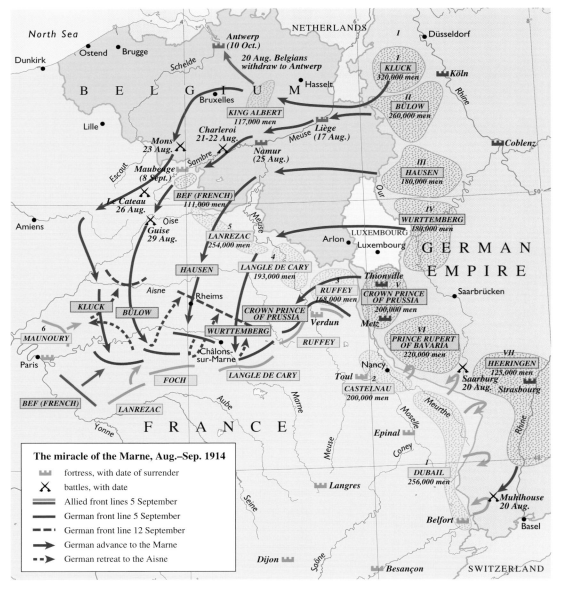

The miracle of the Marne, Aug.–Sep. 1914

- ⌑ fortress, with date of surrender
- ✕ battles, with date
- ▭ Allied front lines 5 September
- — German front line 5 September
- --- German front line 12 September
- → German advance to the Marne
- ⇢ German retreat to the Aisne

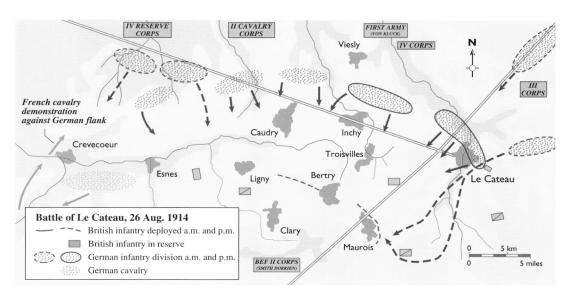

LEFT: Germany was one of the last major powers to adopt the machine gun, but its army enjoyed some significant advantages in 1914. Prepared for siege warfare against French and Belgian forts, it had excellent heavy artillery with its field armies. Artillery and machine guns defeated 19th century style infantry tactics, however gallantly assaults were pressed home.

RIGHT: General Smith-Dorrien's rearguard action at Le Cateau came as a disagreeable surprise to the German army which concluded from the volume of fire, that the BEF bristled with machine guns. In fact, most of the BEF's regulars had earned their marksman's badges (and the extra beer money). The German attack was stopped by 15 aimed rounds a minute from No.3 Lee-Enfields in expert hands.

Battle of Le Cateau, 26 Aug. 1914
- – – – British infantry deployed a.m. and p.m.
- ▢ British infantry in reserve
- German infantry division a.m. and p.m.
- German cavalry

Only the professionals of the BEF used Boer War-style fire and movement, firing 15 aimed rounds in their 'mad minute'. The French lacked experienced NCOs at section level to control infantry fire, but their gunners skilfully laid 'artillery traps' with their *'soixante-quinzes'*, the original and best quick-firing field gun.

The Schlieffen Plan faced enormous logistical difficulties. Soldiers might live off the country, but even the French harvest was insufficient for the masses of horses that armies still required. Deprived of forage, horse-drawn artillery fell behind, and cavalry lost their mobility.

Quick-firing field guns fired four times as quickly as the breech-loaders of 1870, but ammunition could not be improvised. An army corps of 1914 needed 300 tons of supplies a day, delivered by horse-drawn wagons normally expected to march 12 miles a day. Some German units were 80 miles from railheads dependent on war-torn Belgian railways. The Allies, however, fell back on their communications, and could use railways for supply and shifting reserves. The River Marne might have represented the logistical culminating point of the German advance, even without Joffre's strategic riposte.

The sheer numbers of men and guns on both sides prevented a rapid decision, barring levels of incompetence, which the institutionalized professionalism of the French and German staffs made unlikely. Both armies ruthlessly sacked failing commanders, including von Moltke himself. The Army Corps, swollen by extra artillery and ammunition wagons, had become a blunt instrument, occupying so much road it could not deploy and fight on the same day. The sheer weight of the machine prevented the strokes of operational brilliance that had preceded Napoleon's quick victories.

LEFT: A German skirmish line in action. In 1914 rifle companies were uniformly armed and equipped, but as the war continued, they would evolve into combinations of light machine gunners, grenade-throwers and riflemen. It is a paradox that the siege warfare of 1915-16 laid the foundations for modern infantry tactics.

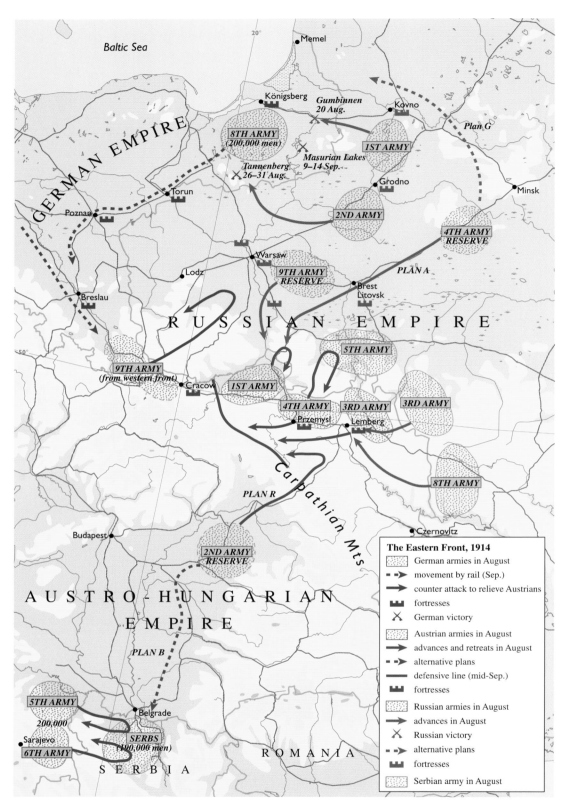

LEFT: Along the far wider frontage of the Eastern Front, manoeuvres were still possible on a grand scale. Russia surprised the Central Powers by assuming the offensive before her mobilization was complete, invading East Prussia and driving the Austro-Hungarian armies back on the fortresses north of the Carpathians. The Austro-Hungarian commander-in-chief changed his mind, first committing the bulk of his armies against Serbia, then withdrawing large forces to fend off the Russians.

Armies individually. General Paul von Hindenberg took over Eighth Army after the unscripted German defeat at Gumbinnen (20 August 1914), with Ludendorff as his General Staff officer. The latter telegraphed ahead to restore the situation, his orders coinciding with those already issued by Eighth Army's existing Chief of Staff, an example of the practical value of common doctrine. Like Joffre before the Marne, the Germans transferred troops from one flank to the other by rail, encouraged by wireless intercepts suggesting First Russian Army would not intervene. German I Corps turned the western flank of Second Army, got behind them and turned north, trapping the whole Army in a pocket near Tannenberg. Their commander shot himself, and 100,000 prisoners surrendered.

Hindenberg and Ludendorff proclaimed a second Cannae, but they had been lucky: initial Russian successes and the slow advance of the German outflanking Corps had drawn Second Army further into the bag. Tannenberg convinced Hindenberg and Ludendorff that Napoleonic envelopment was still possible in the East, offering strategic victory without unacceptable attrition. The two began their climb to absolute power and Germany's ruin. Tannenberg was the result of Russian command failures, not innate backwardness. The subsequent battle of the Masurian Lakes against the surviving Russian Army in the north began well for the Germans, but bogged down by the end of September 1914. It cost Eighth Army 100,000 casualties out of 250,000. Masurian Lakes, not Tannenberg, would be the pattern of the war in the East.

Germany was not Russia's only opponent. The Eastern Front formed a series of salients: Germany in East Prussia; Russia at Warsaw; Austria-Hungary in Galicia to the south. Although their ultimatum to Serbia had sparked off the war, Austria-Hungary was ill-prepared for war. National rivalries within the Empire prevented

The war on the Eastern Front started with one of those brilliant manoeuvres so noticeably absent in the West. The Battle of Tannenberg was the most striking German victory of the war, but it was deceptive. Stalemate and attrition would dominate the Eastern Front as they did the West.

Russian military reform, after the Russo-Japanese War, eroded Schlieffen's strategic margins, leaving less time before

the German Eighth Army in East Prussia came under attack. The Russian First and Second Armies mobilized smoothly, and had overall numerical superiority over the defenders of East Prussia, but woods and lakes divided their advance. They frittered away detachments to protect their outer flanks, and made no use of second line reserve formations. Consequently Eighth Army, which included numerous *Landwehr*, outnumbered the Russian

effective mobilization; Austria fielded fewer battalions in 1914 than in 1866. Like Germany, Austria-Hungary faced a two-front war: against Russia in the East and Serbia in the South. The Germans prioritized one front, and won on the other. The Austrians prioritized neither and lost on both. Serbia distracted Austria's reserve 'B' Staffel from the main threat in Galicia. Serbs and Russians followed similar defensive/offensive strategies. They drew Austro-Hungarian armies forward into salients, then cut them off by attacking the exposed outer flanks. They inflicted enormous losses, especially among the irreplaceable multi-lingual officer corps, who held the Austro-Hungarian army together.

The Eastern Front, with fewer soldiers on twice the front, was never so static as the West. One and a half German divisions held the same frontage in the East as five in France. Poor communications prevented reserves moving swiftly to block gaps in the line. Pushed back into the Carpathians, Austria-Hungary appealed for German help. Hindenberg and Ludendorff flattened the Warsaw salient, but there were no more wholesale Russian surrenders. By year end, Russian gains in Galicia balanced losses in Poland. In the West, the mis-named 'Race to the Sea' followed Allied failures to break through on the Aisne. This series of outflanking moves to the north resembled Grant's attempts to find Lee's flank in the Wilderness, but there were always just enough troops on both sides to extend the line, frustrating hopes of a quick decision. By Christmas 1914 the trenches stretched 400 miles from Switzerland to the English Channel.

The German General Staff, in their professional ivory tower, had started a world war to chastize an obscure Balkan kingdom. Their politically naive invasion of Belgium placed Britain's economic and strategic potential at the disposal of the Entente. Germany faced a two-front war, with no clear idea of how to end it.

ABOVE: The Russian army was not as well equipped as that of Germany in 1914. Russia had modern field guns, like this, seen here before the war; but fewer of them in each division. On the other hand, the Russian naval budget exceeded that of the Germany in 1913 as a new generation of dreadnoughts were laid down at St. Petersburg. Russia's border fortresses were packed with heavy artillery. The Russian army's disadvantages stemmed from poor procurement decisions as much as industrial backwardness.

RIGHT: All armies of 1914 were supposed to dig in when on the defensive, even if their tactical outlook remained offensive. Confronted by the 'storm of steel', soldiers improved their entrenchments, until by the end of the Autumn, the Western Front was an almost continuos line of trenches. Second and even third lines of defence began to appear, with dugouts, communications trenches, saps and listening posts. Few knew it then, but the infantry would be condemned to this troglodyte world for another four years.

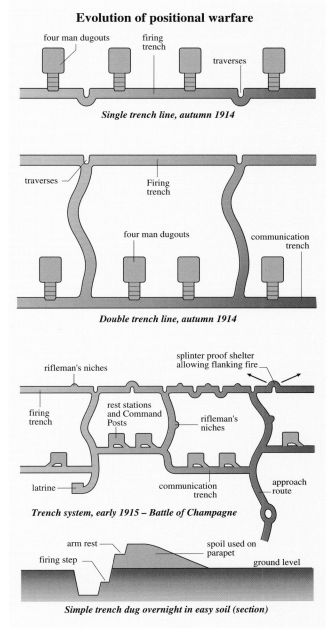

Evolution of positional warfare

Single trench line, autumn 1914

four man dugouts
firing trench
traverses

Double trench line, autumn 1914

traverses
Firing trench
four man dugouts
communication trench

Trench system, early 1915 – Battle of Champagne

splinter proof shelter allowing flanking fire
rifleman's niches
firing trench
rest stations and Command Posts
rifleman's niches
latrine
communication trench
approach route

Simple trench dug overnight in easy soil (section)

arm rest
firing step
spoil used on parapet
ground level

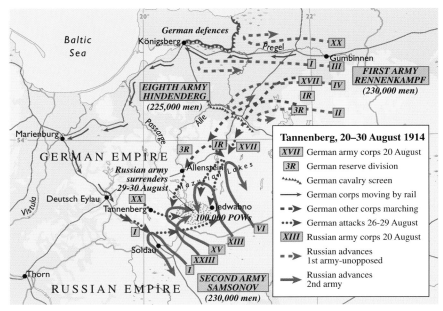

LEFT: The Russian 1st and 2nd Armies failed to coordinate their invasion of East Prussia and, while Rennenkampf was bluffed into immobility, the Germans concentrated every man against Samsonov, who committed suicide when his surrounded army was compelled to surrender.

Baltic Sea
German defences
Königsberg
Pregel
Gumbinnen
EIGHTH ARMY HINDENBERG
(225,000 men)
FIRST ARMY RENNENKAMPF
(230,000 men)
Marienburg
GERMAN EMPIRE
Russian army surrenders 29–30 August
Allenstein
Deutsch Eylau
Tannenberg
100,000 POWs
Jedwabno
Soldau
RUSSIAN EMPIRE
SECOND ARMY SAMSONOV
(230,000 men)
Thorn

Tannenberg, 20–30 August 1914

XVII	German army corps 20 August
3R	German reserve division
⌃⌃⌃	German cavalry screen
→	German corps moving by rail
⇢	German other corps marching
⋯▸	German attacks 26–29 August
XIII	Russian army corps 20 August
⇢	Russian advances 1st army-unopposed
→	Russian advances 2nd army

Offensives in the West

The partial success of the Schlieffen Plan gave Germany the strategic initiative, a choice between offensive or defensive action, on the Eastern or Western fronts. The presence of German troops 50 miles from Paris compelled the French to attack. The tactical imbalance between offensive and defensive made 1915 a year of heavy Allied casualties, for no tangible gain.

The development of trench warfare in late 1914 is less surprising than the war of movement it replaced. Flat trajectory rapid-fire weapons were admirably suited to killing infantry moving in the open. Both sides in the West suffered half a million casualties in the first two months of the war, making the Marne three times bloodier per day than the Somme or Verdun. Infantry dug in, artillery hid behind woods or hills, generals modified pre-war illusions about the offensive. Sir John French, Commander-in-Chief of the British Expeditionary Force and a cavalry general if ever there was, begged for heavy siege guns. Twentieth century firepower made it possible to hold long fronts with only two men per yard, compared with the five needed in the 1870s. Armies had grown so large they could occupy the entire space available, creating an inviolable front without flanks. The Germans constructed trench lines on forward slopes, to secure good fields of fire and observation, relying on strong reserves to seal off any breakthrough. Only the Germans possessed weapons appropriate to trench warfare: howitzers, grenades, signal rockets. The French had neglected howitzers, and hastily stripped their fortresses of heavy guns for the frontline.

Joffre hoped to break through the shoulders of the great German salient that bulged out towards Noyon, and cut the railways running close behind the lines.

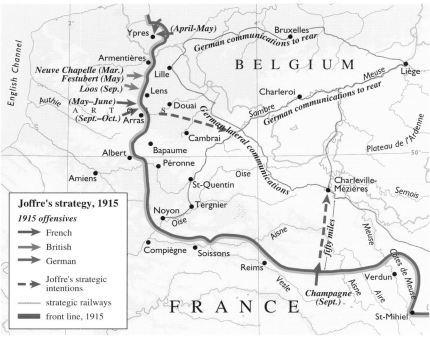

His tactics resembled those of D'Erlon at Waterloo. Massive columns advanced after concentrated artillery had blasted a path through the enemy position. Joffre left no room for initiative or leadership. The two regiments of each brigade followed each other in waves, so close together that 3,600 men formed a mass 1,300 yards wide and 185 deep. Divisions became an unwieldy phalanx that could only go straight ahead, or fall back in disorder. Surprisingly the concept almost worked. Petain's 33rd Corps reached the top of Vimy Ridge on 9 May 1915, but machine gun fire from fortified villages held up progress on the flanks. The 2.8-mile advance in an hour surprised the French command, who had no reserves ready. German infantry arrived in lorries to pinch out the narrow gap in the line. Joffre's September attacks were on a wider front: 22 divisions broke through on a 10-mile front in Champagne. The Germans had learnt too: a second line of trenches concealed on a reverse slope halted the French advance after 2 miles.

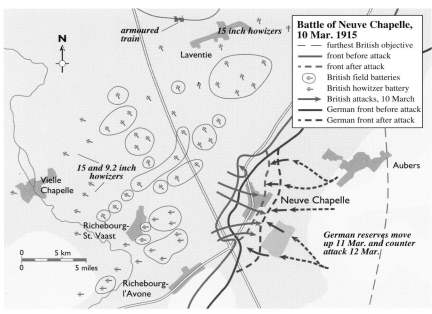

Battle of Neuve Chapelle, 10 Mar. 1915
— — — furthest British objective
———— front before attack
- - - - front after attack
⊖ British field batteries
⊟ British howitzer battery
——▶ British attacks, 10 March
——— German front before attack
- - - German front after attack

N

armoured train

15 inch howizers

Laventie

15 and 9.2 inch howizers

Vielle Chapelle

Aubers

Neuve Chapelle

Richebourg-St. Vaast

0   5 km
0   5 miles

German reserves move up 11 Mar. and counter attack 12 Mar.

Richebourg-l'Avone

LEFT: A single machine gun could inflict terrible losses on infantry struggling to get through gaps in the barbed wire. This German position, destroyed in the second bombardment at Neuve Chapelle, inflicted heavy casualties on the 2nd Cameronians in the opening phase of the attack.

ABOVE: British experience at Neuve Chapelle showed the German line could be penetrated, but the defender's reserves could plug the gap before the attacker could move fresh troops forward. Until this conundrum was solved, no major breakthrough was possible. The last cadres of the BEF were expended in these assaults; larger British operations would have to wait until the Kitchener armies were equipped and trained.

Russo-Japanese trench lines had lacked depth. No one had foreseen that a double line of trenches would be impregnable.

The British offensive at Neuve Chapelle was much smaller than Joffre's, but set a pattern for successful infantry/artillery attacks. The BEF's leadership showed awareness of new tactical conditions, combining methodical preparation and surprise. An unprecedented whirlwind bombardment by 340 guns cut the wire and wrecked the German front line. Tactical novelties included aerial photography, an orchestrated fire plan, and first official use of the term 'barrage'. However, support could not move up quickly enough to maintain momentum. Attacking infantry lost touch with their artillery when German shellfire killed runners and forward observation officers. Neuve Chapelle, like Vimy Ridge, showed how the German front line might be penetrated, starting a debate among the high command. Some hoped better planning or more firepower would produce a decisive breakthrough. Others preferred to wear the

Germans down by a 'bite and hold' strategy, an unacceptable strategy to a public still expecting speedy victory.

The Germans launched only one offensive on the Western Front in 1915. They released clouds of chlorine gas at Ypres, in the first large-scale use of weapons of mass destruction. As so often with new weapons, the inventors were unprepared for their success, especially as the Germans were unwilling to mass reserves near fragile gas cylinders. They owed much of the battle's subsequent success to systematic aerial direction of their heavy guns, as the Allies quickly improvised gas counter-measures. The Germans took half the Ypres salient, but suffered a resounding propaganda defeat. The unbelievable horror of a gas cloud attack confirmed perceptions of Hun beastliness first inspired by atrocities against Belgian civilians. Gas masks transformed soldiers into dehumanized monsters, but human qualities of morale and training remained essential for troops to survive gas warfare.

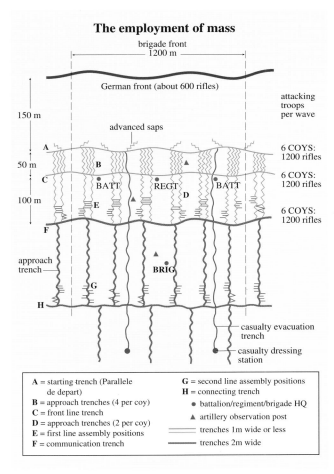

The employment of mass

brigade front
1200 m

German front (about 600 rifles)

attacking troops per wave

150 m

advanced saps

A   6 COYS: 1200 rifles

50 m   B

C   6 COYS: 1200 rifles
BATT   REGT   BATT   D

100 m   E

F   6 COYS: 1200 rifles

approach trench

BRIG

G

H

casualty evacuation trench

casualty dressing station

A = starting trench (Parallele de depart)	**G** = second line assembly positions
B = approach trenches (4 per coy)	**H** = connecting trench
C = front line trench	● battalion/regiment/brigade HQ
D = approach trenches (2 per coy)	▲ artillery observation post
E = first line assembly positions	═ trenches 1m wide or less
F = communication trench	━ trenches 2m wide

ABOVE: French tactics in 1915 relied on the artillery destroying the enemy wire and demolishing the German trenches. A dense mass of infantry would swarm forward to occupy the ground before the enemy could react. It could work, but a pocket of resistance, just a few machine guns, could decimate this inflexible formation.

Gallipoli: The Limits of Sea Power

The stalemate on the Western Front stimulated a search for alternative areas of operations. Over-optimistic expectations of sea power inspired an Anglo-French amphibious attack on Turkey, which joined the Central Powers in October 1914. Deadlock, however, was not confined to the West.

The Entente's confrontation with Turkey showed how railways had strengthened land powers against maritime states. Germany sent advisers and small amounts of technical aid to Turkey, via the Berlin-Baghdad railway, enabling the Turks to distract huge British Imperial forces. Turkish troops in Palestine threatened the British Empire's lifeline through the Suez Canal, while the Basra *vilayet* menaced the oil wells needed by the Royal Navy. Vital to the British, neither area lay near comparable Turkish interests. Turkey could exploit defensive resources of distance, poor communications, and climate to delay British offensives in Palestine and Mesopotamia, shifting reserves between them on interior lines. In April 1916 Turkish troops released by the evacuation of Gallipoli inflicted a humiliating defeat at Kut on a logistically unsound British advance on Baghdad. The Turkish army of 1915 lacked the transport and heavy artillery for large scale offensives, but this was not clear before the failure of Turkish advances in Sinai and the Caucasus (January-February 1915). Turkey lay squarely across the only ice free maritime route to Russia, blocking Russian wheat exports, although the western Allies were too short of ammunition to

spare any for Russia. A successful Allied strike against the heart of the Ottoman Empire could have provided economy of force, avoiding costly offensives in Palestine and Mesopotamia, and possibly preventing the economic collapse that caused the Russian Revolution.

The failure of both sea and land operations at Gallipoli underlined the gulf between strategic vision and operational reality during the First World War. The scheme depended on makeshift expedients: obsolete ships officially regarded as expendable; civilian trawlers impressed as minesweepers; half-trained divisions with incomplete artillery and staffs. A purely naval attack on the Dardanelles flew in the face of experience going back to 1807, and begged the question of what to do if the Turks refused to surrender on the fleet's arrival at Istanbul. Pre-Dreadnought battleships were to silence the Turkish forts at the mouth of the Dardanelles, the straits leading to the Sea of Marmara and the Bosphorus. Trawlers would then clear the minefields for the battleships to engage forts inside the Narrows. Shore bombardment failed to silence Turkish forts permanently. Flat trajectory naval guns were ineffective against the mobile howitzer batteries that hampered mine-clearing

operations. When the fleet attempted to brazen it out on 18 March, unswept mines sank three old battleships, and damaged another two, almost a third of the force. The underwater threat ended the purely naval phase of the campaign. Two months later a U-boat torpedoed two more pre-Dreadnoughts, confirming the dangers of traditional naval power projection in the face of mines and submarines.

The naval bombardments lost any chance of strategic surprise. The Turks held the April landings on the Cape Helles beaches, until nightfall. The red stain in the sea was visible from the air. The debut of Australian and New Zealand Dominion forces at Anzac Cove was more successful, but once ashore, the troops became entangled in razor-backed hills and scrub not apparent from a small-scale map. Rifle, barbed wire and spade dominated the battlefield as in the West, but at Gallipoli the Allies had no continuous line, no high ground for observation, no depth providing escape from enemy fire, and no clean water. Over half the British and Dominion casualties, 145,000 out of 214,000, were from dysentery. The losses from disease associated with every 1914-18 'sideshow' condemn all of them as a way of winning the war on the cheap. The landings at

Map

Gulf of Saros

0 —— 5 km
0 —— 5 miles

Gallipoli

Suvla Bay

British 7 Aug. 1915

Allied bridgehead

evacuated 18–19 Dec. 1915

Sari Bahr

Anzac 25 Apr. 1915

Gaba Tepe

Dardanelles

N

Canakkale

Achi Baba

British 25 Apr. 1915

Krithia

4 knots current

X

Cape Helles W

S

V

evacuated 8–9 Jan 1916

French 25–27 Apr. 1915

French 25 Apr. 1915

The assault on the Dardanelles, 1915–16

- ▪ – – Turkish minefields
- ⌢⌢ Turkish field artillery positions
- ⚓ ⚓ Turkish mobile artillery positions
- → Allied Naval attack, 18 Mar 1915
- *XWVS* British/Dominion assault landings
- → French assaults and diversions
- – – Allied evacuations
- ✳ ✳ British and French naval losses

LEFT: The steamer *River Clyde* run ashore on 'V' beach. The holes cut in her side for unloading can be seen here, together with the walkways down which the troops came ashore.

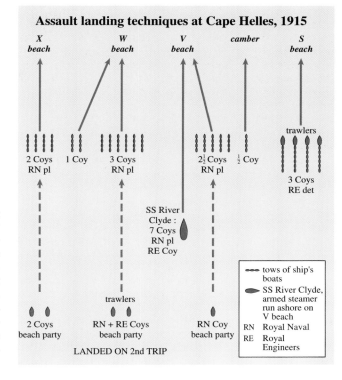

Assault landing techniques at Cape Helles, 1915

X beach	W beach	V beach	camber	S beach
2 Coys RN pl	1 Coy / 3 Coys RN pl	2½ Coys RN pl	½ Coy	trawlers / 3 Coys RE det
		SS River Clyde : 7 Coys RN pl RE Coy		
2 Coys beach party	trawlers / RN + RE Coys beach party	RN Coy beach party		
	LANDED ON 2nd TRIP			

- tows of ship's boats
- SS River Clyde, armed steamer run ashore on V beach
- RN Royal Naval
- RE Royal Engineers

Suvla in August once more showed the futility of amphibious assaults with untrained troops. Only the flawlessly planned and executed evacuation of December 1915/January 1916 showed the impressive capabilities of the staffs, when operating beyond the constraints of bullet, wire, and spade. The rapid technical response to the demands of modern amphibious operations suggest what more careful preparation might have achieved: small cheap monitors replaced battleships for fire support; modified destroyers took over minesweeping; motorized barges or 'beetles' replaced the ships' boats traditionally used for landing troops. The British would not resolve the deeper problems of political/military relations that underlay the disaster until the Second World War. Divisions between Allied statesmen and their professional advisers were as productive of military failure as the political dominance of the German General Staff was of diplomatic disaster.

ABOVE: Without specialist landing craft, the amphibious assault was conducted with ships' boats plus the armed steamer *River Clyde* deliberately run ashore. Preliminary bombardment by warships failed to silence the Turkish guns, dug in on reverse slopes above the beach.

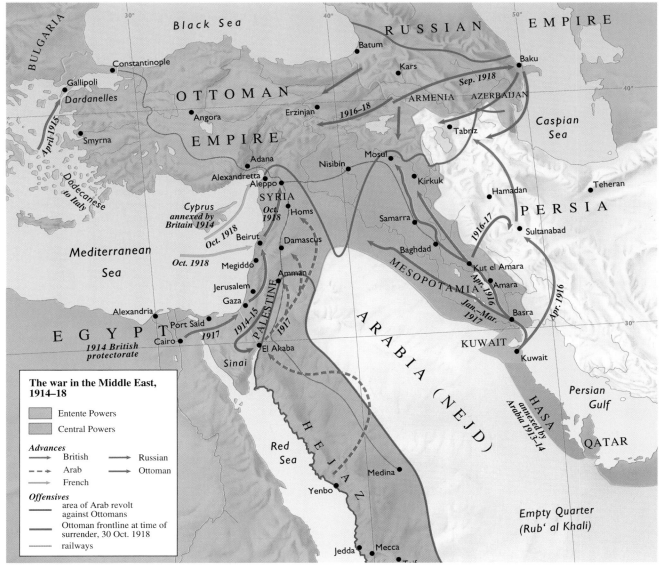

The war in the Middle East, 1914–18

- Entente Powers
- Central Powers

Advances
- → British
- → Russian
- ⇢ Arab
- → Ottoman
- → French

Offensives
- ▬ area of Arab revolt against Ottomans
- ▬ Ottoman frontline at time of surrender, 30 Oct. 1918
- ─── railways

LEFT: The Ottoman Empire entered the war in October 1914, cutting the only ice-free sea route between the western allies and Russia. Its army was short of artillery, but not resolution, and with a leavening of German advisors and deft use of its railways, it beat off successive Allied invasions at Gallipoli and Kut el-Amara.

The Battle Fleets

Apparent inaction at sea contrasted with incessant slaughter ashore. The mightiest fleets ever built disappointed a public expecting a repetition of Tsushima or Trafalgar. Events at sea, however, were crucial to the outcome of the war. Conventional sea power stalemated the Central Powers' surface fleets, securing the Entente's home base from naval attack and free access to the manpower and raw materials of the world.

The Royal Navy possessed significant material and geographical advantages over the Imperial German Navy. The British had 50 percent more Dreadnoughts, with numerous cruisers to blockade German ports, protect British commerce, and escort expeditionary forces. The British Isles physically obstructed German access to the Atlantic, except via the easily blocked Dover Straits, or the Iceland-Faroes gap. The British deployed all their Dreadnoughts to cover the latter, at Scapa Flow and Rosyth. The Grand Fleet's concentration confined the German High Seas Fleet to the North Sea, depriving Germany of the strategic options open to France in the 1790s. Technology favoured the Royal Navy's defensive strategy. Wireless permitted steam warships to concentrate independent of the weather, in response to enemy initiatives, while signal intercepts provided early warning of German intentions. British proximity to the German coast allowed the Royal Navy to exploit the mobility and flexibility of steam power, and eased the process of recoaling.

Like other outnumbered fleets, the High Seas Fleet remained in harbour, inspiring the first air attack on warships in harbour, by RNAS seaplanes on Christmas Day 1914. The Germans expected the British to establish a close blockade, as in previous wars. They hoped mines and submarines would wear down British strength, until a favourable fleet action became possible. However, early losses, including three elderly cruisers sunk together by one U-boat (22 September 1914), persuaded the British to withdraw major units from the North Sea. Such caution was the only responsible strategy, however much it embarrassed junior naval officers or defied Mahan's views on decisive battle as the only worthwhile aim of naval strategy. German cruisers bombarded civilian targets along the east coast of Great Britain in attempts to draw out part of the Grand Fleet. One raid brought on the first action between Dreadnoughts at the Dogger Bank, opposing battlecruisers exchanging hits at an unprecedented 18,000 yards range. However, the refusal of the stricken German cruiser *Blücher* to surrender marked a return to the obstinate savagery of earlier naval wars. The British scored a propaganda victory, but missed vital lessons about anti-flash precautions, or the poor British gunnery and signalling that contributed to the failure to destroy the German squadron.

The battle of Jutland, the only fleet action between Dreadnoughts, resulted from a complex German plan, combining U-boats and Zeppelins, to trap part of the Grand Fleet. Admiral Scheer was himself surprised by the Grand Fleet, forewarned of the German moves by signals intelligence. The Royal Navy had bigger, faster ships with heavier broadsides. German Dreadnoughts were better armoured, with better armour-piercing ammunition and gunnery control. The early stages of the action, between the battlecruisers, showed the structural weakness of the type, two British ships exploding catastrophically. Nevertheless, the remaining British battlecruisers led the High Seas Fleet onto the guns of the Grand Fleet. Despite poor

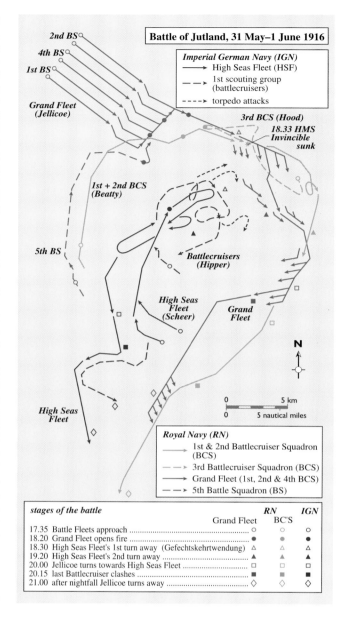

RIGHT: German battle cruisers shelled British coastal ports in the hope of luring an isolated squadron to destruction, but the first major victim was their own cruiser *Blücher*, sunk at Dogger bank, hundreds of her company paraded through Edinburgh in triumph. However, signalling errors deprived Admiral Beatty of a comprehensive victory.

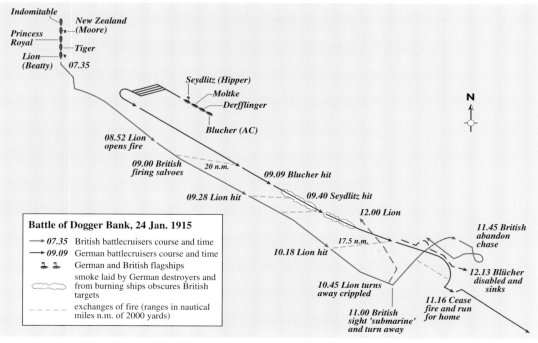

ABOVE: The battlefleets clashed but once, at Jutland, in 1916. Admiral Scheer blundered headlong into the British line of battle twice, his leading ships suffering severe damage. But the action began too late in the day for a sustained gunnery duel and the Germans escaped during the night, their admiral convinced that surface action meant suicide. He told the Kaiser to initiate an unrestricted U boat campaign.

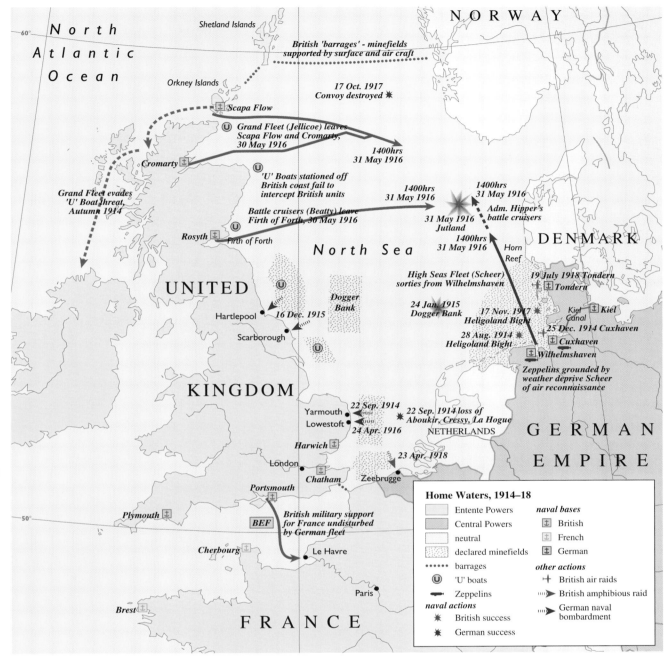

RIGHT: Public opinion in Britain expected the German fleet to be annihilated in 20th century Trafalgar, but the Kaiser forbade his battleships to risk themselves at sea. From its bleak anchorage at Scapa Flow, the British Grand Fleet dominated the North Sea, ensuring an economic blockade of German ports that denied her war economy key resources. In 1916 both fleets tried to trick the other on to minefields or submarine ambushes, preparatory to an engagement: the result was Jutland.

BELOW: Steaming in six compact columns, Admiral Jellicoe had tantalizingly little information on which to decide his deployment. At sea, as on land, weapons technology had outstripped communications, gunnery engagements took place at up to 10 nautical miles but radios were unreliable and signal flags unreadable. With the tactical instinct that marked him out before the war, Jellicoe made the correct deployment that afternoon, crossing the enemy 'T' with potentially decisive results.

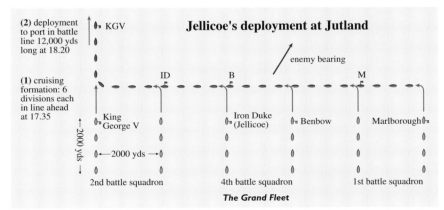

reconnaissance and bad visibility, the British Commander-in-Chief Sir John Jellicoe justified his reputation as the best tactician in the Royal Navy. He twice crossed Scheer's 'T', and placed his fleet

across the German route home. Only nightfall and two very smart 180 degree turns saved the High Seas Fleet. Jellicoe refused a risky night action for which he had no strategic motive.

The battle left the strategic balance unchanged, although British losses in lives and tonnage were double those of the Germans. The Royal Navy improved its signals, safety precautions, gunnery, and night fighting, but Jutland was the last fleet action in the old style, the combatants in view of one another. The battle's indecisiveness, only four Dreadnoughts lost out of 58 engaged, emphasized the limits of the technology. Only visibility limited the range of the 15-inch gun, but ships lacked the signalling and position-finding equipment to coordinate their movements. Fleets were too large and ships too robust, barring careless accidents, to resolve an action in the time available. Before the end of the war the British were planning to break the North Sea stalemate with a futuristic torpedo strike by carrier-borne aircraft.

Commerce Raiders and U-boats

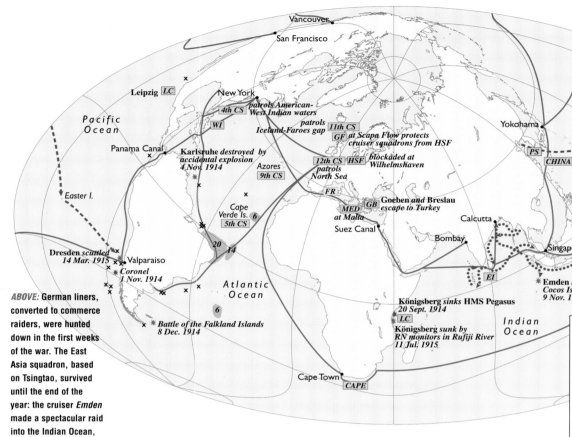

ABOVE: German liners, converted to commerce raiders, were hunted down in the first weeks of the war. The East Asia squadron, based on Tsingtao, survived until the end of the year: the cruiser *Emden* made a spectacular raid into the Indian Ocean, while von Spee's heavy units defeated a British squadron off Chile before their destruction off the Falklands.

BELOW: Unrestricted by maritime law, the U boat campaign was poised to starve out Britain when convoys were instituted and the sinkings suddenly declined. The last year of the war saw U boat losses escalate while only a tiny fraction of convoyed shipping was lost.

The industrial revolution increased seaborne imports of raw materials and food. Nations fighting a total war were bound to interrupt these supplies, regardless of international law. The navally dominant Entente blockaded the Central Powers who pursued a *guerre de course*, the traditional strategy of weaker navies. Technological changes transformed both operations, bringing the weaker side closer to victory than had been possible under sail.

The 1856 Declaration of Paris banned privateers, but allowed commerce raiding by regular warships or armed merchant cruisers. Ten German commerce raiders were at sea on the outbreak of war, leading Entente cruiser squadrons a merry dance

until all were sunk or blockaded. Technology did not favour coal-burning raiders, who lacked the strategic endurance of sailing ships. Wireless distress signals betrayed their latest victim's location, while an all-weather blockade prevented prizes reaching German home ports. The German cruisers were superior to the elderly warships patrolling the sea lanes, but a victory like that at Coronel (1 November 1914) used up half the victor's irreplaceable ammunition. The British responded by detaching battlecruisers from the Grand Fleet, which occupied an interior position between the High Seas Fleet and the raiders. It could therefore act as a reserve for hard-pressed commerce protection cruisers. The Battle of the

Surface raiders and the Allied defence of trade, 1914

———	major sea-borne trade routes
- - -►	von Spee's route
••••►	*Emden's* solo route

naval actions

✳	RN success
✳	IGN success

sinkings in South American waters

✕	individual ships
6	areas of numerous sinkings

abbreviations

CS	cruiser squadron	BB	battleship
CR	cruiser	BC	battle cruiser
LC	light cruiser	GB	gunboat, sloop
AC	armoured cruiser		

Allied trade protection system

▓	British navy squadron
░	French navy squadron
GF	Grand Fleet
5th CS	4 x CR
11th CS	6 x CR
12th CS	4 x CR, 3 x AC (French), 3 x LC (French)
4th CS	1 x old BB, 5 x CR, 1 x LC, 1 x aux. CR
MED	Mediterranean Squadron 3 x BC, 4 x AC, etc.
FR	French Mediterranean Fleet
FP	French Polynesian Squadron 2 x AC
CAPE	Cape Squadron 3 x LC
EI	East Indies Squadron 1 x old BB, 2 x LC, 3 x GB
CHINA	1 x old BB, 2 x CR, 2 x LC, 4 x aux. CR, 1 x CR (French), 16 x GB
AUST	Australia Squadron 1 x BC, 4 x LC
NZ	New Zealand Squadron 3 x LC, 3 x GB
9th CS	4 x CR, 3 x LC, 3 x CR (French), 2 x LC (French)

Imperial German Navy

▓	German squadron
HSF	High Seas Fleet
GB	*Goeben* (BC) and *Breslau* (LC)
PS	Pacific Squadron, including von Spee and *Emden*, 2 x AC, 2 x LC
WI	West Indies Squadron 2 x LC - *Dresden* (joins von Spee) and *Karlsruhe*
LC	2 x LC - *Leipzig* off California, *Königsberg* off East Africa

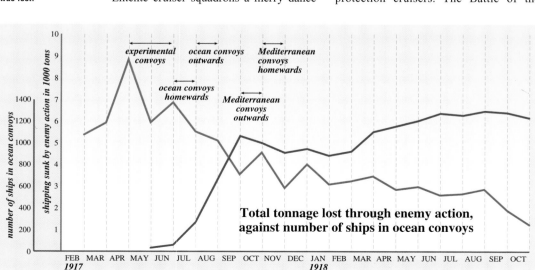

Total tonnage lost through enemy action, against number of ships in ocean convoys

U Boat sinkings in the western approaches, 1917–18

• ships sunk by submarines, May 1917
• ships sunk by submarines, May 1918

the extent of the threat. In February 1917 German naval and military leaders agreed they could not win the war by conventional means, and insisted on a resumption of unrestricted submarine warfare. Statistical analysis suggested U-boats could sink enough Allied shipping to end the war by August. The U-boat offensive was as disastrous a failure of strategic imagination as the Schlieffen Plan. Both guaranteed the entry of powerful enemies into the war against Germany. Both depended on the enemy reacting as predicted.

Unrestricted submarine warfare brought Great Britain to the brink of ruin in April 1917, the only month when U-boats sank the target of 600,000 tons. One in four ships sailing from British ports failed to return, and only six weeks of grain remained in the country. The carnage prompted the Allies to re-allocate shipping, ration civilian food supplies, and re-introduce convoys, the traditional antidote to a *guerre de course*. The Admiralty had rejected convoys, claiming too few escorts and insuperable administrative problems. In practice 30 dazzle-painted ships zig-zagging in formation provided a smaller and more difficult target than the same number of ships scattered singly about the ocean. Convoy escorts, transferred from futile seek and destroy missions, found targets for their new hydrophones and depth charges. Of 880,00 ships convoyed by 11 November 1918, only 436 were lost. Convoys with air cover lost no ships to U-boats at all. The Germans on the other hand lost half their submarine flotilla, with the pick of their crews. The losses contributed to morale problems in the High Seas Fleet whose mutiny precipitated Germany's political collapse in 1918.

LEFT: Most U boat sinkings were achieved in coastal waters, the submarines lying off familiar land falls just like 18th century privateers. Many attacks were carried out by gun, to save torpedoes, but the advent of 'Q' ships led most captains to make their attacks from underwater.

Falkland Islands (8 December 1914) vindicated the battlecruiser as a means of eliminating commerce raiders. Their speed allowed them to stay a safe distance from the German cruisers, whose guns they outranged. The long clear day gave time for the decisive victory that proved elusive in the murky North Sea, ending the surface threat to Allied merchant ships.

German maritime trade, by contrast, was subject to a blockade of increasing rigour. A patrol line of cruisers and armed merchantmen intercepted ships passing between Iceland and Scotland, and redirected those carrying 'contraband' to British ports. The blockade posed no direct threat to life or property, as cargoes were purchased and the ships released. Although the Admiralty had been planning economic warfare since 1906, there was no pre-concerted plan to starve Germany out, like a besieged town. Food was not declared contraband until 1915, after the first unrestricted U-boat campaign began. In 1916 the Allies restricted imports to neutral Scandinavia and Holland to pre-war levels, and refused credit and coal to firms suspected of trading with the enemy. The United States objected, but American trade with the Entente had created a commercial interest in Allied victory. The military effects of the blockade are unclear, although it has been blamed for the deaths of 750,000 German civilians. Nevertheless, economic sanctions remain a popular, 'cheap' foreign policy option.

The only German weapon able to circumvent Allied sea power was the U-boat.

Submarines were too fragile to risk prolonged exposure on the surface to eliminate prizes legally, so they torpedoed merchant ships without warning, even neutrals. The Germans called off the first U-boat campaign, encouraging complacency in the Admiralty, who relied on offensive patrols and defensively armed merchantmen. However, political pressure from America had limited U-boat activities, concealing

RIGHT: By May 1918 the U boats found convoys difficult to locate, and escort vessels with primitive anti-submarine weapons scored an increasing number of kills. British and French aircraft and airships proved highly successful at forcing the submarines to dive, and the first aerial sonar sets were under test by the end of the war.

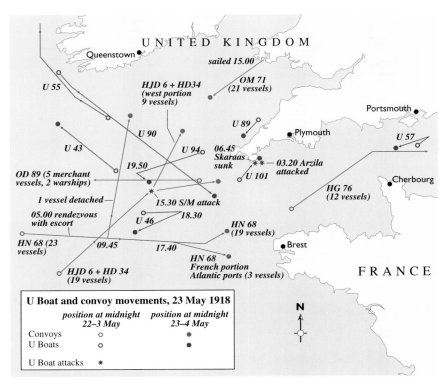

U Boat and convoy movements, 23 May 1918

	position at midnight 22–3 May	position at midnight 23–4 May
Convoys	○	●
U Boats	○	●
U Boat attacks	✳	

War in the East

RIGHT: The main German offensive of 1915 drove the Russians from Poland, their pre-war fortresses proving no obstacle despite the money (and artillery) lavished on them. However, the Russians' ability to withdraw into the strategic depths denied von Falkenhayn the knockout blow he had hoped for.

German troops could move rapidly between Eastern and Western Fronts, on interior lines. The empty spaces of the former appeared to offer more scope for traditional military victory, than the entrenched deadlock in the West. The space that made breakthroughs possible, however, also made them less decisive. The War in the East proved as resistant to a military solution, as the West. Russia's economic and social collapse offered Germany a hollow promise of victory, while infecting her armies with Bolshevism.

After their successful Tannenberg manoeuvre, Hindenberg and Ludendorff aspired to defeat Russia decisively by manoeuvre. They proposed enveloping the Russian Armies in the Warsaw salient, Cannae style. Falkenhayn, Chief of the German General Staff since the failure of the Schlieffen Plan, believed Russia was too large to defeat in a single offensive. He wanted a limited campaign of attrition; the Gorlice-Tarnow offensive of May 1915 was to be a victory for firepower and organization, not manoeuvre. Falkenhayn transferred eight divisions from France to the Carpathian front, deploying 700 guns, one to every 60 yards of front. This was one sixth the density used at Verdun, but sufficed to smash the shallow Russian frontline in a four-hour bombardment. No-man's-land was two miles across, much wider than in France, allowing German infantry to approach the Russian trenches unseen, and capture the shell-shocked defenders. For the first time aircraft strafed headquarters and billets in the Russian rear. In a fortnight the Germans advanced almost 100 miles, an unimaginable distance in the West. Still resisting Ludendorff's grandiose schemes, Falkenhayn exploited north and then east, cutting the Russians' lateral railway through Brest-Litovsk. The offensive petered out in the autumn mud, as the Russians slipped away eastwards. Events had justified Falkenhayn's scepticism about achieving a strategic decision against a numerically stronger enemy prepared to retreat into Russia's endless wastes.

Falkenhayn had not crippled Russia's offensive strength as he hoped. Winter 1915/16 provided a breathing space for Russian industry to make up shortages in rifles and munitions. Material deficiencies persuaded some Russian commanders to seek subtle alternatives to simply piling up masses of shells and men. In June 1916 General Brusilov achieved surprise by attacking on a wide front, with no apparent preparations to alert the enemy. His artillery had saved shells from their daily allowance, while the absence of reserves behind the attacking troops gave no clue of their offensive intentions. After a 24-hour bombardment, Russian infantry patrols tested the defences, a process described as tapping at a wall to find the soft patches.

ABOVE: General Alexei Brusilov masterminded the great Russian offensive later named after him. At the same time as the British and French attacked on the Somme, the Russians achieved complete surprise in a full-scale assault on the Austro-Hungarians. Only massive German intervention saved their allies from total defeat.

Often the Russians surprised Austrian defenders in their dugouts. The Brusilov offensive finished the Austro-Hungarian Army, which never recovered from losing a third of its total manpower in a week. The Germans had to stabilize the front with more divisions from the West, despite the Battle of the Somme. Hindenberg and Ludendorff replaced Falkenhayn, completing the military subordination of Germany's political leadership. The duo pushed through unrestricted U-boat warfare, and introduced the Hindenberg program to maximize munitions output, at the expense of the civilian economy. Army Corps districts became local dictatorships, centrally directed by the *Kriegsamt* or Supreme War Office.

The Brusilov offensive cost the Russians a million casualties, but led nowhere strategically. Another million Russian soldiers deserted. Military failure, however, was not the immediate cause of Russia's leaving the war. There were still 6.5 million troops at the front, when Russia's internal collapse justified pre-war claims that protracted war was economically unsustainable. Wartime inflation had eroded the price paid to Russian grain producers. Peasants refused to market their corn, causing hunger and revolutionary disturbances in the towns. The Germans quietly allowed the Russian Army to disintegrate from within, returning exiled dissidents, such as Lenin, to hasten the process. The Germans reversed Clausewitz's dic-

The Battle of Gorlice-Tarnow and the Russian retreat, 1915

Central Powers (Germany and Austria)
- frontline, 13 May
- frontline, 13 July
- frontline, 29 August
- attacks

9TH German army
7TH Austrian army
SÜD mixed army

Russia
- frontline, 30 September
- fortresses
- **2 Sep.** date of capture by Central Powers

Central Powers: numbers - 1.3 million casualties - 1.0 million

Russia: numbers- 1.75 million casualties- 1.0 million prisoners- 1.0 million of war

BELOW: The harsh terms of the peace treaty dictated to Russia by the victorious Germans in 1918 suggest how ghastly the consequences might have been for western Europe had the Kaiser's armies met with victory there. Ironically, the Germans toyed with removing Lenin and his regime, but eventually supported the revolutionaries who were prepared to make peace on any terms.

The dictated peace - the treaty of Brest-Litovsk

— western border of Russian territory, 1914

☐ Central Powers territory in 1914

— frontline at Armistice 15 Dec. 1917

— furthest extent of Central Powers occupation, 9 Jan. 1918

▨ area of Russia occupied by Central Powers at armistice, 15 Dec. 1917

▨ area of Russia occupied by Central Powers at peace treaty, 3 Mar. 1918

☐ area of Russia independent after Dec. 1917

✊ serious Russian mutinies in Aug. 1917

● principal towns where Bolsheviks took power, Nov. 1917–Feb. 1918

The Brusilov offensive, June–Oct. 1916

— railways

— borders, 1914

front lines

— 4 June

--- 10 June

⋯⋯ mid-July

Russian army

▨ army units, with commanders, (divisions numbers at 4 June)

▷ army unit headquarters

▯ headquarters Southwestern Front (commander Brusilov)

--- army boundaries

→ attacks

Central Powers army

▨ Austrian army units, with commanders

▨ Austro-German unit, with commander

--- army boundaries

---

tum; politics became the pursuit of military ends by other means. Peace was essential to the Central Powers, particularly Austria-Hungary, but unlike the Russians they still had an Army capable of imposing a 'peace of violence'. The Treaty of Brest-Litovsk was an example to Germany's other enemies of what they might expect, if forced to sue for peace. The Central Powers proclaimed 'national self-determination', but only to weaken Russia by detaching Poland, the Baltic States, and Ukraine. Forty divisions remained in the east to assert German control over supplies of wheat, timber, and Romanian oil. Trotsky's policy of non-resistance, 'neither peace nor war', was helpless against unrestrained military power. Russian soldiers voted with their feet, and went home, in the face of a resumed German advance. Economic collapse and revolution brought a total defeat that Russia's enemies had failed to inflict on the battlefield.

The Battle of Verdun

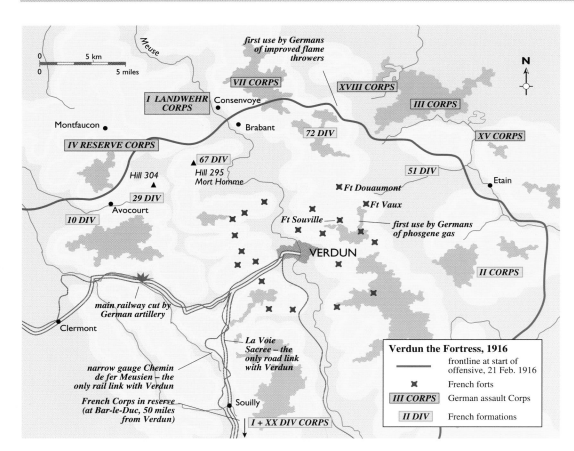

Verdun the Fortress, 1916

——	frontline at start of offensive, 21 Feb. 1916
✖	French forts
III CORPS	German assault Corps
II DIV	French formations

Map labels: Meuse · 0 5 km · 0 5 miles · first use by Germans of improved flame throwers · VII CORPS · XVIII CORPS · I LANDWEHR CORPS · Consenvoye · III CORPS · Montfaucon · Brabant · 72 DIV · XV CORPS · IV RESERVE CORPS · 67 DIV · 51 DIV · Hill 304 · Hill 295 Mort Homme · Ft Douaumont · Etain · 29 DIV · Avocourt · Ft Vaux · 10 DIV · Ft Souville · first use by Germans of phosgene gas · VERDUN · II CORPS · main railway cut by German artillery · Clermont · La Voie Sacrée – the only road link with Verdun · narrow gauge Chemin de fer Meusien – the only rail link with Verdun · French Corps in reserve (at Bar-le-Duc, 50 miles from Verdun) · Souilly · I + XX DIV CORPS · N

LEFT: The 'fortress' of Verdun existed in name only in February 1916 when the Germans attacked. The surrounding forts had been stripped of their guns and garrisons, and it was the more modest dug-outs of the frontline troops that held up the German advance despite an unprecedently heavy artillery barrage. Sustained by a limited road and rail link, the French clung to their positions, bringing on the battle of attrition planned by General von Falkenhayn.

RIGHT: Countless white crosses at the *Ossuaire* testify to the scale of what even the German Official History was moved to call the 'Tragedy of Verdun'. French casualties were 61,000 dead, 101,000 missing and 216,000 wounded; German losses were 143,000 killed or missing and 187,000 wounded.

Falkenhayn needed to end the war in the West before the Allied blockade or the new British armies became effective. He decided to forestall the British military build-up by destroying the French Army through attrition. The resulting battle around Verdun in eastern France was the longest and most terrible of the war. A pitiless rain of shells mocked the efforts of individual soldiers, but paradoxically Verdun forged flexible tactics, based on small units and personal initiative.

Sceptical of prospects for a break-through, Falkenhayn chose the Verdun salient as a symbolic objective that the French could not abandon, but where a series of limited, artillery-heavy attacks could bleed them white. Verdun was the strategic hinge of the Allied line, between the quiet sector in Alsace and more active fronts in Champagne, Artois, and Flanders. Logistically the Germans had 14 railways against a single narrow gauge railway on the French side. Tactically the salient was vulnerable to converging artillery fire, its woods and steep ravines concealing offensive preparations, but Falkenhayn did not intend to win a conventional victory. He starved his subordinates of reserves, relying on an unprecedented bombardment of two million shells to destroy not just the frontline, but the whole zone under attack.

So heavy was the fire that French pilots above the battlefield could not count the muzzle flashes. After an eight-hour bombardment by 1,400 guns, German infantry patrols probed the defences before the main attacks. German air superiority and the absence of the usual advanced trenches ensured surprise, while the short bombardment left no time for French reserves to react. German troops advanced inexorably, seizing the outlying fort at Douamont. For a few hours they held open the way to Verdun.

Falkenhayn's territorial gains revealed the fatal contradictions inherent in a battle of pure attrition. He had no reserves ready to exploit the opportunity of a wider break-through, but the French were no longer within range of the German guns. It took ten days to move these up through their own crater field, allowing time for French reinforcements to arrive. Like other First World War battles, Verdun developed its own momentum. The enemy refused to behave as expected. They voluntarily gave up indefensible ground south east of Fort Vaux, falsifying Falkenhayn's essential premise. Lacking railways the French passed lorries full of troops and stores along La Voie Sacrée from Bar-le-Duc to

RIGHT: This is how a French infantry company formed up for the attack according to the tactics developed in 1916. British and German tactics and organization were very similar. The monolithic rifle companies of 1914 had evolved into all-arms units, using fire and movement to fight their own way forward. 'Modern' infantry tactics were forged in the summer of 1916.

Return of fire and movement

direction of advance

No.1 section — No.2 section — No.3 section

assault sections

20 paces

16 paces

moppers up

(from No.4 sec)   (from 2nd line COY.)

50 paces

reinforcing section

No.4 section (–)

company front 200–300 m

○ grenadiers (bomb throwers)	Voltigeur (riflemen)	⚲ section leader
Fusiliers (light machine gunners)	● rifle grenadier	⚵ company commander
● machine gun number	○ bayonet man	● runner
○ spare number		□ pioneer

The central attack,
Feb. 21–5 1916

voluntary French withdraal

Attack on the flanks,
Mar.– Apr. 1916

Battle of attrition,
May– Sep. 1916

Battle of Douaumont-
Vaux, 24 Oct. 1916

Battle of Louvemont-
Bezonvaux, 15 Dec. 1916

Battle of Hill 304 and Hill 295
Mort-Homme, 20 Aug. 1917

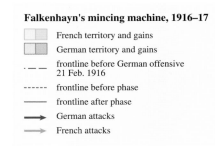

Falkenhayn's mincing machine, 1916–17

	French territory and gains
	German territory and gains
- - -	frontline before German offensive 21 Feb. 1916
------	frontline before phase
———	frontline after phase
→	German attacks
→	French attacks

Verdun, at 14 second intervals, while battalions of territorials continually shovelled gravel into the potholes. For the first time a great battle depended entirely on the internal combustion engine. The British relieved the French Tenth Army at Arras, releasing fresh divisions to be rotated through the mincing machine at Verdun. Falkenhayn widened the front under attack, driving in the French flanks at Mort Homme, Hill 304, and Fort Vaux. He lost the initiative, despite the first use of phosgene gas shells. Falkenhayn could not halt the offensive, lest the 550,000 French troops drawn to Verdun launched a counter-attack. German infantry attacks suffered heavy losses for little gain, as they tried to end the battle before the anticipated Allied offensive on the Somme. Its opening bombardment in June forced Falkenhayn to close down operations at Verdun. He had reduced French participation on the Somme to 12 divisions from the 40 planned, but had similarly depleted German reserves, without achieving the wider aim of knocking France out of the war.

The Germans did not monopolize tactical innovation. The French at Verdun discarded Joffre's inflexible tactics, and perfected artillery techniques to retake much of their lost ground in the autumn of 1916. Generals Nivelle and Mangin attacked in depth to avoid mixing units. They sought surprise by lorrying forward assault troops on the eve of an attack, and not digging extra trenches beforehand. The infantry practised behind the line on taped models of their objectives, every man knowing his place in the battle. They masked German strongpoints, attacking weak spots, such as unit boundaries, behind a carefully timed barrage that advanced 100 yards every four minutes. Heavy guns wrecked the enemy's underground shelters, while a *tir d'interdiction* isolated the survivors. Low-flying aircraft maintained contact with advancing infantry, while new infantry weapons, automatic rifles and grenade launchers, kept the enemy's heads down during the final stages of an attack. Reserves advanced 2,000 yards behind the leading divisions, to rush the German second line before it could be occupied. Mangin's men reached the enemy gun line, taking 115 pieces and 11,000 prisoners. For all its inhumanity and futility in territorial terms, Verdun ended with a demonstration of the value of well-trained infantry acting in close coordination with supporting artillery.

RIGHT: The initial assault failed to take Verdun, but did capture Fort Douaumont. The offensive widened to take in the left bank of the Meuse, but the French line held and a battle of attrition ensued. A final German offensive took Fort Vaux, but with the Somme battles underway, no more troops could be spared to prosecute the offensive. French counter-attacks continued into 1917, retaking the symbolic ruins of the forts.

The Battle of the Somme

BELOW: Popular British attitudes to the First World War remain dominated by first day of the Somme offensive, when 57,000 casualties were suffered for negligible gains. Yet the battle went on for another 141 days and German generals described it as the 'muddy grave of the German army'. A night attack two weeks later captured several key positions, British tactics improved and tanks spearheaded the final battles in September.

Great Britain, alone of the European powers, did not have a large regular army before 1914. Like the Americans in 1861 the British had to raise new armies from scratch. Their inexperienced volunteers suffered terribly against the main force of the German Army on the Somme. However, British material superiority and adaptability turned the Somme into the muddy grave of the pre-war German Army. It laid the foundation for eventual Allied victory.

There was no flank to turn on the Western Front, so the British hoped to create an internal flank by seizing high ground before Bapaume, and rolling up the German trenches towards Arras. The British High Command disagreed over the practicality of a breakthrough. The Army commander responsible for planning the Somme battle wanted to take shallow mile-

deep bites out of the German line, allowing accurate artillery preparation. The Commander-in-Chief, Sir Douglas Haig, was more ambitious, urging attacks up to 4,000 yards deep to penetrate the enemy first and second lines in one bound. This proved too much for the partially-trained British artillery. German positions on the Somme were particularly strong: three trench systems each 500 to 1,000 yards deep, covered by belts of barbed wire 30 yards wide, and studded with shelters 30 feet deep in the chalk, capable of sheltering whole companies from any bombardment. Lock trenches ran front to rear to isolate break-ins. Machine guns hidden in frequent fortified villages and woods swept the open glacis-like slopes. Siege methods offered no cheap alternative given superior German trench warfare capabilities.

The British in 1916 possessed unprecedented material and mechanical resources, which may have dulled their tactical ingenuity. Organization of the rear areas, however, was a logistical masterpiece, including three broad gauge railways, water and accommodation for 400,000 men and 100,000 transport animals, and 7,000 miles of telephone cable to control 1,500 guns. Allied air superiority ensured the preparations remained secret.

The disastrous failure of the initial British attacks on 1 July was tactical in origin. Almost half the 140,000 infantry committed were shot down in no-man's-land; those that reached enemy trenches were cut off by German shellfire, and annihilated by counter-attacks. The BEF suffered the heaviest casualties ever suffered by one army in a single day's fighting. Contributory factors included a late start, which lost the dawn mist, and the infantryman's excessive load, which prevented him closing rapidly with the German trenches. However, many British soldiers were shot down as they went over the top, implying the enemy was waiting for them. The artillery preparation, which had wrecked

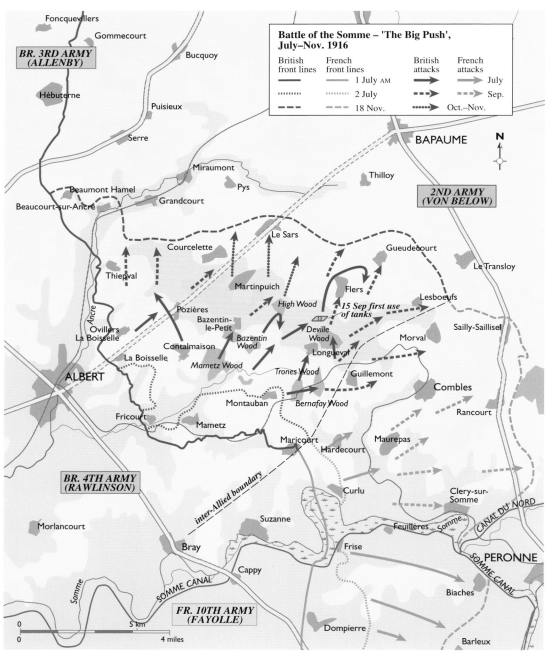

Battle of the Somme – 'The Big Push', July–Nov. 1916

British front lines	French front lines		British attacks	French attacks
——	—— 1 July AM		⇢ ⇢ ⇢	⇢ ⇢ ⇢ July
··········	·········· 2 July		▪▪▪►	▪▪▪► Sep.
– – –	– – – 18 Nov.		●●●►	●●●► Oct.–Nov.

BR. 3RD ARMY (ALLENBY)

Foncquevillers
Gommecourt
Bucquoy
Hébuterne
Puisieux
Serre
Miraumont
Thilloy
BAPAUME
Pys
Beaumont Hamel
Grandcourt
Beaucourt-sur-Ancre
2ND ARMY (VON BELOW)
Le Sars
Courcelette
Gueudecourt
Le Transloy
Thiepval
Martinpuich
Flers
Lesboeufs
High Wood
15 Sep first use of tanks
Pozières
Bazentin-le-Petit
Deville Wood
Sailly-Saillisel
Ovillers
La Boisselle
Contalmaison
Bazentin Wood
Longueval
Morval
La Boisselle
Mametz Wood
Trones Wood
Guillemont
ALBERT
Montauban
Bernafay Wood
Combles
Fricourt
Mametz
Rancourt
Maricourt
Maurepas
Hardecourt
inter-Allied boundary
BR. 4TH ARMY (RAWLINSON)
Curlu
Clery-sur-Somme
Morlancourt
Suzanne
Feuillères
CANAL DU NORD
Bray
Frise
PERONNE
Cappy
SOMME CANAL
Biaches
FR. 10TH ARMY (FAYOLLE)
Dompierre
Barleux

0 — 5 km
0 — 4 miles

N

LEFT: **A 15-in howitzer of the Royal Marines in action during the Battle of the Somme. The overwhelming power of the British artillery came as a disagreeable surprise to the German army: it was the first intimation that Germany would lose the *materialschlacht*.**

RIGHT: **British plans for 1 July 1916 were based on the assumption that the hastily trained volunteers of the 'New Armies' were only capable of simple manoeuvres and that the massed artillery would crush the German defences. Unfortunately the guns fired a high proportion of duds, many German machine gun positions survived, and the German artillery barrage was so effective it destroyed the original British frontline in several sectors.**

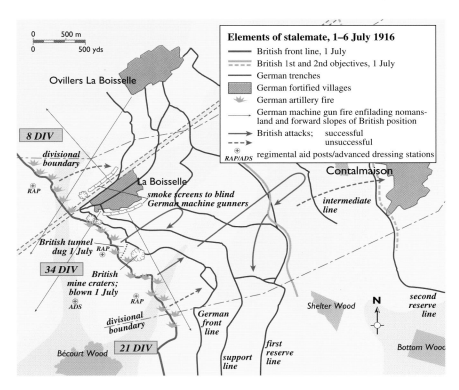

the enemy front line at Neuve Chapelle and Verdun, failed on the Somme. Almost two million shells were fired during a seven-day bombardment, but one in three failed to explode. Most field gun ammunition was shrapnel with a time fuse, less effective for wire-cutting than the instantaneous high explosive used later. There were too few heavy guns, 6-inch calibre or more. The French on the Somme's southern flank deployed one heavy gun every 21 yards, compared with one to 58 yards on the British front. Counter-battery work was patchy. The British had no gas shell, the best means of neutralizing hostile artillery. Infantry-artillery cooperation was poor. Three out of six corps refused to use a creeping barrage on 1 July; the others employed them wrongly. Rare successes by 7th and 18th Divisions followed creeping barrages that prevented the enemy manning his parapet in time to stop the attacking infantry.

The defeat of 1 July confounded British plans, and has dominated later perceptions of the Somme, but the battle lasted another 141 days. Only two weeks after the BEF's blackest day, a British night attack overran five miles of the German second line, after forming up under cover of darkness on white tapes just short of the German positions. Night attacks became common, forcing the Germans to develop counter-measures. In September seven British divisions advanced a mile and a half down the reverse slope of the high ground towards Flers, precipitating the worst German crisis until August 1918. Tanks made their battlefield debut, but the key to British success was improved artillery technique. The Germans' fortified zone had worn very thin. Reserves had fallen to the lowest level before October 1918. Autumn rain saved them. Mud prevented attacking infantry following the protective barrage.

The first day of the Somme showed the impossibility of piercing the German line, but the balance of losses shifted against the defenders as the BEF learned their trade. German infantry became convinced of their inferiority in *Materialschlacht*, whatever their skill as trench fighters. To escape the crushing artillery fire attracted by a visible trench, the survivors crouched in water-logged shell holes, without hot food and unable to evacuate their casualties. They felt abandoned by their artillery and air force, cheering when their own planes were shot down. German commanders unwillingly accepted the need for a less rigid defence, after they had destroyed the last of the peace-trained German infantry in repeated counter-attacks. In February 1917 the Germans withdrew to the Hindenberg line to spare their infantry another Somme battle.

BELOW: **The senior officers involved in the Somme battle had discussed the possibilities of night operations at great length before the war. The possibility of disastrous confusion was a risk accepted on 14 July and the result exceeded expectations: the line was broken and an Indian cavalry brigade came within an ace of taking High Wood. German machine gunners were sabred down by horsemen at once point: not the standard image of the Somme!**

Organization of a British bombing attack

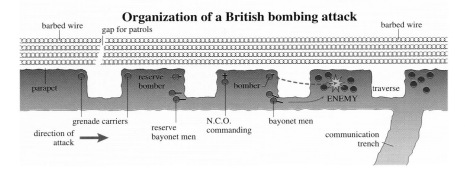

ABOVE: **Combat within the trenches was a specialist art in which 'bombers' (soldiers armed with grenades) were supported by bayonet men (often armed with shovels and revolvers) with riflemen and machine-gunners giving distant cover. Victory in such fights, as future General Erwin Rommel observed, went to the man with the last round in the magazine.**

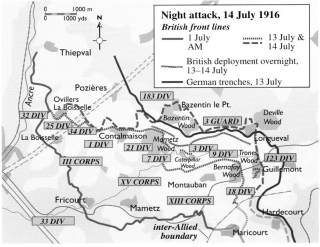

Chapter 8 Restoring Mobility 1917–39

By 1917, the old ways—tactics, operations, strategy, and the highest levels of statecraft—had failed. The search for solutions took place at all levels, from platoon leaders in the trenches, colonels in dugouts, generals in chateaux and leaders in capitals. Changes followed from low-level tactics to national and supranational strategies. This search continued to 1940, when the shape of the new ways of warfare became terribly apparent. In some ways, the questions that were posed in 1917 were never answered.

The answers were all inherent in what had gone on before 1916; most of them dated from before the war. It was apparent that the international system that had evolved since the Congress of Vienna could neither resolve nor win the war. In 1917, two men, previously off-stage, would put forward their own visions of a replacement for it: Vladimir Ulanov Lenin, Russian revolutionary, and Woodrow Wilson, American president. Neither would prevail, but they set up alternatives that would shape the military history of the foreshortened 20th century (1914-91).

Militarily, the emerging technologies of the internal combustion engine and the wireless made new solutions possible. Combined in various different ways, on armoured vehicles, in aircraft, in submarines, they would shape conflicts for the remainder of the century.

In parallel with the changing technologies were new ways to supply the front. 1916 had already seen the introduction of what the Germans called *Materialschlact*. To produce the material required by modern war required the mobilization of national industry, personnel and resources. It was not a war of armies and navies, but of entire nations. It would not be until after 1918 that the rise of supranational ideologies allowed total war to invoke *volk* or the workers of the world as their cause.

National mobilization was part of the solution. In Germany, it ended up with what amounted to a dictatorship under General Ludendorff, with the national economy and everyday life subordinated to the needs of the front. In Britain, mobilization, like conscription, came late, but provided much of the material that led to the eventual battlefield solutions of 1914-18. The United States, later still to mobilize despite its economic strength, had to rely on Allied weapons to equip its divisions.

National mobilization also involved people. Social mobilization required that populations had to be told that this was not simply another dynastic conflict but a war to end war. Ensuring they believed this opened up the world of propaganda and information control that would remain for the rest of the century. Yet while this could spur the

economic base to greater production, it could not counteract the reality of modern war. All the major combatants, except the late-mobilizing British and Americans, had major mutinies and collapsing military morale in 1917-18. While Lenin, Wilson and Ludendorff all tried to implement their national-level solutions, other men in uniform tried to do the same thing on the battlefield. In 1917, the British saw the poten-

tial in improved tactics, including the use of tanks, at Messines and Cambrai. The Germans improved their tactics as well and were able to first apply them at an operational level at the capture of Riga in 1917. After the Russian Revolution, Ludendorff took these tactics and the troops from the East into one last series of offensives to regain the initiative before the Americans arrived. When these failed, the three months

preceding the Armistice demonstrated how far the Allied armies had come from the failures of 1915-16.

Once the audit of battle was closed in 1918, the belligerent nations interpreted the lessons of the Great War very differently. The French looked at the lessons at all levels and built the Maginot Line. The Germans looked at the same lessons and developed the *blitzkrieg*.

The End of the Old: Third Ypres

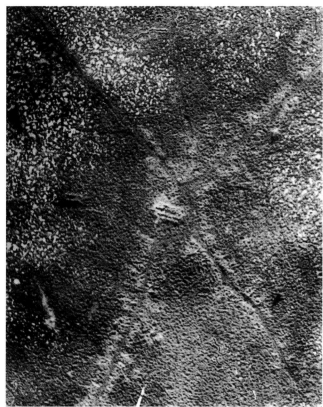

RIGHT: Conceived of as a breakthrough battle to overrun German submarine bases on the Belgian coast, the Third Battle of Ypres pitted a reorganized and tactically advanced British army against the heavily fortified German positions overlooking the city. Haig was deflected neither by the worst summer weather for decades, nor repeated German counter-attacks. The battle petered out here, making Passchendaele synonymous with the 'futility' of war.

ABOVE: A small village on the outskirts of Ypres, Passchendaele was levelled during the battle to which it gave its name. Both sides concentrated large numbers of guns on a narrow front; prolonged barrages left the ground waterlogged and the soldiers floundering in a man-made swamp.

The Third Battle of Ypres – the British Army's offensive in Belgium in the summer and autumn of 1917 – was in many ways the epitome of 20th century land combat. Only Stalingrad and some of the other massive battles in the East in the Second World War matched it in defining what modern war represented.

Third Ypres, like the Somme and Verdun the year before, is also important in that it defined how the Great War would be remembered. Third Ypres was the battle of the mud sea, where heavy rains running down slopes denuded of vegetation turned much of the low-lying areas into quagmire.

Third Ypres is important because it has since defined what people thought about the Great War and, in the years since, the myths have been used to legitimate political, cultural, and societal changes. In that way, the myths have eclipsed what actually happened on the battlefield, just as Homer's *Iliad* has had much greater significance than the realities of Bronze Age Greek warfare.

The Third Battle of Ypres represented the culmination of *Materialschlact*. German veterans of Verdun found it to be worse even than that battle, reflecting both the battlefield conditions and the greater firepower and tactical competence of the British offensive operations in 1917. Like the Somme and Verdun the year before, it also shifted the paradigm of what a battle was meant to be. No longer was it possible to think of battle as a day's business that could be orchestrated by a single great leader, Napoleon at Austerlitz or Wellington at Waterloo. In 1917, modern battle emerged as a process, one as complex and as involved as the industrial societies that made it possible. Even when confined to a relatively limited geographical area, it was no longer a single mind implementing a plan.

The offensive arose from a desire to capture the German submarine bases on the Belgian coast, to cover for the weakened and mutinous French army, and to crack a German army that was thought to be reeling from its losses. Extensive preparations delayed the attack until late summer and prevented any element of surprise, despite Allied air superiority. The bombardment opened on 18 July and continued until zero hour on 31 July. Strong German defences and incessant counter-attacks limited British gains in a series of attacks through September. After regrouping and a change in battlefield command, the British resumed the offensive on 20 September with a series of systematic, limited blows. By October, the new attacks inflicted heavy losses on the Germans, but torrential rains and the need to rush reserves to the Italian front prevented any lasting success. With Passchendaele Ridge finally taken by the Canadian Corps in November, Third Ypres petered out.

LEFT: A British ammunition column picks its way through captured German positions at Hooge, during the battle for Pilckem ridge, July 1917. As the ground deteriorated, re-supply of forward troops became next to impossible, as did the extrication of the wounded.

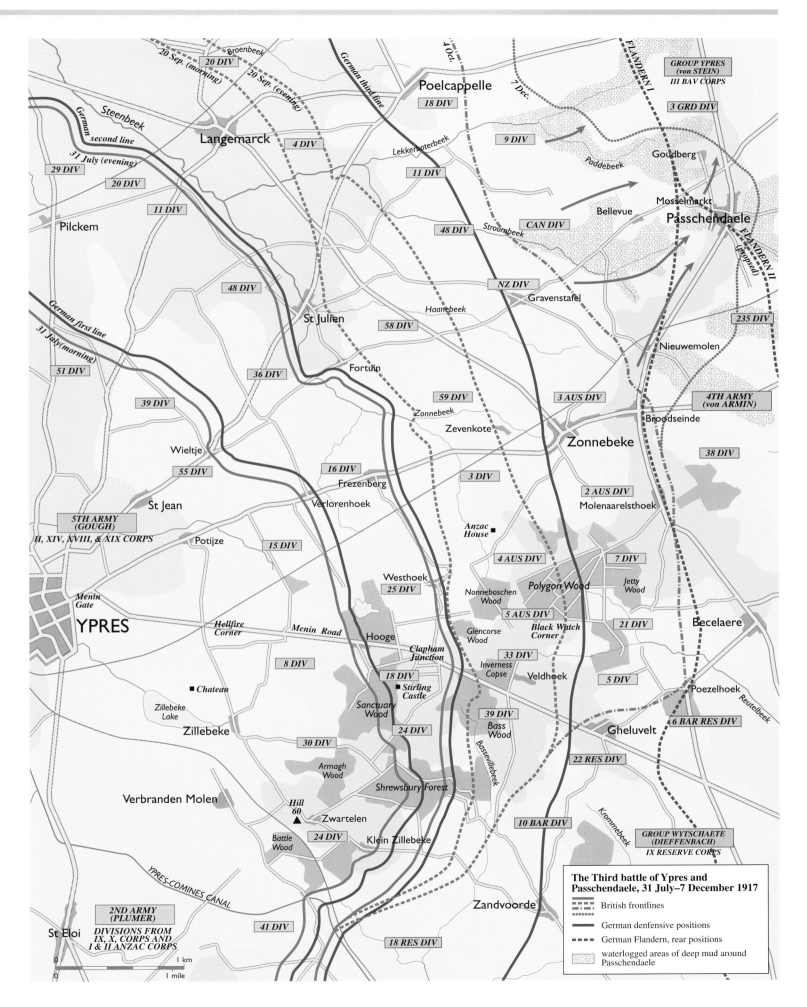

20 Sep. (morning)

20 DIV

20 Sep. (evening)

Broenbeek

German third line

4 Oct.

7 Dec.

GROUP YPRES
(von STEIN)
III BAV CORPS

Poelcappelle

18 DIV

3 GRD DIV

Steenbeek

German second line

Langemarck

4 DIV

Lekkerboterbeek

9 DIV

Paddebeek

Goudberg

31 July (evening)

29 DIV

11 DIV

Bellevue

Mosselmarkt

Passchendaele

20 DIV

German first line

11 DIV

Pilckem

48 DIV

CAN DIV

Stroombeek

FLANDERN II
(proposed)

31 July (morning)

51 DIV

St Julien

58 DIV

Haanebeek

NZ DIV

Gravenstafel

235 DIV

36 DIV

Fortuin

Nieuwemolen

39 DIV

59 DIV

3 AUS DIV

Broodseinde

4TH ARMY
(von ARMIN)

Wieltje

Zonnebeek

Zevenkote

Zonnebeke

38 DIV

55 DIV

16 DIV

Frezenberg

3 DIV

2 AUS DIV

Molenaarelsthoek

St Jean

Verlorenhoek

Anzac
House

4 AUS DIV

7 DIV

5TH ARMY
(GOUGH)
II, XIV, XVIII, & XIX CORPS

Potijze

15 DIV

Jetty
Wood

Menin
Gate

Westhoek

25 DIV

Nonneboschen
Wood

Polygon Wood

5 AUS DIV

21 DIV

Becelaere

YPRES

Hellfire
Corner

Menin Road

Hooge

Glencorse
Wood

Black Watch
Corner

Clapham
Junction

33 DIV

Veldhoek

5 DIV

8 DIV

18 DIV

Inverness
Copse

■ Chateau

Stirling
Castle

Poezelhoek

Zillebeke
Lake

Sanctuary
Wood

39 DIV

Bass
Wood

Reutelbeek

Zillebeke

24 DIV

22 RES DIV

Gheluvelt

6 BAR RES DIV

30 DIV

Armagh
Wood

Bassevillebeek

Shrewsbury Forest

Krommebeek

Verbranden Molen

Hill
60
▲

Zwartelen

10 BAR DIV

GROUP WYTSCHAETE
(DIEFFENBACH)
IX RESERVE CORPS

Battle
Wood

24 DIV

Klein Zillebeke

YPRES-COMINES CANAL

2ND ARMY
(PLUMER)
DIVISIONS FROM
IX, X, CORPS AND
I & II ANZAC CORPS

Zandvoorde

41 DIV

St Eloi

18 RES DIV

The Third battle of Ypres and
Passchendaele, 31 July–7 December 1917

British frontlines

German defensive positions

German Flandern, rear positions

waterlogged areas of deep mud around
Passchendaele

0 ___ 1 km
0 ___ 1 mile

New Approaches: Messines and Cambrai

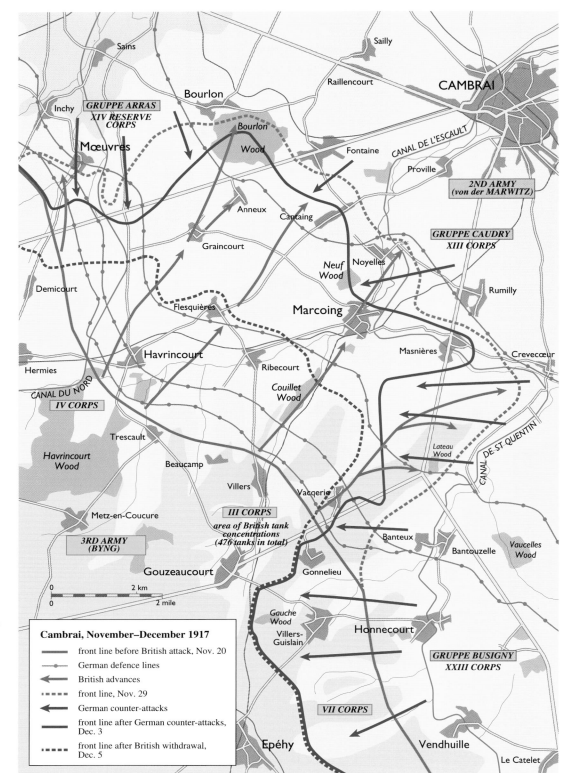

GRUPPE ARRAS
XIV RESERVE
CORPS

2ND ARMY
(von der MARWITZ)

GRUPPE CAUDRY
XIII CORPS

IV CORPS

III CORPS
area of British tank
concentrations
(476 tanks in total)

3RD ARMY
(BYNG)

GRUPPE BUSIGNY
XXIII CORPS

VII CORPS

Bourlon Wood, Fontaine, Cambrai, Sailly, Raillencourt, Sains, Inchy, Mœuvres, Anneux, Cantaing, Graincourt, Proville, Noyelles, Neuf Wood, Rumilly, Demicourt, Flesquières, Marcoing, Havrincourt, Masnières, Crevecœur, Hermies, Ribecourt, Couillet Wood, Lateau Wood, CANAL DU NORD, CANAL DE ST QUENTIN, Trescault, Havrincourt Wood, Beaucamp, Villers, Vacqerie, Metz-en-Coucure, Banteux, Vaucelles Wood, Bantouzelle, Gouzeaucourt, Gonnelieu, Gauche Wood, Villers-Guislain, Honnecourt, Epéhy, Vendhuille, Le Catelet, CANAL DE L'ESCAULT

Cambrai, November–December 1917

— front line before British attack, Nov. 20
•—• German defence lines
← British advances
- - - - front line, Nov. 29
← German counter-attacks
— front line after German counter-attacks, Dec. 3
- - - - front line after British withdrawal, Dec. 5

0   2 km
0   2 mile

RIGHT: Cambrai saw the British Army first coming to grips with the need for tanks and infantry to fight as a combined arms team. This has been, in practice, one of the hardest elements of modern operations and tactics to get right, and was to be responsible for many British defeats in 1941-42.

ABOVE: One of the British tanks that shattered the German frontline at Cambrai in November 1917. The German high command had dismissed the tank as an impractical weapon; now, with only three months to go before their own counter-offensive, they made a desperate effort to build some of their own and repair captured British ones.

Either side of Third Ypres were two smaller British offensives which, if they did not dramatically changed the situation on the Western Front, pointed the way to future changes in war-fighting. Both were important steps in the search for solutions to the modern battlefield.

Messines Ridge formed a German-occupied salient south of Ypres that could enfilade the planned advance into the Flanders Plain that became Third Ypres. To remove this required not a separate 'big push' on the scale of the Somme battles but a limited attack that had to succeed in a limited timeframe. General Sir Herbert Plumer's Second Army was not going to repeat the costly tactics of the Somme. Infantry units practised advancing not in long lines but in smaller, more flexible units. The battle-drill of trench warfare - bombers, bayonet-men, rifle-grenadiers and Lewis gunners working together - was rehearsed before the battle. Officers knew what they were to do through a well-script-

ed plan, coordinated with an artillery barrage. Because the barrage alone could not deliver the massive concentrations of firepower with surprise effect, the British delivered the high explosive to the German trenches by mining. Nineteen mines were dug under Messines Ridge and packed with high explosives.

The 'balloon went up' and the barrage opened on 21 May, but it was not until 0310 on 7 June that the mines were detonated and a massive barrage was 'walked'

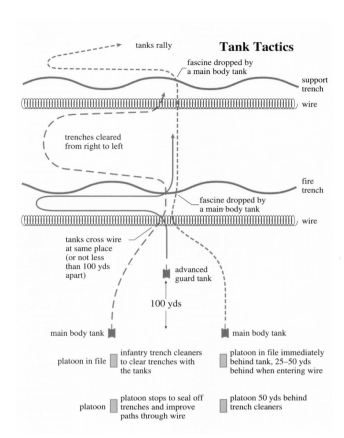

RIGHT: The tanks flattened any wire still standing, making a path for the infantry. The Germans widened their trenches to stop the tanks, but the British responded with ancient technology in the shape of fascines (bundles of saplings secured with wire). These were dropped in the trench, enabling the tanks to cross. These tactics hinged on cooperation between tanks and infantry, although it proved very hard for the two to communicate on the battlefield.

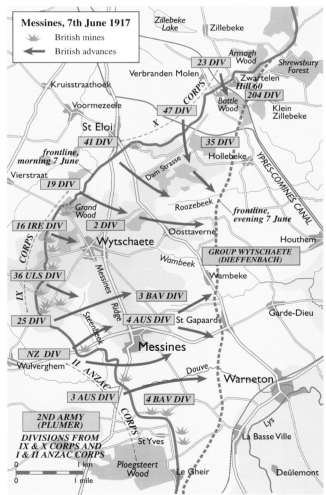

ABOVE: At Messines, the British demonstrated that with new infantry tactics and better coordinated artillery, even the strongest defences could be stormed. General Plumer limited his objectives and opened the assault with 19 gigantic mines, one of which remains unexploded to this day, somewhere beneath the former German frontline.

in front of nine advancing British divisions. By the evening, the Germans had been cleared from the ridge. Further attacks over the following week improved the British position.

The other approach to solving the problems of the modern battlefield stressed the tank. An armoured, self-propelled mount of cannon and machine guns, it could combine both fire and movement, the two key elements of tactics, and could survive the machine-gun fire that dominated the modern battlefield, to close with and destroy the guns themselves, clearing the way for the infantry.

An earlier British plan for a raid with massed tanks through German defences to the railhead town of Cambrai was revived as Third Ypres failed to yield a breakthrough. The Mark IV tank, pushed into production after the success of the original Mark Is on the Somme, was a great improvement but mechanically still very unreliable. The massing of tanks and troops was, thanks to improved artillery tactics, carried out while still retaining some element of surprise. On the morning of 20 November, the artillery fired a short but intense barrage over hours, not days, and the tanks went forward, with seven infantry divisions. The German defences were blown wide open. The cavalry divisions even came forward, seeing their long-awaited chance to exploit the breakthrough.

The vision of 'the green fields beyond' the trenches proved fleeting. Rapidly-arriving German reserves, heavy combat losses and mechanical breakdowns to the tanks, combined with a lack of reserve infantry divisions to follow up - dead at Third Ypres or sent to Italy - meant that the British never made it to Cambrai, the objective that was so close on 20 November. After bitter fighting for Bourlon Wood, the Germans were able to bring up reserves on the flanks of the salient the British advance had created.

Now, it was the Germans' turn to demonstrate their approach to solving the problem of the modern battlefield. On 30 November, their counter-attack hit the British flanks after a brief, intense artillery barrage, mainly with gas shells. The infantry advanced. They included what the Germans styled *stosstruppen*, specialist assault troops used to infiltrate and bypass enemy strongpoints, tactics that had been successful in the taking of Riga earlier that year. Hitting weakened British divisions in the line since the 20th, the Germans soon took back most of their losses and even penetrated the British front line in a demonstration of their offensive power.

Cambrai was to shape debates on the use of tanks for decades thereafter. The lessons were read very differently then, but as 1917 closed and more German troops arrived in the west from the Eastern Front, the Germans believed they had managed to forge a solution to the modern battlefield. The British did as well - between the infantry and artillery of Messines and the tanks of Cambrai - and unlike the Germans, they had the materiel to make it yield victory.

The War in the Air

War in the air was created by emerging technology. The aeroplane had first flown in 1903 and for many years its military potential had been ignored. But in the opening campaigns of 1914, on both the Western and Eastern Fronts, aircraft had brought back vital reconnaissance when the traditional arm of reconnaissance, the cavalry, found its mobility limited by the accurate long-range firepower dominating the modern battlefield.

In the years that followed, aircraft became vital to ground operations, providing reconnaissance and, by 1915, adjusting artillery fire, greatly increasing its accuracy. This led to a need to prevent enemy aircraft carrying out these missions, hence the rise of the fighter. The invention of the synchronized, forward-firing machine-gun gave the Germans an initial advantage in 1915, but after that, despite some costly resurgence such as 'Bloody April' of 1917, Allied numerical superiority normally gave them air superiority. Successful fighter pilots were dubbed aces and publicized by wartime propaganda as knights of the air, traditional heroes in the age of mechanized mass conflict.

Naval operations were increasingly dependent on aircraft. In the early years of the war, the German Navy's fleet of dirigibles gave it a unique scouting force. Later, the British Royal Naval Air Service and Royal Air Force took aircraft to sea, launched first from seaplane tenders but later from warships and the newly-invented aircraft carrier for scouting and attacks on enemy ground targets and ships. Allied aircraft and dirigibles played an important role in the anti-U-boat campaign.

Operations by air forces independent of ground or naval forces started during the

RIGHT: In 1914 the majority of European women in the work force were employed in domestic service, but the demand for military production brought tens of thousands of women into the factories; others served as military auxiliaries.

war. These were the origins of strategic bombing, the idea that aircraft could bypass the enemy's armies and the trenches and strike directly at his means and will to resist, at his industrial heart. These began with attacks by German Zeppelin dirigibles and, later, Gotha heavy bombers on England but were followed, in 1918, by attacks by the Royal Air Force's Independent Force on German industrial targets.

By 1918, air power was established as an integral part of modern war. Air-directed artillery and interdiction and ground attack missions played an important role in halting the German 1918 offensives. The French air force managed to parachute supplies to an infantry brigade cut off by the German advance. German hospitals reported treating soldiers injured by the wheels of very low flying RAF fighter-bombers. When the Allies counter-attacked in the summer of 1918 the German air force mounted the first anti-tank sortie in history, flying all-metal Junkers monoplanes in pursuit of British armour. Sadly, the excellent air-ground cooperation achieved by the British forces was quickly forgotten after the war.

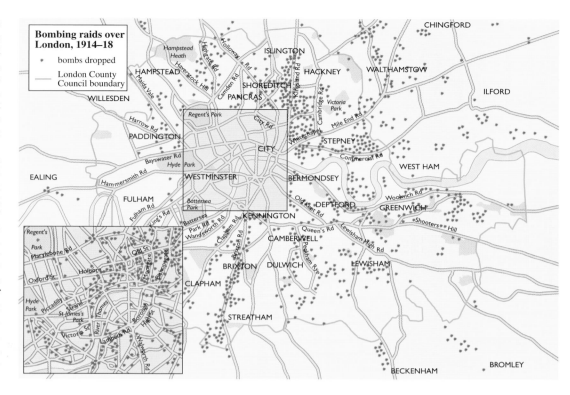

Bombing raids over London, 1914–18
- bombs dropped
- London County Council boundary

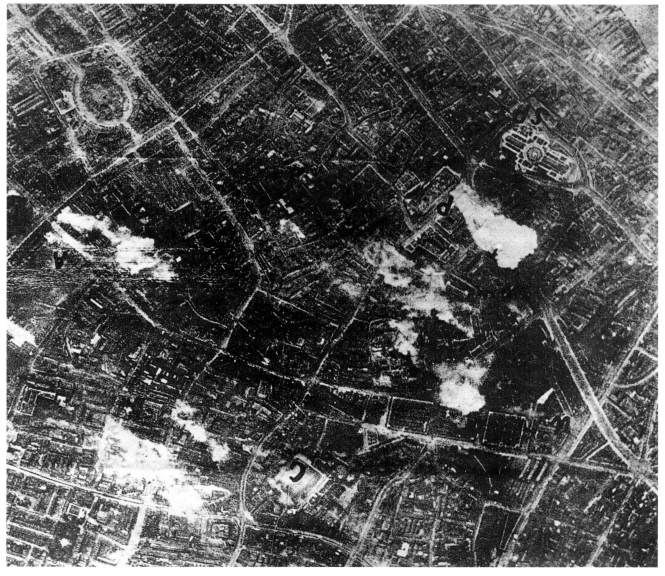

ABOVE: Although notionally aimed at military targets, the first strategic bombing raids conducted by German airships were indiscriminate attacks on major population centres. Airpower visionaries prophesied a future in which precision attacks from the air would achieve instant victory over conventional forces, a theory which would be tested for the rest of the 20th century.

LEFT: A German bomb aimer's view of London, taken in 1917. After the British defences became too dangerous for the airships, the Germans launched a series of raids with Gotha bombers.

The War in the Middle East

ABOVE: Turkish transport destroyed from the air on the Nablus-Beisan road, September 1918. The remorseless bombing of the retreating Turks anticipated later aerial assaults such as that on the Falaise gap in 1944 and the highway out of Kuwait in 1991.

The War in the Middle East was essentially the military story of the end of the Ottoman Empire. After the failure of the Gallipoli campaign in 1915, the campaigns against the Ottoman Empire became "sideshows", condemned by "westerners" as a diversion of resources from the decisive battles in France. These included the Russian campaigns in the Caucasus and Persia, the British campaign in Mesopotamia and, most significantly, the British campaign in Palestine.

These were all uncoordinated and so allowed Turkish resistance to respond to each until 1918, despite only limited German assistance and Turkey's own lack of resources. The two British campaigns were not the result of strategic foresight. The Palestine Campaign grew out of the need to commit forces to Egypt to repulse a Turkish expedition against the Suez Canal in 1915, that in Mesopotamia out of an opportunistic move by the government of India to seize Basra and move up the Tigris on Baghdad.

Fighting in both campaigns during 1916-17 included British reverses: in Mesopotamia, the surrender of a division besieged at Kut; in Palestine, the repulse of two attacks on Turkish positions at Gaza. This underlined the ability of even relatively poor countries to use the machine-gun and the magazine rifle to hold back superior forces. It was only in 1917 that the British invested in building up effective offensive capability in both theatres, which meant logistics infrastructure building. More guns, aircraft, armoured cars and even tanks were diverted to the theatre, along with competent commanders: Allenby in Palestine, Maude then Murray in Mesopotamia. This led to the capture of Jerusalem and Baghdad in 1917.

Despite the collapse of the Russian Army, 1918 saw the rout of Ottoman forces as the British advanced to Mosul in Mesopotamia. And in Palestine, the Battle of Megiddo – the Biblical Armageddon - was one of the best-planned and most decisive combined-arms battles of the war, leading to the fall of Damascus and the end of the campaign.

The war in the Middle East did more, with its post-war treaties and the end of the Ottoman Empire, than create the basis for future conflicts. The Arab revolt and its aftermath showed that the stirrings of nationalism would not be limited to Europe. It demonstrated the ability of modern armies to sustain themselves in combat even in remote areas, and the importance of strategic mobility and logistics that was to be seen repeatedly in the 20th century. It also, in the 1918 defeat of the Turkish forces in Palestine and their successful pursuit, gave a foretaste of the possibility for mobile, combined arms combat, using the internal combustion engine and the wireless, to provide a solution to the modern battlefield.

RIGHT: During the First World War Indian soldiers fought Turks in Palestine because a Bosnian student murdered an Austrian Archduke. Haifa fell to the Jodhpur and Mysore lancers (15th Imperial Service Cavalry Brigade) on 23 September 1918. Until 1917 much of the forces and material diverted to this 'sideshow' were largely irrelevant to the western front: cavalry and obsolete 15-pounder field guns. The victories of 1917-18 stemmed from the creation of a proper logistic structure including a water pipeline and railroad.

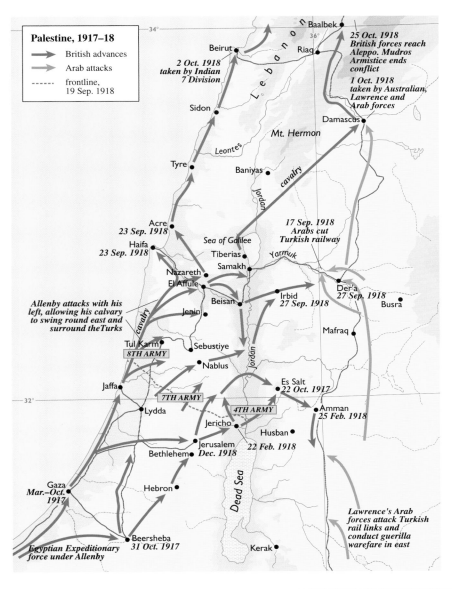

Palestine, 1917–18

→ British advances

→ Arab attacks

- - - frontline, 19 Sep. 1918

Baalbek

25 Oct. 1918 British forces reach Aleppo. Mudros Armistice ends conflict

Beirut

Riaq

2 Oct. 1918 taken by Indian 7 Division

1 Oct. 1918 taken by Australian, Lawrence and Arab forces

Sidon

Damascus

Mt. Hermon

Leontes

cavalry

Tyre

Baniyas

Acre *23 Sep. 1918*

Haifa *23 Sep. 1918*

Sea of Galilee

Tiberias

17 Sep. 1918 Arabs cut Turkish railway

Nazareth

Samakh

Yarmuk

El Affule

Der'a *27 Sep. 1918*

Allenby attacks with his left, allowing his calvary to swing round east and surround theTurks

Beisan

Irbid *27 Sep. 1918*

Busra

Jenin

Mafraq

Tul Karm

Sebustiye

8TH ARMY

Nablus

Es Salt *22 Oct. 1917*

Jaffa

7TH ARMY

4TH ARMY

Amman *25 Feb. 1918*

Lydda

Jericho

Husban *22 Feb. 1918*

Jerusalem *Dec. 1918*

Bethlehem

Gaza *Mar.–Oct. 1917*

Hebron

Beersheba *31 Oct. 1917*

Kerak

Lawrence's Arab forces attack Turkish rail links and conduct guerilla warefare in east

Egyptian Expeditionary force under Allenby

Dead Sea

Jordan

Lebanon

LEFT: The Turkish army proved as stubborn as ever in defence of Gaza, but once their defences were finally outflanked and broken, the British were able to overrun Palestine in 1918. Cavalry, armoured cars, tanks and aircraft all played their part in an increasingly mobile campaign, but the rapid dispersal of the army after the war led the British army to forget much of what it learned there.

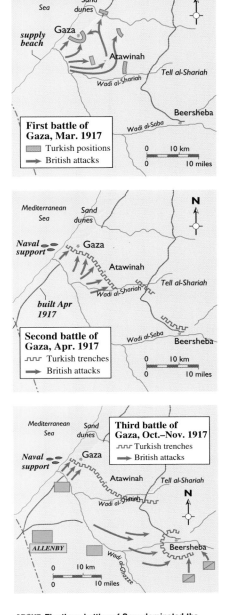

Mediterranean Sea — *Sand dunes*

Gaza

supply beach

Atawinah

Wadi al-Shariah

Tell al-Shariah

Beersheba

Wadi al-Saba

First battle of Gaza, Mar. 1917

▭ Turkish positions

→ British attacks

0   10 km

0   10 miles

N

Mediterranean Sea — *Sand dunes*

Naval support

Gaza

Atawinah

Wadi al-Shariah

Tell al-Shariah

built Apr 1917

Wadi al-Saba

Beersheba

Second battle of Gaza, Apr. 1917

ᴧᴧᴧ Turkish trenches

→ British attacks

0   10 km

0   10 miles

N

Mediterranean Sea — *Sand dunes*

Third battle of Gaza, Oct.–Nov. 1917

ᴧᴧᴧ Turkish trenches

→ British attacks

Naval support

Gaza

Atawinah

Tell al-Shariah

Wadi al-Shariah

ALLENBY

Beersheba

Wadi al-Ghuzze

0   10 km

0   10 miles

N

ABOVE: The three battles of Gaza dominated the Palestine campaign in 1917. The First Battle of Gaza saw British cavalry used to isolate the Turkish positions near the town, but poor staff work – a feature of the first three years of the war in the Middle East – withdrew them as victory was within reach. Second Gaza was launched after the British had extended their railroad to bring up additional troops and Turks has time to entrench. The attack was no more successful than similar efforts on the Western Front. Third Gaza was successful after the British were able to use superior tactical mobility (provided by cavalry) to outflank the Turkish entrenchments while tactical lessons from the fighting in France were used to break through on the coast. The pursuit took the British to Jerusalem and further north.

The German Offensives

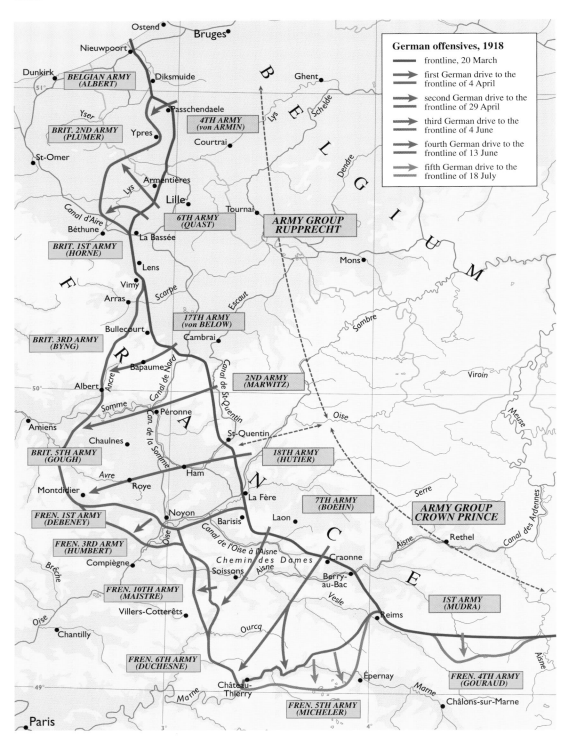

German offensives, 1918

- frontline, 20 March
- first German drive to the frontline of 4 April
- second German drive to the frontline of 29 April
- third German drive to the frontline of 4 June
- fourth German drive to the frontline of 13 June
- fifth German drive to the frontline of 18 July

LEFT: The USA declared war in 1917 but the US Army would take at least 18 months to expand and re-equip for operations in Europe. Germany had one final chance to win the war before the correlation of forces became impossible. In March 1918, reinforced by divisions released from Russia, General Ludendorff began a series of offensives that drove back the British and French, but cost the German army nearly a million casualties. New weapons and tactics were restoring mobility, but the new warfare would be no less deadly.

ABOVE: When German soldiers overran British supply dumps they realized that their generals had lied to them. The Allies had not been brought to their knees by the U-boat blockade; their depots were full of goods not seen in Germany since the middle of the war. Soldiers stopped to loot: the British Army's rum ration playing an unforeseen role in slowing German progress.

The German offensives of 1918 are often characterized as Germany's last chance for victory. In reality, that chance had disappeared some years before. But to General Erich Ludendorff, who by 1918 was de facto dictator of both the German war machine and its war economy, there was no option but to launch one final blow at the western allies - their armies still weakened by the offensives of 1917 - before the United States Army could make its weight felt on the Western Front, the world's largest economy – that of America – mobilized for total war, and the German economy, weakened by the blockade and reduced morale, finally col-

lapsed. To do this, he had troops made available from the collapse of Russia and the tactical improvements developed in 1917 and tested at Cambrai the year before.

Ludendorff planned five successive but basically uncoordinated offensives. The first and largest opened on 21 March, hitting the British Fifth Army on the southernmost part of the British line, which had been taken over from the French the year before. Taking advantage of a massive hurricane bombardment with gas shells and a thick fog, the Germans made tremendous gains in the first day and followed this up by a week of advance towards Amiens that

brought the Germans forward over much of the ground given up after the Somme in 1916. But after a week, heavy casualties, diminishing supplies and the inability to bring the heavy artillery forward brought the offensive to a halt as Allied reserves were brought forward. An attempt to resume the drive, against Arras, was stopped in its tracks.

Ludendorff then launched his second offensive on 9 April, aimed at cutting off the southern flank of the Ypres salient that the British had expanded at such cost in 1917. Again, the Germans made initial gains – though not as spectacular as the month before – and the British were forced

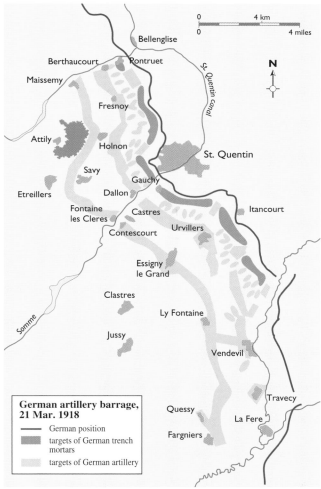

ABOVE: The German 'hurricane' barrage that preceded the 21 March offensive lasted a few hours. While it may have lacked the technical sophistication of those done by the western Allies, it made up for it in mass and intensity and large scale use of gas for suppressive effect. Great concentrations of guns and mortars, directed from the air, focused on defending trenches, artillery positions, headquarters and traffic choke points.

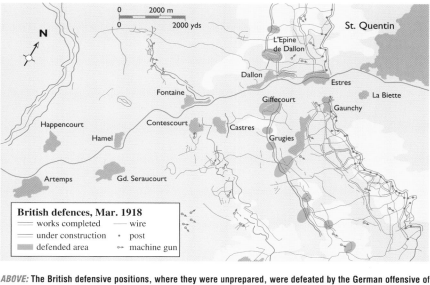

ABOVE: The British defensive positions, where they were unprepared, were defeated by the German offensive of 21 March. This diagram of sector defences near St. Quentin shows much of the reason why. In the line taken from the French, there had been little effort given to constructing a defence in depth. Most of the British forces were near the front lines, subject to being suppressed by German artillery. The deeper positions were not yet completed and, when they were shrouded by gas shells and fog on 21 March, Germans were able to infiltrate between the British strongpoints and continue the advance, leaving them to be mopped-up by follow-on forces.

ABOVE: British artillery positions in the path of the German breakthrough are evacuated, 24 March 1918. His armies starved of reserves by Lloyd-George, Field Marshal Haig was unable to hold the Germans short of the old Somme battlefields. The positions captured at such terrible cost in 1916 had to be abandoned.

to withdraw from the salient. By the end of April, this offensive had also sputtered out, having failed to achieve its goals.

The third offensive, further south, hit the French lines in the Chemin Des Dames along the Aisne on 27 May. This was the fastest and deepest drive of all: 13 miles gained the first day, then Soissons taken and German spearheads were back on the Marne. The next offensive, opening 9 June on the Noyon-Montdidier sector of the French line to the north, was unable to expand the flank of the salient pushed in May and after initial successes soon ground to a halt. The last offensive, an attempt to push over the Marne on 15 July,

gained a sizeable bridgehead across the river but soon hit strong American resistance and, as reserves arrived, was halted within days.

Germany's offensives failed because they lacked the resources of their opponents and because, in the absence of strong planning and coordination (Ludendorff believed instead in improvisation), the Germans' tactical strengths could not be translated to operational strengths. They also lacked the logistics to bring supplies or reserves forward to exploit their successes. The Germans would spend the 1920s and '30s figuring out how to do 1918 again.

The Allied Offensives

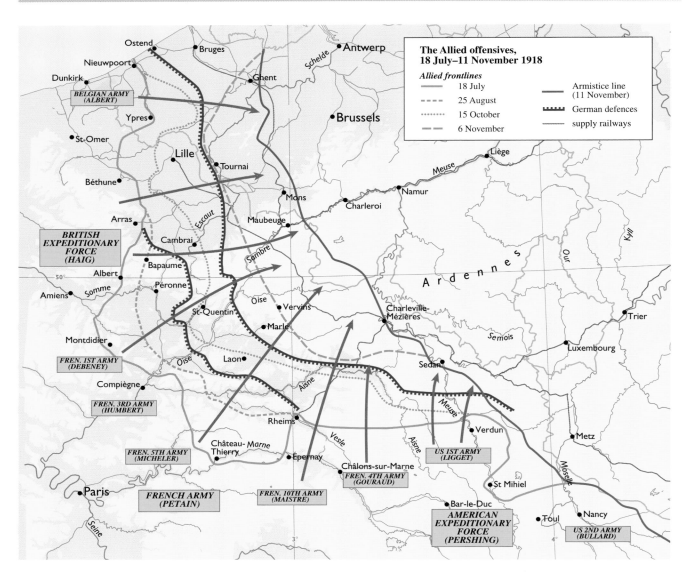

The Allied offensives,
18 July–11 November 1918

Allied frontlines

- 18 July
- 25 August
- 15 October
- 6 November
- Armistice line (11 November)
- German defences
- supply railways

RIGHT: General Ludendorff called it the 'Black Day of the German army': on 5 August 1918 the British broke through near Amiens, their attack spearheaded by 400 tanks. Armoured cars, cavalry and aircraft exploited the gap. The German army failed to seal up the breakthrough and large numbers of German troops surrendered. For the British Army, summer 1918 turned into 100 days of victorious advance, a military achievement destined to be forgotten almost as soon as it was completed.

ABOVE: As the German Spring offensives petered out, the Allies counter-attacked with equal tactical skill but greater resources. The German army was never able to stabilize its front as in previous years: successive Allied attacks ruptured its defences and systematically drove the invader from French and Belgian territory. The German high command accepted defeat and demanded Germany's politicians make peace before the Allied armies crossed the Rhine.

Allied planning had been based on holding the line until a massive 1919 offensive could begin with an expanded American Expeditionary Force. Now, after the German offensives failed, the chance for victory in 1918 appeared to Haig and Foch, the latter now Allied Supreme Commander.

The Allied offensives of July-November 1918 demonstrated an alternative to the German solution to the deadlock on the Western Front. Unlike the German plan, the Allied solution worked, in large part because they had more resources but also because they had worked out a system that was better able to translate tactical victories into operational success that could open up the enemy defences. Despite the terrible losses inflicted by the German offensives, the Allied - especially British - divisions of 1918 were far from the hapless infantry of 1914-16. Tanks, heavy guns, aircraft, combined arms, through planning and logistics support all made the success possible.

The French and Americans attacked the German penetrations in the Marne in July, within days of the German offensive

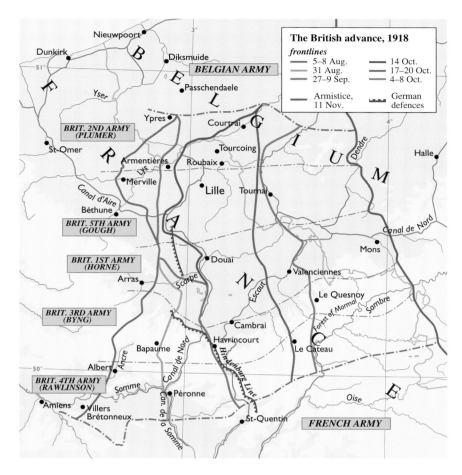

The British advance, 1918
frontlines

▬▬ 5–8 Aug.	▬▬ 14 Oct.
▬▬ 31 Aug.	▬▬ 17–20 Oct.
▬▬ 27–9 Sep.	▬▬ 4–8 Oct.
▬▬ Armistice, 11 Nov.	┅┅ German defences

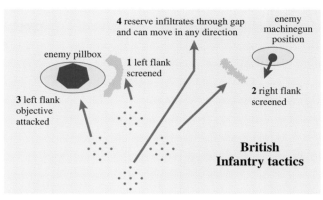

4 reserve infiltrates through gap and can move in any direction

enemy machinegun position

enemy pillbox

1 left flank screened

3 left flank objective attacked

2 right flank screened

British Infantry tactics

ABOVE: From the summer of 1916 British, French and German infantry learned how to combine fire and movement, using light machine guns, grenade-throwers and mortars at company level. The platoon became the basic tactical unit: this diagram is based on the British 1917 manual 'The platoon in the attack'.

starting, while the main British blow, on 8 August, with over 400 tanks, cracked the German front near Amiens. After that, Foch ordered "*tout le monde à bataille*" and their followed a repeated series of blows on a broad front. There was nothing

left for the Germans but retreat when, on 11 November, the political collapse at home that had followed the mutiny of the German Navy, joined by troops and workers, led to the Armistice.

In the end, the events of 1918 demon-

strated the elements that would change war-fighting for the remainder of the century, but it did not by itself usher in these new ways; that would required another world war. The post-war international system did not resemble either Woodrow Wilson's or – in the absence of global revolution – Lenin's vision, but resulted instead in a series of compromises and approaches that led the world from the post-war to a pre-war world. Operationally, while the armies that won the war in 1918 were soon disbanded and many of their capabilities were lost, the technologies that made such capabilities possible would improve greatly over the next 20 years. Tactics would retain the combined-arms and infiltration approaches that had been developed in the last years of the war.

LEFT: Some of the 150 German guns captured by the Canadian Corps at Arras in September 1918. The transition of the Canadian Corps from colonial militia to one of the most professional military units in the world was an outstanding achievement.

BELOW: After the Allied breakthrough in August 1918, German soldiers surrendered in droves. This prisoner-of-war camp near Bapaume holds men captured during the battle of the Canal du Nord, 28 September 1918.

The Russian Revolution and Russo-Polish War

Russia in war and revolution

— boundary of Russian empire, 1914

▲ towns occupied by Entente forces, Aug. 1918–19

--- area controlled by Bolsheviks, Aug. 1918

········· eastern boundary of area controlled by Bolsheviks, Apr. 1919

▨ controlled by Bolsheviks, Oct. 1919

— boundary of areas controlled by anti-Bolshevik forces, Apr. 1920

— deepest advance of Red Army into Poland, Aug. 1920

--- final anti-Bolshevik advance, Oct. 1920

— boundary of Soviet territory, Mar. 1921

← movement of White Russian armies

← movement of non-Russian anti-Bolshevik forces

← anarchist military activities

⊙ centres of Confederation of Anarchist Organizations

○ Makhno's headquarters, 1918–20

— frontiers, 1923

RIGHT: The coup d'etat in November 1917 won the Bolsheviks control of Petrograd, but the capital was menaced by counter-revolutionary forces from the north and west. The Bolsheviks soon transferred the capital to Moscow. Petrograd was rapidly depopulated in the ensuing Civil War. Ironically, the factory workers so crucial to the Bolshevik coup were the first to suffer; thrown out of work as the factories closed, most fled to the countryside.

LEFT: The Russian Civil War was waged by comparatively small armies over vast swathes of territory, coordinated (or not) by telegraph and supported by armoured trains, aircraft, tanks and armoured cars. The strategic mobility and ideological commitment of the Red cavalry played a major part in the Bolshevik victory, creating an inner circle of military and political leaders that would dominate the USSR under Stalin.

The Great War's legacy of the fall of the empires of central and eastern Europe and the rise of ideological states, first the Soviet Union, followed by Fascist Italy and Nazi Germany, had a direct impact on the evolution of war-fighting. Ideology would, in the Second World War, help bring about a return to savagery not seen in Europe since the Thirty Years' War. Ideologically-oriented countries were also intended to bring about the mobilization of all potential resources within the state, much as Luddendorf had tried to do with wartime Germany.

Revolutions present their own form of military requirements which, like everything else in war-fighting, had changed with the Industrial Revolution. The dynamics of Petrograd in 1917 differed from Paris in 1789 - the model so many expected it to follow - because of the impact of the railway and the telegraph. The Leninist concept of the elite mobilizing revolutionary vanguard could be realized in military terms because modern weaponry allowed such a group to implement its policies by force of arms. The organizational development of the modern

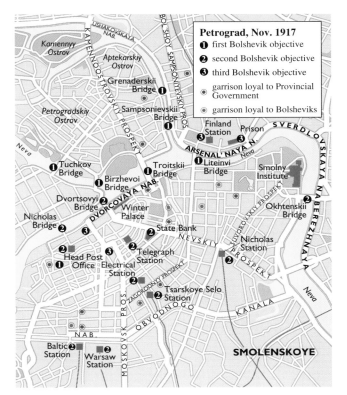

Petrograd, Nov. 1917

❶ first Bolshevik objective
❷ second Bolshevik objective
❸ third Bolshevik objective
⊙ garrison loyal to Provincial Government
⊙ garrison loyal to Bolsheviks

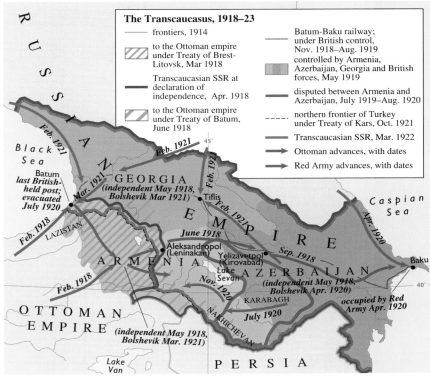

The Transcaucasus, 1918–23

— frontiers, 1914
▨ to the Ottoman empire under Treaty of Brest-Litovsk, Mar 1918
▬ Transcaucasian SSR at declaration of independence, Apr. 1918
▨ to the Ottoman empire under Treaty of Batum, June 1918

— Batum-Baku railway; under British control, Nov. 1918–Aug. 1919
▨ controlled by Armenia, Azerbaijan, Georgia and British forces, May 1919
▬ disputed between Armenia and Azerbaijan, July 1919–Aug. 1920
---- northern frontier of Turkey under Treaty of Kars, Oct. 1921
▬ Transcaucasian SSR, Mar. 1922
➔ Ottoman advances, with dates
➔ Red Army advances, with dates

state allowed the secret police of the Soviet Union broader and deeper reach than that of Napoleonic France.

Militarily, the wars in the East did not offer the preview of future operations and tactics that the Western Front of 1918 did. But they were tremendously important for what they led to. The Soviet Union emerged, with both a supranational communist ideology and the potential for superpower status that had been Russia's for decades. The events also shaped the Soviet way of war - the need for mobile

combat, for operations over widely dispersed fronts - in ways that would endure as long as that country. The multinational intervention by the Allies along the periphery of the Russian Empire, first to continue the war, then to support those fighting the Bolsheviks, was militarily limited. There were few resources available while the Germans were still fighting and, after the Armistice, little spirit for a new conflict.

The end of great wars, like the end of great empires, creates more wars. Once the issue of who would control centralized

state power in the former Russian Empire was established, the next effort was to bring back under its control those peripheral, non-Russian areas that had exerted independence. Poland, with support from France, was able to prevent its re-absorption and check the spread of Bolshevism via the Red Army in its victory in the Russo-Polish War. Elsewhere, the process of military exertion of central authority led to fighting in central Asia during the 1920s and paved the way for its consolidation through the Stalinist terror of the 1930s.

ABOVE: Once secure in the Russian heartland, the Bolsheviks set about reconquering peripheral provinces of the Tsarist Empire that had managed to secure independence during the Civil War. When the USSR tottered and fell 60 years later, the Caucasus was one of the first regions to erupt in a new round of border wars.

LEFT: Royal Marines landed at Murmansk to safeguard the stockpiles of military equipment supplied to the Tsarist government during the war but still sitting on the quayside when the revolution broke out. More troops followed to support a succession of counter-revolutionary leaders, but the Bolshevik regime defeated them all.

The Sino-Japanese Wars

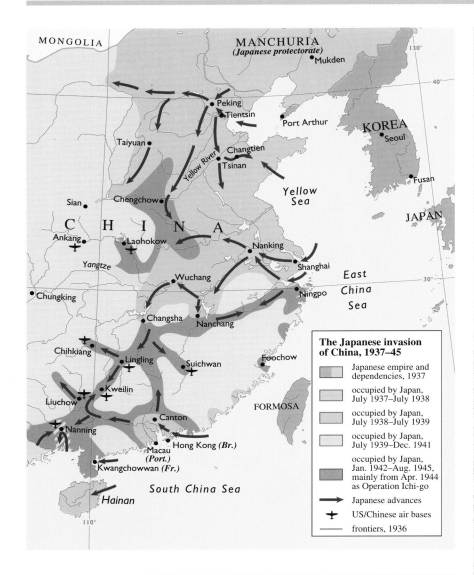

The Japanese invasion of China, 1937–45

- Japanese empire and dependencies, 1937
- occupied by Japan, July 1937–July 1938
- occupied by Japan, July 1938–July 1939
- occupied by Japan, July 1939–Dec. 1941
- occupied by Japan, Jan. 1942–Aug. 1945, mainly from Apr. 1944 as Operation Ichi-go
- → Japanese advances
- ✛ US/Chinese air bases
- —— frontiers, 1936

ABOVE: Japan's occupation of Manchuria in 1931 shattered the cosy belief that the League of Nations could prevent the use of war as an instrument of state policy. No amount of international condemnation stopped the Japanese army in its subsequent invasion of China. Its military operations were conducted with bestial savagery epitomised by the mass slaughter of civilians at Nanking.

Japan's oil sources, 1936–41

- Japanese empire, 1936
- • oilfields
- • oil shale
- • principal refineries
- → Japanese oil routes
- —— frontiers, 1936

LEFT: Entirely dependent on imported fuel, Japan determined to secure the oilfields of the Dutch East Indies. Curiously, Japan made no plans for the security of its supplies if a prolonged war resulted: she had sufficient oil tankers, but few naval escorts and no operational plans for convoying them. The oilfields would be overrun in 1941-2, but US submarines would send her tanker fleet to the bottom by 1944.

By 1914, it had already become apparent that the military history of the world was no longer equivalent to that of just Europe, even though European wars had been fought out on a global stage over the two preceding centuries. Now came Japan's industrialization and entry on the world stage as a military power as a result of the Sino-Japanese and Russo-Japanese Wars.

By 1931, Japan was looking for a solution to its problems and thought it lay in the use of armed force. Japan felt itself a have-not power, with a combination of Western imperialism, closed markets, and racist exclusion preventing it from the type of imperial expansion that the West had carried out in the preceding century and which was now proving increasingly difficult to sustain. The lessons of the Great War had shown that national power was affected by natural resources, and Japan remained resource-poor. Compounding this was the rise of the political power of the Japanese military and an ethos of militarization of society.

LEFT: Japan had enjoyed local naval superiority since 1905. In the 1930s Japan modernized her older warships, like the battle cruiser *Haruna* seen here in 1934, and announced that she would not be bound by naval treaties. New battleships and aircraft carriers followed, openly challenging America. Meanwhile, Japanese naval aviators received valuable combat training in the war with China, flying bombing missions in support of the Japanese army.

This armed force was first applied in the occupation of Manchuria in 1931 (dealing a body blow to another potential "solution" to the problems of modern statecraft, the League of Nations). It was followed by a war against the rest of China, starting in 1937, in which Japan used its superior sea power to occupy ports and coastal areas. Moving inland from these and from Manchuria, the Japanese soon defeated the Chinese armed forces, weak from decades of internal instability. Militarily, perhaps the most significant threat to the Japanese came from guerrilla warfare, most notably practised by the Communist Eighth Route Army.

The Western powers had long opposed the Japanese expansion in China. This led to increasing US support for China in the years before Pearl Harbour. But despite reinforcements of US air power, the Japanese were still able to launch successful offensives in China well into 1944, reflecting in part the Chinese emphasis on preparing for their upcoming civil war rather than devoting resources to defeating Japan.

RIGHT: Passive protest against Japanese rule in Korea during the 1920s was crushed with exemplary brutality. In 1931 Japan struck north into Manchuria, establishing a puppet government and eventually a new land border with Russia. This was disputed and led to battles along the frontier in 1939: shock defeats for the Japanese at the hands of a little known Soviet general, Georgi Zhukov.

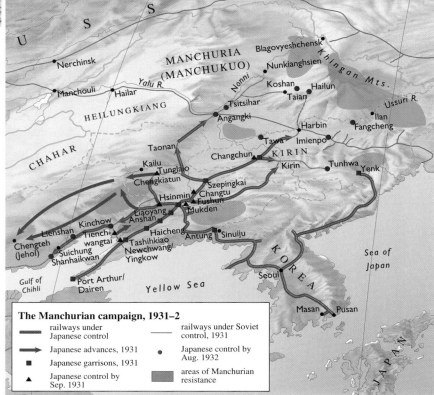

The Manchurian campaign, 1931–2

railways under Japanese control

railways under Soviet control, 1931

Japanese advances, 1931

Japanese control by Aug. 1932

Japanese garrisons, 1931

Japanese control by Sep. 1931

areas of Manchurian resistance

The Spanish Civil War

The Spanish Civil War was, first and foremost, the result of currents in Spanish politics, history, and culture that had endured since the French invasion of 1808. Since then, Spain was seen as increasingly peripheral to the European power system. The loss of most of its colonial empire and its late and limited industrialization compounded this.

When, in 1936, Spaniard once again started to fight Spaniard, the place of armed conflict in the European power system ensured that it would have wider ramifications. The Nationalist rebels were identified ideologically with the Fascist states in Italy and Germany while the Republican government had the Soviet Union as its prime external patron. The weakness of the non-ideological powers and the League of Nations underlined that, at the highest level, ideology was part of the solution of the end of the old order in the Great War.

At the operational and tactical levels other solutions, more developed versions of those seen in 1918, were brought into play. In most cases, this was the result of technological intervention by outside powers, while the bulk of the fighting was Spaniard against Spaniard using older technologies and tactics. Tanks were used in significant numbers but, where not supported by combined arms tactics, they often failed against anti-tank guns or even stalwart infantry, as in 1917-18. Bombers – including the accurate German Stukas – proved important and strategic bombing advocates stressed their efficacy. Anti-aircraft guns – including the German 88mm – were as important in countering the bomber threat. Submarines were able to prey on merchant ships much as in the Great War. Overall, the lessons of Spain were distorted and mythologized, not only by ideologists but also by advocates for military change.

BELOW: The Spanish Civil War began with the first strategic airlift in history: German transport aircraft shuttling Franco's Army of Africa to the mainland where it spearheaded the Nationalist revolt. Although aircraft and tanks were employed by both sides, the fighting was reminiscent of the First World War and many pundits, not least Liddell-Hart, published articles that would be overturned by advent of *Blitzkrieg* in 1939.

RIGHT: The Soviet Union provided military aid to the Republic in exchange for the Spanish gold reserves which were shipped to Moscow. This Russian T-26B was the best tank to see action in Spain, proving far superior to the tankettes fielded by the Italian forces. However, the battles of the Civil War were far closer to 1918 than 1940 and Red Army disbanded its tank corps afterwards. They were not revived until the eve of the German invasion in 1941.

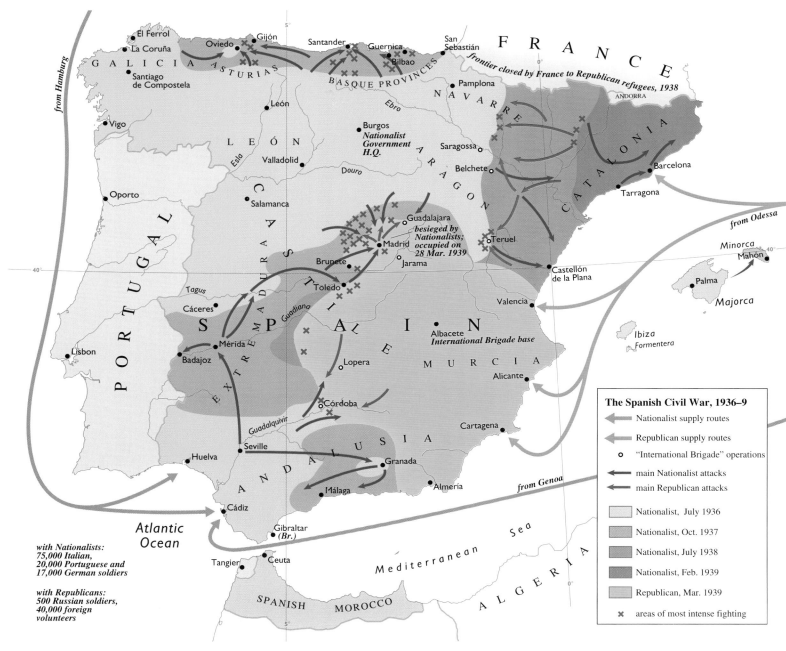

with Nationalists:
75,000 Italian,
20,000 Portuguese and
17,000 German soldiers

with Republicans:
500 Russian soldiers,
40,000 foreign
volunteers

The Spanish Civil War, 1936–9

- Nationalist supply routes
- Republican supply routes
- ○ "International Brigade" operations
- main Nationalist attacks
- main Republican attacks
- Nationalist, July 1936
- Nationalist, Oct. 1937
- Nationalist, July 1938
- Nationalist, Feb. 1939
- Republican, Mar. 1939
- ✕ areas of most intense fighting

LEFT: The Republicans were supplied with 278 Polikarpov I-16 fighters. Introduced in 1935, it was the first cantilever, low wing monoplane with retractable undercarriage to enter service. Such was the pace of technical change, however, that it was obsolete by 1941.

The Gathering Storm

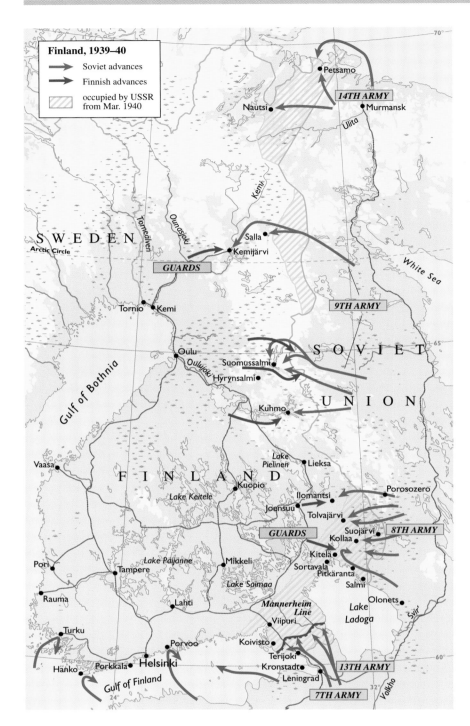

Finland, 1939–40

→ Soviet advances

→ Finnish advances

▨ occupied by USSR from Mar. 1940

LEFT: Its officer corps all but destroyed by Stalin's purges, the Red Army's invasion of Finland met with a series of bloody defeats at the end of 1939. It won in 1940 by sheer weight of numbers; its clumsy performance suggesting to Hitler that it would be no match for the German army.

The years between Germany's re-occupation of the Rhineland and its invasion of France marked the transition from European crisis to world war. These were also the years of re-armament. Within each of the major powers, each service had finite resources and little time to come to grips with fundamental issues. When would the next war break out? What would it be like? Which of the emerging technologies should be invested in and which were immature? What do we need to do to turn this investment into an effective military capability?

No one answered the questions correctly. Some were more wrong than others. The powers all put together and used forces that would prove inadequate when

the "audit of war" started in earnest in spring 1940. What would distinguish the victors from the vanquished were how inadequate these forces were and their ability - a combination of geography, doctrine, and industrial base - to change.

The issue of re-armament dominated Europe in the 1930s, as the powers tried to acquire rapidly improving technologies and – less successfully – merge them with the military lessons of 1918. Yet the resources to support re-armament – including hard currency reserves – were often limited. Those countries that re-armed first, most notably Italy, had to fight the war with mid-1930s technology. Until the invasion of Poland was actually launched, the German services were planning to give themselves

until the 1940s to re-arm. Even when the shooting started, Hitler did not want to pay the political costs of full industrial mobilization which had to await Albert Speer's efforts in mid-war. The Soviets' pre-war investments did not survive the opening stages of the German invasion in 1941. Improvisation – including the evacuation of factories beyond the Urals – would serve the Soviets better than their pre-war planning. The last power to re-arm, the United States, did not have its weight felt on the battlefield until 1944.

No plan survives contact with the enemy. The war plans of the European powers in 1939 reflected not only different doctrines and reactions to both the lessons of 1918 and 20 years of technological progress (the French built the Maginot line, the Germans the capability for blitzkrieg), but also a search for a strategy that could lead, if not victory, then at least to survival. The Germans, for all their operational capability, were strategically bankrupt. Their pre-war plans were not aimed at determining the course of opening campaigns, as the Schiefflin Plan/Plan 17 mis-match of 1914, but rather would contribute to ultimate success, or failure.

The "audit of war" started long before the first shots of 1 September 1939 and included conflicts beyond Europe's borders, notably the Sino-Japanese War and the Italo-Ethiopian War. This latter conflict brought 1930s technology – tanks and mustard gas – into a war of colonial expansion that was intended to boost Italy's sliding international relevance but instead put it on the road to becoming Hitler's junior partner.

Each of Hitler's pre-war deals provided incrementally greater military capability and a correspondingly reduced threat, but none of them, even the Hitler-Stalin pact of 1939, was a strategic solution for Germany. That pact was an expedient that allowed Germany to continue its expansionism through military operations after it appeared inevitable that Britain and France would fight any further expansion follow-

LEFT: While the ground forces were evenly matched, at least in terms of equipment, it was in the air that the British and French were outclassed by the Germans. The French Morane-Saulnier MS 406 fighter (left) only entered service in 1939 but was far inferior to the Messerschmitt Bf-109. The British Fairey Battle bomber (right) was doomed to suffer prohibitive losses attempting to attack German armoured columns in 1940.

ing the post-Munich dismemberment of Czechoslovakia. With neither of its major allies able to take offensive action against Germany, the dismemberment of Poland in 1939 was inevitable.

Stalin, in addition to annexing eastern Poland, added to his buffer by occupying the Baltic States and part of Romania as well. His attempt to occupy parts of Finland led to the Winter War of 1939-40. Finnish resistance was only able to delay inevitable defeat at the hands of the Soviets, but Finnish tactical skills nevertheless allowed them to punish the Soviets on the battlefield. The weakness of the Soviet military – especially in the wake of the Great Purge – was obvious to Germany. What was not so obvious in the limited conflict was its resilience and adaptability.

RIGHT: A Nazi rally in Coburg: the uncanny ability of Hitler to appeal to mutually hostile interest groups helped catapult the Nazi party to power in January 1933. His rearmament programme assumed a European war by the mid-1940s, one intended not just to reverse the result of the First World War but create a racist Empire and exterminate communism.

The campaign plans, 1940

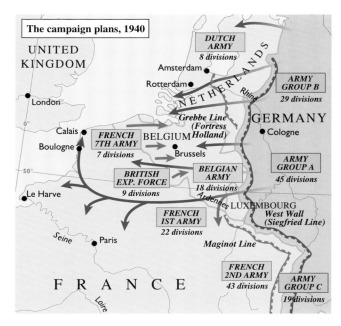

ABOVE: Only at the last minute did Hitler force his high command to adopt a plan hatched by a junior general called Erich von Manstein. Instead of a cautious version of the 1914 plan, Manstein called for the panzer divisions to be concentrated for a breakthrough opposite the Ardennes. The French deployment played into German hands, with next to no strategic reserve held back from the front.

The Polish campaign plans, 1939

Polish forces

German forces

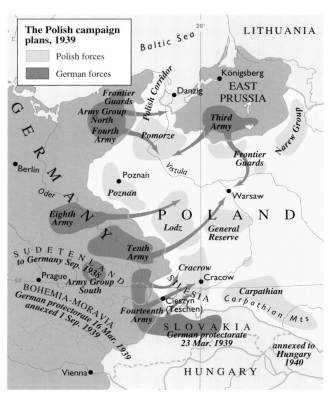

LEFT: The Polish army faced an impossible task in 1939, flanked by East Prussia and the newly created German protectorate in Slovakia. Even so, the speed of the German advance took everyone by surprise.

The Second World War was politically, in many ways, a continuation of the First. The failure of the international system to put in place a stable replacement for the old order that had perished by 1917 became apparent as the transition from a post-war to a pre-war world unfolded.

Militarily, the Second World War was also in many ways a continuation of the First. Not only were the types of weapons and units the same, but also the thinking of generals, admirals and chiefs of state had been shaped by their participation in the earlier war and, often more important, by their observation of its impact after 1918.

Because another world war was unthinkable, the Allies did not effectively prepare for it. They had to deal with the realities of democratic politics, which meant they had to build not on the forces which won the war in 1918 (now long since demobilized) but forces that would avoid the "slaughter of the trenches" that dominated the popular perception of the war. So France built the static defences of the Maginot Line (the ultimate trench system) and Britain invested in strategic options - most notably the concept of strategic bombing, that would ensure that it would never have to repeat its 1914-18 ground combat role.

What made this failure to prepare so critical was the rate of technological change. The years between the two world wars saw the greatest transformation of society and war over the shortest period of time in the modern era. The internal combustion engine and the wireless, both greatly refined by 1918, now could take their role at the centre of the enabling technologies of war-fighting. The wireless' offspring, radar, ensured that the pre-war belief that "the bomber will always get through" was misplaced. Its undersea acoustic counterpart, sonar (ASDIC in its original British incarnation), did much the same for war at sea. By the end of the Second World War, technologies not even anticipated before the war began were introduced, and would shape warfare for the remainder of the modern era: the jet aircraft, the ballistic missile and the atomic bomb.

Warfare in the late industrial age meant that whole economies became military objectives, either through strategic bombing or submarine blockade. Mobilized industrial economies also allowed the fielding and sustaining of massed armies, made possible by conscription (of the

major combatant's only India's forces were all-volunteer). Mass production and sustaining a high quality, standardized product was key to victory, whether the product was a US infantry division or a B-24 bomber from the massive Willow Run plant.

The age of ideology had emerged to replace the progressive, structured world of 1914. This would shape both the descent into war and the course of the war, with the demands of Nazi ideology to overturn the status quo often running counter to sound military judgment. New technologies assisted the ideological powers, with the wireless and cinema proving vital to mass mobilization and social control, while the advocates of Communism and Nazism developed "scientific" principles to justify the socialism and racism, respectively, which lay at their core.

Despite the burden imposed by the overriding need for adherence to ideology - forcibly demonstrated by the purging of the Red Army's leadership by Stalin - the Germans and the Soviets were able to build new armed forces from what remained of their predecessors in the years between the war. The Germans did a better job, having started with better material. They took the infiltration tactic that came so close to victory in 1918, motorized it, and gave it wireless to communicate and aircraft to support it. Journalists - never generals - called the result *blitzkrieg*.

The failure of the Allies to institutionalize the advances that they had made in operational war-fighting in 1918 and to modernize it through the rapidly improving technology of the period doomed their forces to early operational defeat. This was adminis-

tered by German forces that, even if they had not solved the basic strategic bankruptcy of Germany's geopolitical position that had existed since 1915, were certainly highly effective at operations and tactics.

The age of ideology did much to bring about another of the key innovations of the Second World War, the barbarization of warfare. The conduct of a number of the combatants, most notably but not exclusively the Germans on the Eastern Front, ensured that the combination of ideology and technology would lead to the 20th century being the age of man-made mass death. In this way, the conduct of these elements distinguished the Second World War from war as previously waged between European and Europeanized powers since the treaty of Westphalia in 1648.

ABOVE: The quality of Japanese aircraft (not to mention that of their aircrew) would come as a disagreeable surprise to the western allies in 1941. The Mitsubishi G3M entered service at the end of 1936, its operational range of over 1,200 miles was vastly greater than any other bomber in the world. G3Ms flying from Indochina would sink two British battleships off Malaya in 1941.

Blitzkrieg Triumphant

The German campaigns in Europe from September 1939 to June 1941 represented the most complete use of military power to reshape the world since Napoleon. Germany's shift from non-military to military aggression brought in victory after victory.

Those victories demonstrated the quality of the new German armed forces, built for a short, victorious war rather than the massive battles of the previous war. The key element was combined arms panzer divisions. While the quality of German tanks (and their ground weapons in general) was not greatly superior to their enemies (and most of the German Army still relied on the railroad and horse transport as in 1914), they had mastered the new technologies and the operational level of war far better than any of their opponents.

The Germans were also fortunate in their opponents. Poland was in a strategically indefensible position even before the Hitler-Stalin pact of 1939. The only militarily significant opponents were the French and the British. In 1940, they had, in most areas, numerical superiority over the Germans. Where they failed was in two decisive areas. The first was air power. The Luftwaffe was able to seize air superiority and serve as a powerful force multiplier for the ground forces. The second was in the type of combined arms mechanized formations represented by the panzer divisions. The French and British lacked the tanks, tactics and organization to be as effective as the Germans. Even though the British Expeditionary Force had its infantry divisions motorized, the lack of reliable

BELOW: British soldiers await rescue from Dunkirk. Their escape was celebrated as 'the miracle of Dunkirk' while Britain braced itself for invasion, but Churchill reminded the nation that wars are not won by evacuations.

RIGHT: German plans for an invasion of England were improvized in the wake of the French victory. They depended on winning air supremacy, but the integrated air defence of the UK proved impossible to overcome before Autumn weather ruled out a sea crossing.

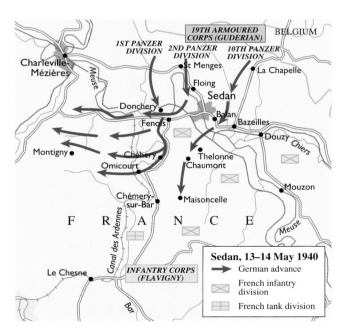

Sedan, 13–14 May 1940
→ German advance
⊠ French infantry division
▭ French tank division

ABOVE: The German assault across the Meuse was achieved through use of 'airborne artillery': waves of dive bombers with the firepower of heavy artillery, but much greater flexibility. French artillery positions were bombed to oblivion, the infantry left to hold off the panzers on their own.

armoured formations limited its operational manoeuvrability.

But the German war machine's limitations became apparent in the months after its greatest triumph, the fall of France. Then, in the Battle of Britain, the Luftwaffe found itself unable to defeat the Royal Air Force. The RAF demonstrated that it was more than an equal in the use of technology, using aircraft on a par with any in the world as part of an integrated air defence system, a new, British creation, made possible by a British invention, radar. The first decisive campaign fought between air forces ensured that Germany's successes would not solve its fundamental strategic problems.

RIGHT: The German army enjoyed few advantages in terms of the quality or quantity of its military equipment. But its mastery of what opponents dubbed 'blitzkrieg' (lightning war) and the superiority of the German air force combined to produce the greatest succession of military victories since Napoleon. It dominated Europe until December 1941 when it stalled in the snow at the gates of Moscow.

Atlantic Ocean

North Sea

15 Apr. 1940
8 June 1940
17 Apr. 1940
2 May 1940
18 Apr. 1940
1 May 1940
9 Apr. 1940
9 Apr. 1940

Narvik
Petsamo *1939–40*
Murmansk
Archangel
Suomussalmi
Namsos
Trondheim
Andalsnes
Bergen
Oslo
Stavanger

N O R W A Y
S W E D E N
FINLAND
Karelia
1939–40
Viipuri (Vyborg)
1940
Helsinki
Leningrad
1940
Stockholm
Copenhagen
DENMARK

ESTONIA
LATVIA
Riga
LITHUANIA *1939*
Vilnius *1940*
Minsk
1940
1939
1940
MEMEL TERR.
Königsberg
Danzig
E. PRUSSIA

German frontlines
Dec. 1941
Sep. 1941
July 1941
Moscow
Smolensk
U S S R
Kursk
Kiev
Kharkov
1939

withdrawal of British army 1 May–June 1940

GREAT BRITAIN
Edinburgh
Dublin
IRELAND
Liverpool
Manchester
Birmingham
Bristol Coventry
London
Plymouth
Southampton
Dunkirk
Hull

NETHERLANDS
Rotterdam
Brussels
BELGIUM
10 May 1940
Hamburg
Berlin
Leipzig
Cologne
GERMANY
Sep. 1939
Prague
BOHEMIA & MORAVIA
Paris
Sedan
Châlons-sur-Marne
Maginot line
Stuttgart
Munich
Vienna
Bratislava
SLOVAKIA
Kutno
Warsaw
Cracow
POLAND
1939
1939

FRANCE
Bordeaux
Vichy
Lyon
SWITZERLAND
Milan
Venice
Genoa
6 Apr. 1941
Budapest
HUNGARY
to Hungary 1940
BESSARABIA
1940
1940

VICHY FRANCE
(under Vichy government 1940–2)
10 June 1940
Marseilles

Zagreb
Belgrade
Sarajevo
YUGOSLAVIA
Ragusa
Ploeşti
ROMANIA
Bucharest
to Bulgaria 1940
Black Sea

PORTUGAL
Lisbon
SPAIN
Madrid
Corsica
ITALY
Rome
Sardinia
Balearic Is.
Adriatic Sea
Sofia
BULGARIA
6 Apr. 1941
Istanbul
ALBANIA
Oct. 1940
GREECE
Thessaloniki
Corinth
Athens
TURKEY
Cyprus
20 May 1941
Crete

SP. MOROCCO
Gibraltar (Br.)
under Vichy government 1940–2
MOROCCO
Mers-el-Kebir
ALGERIA
Tunis
TUNISIA
Taranto
Sicily
Malta (Br.)
Mediterranean Sea

Tripoli
Afrika Korps 14 Feb. 1941
El Agheila
LIBYA
Benghazi
7 Feb. 1941
11 Apr. 1941
Tobruk
11 Sep. 1940
Sidi Barrani
2 May 1941
Alexandria
EGYPT
(under British occupation)

The Axis advance, 1939–41

- Axis territory, 1 Sep. 1939
- Axis co-belligerents
- occupied by Axis after Sep. 1939
- Vichy France and territories
- Soviet annexed territory, 1939–41
- neutral powers
- frontiers, 1 Sep. 1939

- ➤ Axis advances, 1939
- ➤ Axis advances, 1940
- ➤ Axis advances, 1941
- ⬗ Axis airborne landings
- ➤ Allied forces
- ➤ Soviet advances, 1939–40
- ⇢ Allied retreat and withdrawal
- ✳ major cities severely damaged by bombing

The War in North Africa

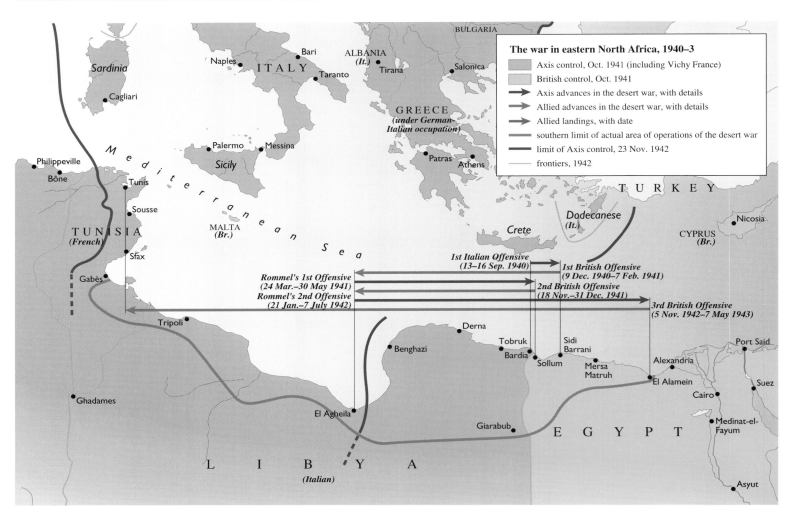

The war in eastern North Africa, 1940–3

- Axis control, Oct. 1941 (including Vichy France)
- British control, Oct. 1941
- → Axis advances in the desert war, with details
- → Allied advances in the desert war, with details
- → Allied landings, with date
- southern limit of actual area of operations of the desert war
- limit of Axis control, 23 Nov. 1942
- frontiers, 1942

1st Italian Offensive (13–16 Sep. 1940)

1st British Offensive (9 Dec. 1940–7 Feb. 1941)

Rommel's 1st Offensive (24 Mar.–30 May 1941)

2nd British Offensive (18 Nov.–31 Dec. 1941)

Rommel's 2nd Offensive (21 Jan.–7 July 1942)

3rd British Offensive (5 Nov. 1942–7 May 1943)

ABOVE: The back and forth movement of the frontline in North Africa was dubbed the 'Benghazi handicap' by Eighth Army cynics, the war raging across Libya and into Egypt as the inspired leadership of General Erwin Rommel compensated for superior British resources. German forces were superbly coordinated, and their commander an indisputable master of modern war.

RIGHT: A Panzer III follows Panzer IIs across the Libyan desert. German tanks were not significantly superior to those of the British, but they were handled with greater skill. Rommel's *Afrika Korps* used anti-tank guns to ambush British tanks, preserving their own for combined arms assaults on infantry and artillery positions.

The war in North Africa and, indeed, the Mediterranean as a whole started off as a sideshow of ill-fated Italian offensives in 1940. It ended up as the major campaign in the west, attracting Britain's strategic reserve, in 1940-43.

The initial 1940-41 campaign saw the defeat of non-mechanized Italian forces, which had invaded Egypt from the Italian colony of Libya. They were defeated by a mechanized British force, permanently reducing Italy to the status of a dependent partner on its German ally and leading to the commitment of German land, sea and air forces, although their numbers remained relatively small until just before their final defeat in Tunisia in 1943.

The war in North Africa was part of a larger Mediterranean campaign which, previewed in the Norwegian campaign of 1940, integrated naval, air and ground forces in a new type of warfare. It included Malta-based British air, sea and submarine forces interdicting the Axis supply routes to North Africa while, in turn, the convoys required to keep Malta fighting in the face of intense air bombardment resulted in some of the most intense air-sea battles of the war. This larger Mediterranean dimension was critical to the war, shaping it at its start by the diversion of British forces to Greece and, at its end, presenting the Allies with the problem of how to use

their hard-won conquest of the North littoral as a trans-Mediterranean springboard against Axis-occupied Europe.

The campaign in North Africa in 1941-43 was dominated by the skill of Erwin Rommel, commander of the German Afrika Korps. But his charisma only compounded the superiority in combined arms mechanized operations and tactics that the Germans had over the British. Once the initial force that had defeated the Italians was dispersed, the British had to learn the business of combined arms mechanized combat - the model for future operations -

in action. By their victory at the Second Battle of El Alamein in 1942, they had learned well enough.

The outcome in North Africa was shaped by two factors that did not easily show up in the orders of battle: logistics and intelligence. Logistics decided the outcome on the battlefield to a greater extent than the most brilliant tactical manoeuvres. British Ultra decrypts of German secure communications, when available, provided excellent intelligence but could often not be made available to the war-fighters in time to be of decisive value.

ABOVE: The war in the desert was described as a tactician's paradise (few terrain features to inhibit manoeuvre) but a logistician's nightmare (few water sources, railroads or airfields). Here, British troops unload water supplies.

RIGHT: The German retreat from Egypt in November 1942 took place in distinctly unseasonable weather, but British commander General Montgomery was nevertheless criticised for his failure to pursue and crush the *Afrika Korps* after the 2nd battle of El Alamein.

BELOW: The Axis presence in North Africa was doomed by 'Operation Torch', an amphibious invasion of Morocco and Algeria for which a large contingent sailed directly from the USA. The signal failure of Germany's submarines to check this onslaught did not auger well for the future of Hitler's European empire. Once ashore, the Allies ground down the Axis army in Tunisia, capturing some 250,000 men in a campaign dubbed 'Tunisgrad' by jaded German officers.

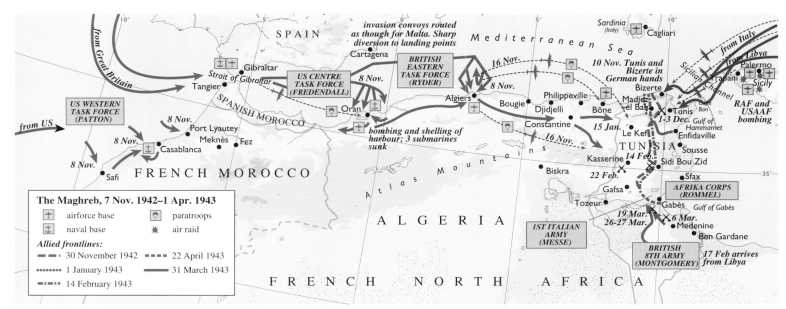

The Maghreb, 7 Nov. 1942–1 Apr. 1943

✠ airforce base	⚓ paratroops
⚓ naval base	✷ air raid

Allied frontlines:
- – – – 30 November 1942
- ••••••• 1 January 1943
- –••–••– 14 February 1943
- ▪▪▪▪ 22 April 1943
- ——— 31 March 1943

To the Spires of Moscow

The German assault on the USSR, June–Sep. 1941

- Germany and her allies, 22 June 1939
- Stalin line
- German attacks
- occupied by Germany and her allies by 9 June 1941
- frontline, 1 Sep. 1941
- occupied by Germany and her allies by 30 Sep. 1941
- under Soviet control on 30 Sep. 1941
- trapped Soviet pockets
- frontiers, early 1941
- **NORTH-WEST FRONT (VOROSHILOV)** Soviet army groups

LEFT: Deep penetrations by the panzer divisions left enormous numbers of Russian soldiers cut off behind the lines. The Stalin line, shown here, was stripped of its mines and guns in 1939 when Stalin pushed the frontier into the Baltic states, Poland and Romania. It was not a serious obstacle in 1941.

The War in the East represented the largest-scale combat operations of the Second World War and many of the most intense. The Soviets long distinguished it as a separate conflict (the Great Patriotic War (from the Second World War of which it was a part. While for decades after 1945 western historians tended to focus on their countries' own combat actions, the German Army suffered some 80% of its total casualties in the east.

The German 1941 invasion of the Soviet Union again reflected the increased importance on strategic surprise that resulted from technological change. Aircraft and mechanized forces could inflict lasting damage swiftly, before the shock effect had worn off. It also showed that the increasing significance and sophistication of intelligence as a counter to surprise – the rise of the wireless meant that signals intelligence and cryptology were now a crucial element of war-fighting – meant nothing if the decision-makers chose to believe their own preconceptions. Hitler was the only man Stalin ever trusted.

The initial months of the invasion saw tremendous advances and volumes of pris-

oners but, as the summer came to an end, increasingly savage if disorganized Soviet resistance and Hitler's shifting of objectives prevented the rapier thrust to Moscow that was thought necessary to bring down the Soviet Union. The *blitzkrieg* forces intended to win a quick, limited liability conflict now found themselves faced by a conflict for which Germany's lack of thorough industrial mobilization had not prepared them. The Soviets were able to evacuate much of their industrial base to the Urals, assuring that future forces could be supported even while those in the field in 1941 were destroyed.

The destruction of the pre-war Soviet forces in the western military districts did not win the campaign. Military improvisation, the arrival of the Soviet strategic reserve from Siberia and the Far East, and the over-stretch of the few German motorized units when the Russian autumn and then winter arrived, brought the advance to a halt.

At the end, the German spearheads actually could see the spires of the Kremlin. But it was too late. In December, the Soviets launched their first major counterattack. Their losses were heavy, but in the end the Germans were forced to give ground in front of Moscow. They would never come as close to the prize again.

The German Plan

ABOVE: The German armies advanced with three lines of objectives, intending to end the year in occupation of Moscow (which Hitler planned to raze to the ground), Leningrad and the industrial heartland of the Donbas. Exercises conducted by General Paulus in late 1940 indicated that the third line was unlikely to be reached for logistic reasons alone. Hitler and his generals gambled on the speedy political collapse of the USSR once the initial invasion was underway.

ABOVE: The German army in Russia had to improvize its winter clothing in 1941. Anticipating victory, only sufficient winter equipment had been ordered for 60 divisions (the intended post-war garrison) and most of that was left in depots as the army brought forward ammunition and fuel for the final attempt on Moscow in December. Survivors of this dreadful episode received a campaign medal that they dubbed 'the frozen meat' award.

LEFT: A Russian prisoner-of-war is searched by two German soldiers. The German invasion cut the Red Army to pieces, capturing about 3 million men in a series of gigantic encirclements. Most of the prisoners were killed during the winter of 1941-2, only a few surviving to be used as slave labourers.

ABOVE: German troops seen in Rostov-on-Don, which was recaptured by the Red Army at the end of 1941. Hitler sacked veteran Field Marshal von Rundstedt for daring to withdraw his shattered frontline units. Successes such this led Stalin to prolong the Soviet counter-offensive and incur severe casualties.

To The Volga and the Caucasus

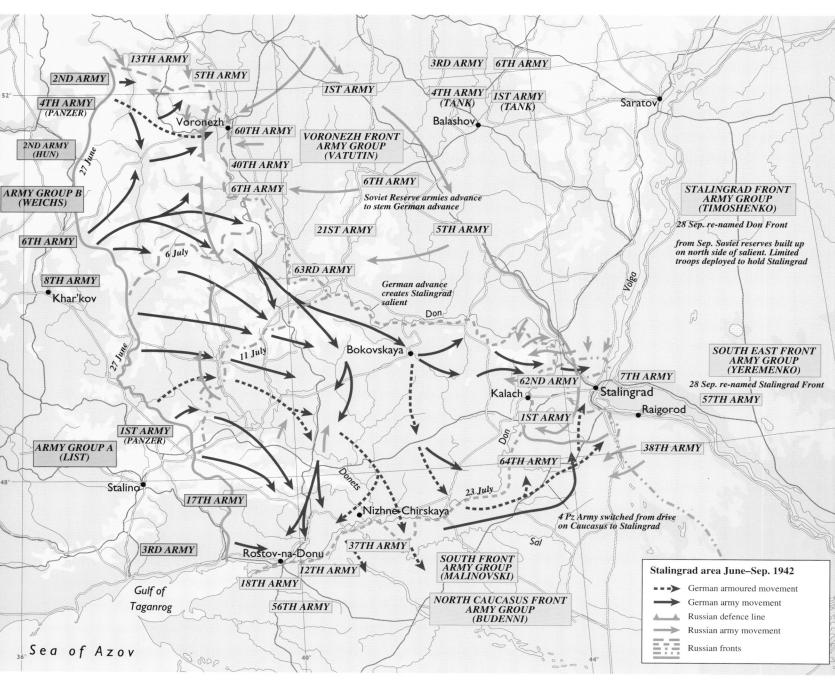

2ND ARMY

4TH ARMY (PANZER)

13TH ARMY

5TH ARMY

Voronezh

60TH ARMY

2ND ARMY (HUN)

27 June

40TH ARMY

6TH ARMY

ARMY GROUP B (WEICHS)

6TH ARMY

6 July

8TH ARMY

Khar'kov

27 June

11 July

1ST ARMY (PANZER)

ARMY GROUP A (LIST)

Stalino

17TH ARMY

3RD ARMY

Rostov-na-Donu

12TH ARMY

18TH ARMY

Gulf of Taganrog

56TH ARMY

Sea of Azov

3RD ARMY **6TH ARMY**

1ST ARMY

4TH ARMY (TANK)

1ST ARMY (TANK)

Saratov

Balashov

VORONEZH FRONT ARMY GROUP (VATUTIN)

6TH ARMY

Soviet Reserve armies advance to stem German advance

21ST ARMY

5TH ARMY

63RD ARMY

German advance creates Stalingrad salient

Don

Bokovskaya

STALINGRAD FRONT ARMY GROUP (TIMOSHENKO)

28 Sep. re-named Don Front

from Sep. Soviet reserves built up on north side of salient. Limited troops deployed to hold Stalingrad

Volga

SOUTH EAST FRONT ARMY GROUP (YEREMENKO)

28 Sep. re-named Stalingrad Front

62ND ARMY

Kalach

7TH ARMY

Stalingrad

57TH ARMY

Raigorod

1ST ARMY

Don

38TH ARMY

64TH ARMY

Donets

23 July

Nizhne-Chirskaya

4 Pz Army switched from drive on Caucasus to Stalingrad

Sal

37TH ARMY

SOUTH FRONT ARMY GROUP (MALINOVSKI)

NORTH CAUCASUS FRONT ARMY GROUP (BUDENNI)

Stalingrad area June–Sep. 1942

- - - ▸ German armoured movement
——▸ German army movement
⊥⊥⊥ Russian defence line
═══▸ Russian army movement
▦ Russian fronts

The Germans did not put their weight into renewing the drive on Moscow that had come so close to success the year before, although in many ways the 1942 campaign opened as a continuation of the year before. The Germans were still able to use their superior capability at combined arms mechanized operations to defeat numerically superior Soviet forces. Increasing German industrial mobilization provided more resources.

The Soviet spring 1942 offensives largely failed, especially at Kharkov, and the Germans were able to follow this up with a planned thrust to Rostov and into the oil-rich Caucasus, an improvised switch to attempting a resource-based strategy. This would require blocking the River Volga's north-south communications at the city of Stalingrad. As in 1941,

operational skill and mobility led to many victories and large numbers of prisoners. But even as the Germans swept down the north shore of the Black Sea to the northern slopes of the Caucasus, they lacked the forces and resources to consolidate these gains against increasing Soviet strength.

The Battle for Stalingrad negated the German advantages as dogged Soviet resistance created a massive house-to-house battle of attrition. While the Germans fed more forces into Stalingrad, without achieving ultimate success, the Soviets began to plan a counter-attack that would cut off both the forces in Stalingrad and those in the Caucasus.

The value of surprise was again demonstrated. Despite excellent reconnaissance and intelligence capabilities, aircraft and

signal intercepts, the power of self-delusion was too strong. The Germans were convinced there was no threat to the vulnerable flanks of the forces committed to Stalingrad. The Soviets put in place an effective deception plan - the first of many - to make sure they remained undisturbed until, on 19 November, the blow fell on weakened forces holding the flanks, many from Germany's poorly equipped client states. Stalingrad was encircled. The forces in the Caucasus escaped the same fate through withdrawal.

Thanks to German indecision and the inability to sustain Stalingrad by airlift, the Soviets were able to defeat attempts to relieve the besieged German forces. The 1942 campaign ended on 31 January 1943 with the surrender of the German headquarters in the Stalingrad pocket.

ABOVE: A German supply column adapted for the Russian winter with locally procured ponies and sleds. In November 1942 the Russian offensive separated the German 6th Army in Stalingrad from its depots of winter clothing.

RIGHT: General Paulus came very close to capturing the city, reducing the Russian bridgehead on the west bank of the Volga to a tiny enclave.

Left: Although the German advance to the Volga caused great concern in Moscow, the presence of the German 9th Army in the salient next to the Soviet capital remained Stalin's chief concern.

**Eastern Europe,
May–July 1942**

→ German advances
—— frontline, May 1942
---- frontline, July 1942

Baltic Sea

Leningrad
Novgorod
Riga
Daugavpils
Volga
Moscow
Gorki
Minsk
Smolensk
U S S R
Briansk
Kiev
Kursk
Voronezh
Don
Kharkov
Dnieper
UKRAINE
Stalingrad
Odessa
Rostov-on-Don
Sevastopol
Black Sea

**The siege of Stalingrad,
Sep.–Nov. 1942**

→ German advances
—— German frontline, 13 Sep.
Soviet frontlines
—— 13 Sep.   —·—· 3 Oct.
---- 27 Sep.   ---- 12 Nov.

6TH ARMY
Orlovka
Orlovka
Rynok
Spartanovka Settlement
Gorodishche
Mokraya Mechetka
Tractor Settlement
Tractor Factory
6TH ARMY
Aleksandrovka
Razgulyayevka Station
Barricades Settlement
Barricades Factory
Gumrak
Red October Settlement
62ND ARMY
Soviet HQ from 17 Sep.
Red October Factory
Soviet HQ 13-17 Sep.
Mamayev Kurgan
Soviet artillery and rocket belt
Hospital
Tsaritsa
Stalingrad No.1 Station
Krasnaya Sloboda
Volga
Grain Elevator
Stalingrad No.2 Station
Sadovaya
Minina Suburb
4TH PANZER
Zelenaya Polyana
Yelshanka
64TH ARMY
Kuporosnoye

World Economies at War

The nature of industrial-era conflict ensured that the Second World War would not be a clash of armed forces, but of mobilized national industries and societies. The realities of strategic war-fighting made not only the war-worker but all citizens legitimate military objectives for bombing or submarine blockade.

All the major Allied powers managed major economic and industrial successes. The Soviet Union managed the evacuation of its industrial base to beyond the Urals. Britain managed the highest degree of industrial mobilization for war of any developed country. The US, starting from scratch, used its industrial strength for prodigies of mass production: a B-24 bomber from the Ford Willow Run plant every hour; Liberty Ships built in 40 days from the Kaiser shipyards. Strategic mobility, the need to keep the sea-lanes open, ensured that the US could truly be, in Roosevelt's epic phrase, the arsenal of democracy. The global nature of this industrial war-fighting – the steelmills of the Great Lakes build the tanks for British soldiers to finally win on Egyptian battlefields – meant that supply routes and resources became critical elements of grand strategy.

Hitler's conquests in Europe gave him access to more industrial and economic capability, but his new economic order in Europe suffered from poor integration and mobilization until the rise of Albert Speer in the German leadership in 1942. Even then, the reliance on the deportation of labour and a heavily bureaucratized command economy meant that Germany never reached the degree of mobilization of Britain or the efficiency of the United States.

Germany was, however, able to continue advancing technology and was able to introduce into combat – although too late and in too few numbers to have a decisive result (the jet fighter, the anti-ship guided missile, the cruise missile and the ballistic missile. But the ultimate linking of economic strength, production capability and technology, the atomic bomb, eluded the Germans.

BELOW: By the time Hitler declared war on the USA, most of the economic resources of Europe were under German control, but overlapping Nazi bureaucracies made for poor industrial management. German military production never matched that of the USSR despite the capture of the Ukrainian coal and steel centres and the dislocation caused by the Soviet evacuation of factory plant to new sites east of the Urals.

The new economic order in Europe, 1940–3

- Axis and Axis-occupied areas, 1942
- coalfields and industrial regions
- other industrial regions
- ⬠ crude oil plants
- ▽ synthetic oil plants
- *678* cost of German war effort borne by occupied or allied states (in RM million)
- ⚓ tonnage of merchant shipping seized by Axis Powers (in thousand tons)

mineral resources:
- ■ bauxite
- ◇ chrome
- C copper
- ◑ magnesite
- ◐ manganese
- ⊕ oil
- ◆ iron ore
- L lead
- ☐ potash
- Z zinc

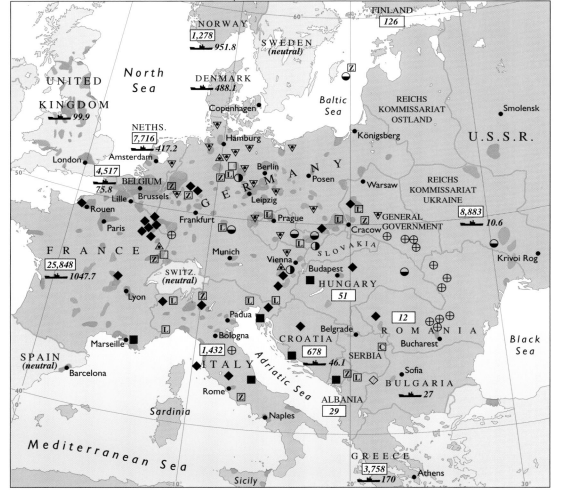

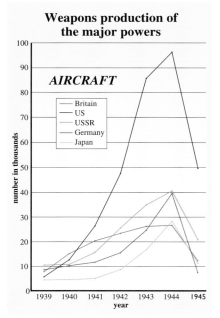

ALASKA
Anchorage
Kodiak
Dutch Harbor

Arctic Ocean

Pacific Ocean

Pearl Harbor

San Diego

CANADA
▲*10 Sep.1939*
△*8 Dec. 1941*
⬩*0.78*

USA
▲ *11 Dec. 1941*
△ *8 Dec. 1941*
⬩*11.49*

Casco Bay

MEXICO
▲*22 May 1942*

BAHAMAS
Key West ■
Guantanamo Bay ■

BR. HONDURAS
Jamaica ■ San Juan Antigua
St Lucia
Port of Spain

GUATEMALA
▲*11 Dec.1941*
△*9 Dec.1941*

NICARAGUA
▲*11 Dec. 1941*

HONDURAS
▲*12 Dec.1942*

EL SALVADOR
▲*12 Dec.1941*

COSTA RICA
▲ *13 Jan. 1942 (Italy)*
△ *8 Dec. 1941*

PANAMA
▲ *13 Jan. 1942*
△ *9 Dec. 1941*

ECUADOR
▲△*2 Feb.1945*

COLOMBIA
▲ *27 Nov. 1943*

Barti

VENEZUELA
▲*16 Feb.1945*

PERU
▲△*12 Feb. 1945*

BOLIVIA
7 Apr. 1943 ▲△

CHILE
▲ *14 Feb. 1945*
△ *16 Feb. 1945*

ARGENTIN
▲△*27 Mar. 1945*

NORWAY
1,278
⚓*951.8*

FINLAND
126

SWEDEN
(neutral)

DENMARK
⚓*488.1*

Z

REICHS KOMMISSARIAT OSTLAND

Smolensk

UNITED KINGDOM
⚓*99.9*

North Sea

Copenhagen

Baltic Sea

Königsberg

U.S.S.R.

NETHS.
7,716
⚓*417.2*

Hamburg

London
Amsterdam

4,517

BELGIUM
75.8
Lille
Brussels
Rouen
Paris

Berlin
Posen
Warsaw

Leipzig

REICHS KOMMISSARIAT UKRAINE

8,883
⚓*10.6*

G E R M A N Y

Frankfurt
Prague

GENERAL GOVERNMENT
Cracow

Krivoi Rog

FRANCE
25,848
⚓*1047.7*

Munich

SWITZ.
(neutral)

Vienna
Budapest

SLOVAKIA

HUNGARY
51

Lyon

Padua

12

Bologna

Belgrade

ROMANIA
Bucharest

Black Sea

Marseille

SPAIN
(neutral)
Barcelona

CROATIA

1,432 ⊕

I T A L Y
Rome

678
⚓*46.1*
SERBIA

Adriatic Sea

Sofia

BULGARIA

⚓*27*

ALBANIA
29

Sardinia

Naples

Mediterranean Sea

GREECE
3,758
⚓*170*

Sicily

Athens

BELOW: The USA was indeed, the arsenal of democracy: building more military aircraft than all other nations combined. German production accelerated after the appointment of Albert Speer in 1942, but not nearly as much as planned. By the time his reforms took effect, the Allied strategic bomber offensive ate deeply into Germany's resources.

Weapons production of the major powers

AIRCRAFT

Legend:
- Britain
- US
- USSR
- Germany
- Japan

number in thousands

year: 1939 1940 1941 1942 1943 1944 1945

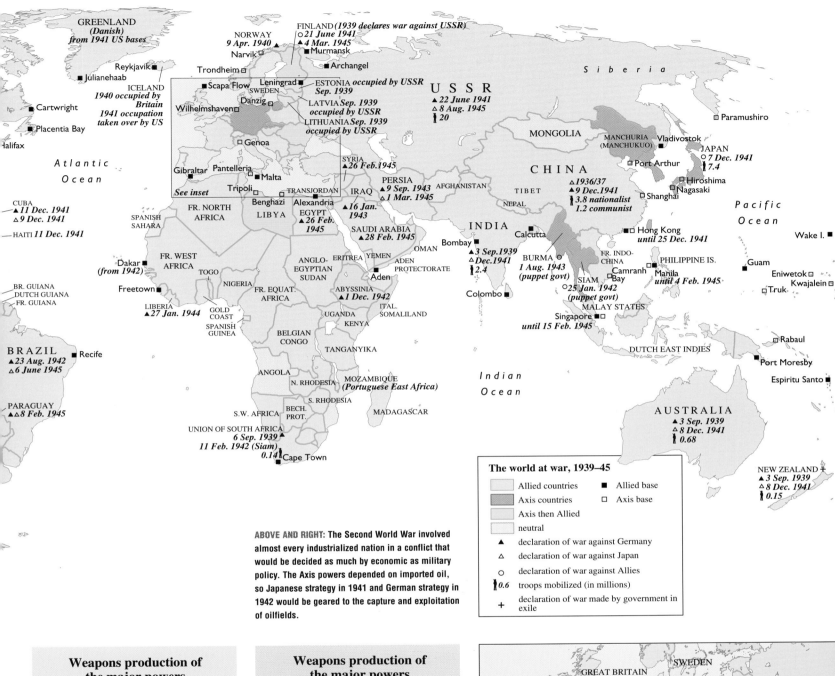

GREENLAND
(Danish)
from 1941 US bases

FINLAND *(1939 declares war against USSR)*
○ *21 June 1941*
● *4 Mar. 1945*
■ Murmansk

NORWAY
9 Apr. 1940 ▲
■ Narvik
□ Trondheim
■ Archangel

S i b e r i a

Reykjavik ■
■ Julianehaab

ICELAND
1940 occupied by
Britain
1941 occupation
taken over by US

■ Cartwright

■ Placentia Bay

Halifax ■

■ Scapa Flow
□ Leningrad
SWEDEN
□ Danzig
Wilhelmshaven ■

ESTONIA *occupied by USSR*
Sep. 1939
LATVIA *Sep. 1939*
occupied by USSR
LITHUANIA *Sep. 1939*
occupied by USSR

U S S R
▲ *22 June 1941*
△ *8 Aug. 1945*
❚ *20*

MONGOLIA

MANCHURIA
(MANCHUKUO) Vladivostok
□ Port Arthur

□ Paramushiro

JAPAN
○ *7 Dec. 1941*
❚ *7.4*

Atlantic
Ocean

Gibraltar ■ Pantelleria
See inset
□ Genoa
□ Malta
Tripoli □

SYRIA
▲ *26 Feb. 1945*
TRANSJORDAN
IRAQ ▲ *16 Jan.*
1943
Benghazi ■
Alexandria
EGYPT
▲ *26 Feb.*
1945

PERSIA
▲ *9 Sep. 1943*
△ *1 Mar. 1945*
AFGHANISTAN

CHINA
△ *1936/37*
▲ *9 Dec. 1941*
❚ *3.8 nationalist*
1.2 communist
□ Shanghai

■ Hiroshima
■ Nagasaki

Pacific
Ocean

CUBA
▲ *11 Dec. 1941*
△ *9 Dec. 1941*

— HAITI *11 Dec. 1941*

SPANISH
SAHARA
FR. NORTH
AFRICA
LIBYA

TIBET
NEPAL

INDIA
Bombay ■
▲ *3 Sep. 1939*
△ *Dec.1941*
❚ *2.4*
Calcutta □

□ Hong Kong
until 25 Dec. 1941

□ Wake I.

● Dakar
(from 1942)

FR. WEST
AFRICA
TOGO

Freetown ■

LIBERIA
▲ *27 Jan. 1944*
GOLD
COAST
SPANISH
GUINEA

NIGERIA

FR. EQUAT.
AFRICA

ANGLO-
EGYPTIAN
SUDAN
ERITREA
YEMEN
Aden ■
ADEN
PROTECTORATE

OMAN

SAUDI ARABIA
▲ *28 Feb. 1945*

ABYSSINIA
▲ *1 Dec. 1942*
ITAL.
SOMALILAND

UGANDA
KENYA

BURMA
1 Aug. 1943
(puppet govt)
Colombo ■

SIAM
○ *25 Jan. 1942*
(puppet govt)

FR. INDO-
CHINA
Camranh
Bay
Manila
until 4 Feb. 1945

PHILIPPINE IS.

Guam ■
□ Eniwetok
□ Kwajalein
□ Truk

MALAY STATES
Singapore □□
until 15 Feb. 1945

DUTCH EAST INDIES

□ Rabaul

■ Port Moresby

BR. GUIANA
DUTCH GUIANA
FR. GUIANA

BELGIAN
CONGO
TANGANYIKA

Indian
Ocean

Espiritu Santo ■

BRAZIL
▲ *23 Aug. 1942*
△ *6 June 1945*
■ Recife

ANGOLA

N. RHODESIA
S. RHODESIA
BECH.
PROT.
MOZAMBIQUE
(Portuguese East Africa)

MADAGASCAR

AUSTRALIA
▲ *3 Sep. 1939*
△ *8 Dec. 1941*
❚ *0.68*

PARAGUAY
▲ *8 Feb. 1945*

S.W. AFRICA
UNION OF SOUTH AFRICA
6 Sep. 1939 ▲
11 Feb. 1942 (Siam)
0.14 ❚ Cape Town

NEW ZEALAND +
▲ *3 Sep. 1939*
△ *8 Dec. 1941*
❚ *0.15*

ABOVE AND RIGHT: The Second World War involved almost every industrialized nation in a conflict that would be decided as much by economic as military policy. The Axis powers depended on imported oil, so Japanese strategy in 1941 and German strategy in 1942 would be geared to the capture and exploitation of oilfields.

The world at war, 1939–45

▭ Allied countries	■ Allied base
▨ Axis countries	□ Axis base
▨ Axis then Allied	
▭ neutral	

▲ declaration of war against Germany
△ declaration of war against Japan
○ declaration of war against Allies
❚ *0.6* troops mobilized (in millions)
+ declaration of war made by government in exile

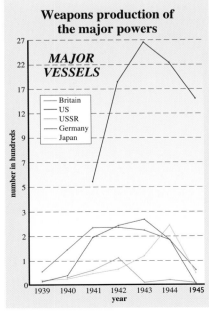

Weapons production of the major powers

MAJOR VESSELS

number in hundreds

Legend: Britain, US, USSR, Germany, Japan

(y-axis: 27, 22, 17, 12, 7, 5, 3, 2, 1, 0)
(x-axis: 1939 1940 1941 1942 1943 1944 1945 — year)

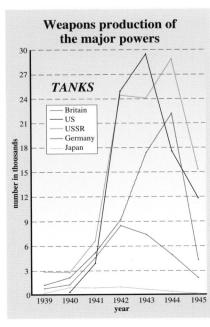

Weapons production of the major powers

TANKS

number in thousands

Legend: Britain, US, USSR, Germany, Japan

(y-axis: 30, 27, 24, 21, 18, 15, 12, 9, 6, 3, 0)
(x-axis: 1939 1940 1941 1942 1943 1944 1945 — year)

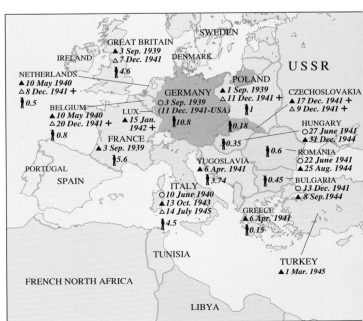

SWEDEN

IRELAND

GREAT BRITAIN
▲ *3 Sep. 1939*
△ *7 Dec. 1941*
❚ *4.6*

DENMARK

NETHERLANDS
▲ *10 May 1940*
△ *8 Dec. 1941* +
❚ *0.5*

GERMANY
▲ *1 Sep. 1939*
(11 Dec. 1941-USA)
❚ *10.8*

POLAND
▲ *1 Sep. 1939*
▲ *11 Dec. 1941* +
❚ *1*
❚ *0.18*

USSR

CZECHOSLOVAKIA
▲ *17 Dec. 1941* +
△ *9 Dec. 1941* +

BELGIUM
▲ *10 May 1940*
△ *20 Dec. 1941* +
❚ *0.8*

LUX.
15 Jan.
1942 +

FRANCE
▲ *3 Sep. 1939*
❚ *5.6*

HUNGARY
○ *27 June 1941*
▲ *31 Dec. 1944*
❚ *0.35*

❚ *0.6*

ROMANIA
○ *22 June 1941*
▲ *25 Aug. 1944*

PORTUGAL

SPAIN

YUGOSLAVIA
▲ *6 Apr. 1941*
❚ *3.74*

❚ *0.45*

BULGARIA
○ *13 Dec. 1941*
▲ *8 Sep.1944*

ITALY
○ *10 June 1940*
▲ *13 Oct. 1943*
△ *14 July 1945*

GREECE
▲ *6 Apr. 1941*
❚ *4.5*
❚ *0.15*

TUNISIA

TURKEY
▲ *1 Mar. 1945*

FRENCH NORTH AFRICA

LIBYA

Strategic Bombing and the Air War in Europe

RIGHT: Only Britain and the USA persisted with the construction of heavy bombers by 1939 and the modest numbers of aircraft available to RAF Bomber Command were not able to inflict serious damage on the German economy before 1942. However, once the new generation of four-engined bombers were in service, the raids became more destructive. By 1943 the bulk of the Luftwaffe was stationed in Germany to defend against Allied air attack, along with some 2 million personnel and thousands of heavy guns. Modern cost benefit analysis suggests the Allied investment in heavy bombers was extremely worthwhile: it cost the German war effort far more to defend against it.

BELOW: An aerial view of the extensive bomb damage in central London shows the remarkable survival of St Paul's Cathedral amid the devastation.

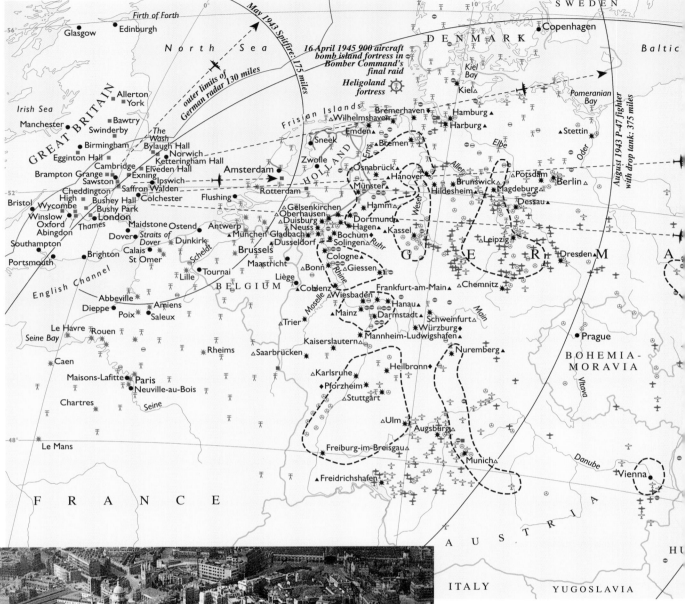

The Battle of Britain had shown that decisive battles could be fought with armies and navies on the sidelines. After the German night-bombing offensive of 1940-41 failed to cripple the British economy, the initiative of the war in the air passed to the British.

Night strategic bombing emerged as the major tenet of British offensive strategy. Using emerging technologies, it offered the chance to strike directly at German industries – and, eventually, cities – and holding out the promise of victory without costly ground battles. But the strategic air war proved costly indeed, not only in terms of aircraft and trained aircrew lost, but in terms of the amount of resources absorbed and diverted from other objectives. It was also highly unsuccessful until mid-1942, when the US Army Air Force started to join the offensive, British production allowed raids of over a thousand bombers on German targets, and navigational aids made area bombing possible.

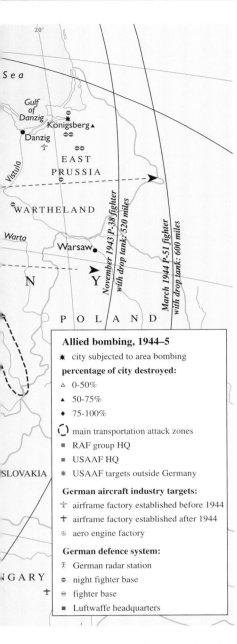

Allied bombing, 1944–5

✳ city subjected to area bombing

percentage of city destroyed:

△ 0-50%

▲ 50-75%

◆ 75-100%

◯ main transportation attack zones

■ RAF group HQ

■ USAAF HQ

✳ USAAF targets outside Germany

German aircraft industry targets:

✿ airframe factory established before 1944

✝ airframe factory established after 1944

⊙ aero engine factory

German defence system:

⊤ German radar station

⊖ night fighter base

⊖ fighter base

■ Luftwaffe headquarters

RIGHT: Parts of the propulsion unit of a V2 ballistic missile that struck Chinatown, Limehouse, London in March 1945. There was no defence against these rockets, apart from overrunning the launching sites. The search for a reliable missile-defence system has continued to the 21st century.

Attempts to secure the airmen's vision of victory through air power in Europe were frustrated. The German air defences, improvised by pulling aircraft and guns off all other fronts, managed to defeat the unescorted US day bombers in 1943 and British night bombers in the climactic "Battle of Berlin" of 1943-44. While the introduction of long range US fighters in early 1944 soon cleared the skies of German fighters, the focus of the strategic bombing offensive shifted to preparation for D-Day before turning to attack the petrochemical industry, which was the most effective part of the bombing.

The success of the strategic bombing offensive remains ambiguous, but its contribution to the Allied victory, while difficult to disaggregate, is also hard to dispute. It introduced independent air operations to warfare and these have since become an integral part of war-fighting by developed countries.

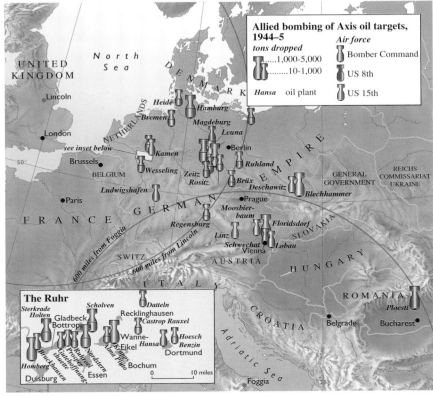

Allied bombing of Axis oil targets, 1944–5

tons dropped

...... 1,000-5,000

.... 10-1,000

Hansa oil plant

Air force

🛢 Bomber Command

🛢 US 8th

🛢 US 15th

The Ruhr

LEFT: The tonnage of bombs dropped on Germany escalated during 1944-45 as the defences weakened and bombers could operate from Italy as well as the UK, with fighter escort flying from France. Improved explosive fillings made the bombs themselves some 30 per cent more powerful than those of the early war period.

The Battle of the Atlantic

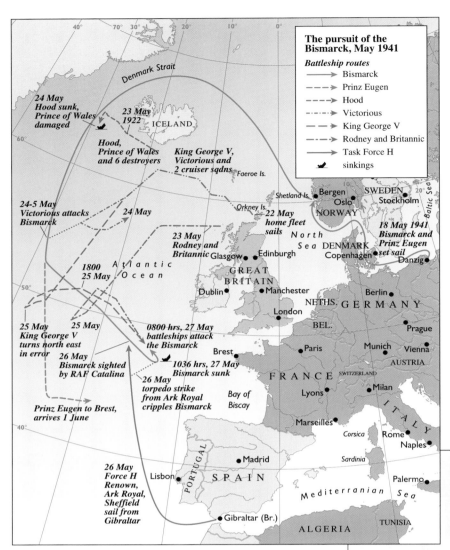

The pursuit of the Bismarck, May 1941

Battleship routes

→ Bismarck
→ Prinz Eugen
→ Hood
→ Victorious
→ King George V
→ Rodney and Britannic
→ Task Force H
⚓ sinkings

24 May Hood sunk, Prince of Wales damaged

23 May 1922 ICELAND

Denmark Strait

Hood, Prince of Wales and 6 destroyers

King George V, Victorious and 2 cruiser sqdns

Faeroe Is.

24-5 May Victorious attacks Bismarck

24 May

1800 25 May At l a n t i c O c e a n

25 May King George V turns north east in error

25 May

26 May Bismarck sighted by RAF Catalina

0800 hrs, 27 May battleships attack the Bismarck

1036 hrs, 27 May Bismarck sunk

26 May torpedo strike from Ark Royal cripples Bismarck

Prinz Eugen to Brest, arrives 1 June

26 May Force H Renown, Ark Royal, Sheffield sail from Gibraltar

Shetland Is.

Orkney Is.

22 May home fleet sails

Bergen, Oslo, SWEDEN, Stockholm

NORWAY

Baltic Sea

North Sea DENMARK Copenhagen

18 May 1941 Bismarck and Prinz Eugen set sail

Danzig

23 May Rodney and Britannic Glasgow, Edinburgh

GREAT BRITAIN

Dublin, Manchester

London

Berlin

NETHS. G E R M A N Y

BEL.

Prague

Brest, Paris

Munich, Vienna

AUSTRIA

F R A N C E SWITZERLAND

Lyons, Milan

Bay of Biscay

I T A L Y

Marseilles

Corsica, Rome

Naples

PORTUGAL

Madrid

Lisbon

S P A I N

Sardinia

Palermo

M e d i t e r r a n e a n S e a

Gibraltar (Br.)

ALGERIA TUNISIA

USSR

UK GERMANY

UNITED STATES OF AMERICA

North Atlantic

AFRICA

SOUTH AMERICA

South Atlantic

ABOVE: Until the USA entered the war, the bulk of U boat sinkings occurred in the North Atlantic, although long-range Type IX U boats had some success off West Africa. Insufficient aircraft were allotted to anti-submarine patrol by the British, and even if they found a U boat, only a single attack resulted in a kill during this period.

ARIGHT: Admiral Dönitz stationed U boats off America's eastern seaboard, anticipating Hitler's decision to go to war. For the first six months of 1942 the U boats enjoyed what they called their 'second happy time' off the USA and in the Caribbean.

ABOVE: German hopes that surface raiders could disrupt the convoys were ended in May 1941 when the *Bismarck* was brought to action and sunk by the Royal Navy. The tragic loss of the battlecruiser *Hood* marred an otherwise successful operation, but the German battle squadron in Brest would never risk itself in the Atlantic after this. Hitler withdrew his heavy units back to Germany and Norway the following winter.

Germany's strategic warfare relied primarily on its submarine force, the U-boats. In 1939, the Royal Navy believed that between the use of the convoy system and the introduction of ASDIC (now known as sonar), the U-boats would not prove the menace they had been in 1917.

The Germans had devised what they believed a counter to both the convoy and ASDIC. The U-boats were to operate not singly, like their Great War predecessors, but in a coordinated wolf pack. U-boats would be called in by others or by aircraft. This put a premium on radio communication. Thus, the British ability to decrypt these signals for much of the war was instrumental to eventual success. Still, the Germans also had success with decrypts and on a number of occasions throughout 1940-43 were able to inflict painful losses on merchant shipping, but they were never able to sever the Atlantic lifelines.

As in the First World War, the German surface navy was unable to defeat the Royal Navy in a major surface engagement. After its role in the invasion of Norway in 1940, its primary mission became commerce raiding. But while the Germans had originally emphasized surface ships rather than

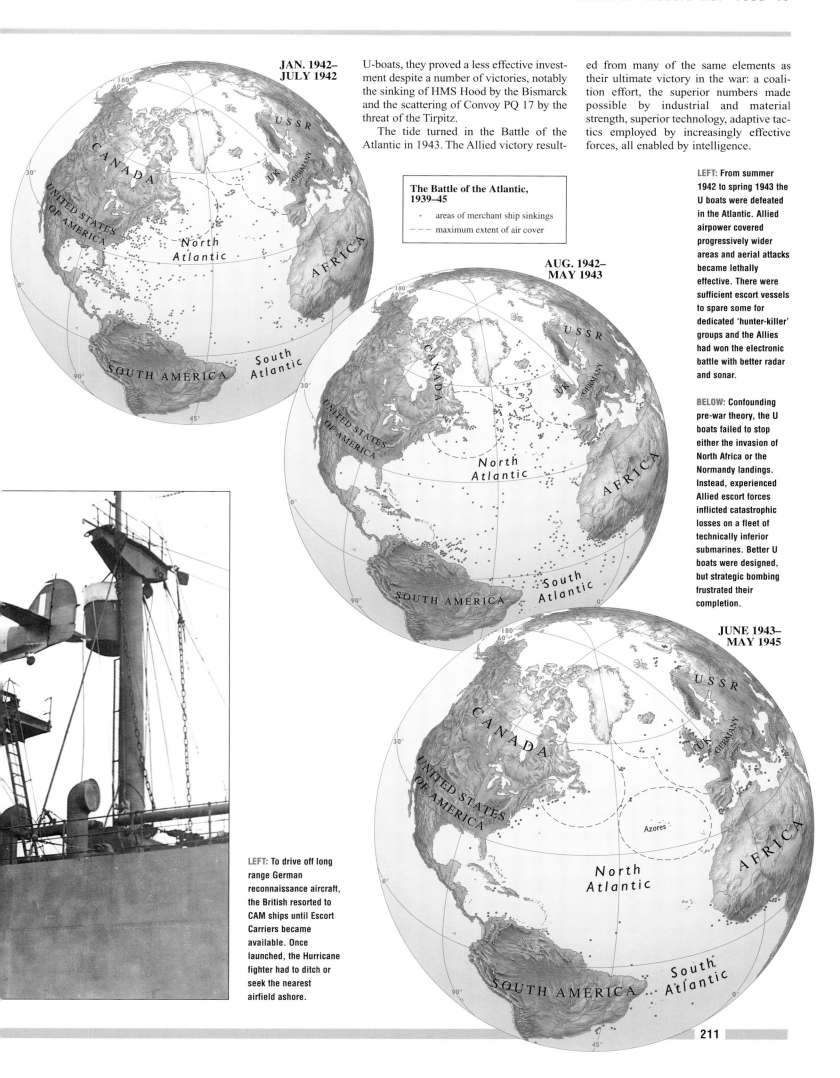

**JAN. 1942–
JULY 1942**

U-boats, they proved a less effective investment despite a number of victories, notably the sinking of HMS Hood by the Bismarck and the scattering of Convoy PQ 17 by the threat of the Tirpitz.

The tide turned in the Battle of the Atlantic in 1943. The Allied victory resulted from many of the same elements as their ultimate victory in the war: a coalition effort, the superior numbers made possible by industrial and material strength, superior technology, adaptive tactics employed by increasingly effective forces, all enabled by intelligence.

The Battle of the Atlantic, 1939–45

· areas of merchant ship sinkings

--- maximum extent of air cover

**AUG. 1942–
MAY 1943**

LEFT: From summer 1942 to spring 1943 the U boats were defeated in the Atlantic. Allied airpower covered progressively wider areas and aerial attacks became lethally effective. There were sufficient escort vessels to spare some for dedicated 'hunter-killer' groups and the Allies had won the electronic battle with better radar and sonar.

BELOW: Confounding pre-war theory, the U boats failed to stop either the invasion of North Africa or the Normandy landings. Instead, experienced Allied escort forces inflicted catastrophic losses on a fleet of technically inferior submarines. Better U boats were designed, but strategic bombing frustrated their completion.

**JUNE 1943–
MAY 1945**

LEFT: To drive off long range German reconnaissance aircraft, the British resorted to CAM ships until Escort Carriers became available. Once launched, the Hurricane fighter had to ditch or seek the nearest airfield ashore.

Soft Underbelly: The Mediterranean Campaign

ABOVE: M4 Sherman tanks in British service seen in Italy in September 1943, shortly after the Allied landings at Salerno. General Mark Clark's hamfisted performance there, combined with the torpid advance of British 8th Army and vigorous German reaction led to stalemate before winter. A protracted campaign ensued up the length of the Italian peninsula.

The Mediterranean Theatre of 1943-45 was the direct result of the Allied victory in North Africa. The invasion of Sicily – bigger than D-Day the following year – was the next step and was seen as required to open the Mediterranean to shipping.

Churchill advocated the invasion of Italy as providing a way into the "soft underbelly" of occupied Europe. This was opposed by the US, which saw it as a diversion of resources away from the coming climactic invasion of France. In the end, the Italian campaign emerged as a strategic compromise. The way it was treated reflected greatly on decision-making within democracies and between democracies, issues in modern-era strategy

that Clausewitz never foresaw.

The Italian campaign proved highly frustrating. It was marked by the hard-fought Salerno invasion and repeated attacks on fortified German positions, most notably that of Monte Cassino. The largest attempt to use Allied amphibious mobility capabilities, the Anzio invasion, failed due to Allied tactical failings. The skilled German defensive tactics and the Italian terrain and weather made sure that the Allies had great difficulty applying the advantages of their superiority in numbers, material, and air power. Indeed, the secondary status of the Italian front made sure this superiority would be limited. It demonstrated how a low-investment strate-

gy, such as that waged by the Germans through most of the campaign, can use operational and tactical skills to negate a stronger opponent.

British interest in the "soft underbelly" applied also to the Balkans. There, the Yugoslav partisan movement represented the largest national rising of the conflict. However, its lack of equipment and preoccupation with establishing post-war political control meant that the Germans were able to keep the lid on the Balkans with a minimum-force, minimum-cost approach. It was the advance of the Soviet Army in 1944 that finally forced the German withdrawal, allowing Greece and Yugoslavia to get on with internal conflicts.

Italy, 1943–5

- ← Allied advance
- — Allied fronts
- — Axis fronts
- ✕ battle
- U.S.
- British
- Canadian
- Polish
- German
- Italian

LEFT: The 'soft underbelly' of the Axis proved nothing of the sort once the Germans occupied Italy. Allied amphibious assaults at Salerno and Anzio failed to break the deadlock as fierce German counter-attacks and lacklustre Allied leadership confined the invasion forces to their beachheads. Both sides believed they were forcing the enemy to devote disproportionate resources to the Italian campaign.

ABOVE: Yugoslavia anticipated its later fate in the 1990s when Germany invaded. Croatian divisions of the Yugoslav army mutinied in support of an independent Croatia, and a Croat state was established under German control. Slovenia and Croatia provided troops for Germany's war in Russia; enough Bosnian Muslims joined the SS for Himmler to form a complete division. Serbia was torn between Monarchist and Communist guerrillas, often more willing to fight each other than the German and Italian occupation forces.

Map labels (Italy, 1943–5):

AUSTRIA — SWITZERLAND — FRANCE

ARMY GROUP C (KESSELRING/VIETINGHOFF)
Alpine Line
advance to cut Brenner Pass road
advance to clear Milan and Turin
Milan
14TH ARMY (LEMELSEN)
Venice
crossed using Fantails and Duplex drive tanks
Verona
10TH ARMY
Turin
Adige (Venetian) Line
Po
Aug. 8 extra divisions (4 from Russian front) designated for defence of Gothic Line
76TH PANZER CORPS
LIGURIA ARMY (GRAZZIANI)
ARMY GROUP SOUTHWEST (KESSELRING)
1ST AIRBORNE CORPS
Modena
crossed by marine boat squadron 9 Apr. 1945
Genoa
Genghis Khan Line
14TH PANZER CORPS
51ST AIRBORNE CORPS
Gothic Line
27 Oct. 1944
Jan.–Mar. 1945 front line
2ND & 4TH CORPS
2ND CORPS
5TH, 10TH & 13TH CORPS
8TH ARMY (McCREERY)
Pisa 25 Aug.
Florence
15TH ARMY GROUP (CLARK)
Ancona 19 July 1944
LIGURIAN SEA
19 July
5TH ARMY (TRUSCOTT)
Arno
10TH ARMY
51ST MTN CORPS
21 June 1944
4 Aug. German forces blow up all but one bridge in Florence and withdraw to N. bank of Arno
14TH PANZER CORPS
76TH CORPS
10TH CORPS
13TH CORPS
2ND CORPS
1ST CORPS
1ST AIRBORNE CORPS
13TH CORPS
20 June 1944
Trasimene Line
FRENCH EXP. CORPS
4TH CORPS
Tiber
Ortona 20–28 Dec. 1943
Viterbo Line
5 June 1944
R. Sangro 27 Nov.–2 Dec. 1943
5 June 1944
13TH CORPS
5 June 1944
5TH CORPS
Rome
76TH CORPS
13TH CORPS
4 June 1944
1ST AIRBORNE CORPS
14TH PANZER CORPS
Monte Cassino 24 Jan.–18 May 1944
Anzio 21 Jan. 1944
8TH ARMY (MONTGOMERY)
Bari 14 Sep. 1943
Gustav Line
6TH CORPS
15 Jan. 1944
10TH CORPS
2ND CORPS
25 Sep. 1943
6TH CORPS (LUCAS)
Napoli (Naples)
US 5TH ARMY (CLARK)
Taranto
Salerno 9–16 Sep. 1943
9 Sep. 1943
10TH CORPS (McCREERY)
15 Sep. 1943
US 5TH ARMY (CLARK)
6TH CORPS (DAWLEY)
13 Sep. 1943
TYRRHENIAN SEA
8 Sep. 1943
10 Sep. 1943
San Stefano Line 23 July 1943
San Frantello Line
Messina 13 July 1943
14TH PANZER CORPS (HUBE)
IONIAN SEA
Palermo
14TH PANZER CORPS (HUBE)
16 Aug.
6TH ARMY (GUZZONI)
10 Sep. 1943
10 July 1943
11 July 1943
8TH ARMY (MONTGOMERY)
7TH ARMY (PATTON)
10 July 1943
10 Sep. 1943
15TH ARMY GROUP (ALEXANDER)

Yugoslavia map labels:

Yugoslavia, 1943
- frontier of Yugoslavia, 1940
- to Germany, 1941
- to Hungary, 1941
- to Bulgaria, 1941
- to Italy directly or as part of Greater Albania, 1941
- Croatia, independent 1941
- German administered
- Italian administered
- frontier between German and Italian zones of occupation in Croatia
- ✕ held by partisans in 1943 on the eve of their offensive
- frontiers, late 1941

ITALY — HUNGARY — ROMANIA — BULGARIA — ALBANIA — GREECE
Trieste, Lubiana (Ljubljana), Zagreb, Pécs, Fiume, Osijek, Vukovar, Novi Sad, BANAT, Belgrade, Bihac, Tuzla, Zara, Sarajevo, SERBIA, Spalato, Goražde, Mostar, Novi Pazar, Nish, MONTENEGRO, Ragusa, Cetinje, Scutari, Vranje, Skoplje, Strumica, Ochrid, CROATIA

Decisive Battles in the East

RIGHT: The collapse of German ambitions in the Caucasus and the loss of the Sixth Army at Stalingrad was followed by a Soviet offensive that briefly recaptured Kharkov. By spring 1943 the Germans had recovered and the army high command urged a third summer offensive in Russia, this time aimed at the Kursk salient.

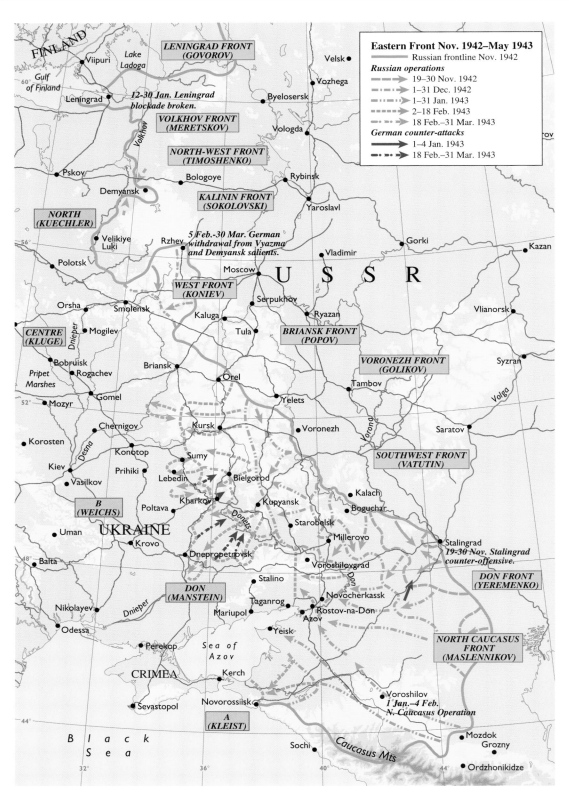

Eastern Front Nov. 1942–May 1943

Russian frontline Nov. 1942

Russian operations
- 19–30 Nov. 1942
- 1–31 Dec. 1942
- 1–31 Jan. 1943
- 2–18 Feb. 1943
- 18 Feb.–31 Mar. 1943

German counter-attacks
- 1–4 Jan. 1943
- 18 Feb.–31 Mar. 1943

ABOVE: The Ilyushin Il-2 'Shturmovik' symbolized the recovery of the Soviet air force. Over 36,000 were built, more than any other military aircraft, and its combination of armour plate and firepower made it a menace to German transport columns and artillery positions. However, their losses to anti-aircraft fire were so high that the position of rear-gunner in an Il-2 was a disciplinary posting.

Despite Stalingrad, as 1943 opened the Germans could point to a number of battlefield successes that could suggest – especially to Hitler but also to senior military commanders – that Germany could regain the offensive initiative. These successes included the halting of a number of Soviet offensives in front of Moscow. One major offensive, Operation Mars, went so poorly that it was retrospectively downgraded to a diversion for Stalingrad. More important was General von Manstein's halting of the Soviet advance that threatened to capitalize on their victory at Stalingrad, one of the best executed manoeuvre defences of the war. In the battles in the Donetz basin and around Kharkov in January-February, von Manstein restored stability to the front.

The Germans decided in the summer of 1943 that they would restart the *blitzkrieg* by cutting off the Soviet-held salient near Kursk. This time, there was no operational surprise. The Germans delayed the opening of the offensive until July, bringing up new Tiger and Panther tanks, but this gave the Soviets time to dig in their defensive forces – with improved tactics learned over the past two years – and carefully plan the commitment of armoured reserves.

In the resulting week-long climax of the Battle of Kursk, the *blitzkrieg*, for the first time, was stopped. It was unable to penetrate into the depths of the Soviet forces as it had in previous years. Where the Germans bludgeoned their way through defensive belts,

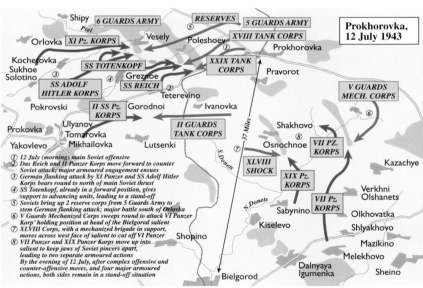

Prokhorovka, 12 July 1943

Shipy · 6 GUARDS ARMY · RESERVES · 5 GUARDS ARMY
Psel · XVIII TANK CORPS
Orlovka · XI Pz. KORPS · Vesely · Poleshoev · Prokhorovka
Kochetovka · Greznoe · XXIX TANK CORPS · Pravorot
Sukhoe · SS TOTENKOPF
Solotino · SS ADOLF HITLER KORPS · SS REICH · Teterevino
Pokrovski · II SS Pz. KORPS · Gorodnoi · Ivanovka · V GUARDS MECH. CORPS
Prokovka · Ulyanov · II GUARDS TANK CORPS · Shakhovo
Yakovlevo · Tomarovka · Lutsenki · Osnochnoe · VII PZ. KORPS
Mikhailovka · XLVIII SHOCK · XIX Pz. KORPS · Kazachye
S.Donets · VII Pz. KORPS · Verkhni Olshanets
N.Donets · Sabynino · Olkhovatka
Kiselevo · Shlyakhovo
Shopino · Mazikino
Melekhovo
Dalnyaya Igumenka · Sheino
Bielgorod

① 12 July (morning) main Soviet offensive
② Das Reich and II Panzer Korps move forward to counter Soviet attack; major armoured engagement ensues
③ German flanking attack by XI Panzer and SS Adolf Hitler Korps bears round to north of main Soviet thrust
④ SS Totenkopf, already in a forward position, gives support to advancing units, leading to a stand-off
⑤ Soviets bring up 2 reserve corps from 5 Guards Army to stem German flanking attack; major battle south of Orlovka
⑥ V Guards Mechanized Corps sweeps round to attack VI Panzer Korp' holding position at head of the Bielgorod salient
⑦ XLVIII Corps, with a mechanized brigade in support, moves across west face of salient to cut off VI Panzer
⑧ VII Panzer and XIX Panzer Korps move up into salient to keep jaws of Soviet pincers apart, leading to two separate armoured actions
By the evening of 12 July, after complex offensive and counter-offensive moves, and four major armoured actions, both sides remain in a stand-off situation

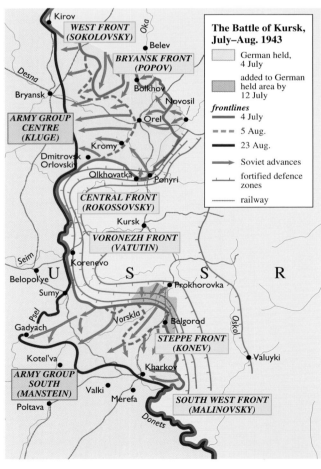

The Battle of Kursk, July–Aug. 1943

Kirov · WEST FRONT (SOKOLOVSKY) · Oka
Belev · BRYANSK FRONT (POPOV)
Desna · Bolkhov
Bryansk · Novosil
ARMY GROUP CENTRE (KLUGE) · Orel
Dmitrovsk Orlovski · Kromy
Olkhovatka · Ponyri
CENTRAL FRONT (ROKOSSOVSKY)
Kursk
VORONEZH FRONT (VATUTIN)
Seim · Korenevo
Belopol'ye · U · S · S · R · Prokhorovka
Sumy
Psel · Vorskla · Belgorod · Oskol
Gadyach · STEPPE FRONT (KONEV) · Valuyki
Kotel'va · Kharkov
ARMY GROUP SOUTH (MANSTEIN) · Valki · Merefa
Poltava · Donets · SOUTH WEST FRONT (MALINOVSKY)

German held, 4 July
added to German held area by 12 July
frontlines
4 July
5 Aug.
23 Aug.
Soviet advances
fortified defence zones
railway

Soviet tank counter-attacks – most notably at Prokhorovka – stopped them.

The Soviets immediately went over to the offensive, which they continued through the summer and autumn. Kiev was liberated and, as winter set in, bridgeheads were pushed over the Dnepr. Von Manstein tried to recreate his successes of the previous winter but failed; his forces were much weaker, the Soviets stronger and more adept. The Soviet war machine was no longer a struggling giant.

ABOVE: The high-water mark of German success in the East: the epic tank battle at Prokhorovka pitted the elite SS panzer corps against the Red Army's new tank armies. Russian losses were horrific, but the German attack had ground to a halt by the time Hitler ordered the battle terminated. The Allies had landed in Sicily.

Invasion and Liberation

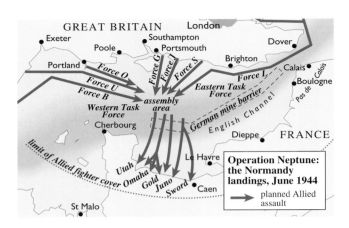

Operation Neptune: the Normandy landings, June 1944
→ planned Allied assault

When the breakout from Normandy finally came, the Allies missed the chance of encircling the German forces opposing them. The manpower, if not their equipment, escaped through the Falaise Gap. As the Allies pursued, liberating much of France, logistics now became the great determinant. Seizing ports such as Antwerp (through a long campaign for the Schelde Estuary) and Marseilles (through the invasion of southern France), lines of communication became seriously stretched and it was a great tribute to Allied logistics capability that they did not break.

A last grab at victory in the west in 1944 came in September, with Operation Market Garden. Three airborne divisions, seizing key bridges, would open a highway across the Rhine for a British armoured corps. Hastily improvised, the plan failed as the Germans defeated the British airborne bridgehead at Arnhem.

Bitter fighting on the German frontier at Aachen, the Huertgen Forest, in Lorraine and Alsace showed that the logistical limitations of the rapid advance and stiffening of German resistance meant there was still much hard fighting ahead.

ABOVE: The cross-Channel assault was protected by fighter cover from bases in England. There was no interference by the *Luftwaffe*, now losing the battle for its own airspace over Germany. German naval resistance was hopelessly outmatched: a handful of destroyers and a dozen submarines against over 700 warships.

The D-Day landings were a triumph of planning and organization, with follow-up support including a harbour to be towed across the Channel and an underwater pipeline. Air superiority was assured; only two German fighters made it over the beachhead on D-Day.

The execution was less than smooth. On Omaha, one of the US beaches, reinforced German defences threatened to halt the invasion until resolute US infantry action took them inland. Opposition on the other beaches, while strong, was less and yet despite the dropping of three divisions of paratroops, the invasion force was unable to seize its first day's objectives, most significantly the city of Caen. Taking it would now require many weeks of hard fighting.

The subsequent Normandy campaign ashore was bitter and frustrating, with the German Army demonstrating its defensive tactics, honed in the east, among the hedgerows. The Allies had planned the invasion itself splendidly, but had left the key operational issue of how to win the battle of Normandy to improvisation.

RIGHT: The greatest amphibious invasion in history, the Normandy landings were preceded by a successful deception campaign that diverted major German forces to the defence of the Calais area. The initial beachhead was not as deep as anticipated, but German counter-attacks were too little and too late to drive the invaders into the sea. The ensuing battle of attrition in the Normandy *bocage* could only have one ending.

Mulberry Harbour

2 miles
high water
low water
floating piers
pierheads move with tide
semi-submerged concrete caisson
sunken vessel breakwater
floating steel caissons

LEFT: The Allied attempt to storm the German-held port of Dieppe failed miserably in 1942. For 'Overlord', the decision was taken to rely on pre-fabricated 'artificial harbours' that could be established on an open beach. The system worked admirably, even after summer storms lashed the beaches in late June.

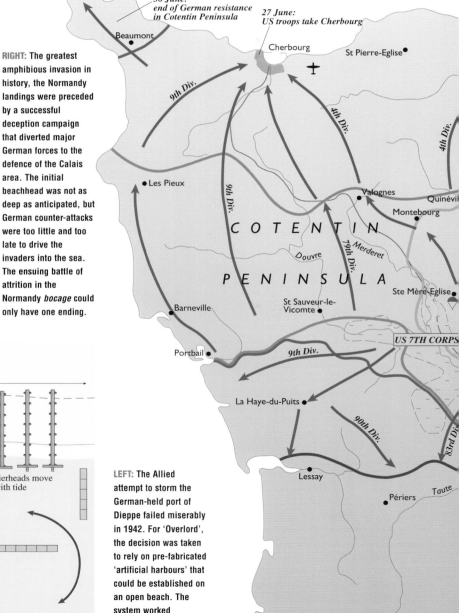

30 June: end of German resistance in Cotentin Peninsula

27 June: US troops take Cherbourg

The Allied advance through France, July–Dec. 1944

→ Allied advances
--- Allied frontlines and date
— planned Allied frontlines
┴ West Wall

BRITAIN
North Sea
London
Portsmouth
English Channel
50°
Cherbourg
Brest
Brittany
Coutances
Avranches
Caen
Vire
Elbeuf
Mortain
Argentan
Lorient
Chartres
Le Mans
Orléans
Loire
FRANCE
0°

The Hague
Amsterdam
Arnhem
NETHERLANDS
Eindhoven
15 Dec.
15 Sep.
Antwerp
CANADIAN 1ST ARMY
BRITISH 2ND ARMY
Brussels
Mons
BELGIUM
Somme
US 1ST ARMY
Ardennes
Cologne
GERMANY
Aisne
Meuse
Marne Verdun
Mainz
Paris
Seine
16 Aug.
US 3RD ARMY
Metz
Strassburg
Karlsruhe
25 Aug.
15 Sep.
Vosges Mts.
US 7TH ARMY
Mulhouse
Belfort
Dijon
Colmar
15 Dec.
SWITZ.

24 July
16 Aug.
25 Aug.
D-Day
D-Day +25
D-Day +60
D-Day +90

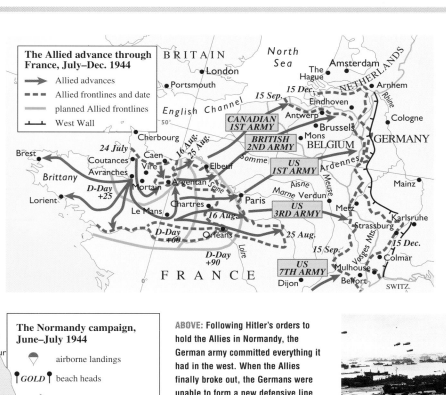

The Normandy campaign, June–July 1944

Barfleur
St Vaast

🪂 airborne landings
🚩GOLD🚩 beach heads
→ Allied advances
✈ airfields
⚓ mulberry harbours
➡ German advance
▨ built-up areas
▢ flooded areas
▨ woodland

front lines
— midnight 6 June
— 10 June
— 18 June
— 1 July
— 24 July

ABOVE: Following Hitler's orders to hold the Allies in Normandy, the German army committed everything it had in the west. When the Allies finally broke out, the Germans were unable to form a new defensive line short of eastern France.

ABOVE: A US Army sergeant searches a captured SS man during the breakout from Normandy. The 1st SS Panzer corps fought with diabolic efficiency but the Allies had complete control of the air: the prerequisite for victory in conventional operations.

ABOVE: Barrage balloons shield the invasion fleet from German air attack, but the *Luftwaffe* was a spent force, unable to make more than a token appearance in the skies over Normandy. The bulk of German aircraft were held back to defend the homeland against the British and American strategic bomber offensive.

UTAH
101 Airborne Div.

US FIRST ARMY (BRADLEY)

21ST ARMY GROUP (MONTGOMERY)

BRITISH SECOND ARMY (DEMPSEY)

Pointe du Hoe
Grandcamp les-Bains
Vierville-sur-Mer
29th Div
US 5TH CORPS
Colleville-sur-Mer
Port-en-Bessin
Arromanches
OMAHA
GOLD
JUNO
SWORD
Bay of Seine

10 June: US troops link
Carentan
Isigny
Aure
2nd Div.
Trévières
Colombières
1st Div.
BRITISH 30TH CORPS
Bayeux Seulles
Creuilly
Courseulles-sur-Mer
Lion-sur-Mer
Ouistreham
Cabourg

St Jean-de-Daye
30th Div
5th Div.
35th Div.
US 19TH CORPS
Forêt de Cérisy
Vire
1st Div.
Drôme
7 June
BRITISH 12TH CORPS
BRITISH 8TH CORPS
CANADIAN 2ND CORPS
BRITISH 1ST CORPS
Ranville
Troarn
Dives

Balleroy
Tilly-sur-Seulles
Caen

St Lô
29th Div.
Gaumont
26–9 June: Operation Epsom
Tourmauville
Bourguébus
18–21 July: Operation Goodwood

Villers-Bocage
Odon
Orne

Defeat in the East

The 1944 fighting in the East saw the Germans driven from the banks of the Dnepr to the Oder River in front of Berlin.

Winter and spring offensives by the Soviets liberated the Ukraine and raised the three-year siege of Leningrad. The most significant of the many Soviet offensives which rippled from north to south in June-August was Operation Bagration, which effectively destroyed the German Army Group Centre in the salient it was holding at Hitler's insistence, pushing the Germans out of Byelorussia and to the banks of the Vistula.

The Soviets next looked to clear their flanks, attacking to clear the Ukraine and then, as Romania and Bulgaria changed sides, into the Balkans. In the north, the surviving German forces were pushed into the Courland peninsula as the Soviets advanced into East Prussia. Finland switched sides: only Hungary would be made to fight to the end.

Then followed repeated offensives against the German centre, hammer blows of the Vistula-Oder operation and the assault on East Prussia. By February 1945, the Soviets were on the Oder.

BELOW: The Soviet air force was able to achieve local air superiority in 1943, and by 1944 the domination of the Luftwaffe was only a memory. Soviet aircraft seldom penetrated far beyond the frontline, but medium bombers like these Ilyushin Il-4s suppressed German artillery positions and interdicted road and rail communications.

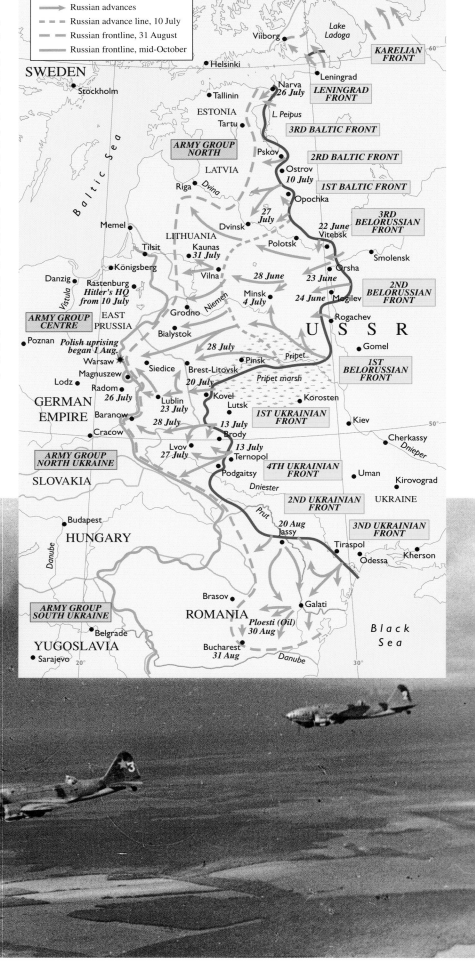

The Soviet summer offensive, June–Oct. 1944

— German frontline, 22 June
→ Russian advances
- - - Russian advance line, 10 July
— — Russian frontline, 31 August
— Russian frontline, mid-October

RIGHT:
The Vistula-Oder operation brought the Red Army from Poland to the gates of Berlin. The German front collapsed, isolated forces fighting their way west in 'moving pockets' or holing up in towns designated as 'fortresses' by Hitler. Russian minor tactics remained crude, their divisions now filled out with released prisoners and slave labourers, but operational direction was ruthlessly competent.

Polish Campaign, 1945

frontlines

——————— 11 Jan.
– – – – – 17 Jan.
–·–·–·– 1 Feb., 8 Feb. (E. Prussia)
····–····– 20 Feb. (Pomerania), 24 Feb. (Silesia)
– – – – 31 March
············· 5 May

➡ German counterattacks
⬤ German pockets
——— pre-war boundaries

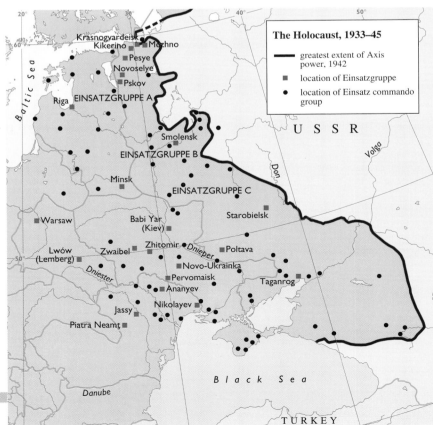

The Soviets were now short of manpower due to massive losses, but their industrial production – with Western aid – increased while that of their opponents weakened. Never as tactically adept as the Germans, the Soviets were able to prevail by mastering the operational level of war. The great breakthroughs of 1944 were made possible not by overwhelming numbers but by massing force at the decisive spot, an approach made possible by intelligence and deception.

The War in the East was a massive one. Battles in which the Soviets suffered hundreds of thousands of casualties were simply never discussed, lost in the "noise" of the clash not only of armies but also of ideologies. The Soviets had realized since 1941 that the Germans' racial ideology meant that defeat would lead to utter collapse, preventing Germany from using the national and political fissures in the Soviet Union against Moscow. Now, the Soviets made sure of the political consolidation of the areas they occupied.

The Holocaust, 1933–45

——— greatest extent of Axis power, 1942
◼ location of Einsatzgruppe
● location of Einsatz commando group

LEFT: Hitler's objective, outlined in *Mein Kampf* and reiterated to his generals in 1941, was to wipe out the Slavic peoples of eastern Europe. He planned a new German empire and the annihilation of the 'Jewish-Bolshevik' menace. In the wake of Hitler's armies came the SS *Einsatzgruppen*, charged with the mass murder of Jews, communists, intellectuals and Russian officers.

Victory in Europe

Germany's ability to shift and reorganize troops, along with the breathing space provided by the failure of Market Garden and the need to clear ports and build up supplies, gave Hitler the chance for a last counter-attack in the West. This, along with the V-1 and V-2 missile attacks, was seen as having given Germany a chance for successes that might divide the Allies.

The resulting offensive, the Battle of the Bulge, achieved some early success, but was soon halted and forced back. Allied offensive operations continued and, with the weather and logistics situations improving, they resumed the offensive. In the spring, a final drive over the Rhine led to resistance crumbling. By 1945, the western Allies and the Soviet Union had widely differing military forces that represented widely different solutions to the problem of waging modern industrial war. These forces not only gained the final victory in the Second World War but shaped those that followed over subsequent decades.

The Soviets continued to attack, in Hungary (site of the last German counter-offensive at Lake Balaton in March), East Prussia, Silesia, Yugoslavia, Czechoslovakia, driving to Vienna by March. But the main Soviet goal was planning and bringing up supplies for the final drive across the Oder to Berlin. This opened in April and, after strong early resistance, the German defences gave way. Berlin was encircled and then reduced, Hitler committing suicide. Soviet spearheads moved West.

The Soviets met US forces on the Elbe, but already the political landscape was being set for another conflict of a different type. Civil wars were in progress in Poland, Greece, and Yugoslavia. Germany was divided into what would, in the following decade, emerge as the western Federal Republic and eastern Democratic Republic.

The defeat of Germany

- ☐ Grossdeutches Reich, 1942
- ← Axis attacks
- ←- - Axis withdrawals
- ← Allied attacks
- major cities under heavy air attack
- ✳ major battle with date
- ✊ partisan/resistance movements
- ● commando raids
- ╲ V1 launching sites
- ╲ V2 launching sites
- — frontiers, 1942

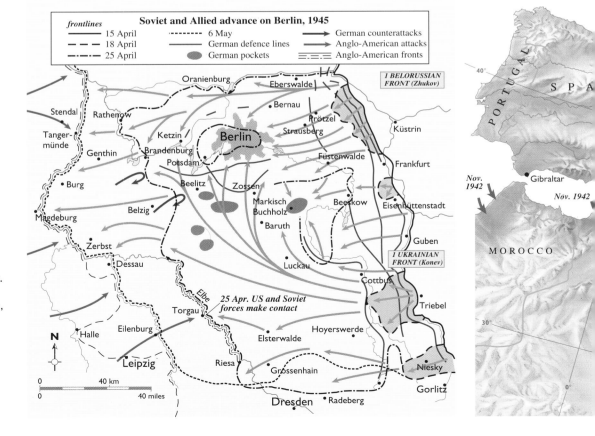

Soviet and Allied advance on Berlin, 1945

frontlines
- —— 15 April
- – – 18 April
- –·–· 25 April
- ········ 6 May
- German defence lines
- ● German pockets
- → German counterattacks
- → Anglo-American attacks
- ══ Anglo-American fronts

BELOW: Peace feelers from Moscow were rejected by Hitler in summer 1941 and again in early 1943. The Allies' insistence on unconditional surrender was never to be tested by a credible peace offer from Germany. The minority of military officers opposed to Hitler fantasized that they could make a separate peace with the western powers, but none of their assassination plans worked. In consequence, the German army resisted to the end, fighting with diabolical efficiency until 1945.

Rising Sun in the Pacific

The opening stages of the Second World War in the Pacific demonstrated many of the themes seen throughout the era: resource war, anti-imperialism, surprise, intelligence, transoceanic warfare (largely unique to this theatre on such a massive scale), and the rise of air warfare.

The origins of the conflict included the demands of industrial-age material war.

Japan needed the resources of Southeast Asia to generate and sustained the forces needed to prevail in its war against China, let alone implement its larger expansionist goals. Japan's shortage of currency, Allied action and US embargoes had cut off access to these resources.

Despite its own repressive occupations of Korea and China, Japan sought to legit-

imize its actions in anti-imperialist terms and indeed it proved that western rule in Asia never recovered from the military defeats Japan inflicted on it in the first six months of the war in the Pacific. The late modern-era "barbarization of warfare" was also apparent in Japanese treatment of Asians and Allied prisoners of war alike.

The importance of surprise in late mod-

LEFT: The Japanese military leadership calculated that it could carve out an empire then defend it so aggressively that the western powers would concede rather than run up an endless casualty bill. However, the Pearl Harbor raid was politically disastrous, Admiral Halsey's echoed the general mood when he swore 'by the time we're done, the only place they'll still speak Japanese will be Hell'.

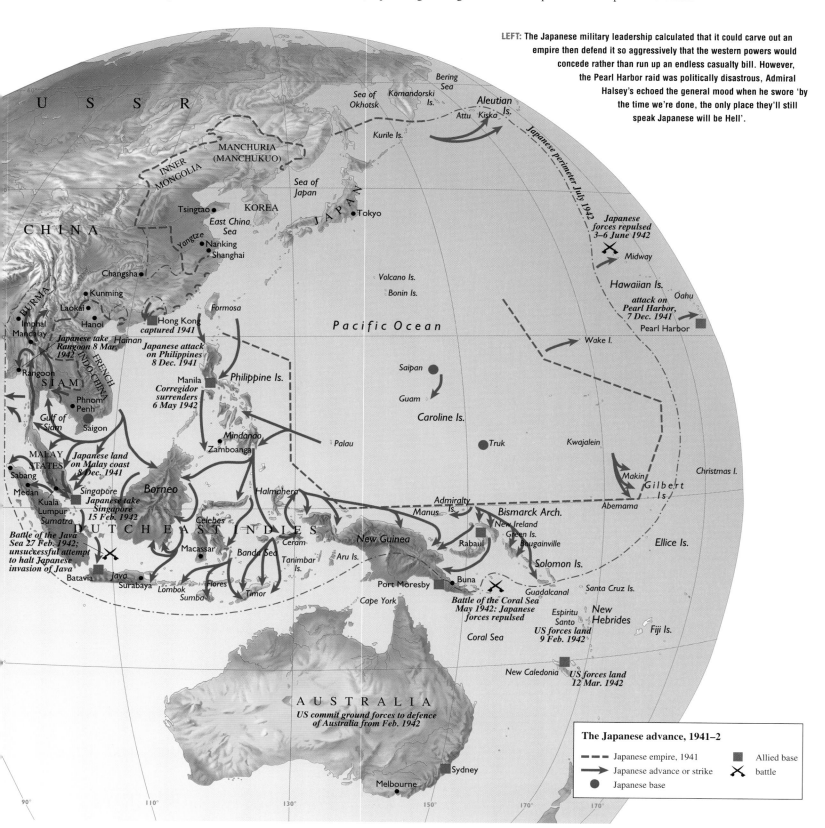

The Japanese advance, 1941–2

- – – – Japanese empire, 1941
- → Japanese advance or strike
- ● Japanese base
- ■ Allied base
- ✕ battle

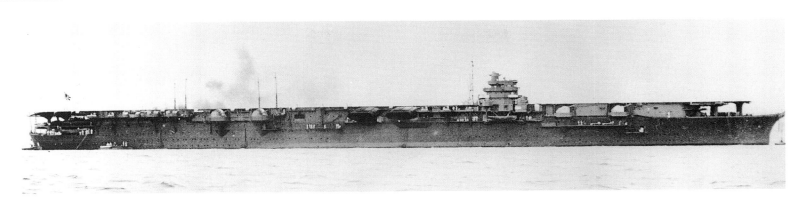

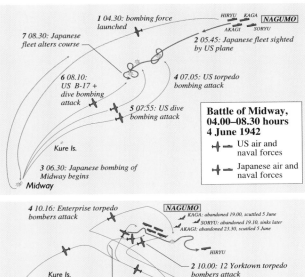

Battle of Midway, 04.00–08.30 hours 4 June 1942

✈— US air and naval forces
✈— Japanese air and naval forces

1 04.30: bombing force launched

7 08.30: Japanese fleet alters course

HIRYU   KAGA   **NAGUMO**
AKAGI   SORYU

2 05.45: Japanese fleet sighted by US plane

6 08.10: US B-17 + dive bombing attack

4 07.05: US torpedo bombing attack

5 07.55: US dive bombing attack

Kure Is.

3 06.30: Japanese bombing of Midway begins

Midway

(08.30–10.30)

4 10.16: Enterprise torpedo bombers attack

NAGUMO
KAGA: *abandoned 19.00, scuttled 5 June*
SORYU: *abandoned 19.10, sinks later*
AKAGI: *abandoned 23.30, scuttled 5 June*

HIRYU

2 10.00: 12 Yorktown torpedo bombers attack

Kure Is.

3 Hornet torpedo bombers refuel at Midway

1 09.20: 29 Hornet + Enterprise torpedo bombers attack

Midway

N

FLETCHER
YORKTOWN
SPRUANCE
HORNET   ENTERPRISE

(10.30–18.00)

N

6 18.00: sinking Hiryu attacked by B-17s

NAGUMO
HIRYU

1 12.05: Hiryu dive bombers attack

3 14.30: 2nd Hiryu torpedo bombing attack, Yorktown hit

Kure Is.

5 17.00: 24 Enterprise dive bombers attack, Hiryu catches fire

2 Yorktown fighters destroy Japanese planes

Midway

HAMMANN
ENTER.
HORNET
FLETCHER
YORKTOWN

4 15.00: Yorktown abandoned, sinks 7 June

SPRUANCE

(17.00 4 Jun–24.00 6 June)

KONDO   **YAMAMOTO**   **NAGUMO**
KURITA

1 Nagumo waits for Kondo + possible US pursuit

4 Hiryu abandoned 01.00 5 June

3 24.00 4 June: Operation Midway cancelled, withdrawal to Japan ordered

Kure Is.

5 5 June: cruisers Mikuma + Mogami collide

7 Enterprise dive bomber attack

8 Mikuma sinks 6 June

6 Spruance persues within Midway air cover

N

Midway

2 Spruance heads for Midway, does not persue

SPRUANCE

LEFT: Japan's run of victories came to an abrupt halt in June 1942 when all four fleet carriers escorting the Midway Island invasion force were sunk in action with the US Navy. US signals intelligence provided timely warning, while Japanese over-confidence led them to disperse their superior forces.

ern warfare was seldom better demonstrated than in the Japanese attack on Pearl Harbour: "the day that will live in infamy", 7 December 1941. Japan had counted on the initial, surprise-generated success to provide six months of victory, and then they would dig in and hold their defensive perimeter, the Greater East Asia Co-Prosperity Sphere. Only when the "victory disease" led them to attack outside the perimeter was their advance decisively halted at the battles of the Coral Sea and Midway. US intelligence failure made possible the Japanese success at Pearl Harbour as much as intelligence success was responsible for the later victories.

The geography of the Pacific meant that navies would be the primary war-fighting assets, but the opening months of the war soon reinforced that aircraft, land- or, more importantly, carrier-based, made naval movement possible. Coral Sea and Midway were the first fleet actions in which opposing surface warships never sighted each other, relying on aircraft to attack and for much of their defence as well.

ABOVE: *Shokaku* was completed after Japan withdrew from arms treaty limitations. Her design incorporated lessons learned from earlier carriers. She and sistership *Zuikaku* formed the 5th carrier division in 1941 and took part in the Pearl Harbor raid.

ABOVE: Loyal to the Vichy regime in France, the colonial authorities in Indochina had no choice but to submit to the Japanese invaders in 1941. Airbases in Vietnam were essential to the Japanese assault on Malaya. Here the Japanese enter Saigon.

Burma

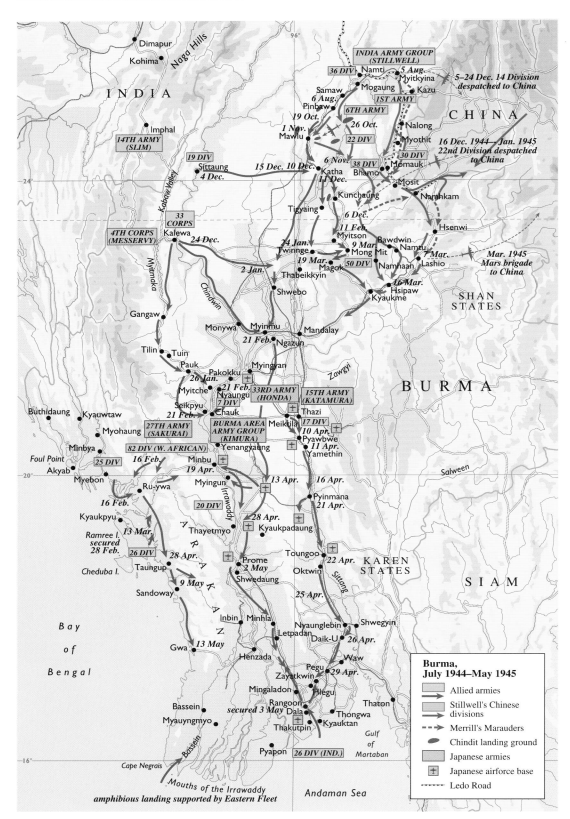

Map labels:

Dimapur, Kohima, Naga Hills, INDIA, Imphal

INDIA ARMY GROUP (STILLWELL)
36 DIV, Namti, 5 Aug., Myitkyina, Kazu, Mogaung
5–24 Dec. 14 Division despatched to China
Samaw, 6 Aug., Pinbaw, 1ST ARMY, CHINA
19 Oct., 6TH ARMY, Nalong
1 Nov., Mawlu, 26 Oct., 22 DIV, Myothit
14TH ARMY (SLIM)
16 Dec. 1944–Jan. 1945 22nd Division despatched to China
19 DIV, Sittaung, 4 Dec., 6 Nov., 38 DIV, 30 DIV, Momauk
15 Dec. 10 Dec., Katha, 11 Dec., Bhamo, Mosit
Kunchaung, Namhkam
33 CORPS, Kalewa, Tigyaing, 6 Dec., 11 Feb., Bawdwin, Hsenwi
4TH CORPS (MESSERVY), 24 Dec., 24 Jan., Twinnge, Myitson, 9 Mar., Mong Mit, Namtu, 7 Mar., Lashio
2 Jan., 19 Mar., 50 DIV, Magok, Namhaan, Mar. 1945 Mars brigade to China
Thabeikkyin, 16 Mar., Hsipaw
Gangaw, Shwebo, Kyaukme
Monywa, Myinmu, 21 Feb., Ngazun, Mandalay, SHAN STATES
Tilin, Tuin, Pauk, Myingyan, Zawgyi, BURMA
26 Jan., Pakokku, 21 Feb., 33RD ARMY (HONDA), 15TH ARMY (KATAMURA)
Myitche, 7 DIV, Thazi
Buthidaung, Kyauwtaw, Seikpyu, 21 Feb., Chauk, 27TH ARMY (SAKURAI), BURMA AREA ARMY GROUP (KIMURA), Meiktila, 17 DIV, 10 Apr., Pyawbwe, 11 Apr.
Myohaung, 82 DIV (W. AFRICAN), Yenangyaung, Yamethin
Minbya, 25 DIV, Minbu, 19 Apr., 16 Feb.
Foul Point, Akyab, Myebon, Ru-ywa, Myingun, 13 Apr., 16 Apr., Pinmana, 21 Apr.
20 DIV, Irrawaddy
16 Feb., Kyaukpyu, ARAKAN, Thayetmyo, 28 Apr., Kyaukpadaung
Ramree I. secured 28 Feb., 13 Mar., 26 DIV, 28 Apr., Taungup, Prome, 2 May, Toungoo, 22 Apr., KAREN STATES
Cheduba I., 9 May, Shwedaung, Oktwin, 25 Apr., Sittang, SIAM
Sandoway
Bay of Bengal
Inbin, Minhla, Nyaunglebin, Shwegyin
Gwa, 13 May, Henzada, Letpadan, Daik-U, 26 Apr.
Pegu, Waw, 29 Apr.
Zayatkwin, Mingaladon, Hlegu, Thaton
Bassein, Rangoon, Dala, secured 3 May, Thongwa, Kyauktan, Thakutpin
Myauyngmyo, Pyapon, 26 DIV (IND.), Gulf of Martaban
Cape Negrais, Mouths of the Irrawaddy, Andaman Sea
amphibious landing supported by Eastern Fleet

Legend:
Burma, July 1944–May 1945
Allied armies
Stillwell's Chinese divisions
Merrill's Marauders
Chindit landing ground
Japanese armies
Japanese airforce base
Ledo Road

LEFT: The British 14th Army absorbed the Japanese 1944 offensive at Imphal and Kohima, then launched the most brilliantly conducted offensive conducted by Commonwealth forces in the war. The Japanese were wrong-footed by the British advance, and the long overdue employment of substantial air and armoured forces in Burma. The race was on to take Rangoon before the monsoon rains turned the roads to liquid mud.

ABOVE: Gurkhas enter Rangoon at the conclusion of one of the British Army's most successful, if largely forgotten campaigns. By summer 1945, the Japanese forces in Burma had been comprehensively outmanoeuvred, isolated and destroyed.

The Japanese advance into Burma in 1942 represented, like the advance into New Guinea at the other end of their would-be empire, a continuation of the offensive tidal wave. The Japanese were able to overcome the initial British resistance of the 1942 campaign. Their victory was assured, despite British reinforcement and even in the absence of strategic surprise, given Japanese air superiority and the tactical superiority of an army experienced in China and in hard training against second-line garrison forces. A major naval raid into the Indian Ocean made an invasion of India appear imminent.

But the mountains and jungles of the Northeast Frontier of India proved an effective barrier, along with Japanese logistics limitations. The Burma front was a low priority for resource allocation on both sides. The British rebuilt their forces and attempted several limited offensives, with varying degrees of success. The Japanese tactical superiority was only slowly countered, through a combination of training a new, predominantly Indian army for the liberation of Burma and the capabilities provided by new technologies, most notably air resupply. This made possible the Chindit operations behind Japanese lines.

These operations led to the Japanese allocating resources – brought forward over the infamous Burma Railway, built across Thailand by prisoners – to a 1944 offensive into India. This was stopped at Imphal and Kohima and, going over to the offensive, the British then liberated Burma in a lengthy campaign which, in its use of both operational manoeuvre and logistics, was one of the most astutely conducted of the conflict. Just as early modern conflict could be waged in remote areas that had acquired strategic value, late modern conflict in these areas was made possible, but only by substantial investments in logistics and adaptation of forces and tactics developed for Europe. The need to adapt to land warfare in Asia would confront all the world's major powers in the years after 1945. Few, if any, would do so as well as the forces that liberated Burma.

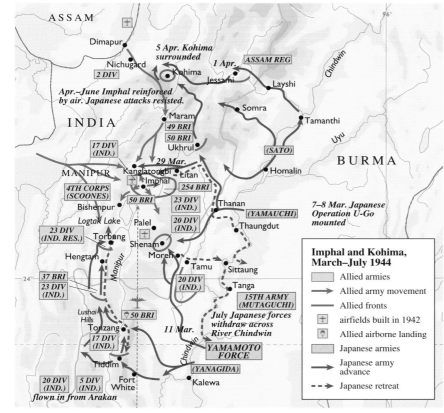

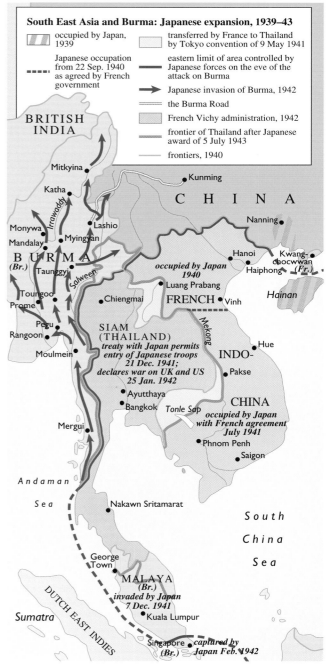

ABOVE: The Japanese offensive over the Indian border was mounted on the thinnest of logistic margins. Once held, then driven back, the remnants of the Japanese divisions had to retreat through the jungle, without any re-supply. Suicide and cannibalism marked the end of Japanese ambitions in south-east Asia.

RIGHT: The Burma campaign followed the Japanese occupation of French Indochina (despite the authorities' loyalty to the Vichy regime) and their entry into Thailand. The Japanese leadership toyed with an invasion of India, and formed a nationalist Indian army, but by the time the Imphal-Kohima offensive began, Japan was losing the war in the Pacific.

Victory in the Pacific

The US counter-offensive against Japan started with the invasion of Guadalcanal in August 1942. It came to its conclusion with the end of resistance on Okinawa almost three years later. The bitter fighting of the island-to-island advance, by-passing many major centres of resistance such as Truk and Rabaul, was made possible by massive naval battles: those of the Guadalcanal campaign, the Philippine Sea, and Leyte Gulf. The Japanese capability to wage war was directly attacked by the US submarine offensive and, starting in late 1944, strategic bombing.

The US offensive required mastering modern amphibious operations, a type of warfare seen as obsolete after Gallipoli. It

The Allied counter-offensive

- → Allied advance
- ⊢ Allied air attack
- ■ Allied base
- ✳ atomic bomb target
- ● Japanese base
- ☒ Japanese base bypassed or neutralized
- ✕ battle

Japanese perimeters
- ········· March 1944
- ─·─·─ October 1944
- ─ ─ ─ August 1945

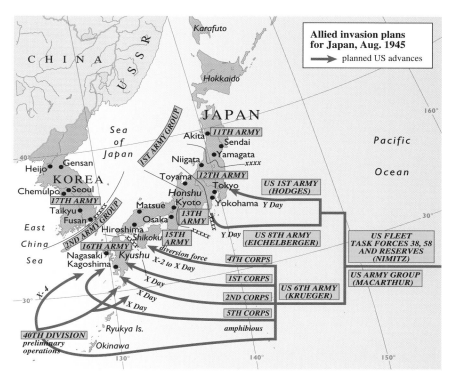

ABOVE: A Japanese flying boat plunges into the Pacific after a dual with an American PBY. Japan began the war with superior aircraft, but was slow to introduce improved types and expand its aircrew-training programmes. By 1945 its aircrew were comparatively poorly trained and most of its aircraft obsolete.

ABOVE: Had the atomic bomb been delayed, or not functioned, a conventional invasion of Japan would have taken place in late summer 1945. Based on the experience of attacking other Japanese-held islands, Allied casualties were estimated at about 500,000 while Japanese losses were expected to soar into millions.

LEFT: The US forces had a choice of routes to Japan. General MacArthur wished to liberate the Philippines, advancing via the Solomons and New Guinea; the US Navy preferred an 'island hopping' strategy aimed directly across the Pacific. In the event, the US had the resources to do both. While these plans unfolded, Japan maintained a substantial field army in Manchuria. Some 750,000 troops remained there until 1945 when the Soviet army demolished the Japanese defences in a week.

required unprecedented investment in logistics, to be able to sustain forces at sea or in distant jungles. All this was made possible by the US's industrial potential and the adaptability of its military and war-fighting institutions. The US was able to overwhelm Japan with only a fraction of its total capability. From the carrier task forces to the base-building bulldozers, it was all an immense triumph of organization, and the levels of strategy, operations, and tactics were high enough to make sure it was effectively applied.

Savage resistance and the introduction of large-scale kamikaze suicide plane attacks marked the last battle of the Pacific War on Okinawa. It became obvious that despite US control of the air and sea, an invasion of Japan would require many months of intense close-quarters combat. The Soviet invasion of Manchuria and the US use of the atomic bomb finally led to the Japanese surrender.

The Bomb was certainly the most dramatic example of the technology and industrial strength that gained the victory in the Pacific. The fact that it had to be used at all also underlined the limits of that sort of strength even against less well equipped and supplied but highly resolute enemies. War termination also was shown to be a key element of effective war-fighting. It is no longer enough to win, but to do so without paying the cost associated with total victory.

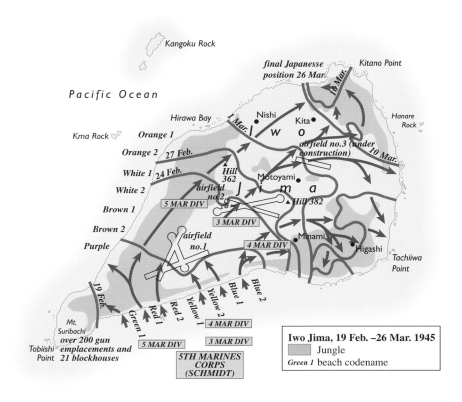

ABOVE: Many armies talk about fighting to the last man and last cartridge, but only the Japanese army has done so consistently. Island garrisons often resorted to bayonet charges in the face of overwhelming US firepower, survivors preferring suicide to surrender. On Iwo Jima they dug extensive tunnel networks, holding out inside Mount Suribachi long after the US flag was famously planted on the summit.

RIGHT: The F-117 Stealth Fighter: symbol of the Gulf War. Built to penetrate Soviet airspace, this distinctive aircraft paved the way for an all-out aerial assault on the Iraqi forces in 1991.

The Cold War differed fundamentally from the many periods of armed and uneasy peace that had been seen since the Industrial Revolution. It was a war fought in an entirely new way as a consequence of the changes in war-fighting brought about by new technologies, most notably the development of nuclear weapons. In the end, what decided the Cold War was a factor that had earlier been considered secondary: economics. The Soviet Union went broke, gave up its empire in Eastern Europe, called off the Cold War, and promptly expired from its own centrifugal forces. And with the Soviet Union so ended the age of ideology and, quite likely, the modern age itself.

The Cold War never saw a direct military conflict between the Soviet Union and the United States and its allies because of nuclear deterrence. The potential cost of direct military conflict was too great to make it a rational tool of 'politics conducted by other means' as Clausewitz had famously identified it. The Cold War was fought through confrontations and crises. It was fought through political means, internal penetration, and even cultural competition. The Cold War was also fought through a series of regional conflicts, all of which took on an East-West orientation even if this was absent in their origins. Regional conflicts in which the United States and the Soviet Union themselves became direct participants - Korea, Vietnam, and Afghanistan - had great influence on the course of the Cold War and its eventual outcome.

The industrial age was coming to an end in the closing years of the Cold War.

The declining percentage of the GDP of the seven OECD countries that came from manufacturing and extraction provided a quantitative edge to the realities of de-industrialization seen in north England or America's 'rust belt'. That other industrial age creation, conscript armed forces, did not long survive it. Britain and the United States abandoned conscription in the 1960s and 1970s respectively. Within a few years of the end of the Cold War, it had ended throughout most of Western Europe as well.

Though the period closed with the transnational ideologies that had dominated the nature of 20th century warfare after 1917 largely coming to an end, the nation state and the modern system that arose from the 1648 Treaty of Westphalia appeared to have an uncertain future. Both multinational and sub-national authorities were sharing the nation state's claims to absolute sovereignty. Meanwhile, the affluence of developed nations meant that mass consumption rather than mass armies was more likely to preoccupy the populace.

The concept of 'modern war' had also diverged. Two models of potential future conflict stand out from the 1990s. The first was the bloody civil war in Rwanda, fought as often with agricultural implements as with Kalashnikovs, in which the 20th century 'barbarization of warfare' was again shown not to be limited to totalitarian states. The second was the NATO air offensive against Serbia in 1999 over the ethnic cleansing of Kosovo, using precision weapons and taking care that no aircrew be lost in action.

BELOW: The first (and last) successful military operation conducted under the United Nations flag, the Korean War saved half the country from communist invasion. Here, Australian infantry hitch a ride on a Centurion tank of the 8th Royal Irish Hussars, June 1951.

The Chinese Civil War and Korea

How wars are fought in a world with nuclear weapons was demonstrated in two Asian conflicts within five years of Hiroshima. Insurgencies (as exemplified by the Chinese Civil War) and limited wars (exemplified by Korea) set a pattern repeated many times – though seldom with such intensity – up to 1991.

The Chinese Civil War represented the implementation of the Maoist paradigm of insurgency. Starting with a Leninist cadre in arms, it culminated (after 1945) with conventional warfare. It presented a way to challenge the West where it was weakest, where its colonial empires were either receding or struggling to hang on. Against insurgency, neither nuclear weapons, nor air power nor the technological warfare evolved from the two world wars could present an effective barrier.

The war in Korea was made possible by the Communist victory in the Chinese Civil War. While its roots were in long-suppressed Korean nationalism, the lasting impact of the Korean War was to define the Communist threat to the West primarily in military terms, of tanks rolling across borders, rather than the internal penetration that had threatened Europe (and claimed Czechoslovakia) in 1945-48. Korea led to the emergence of NATO as a military alliance.

Korea was also a proxy war. It was how the two nuclear-armed superpowers fought. In addition to providing the majority of Communist air power, the Soviet Union provided the material support that allowed the Chinese and the North Koreans to be sustained on the battlefield.

Militarily, the initial North Korean invasion conquered most of the peninsula.

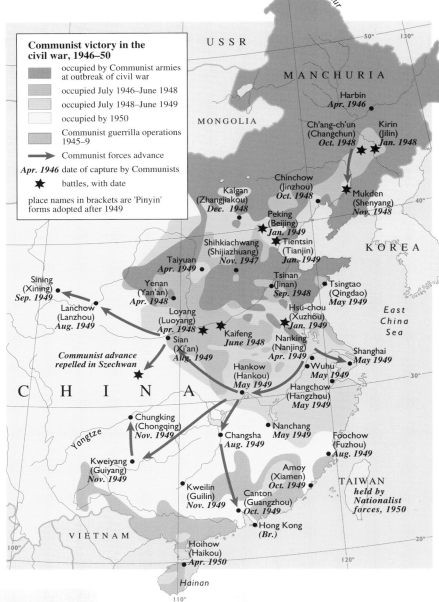

Communist victory in the civil war, 1946–50

- occupied by Communist armies at outbreak of civil war
- occupied July 1946–June 1948
- occupied July 1948–June 1949
- occupied by 1950
- Communist guerrilla operations 1945–9
- → Communist forces advance
- *Apr. 1946* date of capture by Communists
- ★ battles, with date

place names in brackets are 'Pinyin' forms adopted after 1949

USSR
MANCHURIA
MONGOLIA
Harbin *Apr. 1946*
Ch'ang-ch'un (Changchun) *Oct. 1948*
Kirin (Jilin) *Jan. 1948*
Chinchow (Jinzhou) *Oct. 1948*
Mukden (Shenyang) *Nov. 1948*
Kalgan (Zhangjiakou) *Dec. 1948*
Peking (Beijing) *Jan. 1949*
KOREA
Shihkiachwang (Shijiazhuang) *Nov. 1947*
Tientsin (Tianjin) *Jan. 1949*
Taiyuan *Apr. 1949*
Sining (Xining) *Sep. 1949*
Yenan (Yan'an) *Apr. 1948*
Tsinan (Jinan) *Sep. 1948*
Tsingtao (Qingdao) *May 1949*
Lanchow (Lanzhou) *Aug. 1949*
Loyang (Luoyang) *Apr. 1948*
Hsü-chou (Xuzhou) *Jan. 1949*
East China Sea
Sian (Xi'an) *Aug. 1949*
Kaifeng *June 1948*
Nanking (Nanjing) *Apr. 1949*
Shanghai *May 1949*
Communist advance repelled in Szechwan
Hankow (Hankou) *May 1949*
Wuhu *May 1949*
Hangchow (Hangzhou) *May 1949*
CHINA
Yangtze
Chungking (Chongqing) *Nov. 1949*
Changsha *Aug. 1949*
Nanchang *May 1949*
Foochow (Fuzhou) *Aug. 1949*
Kweiyang (Guiyang) *Nov. 1949*
Amoy (Xiamen) *Oct. 1949*
TAIWAN *held by Nationalist forces, 1950*
Kweilin (Guilin) *Nov. 1949*
Canton (Guangzhou) *Oct. 1949*
Hong Kong (Br.)
VIETNAM
Hoihow (Haikou) *Apr. 1950*
Hainan

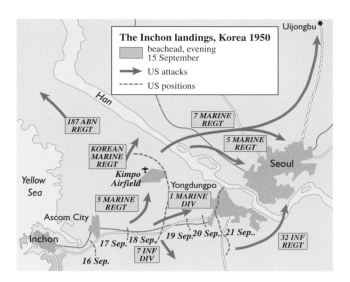

The Inchon landings, Korea 1950
- beachhead, evening 15 September
- → US attacks
- ----- US positions

RIGHT: A British military policeman near the military frontline that ultimately became the frontier between North and South Korea. North Korea outlived its original sponsors and, 50 years later, it remains one of the few old style communist regimes not yet consigned to the dustbin of history.

Forced back to the Pusan perimeter, US and UN reinforcements were able to counter-attack. They were aided by the Inchon landings, deep behind Communist lines, one of the few brilliant operational strokes of the war. The over-optimistic UN offensive had, within a few months, over-run most of North Korea until it too was defeated in a massive Chinese interven-tion. The Chinese pushed south until they, like the North Koreans before them, outran their logistics and were pushed back. Then, by mid-1951, static warfare and truce talks dominated the remainder of the conflict.

Militarily, Korea led to the United States emphasizing nuclear deterrence rather than conventional war-fighting capability. Most pronounced in the late 1950s, it still had not been undone when the next US land war in Asia, in Vietnam, started in the 1960s.

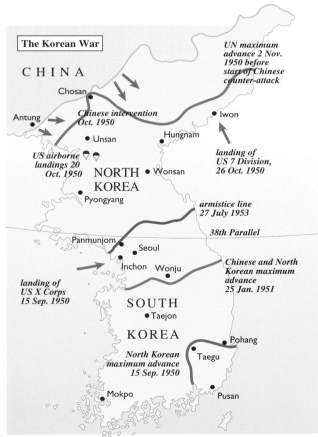

The Korean War

ABOVE: The Korean Civil War became a proxy conflict between the communist superpowers and the United States. Russia provided pilots and military equipment, while China committed hundreds of thousands of ground troops; but the American-led UN forces liberated the southern half of the country by 1953.

The Fall and Rise of Empires – Asia

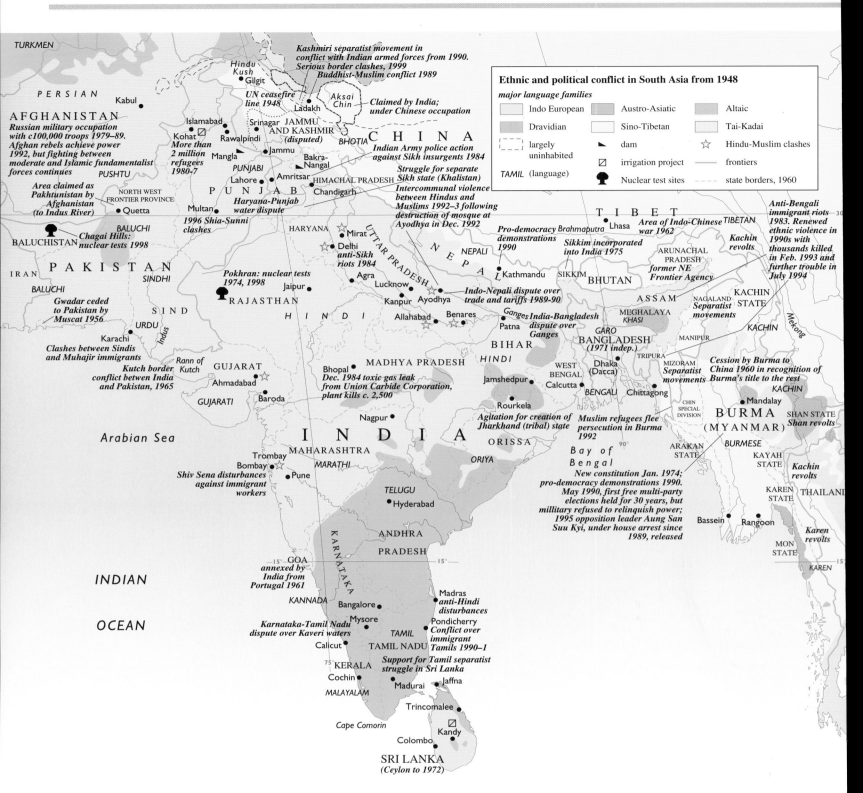

Ethnic and political conflict in South Asia from 1948

major language families

- Indo European
- Dravidian
- Austro-Asiatic
- Sino-Tibetan
- Altaic
- Tai-Kadai
- largely uninhabited
- dam
- Hindu-Muslim clashes
- TAMIL (language)
- irrigation project
- frontiers
- Nuclear test sites
- state borders, 1960

TURKMEN

PERSIAN

AFGHANISTAN
Russian military occupation with c100,000 troops 1979–89. Afghan rebels achieve power 1992, but fighting between moderate and Islamic fundamentalist forces continues PUSHTU

Kabul

Area claimed as Pakhtunistan by Afghanistan (to Indus River)

IRAN

BALUCHI

Chagai Hills: nuclear tests 1998
BALUCHISTAN

PAKISTAN

Gwadar ceded to Pakistan by Muscat 1956

Karachi
URDU
Clashes between Sindis and Muhajir immigrants

SIND

SINDHI

Hindu Kush
• Gilgit

Kashmiri separatist movement in conflict with Indian armed forces from 1990. Serious border clashes, 1999 Buddhist-Muslim conflict 1989

UN ceasefire line 1948
Ladakh
Srinagar
Islamabad
Kohat
Rawalpindi
Jammu
Mangla
PUNJABI
Lahore • Amritsar
Multan •
1996 Shia-Sunni clashes

NORTH WEST FRONTIER PROVINCE
• Quetta

Aksai Chin
Claimed by India; under Chinese occupation

JAMMU AND KASHMIR *(disputed)*
BHOTIA
Bakra-Nangal
Indian Army police action against Sikh insurgents 1984
Struggle for separate Sikh state (Khalistan)

CHINA

HIMACHAL PRADESH
Chandigarh
PUNJAB
Haryana-Punjab water dispute

HARYANA
☆ Mirat
☆ Delhi
anti-Sikh riots 1984
Agra •

Intercommunal violence between Hindus and Muslims 1992–3 following destruction of mosque at Ayodhya in Dec. 1992

Pokhran: nuclear tests 1974, 1998
Jaipur •
RAJASTHAN

HINDI

Lucknow •
Kanpur •
Ayodhya
Allahabad • Benares

UTTAR PRADESH

NEPAL
NEPALI
• Kathmandu

Indo-Nepali dispute over trade and tariffs 1989-90

TIBET

Pro-democracy demonstrations 1990 Brahmaputra
Lhasa
TIBETAN
Area of Indo-Chinese war 1962
Sikkim incorporated into India 1975
SIKKIM
BHUTAN

ARUNACHAL PRADESH *former NE Frontier Agency*

Anti-Bengali immigrant riots 1983. Renewed ethnic violence in 1990s with thousands killed in Feb. 1993 and further trouble in July 1994

Kachin revolts

Rann of Kutch
GUJARAT
Ahmadabad
GUJARATI
Baroda •

Kutch border conflict betwen India and Pakistan, 1965

Bhopal •
Dec. 1984 toxic gas leak from Union Carbide Corporation, plant kills c. 2,500

MADHYA PRADESH

Ganges
Patna •
India-Bangladesh dispute over Ganges
BIHAR
HINDI
Jamshedpur •
Rourkela •

ASSAM
MEGHALAYA KHASI
GARO
BANGLADESH (1971 indep.)
Dhaka (Dacca)
WEST BENGAL
Calcutta •
BENGALI Chittagong

NAGALAND
Separatist movements
MANIPUR

KACHIN STATE

TRIPURA
MIZORAM
Separatist movements

KACHIN

Cession by Burma to China 1960 in recognition of Burma's title to the rest

KACHIN

CHIN SPECIAL DIVISION

Nagpur •
INDIA

Agitation for creation of Jharkhand (tribal) state
ORISSA
ORIYA

Muslim refugees flee persecution in Burma 1992

• Mandalay
BURMA *(MYANMAR)*
SHAN STATE
Shan revolts

Arabian Sea

Trombay ☆
Bombay ☆
MARATHI
• Pune
Shiv Sena disturbances against immigrant workers
MAHARASHTRA

TELUGU
• Hyderabad

ANDHRA PRADESH

Bay of Bengal

New constitution Jan. 1974; pro-democracy demonstrations 1990. May 1990, first free multi-party elections held for 30 years, but millitary refused to relinquish power; 1995 opposition leader Aung San Suu Kyi, under house arrest since 1989, released

ARAKAN STATE

BURMESE

KAYAH STATE
Kachin revolts

KAREN STATE
THAILAND

Bassein • Rangoon •

MON STATE

KAREN
Karen revolts

INDIAN

OCEAN

GOA
annexed by India from Portugal 1961

K A R N A T A K A

KANNADA
Bangalore •
Mysore •
Karnataka-Tamil Nadu dispute over Kaveri waters
Calicut •

TAMIL

Madras
anti-Hindi disturbances
Pondicherry
Conflict over immigrant Tamils 1990–1

TAMIL NADU
Support for Tamil separatist struggle in Sri Lanka

KERALA
Cochin •
MALAYALAM

Madurai •
• Jaffna

Trincomalee •

Cape Comorin

Colombo •
Kandy

SRI LANKA
(Ceylon to 1972)

Just as the end of wars causes new wars, so does the end of empires. The British gave up India without a conflict, but the Netherlands' colonial empire ended only after a lengthy war of independence.

The course of post-imperial Asia was shown in the outcome of two insurgencies. In French Indochina, from 1945-54, the Viet Minh, with the benefits of extensive Chinese aid, were eventually able to implement the Maoist example, starting as guerrillas linking nationalism with Leninism.

In 1953-54, they were able to decisively defeat the French in a conventional battle at Dien Bien Phu. In Malaya, from 1948-60, the British defeated an insurgency aiming at the same result. The British implemented what became the paradigm of effective counter-insurgency, a slow, primarily political process, with military action aimed principally at permitting the evolution of legitimate indigenous institutions. They were able to help defend these against a later, more conventional military

challenge in the confrontation with Indonesia in the early 1960s.

In Malaya, the guerrillas could claim neither foreign arms nor the banner of nationalism. Two communist insurgencies in the Philippines were also defeated despite that country's political weakness.

The component countries of the British Indian Empire opened their independence with mass slaughter and 'transfer of populations'. India and Pakistan have clashed in three limited, conventional wars: 1948 and

RIGHT: A Chinese-built Chengdu F-7 fighter-bomber of the Pakistan air force. China has supplied Pakistan with much of its military equipment, while the Soviet Union supported India. The acquisition of nuclear weapons by India and Pakistan makes a fourth war between them unlikely, but they continue to wage war by proxy in the disputed border state of Kashmir.

LEFT: European empires in Asia could not survive the Second World War. Indian independence was inevitable after 1945, but the haste with which the British withdrew and the gerrymandering that characterized the new state borders contributed to violent religious and ethnic conflicts.

RIGHT: France clung to her colonial empire, but with Chinese military aid, the communist revolutionaries dominated the north of the country and much of the Mekong Delta. The French government shrank from sending conscripts to Indochina, relying mainly on her colonial regiments and the Foreign Legion.

1965, over the disputed state of Kashmir; and in 1971, which led to the creation of Bangladesh. India lost a brief border conflict with China in 1962. India has also, in recent years, been involved in substantial internal security operations including, in the 1980s, one in the island nation of Sri Lanka which, as in Burma, has ongoing ethnic insurgencies. Now, with India and Pakistan both nuclear-armed and the Kashmir issue unresolved, the future of conflict in Asia is likely to make all that has occurred since 1945 seem tame and safe.

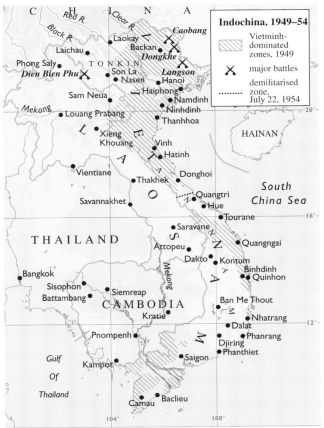

Indochina, 1949–54

- ▨ Vietminh-dominated zones, 1949
- ✕ major battles
- ⋯⋯ demilitarised zone, July 22, 1954

Battle of Dien Bien Phu, 1954

Viet Minh attacks
- → Mar 13–29
- → Mar 30–Apr 9
- → April 10–May 7
- ◠ Encirclement after first attack
- ◻ Viet Minh artillery
- ⬚ French defensive zones
- ➜ French counter-attacks

ABOVE: Overestimating the power of their air force and underestimating the quantity of artillery available to the Viet Minh, the French decision to challenge the enemy to a stand-up battle at Dien Bien Phu backfired hideously. Surrounded by vastly superior forces, the elite of the colonial army was wiped out.

The Fall of Empires - Africa

Conflict in Africa after 1945 was, at first, aimed at the apparently weakened French Empire, leading to risings in Madagascar and Algeria. The French ability to suppress these, plus the counter-insurgency lessons from Indochina, gave the French confidence that they could retain Algeria as a possession as well as a position of influence with other colonies and protectorates that achieved independence. The resulting war in Algeria, eclipsing the previous French colonial conflicts, led to Algerian independence. The French military was never defeated and was winning on the battlefield until the day it lost the war. Politically, the war brought down the Fourth Republic.

The British war in Kenya in the 1950s was much smaller and lacked the political costs of Algeria. The British successfully applied their counter-insurgency tactics developed in Malaya, helped by the insurgents being a tribal minority and lacking external support. But the war still brought home the need for colonial possessions to achieve independence to prevent future conflicts.

Portuguese efforts to hold on to their three colonies of Guinea, Angola, and Mozambique, starting in the late 1950s, lasted until after the government in Lisbon fell in a left-wing revolution in 1974. The Portuguese had also militarily kept the upper hand, fighting effectively despite their limited resources. The end of these conflicts led to civil wars between the participants in the liberation struggle (that in Angola still ongoing in 1999; that in Mozambique halted in the late 1980s). They also increased the pressure on Rhodesia and South Africa.

Rhodesia and South Africa, with tactically excellent armed forces, were militarily undefeated but succumbed to interna-

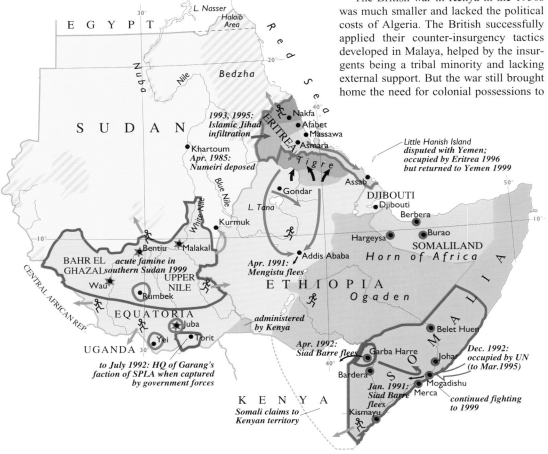

LEFT: Superpower rivalry helped sustain prolonged conflict in the Horn of Africa, Somalia and Ethiopia receiving military aid from the USA and Russia in their struggle for the Ogaden desert. Meanwhile Eritrea fought for independence, ignored by the outside world. Famine and Civil War leave the Sudan in as grim a state as had reached when the British intervened in 1898.

BELOW: The French army and the Algerian rebels drew different lessons from the war in Indochina. Militarily, the French succeeded in containing the guerrillas and even clearing out their urban strongholds, but the political cost was prohibitive. General de Gaulle intervened to make the peace, surviving a coup d'etat attempt by the politicized core of the Army of Africa.

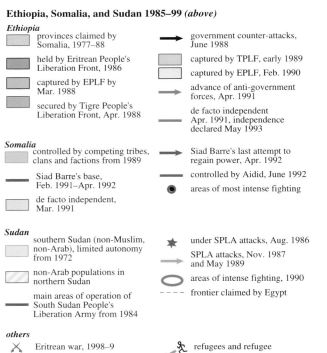

Ethiopia, Somalia, and Sudan 1985–99 (above)

Ethiopia

▨ provinces claimed by Somalia, 1977–88	➡ government counter-attacks, June 1988
▨ held by Eritrean People's Liberation Front, 1986	▨ captured by TPLF, early 1989
▨ captured by EPLF by Mar. 1988	▨ captured by EPLF, Feb. 1990
▨ secured by Tigre People's Liberation Front, Apr. 1988	➡ advance of anti-government forces, Apr. 1991
	— de facto independent Apr. 1991, independence declared May 1993

Somalia

▨ controlled by competing tribes, clans and factions from 1989	➡ Siad Barre's last attempt to regain power, Apr. 1992
— Siad Barre's base, Feb. 1991–Apr. 1992	— controlled by Aidid, June 1992
▨ de facto independent, Mar. 1991	● areas of most intense fighting

Sudan

▨ southern Sudan (non-Muslim, non-Arab), limited autonomy from 1972	★ under SPLA attacks, Aug. 1986
▨ non-Arab populations in northern Sudan	➡ SPLA attacks, Nov. 1987 and May 1989
— main areas of operation of South Sudan People's Liberation Army from 1984	⬭ areas of intense fighting, 1990
	--- frontier claimed by Egypt

others

✕ Eritrean war, 1998–9	🏃 refugees and refugee movements

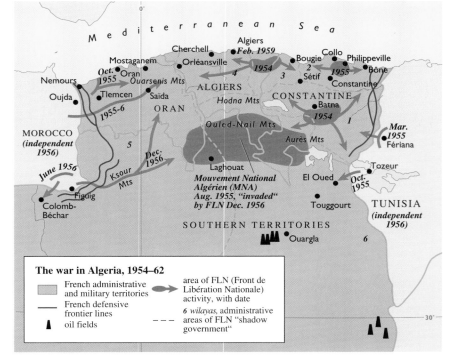

The war in Algeria, 1954–62

▨ French administrative and military territories	➡ area of FLN (Front de Libération Nationale) activity, with date
— French defensive frontier lines	*6* wilayas, administrative areas of FLN "shadow government"
▲ oil fields	---

tional pressure which led them to hand over their countries to representatives of the insurgents they were fighting.

In the 1990s, Africans have largely been fighting Africans in much of the continent. These conflicts include the civil conflicts in the former Belgian Congo (leading to an early UN intervention) and Nigeria in the 1960s. Other civil conflicts have been long-running and bloody, often with foreign intervention: Chad, Sierra Leone, Rwanda, Burundi, and Sudan among many others. More recently, there has been an increasing tendency towards inter-state and well as intrastate conflict in Africa. This is not a new development but the end of Cold War has led to an increasing willingness on the part of neighbouring states to intervene in intrastate conflicts.

RIGHT: Angola's long-running Civil War is replete with Cold War irony: US-owned diamond mines in Cabinda guarded by Cuban mercenaries against local guerrillas sustained by the CIA. South Africa intervened to destroy Namibian guerrilla sanctuaries north of the border; Soviet support for the MPLA gave the Soviet navy a useful base for maritime patrol aircraft.

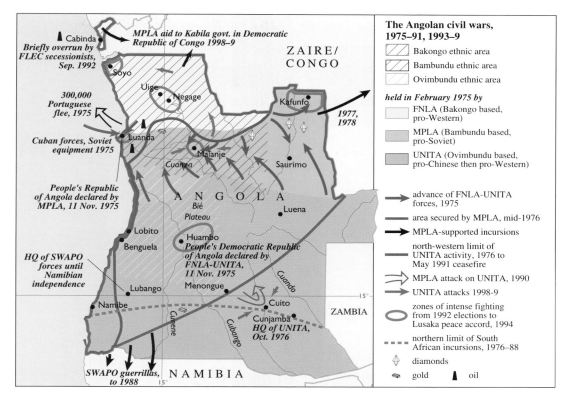

The Angolan civil wars, 1975–91, 1993–9

Bakongo ethnic area
Bambundu ethnic area
Ovimbundu ethnic area

held in February 1975 by

FNLA (Bakongo based, pro-Western)
MPLA (Bambundu based, pro-Soviet)
UNITA (Ovimbundu based, pro-Chinese then pro-Western)

→ advance of FNLA-UNITA forces, 1975
— area secured by MPLA, mid-1976
➡ MPLA-supported incursions
— north-western limit of UNITA activity, 1976 to May 1991 ceasefire
⇨ MPLA attack on UNITA, 1990
⟶ UNITA attacks 1998-9
◯ zones of intense fighting from 1992 elections to Lusaka peace accord, 1994
----- northern limit of South African incursions, 1976–88
◇ diamonds
⬗ gold   ▲ oil

Map labels:
Cabinda
Briefly overrun by FLEC secessionists, Sep. 1992
MPLA aid to Kabila govt. in Democratic Republic of Congo 1998–9
ZAIRE/CONGO
Soyo
Uige
Negage
Kafunfo
300,000 Portuguese flee, 1975
1977, 1978
Cuban forces, Soviet equipment 1975
Luanda
Malanje
Saurimo
Cuanza
People's Republic of Angola declared by MPLA, 11 Nov. 1975
A N G O L A
Bié Plateau
Luena
Lobito
Huambo
Benguela
People's Democratic Republic of Angola declared by FNLA-UNITA, 11 Nov. 1975
HQ of SWAPO forces until Namibian independence
Lubango
Menongue
Cuando
Namibe
Cuito
ZAMBIA
Cunene
Cubango
Cunjamba HQ of UNITA, Oct. 1976
SWAPO guerrillas, to 1988
N A M I B I A

LEFT: Royal Marines in the Congo during international intervention in 1999. The generation of African dictators that came to power in the wake of European withdrawal is now dying off. Since a tank battalion can always trump an election defeat, their successors will stand or fall by military rather than democratic means.

Arab-Israeli Wars

Arab-Israeli conflict started with the waning of the British mandate in Palestine. The Israeli War of Independence that followed demonstrated that the improvised Israeli Defense Forces (IDF) were capable of overcoming the post-imperial armies of its Arab opponents in a low-technology conflict.

The Cold War inevitably invested the Arab-Israeli conflict with a proxy war element. Soviet involvement increased after the 1955 arms deal with Egypt. Israel's pro-western orientation was sealed by its covert alliance with France and Britain to invade Egypt in the 1956 Suez crisis. After the 1967 war, Israel turned increasingly to the US for arms, economic aid and diplomatic support.

By 1967, the IDF was no longer a third-world military force, and US arms increased its already high level of technology. The Israelis seriously studied operations and tactics, resulting in original approaches to low-cost, high-technology warfare.

Starting with the 1967 war, Arab-Israeli confrontations brought about increasing interest in how emerging technologies performed in combat. In 1967, it was the conventional pre-emptive strike, stressing air attacks and armoured forces, by Israel that influenced both Soviet and NATO military

BELOW: Syria's attempt to recapture the Golan Heights ended in bloody defeat in 1973, its masses of Soviet tanks proving no substitute for the better trained and more determined Israeli mechanized units.

RIGHT: In 1956 Britain and France made a secret alliance with Israel and invaded Egypt. But this was not the 19th century, and neither were they the world powers they still aspired to be. Both had to bow to international pressure to withdraw. The humiliation brought down the British government.

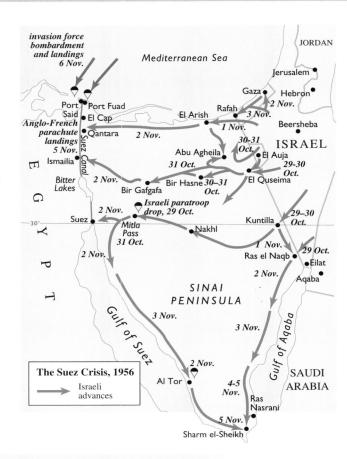

The Suez Crisis, 1956

→ Israeli advances

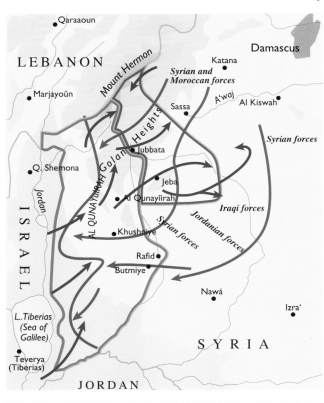

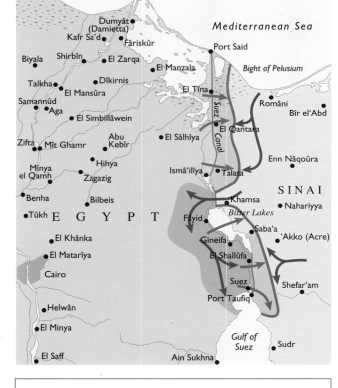

LEFT: Egypt's offensive across the Suez Canal was thoroughly prepared and well conducted. Hasty Israeli counter-attacks were beaten off and new Soviet missile defences inflicted unexpected losses on the Israeli air force. Israeli superiority in mobile operations, plus a bonanza of US military aid, eventually defeated the Egyptians.

The Yom Kippur War, 1973: The Golan Heights

— de facto frontiers before the war
— occupied by Israel at the end of the Six Day War, 1967
→ Arab advances
— furthest Arab advance into Israeli territory
→ Israeli counter-offensives
— Syrian territory held by Israel at ceasefire, 24 October

The Yom Kippur War, 1973: The Suez Canal

☐ occupied by Israel at the end of the Six Day War, 1967
— de facto frontier before the war
→ Egyptian advances
— furthest Egyptian advance into Israeli-held territory
→ Israeli counter-offensives
☐ Israeli territory held by Egypt at ceasefire, 24 Oct.
☐ Egyptian territory held by Israel at ceasefire, 24 Oct.

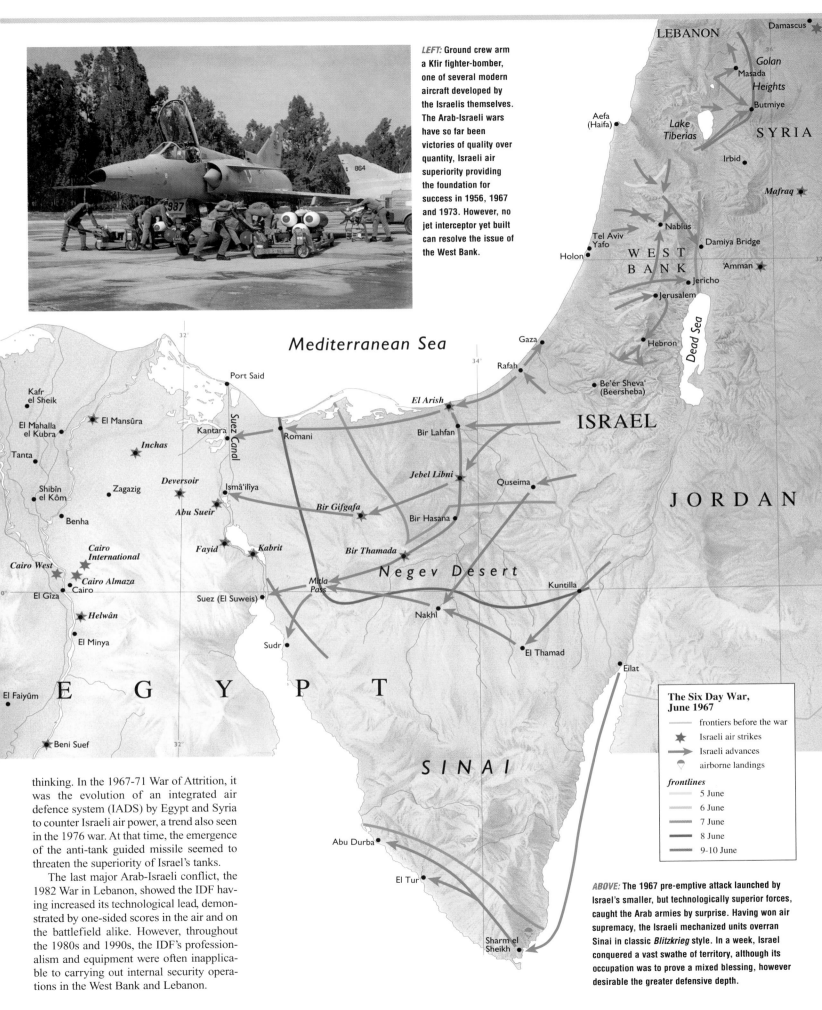

thinking. In the 1967-71 War of Attrition, it was the evolution of an integrated air defence system (IADS) by Egypt and Syria to counter Israeli air power, a trend also seen in the 1976 war. At that time, the emergence of the anti-tank guided missile seemed to threaten the superiority of Israel's tanks.

The last major Arab-Israeli conflict, the 1982 War in Lebanon, showed the IDF having increased its technological lead, demonstrated by one-sided scores in the air and on the battlefield alike. However, throughout the 1980s and 1990s, the IDF's professionalism and equipment were often inapplicable to carrying out internal security operations in the West Bank and Lebanon.

The Six Day War, June 1967

frontiers before the war
Israeli air strikes
Israeli advances
airborne landings

frontlines
5 June
6 June
7 June
8 June
9-10 June

ABOVE: The 1967 pre-emptive attack launched by Israel's smaller, but technologically superior forces, caught the Arab armies by surprise. Having won air supremacy, the Israeli mechanized units overran Sinai in classic *Blitzkrieg* style. In a week, Israel conquered a vast swathe of territory, although its occupation was to prove a mixed blessing, however desirable the greater defensive depth.

The Strategic Balance

The way the Cold War was waged – without direct military confrontation but always in readiness – put a great emphasis on the balance of forces between the opposing sides. While competition in peacetime between military forces was hardly a new thing – witness the pre-1914 Anglo-German naval race – the Cold War placed an unprecedented emphasis on the balance sheet of overall capability of the two principal powers.

The strategic nuclear balance compared the number of nuclear weapons systems that the United States and the Soviet Union could deliver against each other. These consisted of intercontinental ballistic missiles (ICBMs), submarine launched ballistic missiles (SLBMs) and manned strategic bombers. The US nuclear monopoly ended in 1948, but despite fears first of a 'bomber gap', then a 'missile gap', the Soviets were outnumbered in both categories well into the 1960s. The emergence of Soviet nuclear parity and then a potential first-strike capability in the SS-18 ICBM force in the 1970s was one of the reasons the Soviets then thought the 'correlation of forces' had shifted in their favour, only to see it swing back in the 1980s.

The theatre nuclear balance compared Soviet forces that could hit targets such as western Europe and Japan with the forward-deployed US systems and, sometimes, the British and French nuclear deterrents. The NATO decision to revive their theatre nuclear forces in the late 1970s in response to the Soviet deployment of advanced SS-20 ballistic missiles was one of the key events in the Cold War military competition.

The theatre general-purpose forces balance was always in the favour of the Soviet Union. The US nuclear umbrella was the main reason NATO never had to deploy forces to compete on an even basis with those of the Soviet Union. However, starting in the 1970s, the potential inherent in high technology weapons seemed to give NATO forces in then West Germany the potential to even the balance with in-place Soviet and Warsaw pact forces if 'deep attack' operations could keep their reinforcements at bay.

As the Cold War wound down, arms control, be it unilateral, bilateral, or multilateral reduced numbers. The Strategic Arms Reduction (START) agreements were the first to reduce the numbers of strategic systems. The 1987 Inter-mediate Nuclear Forces treaty made the SS-20s and their NATO counterparts extinct. Theatre nuclear systems are now limited to air-delivered or short-range systems. The 1990 Conventional Forces in Europe (CFE) Treaty in Vienna limited conventional forces west of the Urals. It has been revised since the end of the Cold War.

BELOW: **The security of West Germany and western Europe could only be guaranteed by the USA stationing a major army there. The British maintained their 'Army of the Rhine' in northern Germany. A generation of soldiers served their time, preparing for the defence of the inner German border.**

Germany: the Cold War confrontation, 1980

- • Nato bases
- • Warsaw Pact bases

army units
- US
- British
- French
- West German
- East German
- Russian

divisions
- infantry
- armoured infantry
- armoured
- armoured cavalry
- airborne
- artillery brigade
- mountain
- corps HQ
- army HQ

government's internal stability and legitimacy remained limited and was dependent, if not on US troops, then on air support and aid. US combat troops left after the repulse of the 1972 North Vietnamese offensive. US domestic political opposition had started to greatly increase after three years hard fighting showed no end in sight and the cut-off of aid to South Vietnam set the stage for the eventual North Vietnamese conquest of the south in 1975

Further wars in Indochina followed. Cambodia and Laos fell to communist insurgents in 1975. Renaming their country Kampuchea, the Khmer Rouge commenced a revolutionary remaking of society through auto-genocide, with up to a third of the population being killed in three and a half years. Destabilization, ethnic tensions and ideological rivalry with the Vietnamese led to their invasion of Kampuchea. The Chinese, allies of the Khmer Rouge, responded by invading Vietnam, but the Sino-Vietnamese War represented a costly repulse at the hands of an outnumbered Vietnamese force.

The Vietnamese waged a counter-guerrilla war in Cambodia against the Khmer Rouge and non-communist guerrillas throughout the 1980s, trying to keep a friendly government in power in Phnom Penh, but as the Cold War was ending, the Soviet Union could no longer support these operations. The Vietnamese withdrew and a United Nations force moved in and held elections. Despite this, conflict still continued in Cambodia into the 1990s.

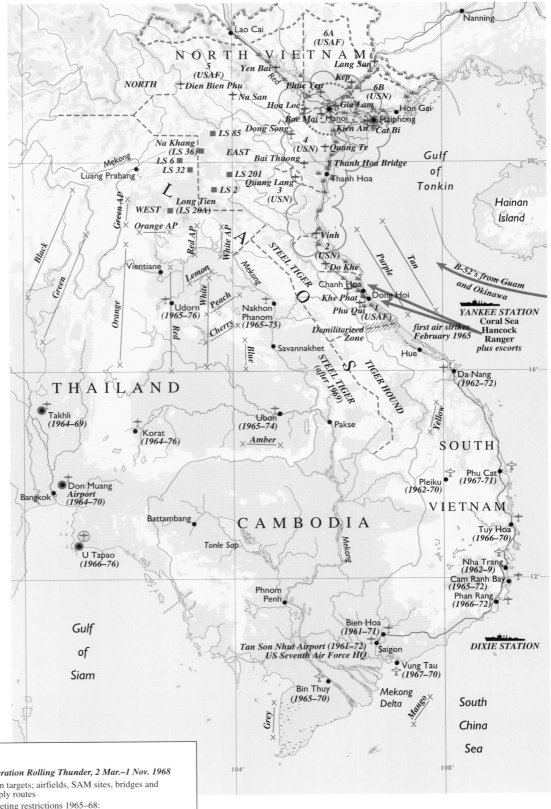

The Vietnam air war, 1965–72

▬▪▬	US 7th Fleet (Task Force 77)
✛	US airbase (jet serviceable)
✛	US airbase (non jet serviceable)
◉	US air tanker base
⊕	US B-52 base
×–×	aerial re-fuelling tracks and anchor points (AP)
WEST	air combat zones (route packages)
✛	North Vietnamese airfield
☐	SAM cover
■	major Lima site
– – –	Chinese buffer zone (prohibited area)

Operation Rolling Thunder, 2 Mar.–1 Nov. 1968
main targets; airfields, SAM sites, bridges and supply routes
targeting restrictions 1965–68:

Hanoi: prohibited zone: 10 nautical miles
         restricted zone: 30 nautical miles
Haiphong: prohibited zone: 4 nautical miles
         restricted zone: 10 nautical miles

Operation Linebacker 1, 8 May–23 Oct. 1972
↯ strikes
fewer target restrictions than Rolling Thunder

Operation Linebacker 2, 19–30 Dec. 1972
✳ strikes
unrestricted bombing; all targets of importance in Hanoi and Haiphong hit

TOP LEFT: **An American soldier among the ruins of Cholon after the Tet offensive, February 1968. This premature attempt to defeat the US forces in a conventional battle cost the Viet Cong and North Vietnamese army severe losses. However, their military defeat was transformed into a political victory; public opinion in America turned against the war.**

ABOVE: **US intervention in South Vietnam prevented a communist take-over in the early 1960s, but the guerrilla war that followed remains controversial. The US forces never lost a major battle, but vocal internal opposition to the war persuaded successive presidents to end US involvement. The impact of daily TV coverage, often graphic images not seen in World War II, had a profound influence on public opinion.**

Soviet Invasions

The Soviet Union waged the Cold War through a number of invasions – including those of Hungary in 1956, Czechoslovakia in 1968 and Afghanistan in 1979 – and the threat of potential ones, most notably that of Western Europe.

The three actual invasions were all aimed at replacing nominally pro-Soviet governments that were not following the course set by Moscow. All three invasions demonstrated the Soviet operational thinking that would also have been seen in an invasion of Europe: pre-empt resistance wherever possible; move to decapitate enemy centres of resistance; stress speed and shock of advance.

In Hungary (after considerable fighting) and Czechoslovakia, the invasions succeeded, after a fashion, but in the long run the political damage caused by the military action outweighed this success. When Moscow's East European empire came apart in 1989, no one was willing to take up arms in its defence. The fall of the Soviet empire itself was to follow in two years. It was economics rather than the clash of arms that decided the Cold War.

Afghanistan was to the Soviet Union what the Boer War was to the British Empire or Vietnam was to the United States. Unlike those, however, the Soviet Union did not survive its frustrating, costly war. Afghanistan has been described as the 'fatal pebble' that finally tripped up the stumbling Soviet colossus. Afghan resistance represented the largest national rising of the century. While the Afghan guerrillas lacked organization and training throughout the war – they did not aim to create their own Dien Bien Phu – they had the advantage of large-scale support from the Soviet Union's Cold War opponents, becoming another proxy war, and strong Islamic faith to provide motivation.

Wars of national liberation have often been followed by civil wars that can prove even more costly and Afghanistan has been no exception. The Soviets invaded in 1979, waged a frustrating firepower-intensive war for many years, and started to withdraw in 1987, completing that withdrawal in 1989. The pro-Moscow government left behind endured until 1992. Since then, civil war between groups incorporating different guerrilla factions has consumed much of Afghanistan.

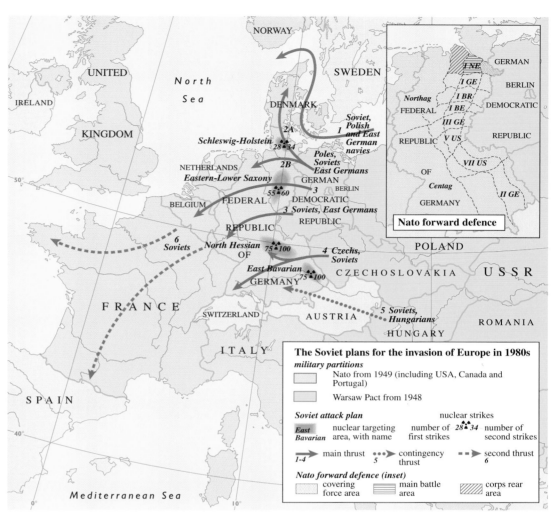

The Soviet plans for the invasion of Europe in 1980s
military partitions

	Nato from 1949 (including USA, Canada and Portugal)
	Warsaw Pact from 1948

Soviet attack plan
nuclear strikes

| *East Bavarian* | nuclear targeting area, with name | number of first strikes | 28 ▲ 34 | number of second strikes |

| 1-4 | main thrust | ●●● 5 | contingency thrust | ---▶ 6 | second thrust |

Nato forward defence (inset)

| | covering force area | | main battle area | | corps rear area |

ABOVE: By 1980 the Soviet forces in Germany had a well prepared plan to invade western Europe, intending to reach the Rhine in a week, blasting their way forward with plentiful use of tactical nuclear weapons. Their East German allies had even struck a victory medal and decided how to rename West German cities. Their operational orders were uncovered when East Germany collapsed.

BELOW: The Soviet invasion of Afghanistan took place over Christmas 1979. Intended as a simple exercise in 'keep your man in the capital', it degenerated into the USSR's Vietnam. Military pundits forecast an eventual Soviet victory, since the Kremlin was immune to public opinion and international condemnation. However, the daunting economic cost of the war and the inability of the vaunted Red Army to overcome the 'bandits' helped bring down the entire Soviet system.

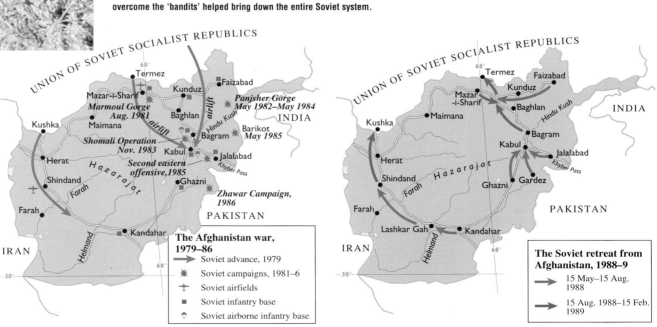

ABOVE: The invasion of Afghanistan in December 1979 was intended as a short, surgical operation to restore a pro-Soviet regime in Kabul. It degenerated into a protracted guerrilla war that the Soviet army was never able to win. Since the withdrawal of Soviet forces, the guerrilla armies have fought among themselves for control of the country.

The Afghanistan war, 1979–86

➔	Soviet advance, 1979
✳	Soviet campaigns, 1981–6
✛	Soviet airfields
■	Soviet infantry base
⬙	Soviet airborne infantry base

The Soviet retreat from Afghanistan, 1988–9

➔	15 May–15 Aug. 1988
➔	15 Aug. 1988–15 Feb. 1989

The Falklands and 1980s Interventions

Western interventions of the 1980s were not directly connected with conflict with the Soviet Union in the last decade of the Cold War but made a contribution to its outcome. Most notable was the British war to reclaim the Falkland Islands after their invasion by Argentina in 1982

The Falklands was not the war (either on the north German plain or the streets of Ulster – for which British forces had trained. As so often throughout history, the war that had to be fought was not the war that had been planned. The result put a premium on improvisation and the logistics capability that, far from being mere 'tail', made victory possible thousands of miles from any base in the South Atlantic. It also underlined the continued importance of quality of military forces, especially when not undercut by technological weakness.

In many ways the Falklands was a low-technology conflict. The British infantry had to fight their way into Port Stanley in a series of hill battles, relying on fine-honed tactics rather than firepower or technological advantage. Infantry patrols carried out reconnaissance that today would be carried out by a UAV. Yet the Argentine Air Force, in its attempt to defeat the British invasion force, failed despite inflicting painful casualties. Brave men in low-technology aircraft lacked the supporting infrastructure of modern air war: the tankers, jamming planes, anti-radiation missiles and the like. Argentina's greatest successes came from the use of Exocet air-launched anti-ship guided missiles.

The US, overcoming the aftermath of its defeat in Vietnam, increased its capability to carry out unilateral actions, including the failed Iranian hostage rescue of 1979, the landing on Grenada in 1983, clashes with Libya in 1981 and 1986, and the intervention in Panama in 1989. There was also the abortive multinational force in Beirut in 1982-83, withdrawn after the US and French contingents suffered heavy losses to suicide terrorist bombings.

These interventions had implications for the course of the Cold War beyond their limited military significance. Along with the policy of supporting those indigenous groups resisting the Soviet Union and its allies – most notably in Afghanistan – these actions demonstrated that the West was not permanently put on the defensive. The Soviets had hoped to achieve this by the shift in the 'correlation of forces' emerging with the attainment of nuclear parity, by Vietnam, and by the potential erosion of support for the military implementation of the strategy of containment the West had tried to implement since the early 1950s. These interventions also showed the way to later 'out of area' actions such as the Gulf War in 1990-91 and Kosovo in 1999.

The Falkands War, 1982

- – – British maritime exclusion zone
- British ships sunk
- Argentine ship sunk
- → main British advance
- ✳ principal engagement with date

night, 15 May Commando raid destroys aircraft, ammunition and fuel dumps — Pebble I.

West Falkland

San Carlos 21 May — Port San Carlos — Douglas

dawn, 21 May — San Carlos Water

beach-heads established by 3 Para, 42 and 45 Mar Cmdo Btns (North) 2 Para, 40 Mar Cmdo Btns (South)

Goose Green 29 May — Darwin

East Falkland

Wireless Ridge 13 June

Bluff Cove 4-8 June — Fitzroy — Port Stanley *Argentine surrender 14 June*

evening, 28 May Argentine garrison surrenders after 12 hour battle

Tumbledown Hill 13 June

4–8 June British reinforcements landed 8 June, landing ships Sir Galahad and Sir Tristram destroyed

ARGENTINA — *South Atlantic Ocean* — See Inset — HMS Sheffield — *Falkland Is.* — **South Georgia** — Punto Arenas — *General Belgrano* — *recaptured by British forces 25–6 April* — CHILE

South Atlantic Ocean

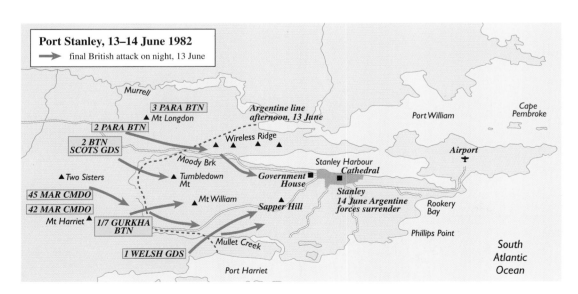

Port Stanley, 13–14 June 1982

→ final British attack on night, 13 June

Murrell — **3 PARA BTN** ▲ Mt Longdon — *Argentine line afternoon, 13 June* — Port William — Cape Pembroke — **2 PARA BTN** — **2 BTN SCOTS GDS** — Wireless Ridge — Moody Brk — Stanley Harbour — Cathedral — *Airport* — ▲ Two Sisters — ▲ Tumbledown Mt — **Government House** — **45 MAR CMDO** — **42 MAR CMDO** — ▲ Mt William — **Stanley** *14 June Argentine forces surrender* — Rookery Bay — Mt Harriet ▲ **1/7 GURKHA BTN** — Sapper Hill — **1 WELSH GDS** — Mullet Creek — Phillips Point — *South Atlantic Ocean* — Port Harriet

RIGHT: A Royal Marine officer brews up, his M16 propped against a rock. The British surprised the Argentines by landing at San Carlos rather than near Port Stanley. This committed them to a foot slog across bleak terrain, but the British were trained to fight in such conditions. Argentina's regular mountain troops remained on the border with Chile.

Battle for Grenada, 1983

Rhode Island

0   10 km
0   10 mile

N

Sauteurs
Victoria
Gouyave
Mount Horne
Pearls Airport
Grenville
Woodford
Marquis
Beausejour
Crochu
Grand Mal
St. George's
Port Salinas Airport
Grand Anse

U.S. forces

▨	mechanised infantry	▨	infantry
▨	heliborne troops	▨	tank forces
▨	paratroopers	▨	engineers

ABOVE: The US invasion of Grenada was ordered to forestall a communist coup. This, and later interventions in Panama, Beirut and Haiti, showed America was prepared to use force despite the debacle in Vietnam. And even a military walkover like Grenada could have useful lessons for the US Army, Navy and Airforce whose coordination would improve considerably by the time of the 1991 Gulf War.

LEFT: Life rafts cluster around HMS *Coventry* after she capsized off the Falklands, sunk by Argentine air force fighter-bombers on 25 May 1982. The British were fortunate that their opponents had to rely primarily on unguided 'iron bombs' because they only had half-a-dozen guided missiles available.

Gulf Wars

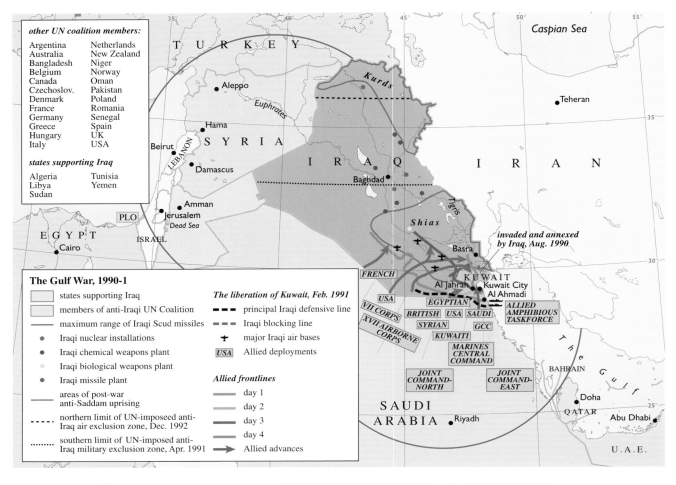

The Gulf War, 1990-1

other UN coalition members:

Argentina	Netherlands
Australia	New Zealand
Bangladesh	Niger
Belgium	Norway
Canada	Oman
Czechoslov.	Pakistan
Denmark	Poland
France	Romania
Germany	Senegal
Greece	Spain
Hungary	UK
Italy	USA

states supporting Iraq

Algeria	Tunisia
Libya	Yemen
Sudan	

- states supporting Iraq
- members of anti-Iraqi UN Coalition
- maximum range of Iraqi Scud missiles
- Iraqi nuclear installations
- Iraqi chemical weapons plant
- Iraqi biological weapons plant
- Iraqi missile plant
- areas of post-war anti-Saddam uprising
- northern limit of UN-imposeed anti-Iraq air exclusion zone, Dec. 1992
- southern limit of UN-imposed anti-Iraq military exclusion zone, Apr. 1991

The liberation of Kuwait, Feb. 1991

- principal Iraqi defensive line
- Iraqi blocking line
- major Iraqi air bases
- USA Allied deployments

Allied frontlines

- day 1
- day 2
- day 3
- day 4
- Allied advances

The regions bordering the Gulf increased in strategic importance with the first oil shortage of 1973-74, following soon after the British withdrawal from the region, although Britain remained involved in the area through a major counter-insurgency conflict in Oman throughout the 1970s. Iran, then under the Shah, increased its armed forces, looking to assure its regional dominance, but the Iranian revolution of 1979 brought a revolutionary Islamic government to power. The hostage crisis of 1979-81 with the US also brought US forces to the region and,

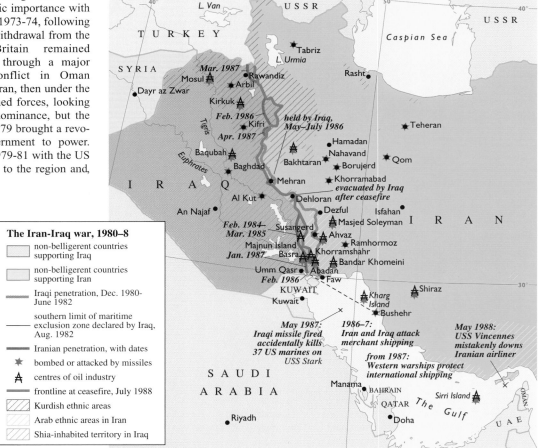

The Iran-Iraq war, 1980–8

- non-belligerent countries supporting Iraq
- non-belligerent countries supporting Iran
- Iraqi penetration, Dec. 1980-June 1982
- southern limit of maritime exclusion zone declared by Iraq, Aug. 1982
- Iranian penetration, with dates
- bombed or attacked by missiles
- centres of oil industry
- frontline at ceasefire, July 1988
- Kurdish ethnic areas
- Arab ethnic areas in Iran
- Shia-inhabited territory in Iraq

May 1987: Iraqi missile fired accidentally kills 37 US marines on USS Stark

1986–7: Iran and Iraq attack merchant shipping

from 1987: Western warships protect international shipping

May 1988: USS Vincennes mistakenly downs Iranian airliner

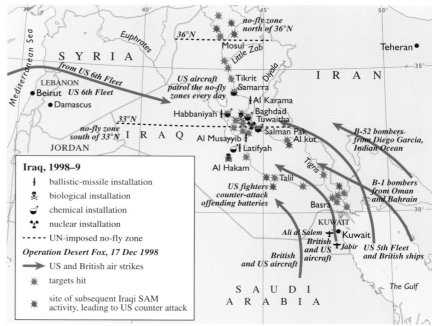

Iraq, 1998–9

✝ ballistic-missile installation

☠ biological installation

⚗ chemical installation

☢ nuclear installation

- - - - UN-imposed no-fly zone

Operation Desert Fox, 17 Dec 1998

→ US and British air strikes

✳ targets hit

✳ site of subsequent Iraqi SAM activity, leading to US counter attack

LEFT: The 1991 Gulf War was the swansong of the dreadnought battleship: here the *Wisconsin* bombards Iraqi positions with her 16-in guns just as HMS *Queen Elizabeth* shelled Turkish defences at Gallipoli. The US battleships were modernized with the addition of Tomahawk cruise missiles as part of President Reagan's naval programme, but have now retired for the last time.

ABOVE: Saddam Hussein was allowed to survive the 1991 Gulf War, but without international consensus on further action against his regime, Britain and the USA have resorted to airstrikes and ballistic missiles to frustrate Iraqi rearmament. However, much of the Iraqi nuclear and chemical weapons development has been undertaken in outside the country. The use of stealth aircraft and cruise missiles makes for dramatic television coverage and evidence of 'action', but its practical value remains questionable.

after the war in Afghanistan started in 1978, superpower tensions. The 'Carter Doctrine' and the organization of the Rapid Deployment Force, later Central Command, put then-weakened US credibility on the line for Gulf stability.

With Iran in disorder, the weaker but aggressive regime of Saddam Hussein in Iraq saw a chance for a military victory and, in 1980, invaded, starting the Iran-Iraq War. The Iraqi attack eventually ground to a halt and, as the revolutionary regime consolidated in Iran and mobilized, that country put more forces in the field, pushing the Iraqis back to their borders by 1982.

The war now changed, with the Iraqis now being seen as the bulwark for the Arab world against the revolutionary Persian hordes. Iraq received the financial and technical backing of the Arab world to rebuild its military. In years of bitter fighting and battles of attrition, the Iran-Iraq war also included the first mutual use of chemical weapons since 1918 and mutual use of ballistic missiles in the 'war of the cities' until Iran, finally exhausted, sued for peace.

With both sides attacking tankers during the Iran-Iraq war, the US escorted ships going to friendly Arab states. There were a number of clashes with the Iranians and one incident – the damaging of a US frigate - involving Iraq. Saddam's goal of regional domination was still unrealized so, in August 1990, Iraq invaded and occu-

pied Kuwait, to which it had long-standing claims, after a dispute over oil production levels. Saudi Arabia and the Gulf states, now threatened by their former protector, asked for foreign help. The bulk of the foreign troops were from the US. Divisions came also from Britain, France, Egypt, and Syria. Aircraft arrived from even more allies.

A lengthy build-up and diplomatic efforts were followed by a 40-day air bombardment and a ground offensive which swiftly evicted Iran from Kuwait. The Gulf War of 1991 was a unique event. It represented a coalition effort not seen since the Second World War. The movement of large-scale mechanized forces from the US, Europe and the Middle East to the Gulf was possible due to the in-place infrastructure and the six months between the invasion of Kuwait and the opening of the land war. While it featured many elements of the digital revolution incorporated in operational and tactical war-fighting, it probably represents at best a transitional stage, with the armed forces of the Cold War and the modern eras fighting their last conventional battle.

The military situation became less clear-cut after the cease-fire. Allied forces intervened to support Kurds in the north of Iraq, but not as Saddam slaughtered Shia opponents in the south. International alarm at Iraq's massive stocks of chemical and biological weapons, the Scud missiles

fired during the war, and how close they had come to a nuclear weapon led to the imposition of an intrusive arms control verification regime. But, through the 1990s, this has failed to end Iraq's capability to produce and use ballistic missiles and weapons of mass destruction.

Limited attacks since 1991, largely by US and British forces, have been provoked by continued Iraqi non-compliance with UN resolutions, especially as to their weapons of mass destruction, and action against the Kurds.

BELOW: Those Kuwaiti forces able to escape the Iraqi invasion joined the coalition forces in Saudi Arabia. Here, a Kuwaiti pilot is interviewed for TV: the US forces demonstrated that they had learned a great deal about media management since the days of the 'five O'clock follies' in Saigon.

Peacekeeping and Peacemaking Operations

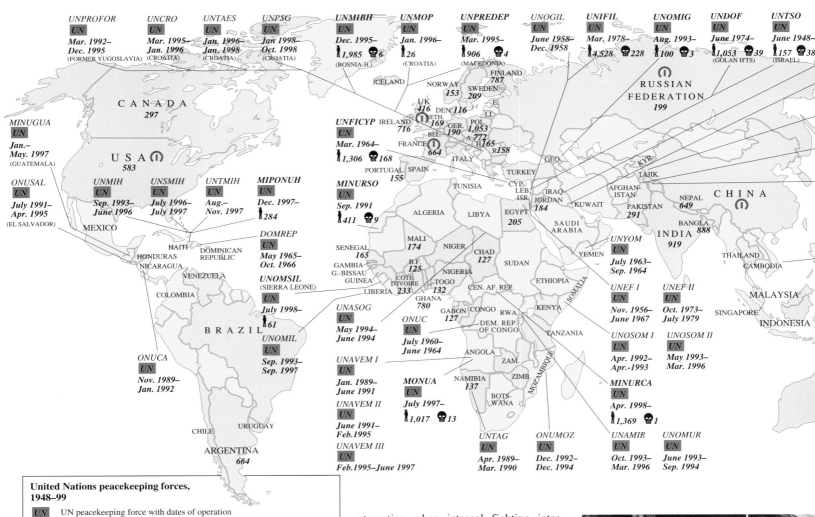

UNPROFOR
UN
Mar. 1992–
Dec. 1995
(FORMER YUGOSLAVIA)

UNCRO
UN
Mar. 1995–
Jan. 1996
(CROATIA)

UNTAES
UN
Jan. 1996–
Jan. 1998
(CROATIA)

UNPSG
UN
Jan 1998–
Oct. 1998
(CROATIA)

UNMIBH
UN
Dec. 1995–
👤1,985 ☠6
(BOSNIA-H.)

UNMOP
UN
Jan. 1996–
👤26
(CROATIA)

UNPREDEP
UN
Mar. 1995–
👤906 ☠4
(MACEDONIA)

UNOGIL
UN
June 1958–
Dec. 1958

UNIFIL
UN
Mar. 1978–
👤4,528 ☠228
(GOLAN HTS)

UNOMIG
UN
Aug. 1993–
👤100 ☠3

UNDOF
UN
June 1974–
👤1,053 ☠39
(GOLAN HTS)

UNTSO
UN
June 1948–
👤157 ☠38
(ISRAEL)

ICELAND
FINLAND 787
NORWAY SWEDEN 209
CANADA 297
UK 416
IRELAND 716
DEN 116
NETH 169
BEL FRANCE 664
GER 190
POL 1,053
A.772
LI
H 165
R 158
GEO
RUSSIAN FEDERATION 199

MINUGUA
UN
Jan.–
May 1997
(GUATEMALA)

UNFICYP
UN
Mar. 1964–
👤1,306 ☠168

PORTUGAL
SPAIN 155
ITALY
TURKEY
CYP.
LEB.
ISR.
IRAQ
JORDAN 184
KUWAIT
GEO
KYR.
TAJIK.
AFGHAN-ISTAN
NEPAL 649
PAKISTAN 291
CHINA
BANGLA. 888
INDIA 919

USA 583

ONUSAL
UN
July 1991–
Apr. 1995
(EL SALVADOR)

UNMIH
UN
Sep. 1993–
June 1996

UNSMIH
UN
July 1996–
July 1997

UNTMIH
UN
Aug.–
Nov. 1997

MIPONUH
UN
Dec. 1997–
👤284

MINURSO
UN
Sep. 1991
👤411 ☠9

MEXICO
HAITI
HONDURAS
NICARAGUA
DOMINICAN REPUBLIC
VENEZUELA
COLOMBIA

TUNISIA
ALGERIA
LIBYA
EGYPT 205
SAUDI ARABIA
YEMEN

MALI 174
NIGER
CHAD 127
SUDAN

THAILAND
CAMBODIA

DOMREP
UN
May 1965–
Oct. 1966

UNOMSIL
(SIERRA LEONE)
UN
July 1998–
👤61

UNASOG
UN
May 1994–
June 1994

SENEGAL 165
GAMBIA
G.-BISSAU
GUINEA
B.F. 125
CÔTE D'IVOIRE 233
LIBERIA
TOGO 132
GHANA 780
NIGERIA
CEN. AF. REP.
GABON 127
CONGO
ETHIOPIA
SOMALIA

UNYOM
UN
July 1963–
Sep. 1964

UNEF I
UN
Nov. 1956–
June 1967

UNEF II
UN
Oct. 1973–
July 1979

MALAYSIA
SINGAPORE
INDONESIA

BRAZIL

UNOMIL
UN
Sep. 1993–
Sep. 1997

ONUC
UN
July 1960–
June 1964

RWA.
DEM. REP. OF CONGO
KENYA
TANZANIA

ONUCA
UN
Nov. 1989–
Jan. 1992

UNAVEM I
UN
Jan. 1989–
June 1991

MONUA
UN
July 1997–
👤1,017 ☠13

ANGOLA
ZAM.
NAMIBIA 137
ZIMB.
BOTS-WANA
MOZAMBIQUE

UNOSOM I
UN
Apr. 1992–
Apr.–1993

UNOSOM II
UN
May 1993–
Mar. 1996

MINURCA
UN
Apr. 1998–
👤1,369 ☠1

CHILE
URUGUAY
ARGENTINA 664

UNAVEM II
UN
June 1991–
Feb.1995

UNAVEM III
UN
Feb.1995–June 1997

UNTAG
UN
Apr. 1989–
Mar. 1990

ONUMOZ
UN
Dec. 1992–
Dec. 1994

UNAMIR
UN
Oct. 1993–
Mar. 1996

UNOMUR
UN
June 1993–
Sep. 1994

United Nations peacekeeping forces, 1948–99

UN — UN peacekeeping force with dates of operation

☐ — countries providing UN peacekeeping troops, 30 Nov. 1998 with number of troops provided (where over 100)

Ⓜ — permanent member of the Security Council

UNMOT — completed peacekeeping missions

forces still operational, Dec. 1998
MONUA operational force

👤 — size of force   ☠ — fatalities suffered to 1998

ABOVE: Many a war has now been re-labelled a 'peace process' but neither linguistic obfuscation nor UN intervention can stop the continued use of violence for political ends. Warfare in the late 20th century was also characterized by irrational motives: ethnic and religious hatred making some wars quite different from the pursuit of 'politics with the addition of other means'.

Peacekeeping and peacemaking are largely about what comes after failure. When wars themselves fail in their aim of achieving political goals by Clausewitz's 'other means', the underlying conflicts remain. Peacekeeping was a product of the end of the Cold War. During the Cold War, the realities of the global balance meant that the use of the military in peacekeeping would either be purely domestic (such as in the British commitment of forces to Northern Ireland, starting in 1969) or in peripheral conflicts when neither superpower had heavy investments in one side (the Congo, Cyprus, south Lebanon). In these years, the use of military observers to assure impartial application of disengagement provisions, was also used.

Post Cold War peacekeeping and peacemaking covers a broad spectrum. Of the interventions into failed states, the multinational force in Somalia stands out as both an example of the potential for humanitarian relief – preventing imminent starvation when internal fighting interfered with food distribution – and of the inevitability that the peacekeepers would become involved in the local fighting, most notably in a bloody battle in Mogadishu with US Army Rangers that prompted the US withdrawal.

Russia's peacekeeping and peacemaking interventions in the former Soviet Union have never been impartial. In Moldova, Georgia, and Tajikistan however, safeguarding Moscow's interests coincided with reducing the level of violence. In Chechnya, attempted secession from Russia was met with an inept attempt to use massed force and intense firepower to defeat resilient and hard-fighting guerrillas. The Russians were forced to grant the Chechens de facto independence, though they have never received international recognition. A resumption of Russia's war in Chechnya remains unresolved.

The most intensive use of international peacekeeping and peacekeeping forces after the Cold War has been in the former Yugoslavia. International forces have operated in Croatia, Bosnia-Herzegovina, Macedonia and Kosovo. In Bosnia, the initial commitment of peacekeepers under UN auspices proved ineffective in halting the conflict; the UN was never set up to be an effective military decision-maker. After the military defeat of Serb forces in

Croatia and Bosnia and a NATO bombing campaign led to the Dayton Accords, UN peacekeepers were replaced by a NATO-led stabilization force. In Kosovo, peacemaking, in the form of a 78-day bombing campaign (notable for its lack of aircrew casualties and use of precision weapons) was followed by peacekeeping in the form of a multinational NATO-led force.

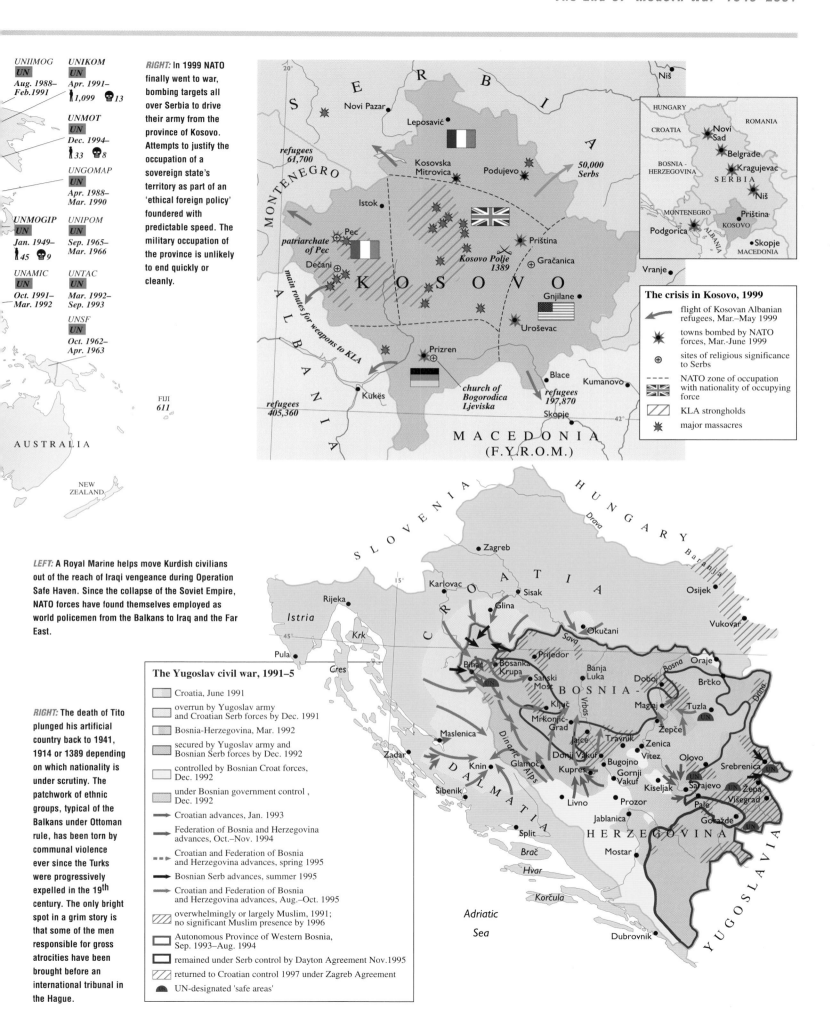

UNIIMOG
UN
*Aug. 1988–
Feb.1991*

UNIKOM
UN
Apr. 1991–
👤 *1,099* 💀 *13*

UNMOT
UN
Dec. 1994–
👤 *33* 💀 *8*

UNGOMAP
UN
*Apr. 1988–
Mar. 1990*

UNMOGIP
UN
Jan. 1949–
👤 *45* 💀 *9*

UNIPOM
UN
*Sep. 1965–
Mar. 1966*

UNAMIC
UN
*Oct. 1991–
Mar. 1992*

UNTAC
UN
*Mar. 1992–
Sep. 1993*

UNSF
UN
*Oct. 1962–
Apr. 1963*

FIJI
611

AUSTRALIA

NEW
ZEALAND

RIGHT: In 1999 NATO finally went to war, bombing targets all over Serbia to drive their army from the province of Kosovo. Attempts to justify the occupation of a sovereign state's territory as part of an 'ethical foreign policy' foundered with predictable speed. The military occupation of the province is unlikely to end quickly or cleanly.

LEFT: A Royal Marine helps move Kurdish civilians out of the reach of Iraqi vengeance during Operation Safe Haven. Since the collapse of the Soviet Empire, NATO forces have found themselves employed as world policemen from the Balkans to Iraq and the Far East.

RIGHT: The death of Tito plunged his artificial country back to 1941, 1914 or 1389 depending on which nationality is under scrutiny. The patchwork of ethnic groups, typical of the Balkans under Ottoman rule, has been torn by communal violence ever since the Turks were progressively expelled in the 19th century. The only bright spot in a grim story is that some of the men responsible for gross atrocities have been brought before an international tribunal in the Hague.

The crisis in Kosovo, 1999

→ flight of Kosovan Albanian refugees, Mar.–May 1999

✶ towns bombed by NATO forces, Mar.-June 1999

⊕ sites of religious significance to Serbs

- - - NATO zone of occupation with nationality of occupying force

▨ KLA strongholds

✴ major massacres

Map labels (Kosovo)

SERBIA · Niš · Novi Pazar · Leposavić · Kosovska Mitrovica · Podujevo · 50,000 Serbs · refugees 61,700 · MONTENEGRO · Istok · Priština · patriarchate of Pec · Pec · Dečani · Kosovo Polje 1389 · Gračanica · KOSOVO · Gnjilane · Uroševac · ALBANIA · main routes for weapons to KLA · Prizren · church of Bogorodica Ljeviska · Blace · Kumanovo · refugees 197,870 · refugees 405,360 · Kükes · Skopje · MACEDONIA (F.Y.R.O.M.)

Inset map labels

HUNGARY · ROMANIA · CROATIA · Novi Sad · BOSNIA-HERZEGOVINA · Belgrade · Kragujevac · SERBIA · Niš · MONTENEGRO · Priština · KOSOVO · Podgorica · ALBANIA · Skopje · MACEDONIA · Vranje

The Yugoslav civil war, 1991–5

▢ Croatia, June 1991

▢ overrun by Yugoslav army and Croatian Serb forces by Dec. 1991

▢ Bosnia-Herzegovina, Mar. 1992

▢ secured by Yugoslav army and Bosnian Serb forces by Dec. 1992

▢ controlled by Bosnian Croat forces, Dec. 1992

▢ under Bosnian government control , Dec. 1992

→ Croatian advances, Jan. 1993

→ Federation of Bosnia and Herzegovina advances, Oct.–Nov. 1994

⇢ Croatian and Federation of Bosnia and Herzegovina advances, spring 1995

➤ Bosnian Serb advances, summer 1995

→ Croatian and Federation of Bosnia and Herzegovina advances, Aug.–Oct. 1995

▨ overwhelmingly or largely Muslim, 1991; no significant Muslim presence by 1996

▢ Autonomous Province of Western Bosnia, Sep. 1993–Aug. 1994

▢ remained under Serb control by Dayton Agreement Nov.1995

▨ returned to Croatian control 1997 under Zagreb Agreement

▲ UN-designated 'safe areas'

Map labels (Yugoslavia)

HUNGARY · SLOVENIA · Zagreb · Drava · Baranja · CROATIA · Karlovac · Sisak · Glina · Osijek · Rijeka · Istria · Krk · Okučani · Sava · Vukovar · Pula · Cres · Bihać · Bosanska Krupa · Prijedor · Banja Luka · Bosna · Oraje · Brčko · Sanski Most · Doboj · Drina · BOSNIA- · Ključ · Vrbas · Maglaj · Tuzla · Mrkonjić-Grad · Žepče · Maslenica · Jajce · Travnik · Zenica · Donji Vakuf · Vitez · Olovo · Zadar · Knin · Glamoč · Bugojno · Srebrenica · Dinaric Alps · Kupres · Gornji Vakuf · Kiseljak · Sarajevo · Žepa · Šibenik · DALMATIA · Livno · Prozor · Pale · Višegrad · Jablanica · Goražde · HERZEGOVINA · Split · Brač · Mostar · Hvar · Adriatic Sea · Korčula · Dubrovnik · YUGOSLAVIA

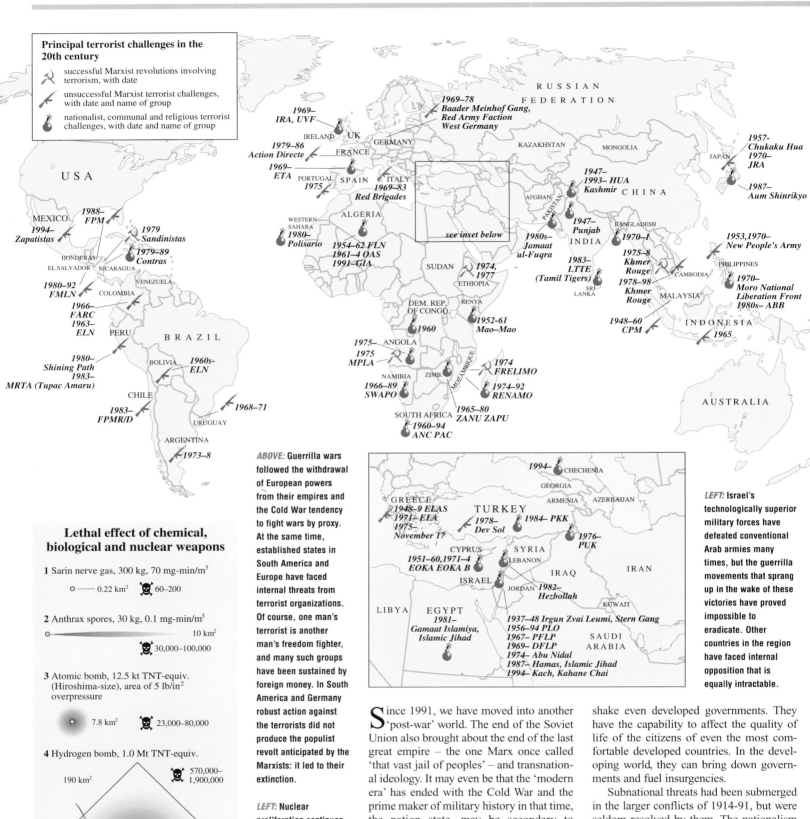

Principal terrorist challenges in the 20th century

⚒ successful Marxist revolutions involving terrorism, with date

🔫 unsuccessful Marxist terrorist challenges, with date and name of group

💣 nationalist, communal and religious terrorist challenges, with date and name of group

USA

1988– FPM
MEXICO
1994– Zapatistas

1979 Sandinistas
1979–89 Contras
HONDURAS
EL SALVADOR NICARAGUA
1980–92 FMLN
VENEZUELA
COLOMBIA
1966– FARC
1963– ELN
PERU
BRAZIL
1980– Shining Path
1983– MRTA (Tupac Amaru)
BOLIVIA
1960s– ELN
CHILE
1983– FPMR/D
URUGUAY
1968–71
ARGENTINA
1973–8

1969– IRA, UVF
IRELAND UK
1979–86 Action Directe
FRANCE
GERMANY
1969– ETA
PORTUGAL
1975 SPAIN
ITALY
1969–83 Red Brigades
WESTERN SAHARA
1980– Polisario
ALGERIA
1954–62 FLN
1961–4 OAS
1991–GIA
SUDAN
1974, 1977
ETHIOPIA
DEM. REP. OF CONGO
1960
KENYA
1952–61 Mao–Mao
1975– 1975 MPLA
ANGOLA
NAMIBIA
ZIMB.
1966–89 SWAPO
1974 FRELIMO
MOZAMBIQUE
1974–92 RENAMO
1965–80 ZANU ZAPU
SOUTH AFRICA
1960–94 ANC PAC

RUSSIAN FEDERATION
1969–78 Baader Meinhof Gang, Red Army Faction West Germany
KAZAKHSTAN
MONGOLIA
JAPAN
1957– Chukaku Hua
1970– JRA
1987– Aum Shinrikyo
AFGHAN
1947–1993– HUA Kashmir
CHINA
PAKISTAN
1947– Punjab
BANGLADESH
1970–1
INDIA
1980s– Jamaat ul-Fuqra
1983– LTTE (Tamil Tigers)
SRI LANKA
1975–8 Khmer Rouge
1978–98 Khmer Rouge
CAMBODIA
1953,1970– New People's Army
PHILIPPINES
1970– Moro National Liberation Front
1980s– ABB
MALAYSIA
1948–60 CPM
INDONESIA
1965

AUSTRALIA

see inset below

ABOVE: Guerrilla wars followed the withdrawal of European powers from their empires and the Cold War tendency to fight wars by proxy. At the same time, established states in South America and Europe have faced internal threats from terrorist organizations. Of course, one man's terrorist is another man's freedom fighter, and many such groups have been sustained by foreign money. In South America and Germany robust action against the terrorists did not produce the populist revolt anticipated by the Marxists: it led to their extinction.

LEFT: Nuclear proliferation continues, despite the efforts of some existing nuclear powers. At the turn of the 21st century, chemical and biological weapons research continues apace: these are alternatives to nuclear bombs within reach of most industrialized countries.

Lethal effect of chemical, biological and nuclear weapons

1 Sarin nerve gas, 300 kg, 70 mg-min/m^3

○ — 0.22 km^2 ☠ 60–200

2 Anthrax spores, 30 kg, 0.1 mg-min/m^3

━━━ 10 km^2 ☠ 30,000–100,000

3 Atomic bomb, 12.5 kt TNT-equiv. (Hiroshima-size), area of 5 lb/in^2 overpressure

● 7.8 km^2 ☠ 23,000–80,000

4 Hydrogen bomb, 1.0 Mt TNT-equiv.

190 km^2 ☠ 570,000–1,900,000

WASHINGTON DC

☠ approximate no. of deaths, assuming 3,000 to 10,000 unprotected people/km^2

1994– CHECHENIA
GEORGIA
GREECE
1948–9 ELAS
1971– ELA
1975– November 17
ARMENIA AZERBAIJAN
TURKEY
1978– Dev Sol
1984– PKK
1976– PUK
CYPRUS
1951–60,1971–4 EOKA EOKA B
SYRIA
LEBANON
IRAQ
IRAN
ISRAEL
JORDAN 1982– Hezbollah
KUWAIT
LIBYA EGYPT
1981– Gamaat Islamiya, Islamic Jihad
1937–48 Irgun Zvai Leumi, Stern Gang
1956–94 PLO
1967– PFLP
1969– DFLP
1974– Abu Nidal
1987– Hamas, Islamic Jihad
1994– Kach, Kahane Chai
SAUDI ARABIA

LEFT: Israel's technologically superior military forces have defeated conventional Arab armies many times, but the guerrilla movements that sprang up in the wake of these victories have proved impossible to eradicate. Other countries in the region have faced internal opposition that is equally intractable.

Since 1991, we have moved into another 'post-war' world. The end of the Soviet Union also brought about the end of the last great empire – the one Marx once called 'that vast jail of peoples' – and transnational ideology. It may even be that the 'modern era' has ended with the Cold War and the prime maker of military history in that time, the nation state, may be secondary to transnational and subnational threats in the future.

Future war will be shaped by a range of post-modern changes in politics, culture and society as well as by technology. Non-state actors have become as powerful on the world stage today as they did in the pre-industrial age. Transnational threats include international crime, narcotics, and even population flow. Organized crime and terrorism have demonstrated their ability to

shake even developed governments. They have the capability to affect the quality of life of the citizens of even the most comfortable developed countries. In the developing world, they can bring down governments and fuel insurgencies.

Subnational threats had been submerged in the larger conflicts of 1914-91, but were seldom resolved by them. The nationalism and violence of Northern Ireland, Serbia and Bosnia-Herzegovina, and elsewhere showed that violence within states was more likely to have an impact on those outside once the damping effects of the Cold War and the firewalls of superpower patronage had been removed.

State threats, however, may well return, more potentially deadly for having access to new weapons technology. The superpowers used the deterrent combination of missiles and weapons of mass destruction to wage a war without mass violence. It is uncertain whether these weapons will have the same effect when interjected in regional rivalries.

Other proliferation is less easy to project. In addition to the widespread information-age technologies now in the world's armed forces – the US Air Force has more computers than personnel – a range of spin-offs is emerging. Intelligence – vital ever since the wireless was introduced – has now grown into 'information warfare', seeking to use these new technologies while denying their benefits to an opponent.

Technological change will affect war in the post-industrial age. The major weapon systems themselves may reflect the more mature technologies of the late industrial age. The US Air Force currently plans to fly its B-52 bombers until they reach 80 years of age.

But even if it is believed that the bombers of the future will look much like those of today, other more dynamic areas will be making fundamental changes in the way wars are fought. Smaller and cheaper microcircuitry, nanotechnology, and biotechnology advances are already finding their way to the battlefield.

The spread of ballistic missiles and weapons of mass destruction – nuclear, biological and chemical – beyond developed nations will likely soon allow even poor, weak countries to threaten rich, strong ones and has motivated the United States to start the development of missile defences.

In the 1990s, war ranged between a highly technological and practically bloodless (for the practitioner) conflict waged in aid of sophisticated statecraft (as in the NATO operations against Kosovo) to simple mass slaughter, largely with axes (as in Rwanda).

ABOVE: Intermediate range ballistic missiles are becoming cheaper and more plentiful and the technology to add a nuclear tip to them is available on the internet. The end of the Cold War has ushered in a new age of anxiety. Who will be the first to employ a live nuclear weapon since 1945?

BELOW: Just as prohibition stimulated organized crime in the USA, attempts to restrict the narcotics business have fuelled international gangs to the point that one Columbian drugs baron offered to pay off the country's national debt in return for his freedom. Many guerrilla armies exploit the drugs trade too: the Shan army in Burma and various Afghan guerrilla groups trade heroin for missiles.

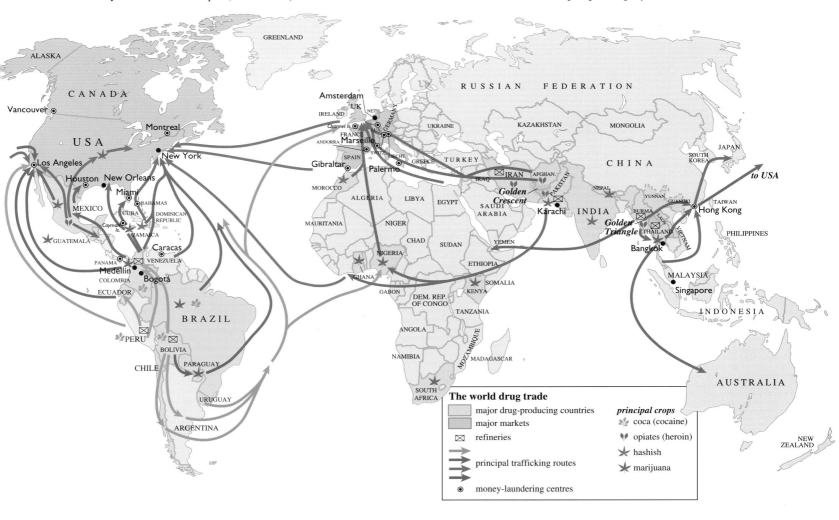

Index